THOMAS MANN
The Uses of Tradition

# THOMAS MANN
# The Uses of Tradition

T. J. REED

OXFORD
AT THE CLARENDON PRESS
1974

*Oxford University Press, Ely House, London W. 1*

GLASGOW  NEW YORK  TORONTO  MELBOURNE  WELLINGTON
CAPE TOWN  IBADAN  NAIROBI  DAR ES SALAAM  LUSAKA  ADDIS ABABA
DELHI  BOMBAY  CALCUTTA  MADRAS  KARACHI  LAHORE  DACCA
KUALA LUMPUR  SINGAPORE  HONG KONG  TOKYO

ISBN 0 19 815742 8

*Printed in Great Britain*
*at the University Press, Oxford*
*by Vivian Ridler*
*Printer to the University*

FOR

ANN, JANE, and MATTHEW

# Preface

TRADITION is an obvious guiding concept for a study of Thomas Mann. There can be few writers whose concern with the legacy of the past, good and ill, was so conscious and intensive, and very few in whose works the materials of a cultural tradition are so prominent. The subject has not been neglected. Influences and affinities, sources and parallels, documented and undocumented, abound in the critical literature. Given the volume and richness of Mann's *œuvre*, the pursuit of these things will keep scholars busy for decades to come.

But a general study of Thomas Mann's relations with tradition need not wait for the completion of such work. On the contrary, existing samples suggest the need for a framework within which to investigate detail, a model of Thomas Mann the traditionalist which will do justice to his procedures as a developing response to his changing times. This study offers such a model. It also offers, because tradition was so important to Thomas Mann at every stage in his life, a coherent general interpretation of his work and thought.

To this end I have drawn on any method apt to increase understanding. Restrictiveness in matters of method seems foolish—in literary study generally, but specifically in the case of Thomas Mann. He requires a pragmatic approach. His texts have an artistic intricacy which demands, and taxes, the formal analyst. But they also frequently had a complex genesis which demands, and rewards, reconstruction. *Der Tod in Venedig* and *Der Zauberberg* especially appear in a new light and can be understood as texts in a more precise way if their genesis is traced. Again, to a degree unusual in a novelist, Mann's underlying purpose was a very personal expression and at times he stated a preference for biographical criticism. Writers who give themselves, he once wrote, want to be recognized for what they are. But this recognition cannot stay within the bounds of Mann's private world because from 1914 on he involved himself more and more in politics. We cannot hope to understand him or his work fully unless we retrace that involvement and its historical background in some detail.

All these approaches—textual, genetic, biographical, political—are indispensable. In recent years many critics have shied away from the genetic and biographical for fear of being labelled 'positivist'. Yet one had better be as positive as one can in those areas of the subject which will allow it. The political approach too, even when it is not being handled in the stereotyped manner which is the latest German fashion, still occasionally provokes demur among critics who turn away from the crudeness of politics and the directness of political messages to the alleged self-sufficient intricacy of art. Yet the relation between art and politics, intricacy and directness, was itself one of Mann's major themes, the tension between them a recurrent dilemma, his solution of the problem—in life and in fiction—an important part of his achievement. To settle for one element only is to impoverish and misrepresent the work of a uniquely responsible modern writer.

It is a pleasure to record the help I have had in preparing this book. The University of Oxford, St. John's College, and St. Catherine's College gave me a total of a year's sabbatical leave. A generous grant from the Leverhulme Research Foundation made it possible for me to work for three months on Thomas Mann's papers in the Zürich Thomas Mann Archive. The Director of the Archive, Professor Dr. Hans Wysling, and his assistants, Fräulein Marianne Fischer and Fräulein Rosemarie Hintermann, did everything to make my stay there as fruitful as possible and have continued to be of invaluable assistance in checking details. Frau Katja Mann, Thomas Mann's widow, has kindly allowed me to quote from manuscript and other materials held in the Archive. For leave to quote other unpublished items in their keeping I am grateful to the Handschriftenabteilung of the Munich Stadtbibliothek and to the Stadt- und Landesbibliothek in Dortmund. The Cotta Archive and the Schiller-Nationalmuseum at Marbach kindly furnished valuable information. The S. Fischer Verlag gave generous permission for me to quote from Thomas Mann's published works *in extenso*.

A number of private individuals have provided further information and stimulus: the late Georg Lukács, Budapest; Dr. Heinz Saueressig, Biberach; Dr. Hans-Otto Mayer, Düsseldorf; Professor Herbert Lehnert, University of California at Irvine; and in particular Professor Hans-Joachim Sandberg of the University of Bergen. Oxford colleagues professing a variety of subjects have given friendly guidance. Fellow Germanists and interested historians have read and commented on individual chapters. For the amalgam of advice and obstinacy which remains I am alone responsible.

It is an especial pleasure to acknowledge permanent Oxford obligations: to the Librarian and staff of the Taylorian Library, whose outstanding resources, facilities, and helpfulness are all too easy to take for granted; to the supervisor who genially guided my first researches, Professor Ernest Stahl; and, oldest and deepest debt of all, to my tutors, Malcolm Pasley and Robert Shackleton.

Finally I must thank my wife for unfailing encouragement despite two more clamorous demands on her attention. To her and them the book is dedicated.

T. J. R.

*January 1973*

# Contents

# List of Illustrations

Illustrations reproduced by kind permission of Frau Katja Mann and the Thomas Mann Archive, Zürich (numbers 1, 3 and 5); Frau Katja Mann and the Heinrich Mann Archive, East Berlin (number 2); Dr. Hans-Otto Mayer and the Universitätsbibliothek Düsseldorf, Sammlung Hans-Otto Mayer (numbers 4 and 7); and Dr. Heinz Saueressig, Biberach an der Riss (number 6).

# References and Translations

REFERENCES by roman and arabic numerals—e.g. iv. 413—are to the *Gesammelte Werke* in 12 volumes published by the S. Fischer Verlag in 1960.

Abbreviations used for the volumes of Mann's correspondence are listed alongside those items in the Bibliography on p. 416.

I have either given the gist of German quotations in my text or, more usually, added an English translation in brackets. This does not apply to German quotations in footnotes unless they are of substantive and not merely corroborative importance.

# Introduction

AT his death in 1955, Thomas Mann had a unique reputation. He was acknowledged not merely as the greatest modern German novelist, but as something like a living sum of German culture.

In part this view derived from his work. It was markedly intellectual and rich in literary and philosophical allusion. It rested, as he often pointed out, on foundations in the art and thought of the nineteenth century—Schopenhauer, Nietzsche, Wagner. From his middle years, Mann began to link himself with the greatest figure in German literary culture, Goethe, and eventually celebrated a 'mystical union' with him in the novel *Lotte in Weimar*, where quotation and allusion, from being a favoured technique, became the continuous substance. As a constant background there were also Mann's essays on German writers and thinkers from the eighteenth down to the twentieth centuries, all of them establishing some intimate affinity with himself and suggesting that his work had systematically drawn nourishment from the traditional canon. All this declared him a *poeta doctus*.

History made him more. It sent him into exile and created a situation in which he could speak the words 'Wo ich bin ist die deutsche Kultur' (Where I am is German culture),[1] not as an arrogant personal claim but as a necessary political act. For the Nazis had narrowed the definition of what was German and what was culture to something crude and chauvinistic; Mann was denying their competence. His declaration must be read with the emphasis on 'ich', and that 'ich' understood in a representative sense.[2] He was not making a complacent claim but stating a programme, anxious that his and other émigrés'

[1] Cf. Heinrich Mann, *Ein Zeitalter wird besichtigt*, Stockholm, n.d. [1946], p.231.
[2] Cf. Mann's letter of 21 Apr. 1933 to Max Mohr: 'Ich kranke im Ganzen nicht an übertriebenem Selbstgefühl — eher im Gegenteil. Aber ich habe die untrügliche Empfindung, dass mit einer deutschen Revolution, die einen Menschen wie mich aus dem Lande stösst, nicht alles ganz in Ordnung sein kann.' Extract in J. A. Stargard's Autographen-Katalog, June 1972, no. 237.

work should make plain the distinction between Nazi Germany
and the Germany which had chosen exile.[3]

A more straightforward equation of Thomas Mann and
German culture was fostered by his public role in America. As
the most distinguished of German literary exiles, he became the
leading anti-Nazi propagandist, a champion of liberal and
democratic values and, increasingly, an authority on things
German. From December 1941 he was Consultant in Germanic
Literature to the Library of Congress. During and immediately
after the war he was appealed to from all sides on every conceivable issue concerning Germany. It was an uncomfortable
position to be in. Whatever he did—and his letters at this time
show exemplary discrimination and diplomacy—he was certain
not to satisfy somebody. Nevertheless, his authoritative status
was unquestioned.

Alongside this he made virtually a new literary career in
America. Alone among the immigrants he was a major success
in translation and his works were deemed 'likely to achieve a
permanent place in the nation's culture'.[4] But his new reputation was subtly different from his European one. It stressed
what was certainly part of his work but arguably not the essential part. It turned him, as he complained himself, into a
'ponderous philosopher'.[5] It concentrated admiration on his
'heritage of culture' (xi. 218). The nuances of his original texts
were not there to distract: cultural matter is what remains
when the volatile element of irony has been driven off by
translation.

His was thus the kind of work, and with his personal background and image he was the kind of writer, to make academics
feel at home. Honorary doctorates showered. His translator
never referred to him but as Dr. Mann, and some critics followed
suit. Full access to his majestic corpus of work would surely have

[3] Cf. to René Schickele, 16 May 1934: 'Sie und ich und mein Bruder . . . müssen
unsere Sache sehr gut machen, damit man einmal sagt, wir seien in dieser Zeit das
eigentliche Deutschland gewesen' (Br. i. 360).

[4] From the citation welcoming Mann to membership of the American Academy
of Arts and Letters in November 1951. Quoted in Hans Bürgin and Hans-Otto
Mayer, *Thomas Mann. Eine Chronik seines Lebens*, Frankfurt-am-Main, 1965 (quoted
henceforth as *Chronik*), p. 232. On the unusual status Mann had achieved in
American letters by 1945, see Walter A. Reichart, 'Thomas Mann: An American
Bibliography', in *Monatshefte* 37 (1945).

[5] To Erika Mann, 6 Nov. 1948 (Br. iii. 55).

to be through a systematic study of the culture whose totality he embodied.

Such study was early forthcoming and has continued to come forth. Sometimes it is in its own way impressive.[6] Yet one may doubt whether it is wholly appropriate, certainly whether it is the most appropriate way to see a writer. It can easily make him seem a mere extension of cultural traditions, his particularity smoothed away. 'Tradition' appears as an elevated continuum almost independent of the individual and the forces of his time, and he himself as a continuator who was effortlessly borne along by it. His knowledge of it is assumed complete, his consciousness of every twist and turn in the development of past thought constant.[7] In some moods, Thomas Mann was not displeased to be seen this way. Beyond doubt he did something to foster the image. Yet in other moods he was aware of the essential misunderstanding and would deprecate the assumptions which readers and scholars made about him and his work.[8] For at heart he knew how a writer really does stand to tradition: that, however real his involvement with it, it remains part of the material which he disposes and is transformed in the process. He moulds it to his needs—artistic, intellectual, social, political.

It is above all through these needs that Mann's work must be approached, and not primarily through the original cultural materials of which he made a highly personal use, nor on the assumption that his work is a neutral medium for their transmission. Thus, not Schopenhauer but what Thomas Mann knew and made of Schopenhauer; not Goethe but Thomas Mann's Goethe and why he saw and needed him thus; not Nietzsche but the successive Nietzsches Mann knew and used, first as a literary beginner, then as a wartime defender of Imperial Germany, later still as a Weimar Social Democrat and finally as an analyst of Nazism and disaster. The title *poeta doctus* is

[6] The foremost example is Fritz Kaufmann, *Thomas Mann: The World as Will and Representation*, Boston, 1957.

[7] For a detailed criticism of these assumptions and their results in the Thomas Mann literature, see my article 'Thomas Mann and Tradition—Some Clarifications', in *The Discontinuous Tradition*, ed. P. F. Ganz, Oxford, 1971.

[8] Cf. to Irita van Doren, 28 Aug. 1951, on the 'tragic illusion' of his encyclopedic knowledge (Br. iii. 218). The most balanced account Mann gave of his culture and its function is in the letter of 29 Apr. 1952 to Hermann Weigand, commenting on Weigand's study of the sources for *Der Erwählte*. See *The Letters of Thomas Mann*, 1970, ii. 639 ff.

wholly apt for Thomas Mann, but it needs to be properly understood. The stress is on the first element.

Recent scholarship has begun to consider Mann in this light and to concentrate on his means of appropriating and using the materials tradition offered. Yet even here, in exact studies very far in spirit from earlier genuflections to a monolithic culture, the old attitudes can paradoxically survive. Mann's practice as an artist and essayist is judged implicitly by his grand image. Any inaccuracies, superficialities, adjustments, misunderstandings, short cuts—all characteristic equally of the artistic temperament and an Alexandrian age—are viewed with a severe eye. *Menschlich* is easily seen as *allzumenschlich*. True, some aspects of Mann's practice have a dubious side. Yet what hardens judgement is the disappointment of expectations. Were those expectations ever proper? Was the Thomas Mann of dignified public occasions and cultural celebrations not also the artist who chose a confidence-man as his confessional mask? Surely, when a scholar remarks that, in the course of Mann's mythological studies for *Joseph*, he never went back to the sources,[9] multiple wrong assumptions are at work—about *Joseph*, about Thomas Mann, about artists and their sources, about art itself. For these assumptions Mann's unique image is to blame.

In short, he now risks suffering a fate which T. S. Eliot foresaw for himself and tried to avoid by disclaiming his reputation for learning and scholarship. 'Better to confess one's weaknesses, when they are certain to be revealed sooner or later, than to leave them to be exposed to posterity.'[10] The revealing of weaknesses may be, objectively, part of the critic's and scholar's job, but he should waste no time on reproofs. He is free to look, having abandoned false expectations, at the organizing structures of thought and artistry with which Mann gave new meaning to the materials tradition offered him.

Materials put to use, uses dictated by need, needs created by changing circumstances: the sequence brings us inescapably to history. For the changing circumstances were not just the internal developments of a creative personality and career, as

---

[9] W. Berger, 'Thomas Mann und die antike Literatur', in Peter Pütz (ed.), *Thomas Mann und die Tradition*, Frankfurt, 1971, p. 97.

[10] T. S. Eliot, 'The Classics and the Man of Letters', opening paragraph.

could be said for example of Goethe's relations with tradition. They were the circumstances of Germany as a society, of the *haute bourgeoisie* Mann sprang from and of the artist guild he belonged to, all of them changed out of recognition in his lifetime. He began as an artist whose last thought was to influence his society or even in any direct way to render it in his work. Literature was a free realm detached from life, its subject matter was 'Life' not as a social reality but as an unchanging metaphysical essence. Only gradually did Mann become aware that the cultural superstructure showed the forces at work in society. Around 1910 he was struggling to clarify this insight, unsuccessfully. War proved how true it was. The Thomas Mann of 1914 believed he was defending that free artistic realm; in reality he was being carried along by the forces governing his society. By the 1920s he understood something of this process and attempted to depict it. By now he was committed to acting upon society, directly and indirectly, as public figure and artist. If he no longer believed in a wholly free realm of art, he did believe in a free faculty, Reason, which should be applied to the task of controlling social existence. Even in this political phase, which lasted through the thirties and forties, his response to the world outside him used cultural tradition as its medium, not just because he was an artist and to speak of culture came easier to him than to speak of economics or policies (though he did this too) but because, in a way possibly unique to Germany, the issues of culture became inseparable from ideology and from that quest for national identity which was a catastrophe for Europe.

Mann's personal dialogue with tradition produced answers radically different from the ones which determined the fate of his country, even though it was the common tradition from which he began. Indeed, nothing more clearly illustrates the neutrality of tradition, its passive availability for present use and misuse, than this divergence. Tradition offers possibilities, for good and ill; the individual selects and uses.

In the process, he may discover an identity of his own. Thomas Mann did. His personal impulses and responses seemed to repeat the patterns of the past, the actions and thoughts of his predecessors. Yet so much lay in the way he read them. Figures and ideas from tradition served the ruse of a mind too modest for self-assertion in directer form. He affirmed himself through them. Then again, tradition had a critical function, posing questions and casting doubt, disciplining that ceaseless self-absorption of Mann's which others found excessive but which was for him eventually a route into other men's concerns. It is his distinction, seemingly simple but an immense achievement, that he did change and learn and correct himself, as few men of his class and background in Germany did.

The resulting life and work are less dramatic than the catastrophe to which heroic inflexibility leads, but that is not a judgement on them, certainly not a negative one. Mann's willingness to learn and adapt appears early. In one of the aphorisms of *Morgenröte*, Nietzsche says that 'we human beings are the only creatures which, if they turn out ill, can strike themselves out like a badly written sentence'. The young Thomas Mann, ardent Nietzschean though he was, noted a more modest alternative in the margin: 'One can always try what filing will do'.[11] It is the proposal of a moralist and a stylist and of a man who returned again and again to the idea that the two are mysteriously linked.

[11] Nietzsche: 'Wir Menschen sind die einzigen Geschöpfe, welche, wenn sie missraten, sich selber durchstreichen können wie einen missratenen Satz', *Morgenröte*, § 274. Thomas Mann: 'Man darf noch das Feilen versuchen.'

# Prelude

But my mind was very young then, and youth I suppose can be easily seduced—even by a negation.

JOSEPH CONRAD, *Victory*

WHAT is literary culture, Thomas Mann asked in 1910, if not a process of learning, taking over, and imitating? One meaning he saw in tradition is the training of the writer's eye by what he reads. He was sceptical about the popular superstition of the unaided original genius. Was it so necessary, was it even possible to write without first having read?[1]

This is the most obvious way in which literary tradition operates and it does so most markedly in the early stages of a writer's career. His learning process may not be easy to reconstruct, since documentary evidence tends to be scarcer and the lack is not made good by later retrospects, not always reliable. Nevertheless, the reconstruction is worth attempting. The writer rarely escapes altogether, and certainly Thomas Mann did not escape, from the effects of his beginnings. They set a course which later correction could only modify. Important clues to the nature of his whole *œuvre* are therefore to be found in the way he embarked on it.

It is well to approach Mann's early stories with the idea firmly in mind that they *are* his earliest, and that they require us to enter sympathetically into the situation of a young man starting to write in the 1890s. Three things then stand out. The young writer's immaturity, which need not be simply assumed, since it can be traced in the content and structure of the stories; the connection between immaturity and the influences, literary

[1] In his notes for the essay 'Geist und Kunst'. The German text of N3 reads: '[Muss: deleted] Kann man schreiben, ohne gelesen zu haben? Steht nicht einer auf den Schultern des Anderen? . . . Das ursprüngliche Genie ohne Lektüre ein Aberglaube. Was ist poetische Cultur, wenn nicht das Lernen, Übernehmen, selbst nachahmen? . . . Tradition. Geschichte. Schulung des Blicks durch Bücher. Es ist doch in allen Künsten so.' The full text in Hans Wysling, *Quellenkritische Studien zum Werk Thomas Manns*, Berne and Munich 1967, henceforth quoted as *Studien*.

and intellectual, which it made him receptive to; and finally the ironic narrative manner which is the result. Mann's irony appears in a new light, less as a calculated literary effect, present uniformly and intentionally in all his work, than as a technical solution produced by the exigencies of those early years. But today's solution then becomes tomorrow's problem, creating both emotional and technical difficulties for the writer. In seeking to solve these in their turn, he is launched into the sequence of adjustments and experiments which are his response to the dual challenge of his talent and his world.

First it is necessary to be clear about the nature of irony. Generally speaking, irony is a device by which the writer hints that his words and his real meaning no longer coincide. He may for example blame a character while using words exclusively of commendation. By sheer excess of commendation or by the jarring repetition of a word or phrase, he manages to make plain to the reader that he is not now speaking with undivided commitment. It is as if he gets off the moving vehicle of his own narrative and watches it from an increasing distance. 'The ironic fiction-writer', Northrop Frye suggests, 'deprecates himself and like Socrates pretends to know nothing.'[2] It would be even truer to say that, rather than pretending to know nothing, the ironic writer pretends to hold no values other than those of his characters. His words would not offend them but his true meaning is clear to his reader. A better description of the ironist, from the same passage of Plato's *Symposium* which Frye presumably alludes to, is that he 'spends all his life in teasing mankind, and hiding his true intent'.[3] Irony is thus a language of secret revolt. But for the secret to be open to the reader, the presence of irony must be signalled by the kind of textual signal already suggested. A critical line has to be crossed perceptibly, by whatever means the occasion offers. By crossing it, the writer implicitly dissociates himself from something he is reporting; equally, he implies in the process a contrasting positive value as the standard by which he chose to do so. This last is not an ethical, but a simple logical requirement, unless the writer is entirely nihilistic. It is crucial to our discussion.

---

[2] *Anatomy of Criticism*, Princeton, 1957, p. 40.
[3] *The Dialogues of Plato*, translated by B. Jowett, repr. Oxford, 1967, vol. 1, pp. 548 f.

These points can best be made by two contrasting illustrations of how irony works. One will be from Thomas Mann, but the first is a passage from Book Third, 'The Downfall', of George Eliot's novel *The Mill on the Floss*.

The Tulliver family's fortunes have collapsed, and in 'The Family Council'[4] we are shown the self-righteousness and grudgingly measured sympathy of their nearest kin. Throughout this chapter such humanity as the relatives show stops well short of solidarity with the Tullivers in their disaster. They make it subtly clear that they remain on the side of a society in which financial ruin is a moral transgression. The one sister, Mrs. Deane, 'a thin-lipped woman who made small well-considered speeches on peculiar occasions, repeating them afterwards to her husband and asking him if she had not spoken very properly', offers jelly, should the doctor order it, for Mr. Tulliver, who lies ill from shock. The offer declares itself as charity beyond his deserving in the words: '"For it is but right he should have proper attendance *while he's ill.*"' Mrs. Tulliver herself is of the same stamp. She may chance now to be on the wrong side of fortune, but her values are those of her sisters. 'Jelly' reminds her only of her 'dozen o' cut jelly glasses upstairs', doomed to be sold up: '"I shall niver put jelly into 'em no more."' The next sister, Mrs. Glegg, arrives wearing 'a costume selected with the high moral purpose of instilling perfect humility into Bessy and her children'; by being short with her husband, 'this superior woman' sets the tone of her role in the family council. Her wrath rises as Mrs. Tulliver presses her kin to buy some of the things she cannot bear to think of as lost to the family, until at last:

'Best things!' exclaimed Mrs. Glegg with severity, which had gathered intensity from her long silence. 'It drives me past patience to hear you all talking o' best things, and buying in this, that, and the other, such as silver and chany. You must bring your mind to your circumstances, Bessy, and not be thinking o' silver and chany; but whether you shall get so much as a flock bed to lie on, and a blanket to cover you, and a stool to sit on. You must remember, if you get 'em, it'll be because your friends have bought 'em for you, for you're dependent upon *them* for everything; for your husband lies there helpless, and hasn't got a penny i' the world to call his own.

---

4 Book Third, ch. 3.

And it's for your own good I say this, for it's right you should feel what your state is, and what disgrace your husband's brought on your own family, as you've got to look to for everything—and be humble in your mind.' Mrs. Glegg paused, for speaking with much energy for the good of others is naturally exhausting.

*Schadenfreude*, and readiness to aid a just nemesis by exacting maximum thanks for minimum gifts and grudged consolation— these are the family values George Eliot reveals. The speakers largely damn themselves out of their own mouths and the writer needs no more than the scenic method to establish their values. But lest this should not sufficiently imply her own, she crosses the critical line in several places, with Mrs. Glegg's 'high moral purpose', and the nothing less than 'perfect humility' which she grimly means to instil; in the phrase 'this superior woman'; and especially in the commentary which takes up that lady's 'for your own good' with almost open sarcasm. The words used, taken literally, compose a judgement Mrs. Glegg would have accepted; the ironic meaning which the repetition signals makes plain her inhumanity. Equally clearly, the phrases which cross the critical line into irony imply a quite different conception of 'high moral purpose', of what is for 'the good' of near relations fallen on hard times, and of the form which truly 'superior' behaviour would take. The obtusest of readers must see, not just what George Eliot dissociates herself from, but at least some glimmerings of the counter-image she is proposing.

The second illustration is the opening of Thomas Mann's *Der kleine Herr Friedemann*:

Die Amme hatte die Schuld. — Was half es, dass, als der erste Verdacht entstand, Frau Konsul Friedemann ihr ernstlich zuredete, solches Laster zu unterdrücken? Was half es, dass sie ihr ausser dem nahrhaften Bier ein Glas Rotwein täglich verabreichte? Es stellte sich plötzlich heraus, dass dieses Mädchen sich herbeiliess, auch noch den Spiritus zu trinken, der für den Kochapparat verwendet werden sollte, und ehe Ersatz für sie eingetroffen war, ehe man sie hatte fortschicken können, war das Unglück geschehen. Als die Mutter und ihre drei halbwüchsigen Töchter eines Tages von einem Ausgange zurückkehrten, lag der kleine, etwa einen Monat alte Johannes, vom Wickeltische gestürzt, mit einem entsetzlich leisen Wimmern am Boden, während die Amme stumpfsinnig daneben stand.

Der Arzt, der mit einer behutsamen Festigkeit die Glieder des gekrümmten und zuckenden kleinen Wesens prüfte, machte ein sehr, sehr ernstes Gesicht, die drei Töchter standen schluchzend in einem Winkel, und Frau Friedemann in ihrer Herzensangst betete laut.

(It was the nurse's fault.—What good did it do that Frau Konsul Friedemann, when the first suspicion arose, earnestly enjoined her to curb such vice? What good did it do that she had a glass of red wine dispensed to her daily, in addition to the nourishing beer? It suddenly became apparent that this girl had descended to drinking the spirit intended for the cooking-stove, and before a replacement had arrived for her, before she could be sent away, the disaster had occurred. When the mother and her three adolescent daughters returned one day from an expedition, they found little Johannes, one month old, lying on the floor, where he had fallen from the swaddling-table, making a horribly faint whimpering sound, while the nurse stood dull-wittedly by.

The doctor, examining with cautious firmness the limbs of the writhing and twitching little being, made a very very serious face, the three daughters stood sobbing in a corner, and Frau Friedemann in her profound anguish prayed aloud.)

The manner of this opening is typical of Thomas Mann's early (i.e. pre-*Buddenbrooks*) stories.[5] It leads into the account of a cripple whose existence, carefully grounded on self-limitation and renunciation of the full pleasures of normality, is finally broken up by passion. From initial accident to final suicide, it is tragic and might claim wholly serious treatment and reception. This is not what it gets in this introduction.

The effect of distance between narrator and subject, the absence of implied sympathy, is unmistakable. This is not just the objective, quasi-scientific reporting of Naturalism—although the motif of alcoholism and the deterministic working out of human fate from a physical defect are superficially Naturalistic, if they are not already a parody of Naturalism. Nor is it simply the pursuit of *unerbittliche Wahrheit* which was one of the literary watchwords of the late 1880s. Distance is also established by notes of irony akin to George Eliot's, albeit less obtrusive. We

---

[5] This is one of the earliest, published in 1897 and probably first written as early as 1894, under the title *Der kleine Professor*. Further examples of the ruthlessly detached manner would be *Tobias Mindernickel* and *Luischen*, but to some degree it is observable in all the early work, even in those stories which have some direct autobiographical basis. There it serves no doubt as a prophylactic against subjectivism and self-pity.

irresistibly add the ironical tone[6] to 'solches Laster', for instance. No doubt Frau Konsul Friedemann did call it a vice, but the narrator's 'solches' lifts the word from a context of conviction and holds it up for our cooler inspection as an attitude. We should need no telling that the Frau Konsul's exhortation was 'ernstlich': the point only needs reinforcing so solemnly if the writer is standing aside and not immediately sympathizing with the character. But are we not to take alcoholism as a vice? Is the good lady's vehemence misplaced?

Again, this is not the point at which we expect to be reminded that beer is nutritious. It is not at all sure this adjective figured in the Frau Konsul's speeches; the narrator is providing information we do not need and thus asserting a right to detach himself from the proceedings and pay attention, rather incongruously, to a trivial general truth.[7]

Perhaps, it seems, the irony is at the expense of the *bourgeoise* as such: even in such grave circumstances, a bourgeois lady's reactions may not command sympathy. Yet even when we turn aside from her, when the narrator faces the circumstances of the accident themselves, knowing the consequences they will have, his irony persists. His rhetorical question 'Was half es . . .?' (and even more its rhetorical repetition) displays the writer's freedom to dispose his stylistic means with little reference, indeed in incongruous disproportion to the content. Rhetoric, from being the proper organizer of passion, has long become its solvent, destroying by overstatement. The grave situation is made less grave by being taken now at too elevated a stylistic level. Similar incongruity lies in the combination of the formal

---

[6] Cf. Frye, op. cit., p. 41: '. . . sophisticated irony merely states, and lets the reader add the ironic tone himself.' Reinhard Baumgart (*Das Ironische und die Ironie in den Werken Thomas Manns*, Munich, 1966, p. 200), suggests that spoken delivery may be needed to bring out latent stylistic irony, and that textual analysis thus has serious limitations. In practice, irony is not so chancy a business, but it is true that reader-receptiveness to the writer's signals may vary. (See below, p. 20, n. 30). Frye's distinction thus has some use, although it fails to take account of the kind of reader who, once sure he has an ironic writer to interpret, sees irony everywhere.

[7] Baumgart points out (op. cit., pp. 23, 199) that the additions to the manuscript of *Tristan* (published in facsimile in 1921) are mainly adjectives, the 'favourite element' of decadent and impressionistic language. But his conclusion that they serve ever greater precision is too simple: remove 'ernstlich' and 'nahrhaft' from the passage under examination, and what we lose is not precision, but ironic distance.

'sich herbeilassen' and the sordid 'Spiritus trinken'. While life suffers, language indulges in almost self-sufficient revels.

There is perhaps no call to speak of irony in the narrator's bald statements of unhappy fact—the whimpering child on the floor, the nurse's stupor—although even this juxtaposition moves towards operatic arrangement. At worst it is coolly uninvolved, as is the precisely observed 'behutsame Festigkeit' of the doctor's examination. But the doctor's facial expression, his 'sehr, sehr ernstes Gesicht'? Is it the doctor himself who exaggerates? Surely it is the stylist, who intervenes between the seriousness of the situation and the reader's potential sympathy, undermining once more by overstatement: a 'sehr, sehr ernstes Gesicht' is not as serious as a 'sehr ernstes Gesicht'. The observing narrator reminds us of his unconcerned presence in every word which is superfluous to the recounting of events.[8] What is more, with this narrative tone once established, even the apparently plain statement can create similar effects, especially if backed up by the artful use of juxtaposition: while the doctor examines and looks grave, the Friedemann daughters stand sobbing as one mechanism in a corner and their mother prays aloud. Here we have a mixture of caricature and melodrama, with a total effect that is far from tragic. There could hardly be a better case of 'a pattern of words that turns away . . . from its own obvious meaning' (Frye, p. 40).

But turns away to what? In quick succession the narrative has dealt with vice, catastrophe, sorrow, prayer. The prelude then ends with hope—once more drawn across the line into irony by the doctor's repetition: 'das Beste hoffen, wie gesagt, das Beste hoffen'. All these are surprising objects for irony. If they are negative, what is positive? In other words, what is at the root of an attitude which can refuse compassion in such a case? Without the fulfilment of a moral implication such as we saw in George Eliot, there is no frame of reference for the reader, who is left disoriented. The objection to this, as already hinted,

[8] Baumgart (pp. 19–27) arrives at a similar conclusion by a roundabout route. He argues that Mann first mistrusts 'big words' (see below pp. 26 ff. on *Enttäuschung*) and consequently aims at a precision which will render reality as it really is. But precision is unfortunately self-defeating when taken to extreme lengths, because increased detail blurs the picture to be presented. As a result, the complexities of language increasingly portray the writer instead of his subject ('subjektivierende Auflösung der kritischen Präzision').

is not a moral one (namely, that a decent author should have positive values) but a practical one concerning the way irony functions as a device. Its negations depend logically on the existence of contrary positions, and if one cannot get back to these through the implications of the ironic phrasing, irony is left as a rhetorical structure hanging in the air. It has a stylistic impact of a purely formal kind.

Significantly, because of the role we shall shortly see him play in the formation of Thomas Mann's early methods, it was Nietzsche who described most clearly the pitfalls of irony. He conceded its use only as a pedagogic means, to disconcert those who were too sure of themselves. Otherwise he thought it a bad habit, an *Unart*. Ironic writers, he argued, count on the silly sort of people who like to feel themselves, along with the author, superior to everybody else, and consider him the mouthpiece of their own presumptions. The habit of irony is harmful because it instils a permanent cocksure superiority ('schadenfrohe Überlegenheit').[9] The habitual and generalized feeling of superiority and of 'knowing better'[10] is not particularized into any specific better value, but exists self-sufficiently. This is a kind of aestheticism, the *Unart* for *Unart*'s sake.

It might be argued that an adequate explanation of the pervasive irony in Thomas Mann's early work would be that he was indeed already a cynic and a nihilist. His 'position' might really have been compounded of negations. If the ironic form leaves the reader disoriented, this accurately reflects the true lack of positive values. This has frequently been the conclusion of readers and critics. Early reviewers complained that Mann left them with a feeling of vertigo,[11] and later criticism has frequently stuck at the same point, seeing these early efforts as a calculated rejection of all positive values and decent emotions. It is certainly true that we observe in Mann the 'flight from feeling that takes place in the fastidious character';[12]

---

[9] *Menschliches, Allzumenschliches*, 1, § 372 (Schlechta i. 642).

[10] The term *wissend* applied to suffering characters, and a claim that they have achieved *Erkenntnis*, figure recurrently in the early stories.

[11] e.g. *Leipziger Tageblatt*, 22 Apr. 1903, reviewing the slightly later *Tristan*: 'In der Fülle der ohnedies kraus genug gestalteten Geschichte sollte eines wenigstens dem Leser einen positiven Halt gewähren, damit ihm nicht . . . wirbelig zu Mute wird.'

[12] R. Peacock, 'Much is comic in Thomas Mann', Inaugural Lecture, Bedford College, London, 1963, p. 7.

but the resultant displays (such as the passage from *Friedemann*) are sometimes taken with grim seriousness as deeply evil, and attacked for their 'implicit amorality'.[13]

These charges must be attended to, but they must also be seen in a new perspective. Both critics quoted are on to something, but the first touches only on the question of temperament, while the second presents us with too systematically wicked a young writer. Temperament is of course a factor, but it must not be seen in isolation from situation; youthful amorality is conceivable, but need not be taken as so sinister with such promptitude. By twenty or so, the writer can scarcely be more than a probationary nihilist.

The appearance of maturity with which the young Thomas Mann comes equipped is put in perspective by a remark G. K. Chesterton made on Browning's first poetic effort: 'It exhibits the characteristic mark of a juvenile poem, the general suggestion that the author is a thousand years old'.[14] The sources and models Mann drew on and openly referred to in his first stories were calculated to create just such an impression. It is not difficult to see how the beginner created literature out of limited and often derivative materials, and by the conscious pursuit of attitudes which would suggest a wealth of disillusioning experience.

Mann's first public defence of his early practice (and as we shall see a key to his later literary methods) was the essay *Bilse und ich* of 1906. In it he attempts to answer the charge of coldness and hostility towards the world he portrays. He argues that the appearance of these things in his work is the product of a dual impulse found in any artist who has been through the school of Nietzsche; not just towards beauty of form, but also towards depth of knowledge (x. 18 f). The passion of all such artists is detailed and objective observation, painful though this may be. And in claiming for literature the right of pitiless objectivity which is commonly accorded to science, Mann uses the phrase 'fröhliche Wissenschaft'.[15] These are unequivocal pointers,

---

[13] R. Gray, *The German Tradition in Literature*, Cambridge, 1965, p. 115.

[14] Quoted by Richard Alewyn apropos Hugo von Hofmannsthal's first play *Gestern*, written at the age of seventeen. See Alewyn, *Hugo von Hofmannsthal*, Göttingen, 1958, p. 165.

[15] Slightly *mal à propos*, since Nietzsche's 'gaya scienza' is the happy state beyond the painful processes of knowledge and the destruction of conventional views,

which direct us to Nietzsche not just as the source of motifs and situations in the early stories,[16] but also as the influence which formed the writer's attitudes towards the world and its reproduction in art. It is possible to follow this process in some detail.

Among the earliest of Mann's preserved writings—contributions to the journal *Der Frühlingssturm* of which he was joint editor at school—there is an essay entitled *Heinrich Heine der 'Gute'* (xi. 711 f.) In it Mann attacks a recent apologist for Heine who had claimed him as a good man, a Protestant, and a patriot. In face of Heine's 'greatness', Mann scorns the predicate 'good'. Real goodness is surely impossible to find in practice (there is only a mixture of egoism and Christian morality), so it is not necessary even to go into the more abstract objections to the concept 'good'. Nevertheless, in passing, he does say what his own philosophical position would be: good and bad, true and false, beautiful and ugly are as non-existent as 'upwards' and 'downwards' are in space. Heine, unlike his narrow-minded defender, was not one of those minds for whom dogmatic straitjackets were made. He was not a 'good', only a *great* man. Greatness is something that transcends mere moral standards.

These are just the sort of views ('vorurteilsfreie Anschauungen') the magazine's manifesto had promised (xi. 545). The protest is ordinary enough for an eighteen-year-old, but the tone and the kind of argument it echoes are Nietzsche's. The young writer clearly knows about Nietzsche and his message: he may have read and partly understood him,[17] he may not have actually read him at all, but he is conscious where, and by whom, the walls of convention have recently been breached and what the weapons are with which to assault the parts left standing. This is unmistakably Nietzsche's influence, whether direct or diffused—the difference at this earliest stage is less important than the direction in which the young writer is influenced. And in this Heine himself, the subject of the article,

while Mann's argument asserts the pain his creative process still brings with it. See Nietzsche, *Vorrede* to *Genealogie der Moral*, § 7.

[16] Discoveries of borrowings from Nietzsche can be found everywhere in the literature on Thomas Mann. The early stories receive a sound first treatment in R. A. Nicholls, *Nietzsche in the Early Work of Thomas Mann*, Berkeley, 1955.

[17] To be in line with Nietzsche's rearrangement of moral terms, the pair of conventional concepts Mann is attacking should be 'gut und böse', not 'gut und schlecht'.

was clearly also a factor. It was most apt that Thomas Mann should use Nietzsche's weapons to defend Heine: Nietzsche was an admirer of Heine, who had anticipated him in more than just the matter of style. This affinity was clear to Thomas Mann, who points out that Heine too scorned conventional morality all his life. This is what made him the young enthusiast's hero— 'meinen Heine'. We know from later references what an established favourite Heine was of the young Mann[18] and the effect this must have had is plain: the scorn of convention here singled out, which squared so well with Nietzsche's aims, the disillusionment with everything Romantic as well as with the materialism of bourgeois society, and not least the merciless irony of Heine's style must all have left their mark.

Heine and Nietzsche, who thus belong together as influences[19] on the young Thomas Mann, very soon occur together again in a revealing way. In the story *Der Wille zum Glück* (1896), with its Nietzschean title, the narrator's friendship with the hero is grounded in their shared feeling that they are different from the rest of their school class: 'Es war das "Pathos der Distanz" dem grössten Teile unserer Mitschüler gegenüber, das jeder kennt, der mit fünfzehn Jahren heimlich Heine liest und in Tertia das Urteil über Welt und Menschen entschlossen fällt' (viii. 44). In a phrase of Nietzsche's, which formulates an attitude derived from reading Heine, the premature worldly wisdom and world-weariness of fifteen are summed up—from the full maturity of twenty-one. With fine double-bluff, the narrator ironizes his earlier claims to precisely the kind of precocious superiority on which his present narration rests.

Once more, it is not clear how direct the derivation from Nietzsche's phrase was. Mann's use of 'Pathos der Distanz', like the title of the story in which it occurs, is again not wholly in line with the meaning Nietzsche gave his concept.[20] For him it meant the confident feeling of superiority which strong, healthy,

---

[18] The *Lebensabriss* speaks of a 'Vergötterung Heine's um die Zeit, da ich meine ersten Gedichte schrieb' (xi. 108). Thomas Buddenbrook is given to quoting Heine —it is one of the things which set him apart from Lübeck business society. (Cf. i. 295, 380.) The foreword to *Bilse und ich* is dated 'München, am 50. Todestage Heinrich Heine's' (x. 11).

[19] Their effect is equated explicitly in the *Betrachtungen eines Unpolitischen* (xii. 88).

[20] In *Antichrist*, § 43. Mann acquired the volume containing this work in 1895, the year before *Der Wille zum Glück* was published.

'aristocratic' men might enjoy; whereas the two figures in *Der Wille zum Glück* are representatives of a 'spiritual', outsider type, set aside by sensitivity and complexity. The technique of quoting and alluding to Nietzsche was an element of modish cultural equipment—his star was in the ascendant at just this time—which helped to establish a sophisticated tone. Its use was more for prestige than precision.

Nevertheless, from 1895 on Mann was acquiring the new complete edition of Nietzsche's works and supplementing such knowledge of Nietzsche as he already had in a more systematic way.[21] From now on, Nietzsche was to dominate his work, providing both the detail of motifs and phrasing and the more fundamental modes of thinking. What Mann said in 1930—that in reading Nietzsche he took nothing literally (xi. 110)—is a product of the political climate of that time; Nietzsche's ideas had acquired associations it was necessary to place at arm's length. One must not be put off by it. It is clear that a number of Mann's problems came to him in the form Nietzsche had given them. He never questioned certain Nietzschean assumptions, like the link between genius and disease. And he did above all take quite literally the injunction, which Nietzsche preached so well by example, not to take anything for granted. The licensing of this attitude, already prepared by Heine, was more important than any specific doctrine in the formation of Mann's literary character, especially as it was imprinted at the formative age when 'human beings have an indubitable tendency to loosen their allegiance to all traditional rites and social norms of their culture, allowing conceptual thought to cast doubt on their value and to look around for new and perhaps more worthy ideals'.[22] The essence of Nietzsche which Mann took in may be summed up in Nietzsche's own description of his works as 'a constant and imperceptible exhortation

---

[21] The Naumann Grossoktavausgabe of Nietzsche began to appear in 1894. Mann's set is in TMA, some volumes with dates of acquisition (viii—1895; iv and v—1896). This publishing event may have intensified his interest. The first notebook entry quoting Nietzsche is datable as 1895, although it is a set of aphorisms from *Jenseits von Gut und Böse*, which did not appear in the GOA until 1899. Among these is § 108, which is the famous declaration that there are no moral phenomena, only moral interpretations of phenomena. Cf. H. Lehnert, *Thomas Mann, Fiktion, Mythos, Religion*, Stuttgart, 1965, pp. 25, 227 f.

[22] Konrad Lorenz, *On Aggression*, 1966, p. 230. Mann stated that he first read *Menschliches, Allzumenschliches* at the age of nineteen ('Geist und Kunst', N 19).

to reverse customary values and valued customs', as a 'school of suspicion and even more of contempt' inculcating 'mistrust of morality'.[23] Seen in this light, all things human deserved to be viewed ironically, as Nietzsche wrote later in the same work.[24]

The lesson that everything is to be questioned and regarded with suspicion necessarily affects statements even in fictional works. Characters, actions, attitudes, implied or expressed values—all will be treated critically, ironically, perhaps cynically. Psychological depths will be sought beneath simple surfaces. The means to perceive these was later summed up in a phrase Mann associated with Nietzsche, 'psychologische Reizbarkeit',[25] itself defined later still as 'the derivation of all good impulses from bad ones'.[26] And in 1897, just when Mann was no doubt reading the newly published volumes of the Grossoktav Nietzsche, *Morgenröte* (subtitled 'Thoughts on moral prejudices') and *Die fröhliche Wissenschaft*, he speaks in a notebook entry of a 'writer who is by birth and formation (*Bildung*) exclusively and fanatically a psychologist',[27] presumably with himself in mind.

Critical reservations about the value of the things which are literature's material suggest an ironical style as the means to treat them; the kind of sweeping negation Nietzsche encouraged points to a constant and implacable irony. If no positive ideal was yet available to contrast with the things irony negated, then it becomes clear how such a passage as the opening of *Friedemann* could come to be written. Even without the example of Heine's or Nietzsche's style, the attitudes they instilled are enough to explain the texture of the young Mann's writing. At the most general level, certain possibilities of realism and epic convention[28] are at once excluded. The imitative impulse in

[23] The first page of the *Vorrede* to *Menschliches, Allzumenschliches*.

[24] *Menschliches* 1, § 252 (Schlechta i. 602).

[25] In the *Lebensabriss* of 1930 (xi. 110), and at various points of the 'Geist und Kunst' notes. The word *Reizbarkeit* means both sensitivity and irritability. Both are clear in Detlev Spinell's letter to Herr Klöterjahn in *Tristan* (viii. 253): he cannot bear the dull unknowing world of life and action around him, with its infuriating *naïveté*, and is driven 'mit qualvoller Unwiderstehlichkeit' to elucidate, express, and bring it to the level of consciousness.

[26] In the manuscript notes for the 1947 Nietzsche essay. TMA Mp. ix. 199/2, fol. 5.

[27] Lehnert, *Fiktion*, p. 18. In retrospect Mann spoke of his early stories as 'leispsychologisches Präludieren' (xii. 89).

[28] I have in mind what Erich Auerbach (*Mimesis*, ch. 1) calls the 'basic impulse of the Homeric style: to represent phenomena in a fully externalized form, visible

realism, the celebrative impulse in epic both depend on the writer's ability to use a word for a thing, to describe an object or state a value, without doubts: to accept, that is, a full correspondence between the word and what it denotes. The word must be, so to speak, positively charged with what is felt and believed about the thing denoted. For the doubter, on the other hand, the word is negatively charged. He can only use it for want of a better means, as a label to identify things from which he must then dissociate himself. The results are recognizably of a kind and all occur in Mann's early stories: ironical paraphrase, pompous or cliché phrasing with implied quotation marks[29] (this is only 'what other people would say'), self-dissociating preambles, euphemisms, polysyllabic humour.[30] All are aimed at avoiding the embarrassment of the plain word, for which the writer will not take responsibility.

More specifically, at the moral level, the adopted attitude either excludes pity as a symptom of weakness (it was an emotion Nietzsche frequently warned against), or finds it simply incompatible with the task of registering whatever comes into view with detachment. Yet pity is clearly something for which the subject matter of all Thomas Mann's early stories gives ample cause. They are full of suffering human beings, yet the treatment these receive suggests that from him that hath not, something more shall be taken away. What is tragic may be presented as if it were comic. An early essay on Thomas Mann by Ernst Bertram compared his mode of narration with the equanimity of a café onlooker and suggested that this meant losing all criteria for distinguishing tragic from comic.[31] A

and palpable in all their parts, and completely fixed in their spatial and temporal relations'; what Schiller and Goethe, in *Über epische und dramatische Dichtung*, called the 'gewisse sinnliche Breite' of epic treatment; and also the relationship of harmony between the narrator and the phenomena of his culture which is apparent in the way the poet of, e.g., the *Nibelungenlied* dwells on the customs and practices of court and knightly life.

29 Cf. Baumgart, pp. 126 f., 'Sprechstil mit Anführungsstrichen'.

30 It is interesting to find a reviewer of Mann's earliest collection censuring the circuitous and formal phrasing—such things as 'ich erkläre mich bereit zu bekennen, dass', 'unterlasse ich nicht zu sagen, dass', 'in Bezug auf', and 'der-, die-, dasselbe'—as 'abscheuliche Schriftsprache'. This, he says, takes up one-fifth of the book and gets on the reader's nerves. *Bonner Zeitung*, 26 June 1898. All these crossings of the critical line into irony, taken seriously, can only seem clumsy.

31 'Das Problem des Verfalls', (1907) reprinted in *Dichtung als Zeugnis*, Bonn, 1967, p. 96.

passage of Nietzsche which caught Mann's attention reads like
a programme for this detached vision. It asks why one should
bother with the theatre when, by looking at everyday life with
a 'third' or 'theatre-eye', one can see much better-acted
tragedy and comedy, however hard to learn the viewing
technique may be:

*Das dritte Auge.*—Wie! du bedarfst noch des Theaters! Bist du noch
so jung? Werde klug und suche die Tragödie und Komödie dort, wo
sie besser gespielt wird! Wo es interessanter und interessierter
zugeht! Ja, es ist nicht ganz leicht, dabei eben nur Zuschauer zu
bleiben, — aber lerne es! Und fast in allen Lagen, die dir schwer und
peinlich fallen, hast du dann ein Pförtchen zur Freude und eine
Zuflucht, selbst noch, wenn deine eignen Leidenschaften über dich
herfallen. Mache dein Theater-Auge auf, das grosse dritte Auge,
welches durch die zwei anderen in die Welt schaut![32]

There could hardly be a clearer statement of the principle
Mann's early stories work on, even down to the difficulties of
remaining a mere spectator, of which much will later be heard
in *Tonio Kröger*.[33]

Even if derivative, Mann's method accorded well with the
literary standards of the 1890s—indeed, he may in part have
been responding to the pressure of this generalized influence.
Through it, the influences of many individual writers filtered
through, some of these confirmed by a direct acquaintance with
their works. Scandinavian and Russian literature were in the
ascendant, as Mann recalls in a retrospect on the literary scene
of his youth.[34] Behind Naturalism there stood, as well as Ibsen,
Tolstoy, and Dostoyevsky, the French influences, Flaubert and
Zola; behind Impressionism, with its analysis of extreme states,
Baudelaire. Analysis predominated in literature, either social or
psychological. While Impressionism dissected extreme states of

---

[32] *Morgenröte*, § 509. The passage is marked in Mann's copy with a cross, which
is common enough in this much-used volume, and with an exclamation-mark,
which is less common, and was probably reserved for particular agreement. Cf.
xii. 521, 'Ausrufungszeichen innigster Zustimmung'.

[33] Tonio Kröger's literary speciality was precisely the mixture of 'Komik und
Elend' (viii. 290), and even at the close of the story, when he has come successfully to terms with his deep-rooted feelings for the representatives of 'normal' life,
he still speaks of his future literary creations as 'tragische und lächerliche Gestalten
und solche, die beides zugleich sind,—und diesen bin ich sehr zugetan' (viii.
338).

[34] *Peter Altenberg*, x. 422 f

mind and feeling to the last nuance, Naturalism dissected the state of society. Neither shrank from extremes, so that indeed extremes began to appear requisite as the norm. One of the liveliest of fashion-makers (or fashion-followers), Hermann Bahr, a little later defined literary talent as the capacity to experience extreme sensations and to give them yet more extreme expression.[35] Thomas Mann quotes the definition in a letter to his brother Heinrich in 1905, and accepts it as true of both of them.[36]

Into such a literary scene it is not difficult to see how the style of the young Thomas Mann might fit, with its cool, detached exploitation of the pathetic, even pathological anecdote. But the conformity is only one more reason for looking closely at the stylistic precocity and show of nihilism, and for wondering whether they served the perhaps conscious purpose of swimming with the stream. The main reason for doubting their genuineness is not that youth and nihilism cannot go together—they do so convincingly in Georg Büchner, for example, who was dead by the age of twenty-four. Yet this comparison is at once felt as a contrast. Büchner's beliefs and attitudes were, we know, paid for in the hard coin of political and scientific experience, as well as wide philosophical reading; his style, especially in his last work, *Woyzeck*, has a firmness and austere purposefulness which is free from effect-seeking. In Mann's early stories, on the other hand, we can discern chinks in the ironic armour which suggest that what we are observing is the attempt to construct a style to match chosen attitudes.[37]

[35] Bahr was himself an early enthusiasm of Thomas Mann's, and Mann's prose piece *Vision* was dedicated to this 'artist of genius'. (Cf. also x. 423.) On Bahr as a literary barometer, see Br. i. 79. In the 1940 Princeton lecture 'On Myself' (*Blätter* 6, p. 11) Mann tells 'wie ich auf der Schule den wunderlichen Prosastil der von Hermann Bahr geführten Wiener Symbolistenschule . . . sklavisch-freudig genau kopierte und *eben darin* [his italics] eine künstlerische Genugtuung fand'.

[36] 'Wir müssen wohl beide, als Neurastheniker vielleicht, eine fatale Neigung zum Extrem haben — was aber auch wieder unsere Stärke sein mag. Bahr, noch immer vortrefflich, hat neulich das "Talent" ganz einfach als die Eigenschaft definiert, "extrem zu empfinden und dies noch extremer auszudrücken"' (Br. H. 35).
—Gottfried Benn, in his *Rede auf Heinrich Mann* of 1931 (the epigraph of which is 'Nihilismus ist ein Glücksgefühl'), said :'Da kamen um 1900 die Brüder Mann und [. . .] brachten die Kunst als die hohe geistige Korruption, was keiner fühlte, die erst zu erfindenden Verfeinerungen . . .' Benn, *Gesammelte Werke*, ed. Wellershoff, vol. i, pp. 411 f.

[37] How anxious Mann was both to be and to appear mature is suggested by the letter of May 1895 to Richard Dehmel asking for an opinion on his second story:

Here and there a sentence may slip through into the text which is worthy of popular fiction at a low level. The central character in *Der Tod* meditates on his past: 'Erinnerst du dich des anmutigen und flammend zärtlichen Geschöpfes unter dem Sammethimmel von Lissabon?' ('Do you remember the graceful and passionately tender creature beneath the velvet sky of Lisbon?' [viii. 71]). This is romantic *Kitsch*, a trap into which the writer has fallen as he labours to eradicate emotional elements from his style. Romantic novelette style of this sort will recur much later (at the end of *Felix Krull*, in Lisbon again!) but by that time it is being exploited as parody—one more way of using language without having to take responsibility for it.

Indeed, parody is so germane to the kind of indirect stylistic means catalogued above (p. 20) that one might well expect to find it at least in embryo in these early stories. *Der Wille zum Glück* offers an intriguing sample. When the narrator-character says to his friend Paolo, who is clearly in love with the young woman they have just visited, 'Und da oben dünkte es mich zuweilen, als trübe — geheime Sehnsucht deinen Blick' (viii. 50), the phrasing seems at first sight another piece of uneradicated romantic style—until one realizes that he is quoting from Heine's poem 'Unterwelt', § 5, and that the dash in Mann's text corresponds to the line-break in the poem. Thus emotion is stated poetically, but the extravagance of poetic speech is partly neutralized by the fact that speaker and listener both recognize the quotation (both, it has earlier been implied, are readers of Heine). The sophisticated indirectness of all this, though strictly the characters', implies similar claims for the author. In fact, the author may even have an edge on the characters in the matter: the following lines of the Heine stanza are:

> Ich kenn es wohl, dein Missgeschick:
> Verfehltes Leben, verfehlte Liebe!

The suggestion of an ill-fated love and a ruined life anticipate the later course of the story. The indirect technique of parody shades over into the allusive technique of quotation. As a final touch of appropriateness, the poem Mann is using is itself an object-lesson in parody, since section 3 of 'Unterwelt' is the

'Glauben Sie, dass "Walter Weiler" meinem Alter von 19 Jahren unangemessener ist, als "Gefallen"?' (Br. i. 6).

place where Heine takes over three stanzas of Schiller's 'Die Götter Griechenlands' into his text.

More revealing than these microsamples which show the young writer struggling to establish a sophisticated style is the whole structure of Mann's first published story, *Gefallen* (1894). A young medical student's love affair with an actress ends when he discovers he has an elderly, paying rival. The framework in which the story itself is inset draws a moral: she who falls today for love will fall tomorrow for money. It is perhaps not an immediately convincing moral, but it gives the story an appearance of being concerned with a social theme[38]—the problem of woman's social status had been 'literary' at least since Ibsen's *Doll's House* of 1879. But beneath this modish surface, the real subject is naïve feeling and its disillusionment, the process of becoming cynical. The two elements, sentiment and cynicism, remain strikingly distinct, which is why Mann could later refer correctly to his story as sentimental *and* cynical.[39] Sentiment dominates the inset narrated past, cynicism the framework narrator's present. Minor touches of humour and irony within the inset story do not substantially affect this division. The separation of the elements stands out all the more because the framework technique, so common in short narrative fiction in German, is not one which Mann later made much use of; also, more strikingly, because the narrator in the framework is described as an ironist whose every nonchalant gesture bespoke worldly experience and contempt for the world (viii. 11), and one would expect more of these qualities to show up in his narration.

The story is an account of his own first disillusionment with life. Its technique may well have derived from literary models so many nineteenth-century stories start from the after-dinner talk of experienced cigar-smoking men —Maupassant's, Turgenev's, later on Conrad's) but the pattern reveals much more than just derivativeness. The external framework, setting things at a distance, objectivizing, even ironizing, is needed to tone down the lyrical voice in which the love-experience is narrated. It may be that irony and cynicism are the only 'right'

---

[38] *Gefallen* was published in a Naturalist journal, M. G. Conrad's *Die Gesellschaft.*
[39] '. . . eine etwas zynische und etwas sentimentale Liebesgeschichte.' In *Geistiges und künstlerisches München in Selbstbiographien*, Munich, 1913, p. 231.

attitudes to life, and a necessary result of experience, but as yet this is known, not felt; it controls the structure of the story but not the texture of the writing. Emotion, compassion are there—as they are in the later reaches of *Der kleine Herr Friedemann*, before the cruel conclusion re-establishes a façade of hardness and mockery. A cool and detached mood encircling the retold events is all there is to negate the romantic content and to assure us of the conversion to wisdom of the original naïve warm-hearted youth: 'Wirklich, von dem "guten Kerl" war nichts mehr an ihm zu merken' reads the final comment, as the embittered Doctor Selten seizes a sprig of lilac (lilac scent having figured largely in his youthful romance) and brutally crushes it: a recrudescence of feeling and a touch of melodrama[40] which, as much as the sentiment of the inset story, belie the cynical attitude which is the story's subject and the author's implicit aim. Irony has not yet begun to seep through into the young Mann's *style*, conviction and expression have yet to become a unity.

By choosing never to republish *Gefallen* in any later collection of his stories, Mann stamped it as a mere *œuvre de jeunesse*. It is all there is to show us the beginnings of his art, aside from the impressionist sketch *Vision* and a handful of poems. Its rejection is as instructive as its structure.

At this point, comparisons with other writers are helpful. Flaubert's much longer process of self-disciplining, aided by a tendency not to throw away anything he had written, produced three stout volumes of *œuvres de jeunesse*. One of these at least, *Novembre* (1842), exemplifies the maturing process even more directly than Mann's *Gefallen*. It uses as a partial framework the old convention of a 'discovered manuscript'. The story is rounded off by someone who 'knew the author'—a device only slightly less awkward than the excuse which Mann's narrator makes for the fluency of his narrative: that he 'used to go in for that kind of thing' (viii. 14). Flaubert's commentator, by his superior remarks on the metaphors and hyperboles of the

---

[40] The title itself is a shade melodramatic. Richard Dehmel, who found Mann's first effort promising, suggested the title *Der Zyniker*, thus acutely seeing that disillusionment was the real subject—'Im Grunde ist auch der Mann gefallen'; yet he also praised the presentation of 'ein Erlebnis in einfacher, seelenvoller Prosa', which again points up the story's disunity. See Richard Dehmel, *Dichtungen, Briefe, Dokumente*, Hamburg, 1963, pp. 169 f.

manuscript and on the inferior writers whose influence they reveal, and further by the suggestion that the work was cut short just when it was on the point of becoming better, dissociates the twenty-one-year-old Flaubert from the faults of his work.[41] The closing section and the work's subtitle 'Fragments de style quelconque' are an attempt to anticipate and disarm attack: the failure to achieve a mature style is to be compensated by the author's own criticism of his immature style. Clearly, Flaubert too was acting on a sense of what would and would not now pass muster as literature. Romantic methods were impossible, subjectivity a literary white elephant. As he wrote later:[42] '*La personnalité sentimentale* sera ce qui plus tard fera passer pour puérile et un peu niaise une bonne partie de la littérature contemporaine.'

This typical dilemma of the young writer is in varying degrees aesthetic—the need to remove or mask subjectivity; and ethical—the desire to deny (or to appear to deny) current values. We find Tolstoy too, in his contriter days, confessing of his early years: 'How many times I cunningly tried to hide in my writings, under the guise of indifference and even light-hearted mockery, those inclinations of mine towards the Good which made the very meaning of my life. And I succeeded: people praised me.'[43] In Thomas Mann's case, we have seen a negative attitude to accepted values forming a literary manner —precociously, but not so fully as to hide all trace of the original 'guter Kerl'; Tonio Kröger, later, admits that he was flattered when critics wrote that he hated or scorned life, but says that it is not true (viii. 302); and we have noted a literary scene which probably contributed a good deal to this formation. The elements are found together in a story whose title and content are almost a programme for Mann's early work: *Enttäuschung* (Disillusion) of 1896.

---

[41] '... si quelqu'un, ayant passé, pour arriver jusqu'à cette page, à travers toutes les métaphores, hyperboles et autres figures qui remplissent les précédentes, désire y trouver une fin, qu'il continue; nous allons la lui donner.' 'J'admire le hasard, qui a voulu que le livre en demeurât là, au moment où il serait devenu meilleur ...' 'Dans sa première jeunesse, il s'était nourri de très mauvais auteurs, comme on l'a pu voir à son style ...' *Œuvres de jeunesse*, Paris, 1910, ii. 243 f.

[42] Letter to Louise Colet of 22 Apr. 1854, *Correspondance*, iv. 61 f. Quoted in Enid Starkie, *Flaubert, the Making of the Master*, 1967, p. 340. See in general her final chapter, 'Flaubert's aesthetic doctrine'.

[43] *Confession*, in *Sobranie sochinenii*, vol. 16, Moscow, 1964, pp. 98 f.

Once again the theme is the process of becoming disillusioned. The young narrator, on a first visit to Venice, meets a man of experience who plaintively tells how 'experience' has always failed to live up to his expectations. He grew up as a small-town pastor's son, in an atmosphere of optimism and pulpit rhetoric, of 'big words' like Good and Evil, Beautiful and Ugly—words which he now hates bitterly, because they are at the root of his sufferings: he has never found anything that corresponded to their early intimations. To every event, his reaction has been: Is that all? No worse—no better?[44] His yearning for 'real' experience has been left unstilled. Even the experience of death, he finally predicts, will be no more impressive. He blames above all the poets whose overstatements inculcate belief in great things—'diese Dichter, die ihre grossen Wörter an alle Wände schreiben und sie mit einer in den Vesuv getauchten Zeder am liebsten an die Himmelsdecke malen möchten' (viii. 65). Nietzsche is discernible again, with his criticism of the naïve language–reality equation[45] and his remark on the way poets have always falsified reality.[46] The 'big words' the stranger rejects are the ones Thomas Mann rejected on Nietzsche's authority in *Heinrich Heine der 'Gute'*, and the stranger's background is deliberately made identical with Nietzsche's. Heine too is close at hand again, though this time as an example of the grand poetic gesture.[47]

Once again, there is some significance in the structure, this time a partial framework. The young narrator begins by confessing that the stranger's words completely confused him; he can only try to reproduce them so as to render the same effect. The responsibility for a disenchanted view of life thus rests, appropriately, on the stranger and his experience as a mature man (the narrator is not sure whether to put his age at thirty or fifty). The young man himself, in his introductory setting of the

[44] Cf. the shoulder-shrugging 'Besser nicht?' with which the cynical story-teller in *Gefallen* receives 'dies von der betreffenden Regie dort oben wenig umsichtig inszenierte Erdenleben' (viii. 12).

[45] Cf. *Menschliches, Allzumenschliches*, I, § 11 on 'Die Sprache als vermeintliche Wissenschaft' (Schlechta i. 453).

[46] Ibid., *Vorrede*, § 1: '. . . zurechtfälschen, zurechtdichten . . . (und was haben Dichter je anderes getan? und wozu wäre alle Kunst in der Welt da?)' (Schlechta i. 437).

[47] Cf. Heine's poem 'Erklärung' (*Buch der Lieder*, 'Nordsee' i. vi) which speaks of dipping a pine tree into Etna and writing with it 'an die dunkle Himmelsdecke'.

scene, seems untouched by disenchantment—the Piazza San Marco in Venice[48] is described in unequivocally poetic manner (viii. 62). Yet this framework, such as it is, is left unclosed: the narrator does not return with a comment or conclusion, the story ends on the stranger's last words. Is his younger hearer still too confused to comment further? Is he leaving the account to speak for itself? He certainly lets pass the opportunity to question the stranger's philosophy. Is he perhaps convinced by it? And is the whole narrative simply a device for putting forward the philosophy of disenchantment? If it is, then the method chosen is telling: the uncertain relationship of narrator and central speaker catches something of the situation behind these early stories, the taking over *en bloc* of a philosophy which by its nature should require a longer and harder novitiate.[49]

But on one point the stranger voices his complaint in a form which seems inappropriate to him and more like the view of the youthful narrator (or author) who is still waiting for experience rather than disillusioned with it. Instead of stating in straight negative terms that language is inaccurate, inflated, hollow, the disenchanted speaker appears to elevate it into a kind of self-sufficiency over against reality and all its disappointments. Contrary to what the poets have said about language—that it is too limited to encompass life—it is life that is poor and limited, language that is abundantly rich. 'Die Sprache, dünkt mich, ist reich, ist überschwenglich reich im Vergleich mit der Dürftigkeit und Begrenztheit des Lebens' (viii. 66). Even if these riches are deceptive and a lie, they are riches. This is an oddly positive way of seeing them (and not at all a Nietzschean way). It might well be the view of one who had early slipped into the shell of a blasé Nietzscheanism which queried the realities behind language, but was aware of his own facility in the use of language; whose scepticism about language concerned the

---

[48] The Venice setting is probably another Nietzsche allusion, unlike the setting for *Der Tod in Venedig* (*pace* Nicholls, p. 14) for which the reasons are quite different, and the choice only accidentally allusive.

[49] It is worth quoting Heinrich Mann's apt account of a similar process in himself: under the influence of a favourite author (Heine once more) 'der junge Mensch glaubt alles schon geschehen und vollbracht, er sieht nicht weiter. Er ist Inhaber des Zweifels, Witzes, Schmerzes seines Toten und nimmt nicht an, ihm bleibe noch zu lernen'. But his first real experience teaches him 'dass er vom Schmerz, ja vom ganzen Leben nur erst kostenlose Proben vorweggenommen hat'. Heinrich Mann, *Sieben Jahre*, Berlin 1929, pp. 278 f.

absolute value of its concepts, but not the possibility of using it constructively. Unlike his major contemporaries, Thomas Mann seems never to have gone through a phase, such as Rilke records in *Die Aufzeichnungen des Malte Laurids Brigge* and Hofmannsthal in *Ein Brief*, in which language as an instrument becomes unusable because of the gulf which opens between it and a radically new kind of reality. Without any such crisis, he was able to draw the less obvious of two possible conclusions from the knowledge that language and reality cannot be equated: not that language must be abandoned, or recreated on the model of some new reality, but that it can maintain—by a variety of expedients—its own ordered world. This is the technical basis of Mann's life-work.

The point at which Thomas Mann drew this un-Nietzschean conclusion from Nietzsche's criticism of language can be plotted with some accuracy. In § 257 of *Morgenröte*[50] Nietzsche states, as part of his recurrent argument on the inherent dangers and limitations of language, that we are dependent on words for the very thoughts we think. We express our thoughts only in those words we already have available—or rather we *only think* those thoughts for which we already have words: '*Worte in uns gegenwärtig.* — Wir drücken unsere Gedanken immer mit den Worten aus, die uns zur Hand sind. Oder um meinen ganzen Verdacht auszudrücken: wir haben in jedem Momente eben nur den Gedanken, für welchen uns die Worte zur Hand sind, die ihn ungefähr auszudrücken vermögen.' Thomas Mann's comment is 'die ihn *schön* auszudrücken vermögen'. He adds it to Nietzsche's paragraph, changing the final full stop into a comma, which indicates that he believes he is extending Nietzsche's statement, or at most correcting his 'ungefähr'. In reality, he is taking Nietzsche's deeply negative view of language and giving it both a positive and an aesthetic turn. It is literary expression he has in mind, as a further comment in the margin against § 257 indicates: 'Beim Gespräch ist es jedenfalls so. Vielleicht aber auch beim *Schreiben*? Und grade beim *gut* Schreiben?'

If we follow Thomas Mann and transfer Nietzsche's thought to the aesthetic plane, it becomes: We express our thoughts only in such fine literary formulation as we have available; or

---

[50] Which, it will be remembered, Mann acquired and was almost certainly reading with intense interest in 1896. Mann's annotation is in an early hand.

rather, we only have such thoughts as we can express in a fine literary formulation. In other words, it is language that dominates in writing, rather than the task it sets out to do or the objects it has to describe. And Mann appears to be simply grasping rather than criticizing the nature of 'good writing'. His comments thus imply that the idea of realism (which is an attempt at moulding language to external reality) has been abandoned, and the limitations of a subjectively determined literary language have been accepted.

This generalization anticipates later developments in Thomas Mann's art. But we can start by relating the idea of the self-sufficient richness of language to the early stories and their already striking 'maturity' and mastery of style. In so far as the maturity is a matter of attitudes, we have already seen some of its components, but there remains the accomplishment which is linked with them, the sheer linguistic virtuosity which so many critics, contemporary and subsequent, have noted.[51] Once again, it is necessary to put ourselves back in the young Mann's situation.

In the lecture 'On Myself' which he gave in Princeton in 1940, Thomas Mann recalled some of his childhood compositions for the puppet-theatre he played with. He describes them as childish nonsense, formal exercises of a play urge which precedes experience and feeling and has to cast about for content:

kindischer, abenteuerlicher Unsinn, dessen Erfindung mit Erlebnis, mit Gefühl nicht das Geringste zu tun hatte. Der reine formale Spieltrieb ist früher da als Erlebnis und Gefühl, zunächst ganz inhaltlos, greift er nach irgendwo entlehnten Scheingehalten, bevor ein wirklicher Lebens- und Erfahrungsgehalt ihm zur Verfügung steht.[52]

The second half of this account is a general proposition, and it is tempting to appropriate it for at least some of the early stories. They are exercises in writing up, with poise and effect, material which has the thinness and implausibility of the

---

[51] The more acute have connected it with the aim and substance of Mann's later work: 'die sinnträchtige konturvolle Kurve des durch und durch gemeisterten Satzes' and 'die sich selbst geniessende und in ihrer All-Macht alle Stoffe und Motive ständig mehr zum blossen Anlass machende Sprache'. Hans Hennecke, 'Der vollkommen gemeisterte Satz', in Hennecke, *Kritik*, Gütersloh, 1958, pp. 151, 158.

[52] *Blätter der Thomas-Mann-Gesellschaft*, 6, p. 10. Quoted henceforth as *Blätter*.

merely anecdotal. In *Gefallen*, for instance, not only the social moral is implausible, so too is the ultimate betrayal of young love after the way the affair has been described. The twist at the end of the story produces the shock not of a surprise denouement, as is no doubt intended, but of fictional inconsistency or arbitrariness.[53] Lacking experience to back his doctrine of disenchantment, the young author has had to construct—in part no doubt from the second-hand experience of literature[54]—an anecdote which will point the desired conclusion. (Where Mann really seems at home, significantly, is in the comic confrontation of the young with the old lover, which gives full scope to his satirical pen.)

A similar impression of the anecdotal and slightly implausible comes out elsewhere. The young artist in *Der Wille zum Glück* has a weak heart and so the parents of the girl he loves will not allow a marriage, even though they esteem him. Years later, the girl's constancy makes them relent; but the young man, who has almost miraculously stayed alive all this time, dies after the wedding-night—not from any physical strain, but from subtle psychological causes: having achieved what he so long desired, he has no further pretext for living. 'Er musste sterben, ohne Kampf und Widerstand sterben, als seinem Willen zum Glück Genüge geschehen war; er hatte keinen Vorwand mehr, zu leben' (viii. 61). This, surely, is melodrama, the striking denouement, the *nouveau frisson* at the expense of verisimilitude. It is typical of the anecdote, which makes the reader say 'Fancy that!', not 'Yes, that's how it really is'. Anecdote can of course become something more by the power of the writing and by the sheer elaboration of convincing detail. The classic example of this would be Kleist, none of whose stories is different in kind from the mere striking anecdotes which he published in his *Berliner Abendblätter*. But the anecdotes which he chose to work up into stories are, against all the odds, developed into compelling visions of real life by a kind of realistic brinkmanship.

In Mann's early stories, on the other hand, the working out tends to reinforce the purely sensational and anecdotal features.

---

[53] It is possible to demand that even surprise be convincing. Cf. E. M. Forster, *Aspects of the Novel*, p. 75.

[54] For the details of Mann's borrowings from Turgenev, cf. my article 'Mann and Turgenev—A First Love', *GLL*, July 1964.

The detached ironic style points up the melodramatic and the abnormal. We are made to look on at a striking but somewhat unlikely event from a distance,[55] not (as in the case of Kleist) put on terms of intimate understanding with it. For example, *Luischen* (written 1896) is the story of an unfaithful wife who makes her docile and doting but ridiculously fat husband perform a song-and-dance act at her concert, dressed up as a fast young 'girl of the people'. The first inkling that his wife is unfaithful dawns on him as he performs, to the piano accompaniment of his wife's lover. He falls dead on the spot. The poor man's sufferings are recounted with elaborate irony,[56] and this ironic aplomb is itself a kind of challenge to the reader to question the truth of the grotesquely incredible anecdote. Even characters within the story are shocked and incredulous at the grotesqueness of Amra's plan.

The story's opening thus takes on a heavy task—that of disarming the reader's disbelief. It tells us that there are marriages which the most practised literary imagination cannot conceive of, and which one must accept as one accepts the unlikely preconditions for a farce in the theatre:

Es gibt Ehen, deren Entstehung die belletristisch geübteste Phantasie sich nicht vorzustellen vermag. Man muss sie hinnehmen, wie man im Theater die abenteuerlichen Verbindungen von Gegensätzen wie Alt und Stupide mit Schön und Lebhaft hinnimmt, die als Voraussetzung gegeben sind und die Grundlage für den mathematischen Aufbau einer Posse bilden. (viii. 168)

This sentence is well worth lingering over as an embodiment of the young writer's situation, reactions, and resources. By a complex double-bluff, it tries to command belief in a fiction by stating that it is a reality which might well not be credible in a fiction. To cap it all, the marriage described in Mann's tale is itself a literary derivative. Turgenev's *Torrents of Spring*, which

---

[55] This is in large measure effected by the technique of what Percy Lubbock in *The Craft of Fiction* calls 'pictorial' as opposed to 'scenic' narration. His remarks on the possible drawbacks of this method (see esp. ch. 7) are very relevant to these stories. See below, p. 54.

[56] E.g. 'Auch ist es an der Zeit, dass ich mich der Wahrheit entlaste, die ich bislang zurückhielt, der Wahrheit nämlich, dass sie ihren Gatten dennoch täuschte, dass sie ihn, sage ich, betrog, und zwar mit einem Herrn namens Alfred Läutner'; or again: 'Nun war, um jedes Herz zu erfreuen, der Frühling ins Land gezogen, und Amra hatte einen allerliebsten Einfall gehabt' (viii. 172, 174).

Mann had been reading not long before he wrote *Luischen*,[57] contains an almost identical pair, the ridiculously fat Polozov and his wife, who feels free to amuse herself with other men. Mann refers to just this detail in a later essay, in terms which link it with his own literary effects. He speaks of the 'elende Komik des Gatten Polosow' (ix. 248), thereby echoing Tonio Kröger's formula 'Komik und Elend'.

Thus, in *Luischen*, Thomas Mann puts before us a story too grotesque to be easily accepted, dependent for its central motif on a literary borrowing, demands that this be taken as true because it is too improbable even for literature, and carries the whole thing off with urbane irony. Gaily ignoring any incredulity the reader may hang on to, the writer pursues his course as resolutely as his 'heroine' pursues hers, and exercises his style on the perverse theme.

We are close here to Bahr's definition of talent—the extreme case recounted in a yet more extreme manner—and thus to *fin de siècle* decadence. In the eleven stories Mann had written by 1900, death, the most extreme and potentially melodramatic ending, and the one which can be used to stop a story short with most conclusive impact, is used in six. (The victims are four men, one child, and a dog.) This has more to do with a literary technique and its limitations than with metaphysics. *Luischen* again is the classic example. At the close, a little Jewish doctor examines the recumbent husband, and to the circle of gentlemen who surround him he says the last word of the story: 'Aus'.[58]

Like this over-use of death as a curtain-line, the constant appearance of savagery and blasé sophistication in stories of suffering like *Luischen*, *Tobias Mindernickel*, and *Der Weg zum Friedhof* is perhaps also as much technique as rooted cynicism. Where the author's fierceness, which we might expect to see turned on events themselves, recoils on their already unhappy victims, it is only in part from a reluctance to show pity and humane feeling, which were among the values we have seen undermined.[59] It is also a matter of a highly developed stylistic

[57] Cf. to Ivan Shmelyov, 4 Jan. 1931 (Br. i. 302).
[58] Cf. the close of Hauptmann's *Hanneles Himmelfahrt* (1893):
    SCHWESTER MARTHA (fragt): Tot?
    DER DOKTOR (nickt trübe): Tot.
[59] Thomas Mann reports to Paul Ehrenberg (postcard of 29 Sept. 1903) on a performance of *The Magic Flute*, whose eighteenth-century values he finds

facility having too little experience to bite on—'experience'
understood technically as a component in the relationship
between form and substance, not just biographically as a
guarantee of 'sincerity'. Lack of experience and its materials
is thus, paradoxically, the root of the 'sophisticated' irony
which is directed at all targets. This is not so much an expert
use of the writer's armoury, but rather the tendency of the raw
recruit to fire at anything that moves. As Mann realized when
he looked back at some of his early pieces in 1910, maturity is
not what they indicate.[60]

Elements of *Luischen* have been referred to above as grotesque.
They can be matched by elements in other stories of this phase,
and our picture of Mann's early fiction can be restated from a
different angle with the help of the concept of the Grotesque.[61]
This is of course not a pejorative term, but a means of defining
the nature of the early stories more closely. Some later thoughts
of Mann's on the subject are very relevant (they occur in the
*Betrachtungen eines Unpolitischen*). Writing there of satire, he
argues that it runs the risk of degenerating into mere mischievous
libel and gross exaggeration if it ignores realities. All art, he
says, is compounded of passivity, (the 'humbly receptive and
reproductive manner of Impressionism'), and activity, (the
'sovereign, explosive, ruthlessly creative outpouring of the
spirit'). Neither is tolerable in entire isolation. Mann's argument states extremes between which he implies a sliding scale:
at the 'passive' extreme are impression, Impressionism, re-
ceptivity to Nature, Realism, Tolstoy; at the 'active' extreme
are expression, Expressionism, the urge towards and the phenomenon of the Grotesque, Dostoyevsky. He then continues:

Lassen wir aber gelten, dass der expressionistischen Kunsttendenz

touching but irretrievably outmoded: 'Rührend, dieser Geist milder und froher
Humanität, der aus Musik und Handlung spricht! "Tugend", "Pflicht", "Aufklärung","Liebe","Menschlichkeit" — die lieben Leute glaubten noch daran! Heute
ist all das angefressen und zernagt . . .' Significantly, on the same card he warns
Ehrenberg against reading Nietzsche. Quoted in Wysling, *Studien*, p. 30.

[60] In a letter of 1910 to Ernst Bertram (Br. B. 8) who was planning a critical
piece on Mann: 'Dass ich frühreif war, werden Sie mir nicht nachsagen. Noch
Äusserungen, die bedeutend später liegen als *Gefallen*, erbringen den Gegenbeweis.'
[61] Wolfgang Kayser's *Das Groteske. Seine Gestaltung in Malerei und Dichtung*, Oldenburg, 1961, gives interesting leads, but discusses Thomas Mann surprisingly little.
Kayser ignores the very early stories, barely hinting (p. 170) at the applicability to
them of Mann's definition of the Grotesque which he quotes.

ein geistigerer Impetus zur Vergewaltigung des Lebens innewohne, so wird man doch der 'Freiheit der Kunst', die hier in Rede steht, gewisse Grenzen ziehen müssen, — sie wird sie sich selber ziehen müssen. Das Groteske ist das Überwahre und überaus Wirkliche, nicht das Willkürliche, Falsche, Widerwirkliche und Absurde. Einen Künstler, der jede Verantwortlichkeit vor dem Leben leugnete; der den Abscheu gegen die Impression so weit triebe, dass er sich jeder Verpflichtung gegen die Lebensformen des Wirklichen praktisch entschlüge und nur die herrischen Emanationen irgendeines absoluten Kunstdämons gelten liesse: einen solchen Künstler dürfte man den grössten aller radikalen Narren nennen.

(But if we allow that the expressionist artistic tendency has in it a more spiritual impetus towards the violation of life, we must surely draw certain limits to the 'freedom of art' which is at issue—it will have to draw them itself. The grotesque is properly something more than the truth (*das Überwahre*), something real in the extreme (*das überaus Wirkliche*), not something arbitrary, false, absurd, and contrary to reality. An artist who rejected all responsibility *vis-à-vis* life, and who went so far in his rejection of impressions as practically to cast off every obligation towards the forms of life as it is, and only allowed the imperious emanations of some absolute art-demon: such an artist would surely be the greatest of all radical fools. [xii. 564 f.])

In context, this is part of Thomas Mann's attack on the social satire of his brother Heinrich and the pro-*Entente* camp in Germany during the war of 1914. It is their picture of Germany which he suggests has lost touch with reality and distorted the truth.[62] But outside the polemical context, it is an interesting theory of balance and imbalance in art and of the Grotesque as one result of imbalance. If we apply the idea of a sliding scale to Thomas Mann's early stories, where do they stand on it? How far is the play of mind and language governed by external realities? How far does creation arise from the mimetic urge, how far purely from the more or less arbitrary expressive urge? Certainly, there is a good deal of sharp observation, but it is hard to call it 'humbly receptive and reproductive' in intention or effect. Rather, the isolated detail Mann picks out usually underlines the narrator's detachment, or gives a caricatural sketch of his characters. A ridiculous or pitiable

---

[62] We might now judge that Heinrich Mann's *Der Untertan*, the classic satire on Wilhelmine opportunism and conformism, ideally fulfilled Thomas Mann's positive conception and gave 'das Überwahre und überaus Wirkliche'.

feature is put under a spotlight—the moisture in the corner of the mouth which Friedemann's sister always has, or her way of shaking when she speaks. This marked tendency to caricature —the visual equivalent of which is the *Bilderbuch für artige Kinder*, with its horrific visions of 'Mutter Natur' and 'das Läben'[63]—could well be described as the 'imperious emanation of some absolute art-demon'. But where Mann's wartime diatribe blames an artist who ignores all obligations to reality, one may say of his own early stories more simply that they are the work of a writer who has not yet acquired such obligations; of one who, imbued with 'modern' ideas and modern literature, but lacking an abundance of first-hand material, has produced glittering but brittle samples of virtuosity. In so far as Mann's apparent savagery of portrayal is a matter of stylistic facility and the tendency of language towards self-sufficient complexity and over-elaboration, its analogies are not with realism or social satire, but with other modern exponents of the Grotesque whose creations are generated by language itself—Christian Morgenstern, for example.[64] The difference is considerable, but is one of degree only. If some essential truth is also stated, it concerns not the external world but the writer's disharmonious relations with it. It should be evident that, in Mann's own terminology, Expression outweighs Impression in these early stories. The label 'realism' will not do at all. Mann's preciseness of observation is only a diversion—in both senses of the word.

[63] This was a book of drawings and literary parodies which Heinrich and Thomas Mann compiled while they were staying in Italy as a present for their sister Carla's confirmation. It was lost in 1933, but samples are reproduced in Arthur Eloesser's 1925 biography of Thomas Mann. Mann's period working for *Simplicissimus* may well have encouraged his penchant for caricature: he saw the connection between his *Bilderbuch* and the *Simplicissimus* style himself (xi. 105 f.); and we now know that at least Herr Permaneder's character was built up around an illustration from *Simplicissimus*. See Paul Scherrer, 'Bruchstücke der Buddenbrooks-Urhandschrift und Zeugnisse zu ihrer Entstehung 1897—1901', *Neue Rundschau* 69 (1958), 287 f.

[64] Kayser, pp. 163 f., discusses the growth of Morgenstern's fantastic figures from language-play. Such independence of reality is an extreme case, but Kayser's phrase 'das Wildwuchernde spracheigener Prinzipien' (p. 222) might be taken as a key to understanding Mann's 'descriptive' language.

# The Making of a Novelist

... fürchten Sie die wachsende Vertraulichkeit mit der Ironie, dann wenden Sie sich an grosse und ernste Gegenstände, vor denen sie klein und hilflos sein wird.

RILKE, *Briefe an einen jungen Dichter*[1]

## I

*Buddenbrooks*, Thomas Mann's only conventional novel, belongs very obviously to the traditions of nineteenth-century realism and draws on its predecessors for inspiration and in details of technique. It is also governed, beneath the realistic surface, by ideas derived from a nineteenth-century speculative tradition; the nature and degree of realism the novel achieves can only be understood when the role these ideas play is clear. In addition, this first novel is related to Mann's heritage of tradition because it is an amazingly complete and sudden solution of the problems which were created for him by his literary and intellectual background, as sketched in the last chapter.

The solution is not a permanent one, but it does become a permanent point of reference in Mann's later work and all his thinking about his art. It lies in the way a balance was for the first time struck between the young writer's stylistic means and a substantial subject to extend them. This balance can in turn be explained by the nature of the realistic approach in general and by the particular possibilities for applying it which were open to Thomas Mann.

*Buddenbrooks* comes closest of all Mann's works to fulfilling the basic realist aim of rendering a recognizable reality. Its techniques are 'receptive and reproductive' to an extent unknown in the preceding stories. In place of the caricaturally sharp observation of detail, ungoverned by any commitment to a consistent large picture and hence essentially piecemeal in

[1] 'If you are afraid of a growing intimacy with irony, turn to great and serious subjects before which irony will be small and helpless.'

effect, there is now a sustained attempt to grasp the totality of a place, a historical span, a group of people, and an ethos. The precondition for this, as for all true realism, was a full and embracing knowledge of the particular reality to be rendered. From at least the time of the Goncourt brothers and Flaubert onwards, writers had met this demand by preliminary study and documentation. The only alternative was for the writer to write only about worlds he already knew intimately, which is clearly a severe limitation. One may write, say, an *Éducation sentimentale* without laboriously accumulating materials, but not a *Salammbô*.

Yet the documenting process has its own limitations and leaves problems to be solved. For the purposes of literary creation, there are different qualities of knowledge. Intensive study and extensive documentation may not produce the same result as intimate familiarity. Such a distinction, between 'two kinds of knowing', has been suggestively drawn apropos Tolstoy. In *War and Peace*, it has been argued, 'things are as he says they are, not because he has found out about them, but because he has drawn instinctively upon his matured awareness, that vast and privileged awareness which his family and position, as well as his own being, had conferred upon him. Knowing in *Resurrection* is by contrast a process of accretion . . .'[2] The distinction is relevant to Thomas Mann because so much of his later work rests on just such a process of accretion, by which the novelist attempts to make himself into an initiate, 'zum Eingeweihten der liebend ergriffenen Welt'. These words are spoken by Goethe in *Lotte in Weimar* (ii. 662) in a passage which, between the lines, tries to suggest the legitimacy of Mann's own montage technique by assimilating it to Goethe's artistic processes.

In writing *Buddenbrooks*, on the other hand, Thomas Mann was able to combine both possible means to realism, the more mechanical supplementing the more intuitive. If he had an intimate familiarity with the Lübeck in which he had grown up —with its topography and even more important its ethos—he also took full advantage of a direct access to the city's past, from its most general character and mood right down to its most minute detail, through the older members of his family.

[2] John Bayley, *Tolstoy and the Novel*, 1966, p. 250.

The extant documentation for *Buddenbrooks*[3] is not great in bulk, certainly not if we compare the masses of preliminary material accumulated later for the Joseph tetralogy or *Doktor Faustus*; it did not need to be. But it does show us how Thomas Mann pursued solidity and precise knowledge at a variety of levels.

There are notes on historical background never used or at most referred to in passing—the attempts on the life of Louis-Philippe in 1835, the title eventually bestowed upon Lola Montez, the 1848 risings in Berlin and Vienna; there are details provided by a legal expert on the conditions for the restitution of a dowry in the event of divorce (used in connection with Tony Buddenbrook's second divorce). Most intriguing of all are Thomas Mann's lists of points 'to be asked about': the mood in Lübeck before 1871; the change-over date from the old to the new currency; corn prices; Lübeck's external policies and relations with the *Zollverein* from 1830 to 1870; the causes of the decline in Lübeck's trade between 1860 and 1875; where the *Bürgerschaft* met; how elections to the Senate worked; when the various local railway lines were opened; the shape of maids' caps; the street lighting; the old goldsmiths' booths; the organization of classes at the Katharinäum; and many others.

To these queries, 'Uncle' Wilhelm Marty sent detailed replies in a long typescript on paper atmospherically headed 'Vice-consulado de Portugal em Lübeck'. The inquiry about corn prices had clearly been angled towards the Pöppenrade episode, since the reply states that the buying of crops before they were harvested was not a normal practice. After conscientious and detailed answers to the many questions on points of fact, Wilhelm Marty goes at some length into the special matter of the decline of a Lübeck corn firm. He explains how serious sudden losses can follow from the bankruptcy of an associated firm and the loss of confidence resulting. But many factors are involved, he says, in a process of gradual decline before some particular circumstance leads to final catastrophe.

It is evident in the novel how useful such informed accounts were. They served to give the writer a firm grasp on the detail of his subject, to back up his feeling for the organism of Lübeck

[3] TMA Mp. xi. 13 Mat. Individual sheets are not numbered.

life. In this they were analogous in function to those careful
tables and schemas in which Mann established the characters'
respective ages in a given year, or kept track of the sequence
of their activities over a number of years, or calculated the
sums of money involved in family transactions, thus securing
the novel's inner consistency. (The notorious time- and age-
discrepancies in Tolstoy's novels show the risks the large-scale
novel is open to.)

It does not matter particularly whether every snippet of
acquired information was then used in the text. One can point
to many places where detailed information is used,[4] but
paradoxically, the more confident the writer's grasp of his subject, the less he will feel compelled to prove it by a display of
knowledge. Fontane once asked his friend Friedlænder for
some names from the Riesengebirge as local colour for a ballad
he wished to write, but did not then include them in his poem.
Still, he claimed, they *were* used, in a sense—the essential thing
had been the awareness of having a firm basis of knowledge:
'es spukt nur hinter der Szene'.[5] It is, indeed, a further difference
between the 'two kinds of knowing', that in the later novels of
Thomas Mann—*Doktor Faustus*, or especially *Der Erwählte*—
every detail acquired is exploited in the text, almost thrust
under the reader's nose, because of a compulsion which was
partly economic. And this display of detail risks having a self-
sufficiency, a lack of integration into the course of the narrative,
a merely decorative imposingness, which make it appear
wooden. By contrast, in *Buddenbrooks* the factual details about
Lübeck life are keyed into the narrative with great deftness;
the narrative imagination absorbs and moulds them to its
purposes.

Take, for example, the street lighting of old Lübeck, about
which Thomas Mann requested information. It is first noticed
when Tony Buddenbrook returns from the Schwarzkopfs
(Book 3, chapter 13). It is there simply 'die über die Strasse
gespannten Öllampen' (i. 157). But in Book 4, chapter 3, the
street lighting takes on a vital role in Lübeck's 1848 rising.

---

[4] e.g. historical allusions very plausibly in Thomas Buddenbrook's morning
conversations with the barber, Book 6, ch. 7.
[5] Quoted in Wolfdietrich Rasch, *Zur deutschen Literatur seit der Jahrhundertwende*,
Stuttgart, 1967, p. 86.

The gentlemen of the *Bürgerschaft* are besieged in their meeting-room by 'the People'. From the preceding chapter we know that the Konsulin is worried about her husband's venturing out into the revolutionary streets—what time will he be back? It gets later and later, as we are reminded by unobtrusive touches, while the situation stays unchanged. At last the Konsul goes out to address the crowd, accompanied by Makler Gosch, who anticipates Schillerian high drama in the confrontation. The People are not as savage as expected, some are sitting on the kerb eating sandwiches—another gentle reminder how late it is getting. Indeed, it is nearly six:

Es war bald sechs Uhr, und obgleich die Dämmerung weit vorgeschritten war, hingen die Öllampen unangezündet an ihren Ketten über der Strasse. Diese Tatsache, diese offenbare und unerhörte Unterbrechung der Ordnung, war das erste, was den Konsul Buddenbrook aufrichtig erzürnte, und sie war schuld daran, dass er in ziemlich kurzem und ärgerlichem Tone zu sprechen begann: 'Lüd, wat is dat nu bloss für dumm Tüg, wat ji da anstellt!'

(It was nearly six, and although dusk was well advanced, the oil-lamps hung unlit on their chains across the street. This fact, this evident and unprecedented interruption of order, was the first thing that genuinely angered Konsul Buddenbrook and it was the reason why he began to speak in a fairly curt and irritable tone: 'Lads, what sort o' gormlessness is this ye're getting up to!' [i. 192])

From this point, the troubles are at an end, within minutes Corl Smolt has stopped answering back and run off obediently to find Konsul Justus Kröger's carriage; the street lighting has helped quell the Lübeck Revolution.[6] It is a perfect example of how the novelist can use his exact knowledge to create authentic background which is yet given so natural a function in the narrative that it loses all appearance of display, historical colour, antiquarian knowledge.

Lübeck had already appeared in Mann's writing to some extent, although it was never named (it is not, for that matter, ever named in *Buddenbrooks*): as the background to *Der kleine Herr Friedemann*, or as the starting-point of *Der Bajazzo*, the

---

[6] It will appear once more with a minor function. Thomas Buddenbrook's go-ahead outlook is later illustrated by his keenness to replace the 'fatalen Öllampen' with gas lighting (p. 361).

most directly autobiographical of the early stories. But it was vague and indifferent background, not realized specifically or in full. With the decision to write a full-length novel, there goes both a unity of purpose and a beneficial subordination of means to the enormous demands of rendering a complex and unified social picture. The technical potential of Mann's 'vermögende Jugendzeit' came to grips with the richness of what lay nearest in his past, 'das Nächstvergangene'.[7]

We can sense something of this in the very first chapter. A new manner has clearly been found. The openings of the short stories had quickly sketched the limited scope in time or place within which a highly concentrated anecdotal interest was to be developed. In contrast, *Buddenbrooks* opens in a leisurely Tolstoyan way, perhaps even consciously emulating the scenic opening of *War and Peace*, with its French dialogue to indicate the social level—Tolstoy, as Mann said, was a great support to him as he laboured at his first novel (x. 592). Far from seeking pungent effects, the observer's sharp eye and pen are now occupied, as they will be frequently throughout the book, with recording details of costume and furniture; the narrator is getting into a longer stride. There will be no short-term shocks or contrived twists, the interest is extensive and panoramic, not intensive and peepshow. If the glitter of verbal irony still shows—the catechism which Tony reels off has just been revised by permission of a 'hohen und wohlweisen Senates' (i. 9)—the allusion also serves the positive purpose of marking a date, 1835, and of beginning to realize the institutions of a particular place.

These institutions, the characteristic order of Lübeck life, its ceremonies and social hierarchy, go far towards absorbing the narrator's irony, which is counteracted by something like that primal epic impulse to celebrate or at least record a way of life. His description of the gifts of bread and salt which the Buddenbrooks receive from friends on moving into their new house (i. 18) is an instance of the lingering over concrete details of a culture which we find equally in Homer, in the

---

[7] Cf. *Betrachtungen* xii. 90, where Mann quotes these words from Goethe's *Dichtung und Wahrheit* and applies them to *Buddenbrooks*: 'Ich hatte . . . in "vermögender Jugendzeit das Nächstvergangene festgehalten und kühn genug zur günstigen Stunde öffentlich aufgestellt".' Goethe was referring to *Die Leiden des jungen Werthers*.

*Nibelungenlied*, in Goethe's *Hermann und Dorothea*. There is also, to be sure, a detached comment on the ostentation which the custom allows: the bread is heavy, sweet, and spiced, the salt comes enclosed in a gold container. The hard money-values underlying all else in this society are a major theme of the novel. Yet even these are not subjected to elaborate stylistic irony. They are too much part of a reality which commands respect. That hallmark of the early stories, indiscriminate verbal undermining, is gone. The narrator dwells on and records the scenes of his family's past. It is a sobering enough general irony that these forms of life and the supremacy of the Buddenbrooks are to prove impermanent in the scheme which he has conceived.

Which he has conceived? But was decline not a part of the given reality in which the writer found his subject? Did the Mann family not decline in much the same way as the Buddenbrooks? 'Um seines "Verfalles" willen ist das Haus überhaupt der Gegenstand geworden', Heinrich Mann wrote in 1935.[8] The novel's true nature will only emerge if we examine this assumption.

## II

We must turn back for a moment to the Thomas Mann of 1897. He has recently completed the story *Der Bajazzo*, significantly the first of his works to be based directly on experience instead of working with grotesque effects or anecdotal impact. It is handled correspondingly as a first-person narrative. It deals with the inner malaise and external failures of a young man of modest independent means living a cultured life on one side from society in Munich—more or less the life Thomas Mann was leading while he strove to establish himself as a writer. Where the early grotesques were self-expressive at most in a symbolic way, in that they were projections of a young man's disharmonious vision of life, *Der Bajazzo* begins a vein of more direct self-expression. The hero is still not an artist—it is often wrongly assumed that Thomas Mann wrote about nothing but artists—but he does have the writer's outward situation, his antecedents, and his problems, and lacks only his talent and

[8] See Br. H. 151.

application. As Mann noted some years later: 'Um ein todver-
fallenes, lebensunfähiges Menschenwesen zu schildern, braucht
ein Dichter nur sich selbst zu geben — unter Weglassung der
schöpferischen Gabe.' (In order to portray a human specimen
doomed to die, inadequate to face life, a poet needs only to
give himself—leaving out the creative gift.)[9]

The new story had been offered to Samuel Fischer, together
with others already published in various places, to make up a
volume. In May 1897 Fischer accepted, requested an option
on Mann's future work, and issued an invitation: 'ich würde mich
aber freuen, wenn Sie mir Gelegenheit geben würden, ein
grösseres Prosawerk von Ihnen zu veröffentlichen, vielleicht
einen Roman, wenn er auch nicht so lang ist'.[10]

No evidence exists that Thomas Mann had up till then planned
a more extensive work; but it is understandable that the suggestion, from such a quarter, should have had the effect it did.
To have anything accepted by the 'Cotta of Naturalism' was
already the fulfilment of a young man's dream (x. 474 ff.); a
virtual commission to write a novel could hardly be refused.

But a novel requires substance. We know where Mann eventually found it, but how—given the literary practice and
materials which we have seen in his preceding efforts—did he
arrive at his decision? One might simply say that he turned to
the one source of ample material that was directly accessible.
But it is possible to be more precise. Mann's own retrospective
account is relevant:

Ich erinnere mich wohl, dass, was mir ursprünglich am Herzen
gelegen hatte, nur die Gestalt und die Erfahrungen des sensitiven
Spätlings Hanno waren, — eigentlich also nur das, [ . . . ] was aus

[9] As an annotation to the chapter on *Werther* in vol. 1 of Bielschowsky's *Goethe*
(TMA, with date 1905). Did Mann perhaps find his own case formulated in the
passage to which he added this reflection? It reads: 'Für den idealistischen Träumer,
der überall das Vollkommene und Unbedingte verlangt, und der überall das
Unvollkommene und Bedingte mit unheimlichem Scharfblick herausfindet und
mit übergewöhnlicher Gemütstiefe fühlt, dem es dazu an jeglicher schaffender
Tätigkeit fehlt, die den ihn quälenden Dissonanzen das Gegengewicht hielte, ist
auf dieser Welt kein Raum.' (For the idealistic dreamer who everywhere demands
that things be perfect and absolute, and who everywhere finds them out with un-
canny penetration to be imperfect and relative, and feels it with unusual depth of
sensitivity, who in addition lacks all creative activity to counterbalance the disharmonies which torment him, there is no place in this world.)

[10] See Paul Scherrer, 'Bruchstücke der Buddenbrooks-Urhandschrift', pp.
258 f.

frischer Erinnerung, aus dichterischer Introspektion geleistet werden konnte.

(I remember well that what I had originally been concerned with was the figure and the experiences of the sensitive latecomer Hanno, in other words really only what could be done from recent memory, from poetic introspection. [xi. 554])

That is, Mann turned to the freshly opened vein which *Der Bajazzo* represented, the direct depiction of personal experience. The idea of a *Novelle* on this theme may even have preceded Fischer's invitation. But how could it be turned into a novel? The problem was one of creating bulk and complexity.

The answer was implicit in the figure of a 'sensitiver *Spätling*', a latecomer. Indeed, it was implicit in the kind of figures he had already used: the Bajazzo, with his typologically divergent parents, his inchoate talents, his unsuitedness for business and burgher life; or even Paolo Hofmann in *Der Wille zum Glück*, with his mixed parentage, artistic ambitions, and precarious health. The fates of these characters were governed by factors whose power was assumed—genetic inheritance and a tendency to decline from physical and social norms which was at the same time a development in spiritual respects. These ideas were commonplaces of the period: Naturalism had made much of heredity, Nietzsche of decline, or in its social and artistic forms 'decadence'. For the young Mann, they were very general explanations of the disharmonies which underlay his early fiction. Conceivably he saw them at first as mere initiating factors, no more important in themselves than the dropping of little Friedemann by the nurse which sets that story in motion. But there was the important difference that they were lengthy processes: if he had so far only concerned himself with the end result, now was the occasion to begin exploring the dimension in which they took place—time, the past. This was where the path to a novel lay.

We cannot document these thoughts as such. But we can document the speed and completeness with which a plan evolved to back up the presentation of Hanno by an exhaustive account of his prehistory. Mann's own later retrospect continues:

Da aber ein epischer Instinkt mich trieb, ab ovo zu beginnen und die gesamte Vorgeschichte mit aufzunehmen, so entstand statt der

Knabennovelle, die sich nicht viel von anderen damals in Deutschland hervorgebrachten unterschieden hätte, ein als Familien-Saga
verkleideter Gesellschaftsroman . . .

(But as an epic instinct impelled me to begin *ab ovo* and include the
complete prehistory, there was born, instead of the story about a
boy, which would not have been so very different from many others
that were being produced in Germany at that time, a social novel
in the guise of a family saga. [xi. 554])

This, like the 'growth of the novel under his hands' of which
Mann was also later to speak on several occasions, is a stylization. But it is the stylization of a real enough process: the
sketching out, within a brief span which we can date, of the
whole generation-sequence, the individual characters, and
many of the details of incident and relationship which are
found in the novel as we have it. The first preparatory notes
for the novel are preserved in a notebook of 1897 and very
early 1898. Within the first few pages, major structural members
of the novel are present—Christian on page 1, 'der kleine
Johann' on the reverse, a sketch for the description of Old
Johann on the third (the second preserved) leaf. In embryo,
the 'gesamte Vorgeschichte'. Leaf 6 verso carries the novel's
opening 'Was ist das', page 19 a sketch of its close, the gathering of female characters 'nach dem Tode des kleinen Johann'.[11]

That Hanno's death is the already planned ending, taken
jointly with the generation scheme which has so quickly sprung
into being, is important. It confirms that the full history of decline was there practically from the first, and also that it was all
along seen, teleologically, from the viewpoint of that ending:
of Hanno's inadequacy to face life and the compensating value
of his accompanying sensitivity. The novel's central theme is
set by the hero of a short study which was compelled by circumstances to strike longer roots. And this theme, although by no
means the only one, is the governing factor in the novel.

Equally significant are two other points about the preparatory sketches. The very first name to occur, with motifs to be
worked out, was Christian. Paul Scherrer thought this important because Christian is the most decadent member (*das
geistig brüchigste Glied*) of the family, and thus proves the
original interest in decline. But this, given Hanno as the starting-

---

11 Scherrer 'Bruchstücke', p. 260 provides the material here analysed.

point, does not need extra proof. What is more important, against the background of Mann's early methods, is the immediate recourse to the one more or less major character in the novel who invited a caricatural treatment of the sort Mann was by now practised at. That is to say, the author's first move is into country where he feels stylistically at home. One might see this as a slight dragging of the foot before he is drawn on, despite himself, to do something new.

This last is also a process we can document. In some other relatively early sketches, Tony Buddenbrook begins to monopolize attention[12]—to such an extent that she almost seems to be becoming the central figure of the novel. This impression remains true of the early sections of the book as finally executed, for not only do we begin with Tony, we have the full treatment of her love for Morten Schwarzkopf and her marriage to Grünlich before ever Christian and Thomas—thematically more important characters—have become of any note. What does this suggest? That once the materials of a family history are taken in hand, some parts may begin to attract undue attention in their own right whatever their relevance to any preordained pattern. Tony Buddenbrook is an example, almost a symbol of the tension in *Buddenbrooks* between chosen theme and material—a tension which proved in the end entirely beneficial.

The pull of a theme; the pull of an old method; the pull of new material: these three factors are at work in *Buddenbrooks*. The upshot is that the seriousness of the theme (and arguably also its intimate importance to the writer, who was exploring his own prehistory as well as Hanno's), together with the volume and dignity of the materials, stimulate new methods and put the old all-too-playful irony in its place; but also that the rich materials, conceived of originally as a medium in which to work out a theme, assert their independent interest to such an extent that, far from being subordinate to that theme, they achieve equal standing and a kind of counterpoint with it. They also bring with them at least one new theme of some importance, which was unavoidably part of a business family's history: the effect of commercial motives on human

---

[12] Paul Scherrer, 'Aus Thomas Manns Vorarbeiten zu den "Buddenbrooks". Zur Chronologie des Romans', in Wysling, *Studien*, p. 10.

living. This is interwoven with the theme of inner decline and strengthens it—which it needs.

For the idea of 'decadence', of a decline in vitality linked necessarily with the rise of intellectuality (or artistic gifts or 'spiritual' differentiation), is shaky by itself. The particular form of heredity theory which ultimately underlies *Budden-brooks* is not a scientific one, and was not so even in Thomas Mann's own day. That is, it was not a Naturalist theory, respectable then, superseded now. Nietzsche is its origin, and it is a mystical assumption, on Nietzsche's authority. If, as Mann said, *Buddenbrooks* set out to present 'die Psychologie ermüdenden Lebens, die seelischen Verfeinerungen und ästhetischen Verklärungen, welche den biologischen Nieder-gang begleiten' (the psychology of waning vitality, the spiritual refinements and aesthetic transfigurations which accompany biological decline [xi. 554]), then it was Nietzsche who pro-vided that psychology: 'Der junge Verfasser von "Budden-brooks" hatte die Psychologie des Verfalls von Nietzsche gelernt' (xi. 556). It is Nietzsche's ideas,[13] so limited in their basis of experience and personal in their angle of vision, that Mann was guided by: general ones in the first instance, like the idea that it is impossible to be an artist without being pro-foundly sick, or that the artist is the final result of the accumu-lated work of generations. These are ideas which Mann was to carry with him for life, but they are never more than assump-tions for which a certain selection of artists provide some sup-port. (Hence Mann's considerable difficulties over digesting the phenomenon of Goethe.) *Buddenbrooks* comes no nearer to demonstrating such a thesis than *Der Bajazzo* had. That 'general explanation' which Mann had accepted in the early stories as a commonplace of his day becomes *artistically* fruitful when extended back into the past in a family history; it becomes no more *intellectually* conclusive. Symptoms of decadence simply have to be scattered, with increasing frequency, over succes-sive generations. The scattering is itself the novel's theme, 'thesis' even, a deliberate dosing with decadence. The experi-ment had to fit the known result.

---

[13] Erich Heller, in his book *The Ironic German*, put the idea about that the 'intel-lectual plot' of *Buddenbrooks* was derived from Schopenhauer. This is demonstrably untrue. See below, pp. 81f.

Thus the crucial and most complex figure in the Budden-brook decline, Thomas, is no less mystified than the Bajazzo was by the malaise he experiences. Like the Bajazzo, he passionately envies and yearns to emulate the unreflectingly happy and successful children of life; like him again, he had the illusion once that he was one of those to whom success comes easily, as a kind of innate gift; and he finally has to recognize, once more like the Bajazzo, that he is not of that type and that he can do nothing about the type he is. It is the complexity of the transition which Thomas represents, from predominant normality to predominant non-normality, that makes him the key figure of the novel. Despite the initial interest in Hanno, it is Thomas to whom Mann later referred in terms suggesting the most intimate involvement: 'der mir mystisch dreifach verwandten Gestalt, dem Vater, Sprössling und Doppelgänger' (xii. 72). 'Father' because Thomas was based on his father, Senator Mann; 'offspring' because he was his literary creation; 'double' because his mixture of bourgeois qualities and 'spirit' was closer to Thomas Mann than Hanno's more extreme state.

There is of course more of the 'offspring' and the 'double' in Thomas Buddenbrook than of the 'father'. He belongs to Mann's scheme of ideas rather than to the reality he was reconstructing. His real-life counterpart, if the testimony of the one unliterary son is to be believed, was neither a tired snob nor in any way 'decadent'—unless refinement and intellect, which he did have, are to be equated *a priori* with decadence. Senator Mann represented the high point of the family's period as *haute bourgeoisie* and his early death ended that phase without any slow process of decline.[14]

But however questionable and 'period' the ideas on which *Buddenbrooks* was based, their elaboration is managed with supreme delicacy and literary tact. If the theme of decline had not had such undue attention from critics, it would be possible to ignore the mystical biology it rests on. Nothing, certainly, should be done to bring this yet more into the foreground. But since it has been so much discussed, it is worth making clear that in its detail as well as in the general guiding ideas, Nietzsche was the great provider. If we leave aside the unhealthy

---

[14] Cf. Viktor Mann, *Wir waren fünf*, Konstanz, 1949, p. 16.

Buddenbrook teeth, the shadows under Buddenbrook eyes, and the veins which show through at Buddenbrook temples, and pass direct to psychological detail, we find in Konsul Jean not just religiosity (doubtless what is referred to when he is said to have had the first ever 'unalltägliche, unbürgerliche und differenzierte Gefühle' in the family [p. 259]), but something more important: a reflective consciousness in the form of interest in the family's history. His father Old Johann never had this: 'Er stand mit beiden Beinen in der Gegenwart und beschäftigte sich nicht viel mit der Vergangenheit der Familie' (he stood with both feet in the present and concerned himself very little with the family's past [p. 56]). Reflection in the form of historical consciousness is pure Nietzsche, the sign of 'angeborene Grauhaarigkeit'.[15] As Nietzsche presents it, it is a symptom of a more general psychological condition, a hampering self-consciousness: activity is undermined by thought, whatever is too much reflected on cannot be performed. So we find that Christian, taking up a post in the family business, expatiates embarrassingly on the joys of the merchant life (p. 270), but after two weeks cannot stick the work. Thomas too, when weary and defeated, recognizes that his early successes were the product of 'Reflexion' (p. 470). Reflection was the only basis for his conscious pursuit of aims he knew were trivial in a world he knew was small; only reflection and a 'sense of poetry' could give these things a (purely symbolic) meaning, summed up in repeated allusions to Goethe's famous lines from the end of *Faust* (pp. 277, 362). This slim reflective defence against reflection finally breaks down.

It is not hard to find other examples of the 'psychology of decadence' woven deftly into the intrinsic interest of episodes. Yet no amount of philosophical source-tracing can demonstrate literary quality. If these details were as obtrusive in the novel as they have become in discussions of it—by Thomas Mann as well as by his critics—it would be a much less fine work than it is. Its salvation from being a mere *roman à thèse* lies in the touch with which ideas and psychological insight were embedded in real character and action—and, once again, in the sheer substantiality of the material subject. For all the skill, *Buddenbrooks* is in a sense a triumph of matter over mind.

[15] *Vom Nutzen und Nachteil der Historie für das Leben*, § 8.

The relationship between theme and substance is epitomized by the balance between title and subtitle. One need only imagine them in the reverse order—'Verfall einer Familie, Geschichte der Buddenbrooks'—to feel the effect which the actual order produces. Moreover, the main title, plain *Buddenbrooks*, has effects of its own, and of a subtlety out of proportion to its terseness. The family name without definite article (contrast Fontane's *Die Poggenpuhls*)[16] is the normal way of referring in German to a family known to one, a part of one's own society. It thus renders the Buddenbrooks immediately real, evoking a community within which the name is one to conjure with. By thus speaking as if with the voice of that community, it is an economic creation of viewpoint. Beyond this, the single word perhaps suggests the omnipresence of the family, its power to fill and dominate the narrative scene, even its existence as a plentiful substance which can absorb attention. The simplicity of the one-word title is, finally, at the furthest possible remove from the rhetorical effects[17] which are sought by a play with grammatical and syntactical forms in the earlier short stories. Some of those stories, it is true, have themselves single-word titles, but they are of very different content. From *Gefallen*, *Gerächt*, and *Enttäuschung* to *Buddenbrooks* is the distance from melodramatic suggestiveness to realistic sobriety.

All this substantiates Mann's later claim that his novel is not a negative book. Contemporaries, arguing perhaps from a general assumption about his literary character rather than from the novel itself, judged it *zersetzend* (undermining, subversive). Mann replied that *Buddenbrooks* was too 'positiv-künstlerisch', too 'behaglich-plastisch' for that (Br. i. 62). Every good book written against life, he went on, is itself an inducement to live.[18] If we stress the word 'good' in that statement, it exactly

[16] Critics frequently misquote the title as 'Die Buddenbrooks'. The distinction between the two forms cannot be made in English, where family names have to be preceded by 'the'. Nevertheless, the translation *Buddenbrooks* adopted by Mrs. Lowe-Porter has something to be said for it, because it catches the other nuances referred to.

[17] As a further contrast, with a rhetoric of inflation this time, not of ironic deflation, there is Galsworthy's title *The Forsyte Saga*.

[18] Quoting Nietzsche, *Menschliches* ii. 16 (passage marked in Mann's copy): 'Alle guten Dinge sind starke Reizmittel zum Leben, selbst jedes gute Buch, das gegen das Leben geschrieben ist.'

catches the counterpoint between the theme of decline and decadence ('against life') and the material substance in which it is worked out. This is not to deny the general—indeed, increasing—pessimism the story-line of the novel imposes, but only to stress the positive effect which is achieved by the *artistic* fusion of this outlook with a demandingly complex reality.

It is thus not certain that 'against life' is a fair description of the final effect of *Buddenbrooks*, as Mann appears by 1906 to have realized. But it does seem to describe the spirit in which he set out to write it, if we can judge by the epigraph he chose for the whole work. It is taken from Platen's poem 'Vision' and has that characteristic Platen note of slightly self-conscious pessimism which the young Thomas Mann seems to have found in tune with his own outlook.[19] The passage reads:

> So ward ich ruhiger und kalt zuletzt,
> Und gerne möcht ich jetzt
> Die Welt, wie ausser ihr, von ferne schaun:
> Erlitten hat das bange Herz
> Begier und Furcht und Graun,
> Erlitten hat es seinen Teil von Schmerz,
> Und in das Leben setzt es kein Vertraun:
> Ihm werde die gewaltige Natur
> Zum Mittel nur,
> Aus eigner Kraft sich eine Welt zu baun.

(And so in the end I grew calmer and cold, and now I should like to view the world, as if outside it, from afar. My timorous heart has suffered desire and fear and horror, suffered its share of pain, and it has no confidence in life. Let it now make mighty nature a mere means of building a world for itself, from its own strength.)

Perhaps the most significant thing about the epigraph is that Mann finally chose to delete it.[20]

[19] In a letter to Heinrich Mann of 1901 (Br. H. 18), he quotes the 'melancholy but radically consoling thought' from Platen that:

> 'Dem frohen Tage folgt ein trüber,
> *Und Alles hebt zuletzt sich auf.*' (Italics Mann's)

A notebook entry of 1898/9 lists four possible Platen epigraphs for *Buddenbrooks*, by page-references only. If one looks through Platen editions to trace which they were, it becomes clear that practically any Platen poem would provide one. Erika Mann reports (Br. iii. 7) that the two or three hundred poems her father knew by heart included some fifty of Platen's.

[20] It occurs, struck through, in the first page of the fragmentary original manu-

Not only Thomas Mann himself, but a number of early critics of *Buddenbrooks* used the term *plastisch* or *Plastik*, especially of the character-depiction.[21] The word suggests a three-dimensional, almost tangible reality as of sculptured figures, but not a statuesque lifelessness. On the contrary, it implies intensely live creations, the work of a true *Dichter*, and is high praise. It was indeed a form of praise Mann was to set great store by later, when critics of his 'intellectual' art denied it him. These early judgements correspond to the argument I have been proposing, that the writer was transformed by the major subject he had taken on. This argument now needs to be made more precise.

## III

Soon after completing *Buddenbrooks*, 'dies Werk dreijähriger Qual' as he called it, Mann gave his account of how the large-scale subject had affected his whole approach to his writing: 'Auf Grösse war . . . während der Arbeit fortwährend mein heimlicher und schmerzlicher Ehrgeiz gerichtet. Mit dem quantitativen ins Kraut Schiessen des Buches wuchs beständig mein Respekt davor, sodass ich einen immer höheren Stil von mir verlangte.' (During work on the novel, my secret and painful ambition was aimed at greatness. The more the book ran away with me quantitatively, the more my respect for it grew, so that I demanded a more and more elevated style from myself.)[22] Together with this higher style, theme and materials stimulated new technical methods and moderated the old. What are these new methods, and in what way are they an advance on the handling of character, theme, and event in the preceding short works?

The techniques in those stories were relatively simple. Straightforward pictorial narration by an omniscient narrator (*Der kleine Herr Friedemann*, *Tobias Mindernickel*, *Der Kleiderschrank*, *Luischen*)

script of *Buddenbrooks* (Scherrer, 'Bruchstücke', 263 f.), which is dated 'Rom Ende Oktober 1897'.

[21] e.g. *Münchener Neueste Nachrichten* 20 Nov. 1901 reporting a public reading from the novel by Thomas Mann: 'greifbare Plastik';or Max Lorenz in the *Preussische Jahrbücher* of 1902: 'für sich aber tritt jede Gestalt in vollendeter Plastik vor Augen'.

[22] To Heinrich Mann, 27 Mar. 1901 (Br. H. 19).

is only insignificantly modified by slight framework elements (*Gefallen, Enttäuschung, Gerächt*, with no completion of the framework in the last two) or by dramatizing the narrator in a minor way as a not very important actor in the story he tells (*Der Wille zum Glück*). Only in *Der Bajazzo*, which I have already suggested was a marked advance, is the first-person narrative a reflection of the story's aim: to give insight into the inner world of the character who is relating his own life and disasters. One further story, *Der Tod*, uses diary form.

These first stages in the personal development of a writer follow very closely the evolution of narrative techniques which can be traced in the history of the novel. What is lacking almost wholly is that range of more sophisticated devices for creating either a sense of immediacy and life (the scenic method, where the narrator effaces himself and forms his material with minimal comment, as a dramatist) or intimacy (the merging of narrator and character in *erlebte Rede* and viewpoint narration).[23]

The effect of these technical limitations has been mentioned: there is a connection (see above, p. 32) between the anecdotal and ironic features of the early stories and their use of pictorial method, which, as Lubbock pointed out, drags in the omniscient narrator and tends to make him conspicuous through the direct reflection of his mind.[24]

This connection is worth pausing over. Was the pictorial method then an ideal form to convey the young Thomas Mann's ironies, whose intellectual background has been sketched in? Or was it rather the case that immaturity of craftsmanship, which limited the writer to these techniques, helped to give an exaggerated impression of pervasive irony? This is an intriguing border-dispute between two critical approaches,

[23] The scenic treatment of the confrontation in *Gefallen* is a worthy forerunner of the Klöterjahn–Spinell meeting in *Tristan*; there is some small use of *erlebte Rede* in the analysis of little Friedemann's misery.

[24] Lubbock, op. cit., pp. 115, 120. Lubbock's *Craft of Fiction* first appeared fifty years ago (1921), and his insights have since been much debated and subtly differentiated (see E. Lämmert, *Bauformen des Erzählens*[2], Stuttgart, 1967, with bibliography). Despite, or even because of this, Lubbock's general theory remains the most useful and flexible in practice. As a first foundation of the aesthetics of the novel (cf. Forster, *Aspects of the Novel*, p. 75) it had the influence, and retains the value, of pioneer works like Lessing's *Laokoon*.

but whatever the answer, one thing is clear: a shift to more 'advanced' methods will alter the effect.

This can be shown happening in *Buddenbrooks*. Against a background of predominantly pictorial narrative, the techniques of greater penetration find their function. The book opens with a scenic fragment, the exchange between Tony and her grandfather, before ever the narrator's voice begins to fill in the social picture. Scenic method goes from strength to strength —Tony's scenes with Grünlich, the 1848 rising, Thomas's confrontations with Christian, Permaneder's arrival and first conversation with the Konsulin, Tony offering Thomas the Pöppenrade harvest deal, Thomas reproaching his mother for giving the dead Clara's inheritance to her husband—the list could be more than doubled. Scenic method goes with whatever is of such vivid interest and plain meaning that the commenting narrator is redundant. Whereas slender anecdote, treated pictorially, left plenty of slack in the virtuoso narrator's hand and resulted in excessive verbal play, the kind of substance which the Buddenbrook subject offered takes the slack up fully and demands the scene.

Even where scenic method is interrupted (and in the scenes listed above it works in phases, not exclusively) the intervening narrative in pictorial form is not playful but fully occupied with the matter in hand, often pictorial in the literal sense of rendering material surroundings, sated with detail. The decision not to use scenic method in places where it seems ideally suitable can itself be subtle policy—e.g. in the Jubilee of the family firm, with Thomas's house brim-full of congratulating Lübeckers, noise, and bustle. Here the more distant pictorial method not only gives a sovereign survey of the whole scene without getting involved anywhere, it also matches Thomas's weariness and distaste for the whole thing. It culminates in two pages which describe the crowd at its thickest, the noise at its noisiest, faces and figures on every side, even the city theatre band playing in the hall—all described in the present tense, as if to ask: will it never end?

Scenic method is half-way to intimacy in that it gives us the character direct, rendering what is spoken and leaving the inner life to be inferred. With someone as spontaneous and heart-on-sleeve as Tony, this is entirely sufficient. What would a closer inspection of her inner life add? Only a confirmation that there is virtually no further substance beneath her familiar mannerisms, her repeated and usually derivative phrases. Hence *erlebte Rede* is not necessary for her, and hardly occurs.[25] The techniques of *erlebte Rede* and narrative from the viewpoint of the character set in with Thomas and grow more intensive with Hanno. The Senator's self-doubts, for example, and his son's sufferings at school are experienced from within.[26] The reason is plain: these later Buddenbrooks are so much more complex than their predecessors that they require deeper probing. Moreover, their complexity is part of the writer's developing theme and also the basis of his sense of solidarity and sympathy with them. And yet these techniques are notably not used for the equally 'late' and complex Christian . . .

At this point, one suddenly realizes how precise is the correspondence between technique and inner meaning in *Buddenbrooks*, how careful Thomas Mann's manipulation of viewpoint was, and how indispensable it is to understand it if we are to grasp the characters, their place in the novel, and the novel's structure. For, looking back, one can see a progression in the handling of character which exactly matches the development of the theme.

Old Johann needed only to be seen from without. Our angle of vision in his case is effectively set by Tony's child's-eye view of him on the opening page. His inner life has the inaccessibility, incomprehensibility even, of another age. His being cannot be refuted, but it cannot be penetrated. If the simple exterior conceals depths, they are not of a kind that lends itself to copious verbal analysis. In his last days and dying moment, he summarizes his experience in the one word 'Kurios!' (p. 73).

Konsul Jean, similarly, is viewed from without, although his more extended role in the action helps to fill out our under-

---

[25] But see below, pp. 64–5, where the technique is used to catch Tony's immediate, and necessarily unspoken, impression of *déjà vu* in a moment of swift action and emotional stress.

[26] Thomas e.g. p. 391, and especially pp. 465 ff., which render Thomas's doubts about his own nature and final, fateful resolution to buy the Pöppenrade crop.— Hanno e.g. p. 484 and especially the accounts of his piano-playing before the family pp. 506 f., and his rising for school, pp. 700 ff. ('Hannos Lever' was one of the earliest motifs in the preparatory jottings for the novel.)

standing (an external, not a particularly sympathetic understanding) of him, and other ways are found to make clear such complexities of motive and feeling as he does have.

Tony has already been placed, in the technical sense. In Thomas, the process of decline and spiritual or intellectual complication reaches its crucial, transitional stage, and accordingly he is treated from within. We eavesdrop increasingly on his thoughts and feelings (which is made even more necessary because of his meticulous keeping up of appearances, 'die Dehors wahren') and the process culminates in the rendering of his Schopenhauer experience. But from Christian, by contrast, we are kept separated by a barrier of reserve in the narrator which matches the distaste which Thomas feels for his brother. Thomas compares Christian's embarrassing *Mitteilerei* to the self-analysis and self-expression of poets (pp. 265 f.) but rejects it because its content in Christian's case is trivially pathological and sordid. The narrator's technique implies a similar judgement, for although he describes Christian's grotesque performances and records his words, he never takes us any deeper into the character. And we would surely have to go deeper in order to understand him fully and sympathetically—unlike the case of Tony's simple character, which is all surface and can be fully rendered by pictorial and scenic technique. Thus Christian inspires for the most part only an unpleasant fascination. He is marked out as an aberration even within the process of decline.

Finally, in the treatment of Hanno—the character and the thematic end towards which the novel moves and out of which it grew—there is expressed the total sympathy which his degree of sensitivity and suffering deserve, and which their link with artistic talent is bound to evoke from a narrator who has accepted unreservedly the Nietzschean doctrine about the nature and origin of artists. By the standards of this novel, which remains basically conservative in its use of the pictorial perspective, involvement with Hanno is, in a discreet way, of the maximum intensity. We see through his eyes deeply enough and long enough to be fully aware of the alternatives to Buddenbrook vitality.

It should be clear from this technical progression that the term *plastisch* for the characters in *Buddenbrooks* (and indeed

in any other literary work which achieves this degree of life)
is misleading in so far as the analogy with visual art suggests
that the effect is managed by external description. It is not.
The great figures of modern literature come alive for us because
their experience is rendered, not their appearance. Is there a
set-piece description of Natasha in the whole length of *War
and Peace*? True, there are physical details of the major characters in *Buddenbrooks* to which our attention is drawn time and
again: Thomas's raised eyebrow,[27] Tony's haughty attitude
with head back and chin in. But these are identifying marks,
not descriptions,[28] and the concentration on them—besides
making for a sense of continuity—is true to the way we see those
we know well most vividly in their mannerisms. Admittedly,
too, there *are* set-piece descriptions of people in *Buddenbrooks*,
but they tend to be of minor figures, and the effect is often on
the edge of caricature, like the descriptions in the early stories.[29]
Certainly that is the result if a corresponding inner life is in no
way added to complement the externals. Description alone
can only give us the human being as an object, his human
substance needs other approaches. Hofmannsthal put the truth
of the matter perfectly in his aphorism: 'Das Plastische entsteht
nicht durch Schauen, sondern durch Identifikation.'[30]

Even where such identification does not occur, there is still
a dampening down, if not a putting by, of irony. Satire and the
grotesque do still have a place—the Konsulin's religious
gatherings ('Jerusalemsabende'), the ugly daughters of Uncle
Gotthold who are reminiscent in detail of little Herr Friedemann's sisters, Christian's more extreme oddities, the death of
the diabetic James Möllendorpf from furtive cake-eating in a
hired room in a poor quarter, and the almost Dickensian
masters at Hanno's school. But their effect is diluted by the

---

[27] Incidentally one of Thomas Mann's own mannerisms, as mentioned by Erika
Mann, Scherrer, 'Bruchstücke', 276.

[28] Bayley, op. cit., pp. 73 and 113, writes illuminatingly about this distinction in
Tolstoy's work.

[29] e.g. the description of Pastor Tiburtius, p. 283. Gerda Arnoldsen-Buddenbrook
is a special case. The striking description of her beauty is never complemented by
'inner' presentation. But the limitation to impassive, statuesque beauty—'morbide
und rätselhafte Schönheit' (p. 343)—is itself part of Gerda's character. There are
surely depths in Tony's comment when she hears Gerda playing the violin in
another room: 'O Gott, dieses Weib . . . sie ist eine Fee!' (p. 427).

[30] *Aufzeichnungen*, Frankfurt, 1959, p. 73.

broad context in which they occur, in much the same way as the narrator's sharp observations of detail are often marginal to some absorbing scene: the semi-educated bourgeoisie mispronounce foreign words ('Kongflick', 'Infamje') but this is only a tiny stroke in the depiction of a Buddenbrook dinnerparty or a political upheaval. Moritz Heimann, the chief reader of the Fischer Verlag, thought that the satirical and grotesque elements supported rather than disturbed the large epic form.[31] Rilke, in a remarkable review of *Buddenbrooks*, praised the objective epic presentation within which even the crueller details came to appear necessary and in place.[32]

This has brought us back to our central theme, the absorption of irony in the rescuing format of the full-length novel. It is most marked in the treatment of the major characters, who are too large and real for the ultimately precarious irony of the early stories to find a hold. In general there is little verbal over-elaboration in *Buddenbrooks*. Where it does occur, it is a means of characterizing the pompous Grünlich, who speaks and writes a comic *Papierdeutsch*. Even Tony's foibles are only gently made fun of, not exposed to elaborate verbal ridicule. They are evoked with the affectionate tolerance of one who has learned to make allowances. Tony's character, with its reallife core in the character of Elisabeth Haag-Mann, was aesthetically rich though psychologically not complex. It offered creative scope—or, put the other way round, demanded scenic presentation. Thus, if the question 'who was who' has less fascination for us than it had for contemporary Lübeckers, who read the book again and again until they 'had them all',[33] the fact remains relevant that there were real-life models. It was a factor in the making of the novel, and of the novelist.

[31] Thomas Mann quotes part of Heimann's verdict in a letter to his brother Heinrich in 1901 (Br. H. 19). Part of Heimann's original *Gutachten* is preserved in TMA.

[32] Rilke, *Sämtliche Werke*, ed. Zinn, vol. v, p. 579. The contrast between Mann's early stories and *Buddenbrooks* is borne out by Rilke's further comment that 'nirgends, über die Ereignisse hinweg, ein überlegener Schriftsteller sich zu dem überlegenen Leser neigt, um ihn zu überreden und mitzureissen'.

[33] Cf. Klaus Schröter, *Thomas Mann im Urteil seiner Zeit. Dokumente 1891 bis 1955*, Hamburg, 1969, p. 23.

## IV

If excess irony has largely disappeared, something akin to it—
a maturer and more acceptable form of irony—remains, both in
the detailed treatment and the larger structures of the novel.
At the level of detail, it is fastidiousness, self-discipline, 'eine
Art geistiger Zucht, Disziplin, "*Haltung*", artistischer Würde'.[34]
It is what, in *Buddenbrooks*, prevents too complete an involvement of the author with particular characters, or his too
complete absorption in the recreated material world of Lübeck.
Sympathy with certain characters could have become sentimen-
tality, absorption could have become descriptive wallowing.
They do not do this firstly because an over-all narrator-
perspective is regularly asserted, the techniques for creating
immediacy and intimacy are given strict limits within the
setting of a more conservative pictorial convention. But in
addition new ways were devised to keep sympathy in check
where it was strongest. The indirect account of Hanno's death
through the montage of bare fact about the course of typhus
is a celebrated and brilliantly successful instance. It does not
return to the callousness of the early tales, but it avoids a tear-
jerking climax. Equally good, if less obvious, is the conclusion
of Hanno's piano recital before the family. After the abrupt
ending of his composition (*abbrach*), the sympathetic involvement with the playing might have modulated into a moving
account of the family's incomprehension, of Hanno's total
isolation. But the scene is dissolved in humour—the humour of
Tony's love for the boy and the incongruous form her enthusiasm
takes: '"Gerda, Tom, er wird ein Mozart, ein Meyerbeer, ein
..." und in Ermangelung eines dritten Namens von ähnlicher
Bedeutung, der ihr nicht sogleich einfiel, beschränkte sie sich
darauf, ihren Neffen, der, die Hände im Schosse, noch ganz
ermattet und mit abwesenden Augen dasass, mit Küssen zu
bedecken.' ('Gerda, Tom, he will be a Mozart, a Meyerbeer,
a . . .' and in the absence of a third name of equal significance,
which did not at once come to mind, she confined herself
to covering her nephew with kisses as he sat there with his
hands in his lap, still quite exhausted and his eyes far away
[p. 507].) Mozart and Meyerbeer—and a name of 'equal' signi-

[34] Letter of 23 May 1904 to Samuel Lublinski (Br. iii. 450).

ficance! The chapter closes with Thomas's reply; Gerda's reaction to the pairing we are left to imagine. Hanno is left with his far-away look, but the reader is back in the ordinary world.

Similarly with Thomas. Against the sympathy inspired by his —thematically important—divided inner self must be set the impartial account of the effect it has on his relations with his family: his harsh and clumsy alienation of Hanno, his self-righteousness towards Christian. The brothers' row after the death of the Konsulin shows this balance well: Christian's accusations make a strong case against Thomas, which he accepts. But what he is accused of—coldness, self-righteousness, egoism—sprang all along from the fear of becoming like Christian, for which he felt the potentiality within him. This admission (p. 580) is at the thematic heart of the novel, but the result in human terms is presented wholly objectively.

The devices which Thomas Mann uses to avoid overabsorption in the material richness of the setting can also be pinpointed, though they are even more unobtrusive, often tiny details: the brevity of the vignettes in the prolonged scenic opening of the novel,[35] where we are taken from one area to another of the social gathering without being allowed to get involved too deeply in any; the delicate fade-out into '. . .' with which six of the ten chapters covering this grand party end, distancing the numerous characters and their conversations by something like a *Verfremdungseffekt*; the reflections on rich men's eating and sudden dying which are induced in Doctor Grabow by the young Christian Buddenbrook's eating himself sick; or the seemingly simple descriptive sentence: 'Man sass auf hochlehnigen, schweren Stühlen, speiste mit schwerem Silbergerät schwere, gute Sachen, trank schwere, gute Weine dazu und sagte seine Meinung' (they sat on high-backed, heavy chairs, ate heavy, good food with heavy silver implements, drank heavy good wines with it, and spoke their minds [i. 31]), which recreates and yet simultaneously makes the things recreated recede into the distant past, so that we see them as through a kind of historical telescope. (The effect is achieved

---

[35] It is instructive to observe how these delicate effects are ruined by the physical presentation of the text in the English translation of *Buddenbrooks*, which starts every short chapter on a fresh page, under a heavy decorated rule, instead of running on easily as the German text does.

not just by the repeated *schwer*, but by the word *man*, which both generalizes about all those present and suggests that this is the way 'people' lived once.)

Such discipline on the author's part creates, in comparison with the early stories, the effect of a neutral rather than a sharply hostile narrator. No more is needed, because the larger novel-form has techniques which make it unnecessary to use those fiercer forms of immediate verbal irony. Compressed, pointed effects yield place; the narrator's point can be made more subtly over a longer span. Any criticism or undermining of the characters and the values they hold can be carried out gradually without the narrator's declaring his hand so crassly. This is the second form which irony takes on. The tactics of ironic formulation give way to the strategy of ironic structures. The aim is still to undermine critically, with the difference that now there is a real target and a recognizable moral alternative to what is criticized.

Firstly there is the religious sentiment of the Konsul, almost always juxtaposed, without comment, with thoughts of financial gain for the firm and the family. His high-minded scruples first appear in his role of unwilling mediator between old Johann and the estranged son of his first marriage, Gotthold. After all the younger Johann's expatiation on family feeling, on the need to retain God's blessing by family unity, after his concern to act justly in a situation which gives him every chance to influence his father against Gotthold, all of this culminating in the father–son discussion after the dinner-party which opens the novel: after all this build-up, and some final moral-religious reflections, there is a pause. Old Johann can scarcely see his son in the dying candle-light, he asks what he is doing. Calculating, the Konsul answers drily (p. 50). His calculations make it plain that the settlement Gotthold wants would do undue harm to the firm. The Konsul's conclusion is energetic, not morally reflective: '"Nein, Papa!" beschloss er mit einer energischen Handbewegung und richtete sich noch höher auf. "Ich muss Ihnen abraten, nachzugeben".' ('No, father!' he concluded with an energetic gesture of the hand and drew himself up still further. 'I must counsel you not to yield.') In neutral narrative language and direct reported speech, the decisiveness of the business motivation is established.

Later we hear of the extreme diligence of the Konsul, 'der mit zusammengebissenen Zähnen arbeitete und manches Gebet um Beistand in sein Tagebuch schrieb; denn es galt, die bedeutenden Mittel wieder einzubringen, die beim Tode des Alten der "Firma", diesem vergötterten Begriff, verlorengegangen waren' (who worked with clenched teeth and wrote many a prayer for support in his diary; for it was imperative to regain the considerable sums which the 'firm', that deified concept, had lost at the old man's death [p. 77]). The stylistic pointers—*denn* (for) and *vergöttert* (deified)—are not obtrusive, certainly not heavily ironic. What is done is done by juxtaposition, and by the echoes it awakens of the previous incident.

When the Konsul puts pressure on Tony to marry Bendix Grünlich, we are well prepared to understand his motivation. Much is made of the idea of duty—to the family, and religious duty—to the point where the local pastor is put up to preaching fiercely on the text that a woman shall leave her father and mother and follow her husband. The hard fact is that Grünlich is thought a good match, with his 'lively business'. Little else matters. Even when the Konsul seems most understanding towards his daughter, as when, on first broaching the subject, he urges that things be proceeded with slowly—'Das alles kann mit Ruhe erwogen werden, *muss* mit Ruhe erwogen werden [. . .] Es gibt da viele Dinge zu überlegen . . . '(p. 105)— what he really means is that time is needed to make inquiries into the solidity of Grünlich's firm, inquiries which those in Hamburg, deeply engaged themselves by Grünlich's debts, will answer with lying reassurances.

The Grünlich episode is a second, and related, ironic structure, a *tour de force* even within the uniformly high performance of *Buddenbrooks*. As in a good detective story, all the clues are given, but not forced on the attention of the reader. Every action of Grünlich's has a plausible motive (which the Buddenbrooks believe) and is also compatible with the hidden one: the need to marry a daughter of some major firm to save his shaky enterprises. It is the kind of episode most enjoyed on second reading, where the double motivation, appearance and reality, can be savoured in detail: Grünlich's proprietorial air towards Tony after their engagement ('er betrachtete sie lediglich mit einer heiteren Besitzermiene' [p. 163]), the immediate decrease in his attentiveness after the marriage, the increasing demands of his 'lively business', the way Tony is kept from contact with local people, stranded without a coach of her own in an out-of-town villa, not taken into society, not encouraged to talk to people—can Grünlich be jealous? Visiting parents are so monopolized by Grünlich that they have no chance to call on their relatives locally. And finally Kesselmeyer, the banker who is always in and out of the Grünlich house, has a habit of patting Tony's cheek and saying what a blessing from above it was for Grünlich when he acquired her. All the clues become apparent as such on the day of reckoning, but are unforced in themselves and give the episode a perfectly managed double nature. It is managed with most virtuosity in the two scenes in which Grünlich makes appeals to Tony—first to marry him, then not to leave him. This is the culmination of the 'proposal' scene:

'Tony . . .', wiederholte er, 'sehen Sie mich hier . . . Dahin haben Sie es gebracht . . . Haben Sie ein Herz, ein fühlendes Herz? . . . Hören Sie mich an . . . Sie sehen einen Mann vor sich, der vernichtet, zugrunde gerichtet ist, wenn . . . ja, der vor Kummer sterben wird', unterbrach er sich mit einer gewissen Hast, 'wenn Sie seine Liebe verschmähen! Hier liege ich . . . bringen Sie es über das Herz, mir zu sagen: ich verabscheue Sie —?'
'Nein, nein!' sagte Tony plötzlich in tröstendem Ton. [. . .]
'Nein, nein', wiederholte sie, indem sie sich ganz ergriffen über ihn beugte, 'ich verabscheue Sie nicht, Herr Grünlich, wie können Sie dergleichen sagen! . . . Aber nun stehen Sie auf . . . bitte . . .'.
(pp. 111 f.)

And in the second scene, we find this:

'Antonie . . .!' sagte er. 'Sieh mich hier . . . Hast du ein Herz, ein fühlendes Herz? . . . Höre mich an . . . du siehst einen Mann vor dir, der vernichtet, zugrunde gerichtet ist, wenn . . . ja, der vor Kummer sterben wird, wenn du seine Liebe verschmähst! Hier liege ich . . . bringst du es über das Herz, mir zu sagen: Ich verabscheue dich —? ich verlasse dich —?'
Tony weinte. Es war genau wie damals im Landschaftszimmer. [. . .]
'Steh auf, Grünlich', sagte sie schluchzend. 'Bitte, steh doch auf!' Und sie versuchte, ihn an den Schultern emporzuheben. 'Ich verabscheue dich nicht! Wie kannst du dergleichen sagen! . . .'
(pp. 230 f.)

(1. 'Tony', he repeated, 'see me here . . . This is what you have brought me to . . . Have you a heart, a feeling heart? . . . Listen to me . . . You see before you a man who is destroyed, ruined, if . . . nay, who will die of a broken heart', he interrupted himself with a certain haste, 'if you spurn his love! Here I kneel . . . can you find it in your heart to say to me: I abhor you—?'

'No, no!' said Tony suddenly, in a consoling tone. [. . .]

'No, no', she repeated, bending over him quite moved, 'I do not abhor you, Herr Grünlich, how can you say such a thing! . . . But now do stand up . . . please . . .'

2. 'Antonie . . .!' he said. 'See me here . . . Have you a heart, a feeling heart?' . . . Listen to me . . . you see before you a man who is destroyed, ruined, if . . . nay, who will die of a broken heart if you spurn his love! Here I kneel . . . can you find it in your heart to say: I abhor you—? I am leaving you—?'

Tony wept. It was exactly like that other occasion in the Landscape Room.[. . .]

'Stand up, Grünlich', she said, sobbing. 'Please, do stand up!' And she tried to raise him up by the shoulders. 'I don't abhor you! How can you say such a thing! . . .')

The words 'It was exactly like that other occasion . . .' mean precisely what they say. Not only are the situations similar, but the words the characters speak are virtually identical, and so are their gestures, which the author accordingly describes in exactly the same terms. 'It was exactly like that other occasion . . .' is the author's commentary on his own device, as well as being a rendering of Tony's thoughts in the form of *erlebte Rede*.[36]

The point of the device is not to show, in a Naturalist-deterministic spirit, that people's reactions to similar situations are identical, but to bring out the consistency of Grünlich's motives, which are commercial. Any difference between the two scenes is inessential, a matter of merely superficial changes like marriage. In both cases, Grünlich is really pleading for financial rescue, which only the Buddenbrook credit can secure. His words, 'destroyed, ruined', have the ambiguity inherent in the whole episode. Technically, the repetition of

[36] The *Buddenbrooks* materials include a sheet which was used to construct the second scene by transferring the verbal formulations from the first. It has three passages in it: a sketch for the description of Kesselmeyer on p. 228; then Grünlich's speech in its later form (with familiar address); finally, the description of Grünlich's entrance which begins 'Mit raschen Schritten, die Arme ausgebreitet . . .', also common to both scenes (pp. 109, 230), but with the verb 'kam er auf sie zu' which occurs only in the first.

these identical formulas completes a structure, linking two scenes which lie over a hundred pages apart, at the beginning and end of Grünlich's confidence trick. Morally, it reminds us that Tony the person meant nothing to him at any stage, and was torn away from Morten Schwarzkopf merely to keep Grünlich solvent.

Yet although these points are made by use of a verbal repetition, the effect is not like that of the ironic formulas in the early tales. It is only the last touch to a portrayal which depends on accumulation and connection, and which has had to be conducted with restraint: too pointed a verbal irony at any stage would have weakened the final effect. An ironic structure of this kind would be impossible in a short work. The very gentleness and unobtrusiveness of the clue-scattering requires, among other things, the intervention of other unrelated episodes to act as a distraction (e.g. the 1848 incident already discussed).

But the discussion of technique has now led us to a surprising conclusion. Once given the vicissitudes of real figures within a major subject, the 'immoralist' Thomas Mann turns out to be a moralist. In the analysis of Konsul Johann Buddenbrook's guilty feelings towards his daughter, and in the description of the action which follows (the final negotiations with Kesselmeyer and Grünlich) the catastrophe of Tony's first marriage is rounded off with full moral restitution. The lesson that people's lives ought not to be sacrificed to the 'deified concept of the firm' emerges clearly—at least as clearly as any moral issue in Fontane, if not as explicitly as those in George Eliot.

As such, it is part of a theme which the novel persistently returns to, that of the conflict between commercial interest and human feeling. It can be heard, unobtrusively, in small details like the report of old Madame Kröger's death, where the narrator's phrasing renders the way of thinking, perhaps even the words, normal in Buddenbrook society: 'Man musste den Verlust der alten Dame mit Fassung ertragen. Sie war steinalt geworden und hatte zuletzt ganz einsam gelebt. Sie ging zu Gott, und Buddenbrooks bekamen eine Menge Geld, volle runde hunderttausend Taler Kurant, die das Betriebskapital der Firma in wünschenswertester Weise verstärkten.' (The loss of the old lady had to be borne with composure. She had reached a ripe old age and at the end had lived quite alone. She was taken by the Lord, and the Buddenbrooks got a great deal of money, every bit of a hundred thousand thalers, which reinforced the firm's working capital in the most eminently acceptable way [p. 236].) It becomes explicit in Thomas Buddenbrook's reflections on the brutal cruelty of business life (p. 469) and is scenically demonstrated in his furious reproaches to his mother for giving up the dead Clara's inheritance to her husband, in the course of which he states as his justification what is surely itself the indictment of business mentality: 'meine Eigenschaft als Sohn [wird] zu Null, sobald ich dir in Sachen der Firma und der Familie als männliches Oberhaupt und an der Stelle des Vaters gegenüberstehe' (my capacity as your son becomes null and void as soon as I stand before you in matters which concern the firm and the family, as its male head and in father's stead [p. 432]).

These criticisms culminate in the ironic coincidence whereby Thomas's most ruthless act as a businessman, the Pöppenrade deal, ends in disaster on the very day of the firm's hundred-year jubilee: the day on which the Konsulin has once again thanked God for his support, and the other members of the family have presented Thomas with a plaque bearing the founder's exhortation to do only such business by day as will allow easy sleep o' nights. Yet where, given the brutality of business life, can a line be drawn? As in the case of Hugo Weinschenk's insurance practices, where a swindle is an almost imperceptible extension of accepted *Usancen*, the judgement on Thomas's action seems a creeping indictment of business life as such.

The rich seam which this critique of commercialism offered is yet another illustration of how the material subject saved *Buddenbrooks* from being a schematic *roman à thèse*. For the author, the relationship between his 'decline' theme and the theme of commercialism was that between two different levels of reality. As we saw, he shows piety and high principle to be a superstructure, in the Marxian sense, underlying which are economic interests and an unquestioning acceptance of the existing social order. The Konsulin prays for the poor, and can start on the first course of her Christmas dinner, carp in butter sauce and old Rhenish wine, with a good conscience (p. 543). But this ironic revelation of the reality beneath the religious superstructure is for him only a first stage: socio-economic reality is itself in turn a superstructure, beneath which forces yet more 'real' are at work.

These forces are briefly brought to our attention in the opening pages of the novel when the sad falling off of the Ratenkamp firm and family (it is the Ratenkamps from whom the Buddenbrooks have just bought their new house in the Mengstrasse) is discussed at the celebration dinner, a kind of skeleton at the feast. Konsul Jean states his view that the dishonest partner Geelmaack who completed the Ratenkamps' ruin was less a cause than an effect. Ratenkamp was subconsciously looking for someone to bear part of the responsibility for his ruin, because he could feel the irresistible force of decline. 'Diese Firma hatte abgewirtschaftet, diese alte Familie war passée' (the firm had had its day, the family was *passé* [p. 24]). Fate is thus not the sum of human actions, but a higher force affecting them. For the purposes of the social occasion being portrayed, this theory is dismissed by Old Johann Buddenbrook's remark that it is just a bee in his son's bonnet—'so eine von deinen idées' (p. 25); but for the purposes of the novel, it sets a tone and creates a sense of epic premonition.[37] The point is made that economic causes are only the realization of others less tangible. In *Buddenbrooks*, the action of Fate, in the particular 'period' form of decline,[38] merely takes on the outward dress of commercial occasion. The criticism of mercantile morality then lay near to hand as a reaction to the material subject. Moral criticism operates on the substance of episodes, it is not what determines their function in the thematic development. Thus, even so commercial a thing as Thomas's ruthlessness over the Pöppenrade affair has its thematic importance as an attempt to prove to himself that he is a hard man of action, and not an overscrupulous dreamer; it springs directly from the self-doubts which are his heritage in the process of decline. The decline itself, determined by forces to which morality is irrelevant, must not be seen as a moral judgement or nemesis on the family.

[37] Cf. the words used of Ratenkamp in his last phase—'Er war wie gelähmt', 'er ging wie unter einem Drucke einher' (p. 24)—with the phrase in Mann's notes which sums up Hanno's last days: 'Steht zuletzt beständig unter dem Eindruck des Endes, der Auflösung, des Verfalles . . .'

[38] Cf. *Blätter* 6, p. 17: 'die naturalistisch-fatalistisch empfundene Geschichte eines Verfalls . . .'

But however clear this relationship between levels of reality for the author, the final effect on the reader is less clear-cut. At the very least, commercialism becomes a theme in its own right. It interweaves with the theme of decline, as when Thomas takes Gerda to wife for reasons which include business considerations (p. 290) and thus contributes to the decay in Buddenbrook vitality. She, presented with such deft dramatic irony as 'die Mutter zukünftiger Buddenbrooks' (p. 304), will bear only Hanno. And the two themes are joined in a symbolic tableau at the Jubilee celebrations when the family present Thomas with the inscribed plaque. It is to be handed over by Tony and Hanno—Tony, the victim of family and firm in her failed marriages,[39] Hanno the victim of the very different forces of biological decline: 'Tony trug die Tafel beinahe allein, da Hannos Arme nicht viel vermochten, und bot in ihrer begeisterten Überanstrengung das Bild einer entzückten Märtyrerin' (Tony bore the plaque almost alone, since Hanno's arms could do little, and presented in her enthusiastic over-exertion the tableau of a rapt female martyr [p. 481]). A martyr to the interests of the family, and a decadent scion it has thrown up, both borne down by the emblem of its hundred years' activity: here the two themes meet on an equal footing.

## V

The distinction insisted on throughout this chapter, between the shape and the substance of *Buddenbrooks*, its structure and its texture, thesis and materials, is vital. The novel was based from the first on pessimistic *a priori* conclusions, with the rise of artistic sensitivity (itself to be brutally cut off before fulfilment) as the only compensation. All this was in tune with the deliberate nihilism of the early stories. Yet the execution of the novel, spread over three years, gave the writer compensations

[39] Tony's marriage to Permaneder, entered into after so much doubt, is an effort to make good the blemish on the family brought by her first marriage. Thomas, she knows very well, expects her to take the first at all respectable candidate. Tony's daughter Erika, in her turn, has little choice but to marry Weinschenk, because of her mother's very limited social contracts as a divorcee. (The pair are ironically described as 'von Gott ersichtlich füreinander bestimmt'—plainly destined for each other by God [p. 440].) A clear thread thus connects all Tony's marital disasters and places the blame for them with 'firm and family'.

of another sort. By extending him, as he himself described,[40] it largely restored those possibilities of language which the early stories had denied. The flimsy lives which had there been set up, Aunt-Sally-like, for nihilism to destroy gave way in *Buddenbrooks* to lives of more resistant stuff. The texture of the writing changes accordingly. Language is no longer played with. Words have regained a value, because they have the backing of a reality independent of the writer's arbitrary imagination—a reality which, despite his status as an artist and 'outsider', despite his having condemned it to a thematic death, he still respects. What we repeatedly hear in the novel is what Tony Buddenbrook sensed when she perused the family records: 'eine ohne Übertreibung feierliche Vortragsweise . . . einen instinktiv und ungewollt angedeuteten Chronikenstil,[41] aus dem der diskrete und desto würdevollere Respekt einer Familie vor sich selbst, vor Überlieferung und Historie sprach' (a tone which was solemn without exaggeration . . . an instinctive and involuntary hint of the chronicle style, in which could be heard the discreet and thereby all the more dignified respect of a family for itself, for tradition and history [p. 159]). For all the moral criticism of the mercantile world, for all the ironic undermining of its values by uncommentated quotation of the words and concepts current in it, there remains a strong element of this respect in the texture of *Buddenbrooks*. For all his problematic relations with *Bürgertum*, Thomas Mann remained proud of his origins[42] and deeply influenced by their ethos, as he was aware. In 1905, long before the full description of that awareness in *Lübeck als geistige Lebensform* (1926), he concluded his first reply to accusations from Lübeck that he had written a scandalous *roman à clef* with the words:

> Ohne Familien- und Heimatsinn, ohne Liebe zu Familie und Heimat, werden Bücher wie 'Buddenbrooks' nicht geschrieben; und wer mich kennt, wer gewisse Arbeiten von mir gelesen hat, die auf dieses Buch folgten, der weiss, wie tief ich, trotz aller Künstler-Libertinage, ein Lübecker Bürger bin.

[40] In the letter to Heinrich Mann (Br. H. 19) quoted above, p. 53.

[41] Rilke and Lublinski both drew attention to the chronicle style of the narrative.

[42] To the annoyance of some critics. See Alfred Kerr's satirical verses 'Thomas Bodenbruch', in Kerr, *Caprichos*, Berlin, 1926, p. 168, esp. the lines 'Sprach immer stolz mit Breite / Von meiner Väter Pleite'.

(Without a feeling for family and native town, without love for them, books like 'Buddenbrooks' cannot be written; and anyone who knows me, and has read certain works of mine which followed that novel, knows how deeply I have remained a Lübeck burgher, even if I am a 'free-thinking artist'. [xi. 549])

True, in *Lübeck als geistige Lebensform* Mann denies that he set out to glorify Lübeck in his novel, and even claims that the reality of the city, its 'örtlich-stoffliches Teil', inspired him with no enthusiasm. But an uncritical acceptance of the Lübeck world need not be imputed to him, and was not required as the foundation of his novel. It was enough that he had a full familiarity with the place he sprang from which claimed, almost despite himself, a sustained seriousness of treatment. Perhaps the most exact statement on the matter occurs in Mann's defence of another Lübeck artist, Fritz Behn, in 1913:

Der Knabe mag die Heimat verachten, der ungeduldig und unbewegt ins Weite stürmt . . . Und doch, wie sehr er sich ihr entwachsen dünken, wie sehr er ihr entwachsen möge: doch bleibt ihr übervertrautes Bild in den Hintergründen seines Bewusstseins stehen oder taucht nach Jahren tiefer Vergessenheit wunderlich wieder daraus hervor: was abgeschmackt schien, wird ehrwürdig . . . .'.

(The boy may despise his home-town when he storms off, impatient and without a qualm . . . And yet, however much he may think he has left all that behind him, however much he may really do so, its deeply familiar image remains at the back of his mind or emerges from it in some bizarre way after years of oblivion; what once seemed ridiculous now becomes venerable . . . [xi. 738])

Though the young writer's escape from Lübeck made him an outsider, he is far from being one entirely in his fictional return. To borrow again from Bayley on Tolstoy, whereas Balzac or Proust are 'showing us over their acquired territories', Thomas Mann in this instance 'belongs to his'.[43]

Yet as we have seen, making *it* belong to *him*, in a literary sense, was dependent on the acquisition of a broad range of new techniques. Here his nineteenth-century predecessors in the large novel form were an indispensable aid. It is of course impossible to locate a precise source for every technique used in *Buddenbrooks*. Though new to Thomas Mann, they were

[43] Bayley, op. cit., p. 210.

widespread in nineteenth-century fiction and hence Mann could acquire them without at the time being aware of each specific debt. He was to speak later of the Naturalistic means used in *Buddenbrooks* and of the influences from all sides, from France, England, Russia, and the Scandinavian lands, which he eagerly learned from (xi. 553 f.). He also gives us some leads as to their respective roles.

The solution to his most basic problem of how to achieve novel length as such, when his genre to date had been the short story, was offered by the Goncourt brothers' novel *Reneé Mauperin* which he read in Rome. The grace and clarity of composition, the arrangement in short chapters, gave him the courage to say to himself 'You can do that too'.[44] This is the root of that method of persistent application, the piling up of many individual inspirations into a work of stature, which Mann was to practise throughout his career and to celebrate as the moral victory of will over slender means, producing a result which the public could take for the product of sheer power.[45]

But Mann's original intention, as we know, was not to push this mode of creation to the lengths which *Buddenbrooks* finally reached. He planned a novel of some 250 pages, modelled on the family novels of the Norwegians Kielland and Lie— Scandinavian writing was the height of fashion in this period of foreign influence ('für Deutschland eine Zeit literarischer Lufterneuerung aus dem Ausland' [xi. 550]), and Lübeck, with its obvious Nordic affinities, required little stylization to fit in with the trend.

It was only subsequently, when the unplanned 'swelling' of the novel began, when it declared its own 'ambitions', that the search for outside help became crucial. As the task threatened to be too much for the young writer, he sought aid and support from the 'giants of the declining nineteenth century'—

---

44 *Blätter* 6, p. 13.

45 Cf. *Der Tod in Venedig*: 'in kleinen Tagewerken aus aberhundert Einzel-inspirationen zur Grösse emporgeschichtet' (piled up in short daily stints from hundreds and hundreds of individual inspirations to make a work of stature [viii. 452]). Lorenz, in the *Preussische Jahrbücher* of 1902, made the perceptive comment: 'Ein Meister der Skizze hat einen Roman von 1000 Seiten geschrieben.' Ironic, in view of the Goncourt connection, is the first French reaction to *Buddenbrooks*: 'une succession bousculée de scènes rapides, de visions brèves . . . Une incohérence pénible à nos intelligences latines'. Maurice Muret, *Journal des Débats*, 24 Mar. 1908.

which meant above all Tolstoy. He read *Anna Karenina* and *War and Peace* to gain strength for a task which could only be mastered 'in beständiger Anlehnung an die Grössten' (in constant imitation of the greatest writers).[46] No further details are vouchsafed. One is left to imagine what the particular effects were of an influence which Mann later summed up in the words 'erschütternd, stärkend, die Ansprüche steigernd' (shattering, strengthening, raising the level of one's requirements), and what particular artistic possibilities among those touched on above were derived from Tolstoy's 'ungeheure plastische Kraft'.[47] Contemporary critics, at any rate, realized that Tolstoy was not an unreasonable term of comparison for the achievement of *Buddenbrooks*: if Hanno's piano improvizations called to mind D'Annunzio, the death of the Konsulin was worthy of Tolstoy.[48]

The English contribution is named as Dickens (x. 838)—no doubt his humour, which was also the contribution of the *plattdeutsch* works of Fritz Reuter. Mann occasionally mentions the symbolism of Ibsen as a further influence, but without being more specific (xi. 551). Still other influences are a matter for conjecture. The Konsul's death at the high point of a storm echoes the use of weather climaxes in Turgenev's *Torrents of Spring*, which Mann so much admired and later referred to as 'feinste Naturempfindlichkeit' (ix. 248). It also seems inconceivable that there was no side-glance at his beloved Fontane, when one thinks of the romance between Tony and Morten Schwarzkopf, the end of Thomas's affair with Anna, and—most marked of all—the treatment of the Buddenbrook family outing which leads up to Permaneder's proposal to Tony. (Fontane's outings are so crucial that, although apparently part of the 'matter' of his novels, they acquire the status of a technique.) Indeed, Tony is a character inviting treatment *à la* Fontane—the whole Grünlich episode can be read as a comic reversal of *Effi Briest*, which Mann had read in 1896.[49]

[46] *Blätter* 6, p. 13.

[47] *Die Zeit*, Vienna, 8 Sept. 1908, in a collection of tributes for Tolstoy's eightieth birthday. The piece has not been republished.

[48] Eduard Goldbeck, 'Der Kampf mit dem Leben', Wochenbeilage des *Leipziger Tageblattes*, 11 Apr. 1904.

[49] Cf. Schröter, *Dokumente*, p. 474, n. 51, and x. 838. For later detailed allusions to and borrowings from Fontane in Mann's writings, esp. in *Felix Krull*, see H. H. Reuter, *Fontane*, Berlin, 1968, vol. 2, pp. 977 ff.

There remains one other artistic influence which all Mann's accounts of *Buddenbrooks* insist on, and which gives new insight into his relations with tradition. That is the influence of Wagner's music.

It seems at first sight surprising that literary work should have been influenced by music. It is difficult to translate any specifically musical device into literary terms, and the designations for such devices (modulation, say, or counterpoint) can be applied to literary composition and effects only as metaphors. What they refer to is likely to have been determined by quite other factors than the emulation of a musical model. For instance to speak of the rise of artistic sensibility and simultaneous decline of vitality in the Buddenbrooks as a 'counterpoint' would be merely to give a suggestive description, not a technical insight.

In the case of the leitmotiv, moreover, we are not dealing with a specifically musical device at all. The name itself may have been new in the nineteenth century, coined to describe Wagner's practice, but the thing itself—the repetition of identical material as a means of characterization or as a structural 'reminder'—was a *literary* device as old as literature itself, going back to the *topos* of early epic poetry. Wagner's appropriation of the technique for his music drama was late and nobody who was at all well read could be struck by it as something new. Thomas Mann was not. He writes in his *Versuch über das Theater* (1908) that he cannot see how anyone can think the leitmotiv a dramatic device: it is profoundly epic, of Homeric origin (x. 27). And even without the recollection of Homer, it was impossible not to learn the method from more modern sources. Tolstoy makes use of it in the recurring descriptions of characters in *War and Peace*, and the Danish writer Herman Bang, at that time highly regarded in Germany and by 1902 certainly a particular enthusiasm of Thomas Mann's, was a virtuoso in the exploitation of the technique.[50] Thus the use of the leitmotiv needed no cue from Wagner. Significantly, the conversations on Wagner and his technique which occur within the novel (pp. 498 f.) give us no sense of

---

[50] See Ernst Alker, 'Über den Einfluss von Übersetzungen aus den nordischen Sprachen auf den Sprachstil der deutschen Literatur seit 1890', in *Stil- und Formprobleme in der Literatur*, Heidelberg, 1959, p. 457. Cf. Br. i. 36.

being—as so many passages in Thomas Mann are—meant to be understood also as self-commentary.

What was there then to be *learned* from Wagner's musical practice? Nothing, as Mann himself admitted in a note on Wagner's art written in 1911. He had, as a prose narrator and psychologist, nothing technical (*Direktes und Handwerkliches*) to learn from the *symphonischen Theatraliker* (x. 840). Yet he goes on, in a characteristic way, to add that the ultimate unity of art, quite apart from Wagner's own programme of mixing the arts, makes Wagner instructive and nourishing (*lehrend und nährend*) for any artist; and his personal view of Wagner as essentially 'epic' gives Mann a sense of direct and intimate relationship with him. Thus the clear statement denying Wagner's relevance in technical matters is blurred sufficiently for parallels between *Buddenbrooks* and the *Ring* to be drawn after all: 'Wirklich ist es nicht schwer, in meinen 'Buddenbrooks', diesem epischen, von Leitmotiven verknüpften und durchwobenen Generationenzuge, vom Geiste des 'Nibelungenringes' einen Hauch zu verspüren.' (It is indeed not hard to detect in my 'Buddenbrooks', that sequence of generations connected and woven through with leitmotivs, a breath of the spirit of the 'Ring' [x. 840].) This conclusion, at once so sweeping and so vague ('detect . . . breath . . . spirit') becomes the basis for the many subsequent references to Wagner as a direct source for and influence on *Buddenbrooks* and its compositional method.[51] Later there is added the suggestion of a parallel between the genesis of the novel, with its filling in of the complete prehistory of Hanno, and the genesis of the *Ring* tetralogy, with its progressive exploration further back into the prehistory of *Siegfrieds Tod* (e.g. xi. 381).

The purely coincidental nature of this last parallel is illuminating. It gives us the clue to why Mann modified the plain statement that there was nothing technical to be learned

---

[51] 'Der deutsche Einfluss . . . kam von Fritz Reuter und Richard Wagner' (xii. 89, 1917); 'Quellen wie . . . Richard Wagners Motivtechnik und symphonische Dialektik' (*Blätter* 6, p. 15, 1940); 'Bildungserlebnisse . . . die motivische Musik von Wagners "Nibelungen" . . . strömen in das Werk ein' (xi. 550 f., 1940); 'niederdeutsche Humoristik und die epische Motivtechnik Richard Wagners gingen darin eine wunderliche Verbindung ein' (xi. 554, 1949).—Mann's lifelong re-use of conclusions once reached, with minimal variations in wording, means that later statements rarely add authority to earlier ones, on which they simply depend.

from Wagner. This was simply not adequate to express the kind of feeling Mann had for his predecessors in German culture. Admiration fathered in him the wish to establish in some way a personal connection with them. Wagner's was a name to conjure with; any ground for linking it with his own was welcome. The similarity of technique would do very well, even if Mann had never needed actually to go to Wagner to learn it. In due course, this too would come to be rather hazily asserted, Wagner would join the list of influences on *Buddenbrooks*.

Of course, in a general way, as an object of emulation, a standard of achievement, Wagner exerted an influence. Mann speaks in 1911 of the way Wagner's name for long overshadowed all his work and his thinking about art; all artistic striving seemed to be epitomized in the name Wagner. But this is a matter simply of ambition—the ambition to achieve large-scale work, or success.[52] *Buddenbrooks*, the first of Mann's works to do both, was the first one to be linked with Wagner's name. The relatively slight early stories never were, even though they had already made ample use of the leitmotiv.

It was arguably the success of *Buddenbrooks* and the terms on which reviewers drew for comparison that gave its author the assurance to see his work in connection with such a great name. Indeed it seems likely that the Wagner parallel was actually suggested to him by one of the early reviews. The *Münchener Neueste Nachrichten* of 24 December 1901 commented: 'Spezifisch Wagnerisch ist die eminent episch wirkende strenge Durchführung des Leitmotivs, die wörtliche Rückbeziehung im Wechsel der Generationen über weite Strecken des Buches hin.' (Specifically Wagnerian is the eminently epic effect of a rigorous use of leitmotivs, the verbal reference back, over great stretches of the book, from one generation to the other.) Not only the main point here, but details of the wording anticipate Mann's earliest declarations of indebtedness to Wagner—the one of 1904, which describes 'das Motiv, das Selbstzitat, die autoritative Formel, die wörtliche und gewichtige Rückbeziehung über weite Strecken des Buches hin' as

[52] Cf. x. 837, on his 'Sehnsucht, wenigstens im Kleinen und Leisen "auch dergleichen zu machen"', and x. 895 (and often) 'unseren Werkinstinkt zu stacheln ist niemand besser geschaffen als er'.

'diese wagnerischen und eminent nordischen Wirkungsmittel' (x. 838), or that of 1911 which declares that such methods are essentially epic. This evidence is not conclusive, but it is strongly suggestive. Sensitive to critical appraisal of his work as the young novelist was, he probably took over this critical comment as he took over others.[53] If critics did not find such parallels extravagant or incongruous, his own need for support might well take the form of claims to affinity.

Yet this particular claim to affinity was not all self-congratulation. Mann's admiration for Wagner had a critical element from the very first. He read Nietzsche's writings on Wagner at the age of nineteen,[54] and the suspicion which inevitably resulted—of Wagner's methods and motives, of his effects on German culture and later politics—remained with Mann permanently. Taking over Wagner as akin to himself meant taking over this suspicion. Thus what Mann says in the *Betrachtungen eines Unpolitischen* about having learnt the very nature of artistic effect and artistic formulation from Wagner can also be put critically: the effect-seeking of the artist is part of his charlatanry and illusionism, and hence a self-reproach for one who feels, like Tonio Kröger, that he has sacrificed human substance and human relations to his art. The ambivalence appears in early letters. During his courtship of Katja Pringsheim, Mann worked hard to persuade her that irony and coolness in art did not mean, as people supposed, an unfeeling personality:

Und wenn einer zu pointieren und mit seinen Mitteln zu wirtschaften versteht, so muss er ganz unbedingt ein gemütloser Blender sein. Mich wundert immer, dass man Wagnern nicht längst für einen eiskalten Faiseur erklärt hat, weil er den Liebestod an den Aktschluss setzt . . .

(And when a writer knows how to make a point and manipulate his means, he necessarily has to be a heartless hoodwinker. I am always amazed that people haven't long ago written off Wagner as

[53] The review is among his own early collection, which became the basis for the Ida Herz collection. His references to Wagner in 1904 include the sardonic remark that nobody has yet noticed any connection, despite the title of his latest book (i.e. *Tristan*). Has he by now forgotten the review, or is this a kind of double bluff? For other instances of Mann's taking over judgements on himself and his works, see below, p. 100, footnote.

[54] Cf. 'Geist und Kunst', N 19.

an ice-cold contriver because he puts the 'Liebestod' at the end of
the act . . . [Br. i. 52])

On the other hand, replying in 1910 to Hermann Hesse's
criticisms of *Königliche Hoheit*,[55] Mann put down what Hesse
called its manipulation or incitement of the audience (*Antrei-
bereien des Publikums*) to the influence of Wagner, and wondered
whether he had not been corrupted for good by that 'exclusive yet demagogic art'. He admits his ambition to make
popular appeal compatible with subtler effects, a dual aim
which was to govern his work for a lifetime.[56]

There was one other affinity between Mann and Wagner as
creators which, to a disciple of Nietzsche, was bound to appear
in a dubious light, namely their relation to the large-scale work.
Mixed with Mann's pride in the achievement of major form
by a process of building up small elements and inspirations
there is a note of unease, which sprang from the belief that by
the highest ideals of creativity this process was inorganic. It
was close to what Nietzsche had indicted as 'decadent' literature:[57] not literature produced by those whom decadence in
the vital sense had refined into artists, but literature which was
weak and unvital *qua* literature. Mann had been called a
'master of the sketch who has written a novel'. Nietzsche in a
sublime paradox had called Wagner the greatest miniaturist of
music.[58] The effort to come to terms with this aspect of his art
is at the centre of Mann's thought for two decades during which
he alternates between self-doubt and self-affirmation, a critique
of and an apologia for 'modernity'.

These are the main influences Mann himself named. In a
more general way, one can think of the whole nineteenth-
century realistic tradition as 'there' in the background, though
the relation may not be simple dependence.[59] Some contri-

---

[55] Hesse's perceptive review, relevant to far more of Mann's work than the
novel it treats, is reprinted in the Mann–Hesse correspondence, pp. 207 ff.

[56] Br. iii. 457.

[57] Cf. *Der Fall Wagner*, § 7 on the loss of organic life in literary texts, concluding
with: 'Das Ganze lebt überhaupt nicht mehr: es ist zusammengesetzt, gerechnet,
künstlich, ein Artefakt' (Schlechta ii. 917).

[58] Ibid., p. 918: 'Unsern grössten *Miniaturisten* der Musik'.

[59] For example, an attempt to establish the ways Theodor Storm contributed
to Mann's early writing in fact brings out most effectively the ways in which Mann
has left behind the cosier moods of nineteenth-century narrative. See Günther

butors never received acknowledgement.[60] Mann's selectivity
in matters of influence could exclude real ones as well as including those with vaguer claims like Wagner.

Finally what about the two much-discussed philosophical
influences on the novel, Nietzsche and Schopenhauer? Approaching this subject it is well to remember the half-truths
and confusions of the Wagner case, especially when Mann's
own hints have been taken up a shade uncritically by students
of *Geistesgeschichte*. An appropriate lead-in to it is the *Betrachtungen* passage which links all three, Schopenhauer, Nietzsche,
and Wagner, in an apparently unresolvable amalgam:

Schopenhauer, Nietzsche und Wagner: ein Dreigestirn ewig ver-
bundener Geister . . . Tief und unlösbar sind ihre Schöpfer- und
Herrscherschicksale verknüpft. Nietzsche nannte Schopenhauer
seinen 'grossen Lehrer'; welch ungeheueres Glück für Wagner das
Erlebnis Schopenhauers war, weiss der Erdkreis; die Freundschaft
von Tribschen mochte sterben, — sie ist unsterblich . . . Die drei sind
eins. Der ehrfürchtige Schüler, dem ihre gewaltigen Lebensläufe
zur Kultur geworden, möchte wünschen, von allen dreien auf einmal
reden zu können, so schwer scheint es ihm, auseinanderzuhalten,
was er dem einzelnen verdankt. Wenn ich von Schopenhauer den
Moralismus — ein populäreres Wort für dieselbe Sache lautet
'Pessimismus' — meiner seelischen Grundstimmung habe, jene Stim-
mung von 'Kreuz, Tod und Gruft', die schon in meinen ersten Versuchen hervortrat: so findet sich diese 'ethische Luft', um mit
Nietzsche zu reden, auch bei Wagner . . . Wenn aber eben diese
Grundstimmung mich zum *Verfalls*psychologen machte, so war es
Nietzsche, auf den ich dabei als Meister blickte . . .

(Schopenhauer, Nietzsche and Wagner: a triple constellation of
eternally connected spirits . . . Their destinies as creators and
dominators are profoundly and inseparably linked. Nietzsche called
Schopenhauer his 'great teacher; what an enormous stroke of
fortune the experience of Schopenhauer was for Wagner, the whole
world knows; the Tribschen friendship might die,—it remains
immortal . . . The three of them are one. The reverent disciple, for
whom their mighty careers represent a culture, could wish to speak
of them all simultaneously, so difficult does it seem to him to keep
separate what he owes to each individually. If I have from Schopenhauer the moralism—a more popular word for the same thing would

Weydt, 'Thomas Mann und Storm', in R. von Heydebrand and K. G. Just (eds.),
*Wissenschaft als Dialog*, Stuttgart, 1969.

[60] Cf. Klaus Schröter, *Thomas Mann*, Reinbek, 1964, pp. 35 f. on Paul Bourget.

be 'pessimism'—of my basic attitude of mind, that mood of 'cross, death, and the grave', which is already present in my earliest writings: then this selfsame 'ethical atmosphere', to quote Nietzsche, can also be found in Wagner . . . But if it was precisely this basic outlook that made me into a psychologist of decline, Nietsche was the man whom I looked to as my master. [xii. 79])

Now it is certainly true that Schopenhauer, Nietzsche, and Wagner make up a coherent chapter in German intellectual and cultural history in the way Mann indicates. Nietzsche took over Schopenhauer's basic analysis (though not his evaluation) of the relationship between life and intellect. Wagner derived inspiration from Schopenhauer in the writing of *Tristan*. Nietzsche found in Wagner, for a time, the embodiment of his ideals for a rebirth of German culture and especially tragedy. His subsequent disillusionment produced those hostile accounts of the 'Wagner case' and the (perhaps unduly) generalized critique of the Artist which were to colour Mann's own view so strongly. Thus the three names make a closely woven tradition, which Mann is perhaps attaching himself to in yet another way when he remarks somewhat disingenuously that Nietzsche has 'not yet' found his artist as Schopenhauer did in Wagner.

The attraction of such historical interconnectedness, the richness of cross-reference between the members of a distinct tradition, is presumably what made Mann unable or unwilling to disentangle at this point the precise influence each had on him. As we saw him do with Wagner, so again with Schopenhauer he slides from 'essential' affinities into assertions of direct dependence. He claims that he actually 'has from' Schopenhauer the basic pessimism of his outlook. Yet Mann read no Schopenhauer until well on in the composition of *Buddenbrooks*.[61] Schopenhauer's philosophy can hardly have determined even the pattern of that novel, let alone the mood of the stories written earlier still. What Mann is aiming at here, as so often when he discusses his antecedents and his place in traditions, is wealth of connection, not autobiographical accuracy.

It is possible to understand the 'traditionalist' need from which such generalizations sprang—and to make this insight

---

[61] Probably autumn 1899, and perhaps as an effect of reading Nietzsche's *Schopenhauer als Erzieher*, which appeared in GOA, vol. i in 1899.

fruitful for an interpretation of Thomas Mann—while still wishing to get the facts right. Indeed, only by getting the facts right can we know what needs interpreting on these lines. What are the facts about the philosophers and *Buddenbrooks*? Thomas Buddenbrook's reading of Schopenhauer occurs in part 10 of the novel, more than four-fifths of the way through it. This accords with Thomas Mann's two accounts of his own reading of Schopenhauer and of the way he at once transferred his experience to the book. He stresses that the composition of *Buddenbrooks* was already well advanced, that it was time to prepare Thomas Buddenbrook for death, that the young writer was delighted to have an opportunity to use this intense experience straight away in his nearly completed fictional work.[62]

Besides the main Schopenhauer episode, there are unmistakably elements of Schopenhauer's thought in two passages concerning music, the description of Hanno's performance before the family and a conversation between Gerda and Thomas on musical taste. Both use the concept of a transitory and illusory moment of happiness towards which the Will strives.[63] To these might be added the description of the organist Edmund Pfühl, whose gaze, when playing, 'die Dinge träumerisch zu durchschauen und jenseits ihrer Erscheinung zu rühen schien' (seemed dreamily to see through things and to rest somewhere beyond their appearance [p. 495])—conceivably a reference to Schopenhauer's view that music is a direct expression of the ultimate reality of the Will and not, like the other arts, a mere response to the phenomena (*Erscheinung*) in which the Will is

---

[62] 'Und welch ein Glück, dass ich ein Erlebnis wie dieses nicht in mich zu verschliessen brauchte, dass . . . dichterische Unterkunft unmittelbar dafür bereit war. Denn zwei Schritte von meinem Kanapee lag aufgeschlagen das unmöglich und unpraktisch anschwellende Manuskript . . . welches eben bis zu dem Punkte gediehen war, dass es galt, Thomas Buddenbrook zu Tode zu bringen' (xiii. 72). Cf. also xi. 111: 'die Möglichkeit . . . mein überbürgerliches Erlebnis in das zu Ende gehende Bürgerbuch einzuflechten'.

[63] Of Hanno's playing: 'Noch ein letztes, allerletztes Auskosten dieser drängenden und treibenden Sehnsucht, dieser Begierde des ganzen Wesens, dieser äussersten und krampfhaften Anspannung des Willens, der sich dennoch die Erfüllung und Erlösung noch verweigerte, weil er wusste: Das Glück ist nur ein Augenblick' (pp. 506 f.).—And Gerda to Thomas: 'Was freut dich in der Musik? Der Geist eines gewissen faden Optimismus . . . Schnelle Erfüllung jedes kaum erregten Wunsches . . . Prompte, freundliche Befriedigung des kaum ein wenig aufgestachelten Willens' (p. 509).

D

objectified. All three passages are likewise relatively late in the novel and hence fit well enough what Mann said about Schopenhauer, for that need not be taken to mean that Thomas Buddenbrook's death was the very next thing to be taken in hand.

Nothing else in the novel requires us to invoke Schopenhauer in order to clarify or deepen our understanding.

What Erich Heller says about the genesis of *Buddenbrooks*— that it 'derives its intellectual plot from Schopenhauer', that it is a 'philosophical novel in the sense that the imagination which conceived it bears the imprint of Schopenhauer's thought'[64]—is wholly disposed of by Mann's own accounts. Hence Heller's whole interpretation of *Buddenbrooks* by reference to Schopenhauer's general thesis of the intellect, with its products, art and saintliness, rebelling against the life-force which has gradually evolved it—this whole interpretation, stimulating though it is, rests on an oversight.

Of course the correspondence between the line of development in *Buddenbrooks* and the general pattern of Schopenhauer's thought is not in every sense a coincidence. Mann's ideas were derived from the theory of decadence current in the period and in particular from Nietzsche. The young author of *Buddenbrooks* 'learned the psychology of decline from Nietzsche', as he said. This explains perfectly well why the development in *Buddenbrooks* could appear Schopenhauerian: the similarity between Nietzsche's system and Schopenhauer's, from which it derives its general shape, means that any derivative of the one will be bound to resemble the other. Where the two philosophers diverge is in their valuation of 'vitality' (*Leben*) and 'intellect'. Mann's own valuation of these things is no clue to where his direct allegiance and indebtedness lay. It depended clearly enough on his own experience as a *fin de siècle* artist and it is in any case an ambivalent valuation.

The case is surely plain enough. If academic critics sometimes seem intent on rescuing at all costs the theory of a Schopenhauer influence,[65] this is a symptom both of the type of reputation

---

[64] *The Ironic German*, 1957, pp. 30, 27.

[65] e.g. Jürgen Scharfschwerdt, *Thomas Mann und der deutsche Bildungsroman*, Stuttgart, 1967, p. 67. Scharfschwerdt notes the passages on music mentioned above, but quaintly adds that Tony Buddenbrook embodies Schopenhauer's conception of genius. Lehnert, *Fiktion*, p. 36, argues that Schopenhauer's philosophy

which Thomas Mann came to have, with erudition *per se* and the continuing of tradition as a major element in it, and also of a *Geistesgeschichte* which is simply unwilling to forgo any connection between great and great.[66] Hence even Thomas Mann's clear statements on the chronology and effect of his reading of Schopenhauer have to be neutralized in order to maintain the less valid part of his image.

The Schopenhauer case has further ramifications. The unrepresentativeness of that chapter of *Die Welt als Wille und Vorstellung* which is the core of Thomas Buddenbrook's reading ('Über den Tod und sein Verhältnis zur Unzerstörbarkeit unsers Wesens an sich'), its tendency if taken in isolation to run counter to Schopenhauer's general argument, leads Thomas Buddenbrook—as it had perhaps led Thomas Mann—to misunderstand that argument. It inspires in him a hope of mystical union after death with all the more harmonious, powerful embodiments of life. Perhaps a shade embarrassed by the misreading he had lent his character and called the 'essential' in Schopenhauer ('das eigentlich Wichtige' [p. 655]), Mann later tried to make it plausible by suggesting that a striving for erotic union is what Schopenhauer is more profoundly and 'really' about than the negation of the lifeforce he so lucidly and repeatedly preaches. As an alternative explanation, Mann took over the discovery by critics[67] of a Nietzschean admixture to Thomas Buddenbrook's (and perhaps his own) reading of Schopenhauer. 'Hier dachte freilich einer, der ausser Schopenhauer auch schon Nietzsche gelesen hatte' (ix. 561). The misreading makes it quite plain that there was no intention of making that episode a 'consummation' for a Schopenhauerian 'syntax of ideas'[68] in *Buddenbrooks*, since

was somehow 'there' even before Mann read it because (i) he had possessed the volumes (uncut) long before opening them; (ii) there are isolated Schopenhauer quotations in an early notebook, almost certainly, Lehnert agrees, from secondary sources; and (iii) Nietzsche makes frequent references to Schopenhauer. But the reading of Nietzsche is precisely what makes the whole Schopenhauer hypothesis unnecessary, for reasons outlined above.

[66] Cf. above, Introduction, p. 3.

[67] e.g. Wilhelm Alberts in the *Buddenbrooks* chapter of his book *Thomas Mann und sein Beruf*, Leipzig, 1913, a work which Mann certainly knew, if only because its publication set off the hilarious public protest by Onkel Friedl ('Christian Buddenbrook') against the long years of notoriety his nephew's book had brought him.

[68] *The Ironic German*, p. 57.

an untypical chapter and a misunderstanding of an argument
are an inept consummation of that argument's effect; while
Mann's later adjustments illustrate the dilemmas of a writer
caught in the meshes of *Geistesgeschichte* by the simple fact of
having used an experience which happened to be the excitement
of reading Schopenhauer.

It would be tedious to follow all this out in detail. I have had
to say this much to unpick some of the strands of 'tradition'
plaited by Thomas Mann and his critics. This has meant
wandering from the central concerns of a reader of *Buddenbrooks*.
He must be recommended to keep a sense of proportion; to take
seriously the ideas which were current at the time Mann wrote
the novel, especially where there is clear internal and external
evidence that particular ideas were important; and not to read
the Schopenhauer episode as part of an intellectual plot except
in the sense that it is itself the finely conceived culmination of
Thomas Buddenbrook's history as a divided burgher. The
reader can safely take *Buddenbrooks*, whatever may later be true
of the complex weave of *Der Zauberberg* and *Doktor Faustus*, as
a novel in the nineteenth-century manner, concerned with
story, character, psychology, and moral criticism, all of which
give substance to a general thesis. The Thomas Mann of
*Buddenbrooks* is not yet predominantly a novelist of ideas. His
ideas are buried in that rich substance, fused with it successfully if involuntarily. We separate them out and stress them only
to the detriment of the novel.

Only by taking *Buddenbrooks* on these terms as a successful,
if highly sophisticated and late essay in nineteenth-century
realism do we grasp the novel's significance in Thomas Mann's
career, in his thinking about his art, in his ambitions for future
works. In retrospect, the novel and his composition of the novel
came to appear transfigured, ideal. It represented for him a
standard of achievement and a solution to problems of technique
and balance which was exemplary. Substance, so problematic
in his later works, was there in this first masterpiece in plenty,
enough to extend the writer technically, and apt to express his
ideas not allegorically but in full fictional fusion. Immediately
after finishing the book, he wrote to Heinrich of the three
years of torment it had cost him. But by 1905, the failure of his
drama *Fiorenza* could make him long for the days of 'Budden-

brook *naïveté*' (Br. H. 35). By 1910 he is asking if he has achieved sufficient *Plastik*—the characteristic associated with *Buddenbrooks*—to be in a position to criticize, for reasons we shall see, the *Plastik* principle. By 1917, in the general attempt to set off superficial *Entente* rationalism against the profounder, more organic German culture, *Buddenbrooks* has become a Gothic ideal, a natural growth, not a construction.[69] No later work of Mann's has this status, all are constructed, composed, with a glance over the shoulder at that first triumphant achievement and an occasional attempt to persuade himself he had again achieved something comparable. In old age, Mann was to reflect that perhaps only *Buddenbrooks* would last, that his later works were simply more-or-less respectable ways of filling in the time after his real task was complete.

In this last point, it is hardly necessary to say, he was wrong. Different though his later work is, it can be rejected thus sweepingly only on some such simplistic principle as his many anti-intellectualist critics, often politically motivated, were to use. Yet we do well to remember the status which his first novel always had for Thomas Mann. It is the key to what he tried to do subsequently and a measure of his problems, experiments, and achievements.

---

[69] '... geworden, nicht gemacht, gewachsen, nicht geformt und eben dadurch unübersetzbar deutsch ... die organische Fülle, die das typisch französische Buch nicht hat ... kein ebenmässiges Kunstwerk, sondern Leben' (xii. 89).

# The Making of Illusion

PHILETYMUS. But this Art is what we Dullards call Theft, who call a Fig a Fig and a Spade a Spade.
PSEUDOCHEUS. O Ignoramus in the Law! Can you bring an Action of Theft for Trover or Conversion?

ERASMUS, *Familiar Colloquies*

## I

IN 1904 Thomas Mann gave a public reading in his native city. The Lübeck *General-Anzeiger* reported it and voiced its view of the by now famous *Buddenbrooks*:

We find this type of artistic creation lacking in taste—not to use another, stronger term; for the people concerned are entirely defenceless against such an undertaking and cannot but feel injured when they are described in the novel with their foibles, great and small. The author has duly found little sympathy for the most part among our townspeople. That of course was no reason for not taking a look at him.

Injured or no, some Lübeckers handed Thomas Mann a laurel wreath, complete with bow in the city colours. This too inspired only acid comment from the local organ:

Herr Mann, whose fame has given him a certain superiority of manner, was evidently very pleased with this ovation. Did it perhaps also bore him, like the wreaths presented to the child prodigy in his story?[1] At all events, the evening was quite an interesting one; we have at least seen the celebrated Thomas Mann, and that is after all something, many may think.

This Lübeck's-eye view aptly introduces Thomas Mann's first appeal to the authority of tradition, for it was attitudes like these that provoked him to a public stand on an issue of literary principle. His ambivalent feelings about his burgher background made him sensitive to Lübeck opinion, and in the

---

[1] Cf. viii. 343. Mann read *Das Wunderkind* as part of his programme.

following year a Lübeck libel action against a writer gave wider publicity to the kind of objections quoted above. *Buddenbrooks* was referred to several times in the proceedings, and mentioned by the prosecution in the same breath with a novel which had recently caused a scandal, Fritz Oswald Bilse's *Aus einer kleinen Garnison* (1903). This work was, in Thomas Mann's view, little more than a thinly disguised libel, and he protested against the guilt-by-association, briefly in a piece entitled *Ein Nachwort*, and at greater length in the essay *Bilse und ich*. Both appeared in newspapers[2] because they were meant to set right popular misconceptions and would have seemed platitudinous in a literary journal. Nevertheless they have an interest beyond this limited intention. They show us new literary possibilities branching out from the traditional practice which Mann set out to defend.

The first piece is brief and its argument simple. I should not have appeared for the defence, Mann says, because I could not support the contention that the use of living persons in a novel is unconscious. It was not so with *Buddenbrooks*. But if all the books which use living persons for artistic purposes are to be called 'Bilse' works, this will mean branding much of what is greatest in world literature. Mann quotes the obvious example of *Werther*. He denies that it is presumptuous to link his name with Goethe; it is simply a matter of which of the two, Goethe or Bilse, he is nearer to. Bilse was a libellist with no talent; Goethe was aiming higher. *Buddenbrooks*, like *Werther*, was an attempt at art. That is the crucial distinction.

*Bilse und ich* adds further authorities: Turgenev, with his use of living persons in *A Sportsman's Sketches* and *Fathers and Children*; Wagner and Schiller, in works not specified; and Shakespeare, with his real model for Falstaff. But great names from the past provide only support, not theoretical justification. What actually justifies their practice and constitutes 'art' is, in Mann's view, what the writer himself contributes, what he makes *of* his material. He calls it, at different points in the essay, 'Beseelung', 'Durchdringung und Erfüllung des Stoffes mit dem, was des Dichters ist', and 'subjektive Vertiefung des Abbildes einer Wirklichkeit' (bestowing of a soul; permeation

---

[2] Respectively in the *Lübecker General-Anzeiger* of 7 Nov. 1905 and the *Münchener Neueste Nachrichten* of 15 and 16 Feb. 1906.

and filling of the material with something of the poet's; subjective deepening of the image of reality). Once this process has occurred, what the poet has taken over is no longer what it was in reality. It is philistine to think it is still the same, try to reclaim it, or be enraged by its use.

So far, Mann's sprited defence is a classic statement of fundamentals. His insistence on a separate aesthetic category and his warding off of attempts to treat elements within the work of art as if they were unaltered reality are akin to the *Schein* theory of Weimar Classicism; but the word *Schein* is nowhere used, and it seems the need to defend himself has made him work out his own common-sense principle from the examples of great writers who sprang to mind. From them all, he derives the generalization that it is precisely the great writers who have not been strong on imaginative invention, preferring to use the materials of reality ('statt frei zu "erfinden", sich lieber auf etwas Gegebenes, am liebsten auf die Wirklichkeit stützten' [x. 13]). Applied to *Buddenbrooks*, which was the starting-point of the essay, Mann's argument is a full vindication. However much Lübeck and the Buddenbrooks retain an independent vitality and interest, they clearly also serve to convey Mann's own ideas and mode of experience. And equally, the identification between author and characters in *Buddenbrooks* is a legitimate example of what he sees in Shakespeare's creations, Othello or Shylock: 'das innere Einswerden des Dichters mit seinem Modell' (p. 17).

But there are points in Mann's argument where more is suggested than his chosen examples will substantiate, for instance, when he says that the real Lübeck has *nothing* to do with the Lübeck of his re-creative imagination (pp. 15 f.). Or when, speaking of characters based on real-life models, he reduces the models to mere masks through which the writer presents problems which are his, not theirs (p. 17). This too is a kind of identification, but a rather different kind from the Shakespeare examples, or from Mann's own achievements in *Buddenbrooks*. For the crucial question about any artistic *Einswerden* is, whose identity is to swallow up whose? Or is there to be a mutual adaptation? If there is identification in Tolstoy's portrayal of Pierre and Prince Andrei, or even of Natasha, and in Flaubert's of Emma Bovary; if there is something very similar in Thomas Mann's portrayal of Hanno and

Thomas Buddenbrook and even at times Tony, then these are cases where authorial identity is yielded, at least partly, to the characters' own. The writer feels his way into the character. And this is ultimately what we understand by 'realism': not a photographic, factual presentation but a fusion of idea and reality. If characters, or places, are left with no vestige of the reality they originally possessed, what is created is not realism. *Buddenbrooks* undoubtedly is realistic by this criterion.

What made Thomas Mann push his argument so much further than he needed in the direction of absolute autonomy and art for art's sake? The answer lies not in *Buddenbrooks*, but in his work since that novel. When he speaks of living models as mere masks through which to work out his own problems, he almost certainly has in mind the fuss Arthur Holitscher made over the borrowing of his features for Spinell in *Tristan*,[3] and possibly also the near-scandal surrounding the composition and withdrawal of the story *Wälsungenblut*.[4] For 'identification' in these stories, unlike Mann's practice in *Buddenbrooks*, is not a fusion with, but a hollowing out of the real-life model— or so Mann was forced by the unpleasantness of the characters in his two stories to argue. When he says that *Bilse und ich* is concerned with human relations rather than literature we must imagine in the background a father-in-law for whom *Wälsungenblut* had been 'too close to reality not to be very offensive in its deviation from reality'.[5] But more important than these private embarrassments is the shift of aesthetic method over against *Buddenbrooks*. Reality is now entirely disponible material. The writer claims sovereign rights over it, but no obligations to render its actual nature.

Thomas Mann only apparently justifies this practice by

[3] Cf. Holitscher's account of how Thomas Mann watched him through opera glasses from his window, repr. in Schröter, *Dokumente*, p. 16. Mann's declaration in a foreword to the book publication of *Bilse und ich*, that he has only contempt for an *artist* who cannot keep art and reality in their separate categories, is presumably aimed at Holitscher. See x. 10 and 18.

[4] Hence the allusion 'die Wirklichkeit . . . mag als Person sein Nächstes und Liebstes sein' (x. 16). For full details of the affair see Br. H. 265 and the decidedly *pro familia* account by Klaus Pringsheim, 'Ein Nachtrag zu "Wälsungenblut"', *Neue Zürcher Zeitung*, 17 Dec. 1961.

[5] George Henry Lewes's phrase apropos the Kestners' reaction to *Werther* (*Goethe*, Everyman, p. 159). This is much nearer the mark than Mann's idea of Lotte and Albert realizing that Goethe had given them a 'higher, more intense and more lasting life than they led in bourgeois reality' (xi. 547 f.).

leading over to it from the less problematic kind: Goethe is in both Tasso and Antonio, Shakespeare in Othello and Shylock, Turgenev in Bazarov and Pavel Petrovich. Does this not remove, he asks, all suggestion of an arbitrary usurpation by the poet? The answer in the rather different case of Mann's offending stories is not so straightforward as the rhetorical question implies.

Nor is it straightforward in the case of one other almost imperceptible shift of argument in this essay. Discussing Shakespeare's borrowings, Mann includes not only real-life models, but other kinds of material which are nothing to do with a writer's primary experience. The piece *Ein Nachwort* had said of its one witness from the past, Goethe, that he was once merely 'irgendein junger Mann aus Frankfurt, der "schrieb", der sein Leben dichtete, die Eindrücke, die er von Welt und Leben gewann, in Büchern gestaltete' (some young chap from Frankfurt who 'wrote', who made poetry from his life, who gave form to his impressions of life and the world in books [ix. 548]). This is an apt enough example in a defence of Mann's own exploitation of primary experience in *Buddenbrooks*. But the later piece shifts to stating a more general principle: 'Schliesslich, ob nun die Geschichte, die Sage, die alte Novellistik, ob die lebendige Wirklichkeit selbst das "Gegebene" ist, worauf ein Dichter sich stützt, — gilt das nicht, im Wesen, gleichviel?' (And in the end, whether it is history, saga, older stories, or live reality that a poet bases his work on—isn't it essentially all the same? [x. 14])

This no longer concerns how not to give offence to living persons or the translating of primary experience into literature at all, but states the writer's freedom to draw on any source for the substance of his works—to which he will then give a 'soul'. If *Buddenbrooks* represented what may be termed a 'normal' relationship between writer and reality, a creative reaction to experience which—whatever the torments of the compositional process—can still be called spontaneous, then these theories which ostensibly spring from *Buddenbrooks* are the first formulations of a radically different aesthetic which grew out of the problems Thomas Mann was left with after completing *Buddenbrooks*. Since this is the aesthetic on which all his later large-scale works rest, there is some value in a close examination of its beginnings.

II

The characteristic of Mann's earliest stories was an imbalance
between form and substance, a paucity of narrative matter to
absorb and develop the stylistic means. We saw how *Buddenbrooks* solved this problem. But it was a solution which exhausted its own potential. The family and its Lübeck past were
a rich vein, its later stages were materials of direct experience
such as Mann had till then barely experimented with; but the
shape of the 'intellectual plot' within which they were presented
had cut them off short. The Buddenbrooks were not good for
a sequel in the manner of Freytag's novel-sequence *Die Ahnen*,[6]
nor was Thomas Mann the kind of writer to settle permanently
for *Heimatkunst*, exploring the Lübeck past for its own quaint
sake. Nor, given the level of achievement of *Buddenbrooks*, was
it conceivable that he should go back to the arbitrary constructs
of his early days for long. (It is arguable that *Der Weg zum
Friedhof*, written as a 'chaser' immediately after *Buddenbrooks*,
is one such.) But what experience was to hand as grist for the
literary mill? Only the experience of being cut off from normal
experience, and this reason for lacking external themes had to
become itself a theme.

Tonio Kröger's emotional discomforts have been too much
discussed to need insisting on. His yearning to be reunited with
'normal' life in all its seductive banality is the vestige of
natural feeling which his *fin de siècle* view of art (stated in the
conversation with Lisaweta Iwanowna, but queried by the
whole story and finally invalidated) has not killed off. His
situation as an observer, set apart from the world, not involved
in its activities, seeing through its values, bound by none of
the usual ties, constitutes his problem: how to live a negative,
insubstantial existence. This was no doubt one sense in which
Mann understood Nietzsche's comment on the artist as
eternally cut off from reality: 'in alle Ewigkeit von dem

---

6 Freytag's 'series of freely invented(!) stories' was to fill in the prehistory of a
more triumphantly conceived German present than Thomas Mann's. Freytag
planned it to move from the very earliest times 'gradually down to the last descendant . . . a fresh young fellow who still goes his way under the German sun, without
much worrying his head about the deeds and the sufferings of his forebears'.
(Foreword to *Ingo und Ingraban*, 1872.)

"Realen", dem Wirklichen abgetrennt'.[7] But Nietzsche's comment, like Tonio Kröger's situation, has implications for the artist's creativity, not just his social existence. What work of substance can grow from the experience of insubstantiality? Only a work about this problem itself. The life of the artist—and *Buddenbrooks* had certainly established in every sense that Thomas Mann was an artist—had to become the theme. Clearly the theme has drawbacks. It makes literature possible at the price of becoming ever more introverted. The writer never ventures beyond the examination of his own craft and the difficulties of its practitioners.[8] Infinite regress is always at hand. Yet this theme dominates practically all Mann wrote or planned between *Buddenbrooks* and *Der Zauberberg*. Even in works which seem to be 'about' something external to the writer—the Florence of Lorenzo de' Medici and Savonarola, the life of Frederick the Great, or a prince, or a confidence trickster—the author's point of contact with his subject proves to be some analogy which it offers with the life or work of a writer.

For instance, beneath the efforts of the fanatic Savonarola to overcome the sensuality of Florence by his pure spirituality, there lies at no great distance below the costumed surface the theme of literature as the art of pure spirit which, unlike the superficial plastic arts with their superficial exponents, can penetrate human suffering and the complexities of existence. This conflict was first sketched in the story *Gladius Dei*, in the Munich setting which provoked it. The drama *Fiorenza* puts it in terms which are crucial in Thomas Mann's thinking about the functions of literature. Savonarola's art as a preacher fails to be 'plastic' (viii. 986 f.). Instead it pursues insight and knowledge (*Erkenntnis*) of the depths of shame and suffering. Savonarola is a genius, the decadent product of a good *Bürger* family who has escaped from parents and profession into sanctity (literature). So one of Mann's working notes reads.[9]

[7] *Zur Genealogie der Moral*, 'Was bedeuten asketische Ideale?' §4. In Mann's copy (GOA vol. vii. 404) probably acquired in 1899, the passage is marked with a cross.
[8] In 1901 *Tonio Kröger* was to be called simply *Literatur* (Br. H. 14), which is some indication of how self-sufficient the subject was felt to be.
[9] 'Aus Ferrara, aus guter und hoch angesehener Bürgerfamilie gebürtig. Statt auch seinerseits einen bürgerlichen Beruf zu ergreifen, entweicht dieser geniale Verfallstypus seinen Eltern ins Kloster, in die Heiligkeit (die Literatur) . . .' TMA Mp. xi. 13b Mat., sheet headed 'Savonarola'.

Even the political and military career of Frederick the Great exemplifies something which literature also demands, the disciplined ethic of achievement (*Leistungsethik*) and the practical maxim of 'sticking at it' (*Durchhalten*), which were Mann's as well as Frederick's and were later to be Gustav von Aschenbach's. Indeed, when Mann passed on the Frederick project to his fictional character, he also passed on his own motive for wishing to write a novel on this subject: the desire to celebrate the stoic virtue which turns weakness into strength by sheer heroic effort (viii. 451). This may seem a tenuous link to inspire a whole historical novel. Perhaps the tenuousness is one reason why the plan was never executed. Mann's link with the historical figure had become firmer when he came to write his Great War essay, *Friedrich und die grosse Koalition*; not because Mann had found new elements in Frederick, but because in 1914, like most European men of the pen and the spirit, he had briefly become something of a militarist.

The tendency of writers in Europe at the turn of the century to write about writers is open to the charge of narcissism. But the more acute disadvantage for Mann lay in the particular way he experienced the literary life. Separation, alienation, yearning, distance, were ethereal themes. They needed a medium in which to be realized. The emotional problem thus went hand in hand with a technical problem. Without the means to realize the theme, the alternative that threatened was self-absorption to the point of solipsism. Thomas Mann's whole subsequent work was a struggle to avoid this.

The materials of the writer's day-to-day existence were clearly a thin source. *Tonio Kröger* uses what little there was of post-Lübeck experience so openly and directly, and ends with so final a statement on it, that it leaves little to take further. These elements do not even make the main contribution to the story. Its best effects are resonances from the more self-sufficient structure of *Buddenbrooks*.[10] And if the opening sections of *Tonio Kröger* are already dependent, echo-like, on the novel, the later sections are in turn echoes of echoes. The story is a delicate essay in the pathos that can be produced by

[10] Cf. xii. 90 on *Buddenbrooks* as a violin whose 'acoustic inner space' would add resonance to his playing, and of *Tonio Kröger* as a 'prose-ballad . . . played on the home-made instrument' of the larger novel.

a steadily attenuated reality. The writer's life *as a writer*, when he is not returning to home places or holidaying in Denmark, offers no motifs remotely as stirring as the lost northland: only painter's fixative and the scent of spring and the poignancy of their uneasy mixture. The need is evident—for Renaissance Florence, or eighteenth-century Prussia.

Artistically, such casting around for a way to broaden and body out the theme has its own pitfalls. How *Friedrich* would have turned out, we cannot tell. But *Fiorenza* was, in Mann's own words, a fiasco, and for reasons rooted in the methods that created it.[11] As a Renaissance drama—yet another Renaissance drama[12]—it is difficult to take seriously. Its plaster-statue figures, its melodramatic gestures, its stylized speeches and purple passages, with pentameters either creeping into or not wholly eradicated from the prose: all these things are barely credible from the author of, say, *Tristan*. It is the Case of the Absent Ironist. The dramatic form excludes the sophisticated narrative voice and the array of syntactical means[13] which would clear him of responsibility for the excesses of his figures. Without these, the characters must speak their own minds direct, and the ones who bear some intellectual message like Lorenzo and Savonarola must do so with vehemence. If one cannot take the reconstructed Florence seriously, from the seriousness of the protagonists one cannot escape. That is the measure of the gap between the essential theme and the extraneous materials.

In a work so sharply divided, where the bulk of the matter is meant to illustrate but in fact partly obscures the theme, is the reader not best advised to ignore the theme? This would then simply have been the author's private impetus, leading him and us to the Florentine subject. Unfortunately, this will not work. A reader can hardly miss sensing special intentions, a portentousness which points beyond the overt plot. And without these, the subject hardly stands up alone. But it might be argued that a less unsuccessful work would allow the author

---

[11] '. . . diesem Fiasko in dem Bemühen, eine geistige Construction mit Leben zu erfüllen'. To Heinrich Mann, 18 Feb. 1905 (Br. H. 35).

[12] Cf. Hofmannsthal's letter to Richard Strauss of 27 Apr. 1906 on the prevalence of bad Renaissance dramas.

[13] In Baumgart's phrase (op. cit., p. 118) 'das erzählende Oberbewusstsein'.

and his theme to be invisible in his creation, even if everywhere present. This might be so, but it is a hypothesis which Mann's practice in the 1900s cannot illustrate. Both his more ambitious works of this period fail in the same way. Read without attention to their theme, they are inadequate; read with it, they are unintegrated. Moreover, if one is to understand Thomas Mann as he wished and tried to be understood, this manner of reading again will not do. As he wrote in his essay on Chamisso: 'Dichter, die sich selbst geben, wollen im Grunde, dass man sie erkenne; denn nicht sowohl um den Ruhm ihres Werkes ist es ihnen zu tun, als vielmehr um den Ruhm ihres Lebens und Leidens.' (Poets who give themselves want basically to be known for their own sake; for they are not so much concerned with the fame of their work as with the fame of their life and suffering [ix. 54].) In *Fiorenza*, the vehemence of the writing is aimed at making its true meaning shine through. And in general, whenever Mann had an opportunity to comment on one of his works, he laid bare its real message. The primacy of this aim is constant. The message is not a mere pretext for treating a subject, which then becomes artistically self-sufficient. Rather, the material subject serves the personal statement. It is in this sense that Mann called his work 'essentially lyrical'.[14] The writer's subjective concerns are stated indirectly via his subject.

The other ambitious work of this period makes the issue clear, and shows Mann laying the foundations for his mature work. The novel *Königliche Hoheit* is once more on the literary theme, and once more (as in *Fiorenza*) not by direct confession but by the use of realia which seemed to offer an analogy. The realizing process in this case is an example of literary self-generation. From *Tonio Kröger*, itself in a sense derived from *Buddenbrooks*, one motif, itself a literary derivative, is taken and elaborated into a new treatment of the outsider theme. *Tonio Kröger* used the motif of the lonely King Philipp from Schiller's *Don Carlos* very delicately to suggest the loneliness and betrayal of which the young Tonio is getting his first taste. After writing that *Novelle*, Thomas Mann became increasingly taken with the idea that

[14] 'Und ich bin ja ein Lyriker (wesentlich).' Letter to Kurt Martens, 28 Mar. 1906 (Br. i. 62).

the life of a prince, with its insubstantial formality, lack of practical use, and unhappy isolation, was very like the life of a writer. The idea, only one of many in *Tonio Kröger*, was brought home to him particularly when a painter sent him an epitome of his story, a picture of the Spanish king sobbing high on his throne. To write about a prince and his life would provide, if the materials could once be acquired, a solid world in which to embed the real theme. Little else contributed (though Mann's marriage inspired the happy ending); the novel is a remarkable expansion of a tiny original idea.

The resulting work hides its own impulse and intention at least as much as it reveals it. It was taken at the time (and still occasionally is) to be a straightforward Ruritanian tale. As such it has a certain not very distinctive charm. The critics understandably thought it surprisingly lightweight, from the author of *Buddenbrooks*.[15] Mann's reaction, when an occasion offered for making it public, was unequivocal. It was the meaning that counted; if he had been too successful in disguising his theme, he was quick to uncover it. Answering criticisms from a real prince of the way royalty and court life were portrayed in the novel, he made his deeper intentions clear and mocked at critics who had not seen through the text to the confessions of a poet, but had concentrated on the mere allegorical costume. Yet he also maintains that this 'costume' was accurate, thanks to his training as a Naturalist. He can see, he admits, why it was misunderstood: 'Ich verstehe, dass die Detailmenge, die zu arrangieren ich mich nicht verdriessen liess, dass die Akribie eines Schriftstellers, der durch die naturalistische Schule gegangen ist, über die innere Natur des Buches täuschen konnte.' (I can understand that the mass of detail which I took the trouble to arrange, the concern for accuracy of a writer who had been through the Naturalist school, could be misleading about the book's inner nature [xi. 570].)

The criticisms to which Mann's experiments in this decade are open are implied in these words. When the 'real' point was explained, critics were harder still on the book. They had found a court novel trivial from the author of *Buddenbrooks*; they

---

[15] Cf. xi. 573: 'er wurde . . . absolut und relativ zu leicht befunden . . .'

found his underlying purpose pretentious.[16] (He later admitted himself that it had an element of vanity.[17])

More important from the artistic point of view, the elaborate execution is out of all proportion to the value of the idea. Where in *Tonio Kröger* the symbolic juxtaposing of the boy's suffering and the betrayal of King Philipp by Posa was effective in an unobtrusive way, the working out of the Prince–Poet parallel as a three-hundred-page allegory becomes, once the point is grasped, tediously emphatic. Dominated as it is by the ever-present intellectual formula, the novel never achieves life.

Mann's reply to the real prince was written in 1910. The year before he had written an apologia for allegory to Hugo von Hofmannsthal. Hofmannsthal had used the word allegory of *Königliche Hoheit*—aptly, for when the substance of a work is there only to encode a message, it is the proper word. With due consistency Thomas Mann viewed his materials after use in the same way he had viewed them before use, as inessential. Though he defended it, the realistic detail, the legacy of Naturalism, was secondary. The meaning mattered, not the means.

To Hofmannsthal Mann wrote as follows:

Sie brauchten auch das Wort Allegorie, und dieses Wort ist ja ästhetisch recht sehr in Verruf. Mir scheint trotzdem die poetische Allegorie von grossen Massen eine hohe Form zu sein, und man kann, scheint mir, den Roman nicht besser erhöhen, als indem man ihn ideal und konstruktiv macht.

(You also used the word allegory, and this word is of course aesthetically very much discredited. But the large-scale poetic allegory still seems to me an elevated form and one cannot, it seems to me, elevate the novel better than by making it a construction to bear ideas. [Br. i. 76])

*Konstruktiv* and *ideal* are the key words, which need precise

---

[16] Mann's materials for 'Geist und Kunst' (TMA Mat. I, 'Abhandlung über das Literarische') include a cutting from a review which comments on Mann's revelation: 'Mit dieser überraschenden Erklärung nimmt Thomas Mann seinem anmutigen Buch jede Bedeutung für das Publikum und setzt an die Stelle einer interessanten Tatsache deutschen öffentlichen Lebens das kokette Spiel der Selbstbespiegelung eines Poeten, der der Aussenwelt absichtsvoll gleichgültig und geringschätzend gegenübersteht.'

[17] '. . . eine Idee, die sich überall spiegelt und zwar wohl etwas eitel spiegelt.' To Paul Amann, 8 Oct. 1916 (Br. A. 48).

glossing because they are the basis for Mann's developing methods. They crop up again in his reply to the prince. He there speaks of court life as the allegorical costume (*allegorisches Kleid*) for intellectual intentions (*ideelle*[18] *Absichten*)—much as he had earlier, in *Bilse und ich*, referred to Shakespeare's use of naïve Italian plots 'als buntes Kleid, als sinnliches Mittel zur Darstellung eines Erlebnisses, einer Idee' (as a coloured costume, a sensuous means for the presentation of an experience, an idea [x. 15].) A prince, living his life in the milieu which Mann had appropriated, would naturally object to 'das Konstruktive, das Absichtliche meines Buches' (the constructive and intentional element). These words must refer to the act of taking over constructional materials for a purpose. They cannot refer to any presumptuousness in that purpose itself, the equating of the Poet with the Prince, because that was a point the exalted personage had not grasped.

Mann's new principle, then, is the arrangement of a mass of constructional material in obedience to some intellectual formula. And what does he mean when he speaks of 'elevating' the novel form? Essentially, establishing its pretensions to serious consideration as a genre, alongside lyric and drama. Mann was sensitive about the German tendency to take only these more venerable genres seriously. Much of his *Versuch über das Theater*, written in 1906, is an attempt to undo this prejudice. In 1910 he calls Fontane the father of those who are trying to get equal recognition for the novel, in the teeth of an outdated but diehard doctrine ('einer überholten, doch zählebigen Ranglehre zum Trotz').[19] In 1913, he is still complaining that many theorists of literature remain convinced of Schiller's dictum that the novelist is only the half-brother of the poet.[20] Perhaps he was provoked to these repeated declarations by the austere attitude of arbiters of culture like Stefan George and Rudolf Borchardt. A typical reaction of the George circle is the 1918 dismissal of both Fontane and Thomas Mann as 'ephemere

[18] *Ideell* is more correct than *ideal* in this meaning. It seems clear from a comparison of the three passages concerned that Mann means the same thing in each, and the usage in his letter to Hofmannsthal is simply less precise.

[19] In a newspaper comment on the unveiling of a Fontane memorial in Berlin, quoted in H. H. Reuter, *Fontane*, Berlin, 1968, i. 34.

[20] Funeral oration for Friedrich Huch (x. 409). Schiller's phrase occurs in *Über naive und sentimentalische Dichtung*.

Jahrzehntemänner' (ephemeral men of a decade) when measured against poetry which is truly 'schicksalhaft' (fateful).[21] More specifically, the attempt to elevate the novel meant rescuing it from the limitations of nineteenth-century realism, especially from the excesses of its latest phase, Naturalism. *Buddenbrooks* is already far more than just a Naturalistic novel, but this was not apparent to all its readers. Not everybody could distinguish its use of reality, its intellectually underpinned re-creation of reality, from the mere wallowing in real and sometimes sordid detail which Naturalist writing offered. When an acquaintance disliked the leitmotivs, failed to notice the part played by music, and ignored Thomas Buddenbrook's adventure with Schopenhauer, Mann could only ask despairingly whether he was really no more than a describer of good dinners.[22] His own view was stated by the reviewer who called *Königliche Hoheit* a declaration of war on Naturalism: Thomas Mann, the 'worshipper of matter', had become a 'worshipper of the idea'. The world of the new novel was small, but it had 'an earnest symbolic grandeur'.[23]

Mann's retrospect on *Königliche Hoheit* confirms this view of his aims and the direction they were leading in. He wrote in 1947:

Was mir künstlerisch am Herzen lag, war die geistige Auflockerung und Durchhellung eines vom neunzehnten Jahrhundert ererbten und in 'Buddenbrooks' treulich geübten massiven und durchaus lebensernsten Naturalismus, seine Erhöhung und Erheiterung zum symbolischen, für das Ideelle transparenten geistigen Kunstwerk. In dieser Richtung war 'Königliche Hoheit' ein Fortschritt . . . Ohne sie [sind] weder der 'Zauberberg' noch 'Joseph und seine Brüder' zu denken.

(My artistic interest lay in letting a little light and intellectual flexibility into the massive and wholly earnest Naturalism which I had inherited from the nineteenth century and faithfully practised

[21] Phrases of Friedrich Gundolf's, quoted by Reuter, op. cit., i. 145.

[22] 'Gewundert hat mich aber, dass Sie das "Ausserordentliche", das "Transzendentale" in dem Roman "vergebens gesucht" haben. Und die Musik? Und Thomas Buddenbrooks Abenteuer mit Schopenhauer? Bin ich wirklich nur ein Schilderer guter Mittagessen?' Unpublished letter of 16 Feb. 1904 to Eugen Kalkschmidt, Munich Stadtbibliothek manuscript collection. Cf. x. 837.

[23] Georg Martin Richter, in *Münchener Neuste Nachrichten*, 28 Oct. 1909. Mann had known Richter since 1901, and the statements of principle in this review can fairly be taken as straight from the horse's mouth. Cf. below, p. 117, note 52.

in 'Buddenbrooks'; in brightening and elevating it into an intellectual
work of art in which ideas could clearly show through. In this
direction 'Royal Highness' was a step forward . . . Without it
neither 'The Magic Mountain' nor 'Joseph and his Brothers' is
conceivable. [xi. 574].

This 1947 wording echoes the formulations of 1909 and 1910.
The transcending of Naturalism has become so much the point
to be made that *Buddenbrooks* is now seen wholly, and simpli-
fyingly, as a Naturalist work.[24] But the importance of *Königliche
Hoheit* as the first stage in a consistent development which
later produces Mann's major intellectual constructions is amply
confirmed.


## III

We now have a picture of the aesthetic of constructivism which
was to make up for the unrepeatability of *Buddenbrooks*, and
some idea of the literary value it set out to achieve. By the
Chinese-box principle which literature about literature entails,
*Königliche Hoheit* tells us in more detail about its own compositional method. The author's confessional urge and the demands
of allegorical completeness together lead to a statement on how
the writer works, duly encoded into a princely equivalent. It
is given in the chapter 'Der hohe Beruf' (*The High Calling*),
which departs from the story-line to review Prince Klaus
Heinrich's customary tasks. His daily life, itself 'without proper
reality' (ii. 159), consists in adding the final ceremonial touch
to the real and useful activities of ordinary people. To do this,
whether it is laying a foundation-stone, visiting a festival, or
inspecting an exhibition, his role requires that he show an
easy familiarity with the substance of what is going on. He
creates this illusion by the apt display of what in fact is a mere
smattering of knowledge. At a gymnastic festival, he 'used in
quick succession several technical expressions' which he
remembers from school, 'pronouncing them with great ease

<hr>

[24] Mann's view of *Buddenbrooks* as Germany's 'first and perhaps only' Naturalist
novel (xii. 89) probably derives originally from Samuel Lublinski's *Die Bilanz der
Moderne* (1904). Lublinski uses the formula in his section on Thomas Mann which
also yielded the Saint Sebastian image for *Der Tod in Venedig*. (Cf. viii. 453: 'hatte
schon frühzeitig ein kluger Zergliederer geschrieben . . .'.)

and confidence (*Geläufigkeit*), hiding his left hand' (ii. 161). His hand was damaged at birth and would make plain that his knowledge of gymnastics was not based on experience. In such situations the Prince must beware of using a technical formula from the wrong milieu. At a shooting competition he uses the marksman's greeting, whispered to him by his adjutant at the last moment. Should he chance to use the miner's greeting among marksmen, or the huntsman's greeting among miners, it would destroy 'die schöne Täuschung der Sachkenntnis und ernsten Vorliebe' (the beautiful illusion of specialist knowledge and genuine predilection [ii. 162]) by which the good people are otherwise convinced. This illusion has to be created by acquiring in advance whatever will be needed— and preferably *just as much* as will be needed, no more. The method is generalized in these words:

> Überhaupt bedurfte er zu seiner Berufsübung gewisser sachlicher Kenntnisse, die er sich von Fall zu Fall verschaffte, um sie im rechten Augenblick und in ansprechender Form zu verwenden. Sie betrafen vorwiegend die auf den verschiedenen Gebieten menschlicher Tätigkeit gebräuchlichen Kunstausdrücke sowie geschichtliche Daten, und vor einer Repräsentationsfahrt machte Klaus Heinrich daheim in Schloss 'Eremitage' mit Hilfe von Druckschriften und mündlichen Vorträgen die nötigen Studien.

> (In general he needed for the exercise of his calling certain factual knowledge which he acquired as circumstances demanded, making use of it at the right moment and in an appealing form. It was largely a matter of the accepted technical terms and historical data connected with a particular field of human activity, and before any such ceremonial mission Klaus Heinrich did the necessary studying at home in the Hermitage with the aid of printed matter and oral reports. [ii. 162].)

The result is that when unveiling a statue of his father in the town of Knüppelsdorf, he can make 'a speech in which everything he had noted down about Knüppelsdorf found its place, and which produced in all present the agreeable impression that he had been principally concerned his whole life through with the historical vicissitudes of this important centre' (ibid.). He concludes his speech with a feeling of being drained dry (*Ausgeleertheit*), but is happily secure in the knowledge that no one was allowed to ask him any further questions, 'for he would not for the life of him have been able to say a single word more about Knüppelsdorf'.

Essential points about the writer are reinforced (*Königliche Hoheit* is nothing if not thorough) in a scene where the Prince actually meets a poet. Heinrich Mann thought it a flaw in the allegory that an actual poet should hold converse with his own symbol.[25] It is a further pointer to the transcendent importance of the theme for Mann that he took this chance of underscoring it, even against the artistic proprieties. Klaus Heinrich is of course unaware of the poet's way of life as a parallel to his own. When he has to present a prize to a poet who has celebrated life in its most wild and amoral forms, he expects to find a wild and amoral individual. Axel Martini, asthmatic, delicate, and abstemious, disillusions him, repeating many of Mann's by now familiar *idées fixes*—the causal link between physical weakness and talent, the 'profession' of literature as merely the inability to do anything else, etc. But he makes his most important point when the prince asks whether he has not suffered hardship, hunger for instance. Not at all, says the poet. That is the popular view, but the truth is 'dass es nicht sowohl der wirkliche Hunger, als vielmehr der Hunger nach dem Wirklichen ist . . . he, he . . . was das Talent benötigt' (that it is not so much real hunger as hunger for the real . . . ha, ha . . . that talent requires [ii. 177]).

Once more and in caricatural form the popular idea of literary creation is denied, and the gap between real experience and literary creation is put thus extremely, as if it were a norm worth affirming. One is reminded of Mann's definition of irony, in the essay on Chamisso of 1911, as the business of making a superior virtue out of necessity ('aus einer Not eine Überlegenheit' [ix. 56]).

In many respects, *Königliche Hoheit* repeats the patterns of *Tonio Kröger*. If Mann had written it in 1903, when he first had the idea, it would have been even closer, and it seems likely that he abandoned the early fragments because of this essential proximity.[26] New experience, his marriage in 1905 to Katja Pringsheim, provided the one authentic new turn the

---

[25] See Br. H. 77, Thomas's reply of 3 June 1909, and the letter of 25 July 1909 to Hofmannsthal quoted above.
[26] Cf. Wysling, *Studien*, pp. 71 and 101.

story takes, and made possible a happy ending of a solider kind than the mere fruitful tension which was the final word of *Tonio Kröger*. In his personal life, the coldness and lack of human feeling Thomas Mann had been accused of is thus overcome, the emotional aspect of the 'separation' problem is settled.[27] But there is no such conventional happy ending for its technical aspect. Instead there is the principle of constructivism and allegory. Through the veil of its own allegory, *Königliche Hoheit* talks frankly about this method. It was one which had already been employed to some extent in *Schwere Stunde* and *Tristan*,[28] and even earlier in the typhus chapter of *Buddenbrooks*, which was based on an encyclopedia article—a technique Mann later called 'eine Art von höherem Abschreiben' (a kind of higher cribbing).[29] But by 1910, the method has been systematized into a programme for the building up of literary structures by an exactly calculated acquisition of materials under the direction of an intellectual formula.

What are we to make of this declared method? A lot will depend on the success with which it is handled, for which there are various criteria. But is it, initially, open to criticism in principle? How does it stand in relation to the aesthetics of the novel as previously practised? Is what Mann reveals so very different from the problems and techniques common to novelists: the coherent organization of a work, the material study of the subject it treats?

Some distinction can be drawn between Mann's programme and the documentation process which became common with nineteenth-century novelists as their subjects grew in scope. Such documentation—and this is still true of *Buddenbrooks*—is aimed at the convincing portrayal of the real subject. Mann's new aim, so far, was only a materially supported presentation of himself. True, we can find something of any novelist in his choice of subject and the way he treats it—Flaubert's contempt for the *bourgeoisie* is still plain in the exotic setting of *Salammbô*. But that is only a component, not a central message, and

---

[27] This does not mean it is disposed of as a theme. It recurs in *Joseph* and *Der Erwählte* and, at its most extreme, in *Doktor Faustus*.

[28] See W. Berendsohn, 'Ein Blick in die Werkstatt', *Neue Rundschau* 1945.

[29] To Theodor Adorno, 30 Dec. 1945 (Br. ii. 470). From the phrasing, it seems likely that Mann used the typhus article in *Meyers Konversations-Lexikon*, edition of 1897.

*Salammbô* remains a novel about ancient Carthage. Mann's position is an extreme one, both in the completeness with which the intellectual element dominates the material, and in the limited, purely subjective reference of the intellectual formula once one gets through to it. There is no question, as there is later in *Der Zauberberg* or *Doktor Faustus*, of the intellectual formula's having a wider reference. Nor is there any question of its stimulating so much interest in the material it is to inhabit that this material takes on an independent life, so that the work would become an attempt to render realistically the chosen area of existence. The prince's life cannot have offered a serious challenge to the basic urge of a realist, if we accept that this is 'the passion of understanding, the desire for rational penetration and imaginative appropriation, the driving force towards the resolution of the mystery of living'.[30] Both Mann and his readers were right—they in being puzzled at the lightweight, novelettish story, he in feeling that it required its 'real' theme to raise it at all above the ordinary.

Equally extreme in Mann's approach is the relationship between acquisition and exploitation of extraneous materials. Unlike Flaubert's detailed preparatory studies, which can lay claim to throughness and are an attempt to get deeply into his subject,[31] Mann makes it clear that the minimum possible study is to yield the maximum possible return: the thinnest skimmings from a subject, duly transferred, are to create the impression of a surface under which lies solid substance. Indeed, in the later developments of the technique for which Mann used the term montage, it is often only by the merest syntactical details—the changing of direct into indirect speech, the substitution for one word of its approximate synonym— that the ready-verbalized material is altered; so that in a sense the identical surface, with its implied substance, is simply shifted from its source to the context of a fictional work.

Yet when laying down the programme for this, Mann is not consciously confessing a weakness. If anything, a certain ironic glee informs his account, as well as a high degree of honesty. (In general, the honesty with which Mann's dilemmas over

---

[30] Erich Heller, 'Imaginative Literature 1830–1870', in the Cambridge Modern History, vol. x, ch. 7, p. 159. The definition fits *Buddenbrooks* well enough.
[31] See Enid Starkie, *Flaubert, The Making of the Master*, p. 338.

technique all became at some stage the subject matter of his fiction makes his work an account of the Artist in a more interesting sense than the cliché about the 'problem of the Artist' usually connotes). This suggests that he did not think his practice abnormal or peculiar to himself. According to *Königliche Hoheit*, which is a little more positive than *Tonio Kröger* in that it gives the artist a function in society, his particular gift to his fellow men is form: he shows them their everyday reality under the aspect of form, teaches them that there is something 'higher' than mere practical matters.[32] But what does the artistic conferring of form turn out to be? Not that the artist moulds and reworks his subject at a deep level of the mind or personality, not that he expresses the essentials of something he has fully assimilated, but that he picks up some deceptively knowing phrases and by using them is able to present a thin skin as solid substance. Knowing the artist's self-avowed unsatisfactory nature and the makeshift means he uses, it is hard to feel that 'the gift of form' carries any superior value. Mann relies on the notion as a traditional attribute of art, but it is here very much diluted. What the artist creates is an illusion, but not in the sense in which 'illusion' is the basis of art as such —that is to say, the appearance that something is present to the imagination when it is not 'really' there. Illusion in this sense is merely a matter of convention, of the agreed means by which a picture of reality is rendered in a particular art at a particular time. Mann's technique goes well beyond this. How far beyond, can be shown if we briefly compare it with the aesthetic principles of Weimar Classicism, in which illusion or semblance (*Schein*) was also a central concept. The comparison is all the more appropriate because of the customary association of Mann with Schiller and Goethe. It has even been specifically

---

[32] See ii. 169 f.: 'Dieser gemeine Mann, dessen Sinn sonst am Boden haftete, der ausser dem handgreiflichen Nützlichen nichts, wohl nicht einmal die alltägliche Höflichkeit in Bedacht nahm und auch hierher um einer Sache willen gekommen war, — er erfuhr in seiner Seele, dass es etwas Höheres gäbe als seine Sache und die Sache überhaupt, und erhoben, gereinigt, mit blindem Blick und noch immer das Lächeln auf seinem geröteten Antlitz, ging er von dannen.' (This common man, whose thoughts were normally on lower things, who thought of nothing but the tangibly useful, probably not even of everyday politeness, and had come to audience over some practical matter—he learned in his soul that there existed something higher than that matter, and higher than practical matters generally; and raised, purified, with unseeing eye and a smile still on his flushed face, he went away.)

argued that his methods are an exact continuance of their aesthetic doctrine,[33] and if this were true it would be an important part of his creative use of the past.

The question at issue is principally: how does the artist convert reality into art and what is the status of the illusion or semblance which he presents in his work? On this Goethe and Schiller evolved views which seem such basic common sense that to call them a 'doctrine' sounds an exaggeration. This is only because they have since been so fully accepted. It is necessary to realize that, in their time, they were pleading a new cause. But it is also necessary to beware of thinking, converted as we already are to their basic doctrine, that they meant something more sophisticated than they did by the term *Schein*.

Their cause was simply the recognition of aesthetic experience as an independent category, a way of looking at things which was totally different from the purposeful or utilitarian way. This is a distinction which Kant had introduced in the *Kritik der Urteilskraft*, and some of the most striking of Schiller's theoretical formulations are restatements of this idea from a different angle. Thus the concept of *Schein* translates what for Kant was a state of mind into an aspect of the object viewed. Although *Schein* is 'in the eye of the beholder' (*des Menschen Werk*), Schiller uses it to mean the face things wear when they are being looked at with what Kant called 'disinterested pleasure' (*interesseloses Wohlgefallen*). When Schiller insists, in what seems in places an extreme manner, on the independence of this pure aesthetic aspect,[34] it is because as yet the idea had not been grasped or accepted by his contemporaries: the crude approach of applying extra-artistic criteria to artistic phenomena, treating what is in the work of art as if it were in the real world, could still be observed in the eighteenth century— for instance, the theory of didactic art in its crudest form, or the moral disapproval which was aroused by certain subjects regardless of their artistic treatment, or—even more basic— Gottsched's idea that a play ought ideally to last exactly as long on the stage as the action would take in real life. But in the work of art, according to the *Schein* principle, we are not dealing with the thing itself, only with its pure appearance.

[33] E. M. Wilkinson, 'Aesthetic excursus on Thomas Mann's *Akribie*', *GR* 31 (1956).    [34] Especially in the 26th of the *Aesthetic Letters*.

Yet the absence of its 'reality' does not mean a loss of its richness and complexity, nor does it imply that art involves peeling off the 'mere' appearance of things in a facile manner. It only implies the absence in the reader of certain kinds of practical claim on the object before him. There is no question of art presenting an illusory appearance: it presents *only* the appearance, but of the real world.[35]

This is a crucial distinction, and naturally Schiller had to defend his idea of 'semblance' against the suspicion that it was a deceptive appearance, an illusion in the pejorative sense. To satisfy those for whom a realm of pure aesthetic appearance was unfamiliar or unacceptable, and the term *Schein* ambiguous, he had to explain that legitimate aesthetic semblance must be honest (*aufrichtig*), that is, it must declare itself to be semblance, and not set itself up as reality.[36] Thus *trompe-l'œil* painting, to use an example not Schiller's, would be not an aesthetic semblance, but a deception. Anything which a work of art suggests about itself, but which is not true, disqualifies it from being *Schein* in Schiller's sense. *Schein* is not a misrepresentation of reality nor a substitute for reality, but the outward aspect of reality, viewed for its own sake. The artist takes the pure percept and plays with it, thus both setting his fellow men an example of freedom from material preoccupation and providing them with an object on which to exercise their play instinct. How much sheer hard work this preparation entails for the artist in the mastering of his material is evoked in a striking way by stanzas 8 and 9 of Schiller's poem 'Das Ideal und das Leben'.[37] There is no short cut to the lightness and immateriality which is paradoxically the result in the perfected work of art, it is achieved by a struggle ('Und beharrlich ringend unterwerfe / Der Gedanke sich das Element,). On the one hand, hard work on the stubborn real material for the work ('des Meissels schwerem Schlag', 'des Marmors sprödes Korn'); on the other, a final form which shows no sign of the struggle and is as if born from Nothing, 'wie aus dem Nichts entsprungen'. This birth of form from mastered substance is a matter of balance and fusion. The famous maxim from Letter 22, that the secret of art lies in the extermination ('Vertilgung') of matter through form, is only one side of the question, forcefully stated in an attempt to keep reality in its place. The consciously provocative phrasing is put in perspective by Schiller's definition of beauty in Letter 15 as 'lebende Gestalt' (living form). There, with an eye on the ideal rather than on the need to correct his age, Schiller puts equal stress on the antithetical concepts of form and matter and conceives of beauty as their interpenetration.

How does Thomas Mann's practice as described in *Königliche Hoheit* stand in relation to these normative theories? What kind of illusion does he conceive art as? Rather than a process of struggle and assimilation which will produce an 'honest' illusion, he gives an account of how to create the illusion that such a process has been gone through. The method has only a distant resemblance to Classical aesthetics. It is mischievously sketched in the Prince's story, but will later become increasingly a crisis rather than a joke. The maximal exploitation of limited materials, often ready formulated in printed sources, the absence of any but a superficial assimilation by the artist, becomes eventually that complete loss of direct knowledge of the world which the monkish narrator in *Der Erwählte* ruefully confesses. Only words are left, for he knows nothing of the knightly customs he describes in such an apparently specialist manner: 'Ich tue nur so, als wüsst ich recht zu erzählen, wie Junker Wiligis gezogen wurde, und wende Worte vor.' (I only pretend to know how to relate properly the way young Lord Wiligis was educated, and put up a screen of words [vii. 24].) From an aesthetic which took the real world as its starting-point, the novelist has progressively created a situation in which his contact with reality is tenuous and distant. His argument from *Buddenbrooks* never more than apparently legitimized what was to follow it; and if *Buddenbrooks*, which meets Schiller's criteria, is set directly beside *Der Erwählte*, which is the logical conclusion of the constructivist method, then the effect can only be one of extreme contrast.

## IV

Mann was never under any illusions about his own illusionism. The story of the confidence-man Felix Krull, begun in 1910 immediately after *Königliche Hoheit*, has at its centre the idea of art as deceptive illusion. Tonio Kröger had nearly been arrested as a criminal on his return home to the north, and had felt the higher appropriateness of the error. Thomas Mann, collecting notes and materials for *Krull*, was surprised to find how much of his inner experience was relevant to the account of Krull's deceptions.[38] This opportunity to tap personal experience direct gave the new subject its potential; it was an allegory which would need less 'constructing' than that of the prince. Illusion was nearer the core of art than the mere formality of artistic existence which had been the point of *Königliche Hoheit*. Hence Krull's early insistence, no doubt seriously meant through all the elaborate playfulness of the first-person form and the parodying of revered autobiographies, that 'alles, was ich mitzuteilen habe, sich aus meinen innersten Erfahrungen, Irrtümern und Leidenschaften zusammensetzt und ich also meinen Stoff vollkommen beherrsche' (everything that I have to relate is made up of my innermost experiences, mistakes, and passions, and I am thus in perfect command of my material [vii. 265]).[39]

Inevitably, Mann then introduces other of his stock *aperçus* about the artist. They sometimes seem incongruous in what is ostensibly the autobiography of a criminal, although even this can turn into a piquant literary effect, as when Krull claims that all his 'achievements' are the product of a 'moral' victory over himself: 'ein Produkt der Selbstüberwindung, ja . . . eine sittliche Leistung von hohem Range' (p. 299). But it is the illusion common to the activity of artist and trickster that

[38] '. . . ich bin manchmal überrascht, was ich dabei aus mir heraushole'. To Heinrich Mann, 10 Jan. 1910 (Br. H. 83).

[39] Cf. p. 293, with echoes of the argument from *Bilse und ich*. Krull denies that he is trying to create suspense or artistic proportion in his narrative, leaving such considerations to writers 'die aus der Phantasie schöpfen und aus erfundenem Stoff schöne und regelmässige Kunstwerke herzustellen bemüht sind, während ich lediglich mein eigenes, eigentümliches Leben vortrage und mit dieser Materie nach Gutdünken schalte' (who create from imagination and are intent on making beautiful and regular works of art from invented material, whereas I am merely presenting my own peculiar form of life and disposing this material as I see fit).

gives life to the new revelations. Krull's first public imposture, acting out, with muted violin, the role of a child virtuoso, his elaborately feigned illnesses which regularly free him from school, his later even more elaborate faking of epileptoid symptoms (carefully read up in a technical work beforehand) which convince the army medical board[40]—all these deceitful shows aim to create the illusion of substance. They are repeats of the chapter 'Der hohe Beruf' in *Königliche Hoheit*, more outrageous as befits a con-man, but not essentially new.

Yet *Felix Krull* does break new ground, taking the theme of deception beyond mere confessional hide-and-seek to something like a metaphysics of illusion. This happens in the most striking episode of the 1911 fragment, Krull's meeting with an operetta star (once more, as in *Königliche Hoheit*, direct inspection of an artist within the framework of the allegorical structure).

Felix has two views of Müller-Rosé, one immaculate and ideal in his stage incarnation, the other vulgar and sordid behind the scenes. But this is not simply a showing-up; it is the start of a slightly desperate apologia for the more problematic side of art. For Krull's reflections as he stands in the dressing-room and looks at the actor's pimply body are on the value of illusion and mankind's need for it. Is the true form of the glow-worm necessarily the daytime one, when it lies in the palm of your hand, insignificant and without brilliance? Krull thinks of all those rapt faces in the audience which were turned up-wards to watch the glamorous artist's performance. They attest Müller-Rosé's indispensable function in the economy of life ('eine für den Haushalt des Lebens unentbehrliche Einrichtung' [p. 294]). The wording already suggests Nietzsche's view of art as a palliative for the horror and tragedy or even mere nothingness of life, an illusion necessary if mankind is to go on living at all. Even in a German music-hall, far from the heights of tragic drama with which Nietzsche was concerned, the idea remains relevant.

If we look at the 1911 note which sketched this meeting, we find confirmation that this is indeed the philosophical region Mann is moving in, and we also find a yet more far-reaching exposure of illusion. The note examines the instinct, or appetite,

---

[40] Although not published until 1937, this was among the episodes completed relatively early. Cf. letter to Paul Amann, 11 July 1917 (Br. A. 61).

which inspires Krull's deceptions, a yearning for the world
which rests on illusion every bit as much as does the world's
acceptance of the appearances he constructs:

> . . . Aber auch seine Sehnsucht nach der Welt ist das Werk eines
> Betruges von seiten der Welt, das *Blend*werk des Schleiers der Maja.
> (früher Besuch im Variété. Operette? Weinen.) Es ist ein erotisches
> Betrugsverhältnis auf Gegenseitigkeit. Er hat von der Welt das
> Blenden gelernt und macht sich zum Ideal, zum Lebensreiz, zur
> Verführung ihr gegenüber — worauf sie gründlich einfällt. Alle
> fliegen wie die Mücken ins Licht. Die Welt, diese geile und dumme
> Metze will geblendet sein — und das ist eine göttliche Einrichtung,
> denn das Leben selbst beruht auf Betrug und Täuschung, es würde
> versiegen ohne die *Illusion*. Beruf der Kunst.

(But his yearning for the world is itself the result of deception on
the world's part, the *false* show of the veil of Maya. (early visit to
the music-hall. Operetta? Weeping.) It is a relationship of erotic
deception, and mutual. He has learnt hoodwinking from the world
and makes himself into an ideal, a stimulus to life, a power of
seduction *vis-à-vis* the world—and she falls into his trap. They all
fly into the flame like moths. The world, stupid lascivious whore
that she is, want to be hoodwinked—and that is a divine ordinance,
for life itself rests on deceit and trickery, it would dry up without
*illusion*. Calling of art.)[41]

'Blendwerk der Maja', 'Schleier der Maja', are terms for the
illusory character of all appearance which Schopenhauer borrowed from Indian religious philosophy and which Nietzsche in
turn took over from him. In the early 1900s, Mann was sufficiently struck by this idea to plan a full-scale novel called 'Maja'.
(The brief *Anekdote* of 1908 hints at what he had in mind,
rather crudely combining the schematism of allegory with the
sensationalism of anecdote.) Here, in the note for *Krull*, the
belief in illusoriness is put as radically as by Schopenhauer,
the pessimism[42] goes deeper than mere scepticism about the
artist's relations with his gullible audience. His activity is
valueless because it is a response to an illusory world; his
efforts are pitiful in advance. His techniques and his achievements are merely emulation of the world's deceit, and their
purpose is to help maintain a life which has been seen through.
If the radical pessimism is akin to Schopenhauer's, the resolve

[41] Scherrer, *Blätter* 1, p. 5.
[42] Hence perhaps the motif of weeping, not used in the text.

to go on serving illusion, if necessary by the creation of yet more illusion, is an exact equivalent to Nietzsche's 'transcending' of Schopenhauer, which takes the continuation of life as an overriding value.[43] But such a resolve can only be tragic for an artist. Illusion, stripped of its glamour and its humorous treatment, is deeply disquieting. Is this, as Scherrer suggests, itself a major reason why Mann did not go on with *Felix Krull*? Was the revelation too deep, the insight too uncomfortable? Had the artist cut away too much of the ground under his own feet, or (in the image of a later story) come too near to the abyss? He might still have ambitions to conquer the world, but he now knows both how little value the world's appearances have and how little value there is in the means of conquest at his disposal. Certainly the idea of a devoted realism becomes meaningless, even ludicrous.

Krull describes the meeting with Müller-Rosé as one of the decisive impressions of his life: 'wie er damals die Menge und mich zu blenden, zu entzücken verstand, das gehört zu den entscheidenden Eindrücken meines Lebens' (p. 287). And he promises to explain the full significance of the word 'blenden': 'Ich sage: zu blenden, und ich werde etwas weiter unten erklären, wieviel Sinn dieses Wort hier umschliesst.' No such gloss is in fact ever given. But we hardly need it, for the word[44] and its variants have cropped up in so many of Mann's statements on art. He had written to Katja Pringsheim denying that he was a 'gemütloser Blender'; the subject who had audience with the prince came away 'mit blindem Blick'; *blenden* is what Müller-Rosé did to the audience; *blenden* is what Krull does to the world, having learnt the art from the world's own *Blendwerk*.[45] The implications should be clear enough: a type of illusion far more extreme and more frankly deceptive than the Classical *Schein*; a theory more sceptical about the reality of appearance

---

[43] Schopenhauer on the contrary saw art as a first step towards Man's liberation from the tyranny of the life-force. Nietzsche called this a 'scandalous misunderstanding' (Schlechta iii. 755).

[44] Its literal meaning, like that of *Schein*, is visual: to blind, dazzle with light.

[45] The words *blenden* and *verblenden* continue to occur throughout *Krull* (i.e. the 'first part of the memoirs', completed in the 1950s). For example, Krull's display of linguistic virtuosity—French, English, and Italian in quick succession—is a matter of making 'aus einem Nichts von Material etwas für den Augenblick hinlänglich Verblendendes' (vii. 415).

itself; an aesthetic concerned with the creating of autonomous illusion, whose criterion is success in deceiving, whose justification is men's need to be deceived, whose tragedy is the recognized valuelessness of the deceit.

This is the art Mann is aware of practising. His choice of a criminal figure implies a more critical view of it than the choice of a prince. But this critical realization was no reason for ceasing to pursue the artistic techniques which first brought home to him art's illusory nature. On the contrary, it is most important for being a usable thematic novelty—which needs in its turn, despite the close correspondence between the inner experiences of artist and criminal, some bodying out. The collecting of 'high life' documentation duly began in 1911, newspaper cuttings, brochures, pictures from illustrated papers, all sorted under headings like 'Kur- und Lustorte', 'Elegante Festlichkeiten', 'Hôtel. Reise', 'Sport'. The world Krull was to move in needed acquiring, just as some kind of story-line needed to be constructed, that is to say invented. Mann had the 'psychological material', as he wrote to Heinrich on 17 February 1910, but lacked a plot: 'es hapert mit der Fabel, dem Hergang'.[46] This difficulty, and not just the strain of keeping up the parodistic style, is surely one reason why the work was abandoned.

## V

Can we be sure that the programme of constructions to serve ideas, with all the illusory means those constructions would require, was really a programme for the future, and not just a temporary expedient in a not very happy phase of Mann's work? The retrospect of 1947 described *Königliche Hoheit* as a forerunner without which *Der Zauberberg* and *Joseph* would not have been possible. There are two further pieces of evidence, each connected with one of these later novels. The first is a passage of the *Betrachtungen eines Unpolitischen* where Mann discusses the characteristics of an artist which may account for

---

[46] This is not incompatible with the fact that in a general way Krull's 'career' had been planned, on the basis of the confidence-man Manolescu's memoirs *Ein Fürst der Diebe* (1905). See Wysling, 'Thomas Manns Pläne zur Fortsetzung des "Krull"', *Fischer Almanach 1967*, p. 21.

his attitudes to politics. It is part of the massive attack on Heinrich Mann for the 'facile', rationalistic, unpatriotic stand he made in 1914, as a pro-*Entente* critic of Germany. In contrast to this 'superficiality', Thomas Mann takes the example of the artistic conscience, the belief in the need for proper competence in what one is doing. This is what has made German artists stay out of political life—professionals themselves, they believe in leaving politics to professionals:

Dieser Spielart des Tätigen ist der Sinn für Können und Meisterschaft, der Abscheu vor der Stümperei am tiefsten eingeboren: souveräne Beherrschung der Materie scheint ihm Voraussetzung aller Kunst, denn diese bedeutet ihm Vertilgung des Stoffs durch die Form. Was Wunder, dass er nur zu bereit war, der Betörung durch das deutsche Dogma vom 'Fachmann' zu erliegen und politischem Quietismus zu verfallen? Dennoch ist gerade er der Demokratie unentbehrlich, — unentbehrlich im Kampf gegen jenes fortschritthemmende Dogma, kraft einiger Eigenschaften, die seinem Abscheu vor der Stümperei die Waage halten. Ist er nicht fast immer ein Arrangeur von Instinkt? Versteht er sich nicht auf das Blenden? Weiss er nicht aus wenigem viel zu machen, — gleich seinem Milchbruder, dem Journalisten, diesem gewiegten Saucen-Koch, der aus einer ganz kleinen Information einen Leitartikel von fünf Spalten anrichtet? Sachkenntnis zu schauspielern: gehört das nicht am Ende zu seinen Grundtrieben? Als Romanschreiber zum Beispiel, — legt er dir nicht, wenn's ihm die Komposition zu stärken scheint, ein ganzes Kapitel über Nationalökonomie hin, das aussieht, als habe er nie etwas anderes getrieben? Ein wenig Lust nur an rednerischer Rippenatmung, ein wenig Begabung für Schmiss und Schmalz hinzugenommen, — was fehlt zum demokratischen Politiker, zum Überwinder des 'Fachmannes'?

(This variety of the active man [the artist] has the most deeply innate feeling for ability and mastery, an abhorrence of bungling: a sovereign control of the material seems to him the precondition of all art, for art to him means the consuming of the material by the form. Is it any wonder that he was only too ready to yield to the seductive German dogma of the 'specialist' and fall into political quietism? Nevertheless, it is precisely he who is indispensable to democracy—indispensable in the struggle against that antiprogressive dogma by reason of certain qualities which balance out his abhorrence of bungling. Is he not almost always an instinctive 'arranger'? Is he not an expert at hoodwinking? Is not his *forte* making much out of little—like his foster-brother the journalist, that practised cooker-up of sauces who can make a five-column leader out of one little bit of information? Play-acting expert knowledge—is that not after all one of his basic instincts? As a novelist, for example—is he not likely to put in, if he thinks it will strengthen the composition, a whole chapter on economics that looks as if he had never specialized in anything else? All that's needed is the addition of a little throwing out of the chest, a little flair for dash and cheap sentiment—and you've got your democratic politician, the 'specialist' has had his day. [xii. 301 f.])

It is strange at first sight that both the instincts Mann here refers to are in some sense his own. The idea of 'form consuming material' is the famous quotation from Schiller's *Aesthetic Letters*. He had used it once to explain how *Buddenbrooks* sustained interest despite its great bulk.[47] But the tendency to 'play-act expert knowledge' (*Sachkenntnis zu schauspielern*), which is clearly set against this, is the practice described in *Königliche Hoheit*, and Mann has that novel in mind. It is there that he himself introduced a 'chapter on economics'[48] which may create in the reader, as Klaus Heinrich's speeches created in his subjects, an illusion of full expertise. The terms Mann uses are telling: 'arranger' (*Arrangeur*) has the pejorative nuance of the French borrowing; 'hoodwinking' (*Blenden*) is familiar already. But what is most important is the way in which Thomas Mann draws a firm line between the two artistic practices, so that they can hardly be related to each other in the same aesthetic theory. On the one side is real mastery, summed up in Schiller's famous phrase, which had earlier been quite rightly applied to *Buddenbrooks*. On the other side is apparent mastery, the simulation of that process, an example taken from *Königliche Hoheit*, and

---

[47] In a rather schoolmasterly letter of 3 Dec. 1906 to Hans Brandenburg, on the faults of his novel *Erich Westenkott*. After quoting a comment on *Buddenbrooks* by a reader who 'was not bored, and wondered on every page why not', Mann criticizes Brandenburg's failure to turn matter into art: 'Also, nicht Alles in Ihrem Buch ist hoch genug gehoben, um als Kunst zu wirken; oft fehlt die Läuterung; und eine naturalistische Gegenständlichkeit liess mich oft sehnsüchtig an Schillers Künstlerweisheit denken: "Darin besteht das eigentliche Geheimnis des Meisters, *dass er den Stoff durch die Form vertilgt.*"' (Italics Schiller's.) Brandenburg's attempts to make use of recurrent phrases (leitmotivs) are recognized as 'Versuche einer kunstvolleren Machart' but condemned because they 'wirken oberflächlich angelernt und bleiben im Äusserlichen stecken'. All Mann's ambitions and intentions discussed above—the 'elevation' of the novel, the desire to escape from Naturalism, the leitmotiv as a step in that direction—are confirmed in his critical reactions to another man's works.

[48] The chapter 'Das Land', esp. ii. 36–41. Perhaps also the chapter 'Die Erfüllung', esp. pp. 288 ff.

a phrase summing up the method which that novel inaugurated. On the one side, very much what Schiller meant by *Schein*, an honest illusion such as Mann's first novel created; on the other side a construct to replace such semblance—the illusion of an illusion. Mann's distinction should suffice to prevent misunderstanding of his post-*Buddenbrooks* techniques as an application of the principles of Weimar Classicism.

Mann wrote this account in the middle of the long-drawn-out genesis of *Der Zauberberg*, when the wartime pressures had pushed the novel to one side but it was still much in his mind. This makes it legitimate to view that massive construction, technically speaking, in the light of the 'constructivist' aesthetic. Can we do the same with the even more massive Joseph novel? The second piece of evidence is Mann's account of the kind of illusion he created in that work. He tells how his typist reacted to the first volume of the tetralogy with the words: 'Well, now we know how all that really happened.' Mann comments:

> Das war rührend; denn es hat sich ja gar nicht zugetragen. Die Genauigkeit, die Realisation sind Täuschung, ein Spiel, ein Kunstschein, eine mit allen Mitteln der Sprache, der Psychologie, der Darstellung und dazu noch der kommentierenden Untersuchung erzwungene Verwirklichung und Vergegenwärtigung, deren Seele, bei allem menschlichen Ernst, der Humor ist.

(It was touching; because 'all that' didn't of course happen at all. The exactitude, the realization are a deception, play, an artistic semblance, a real presence forced into existence by every means at the disposal of language, psychology, presentation and, on top of all, a commentating investigation, and the soul of it all, despite its human seriousness, is humour. [xi. 655])

In particular, the last element, the 'commentating investigation' (historical, theological, philosophical, archaeological, of which the Joseph novels are full) is picked out as a means towards the total artistic effort. 'Die Erörterung gehört hier zum Spiel . . . ein Beitrag zur Schein-Genauigkeit.' (The discussion is here part of the play . . . a contribution to the illusion of exactitude.)

It is understandable that certain words—*Kunstschein, Spiel*—should suggest a similarity to Classical aesthetic principles.[49]

---

[49] It was this text that set Professor Wilkinson to comparing Mann's and the Weimar aesthetic in the article cited above.

But on examination the *Kunstschein* and the *Schein-Genauigkeit*
turn out to be different kinds of illusion from Schiller's. They
are avowedly substitutes for, not aspects of, reality. All Mann's
terms if taken together agree on this—*Realisation, Verwirklichung,
Täuschung,* and especially *erzwingen.*[50] It is not Schiller or Goethe
whose neighbourhood we are in, although in so far as Mann
came across their aesthetic views, he clearly felt himself encouraged by a surface similarity.

Whose neighbourhood then is it? In one of his notes for the
essay 'Geist und Kunst', Mann weighs up the possible relationships between ideas and life in the creative process, and
makes a passing reference to 'Nietzsche on the parodistic
element in artists' writings', adding the source: *Menschliches*
ii. 123.[51] In that section of 'Der Wanderer und sein Schatten',
Nietzsche calls serious learned writing forbidden ground for
artists, with their disorderly and often ill-equipped minds. If
they do try to write 'seriously' in this area, all they produce is
an inadvertent parody of seriousness—and thus by coincidence
do the very thing which is their proper office: parody the
inartistic and the scientific character. The artist, *qua* artist,
should have no other relationship to learning than parody.
Clearly, something very like this is what Mann is saying when
he talks of the 'illusion of exactitude' in his Joseph tetralogy.
His real source and affinity are, once again, Nietzsche and
Nietzsche's Artist.[52] To establish Mann's relationship to the
aesthetic philosophy and methods of periods further back in the
past than his direct source would involve examining the way
in which these were adapted or distorted in the decades which
separate him from Goethe and Schiller. No unbroken line joins

---

[50] In contrast to *bezwingen*, the word which would apply to the mastering of
experience in literary form. Cf. the letter to Walter Opitz of 5 Dec. 1903: '. . . o
Zeit, da man . . . in Briefen seine Erlebnisse bezwang und gestaltete . . .' (Br. i.
39).

[51] Note 46, Wysling, *Studien*, p. 174.

[52] Further confirmation is supplied by Richter's review of *Königliche Hoheit* which
says of Mann's methods: 'er denkt nur an seine Aufgabe, fast möchte man sagen
wissenschaftliche Aufgabe. Denn . . . er beobachtet und schildert mit den Allüren
des forschenden Historikers. Allüren, sage ich, denn das Instrument der wissen-
schaftlichen Analyse wird mit unverkennbarer Ironie gehandhabt'. (He thinks
only of his task, one might almost say, scientific task. For he observes and describes
with every appearance of being a research historian. I say 'appearance', for the
instrument of scientific analysis is handled with unmistakable irony.)

Thomas Mann's art to theirs, however much and in whatever causes he may have chosen to invoke them.

What I have been describing is the basis which Mann perforce began to lay early on for his later *œuvre*. This remains true to the pattern, with all its strengths and weaknesses. As Mann wrote at the end of his life, he had made for himself his own kind of novel out of his gifts and profound shortcomings (*Begabungen und profunden Unbegabungen*), and could thus not fail to excel at it.[53]

For the moment, the prospects seem arid. The organic richness of *Buddenbrooks*, its balance between substance and idea, lie behind the writer. His new method seems unlikely to achieve results of comparable quality. But it would be unfair to judge it on its first product, *Königliche Hoheit*, or on the unpublished 1911 fragment of *Felix Krull*. The court novel reveals the sources and nature of the programme that created it, but in itself gives no more than a hint of its possibilities. *Königliche Hoheit* is just too simple an allegory to do more. Its fault lies in the sheer paucity of intellectual content: a single idea developed from an image, a symbolic bee in the writer's bonnet, with no reference beyond himself.[54]

But its limitations are not the limits of intellectual experience as such. For a novelist to whom intellectual positions and issues were almost more real than external events, and in whose life intellectual crises and conflicts were the main events, the aesthetic method he had evolved was open to infinitely more complex and worthwhile exploitation. *Königliche Hoheit* gives us insights into the nature of *Der Zauberberg* much as the tiniest model hints at the final massive sculpture. Whereas the quality and richness of a material subject had been the major factor in *Buddenbrooks*, it is the scale and richness of intellectual experience that determine the later achievements of a uniquely intellectual novelist.

[53] To Karl Kerényi, 5 Dec. 1954. Mann is adapting what Schiller once said of his dramas.

[54] However much he may have tried after the event to interpret into the novel other than self-concerned themes. Cf. xi. 570 and xii. 97 on the 'democratic' implications which Heinrich Mann and Hermann Bahr encouraged Thomas Mann to see there.

# Art and Intellect

Niemand bleibt ganz, der er ist, indem er sich erkennt.

THOMAS MANN[1]

SELF-JUSTIFICATION and self-criticism mingle uneasily in Mann's writing throughout the decade following *Buddenbrooks*. This is the most complex phase of his work to unravel, although perhaps for this reason not the most happy artistically. If we grasp its essentials, we have grasped not only *Der Zauberberg*, the first work to treat the conflicts of this period with artistic freedom and thus transcend them, but also *Doktor Faustus*, which returns to them to pass a final judgement, coloured by the experience of later political events which had their roots in that decade.

Fictional and direct statements from *Tonio Kröger* onwards make up a single argument culminating in *Der Tod in Venedig*. That work shows Thomas Mann on the brink of a decision which the pressures of wartime soon afterwards precipitate, and which only a cooler atmosphere will subsequently allow to be reversed. At each stage in this development, impulses and models from the past play a vital role, as well as the fields of force of the contemporary literary scene.

The central issue is the right to criticize, the validity and value of criticism in the context of society or of life generally. For Thomas Mann at the time of his first novel, art *was* criticism of life in very much the sense Matthew Arnold gave to that phrase. *Buddenbrooks* makes this clear in two ways. First, it is itself informed by critical insight. Its outstanding quality is the way a clear-sighted analysis of people and setting is combined with their ample re-creation, so that justice is done to the subject in two quite distinct senses. Secondly, the type of artist shown evolving within the novel, far from being a *fin de siècle*

---

[1] No one who examines himself closely can remain quite the same as he was (xi. 90).

aesthete, is marked out by his critical perceptiveness. Hanno's talent may be for music, but he also has an acuteness of moral perception, a precocious clarity of vision, which is connected with his experience of suffering (p. 514). His eyes see too deep, he is disturbed by things which other people take for granted (p. 469), he sees more than he is meant to—for example, the strain and artificiality of the social round on which his father insists on taking him, as a form of training (p. 627). Hanno's one recorded moment of true contact with his father comes when Thomas's mask slips to reveal suffering, which Hanno can recognize and understand (p. 650). Finally, that account of a typical day at school, a feast of unpleasantness, gives full scope to Hanno's moral perception. He sees through the behaviour of teachers, the ineffectual and distorting methods of education, and the perverted values which the Prussianized school inculcates. The viewpoint technique in this section of the novel unites author and character in a single critical vision.

Other characters have a measure of perceptiveness, but its limits are significant. Thomas sees how relative are the Lübeck absolutes, but is lost because he has none of his own to put in their place. His perceptiveness is spasmodic; he can be grossly insensitive, especially towards Hanno. Christian's perceptiveness is a dead end. He peers into his abnormal sensations but with no moral result; he is satisfied, gratified even, to have insights and retail them *con amore*. Only Hanno is constantly and critically perceptive. The trio illustrate the potential and the problems of perceptiveness. Christian's indiscretions ('Mitteilerei', 'Intimstes nach aussen kehren' [p. 265]) parallel the fascination of decadent writing with the analysis of abnormal states for their own sake. Thomas is sarcastic about his brother's urge to wallow in such description.[2] At the other extreme, his own capacity for insight is limited, even deliberately resisted, as not proper in a burgher. Only in Hanno is perceptiveness given both freedom and purpose.

The cool, penetrating, incorruptible view is the feature of Mann's early writing which most struck his contemporaries. 'I have rarely seen clearer eyes than Thomas Mann's,' wrote a reviewer. 'That is, I have not seen the eyes themselves, only

---

[2] Cf. i. 545. Christian calls the feelings which go with a hangover 'sonderbar und widerlich zu gleicher Zeit'. Thomas retorts: 'Grund genug, sie zu beschreiben.'

what they have seen.'³ But the same point could sometimes be made a reproach, the coolness called coldness, the objectivity set down to a lack of human feeling. Mann took this to heart. He was aware enough of his own reserved nature. In his relations with Paul Ehrenberg, which were at their height in 1902, and later in his courtship of Katja Pringsheim in 1904, he had to urge that the man behind the writing was no heartless monster.

Hence *Tonio Kröger*, with its outburst against the 'curse' of literature and the sacrifices art demands: the sufferings of being a detached observer and the disgust which too much insight brings (*Erkenntnisekel*). This vindicates the writer as a human being. It becomes public knowledge that he suffers for his art and secretly yearns for a normal existence. This would correct the impression that Thomas Mann was cold and perhaps also flatter any 'normal' person to whom Mann's art meant anything—Paul Ehrenberg for instance—with the idea that love for ordinary people was its ultimate inspiration and, in ways not explained, the guarantee that it would be of more than ordinary quality.⁴ But the outburst signals no change of direction in practice. Tonio Kröger's last stated intention is to write about figures who are both tragic and ludicrous (viii. 338). For this purpose, technically speaking, the writer must go on with his precise observation and exact phrasing; they remain, uncomfortable or no, inseparably part of literature. Tonio Kröger's wistful injunction, 'Still, still und kein Wort, keine Worte!' (viii. 308) could only be temporary.

*Bilse und ich* is likewise concerned to explain away the impression of hostility left by the writer's critical perceptiveness and thus clear up a misunderstanding between literature and bourgeois reality. It confirms what can be inferred from Mann's practice about the effect Nietzsche had on him; it places what in *Tonio Kröger* is an emotional issue in a broader literary context; and it provides the concept on which Mann's inner and outer debates were to centre for some time, the concept of *Kritik*.

Mann speaks of a whole European school created by Nietzsche in which the borderline between art and criticism—'Kunst und Kritik'—is fluid. The school contains critics of a creative

³ Edgar Steiger in *Freistatt* 17, 1903.
⁴ Cf. viii. 338 on the condition for raising a mere *Literat* to the level of a *Dichter*.

temperament and creative writers with an extreme critical discipline of mind and style. He calls the resulting mixture critical creativity ('dichterischer Kritizismus'). Its uncompromising pursuit of knowledge through observation and its critical incisiveness of phrasing ('die Rücksichtslosigkeit der beobachtenden Erkenntnis und die kritische Prägnanz des Ausdrucks' [x. 18]) are what strikes the reader as cool and hostile.

The concept *Kritik* is taken not so much from Nietzsche's vocabulary as from his practice, that ability to penetrate beneath the surface of things to the probably unpleasant truth of which he was a master. Increasingly Mann felt this affinity between Nietzsche's practice and his own 'critical' writing, the importance of criticism as literature's defining element, its crucial role in the education and intellectual hygiene of society.

Not that criticism meant for him primarily social criticism. It was deeper and more general than this, as a note for *Fiorenza* makes clear:

Bei dem geborenen Protestanten u. Märtyrer handelt es sich gar nicht um die Sache, sondern um ihr Temperament, ihre physiologische Veranlagung. Sie würden protestieren, wie auch immer sie die Welt angetroffen hätten. Das Protestieren, *unkünstlerisch wie es ist*, gehört zur 'Literatur', (Opposition, Ironie, Nihilismus). Der Künstler kritisiert nicht, nimmt auf, gibt sich hin, lässt sich von den Tatsachen, den Erscheinungen besiegen, sagt immer Ja, spiegelt wieder, ohne Reflexion. [Added in the margin] Kritik der Sitten, Kritik des Lebens (Pessimismus) Mut gegenüber dem Bestehenden, Üblichen.

(The born protestant and martyr is not concerned with the cause, it is a question of temperament, of physiological endowment. They would protest no matter how they found the world. Protest, *inartistic as it is*, is the nature of 'literature', (opposition, irony, nihilism). The artist does not criticize, he receives impressions, gives himself fully, lets facts and phenomena conquer him, always accepts, mirrors things without reflecting on them. [Added in the margin] Criticism of morals, criticism of life (pessimism) courage *vis-à-vis* what is established and accepted.)[5]

So general was the sense Mann gave to the term about this time that he could make the simple equation: 'Kritik ist Geist'

---

[5] TMA Mp. xi. 13b Mat., sheet headed 'Savonarola'. The notes for *Tonio Kröger* similarly describe Tonio as suffering from the first, even as a boy, from his 'literary opposition', which means the outsider's critical view, his 'being opposite life' as a spectator, rather than any activism. Cf. Wysling, *Studien*, p. 53.

(criticism is mind),[6] adding 'der Geist aber ist das Letzte und Höchste' (mind is the ultimate and highest instance).

Nevertheless in the years following *Bilse und ich* Mann's concept acquired connotations from the cultural scene and the society Mann saw around him, and from the historical figures he turned to for support. From these two sources, as well as from introspection, he evolved a view of the role of critical intellect in art. A defence of the critical artist was the aim of 'Geist und Kunst', the essay project he worked at between spring 1909 and some time in 1910.

The *Fiorenza* note hints at the issues, implying a partial conflict between literature and art. Protest is an essential part of literature, yet protest is inartistic. This means that literature, if true to its own nature, tends away from art. The artist on the other hand (clearly this does not now include the writer at all) abstains from criticism and from any form of reflection about what he sees. The terms 'art' and 'literature', in the special senses which Mann's note implies, are being set against each other. Literature of course still remains art in a general sense. Mann is not advocating that it should be turned to the production of moral tracts, only saying that its defining element is a moral awareness of life in all its depths. Beauty as well as knowledge has a place in literature—the artist of the 'Nietzschean school' was said to have the twofold aim of 'tief erkennen' and 'schön gestalten'; but one element needed stressing in the particular circumstances of Germany at the turn of the century.

The text of *Fiorenza* enlarges on the conflict between two types of art, and places them in relation to society. The artists at Lorenzo de' Medici's court create beauty for their great patron, they embellish his festivals in return for their keep. They can ignore the dungeons in which men languish while dancing and feasting go on above. In contrast, Savonarola is the radical man of the spirit, who attempts to convert a Florence wallowing in sensual pleasures. His art (that he should refer at all to his 'art' is a plain enough hint that the whole construction is a vehicle for Mann's views on literature) is very different:

Meine Kunst ist heilig, denn sie ist Erkenntnis und ein flammender Widerspruch. Früh, wenn der Schmerz mich befiel, träumte mir von

---

[6] In his answer to a questionnaire on attitudes to criticism sent out in 1905 by the journal *Kritik der Kritik*.

einer Fackel, die barmherzig hineinleuchte in alle fürchterlichen
Tiefen, in alle scham- und gramvollen Abgründe des Daseins, von
einem göttlichen Feuer, das an die Welt gelegt werde, damit sie
aufflamme und zergehe samt all ihrer Schande und Marter in
erlösendem Mitleid. Es war die Kunst, davon mir träumte . . .

(My art is holy, for it is knowledge and a flaming protest. Early
on, when pain attacked me, I dreamt of a torch which would cast
merciful light into all the terrible depths, all the shameful abysses
of existence, of a divine fire which would set the world alight so
that it would flare up and be destroyed with all its shame and torment in saving pity. It was art of which I dreamt . . .[viii. 1060]).

Savonarola and the Renaissance artists at Lorenzo's court are
worlds apart; they are trivial hirelings, while he has a high
spiritual mission. How serious the dramatist's commitment to
the idea of a purifying mission is can be sensed from the
embarrassing rhetoric of the piece alone.[7]

The play is a masked attack on the cultural values of Munich
in the early years of the century. In unmasked form, with the
modern Munich setting, the short story *Gladius Dei* (1902) had
the same aim. Both had a reference beyond Munich to the
situation of the arts in Wilhelmine Germany at large, where
there was a sharp division between the fashionable portraitists
and pseudo-classical architects favoured with Imperial patron-
age and the more modern and socially radical artistic movements like Naturalism.[8] However general Mann might insist
his conception of 'critical' literature was, it was bound to become specific—in the form of satire, or didacticism—when
seen in the context of a particular society and brought up
against particular opposing forces.

What these are becomes clear in 'Geist und Kunst'. In an
early note[9] Mann refers to the innate hostility of Germans to
literature. The Munich attitude is typical: literature is looked

[7] It is confirmed by Mann's retrospective comments of 1917 (xii. 93), as well as
by the union of author and character in another working note for the play: 'Alles
Wissen, alles *Gewissen*, alle melancholische Einsicht ist auf unserer, der priester-
lichen Seite' (all knowledge, all conscience, all melancholy insight is on our side,
the priestly side). MS. cited, sheet headed 'Savonarola'.

[8] Cf. Hans Schwerte, 'Deutsche Literatur im Wilhelminischen Zeitalter',
*Wirkendes Wort* 14 (1964), 254 ff.

[9] References with the N-prefix are to the individual notes. Notes 1–118 are
numbered by Thomas Mann, the remaining notes (119–52) are so numbered in
Wysling, *Studien*, pp. 123–223, where the manuscript is printed entire.

at askance, mistrusted, seen as the antithesis of art. It is in the situation of Savonarola in *Fiorenza*, 'Geist gegen Kunst' (N 31). Only in Berlin does it have any better standing, because of the influence of Jews, the 'people of the book' (N 10). Accordingly, the very words 'literary' and 'man of letters' have become terms of abuse in Germany. By *literarisch* people mean whatever has no contact with life and is not a direct, spontaneous response to it (N 43, N 3). They declare it is no art at all: 'Literatur gleich Unkunst' (N 27).

This last note specifies one of their authorities for doing so: Wagner. 'Der neueste Mode-Unsinn, der übrigens von Wagner her durchgesickert ist' (the latest fashionable nonsense, which incidentally has seeped through from Wagner). Wagner is now an accepted classic, and his word carries weight—in this case, his facile contempt for any 'mere' literature, i.e. texts not accompanied by (his) music. Mann quotes Wagner's references to *Literaturlyrik* and *Literaturdichtung*, and counters them with examples of 'mere' literature: *The Odyssey*, *The Divine Comedy*, *Don Quixote*, *Gil Blas*, *Dead Souls*, *Hamlet*, the *Comédie humaine*, *Faust* (N 97), or again Goethe's lyrical poems and the plays of Shakespeare, Schiller, Kleist (N 76). He repeatedly makes clear that Wagner was in no position to be patronizing about literary art, given the often ludicrous level of his own libretti (N 14, 25, 76, etc.). In much the same way, the Germans of Mann's day have no right to reject something —literature—about which they understand so little (N 35, 36).

However far Wagner's operatic *Gesamtkunstwerk* fell short of literary criteria, it swept all before it by its sensuous music. Nietzsche saw Wagner's art as an unscrupulous onslaught on the senses, inspired by a hatred of intellectual clarity—'es gab nie einen solchen *Todhass* auf die Erkenntnis'.[10] Mann means much the same when he calls Wagner a demagogue (N 10). That he was a successful one is shown by the general acceptance of the view that art is a thing of the senses. So dominant has this view become that it has reversed the old idea that German art was deep, spiritual, intellectual, as against the art of the Romance peoples which was plastic and sensuous. It is now the other way about, and the Germans have gone to extremes in their rejection of intellect and its works: 'Wir treiben das

[10] *Der Fall Wagner*, Nachschrift.

"Künstlerische", gründlich wie immer, gleich bis zum Animalismus' (thorough as always, we take the 'artistic' straight to the lengths of animalism [N 29]). This explains the status that the plastic arts enjoy, as pilloried in *Fiorenza* and *Gladius Dei*. It explains the attempts of the contemporary theatre to 'free' itself from literature and become nothing but lavish settings and the physical talent of the actors (N 54, 39). All this is part of an elaborate anti-intellectual snobbery.

Yet nowhere is literature and its critical perspicacity more needed than among Germans:

> Notwendigkeit der 'Literatur', zumal bei uns: Erweckung des Verständnisses für alles Menschliche, Sittigung, Veredlung, Besserung, Schwächung dummer Überzeugungen und Werturteile, Skeptisierung, Humorisierung. Was das Moralistische betrifft, *zugleich* Verfeinerung und Reizbarkeit einerseits und Erziehung zum Zweifel, zur Gerechtigkeit, Duldsamkeit, *Psychologisierung*.

(Necessity of 'literature', especially in this country: development of an understanding of human nature, moral education, refinement, improvement, weakening of stupid convictions and value-judgements, growth of scepticism and humour. As far as morality is concerned, *at the same time* development of a subtler sensitivity and education in doubt, justice, tolerance, *psychologization*. [N 20])

Psychological understanding, as Nietzsche had so often complained,[11] is what Germans lack. 'Es fehlt in Deutschland an Psychologie, an Erkenntnis, an Reizbarkeit, Gehässigkeit der Erkenntnis, es fehlt an kritischer Leidenschaft.' (There is no psychology in Germany, no deeper knowledge, no sensitivity, no bite to analysis, there is no critical passion [N 19].) This after all is why a charlatan and demagogue like Wagner could rise to the status he now has, despite the fundamental shortcoming in his character which Mann sums up as his 'lack of literature' (N 97). The term 'literature' here means little less than integrity, moral conscience, critical self-awareness— a broadening of the sense which is a key to Mann's whole argument.

But there was one German who did see through Wagner, and he accordingly becomes the great example and patron saint of

---

[11] Cf. *Jenseits von Gut und Böse*, § 254; foreword to *Nietzsche contra Wagner*; *Ecce Homo*, section on *Der Fall Wagner*, § 3.

the critically perceptive. It is Nietzsche, whose rejection of Wagner after their intimate friendship was the effect of all those qualities in him that Wagner lacked: 'die Reinheit, psychologische Reizbarkeit, Wahrheitsliebe des Literaten, des Menschen der Erkenntnis' (the purity, psychological sensitivity, love of truth of the man of letters, the man of insight [N 32]).

In re-enacting, as he clearly does in 'Geist und Kunst', the controversy between Wagner and Nietzsche, Thomas Mann is firmly on Nietzsche's side, despite his own fascination with Wagner's art. (He always maintained that his love of Wagner was quite compatible with critical clarity about him.) And the re-enactment is not merely made possible by a personal involvement with two figures to whom he was in different ways devoted. It is made necessary by the continued relevance in German culture of the issues which Nietzsche first raised. His prophetic warnings about the dangers of Wagner have gone unheeded. Wagner is a major cultural influence and the direction in which his influence moves the arts, the theatre, the public attitude towards artists and towards the spurned art of letters, seems as undesirable to Thomas Mann as the seeds of these developments appeared to Nietzsche.

Nietzsche's prophetic clear-sightedness is a great part of the achievement which leads Mann to ask how people can possibly still say after Nietzsche that the critical writer is inferior to the pure creative writer, the 'Dichter und Künstler' (N 40). Germans make altogether too much fuss about the *Dichter* as against the mere *Schriftsteller* (N 47). It is a distinction which especially rankles with Thomas Mann, because he has by this time often had to suffer from it. Within the cultural scene his notes re-create, the honorific term *Dichter*, always an arbitrary judgement, was accorded only to writers whose work offered some analogy with the visual beauty, sensuousness, unintellectual immediacy of the plastic arts and could be given the accolade *plastisch*. In other words, literature could be acceptable—at the price of abstaining from the moral-critical element which Mann saw as its *raison d'être*. It was then *Dichtung*, not *Literatur*; *Plastik*, not *Kritik*. This kind of writing would also qualify, in the anti-intellectual climate of the times, as *Kunst*, something scarcely removed from the beautifying activities of Lorenzo de' Medici's *Künstlervölkchen*.

Even in his most purely re-creative work to date, *Budden-brooks*, Mann was anything but a beautifier of life's surface. His first novel had frequently been paid the compliment that it had a good deal of *Plastik* in it, but since then the term had been more often used as a stick with which to beat his work. No doubt this strengthened his commitment to the critical-intellectual side of the debate, giving him an additional motive for attacking 'anti-literary simplemindedness' (N 11). Having asked himself (N 33) whether he had enough *Plastik* to his credit to be arguing from a position of strength —surely it was not necessary to have first written *War and Peace* and *Anna Karenina?*—he could campaign against all those snob terms which made facile judgements easy—*Plastik, Dichter, Kunst*; and stand up for their unpopular opposites—*Kritik, Schriftsteller, Literatur*.

He then tries a number of approaches. He pooh-poohs the whole *Dichter/Schriftsteller* distinction. He accepts it, but only to polemicize in the spirit of *Fiorenza* against the currently favoured term, describing the *Künstler* (*Dichter*) as the great man's Fool and flatterer (N 121), and declaring that the value of the *Schriftsteller* to humanity is far greater:

> Was, wo wären wir, wäre die Menschheit ohne ihre grossen Fürsprecher, die Schriftsteller! Verdankt sie ihnen nicht mehr, als den Dichtern, die, Künstlerkinder, die sie sind, allzu oft nur dem Vergnügen, dem Genuss der Herrschenden gedient haben?'

> (What, where should we be, would humanity be, without its great advocates, the writers! Does it not owe them more than it owes the poets who, artist-children that they are, have all too often merely served the pleasure and enjoyment of the rulers? [N 41])

It was surely time to speak up for the *Schriftsteller*, with their knowledge of the world and the human heart, and claim for them the title of *Künstler*, even if they did not work by direct sensuous presentation, but used words to express and to designate precisely (N 27).[12]

Would this make intellectualism any more palatable to Mann's audience? Why not also show that *all* modern art was necessarily intellectual, and that the ideals of unconscious creativity and pure spontaneous inspiration were illusions? The

---

12 An echo of the passage in *Bilse und ich* on 'kritische Prägnanz der Bezeichnung'.

lack of 'critical passion' in Germany meant that people knew nothing of what lay behind the surface of modern art—the work of Strauss, Mahler, George, Hofmannsthal, Wedekind (N 19), or Max Reinhardt (N 102). There is not even, Nietzsche apart, any real criticism of Wagner, who is now sacrosanct (N 53). Yet all these men have secret weaknesses, and tricks to make up for them. Wagner himself is far from being all he seems, and all that his popular legend has made him. His apparent simplicity is refined calculation, his 'popular' quality is not a matter of spontaneous naturalness but of deliberate demagogy. It is these discrepancies that make him for Thomas Mann, as for Nietzsche, *the* problem of modern art: 'das Problem der Modernität selber' (N 53).[13]

This lifting of the curtain to show what lies behind modern art is typical of Thomas Mann, but it is meant as an appeal rather than a debunking. Intellectualism is to be made respectable by showing that there is simply no alternative in modern times. Another method lay in showing that it was not limited to modern times either: great and respected literary figures and movements of the past could be quoted as authorities. Mann records Lessing's crisply expressed view of the place which reason has in creation: 'Wer richtig räsonniert, erfindet auch; und wer erfinden will, muss räsonnieren können. Nur die glauben, dass sich das eine von dem anderen trennen lasse, die zu keinem von beiden aufgelegt sind.' (The man who can reason properly can invent; and anyone who wants to invent must be able to reason. The only people who think that the one can be separated from the other are those who have no inclination for either. [N 80])[14]

Mann's second authority is the whole Romantic movement. His note reads:

*Romantik* und Kritizismus (Schriftstellertum). Schlegel. Wackenroder. In der ganzen Romantik ist der *Geist*, die Ironie die Hauptsache. Sie ist tief literarisch. Tieck. Wackenroder, ein Standard Werk der Romantik, ganz analytisch-schriftstellerisch. Unnaiv. Ebenso Lucinde. Die Romantiker im Ganzen keine starken Plastiker: philosophisch. Ihre Naivität ist Raffinement. 'Welch ein Wissen vom Dichterischen, von Sprache und Bildung . . .' (Gundolf).

---

[13] Cf. Nietzsche, *Vorwort* to *Der Fall Wagner*: 'Wagner *resümiert* die Modernität.'
[14] Quoting *Hamburgische Dramaturgie*, 96. Stück.

(*Romanticism* and the critical ('literary') approach. Schlegel. Wackenroder. In Romanticism generally, *intellect*, irony is the main thing. Romanticism is deeply literary. Tieck. Wackenroder, a standard work of Romanticism, entirely analytical and literary. Un-naïve. Lucinde the same. The Romantics on the whole not strong on 'plastic' effects: philosophical. Their *naïveté* is calculated. 'What a knowledge they show of the nature of poetry, of language and culture . . .' (Gundolf). [N 42])[15]

Schiller is yet another name Mann appeals to. Schiller's declared ambition was to be a great *Schriftsteller* (N 10),[16] his dramatic talents were *rhetorisch-idealisch-kritisch* (N 117), and he was by his own admission a 'barbarian' in regard to the visual arts (N 37). Would these authorities not add weight to Mann's argument—perhaps especially the Romantics, in whom there was a revival of interest around 1900?[17]

But the question is whether any arguments for clarity and reason, however clear and reasonable, would have an effect on readers who needed persuading that such things mattered. Mann's authorities and the points he makes are impressive, but could be only piecemeal attacks on very deep-rooted attitudes, of which the dominant cultural preferences were merely symptoms. Beneath the 'fashionable snobbery against literature and the man of letters' (N 12), beneath the aversion to consciousness in the creation of art and to analysis as the substance of art, there lay a general mistrust of intellect as the enemy of vitality and the cause of decadence. It is ironical that what Mann was ultimately up against was the very idea which is at the base of his *Buddenbrooks*; ironical too that the thinker above all others responsible for the spread of this idea was Nietzsche, who figures in Mann's argument as the hero of the critical intellectual writer. But to find Nietzsche on both sides of the same controversy is not uncommon, given the nature

---

[15] What Mann sought and found in the Romantics is clear from his copy of Ricarda Huch's *Blütezeit der Romantik*, Leipzig 1899, in TMA. Passages marked and underlined concern predominantly the Romantics' intellectuality and ironic self-consciousness, and also their ultimate aim of regaining a higher simplicity via intellectual complexity. Mann's tribute to Ricarda Huch on her sixty-fifth birthday centres on this study, especially her declaration that the novel is the perfect vehicle for the post-Romantic ironic consciousness—a rehabilitation after Mann's own heart. See Huch, op. cit., p. 319, and Mann x. 433.

[16] Mann's source is the *Marbacher Schillerbuch*, one of his sources for *Schwere Stunde*, p. 23.

[17] Cf. Soergel-Hohoff, *Dichtung und Dichter der Zeit*, Düsseldorf, 1964, i. 706.

of his thought. The oscillation in Nietzsche's values between a ruthless unmasking of truth and a resolute defence of life against the unmasking intellect is well known. It is re-enacted in Thomas Mann's life and work. Indeed, the self-criticism in *Tonio Kröger* is a first sign of the literary intellectual recoiling from his own aims and methods. Probably the cultural background which 'Geist und Kunst' reflects was already a factor in Tonio Kröger's unease. By 1900 reactions had set in against the extremes of psychology, analysis, and literary self-dissection of Naturalism and Impressionism; manifestos had been published appealing for a turn away from these unhealthy concerns to a new idealism, reinvigorated by the fresh air of the German provinces, a literature accessible to good ordinary German people instead of one restricted to coteries of *Literaten* in the cafés of Berlin and fostered by the latest 'isms' imported from Paris. Warmth of heart, not cold cerebral analysis; the expression of whole healthy (*tüchtig*) men, not specialized, immature, inbred writers; an affirmation of the positive side of life, not a constant nagging criticism— these were the values preached by Friedrich Lienhard, the initiator of what came to be known as *Heimatkunst*. His complaints about modern writing anticipate Tonio Kröger's self-reproaches. They are relevant not because Thomas Mann necessarily knew and attended to Lienhard's essays and speeches in particular,[18] but because they typify the external pressures to which Mann was sensitive. Similar impulses and ambitions inspired cultural societies like the Werdandi-Bund and the Walhalla-Gesellschaft, the first of which Thomas Mann dismisses as 'drooling with idealistic garrulousness' (N 18).

But if these critics of decadence were not, at least by the period of 'Geist und Kunst', all taken seriously, there were other, greater critics of decadence who were. Tolstoy, for instance, whose onslaught on modernism in *What is Art?*[19] and other essays carried an authority which the crudity of its argument

[18] It is quite likely that he did, nevertheless. He had contributed reviews to a journal founded by Lienhard in the 1890s under the title *Das Zwanzigste Jahrhundert*. In 'Geist und Kunst' he takes up points made in a recent article of Lienhard's (N 91). Practically all the key words against which Mann polemicizes in his essay notes are found in Lienhard's writings. Cf. the collection of essays grouped under the title *Neue Ideale* (5th impression, Stuttgart, 1920).

[19] German edition, 1902.

could not wholly destroy. 'Tolstoy on modern art' was avowedly one of Mann's favourite books (N 19). The spirit in which he took it is hinted by a letter to Heinrich Mann in 1900: he writes that his 'Tolstoyism' almost makes him feel that such things as rhyme and rhythm are wicked (Br. H. 4). He has clearly taken to heart Tolstoy's message that the complexity and refinement of modern art serve immoral ends. And in a different way from Tolstoy, Mann's critical hero Nietzsche also pointed an accusing finger at him, with his sceptical insights into the spiritual economy of artists. In particular his distinction between artists who create from superfluity and vitality and those who create from a hatred of life[20] must have struck at Thomas Mann. It was a distinction which paved the way for that delightful paradox that Wagner was truly a miniaturist and that, lacking the capacity of organic creation (*organisches Gestalten*), Wagner concentrated on the invention and elaboration of detail and raised this necessity to a dramatic principle ('er setzt ein Prinzip an, wo ihm ein Vermögen fehlt'). Just such a concentration on detail, to the neglect of the life of the whole, is Nietzsche's definition of decadence: the parts become self-sufficient, the whole is no longer a whole. It is composite, calculated, artificial, an artefact ('zusammengesetzt, gerechnet, künstlich, ein Artefakt').[21]

Whether Nietzsche was right or wrong about Wagner, what he says exactly fits Thomas Mann's view of himself: the concentration on detail, the building up of a massive whole out of many discrete parts, the absence of a cohesive force of 'genius' to make the hard slog easier; even the point that these shortcomings are restated in the guise of principles.[22] Against Nietzsche's accusation, Mann could only set his belief that *all*

---

[20] Cf. *Nietzsche contra Wagner.* 'Wir Antipoden': 'In Hinsicht auf Artisten jeder Art bediene ich mich jetzt dieser Hauptunterscheidung: ist hier der *Hass* gegen das Leben oder der *Überfluss* an Leben schöpferisch geworden? In Goethe zum Beispiel wurde der Überfluss schöpferisch, in Flaubert der Hass: Flaubert, eine Neuausgabe Pascals, aber als Artist, mit dem Instinkt-Urteil auf dem Grunde: "*Flaubert est toujours haïssable, l'homme n'est rien, l'œuvre est tout*" . . .'

[21] All these quotations are from *Der Fall Wagner*, § 7.

[22] Mann's classic confessional statement on his method is the description of Gustav von Aschenbach's in *Der Tod in Venedig* (viii. 452). Unsuspecting readers took Aschenbach's works for the product of a powerful force and a flow of creative impulse, whereas they are built up in layers, in short bursts of work, from hundreds and hundreds of separate inspirations.

modern art was necessarily like this. Reinhardt for example gave him the reassurance that it could still achieve a kind of greatness:

Der Fall *Reinhardt*: für mich ein künstlerisches Erlebnis hohen Ranges. Es ist nämlich ein ermutigendes, michselbst bestätigendes Erlebnis. Dass *Modernität*, dass Kleinheit, Detail-Addition, Geniemangel, Intellektualität, verbunden mit Zähigkeit, Arbeit, Willensdauer, sich mit Glück an Aufgaben grossen Stiles wagen darf: der Fall Reinhardt beweist es.

(The *Reinhardt* case: for me an artistic experience of the first rank. For it is an encouraging experience, which gives me confirmation. That the modern approach, minuteness, accumulation of details, lack of genius, intellectuality, allied with tenacity, work, endurance of will, can successfully go in for ambitious tasks—the Reinhardt case proves it. [N 102])

So we have a picture of a writer defending positions which are open to criticism, for reasons he is more aware of than most people because his essentially critical mind cannot but be self-critical too. His affirmations and self-assertion thereby become a symptom of uncertainty: 'Die Neigung zu einem scharfen, polemischen, herausfordernden streitsüchtigen Ton . . . gerade die Folge der Skepsis, ein Übertönen des Gewissens' (the tendency to a sharp, polemical, challenging belligerent tone . . . the consequence, precisely, of scepticism, a shouting down of one's conscience [N 144]). Mann also recognized that many of the features of his age which he was critical of were present in himself (N 19), a fifth column behind his apparently firm defence of the critical intellect in literature. The important question becomes, what positive action can be taken? In what ways can the self-critical writer consciously guide his own literary career? What will be the result of the dialectic between those characteristics he has developed, and is prepared to stand up for, and the pressures of his day? For its pursuit of other gods than his does affect the practical question of finding a continuing audience for what he writes.

A number of notes for 'Geist und Kunst' are straws in the wind. The ones quoted so far make up an argument for an 'intellectualist' view of literature, but this emphasis was necessary because of the exaggerations of a current fad, 'eine törichte, national bornierte Zeitströmung' (N 27). Mann also had nevertheless some attachment to the 'plastic' element in literature, to the principle of 'schön gestalten' as well as that of 'tief erkennen'. He believed he had a good deal of 'plastic' achievement to his credit and wanted it recognized. It would therefore not do to present an account of literature too one-sidedly intellectual.

This is why, besides arguing that the *Dichter/Schriftsteller* distinction is invalid, he can also try to appropriate the title *Dichter* for the analytical school; why besides satirizing the *Künstler* as a time-server, he claims the title *Künstler* for the scorned *Literat*, and the term *Kunst* for what he produces. This readiness to accept the criteria implied in the cant terms of anti-intellectualist criticism shows that Mann was right when he perceived the trends of the time in himself too. It is not mere tactics that makes him adopt these terms and manipulate them in such a way as to make his kind of literature qualify for them.

This tendency comes out especially clearly in Mann's treatment of the term *Plastik*, which—besides some polemic against it, and besides the historical evidence that it is not necessary to literary greatness ('die Romantiker im Ganzen keine starken Plastiker' [N 42])—he also tries to redefine:

> *Bornierter Begriff des 'Plastischen'*: Auch das blosse Wort kann plastisch sein, auch das gesprochene. Auch einen rein geistigen Stoff, nicht nur eine Fabel, Handlung und 'Charaktere' gilt es zu gestalten. Auch das rein schriftstellerische Produkt ist eine Objektivierung, eine Verwirklichung, Ausscheidung, Begrenzung, Verkörperlichung, ein Fertigwerden mit dem Unendlichen . . .

> (*The concept of 'plasticity' too limited*: the mere word, even the spoken word, can be plastic too. Purely intellectual material has to be given form too, not just plot, action, and 'characters'. The 'writer' too has to objectivize, realize, eliminate, limit, render corporeal, come to terms with an endless material . . .[N 104])

In another note Mann quotes two well-known aphorisms on the limitations of language and its inadequacy to grasp complex realities[23] and comments: 'Gerade der Schriftsteller, der dies nicht vergisst, der also *bewusst spielt* ist ein Künstler so gut wie

---

[23] 'Sobald nämlich unser Denken Worte gefunden hat, ist es schon nicht mehr innig, noch im tiefen Grunde ernst' (Schopenhauer); and Goethe's
   'Ihr müsst mich nicht mit Widerspruch verwirren,
   Sobald man spricht, beginnt man schon zu irren.'
Mann found both aphorisms in Schopenhauer's *Über Schriftstellerei und Stil*, § 4.

der Plastiker.' (Precisely the writer who does not forget this, who *consciously plays*, that is, is an artist every bit as much as the 'plastic' creator [N 68].) The redefinition here begun is perfected in a later comment on the same aphorisms:[24]

Das kann der schreibende Künstler (der Plastiker) der alles rund, alles von allen Seiten sieht, nicht vergessen, und er schätzt den Geist und die Wahrheit zu hoch, als dass er glauben könnte, es je vergessen zu dürfen. Daher seine beim Schreiben so viel stärkere Hemmungen.

(That is something that the writing artist (the plastic creator) who sees everything round, everything from every side, cannot forget, and he has too high an esteem for mind and truth to be able ever to think he may forget it. That is why his inhibitions when writing are so much stronger. [N 143])

A reconciliation and fusion of the two sides is here complete. The awareness of complexity which characterizes the intellectual appears as the reason why he produces a many-sided, intellectually neutral work of art. This is already a shift of position from the straightforward view that moral criticism was the function of literature. That there is still another type of artist in Mann's mind as a term of comparison is plain from the reference to 'stronger inhibitions'—stronger, that is, than any the spontaneous, carefree creative artist may have. Mann's avowed Flaubertian difficulties with the compositional process here get a reinterpretation so as to bring them under the term *plastisch*. Finally, in the phrase 'der schreibende Künstler (der Plastiker)', the reconciliation between the intellectual artist and the ideals of his age has become an accomplished fact.

What are the practical implications? An immediate one is that the essay on 'Geist und Kunst' is not going to be completed. The writer has come too far from his initial positions, shifted the meaning of his terms and his allegiance too much ever to forge a single argument from his notes. He has recoiled from too extreme an intellectualist account of literature. He has also realized that the unhappy effect of attacking the sillier fringes of anti-intellectualism would only be to fall out with his times—'sich mit der Zeit verfeinden, was unglücklich macht' (N 112).

[24] To which is added a further dictum of Goethe's, 'Der Mensch, indem er spricht muss für den Augenblick einseitig werden'.

Broader implications for Mann's artistic development are confirmed in the longest and most interesting note of the whole project, which gives us the framework within which to understand the complexities of his situation in 1910:

Die neue Generation, jenseits der Modernität. Ich weiss nicht, wie es in der Malerei, der Musik steht (Strauss scheint mir nur zur Psychologie der Modernität Wert zu haben). Aber in der Literatur höre ich es überall pochen. *Speyers* Novelle.[25] Fühle da viel Neues, Zukünftiges, Junges, Symptomatisches, viel 'neue Generation', viel 'Heraufkommendes'. Gesundheit, kultivierte Leiblichkeit, vornehme Natur, vornehmes Wohlsein u. dergl., in diesem Falle noch dem Lächeln ausgesetzt durch den Snobismus eines jungen Juden. Die Arbeit auf dem Felde (die seine Leidenschaft unter ihn bringt). Das Wandern und Schlafen im Freien. Die Tennispartie. Der Ritt. Das Brausebad. Das Alles um seinerselbst willen da, stolz betont, stark empfunden. Ich rieche Morgenluft. Im Verhältnis zur Natur, zur Landschaft, zum Wandern: viel echte und unmittelbare Romantik: reine, unverhunzte Gefühlsintensität. 'Man muss das Leben mit gesunden Händen anfassen'.[26] Das hätte vor 10 Jahren kein junger Novellist geschrieben. *Ich*—grub mit 20 Jahren Psychologie: kein Unterschied der Bedeutung das, sondern einer der Generation. Interessant, interessant—und beunruhigend. Nicht durch beklemmend viel Talent kann diese Jugend den Baumeister Solness fürchten machen, aber durch dies Neue. *Hier* ist unsere Gefahr, rascher zu veralten, als nötig wäre. Das Interesse, das, au fond, die Generation beherrscht, zu der Hauptmann, Hofmannsthal und ich gehören, ist das Interesse am Pathologischen. Die Zwanzigjährigen sind weiter. Hauptmann sucht eifrig Anschluss. Jemand sollte zählen, wie oft im Griechischen Frühling[27] 'gesund' vorkommt. Auch Hofmannsthal wird sich auf seine Art zu arrangieren suchen. Die Forderung der Zeit ist, alles, was irgend gesund ist in uns, zu kultivieren.

Einfluss Whitmans auf die jüngsten grösser, als der Wagners.—

Wir um 70 Geborenen stehen Nietzsche zu nahe, wir nehmen zu unmittelbar an seiner Tragödie, seinem persönlichen Schicksal teil (vielleicht dem furchtbarsten, am meisten Ehrfurcht gebietenden Schicksal der Geistesgeschichte). Unser Nietzsche ist der Nietzsche *militans*. Der Nietzsche *triumphans* gehört den 15 Jahre nach uns Geborenen. Wir haben von ihm die psychologische Reizbarkeit,

---

[25] Wilhelm Speyer, *Wie wir einst so glücklich waren*, Munich, 1909.
[26] Speyer, op. cit., p. 88.
[27] Hauptmann's travel memoir *Griechischer Frühling* appeared in 1907.

den lyrischen Kritizismus, das Erlebnis Wagners, das Erlebnis des Christentums, das Erlebnis der Modernität, — Erlebnisse, von denen wir uns niemals vollkommen trennen werden, so wenig, wie erselbst sich je vollkommen davon getrennt hat. Dazu sind sie zu teuer, zu tief, zu fruchtbar. Aber die Zwanzigjährigen haben das von ihm, was übrig bleiben wird, sein Zukünftiges, seine gereinigte Nachwirkung. Für sie ist er ein Prophet, den man nicht sehr genau kennt, den man kaum gelesen zu haben braucht und dessen gereinigte Resultate man doch instinktweise in sich hat. Sie haben von ihm die Bejahung der Erde, die Bejahung des Leibes, den antichristlichen und antispirituellen Begriff der Vornehmheit, der Gesundheit und Heiterkeit, Schönheit in sich schliesst . . .

(*The new generation*, beyond 'modernity'. I do not know how things stand in painting or music (Strauss seems to me of value only for the psychology of modernity). But in literature things are stirring everywhere. *Speyer's Novelle*. I feel in that much that is new, the coming thing, young, symptomatic, a lot of 'younger generation' and 'new wave'. Healthiness, cultivated physical element, aristocratic nature, aristocratic well-being, and the like, in this case somewhat exposed to ridicule by the snobbery of a young Jew. The work in the fields (which subdues his passion). Hiking and sleeping out of doors. The tennis match. The ride. The shower. All that described for its own sake, proudly emphasized, strongly felt. I sense fresh beginnings. In the relationship to nature, landscape, hiking: a great deal of genuine and spontaneous romanticism: pure, unspoiled intensity of feeling. 'One must seize hold of life with healthy hands'. Ten years ago no young novelist would have written that. *I*—was working the 'psychology' mine at twenty: that is not a difference of stature, simply of generation. Interesting, interesting— and disquieting. It isn't any oppressive amount of talent in these young writers that can make Master-Builder Solness afraid, but they do have this new approach. *Here* lies the danger that we may become *passé* sooner than would be necessary. The interest which, at core, dominates the generation which Hauptmann and Hofmannsthal and I belong to is the interest in things pathological. The twenty-year-olds are beyond this. Hauptmann is keenly looking for a way to join in. Somebody ought to count up how many times he uses the word 'healthy' in his *Grecian Spring*. Hofmannsthal too will try in his way to come to some arrangement. The demand of the times is to cultivate anything in us that can be called healthy.

Influence of Whitman on the youngest people is greater than that of Wagner.

We who were born around 1870 are too close to Nietzsche, we participate too directly in his tragedy, his personal fate (perhaps the most terrible, most awe-inspiring fate in intellectual history). Our Nietzsche is Nietzsche militant. Nietzsche triumphant

belongs to those born fifteen years after us. We have from him our
psychological sensitivity, our lyrical criticism, the experience of
Wagner, the experience of Christianity, the experience of 'modernity'—experiences from which we shall never completely break
free, any more than Nietzsche himself ever did. They are too precious for that, too profound, too fruitful. But the twenty-year-olds
have from him what will remain in the future, his purified after-
effect. For them he is a prophet one doesn't know very exactly,
whom one hardly needs to have read, and yet whose purified
results one has instinctively in one. They have from him the affirmation of the earth, the affirmation of the body, the anti-Christian and
anti-intellectual conception of nobility, which comprises health
and serenity and beauty . . . [N 103])

Beneath all the cultural tendencies he had traced and
labelled variously *Gesundheits- und Durchsonnungstendenz* (N 91),
or *Regenerationsgedanke* (N 109), or *Renaissance* (N 150), Mann
saw ultimately a 'yearning for life', a 'glorifying of the body'
(N 72). In Speyer's treatment of things physical he sees the
literary potential of this trend. He also watches, acutely and
without illusions, the reactions of his major contemporaries
to the fact that their generation is no longer automatically in
the forefront of literary change. He sees clearly what the times
require if one is not to be ousted, like Ibsen's Master-Builder,
by younger men. In all this, he is the practical critic. Insight is
to serve action, the cultural diagnosis will serve the conscious
guidance of his own career.

But at the same time, characteristically, Mann attempts to
understand the issues he is involved in as exhaustively as he
can. Watching current trends, he also probes for their antecedents (Nietzsche) and distinguishes illuminatingly the type of
influence Nietzsche had on two successive generations. Further
back still, he relates what he observes to other names—Darwin
(N 49), Rousseau (N 109); he seeks parallels for the antitheses
of his day in Schiller's *naiv* and *sentimentalisch* concepts, in
Schopenhauer's *Wille* and *Vorstellung*, and at the very roots of
European culture in the conflict of heathen and Christian
thought, the latter traced even further back to its roots in
Platonism.[28] He lists these and other concept pairs in a note
headed *Gegensätze*:

[28] Doubtless with Nietzsche's *mot* in mind that Christianity is 'Platonism for the
people'. (*Vorrede* to *Jenseits von Gut und Böse*.)

Geist und Natur
Geist und Kunst
Kultur und Natur
Kultur (Zivilisation) und Kunst
Wille und Vorstellung
Naiv und sentimental
Realismus und Idealismus
Heidentum und Christentum (Platonismus)
Plastik und Kritik  (N 124)[29]

Here, Mann was striving to synthesize out from a confusing multiplicity of time-honoured terms one underlying antithesis. Perhaps the failure to do so was a further reason for not completing his essay. Yet he retained a sense that some such illuminating principle existed. Of all the formulations he toyed with, Schiller's seemed most like the definitive statement. In a brief comment on *Fiorenza* written shortly after abandoning the 'Geist und Kunst' project, Mann said that the antithesis his play treated was ultimately (*zuletzt*) the one which Schiller formulated in the concepts *naiv* and *sentimentalisch* (xi. 563). And in later references to Schiller's essay, he usually remarks that it makes all other aesthetic essays superfluous because it contains them in itself (ix. 177 etc.).

'Geist und Kunst' was Thomas Mann's first defeat by the antithetical approach on which all his work so far had been based. In part the issues were too vast, in part his own position was too unstable to allow final statement. What happens next?

The shift of attitudes perceptible in 'Geist und Kunst' is echoed here and there in his letters and essays. There are hints that he is on the brink of change. Then, in the experiences of his stay in Venice in 1911, he finds the ideal subject matter in which to embody the issues which have been taxing him and which he has so far not made himself master of. In Gustav von Aschenbach he sketches an artist and an artistic development closely related to the situation he sees himself in, but fifteen years on, with the decisions taken and the changes accomplished. In

[29] A line down the left-hand margin cuts in under the fourth pair of terms and runs down the centre of the last five pairs, indicating that from 'Wille und Vorstellung' onwards the positions must be reversed to bring all the terms that belong together on to the same side. See the plate reproducing this sheet in *Oxford German Studies*, 1 (1966), 54.

the *Novelle's* final form, he also shows the risks and the eventual tragedy which flow from that particular artistic development. First the signs of change. The one thing a Master-Builder cannot do when challenged by youth is vie in youthfulness with his challengers. Just as there was no possibility that the author of *Tonio Kröger* would become a *Heimatkünstler*, so now it is impossible for Thomas Mann to write in the fresh sensuous style which impressed him in Speyer's work. But the process of growing more mature, of becoming the established older generation offered an alternative which would not be much less in tune with the times. For the psychological extremism of Mann's work to date could be felt as the characteristic of a young man (he was only thirty-five in 1910) which still left open other paths of development. 'Psychology' might become a thing of the past, the critical free-thinker might settle down to quieter, mellower modes of literary creation.

In 1911, just before the start of work on *Der Tod in Venedig*, Mann wrote an essay on Chamisso, the author of one of the oldest 'outsider'[30] stories in literature, the tale of Peter Schlemihl who lost his shadow. Yet the problematic author did not remain for ever problematic:

. . . Chamisso, nachdem er aus seinen Leiden ein Buch gemacht, beeilt sich, dem problematischen Puppenstande zu entwachsen, wird sesshaft, Familienvater, Akademiker, wird als Meister verehrt. Nur ewige Bohemiens[31] finden das langweilig. Man kann nicht immer interessant bleiben. Man geht an seiner Interessantheit zugrunde oder man wird ein Meister.

(Chamisso, after making a book out of his sufferings, hastens to grow out of the problematic chrysalis stage, settles down, becomes father of a family, an academic, is revered as a master. Only eternal bohemians think that is boring. One cannot remain permanently interesting. One is ruined by one's 'interestingness' or one becomes a master. [ix. 57])

*Peter Schlemihl* is a lovable but, Mann stresses, a youthful work.

A letter of the following year echoes these trains of thought. Mann is giving a younger writer his opinion of his books, and explains why he cannot feel full sympathy with them. Too much that they contain reminds him of his former self:

---

30　Mann interprets Schlemihl's shadow as a symbol of social integration ('bürgerliche Solidität und menschliche Zugehörigkeit' [ix. 56]).

31　Probably a reference to Heinrich Mann. See below, pp. 195 ff.

. . . wenn ich für das Buch [. . .] die rechte freudige Teilnahme nicht aufbringe, so liegt das daran, dass Vieles darin mich allzu sehr an mich selbst von vor 15 Jahren erinnert, an überwundene oder um mich weniger heroisch auszudrücken an über*standene* Zustände die wiederzuerkennen, bei Anderen wiederzufinden mir eher peinlich als erquicklich sein muss. Bedenken Sie: ich werde siebenunddreissig! Da fängt man heutzutage an, akademische Neigungen zu spüren . . . Nun, halten Sie mich noch nicht für ganz verkalkt! Aber es ist etwas an dem, was ich sagte. Ich meine eine gewisse psychologische Überreiztheit, eine gewisse Unverschämtheit der Erkenntnis, eine gewisse Boshaftigkeit der Dialektik — es ist schwer, das so beiläufig zu sagen. Ich bekenne Ihnen eine lebhafte Antipathie gegen junge Leute . . .

(If I can't muster the proper pleasurable sympathy for your book, the reason is that much in it reminds me excessively of myself of fifteen years ago, reminds me of circumstances I have struggled through, or to put it less heroically *got* through. Finding them and recognizing them in other people is inevitably painful for me rather than cheering. Just think: I'm nearly thirty-seven! These days people at that age begin to feel academic inclinations . . . Well, don't think I'm quite fossilized yet! But there is something in what I said. I am thinking of a certain psychological overwroughtness, a certain shamelessness of analytical probing, a certain maliciousness of argument—it is difficult to put it into words just like that. I will confess to you that I feel a lively antipathy for young people . . . [Br.i.96])

These two passages are very revealing. The first sets up a theory that writers naturally grow out of their problematic phase. But its images tell us a lot: 'master' has connotations not just of literary quality, but of the socially integrated and respected guild-craftsman,[32] its associations are training and ambition rather than organic growth. And the other, organic image of emergence from the chrysalis is belied by the suggestion of a deliberate haste to achieve this crucial development.

In the letter to Ehrenstein on the other hand Mann struggles to keep some ironic distance from an attitude in himself which he is strongly aware of, and which he finds hard to state though impossible to dismiss. What he was still defending in 'Geist und Kunst' under the name 'psychologische Reizbarkeit' he is now deprecating as 'psychologische Überreiztheit'; 'Gehässigkeit der Erkenntnis' has become 'Unverschämtheit

---

[32] See O. Seidlin, 'Stiluntersuchung an einem Thomas-Mann-Satz', now in his *Von Goethe zu Thomas Mann*, Göttingen, 1963.

der Erkenntnis'. This implies that penetration is yielding to discretion as a literary ideal, it hints that a Nietzschean veil is to be drawn over things better not seen. As Nietzsche wrote in the epilogue to *Nietzsche contra Wagner*:

> Wir wissen einiges jetzt zu gut, wir Wissenden: o wie wir nunmehr lernen, gut zu vergessen, gut *nicht*-zu-wissen, als Künstler!... Nein, dieser Wille zur Wahrheit, zur 'Wahrheit um jeden Preis', dieser Jünglings-Wahnsinn in der Liebe zur Wahrheit—ist uns verleidet: dazu sind wir zu ernst, zu lustig, zu gebrannt, zu *tief*... Heute gilt es uns als eine Sache der Schicklichkeit, dass man nicht alles nackt sehn, nicht alles verstehn und 'wissen' wolle. *Tout comprendre, c'est tout mépriser*... 'Ist es wahr, dass der liebe Gott überall zugegen ist?' fragte ein kleines Mädchen seine Mutter: 'aber ich finde das unanständig'—ein Wink für Philosophen!...

> (We know certain things too well now, we knowing ones: Oh how can we learn instead to forget well, *not-to-know* well as artists! No, this striving for truth, truth 'at any price', this young men's madness in love with truth is not for us: we are too serious, too gay, too wily, too *profound*... It is a matter of propriety for us today not to try and see everything naked, understand and 'know' everything. *Tout comprendre, c'est tout mépriser*... 'Is it true that the Lord is present everywhere?' a little girl asked her mother. 'But I think that's improper'—philosophers please note!...)[33]

The same page of Nietzsche's text contains his famous formulation 'Olympus of illusion' to describe the way the Greeks masked a terrible reality with beauty. It affirms their profoundly knowing superficiality ('diese Griechen waren oberflächlich—*aus Tiefe*') as against the attitude of probing doubt and suspicion, the 'Abgrund des grossen Verdachts'. When one has been through such a 'suspicious' phase, one has a new taste, a 'second taste' as Nietzsche put it, for a beauty of the surface.

[A rejection of knowledge and psychological probing, which are summed up in the image of an 'abyss'; a reborn taste for the beauties of the surface; the view that analysis is essentially a youthful excess: all this, along with much else from Mann's inner debate in 'Geist und Kunst', becomes the material out of which the literary character and career of Gustav von Aschenbach are constructed.] Hauptmann's response to the demands of

[33] Section 2 of the epilogue to *Nietzsche contra Wagner*. Mann quotes from this section in N 43.

the age had been abrupt and obvious: 'Hauptmann plötzlich ein Grieche!' (Suddenly Hauptmann is a Greek!) as Mann wryly commented on *Griechischer Frühling* (N 84). His own subtler way 'sich zu arrangieren' was the tentative renunciation of psychology and analysis, on the grounds that this was part of a process of maturing.

Was this simply opportunism? Perhaps not to the extent it first appears. It is true that the discussion in N 103 is almost cynically clear-sighted about the relations between writers and the cultural climate of their day. The changes that take place within the 'Geist und Kunst' notes—begun in 1909, abandoned by 1911—seem sudden, the self-adjustment all too deliberate. But the case is more complicated. Mann's inconclusive work on the essay proves his belief that one finds out about oneself by writing. Positions one may have genuinely thought one held whole-heartedly turn out to be less than firm. 'Geist und Kunst' is a stock-taking operation, and some of the stock is old— *Tonio Kröger* is already well in the past, *Fiorenza* in conception even further back (*c.* 1900). Formulations and intellectual conclusions from these works were taken over as starting-points for 'Geist und Kunst' as if they were permanent achievements. Work on the essay showed Mann how much less clear his position really was. It proved that any answers already sketched had been partial or temporary. Everything was again in flux. It would take firm shape again in the complex crystal[34] of *Der Tod in Venedig*.

[34] Mann's own image for the work (xi. 123).

# The Art of Ambivalence

So ein Kunstding ist ja schwer auf eine einzige Formel zu bringen,
sondern stellt ein dichtes Gewebe von Absichten und Beziehungen
dar, das etwas Organisches und darum durchaus Vieldeutiges hat.

THOMAS MANN[1]

## I

IN *Der Tod in Venedig*, Thomas Mann returns from excursions
into allegory and once more writes directly about a literary
artist. But the directness is not that of *Tonio Kröger*. There he
was expressing lyrically his immediate experience, formulating
and coming to terms with what he had gone through. In the
figure of Gustav von Aschenbach, by contrast, he experiments[2]
with a possible future, with 'how it would be if . . .' Author and
character have of course a great deal in common—racially
mixed ancestry, disciplined bourgeois background, slow and
tortured compositional method, concentration on a certain type
of character, residence in Munich, Upper Bavarian country
house, and many other details: without such initial similarities,
the fictional experiment would not have been relevant to
Thomas Mann. But the most important indication of how the
character is related to his author is their difference in age.
Aschenbach in the story is over fifty (fifty-three according to
one of Mann's working notes).[3] Thomas Mann when he wrote
the story was thirty-six.

Aschenbach has accomplished much that Mann had not. He
has achieved a greater eminence, he bears the *particule de
noblesse*, his works provide stylistic models for school use, he is
a pillar of the cultural establishment. He has written more than
Thomas Mann, in fact he has completed all Thomas Mann's

---

[1] 'An artistic object like this is of course difficult to reduce to a single formula;
it represents a dense web of intentions and relationships which has something
organic and thereby extremely ambiguous about it'. Letter to Elisabeth Zimmer,
6 Sept. 1915, (Br. i. 123).

[2] The word is Mann's own. See below, p. 176.

[3] TMA Mp. xi. 13e, fol. 24. Mann takes 1911 as the basis for his calculation.

abandoned projects: 'Maja', 'Ein Elender', the Friedrich novel, and most notably an essay 'Geist und Kunst', which competent judges compare on an equal footing with Schiller's *Über naive und sentimentalische Dichtung*. This last detail is important because Aschenbach has taken conscious decisions about the course of his career in which we can recognize, if we approach Aschenbach's story from the angle of Mann's own 'Geist und Kunst', solutions to the dilemmas which that project revealed.

We are given a clear picture of Aschenbach's development and its psychological background. Attention is focused particularly on the way his early analytical, 'problematic' work, his pursuit of *Erkenntnis*, has yielded in mature years to the very opposite: a rejection of knowledge and of the 'improper psychologism' of the age, and an associated increase in his feeling for external beauty, a deliberate pursuit of 'classical' style. 'Psychology' was an indiscretion of youth, its supersession is the act of a grown man: '. . . gewiss ist, dass die schwermütig gewissenhafteste Gründlichkeit des Jünglings Seichtheit bedeutet im Vergleich mit dem tiefen Entschlusse des Meister gewordenen Mannes, das Wissen zu leugnen, es abzulehnen, erhobenen Hauptes darüber hinwegzugehen' (it is certain that the most gloomily conscientious thoroughness of the youth is mere shallowness in comparison with the profound decision of the matured master to deny knowledge, to reject it, to pass it over with raised head [viii. 454]).

Wording and idea here echo the epilogue to *Nietzsche contra Wagner*, as does the phrase 'unanständiger Psychologismus' a few lines further on, and the description of 'Ein Elender' as 'die Abkehr . . . von jeder Sympathie mit dem Abgrund, die Absage an die Laxheit des Mitleidssatzes, dass alles verstehen alles verzeihen heisse' (the turn away . . . from all sympathy with the abyss, the renunciation of the laxity contained in the maxim of compassion, that to understand all is to forgive all). What Nietzsche expressed in one of his characteristic swings away from analytic thought has become the basis for Aschenbach's motivation. We are not told that Aschenbach has been affected by the anti-intellectual fashions of early twentieth-century Germany which that component of Nietzsche's thought had inspired, but the relevance of this central 'Geist und Kunst' problem is obvious. It hardly needs the confirmation provided

F

by the fact that a handful of notes from 'Geist und Kunst' reappear among the work-notes for *Der Tod in Venedig*.[4] Mann's Chapter Two, from which all the above details come, is almost an obituary of Aschenbach. In its abstract way it provides an advance explanation of his fate, for it warns expressly against the dangers of Aschenbach's decision: moral resoluteness 'beyond knowledge' is an oversimplification and hence an open door to immorality. Beauty of form, to which Aschenbach is now devoted, is also potentially immoral in so far as it claims primacy over moral judgements (viii. 455). This is a remarkably clear statement of the issues which the story embodies. But how does it embody them?

Firstly by showing how Aschenbach's fatal infatuation grows out of his new aesthetic taste. He begins by admiring the boy as if he were a work of art. Tadzio on his first appearance reminds Aschenbach of Greek sculpture 'of the noblest period' (469), his flowing locks recall the famous statue of a boy drawing a thorn from his foot (470). Aschenbach's sober approval is that of a connoisseur of beauty—'fachmännisch kühl' (474). Tadzio on the beach is seen as a figure in a picture, against the horizontal of the water's edge (475), with the sea behind him as 'foil and background' (489). This aesthetic pretext persists into Chapter Four, even after Aschenbach's abortive effort to escape from Venice. He has admitted to himself by now that it was really Tadzio he could not bear to leave, but the attention he devotes to the boy is still aesthetic, even religious: 'Andacht und Studium' (488).

It reaches its height, and at the same time is most explicitly linked with Aschenbach's own creative aims, in the writer's meditations as he observes Tadzio on the beach. After an introduction again packed with sculptural phrases—'den zart gemeisselten Arm', 'die feine Zeichnung der Rippen', 'Achselhöhlen glatt wie bei einer Statue', etc.—we have this:

Welch eine Zucht, welche Präzision des Gedankens war ausgedrückt in diesem gestreckten und jugendlich vollkommenen Leibe! Der strenge und reine Wille jedoch, der, dunkel tätig, dies göttliche Bildwerk ans Licht zu treiben vermocht hatte, — war er nicht ihm, dem Künstler, bekannt und vertraut? Wirkte er nicht auch in ihm, wenn er, nüchterner Leidenschaft voll, aus der Marmormasse der

4 fol. 29.

Sprache die schlanke Form befreite, die er im Geiste geschaut und
die er als Standbild und Spiegel geistiger Schönheit den Menschen
darstellte?

(What discipline, what precision of thought was expressed in this
outstretched and youthfully perfect body! But the pure and austere
will, whose mysterious action had been able to thrust this divine
creation into the light—was it not known and familiar to him, the
artist? Was it not equally at work in him, when, filled with a sober
passion, he freed from the marble mass of language the slender form
which was his inner vision and which he presented to men as a
statue and mirror of spiritual beauty? [p. 490])

Here the 'statuesque' language used of Tadzio is linked with
the nature of Aschenbach's literary creations.[5] One could
hardly have a more evident attempt to present literature as
*Plastik*. It is clear what kind of ideals have dictated Aschenbach's
pursuit of *Klassizität*.

But his admiration for the boy's beauty might have stayed
within aesthetic bounds. It is the rejection of critical analysis—
the concomitant of his mature artistic tastes—that proves fatal.
This is the second way in which the story embodies the issues
set out in Chapter Two. Aschenbach has no eye for his own
underlying motives. Long before he has given up all pretence
and admitted that he loves Tadzio (end of Chapter Four),
doubt has been cast on his motives. Then, just before his admission, he fails to speak to the boy—an action which might have
dispelled his intenser feelings and established a normal relationship. We are told that he did not want to, his intoxication is
too dear to him. This refusal to be sobered is called immoral
(*Zügellosigkeit*), but Aschenbach has no mind for such things:

Aschenbach war zur Selbstkritik nicht mehr aufgelegt; der
Geschmack, die geistige Verfassung seiner Jahre, Selbstachtung,
Reife und späte Einfachheit machten ihn nicht geneigt, Beweg-
gründe zu zergliedern und zu entscheiden, ob er aus Gewissen, ob
aus Liederlichkeit und Schwäche sein Vorhaben nicht ausgeführt
habe.

(Aschenbach was no longer disposed to self-criticism; the taste,
the intellectual constitution of his years, self-esteem, maturity, and

---

5 Luchino Visconti's film of *Der Tod in Venedig*, so faithful in atmosphere and
period detail, breaks this vital link by making Aschenbach a musician, probably
on the false assumption that Mann was 'really' writing about Mahler, whose
external appearance he borrowed for his protagonist.

late simplicity made him disinclined to analyse motives and to distinguish whether he had failed to carry out his intention from conscience or from weakness and dissoluteness. [p. 494])

The verdict on this late failure reflects back on Aschenbach's many preceding failures (or refusals) to suspect passionate motives beneath the aesthetic pretext.

These precise links between Aschenbach's loss of control and his artistic development settle one question critics have sometimes raised. Why did his downfall have to be brought about by a homosexual passion? Why not—since the Venice episode is only the external fulfilment of a psychological process which has begun before he ever leaves Munich—why not a passion for cards? or drink? or a woman? The answer is that these would not have followed from Aschenbach's particular state of mind. The first two would have been crude irrelevancies, the third would have served only if it could be shown to grow from an admiration initially aesthetic. But it is hardly possible for the sexual element in female beauty to be overlooked, even by one who has put aside psychology. Only male beauty could so insidiously transform cool appreciation into passion. This justifies the central encounter in *Der Tod in Venedig* as part of the artistic whole, although it would be wrong to speak as if Mann deliberately chose it for this reason. Like so much else in the remarkable genesis of the work, it was something given, which fused perfectly with other given elements.

From the point where he avows his true feelings, Aschenbach goes from bad to worse. His reverent study of Tadzio's godlike beauty becomes frank pursuit of an idol (*Abgott*). Judgement is implicit in the mere narration of his actions, and still more in the descriptions of his state—sweating, desperate, cosmetically rejuvenated. It is made explicit in the participle-nouns which increasingly replace Aschenbach's name: *der Betörte, der Verwirrte*, etc. These establish the author's distance from his character succinctly and unequivocally. Indeed, Mann dissociates himself from Aschenbach more obviously than from any of his other protagonists. Towards the close he even treats him with open sarcasm, in the passage beginning 'Er sass dort, der Meister, der würdig gewordene Künstler, der Autor des "Elenden", der in so vorbildlich reiner Form dem Zigeunertum und der trüben Tiefe abgesagt, dem Abgrunde

die Sympathie gekündigt und das Verworfene verworfen hatte
. . .' (He sat there, the master, the artist who had achieved
dignity, the author of 'A Miserable Specimen', who in such
exemplarily pure form had declared his rejection of bohemianism and the murky depths, renounced all sympathy with the
abyss, and called depravity by its name . . . [p. 521]). The gap
between Aschenbach's claims to public respect and his present
behaviour amount to an emphatic judgement.

It is a shade too emphatic for the reader accustomed to
Mann's ironic temper. Where are the reservations usually felt
in every inflection of his phrasing? The finality with which
Aschenbach's case is settled is positively suspicious. Is it not
very like the 'Wucht des Wortes, mit welcher das Verworfene
verworfen wurde' (p. 455)—i.e. Aschenbach's own moral
decisiveness which has since proved so dubious? Is it not
crudely direct beside the informed survey of Aschenbach's
development in Chapter Two, which surely practises the maxim
he rejected: 'Tout comprendre, c'est tout pardonner'? And did
Mann not later write, in a letter exhaustively analysing the
genesis and attitudes of *Der Tod in Venedig*, that the moralistic
standpoint was one to be adopted only ironically?[6] There are
depths to be sounded under the polished surface of the story.

## II

*Der Tod in Venedig* records the phases of a real experiment; it
is not a mere mental construct, manipulating an imagined
character through arbitrarily chosen adventures. To begin with,
Thomas Mann's own Venetian experiences in 1911 were close
to Aschenbach's, at least in embryo. The figure in the Munich
cemetery, the sordid ship from Pola to Venice, the aged dandy
on board it, the unlicensed gondolier, Tadzio and his family,
the attempt to leave Venice foiled by a misdirection of luggage,
the cholera epidemic, the honest English clerk at the travel
bureau, the street singer—everything was provided by reality,
not invented for the later fiction. It all had an 'innate symbolism'
(xi. 124).

Equally real was the literary standstill which Mann makes
the motive for Aschenbach's journey. Thomas Mann's work in

[6] To Carl Maria Weber, 4 July 1920 (Br. i. 177).

the first decade of the century was in general in a transitional phase, and failure arguably outweighed success: *Fiorenza* and *Königliche Hoheit* had fallen far short of what was expected of the author of *Buddenbrooks*, the projects for 'Maja', 'Ein Elender', the Friedrich novel, and 'Geist und Kunst' had all been abandoned, and now *Felix Krull* was hardly moving. In the early months of 1911 Mann wrote very little. Reporting this to Heinrich late in March, he speaks of his present low vitality— 'eine momentane Erschöpfung des Centralnervensystems' (Br. H. 95); the same letter announces a planned holiday in Dalmatia. In mid-May he leaves with his wife for the island of Brioni, but moves to Venice for a short stay from the 26th to 2 June. The first news of the new work comes in a letter to Philipp Witkop on 18 July 1911: he is at work on a 'recht sonderbare Sache, die ich aus Venedig mitgebracht habe, Novelle, ernst und rein in Ton, einen Fall von Knabenliebe bei einem alternden Künstler behandelnd. Sie sagen "hum, hum!" Aber es ist sehr anständig' (an exceedingly bizarre thing I brought back from Venice, a *Novelle*, serious and pure in tone, treating the case of an elderly artist's passion for a boy. 'Hm, hm!', you say. But it is all very proper).

This jaunty tone is gone altogether the next time Mann reports on progress. He writes to Ernst Bertram on 16 October 1911 that he is 'von einer Arbeit gequält, die sich im Laufe der Ausführung mehr und mehr als eine unmögliche Conception herausstellt und an die ich doch schon zuviel Sorge gewandt habe, um sie aufzugeben' (tormented by a project which in the course of execution has turned out more and more to be an impossible conception and on which I have nevertheless spent too much trouble to give it up now).[7] At the beginning of April he has hopes of finishing the story by the end of the month; although he thinks Heinrich may not approve of it as a whole, he is sure it has 'individual beauties', and is especially pleased with a 'classicizing' chapter (*antikisierendes Kapitel*— letter of 2 April 1912). But by the 27th, problems again dominate. Although publication arrangements are already well in hand,[8] Mann writes to Heinrich that he cannot round the story

---

[7] The editor of the correspondence between Mann and Ernst Bertram mistakenly refers this (Br. B. 204) to *Felix Krull*.
[8] See letter to Kurt Martens, 14 Feb. 1912.

off: 'ich kann den Schluss nicht finden'. And on 3 May he speaks once more of being 'schrecklich angestrengt und besorgt, einer eigenen Arbeit wegen, an die ich — vielleicht instinktloser Weise — beinahe ein Jahr gewandt habe und die nun so oder so fertig werden muss' (terribly strained and worried about a work of my own on which—perhaps I should have known better—I have now spent nearly a year and which must now be finished one way or another).

This is not a picture of issues easily mastered or of an experiment which yielded its conclusions straight away. That is hardly surprising if we remember Mann's difficulties over 'Geist und Kunst'. And if the Venice stay had provided material for working out these teasing problems in fictional form, new factors had added to their complexity. The clearest way to present the matter is to reconstruct the genesis of the story.

The clues Mann provides are suggestive and, although not precise as to time, help us to see essentially what occurred. Our knowledge of his sources and of the dates at which he came upon them also helps. The purpose of our reconstruction, which may seem at times to be suggesting 'earlier versions' of the text (there is some evidence for this) is to point up the possibilities— both literary and moral—of each contribution to the story in such a way that its final form can be grasped in all its richness of reference, and appreciated as a solution which was anything but facile.

The threads we have to follow are drawn together by Mann himself in his letter of 4 July 1920 to Carl Maria Weber. The ethos Mann discerned in Weber's poems led him to declare his own attitude to homosexuality, about which *Der Tod in Venedig* had left room for misunderstanding. Mann says that he would not wish to give the impression of rejecting a type of feeling which he honours, which almost of necessity has more spiritual value (*Geist*) than the so-called normal type, and which he is himself no stranger to. He then goes at length into the reasons why his story nevertheless appears to reject it.

First there is the nature of his artistic processes. He distinguishes between the 'Dionysiac spirit of irresponsible-individualistic lyrical effusion' and the 'Apolline spirit of epic with its moral and social responsibilities and objective limitations'. In other words, between the urge to express private and

personal feeling, and the requirements of the more p      e
of prose narrative. It may not be permissible to endoɪ·    ᴐber
prose what one feels a private enthusiasm for. In fact, iᴄ may not
be possible, for the execution of the literary conception has its
own corrective influences, which Mann calls a 'painful process of
objectivization'. He says that *Der Tod in Venedig* finally strove
for a balance between sensuality and morality, analogous to
Goethe's achievement in *Die Wahlverwandtschaften*. But in its
origin, and still at its core, the story is essentially 'hymnic'.

Mann refers Weber to his account of hymnic origin and
objectivization already published in 1919, in the *Vorsatz* to
*Gesang vom Kindchen*. That opens with Mann's old nagging
question: 'Bin ich ein Dichter?' (viii. 1068). There follows his
defence of the prose moralist as a 'poet', familiar from 'Geist
und Kunst'. But what comes next is the confession of a past
shame which still rankles, a secret defeat, a never-avowed
failure. He means the writing of *Der Tod in Venedig*. These are
the lines quoted in the letter to Weber:

> Weisst du noch? Höherer Rausch, ein ausserordentlich Fühlen
> Kam auch wohl über dich einmal und warf dich danieder,
> Dass du lagst, die Stirn in den Händen. Hymnisch erhob sich
> Da deine Seele, es drängte der ringende Geist zum Gesange
> Unter Tränen sich hin. Doch leider blieb alles beim Alten.
> Denn ein versachlichend Mühen begann da, ein kältend
>       Bemeistern, —
> Siehe, es ward dir das *trunkene Lied* zur *sittlichen Fabel.*

> (Remember? Intoxication, a heightened, exceptional feeling
> Came over you as well on one occasion, and threw you
> Down, your brow in your hands. To hymnic impulse your spirit
> Rose, amid tears your struggling mind pressed urgently upward
> Into song. But unhappily things stayed just as they had been:
> There began a process of sobering, cooling and mastering—
> Lo! there came of your *drunken song* an *ethical fable.*)[9]

Clearly Mann's Venice experience—what he calls a little further
on 'ein persönlich-lyrisches Reiseerlebnis'—originally inspired an
affirmative rather than critical treatment, perhaps even in verse
(*Gesang*) rather than prose.[10] The hexameters in the text of *Der*

---

[9] viii. 1069. Italics only in the text of the letter.
[10] Thereby repeating the case of *Tonio Kröger*, which was preceded by a fragmentary lyrical treatment of the story's theme. See Wysling, *Studien*, p. 31.

*Tod in Venedig* could be remnants of this treatment. At all events, the failure to carry the project out in that form still rankled in 1919—even though the final form of the story had turned the shortcoming into a virtue and reaped praise (viii. 1069). The heights of *Dichtertum* were not scaled. In his letter Mann names other factors at work in the story's development: first, his Naturalist background, so alien to the younger generation Weber represents, which made him see the 'case' in a pathological as well as a symbolic light. This clearly echoes the lengthy discussion of the two literary generations and the supersession of Naturalism in N 103 of 'Geist und Kunst', but now from the viewpoint of one who is resigned to being what he is, who knows that he cannot deny his past and his intellectual roots. This much his experience of the 'objectivizing process' taught him, for it was rooted in the 'necessities of his nature'. Secondly, there was his personal mistrust of passion as such, a Protestant and puritanical burgher trait which he shares with Aschenbach, and which counteracted any 'Greek' view of homosexual love. The real subject of his fable, he says, was the confusion and degradation caused by passion, a theme he had previously thought of treating in a renarration of the aged Goethe's love for the seventeen-year-old Ulrike von Levetzow.

In the rest of the letter, Mann develops the idea that the erotic attraction of *Leben* for *Geist* need not correspond to the attraction between the sexes. He sums it up with a quotation from Hölderlin's poem 'Sokrates und Alkibiades': 'Wer das Tiefste gedacht, liebt das Lebendigste' (whose thought deepest has probed, most loves vitality). And he makes the judgement on homosexual love depend on the nature of the individual instance: it is morally neutral until it shows its value in its works.

This remarkably frank self-interpretation suggests why the 'bizarre thing' Mann brought back from Venice gave him such trouble in the composition, and fills in the background to the letters quoted above. By July 1911 the work was already to be a *Novelle*, though not yet necessarily a 'moral fable': the 'purity of tone' and the 'propriety' may at that stage have meant something other than adverse judgement on Aschenbach. By October of that year the difficulties have set in, Mann finds he is working with an 'impossible conception'. This surely is the point at which an affirmative treatment was abandoned. It had proved impossible 'in the course of execution'—the letter to Bertram dates the turning-point which *Gesang vom Kindchen* and the retrospective letter to Weber describe in general terms. So we have a picture of a diametrical change in the conception of *Der Tod in Venedig*. Is it compatible with Mann's other statement, that the 'real subject' of his fable, the confusion and degradation which passion causes, was a theme he had long intended to treat? This is certainly true. As early as 1905 a notebook jotting for a future story reads:

Der erhöhte Respekt vor sichselbst, das gesteigerte sich Ernstnehmen [. . .] die Neigung, sich als nationaler Faktor, sich überhaupt national zu nehmen, der Blick auf die Literaturgeschichte etc. Das ist *darzustellen*, damit es nichts Gemeinsames und nur Typisches bleibe. (Ich will keine Figur sein). Das Leid und die tragische Verirrung eines Künstlers ist zu zeigen, der Phantasie und 'Ernst im Spiel' genug hat, um an den ehrgeizigen Ansprüchen, zu denen der Erfolg ihn verleitet und denen er zuletzt nicht gewachsen ist, *zu Grunde geht* [*sic*].

(The increased respect for oneself, the intensified taking of oneself seriously [. . .] the tendency to take oneself as a national factor, as national in any way, the eye on literary history, etc. That is something to be *portrayed*, in such a way that it has nothing in common [viz. with TM himself] and remains merely typical. (I do not want to be a figure). The suffering and the aberration of an artist must be shown who has enough imagination and 'seriousness within artistic play' to be brought low by the ambitious claims which success leads him to make for himself and which in the end he is not up to.)[11]

The precariousness of the Artist's claim to dignity and public respect was thus a theme awaiting embodiment. But this does not mean it was from the first the keynote of the new story. Rather, it was an old theme towards which the working out of the story increasingly gravitated. Mann was in this case, it is plain from his accounts, a reluctant moralist.

Picture him as a writer at a cross-roads in his development, with the doubts and possibilities of the 'Geist und Kunst' essay in his mind, with his work seemingly much in need of a revivifying impulse. In Venice he has an intense emotional experience. It inspires him to treat it in a form which is far from his usual literary stock-in-trade and is thereby a kind of creative rebirth: in place of cold analysis and Apolline epic form, an impassioned outpouring, lyrical and Dionysiac. Tadzio is celebrated hymnically, the passion he inspires is affirmed because it is fruitful. In a milder way, *Tonio Kröger* asserted that the basis of true *Dichtertum* was emotional. Now the emotion goes deeper: it is nothing less than Nietzsche's Dionysiac spirit, described in the *Geburt der Tragödie* as indispensable for great art.

These elements are visible in the late dream orgy with the coming of the Stranger God. But long before that point, Mann has placed his clues. The phrase which describes Aschenbach's feeling when he sees the Munich stranger, the 'seltsame Ausweitung seines Innern' (strange dilation within him [p. 446]) is taken from the same account of the Thracian Dionysus' orgies which yielded such graphic details for Aschenbach's dream.[12] From the very first, the process of bringing his feelings alive is Dionysiac. The encounter with Tadzio will complete this process.

The literary rebirth is a different thing from the all-too-deliberate rebirth Aschenbach had constructed for himself. It casts doubt on it, precisely, as too deliberate—'eine gewollte Klassizität' (455). Yet it also in a way supplements it (or in the case of Mann himself, who had not yet taken Aschenbach's mature decisions, replaces it). To both, as lovers of external beauty—the one on principle, the other through chance encounter—a new poetic strength was granted. This was clearly one solution to the problems of which way to turn, raised in 'Geist und Kunst'.

Could it be carried through? Intoxication is a difficult condition to maintain, at least as a basis for creativity. Mann had always considered himself an 'Apolline' creator, mistrusting inspiration, preferring discipline. His favourite images for his art, the lyre and the bow, were Apollo's attributes. If he now tasted intoxication for once, it was almost certainly short-lived. The short prose piece he wrote on Wagner while he was

---

[12] Erwin Rohde, *Psyche*, extensively excerpted in Mann's work-notes. The idea of *Ausweitung* comes in Rohde's discussion of the spiritual aims of the Thracian Dionysus' orgies: closest possible contact with the god, a state of 'mania' (xi. 13e, fol. 8). *Manie* is Aschenbach's later condition (499).

Rohde was of course a friend of Nietzsche's, which probably stimulated Mann's interest in his mythological study.

actually in Venice speaks of the ideal art of the future as cooler than Wagner's and not relying on *Rausch* (x. 842).

But it also speaks of a healthier art and of a new classicism—very much the ideals which Aschenbach pursued, and the ideals of the times. For these things equally Tadzio's beauty could serve as an inspiration: a work of celebration was still possible. But if the celebration was not to be drunken and Dionysiac, what was it to be?

The answer is: Platonic. This brings us to the most important source for *Der Tod in Venedig*. The text is rich in phrases, images, and ideas from Plato's *Symposium* and *Phaedrus* and from Plutarch's *Erotikos*, a much later dialogue essentially Platonic in style and theme.[13]

The technique of weaving in quotation and allusion to famous texts was one Mann had practised skilfully before, not merely to decorate his fiction but to add a dimension of meaning to what was being narrated. The references to *Don Carlos* in *Tonio Kröger*, the retelling of the Tristan story as a burlesque, in different ways place the characters' experience in a broader context than that of the immediate fiction. This is true to a yet greater extent of the Greek sources in *Der Tod in Venedig*. Even before being exploited for literary effect, they clearly helped Mann himself to a deeper, more generalized understanding of his theme. If the fate of Aschenbach embodies problems connected with the literary scene of the 1910s and Mann's place in it, the Greek dialogues placed these problems in a wider framework still. For where Mann had been concerned with a fashionable emphasis (*Zeitströmung*) on external beauty in the Germany of his day, and with a defence of intellect in art, the Platonic dialogues stated an all-embracing and timeless theory of the relationship of beauty to men's spiritual and intellectual life, ideally reconciling the two. They also discussed the kinds of love beauty provokes, its potential inspiring quality and potential dangers. And since they are mainly about homosexual love, they were precisely relevant to the subject which Mann's Venice encounter had presented him with. They provided an altogether more profound explanation of Aschenbach's artistic development and his passion, and clear criteria for judging it.

[13] There is also one quotation from Xenophon's *Memorabilia of Socrates* (p. 477) as well as a number of thematically less important ones from Homer and Virgil.

Plato and Plutarch see beauty in a religious light. It is a reminder to men of the vision which was vouchsafed to each soul before its birth into the world: a vision of ultimate reality, Plato's realm of Forms, or Ideas, where goodness, wisdom, truth exist unchanging in absolute perfection. Men forget this vision to varying degrees, and cannot be directly reminded of some of the absolutes—Reason, Virtue, Justice, are not objects of the senses. (If they were, the love they would inspire would consume men utterly.) But Beauty is by its nature sensible, the only absolute that is. It thus becomes the vital link between men in their earthly existence and the higher realm. When a man whose soul is not already too corrupted by the world sees an object of beauty, he is reminded with a shock of that realm, his spiritual wings (in Plato's image) grow strong. The value of beautiful forms lies not in themselves, but in the higher reality they partake of and point to. In another image, which Mann uses in his text, Plutarch speaks of the solid shapes to which teachers of geometry have to resort when their pupils are not yet capable of abstract intellectual concepts. In the same way, he says, heavenly love has provided men with beautiful reflections of the divine, pointers in the corrupt world of sense to a world which is beyond sense and beyond corruption.[14]

This is why there need be no conflict between a love of external beauty and a devotion to things intellectual and spiritual: the one stands for the other, has its meaning from it, leads back to it. But this is the ideal. There are problems in practice. Beauty, being sensuous, may stimulate a purely sensuous response. The uninitiated and corrupt will desire to possess and enjoy the particular beautiful object. This sort of fulfilment thwarts the true purpose of beauty, which is to be a means, not an end in itself. For Plato (though not for Plutarch) the love of men for women seemed necessarily to come into this lower category, having the earthly purpose of procreation. Procreation was necessary, but a relationship which had only this aim might not leave room for spiritual development.

So it seemed obvious that the spiritual potential lay in love between men. Since it was a relationship that could not procreate physically, it was free to create in the spirit. It could inspire poetry or philosophy, it could further the education of

[14] *Erotikos* 765 a. Cf. viii. 490.

the young, it could inspire bravery in war. All these were noble in themselves and it was thought noble to pursue them. They were what the *Symposium* calls children of the mind rather than the body and they promised immortality of a different order. Men ambitious for fame, poets among them, would make greater sacrifices for these than for bodily children.

But the spiritual potential of homosexual love was not a guarantee of fulfilment, any more necessarily than in the case of heterosexual love. It could as easily stop short at earthly gratifications. Its advocates in the Platonic dialogues take account of this possibility, familiar enough to the Greeks, and duly speak of lovers as ignoble or noble, depending on whether their love is a mere present enjoyment or a starting-point for higher achievement. The lover's behaviour is a measure of his human quality and a condition of his right development.

We can follow Mann's assimilation of these doctrines through the markings in his copy of the *Symposium*[15] and through his extensive excerpts from all three dialogues in his work-notes. The relevance to Aschenbach's situation is obvious. Will he see in the individual boy Beauty itself, will the sight strengthen his 'spiritual wings'? Will it inspire him in his writing? Will it spur him in the pursuit of fame, through his 'spiritual children', his works? Will it point him onwards to the realm of ultimate Beauty?

The text of *Der Tod in Venedig* contains passages corresponding to each one of these questions. Mann used, very deliberately, material from Plato and Plutarch to construct the situations in which Aschenbach's love of beauty is tested. We have seen that his appreciation of Tadzio is at first markedly aesthetic, and that this was a link with the aesthetic preferences of his day, in response to which he had developed a classicizing taste. But the Platonic doctrine gave this taste a deeper grounding, and the text shows it. When Aschenbach lingers before going in to dine on the first evening in his Venice hotel, it is because Tadzio's family has not gone in yet. He is satisfied to have *das Schöne* to look at—the Beautiful itself in its chance embodiment (p. 471). During the meal he occupies his mind with philosophical reflections, which Tadzio has inspired, on the relationship between the General and the Particular in human beauty (*das*

15 Platons *Gastmahl*, verdeutscht von Rudolf Kassner, Jena, 1903.

*Gesetzmässige* and *das Individuelle* [p. 472]). Although his reflections lead him nowhere, they are exactly on the central Platonic theme. For behind the theory of Forms and an absolute realm, Plato is dealing with just this question: the absolutes are related to earthly objects as the General to the Particular. (Plato speaks in the *Phaedrus* of an Idea as 'a unity gathered together by the reason from many particulars of sense'.)[16]

Even more clearly Platonic is the long reflection that follows Aschenbach's comparison of the boy's statuesque beauty with the plastic form of his own works. Once more a contemporary touch, once more taken deeper in Greek terms. In the figure at the water's edge, Aschenbach sees Beauty itself: '. . . glaubte er mit diesem Blick das Schöne selbst zu begreifen, die Form als Gottesgedanken, die eine und reine Vollkommenheit, die im Geiste lebt und von der ein menschliches Gleichnis hier leicht und hold zur Anbetung aufgerichtet war' (he believed that with this glance he comprehended Beauty itself, form as a divine thought, the one and pure perfection which lives in the spirit and of which a human likeness was here set up, graceful and light, for adoration [p. 490]).[17] Images from Plato and Plutarch at this point come thick and fast: the 'geometry teacher' simile, then Aschenbach's mental reconstruction of the setting of the *Phaedrus* and long quotations from that dialogue, in the phrasing of the Kassner translation which Mann used. Intermingled are other literary echoes: Socrates and Phaedrus, 'der Weise beim Liebenswürdigen', recall Hölderlin's 'Und es neigen die Weisen / Oft am Ende zu Schönem sich' (Wise men often incline to / Something beautiful at the last);[18] the paragraph that describes Aschenbach writing in Tadzio's presence opens appropriately with an echo from August von Platen's epigram on Venice entitled 'Rückblick'.[19]

---

[16] 249 c.

[17] The work-note corresponding to this passage is more Platonic still in its wording: 'Er schaut die ewigen Formen, das Schöne selbst, den ewigen Grund, dem jede schöne Form entquillt' (he sees the eternal Forms, Beauty itself, the eternal ground from which every beautiful form springs [xi. 13e, fol. 18]).

[18] The poem 'Sokrates und Alkibiades' referred to in the letter to Weber.

[19] Mann's text: 'Glück des Schriftstellers ist der Gedanke, der ganz Gefühl, ist das Gefühl, das ganz Gedanke zu werden vermag' (p. 492). Platen's epigram ends with:

'. . . es wird in der Seele des zärtlichen Schwärmers
Jedes Gefühl Sehnsucht, jeder Gedanke Gefühl.'

Aschenbach writing in view of Tadzio as the boy plays on the beach: this episode corresponds obviously to the idea that love could inspire poetry. Mann's work-notes confirm that it was meant so. The text's simple suggestion 'dass Eros im Worte sei' (that Eros is in the word [p. 492]) goes back to passages in Plutarch and Plato which speak of love as the poet's teacher, and of the impossibility of shining in the arts without love's inspiration. Mann's excerpts clearly prepared this episode in the *Novelle*, for they include the words 'Arbeit am Strande' (work on the beach).[20] And in a striking reinterpretation of Aschenbach, erotic inspiration in the highest sense is read back into his whole literary career: 'Nur der glänzt in der Kunst, den Eros unterweist. Auch seine Kunst war ein nüchterner Dienst im Tempel zu Thespiä. Eros ist immer in ihm gewesen. Tadzio war immer sein König. Auch seine Liebe zum Ruhm war Eros' (A man can only shine in art if Eros instructs him. His art too was a sober service in the temple of Thespiae [a temple to Eros mentioned in Plutarch's *Erotikos*]. Eros was always in him. Tadzio was always his king. His love of fame was Eros too).[21]

These notes are far from having the critical tone Mann's story finally acquired. Are they merely a preparation for constructing the awareness of classical parallels in Aschenbach himself? Taken by themselves, they do not suggest this. Rather they show how much more deeply and sympathetically it was possible to understand Aschenbach in the light of Platonic doctrine: his ascetic life a self-sacrifice to a higher form of love, his ambition one of those noble sublimations of the love of beauty, Tadzio a late embodiment of the ideal he had always served.

Finally, there is the question whether Tadzio will point Aschenbach on, not just to Beauty itself and its nobler pursuits, but to an absolute realm of spiritual things. Once more, Mann constructed a passage to embody and answer this question. It is the final scene, Aschenbach's death on the beach. He is, as always, watching Tadzio, who is alone at the water's edge after the scuffle with Jascha. Cut off now even from companions, he seems an almost freely floating figure against the background

---

[20] xi. 13e, fol. 20. The note reads: 'Eros und *Wort*. Im Werk — da weiss er sicher zu lenken. [. . .] Die Arbeit am Strande.' (Eros and *word*. In the work—there he is a sure guide. [. . .] Composing on the beach.)    [21] fol. 20.

of the sea—'eine höchst abgesonderte und verbindungslose Erscheinung, mit flatterndem Haar dort draussen im Meere, im Winde, vorm Nebelhaft-Grenzenlosen' (p. 524). And just as Aschenbach collapses, Tadzio has adopted a statuesque pose and seems to be beckoning: 'Ihm war, als ob der bleiche und liebliche Psychagog dort draussen ihm lächle, ihm winke; als ob er, die Hand aus der Hüfte lösend, hinausdeute, voranschwebe ins Verheissungsvoll-Ungeheure. Und wie so oft, machte er sich auf, ihm zu folgen.' (It seemed to him as if the pale and lovely conductor of souls out there were smiling to him, beckoning him; as if, taking his hand from his hip, he were pointing out, drifting on before him into the vast promising spaces. And as so often he rose to follow him.)

This crucial, because final, passage is based exactly on Plato's image for the realms into which the spiritual initiate progresses. Diotima's speech to Socrates in the *Symposium* traces a man's spiritual development from love of a single beautiful body to love of all physical beauty, then to love of spiritual qualities, of the beauty in laws and institutions, and ultimately to a vision of absolute Beauty itself. This is the final initiation and reward. Here is Kassner's translation, excerpted by Thomas Mann:

. . . und so im Anblick dieser vielfachen Schönheit nicht mehr wie ein Sklave nach der Schönheit dieses einen Knaben verlange und dieses einen Menschen Schönheit wolle und gemein sei und kleinlich, . . . sondern, *an die Ufer des grossen Meeres der Schönheit gebracht,* hier viele edle Worte und Gedanken mit dem *unerschöpflichen Triebe nach Weisheit* zeuge, bis er dann stark und reif jenes einzige Wissen, das da das Wissen des Schönen ist, erschaue. . . . Ja, Sokrates, wer immer von dort unten, weil er den Geliebten richtig zu lieben wusste, empor zu steigen und jenes ewige Schöne zu schauen beginnt, *der ist am Ende und vollendet und geweiht.*

(. . . and so, seeing this manifold beauty, long no more like a slave for the beauty of this one boy and desire this one human being's beauty and be common and petty . . . but, *brought to the border of the great sea of beauty,* here beget many noble words and thoughts with the *inexhaustible urge for wisdom,* until he then, strong and mature, has a vision of that unique knowledge which is the knowledge of beauty . . . Yes, Socrates, whoever has been able to ascend through right loving of the beloved and begins to see that eternal beauty, *he is at the end and perfected and initiated.*)[22]

[22] Kassner, pp. 62–4. Work-notes, fol. 16, with Mann's underlinings.

There is no better guide to higher things than Eros, Diotima continues. *Der Tod in Venedig* contains elements which suggest it was constructed to show just this. It is even possible to see Tadzio in the role of Eros—the god Plato calls young and delicate[23]—before his function as Aschenbach's guide to death made the analogy with Hermes, conductor of souls to the underworld, seem more appropriate.[24]

As Mann later said (xii. 98), the death of a character is not in itself a judgement on what he stands for. One need only think of Hanno Buddenbrook. Aschenbach's death, so exactly embodying the Platonic theory of ascent to ever higher spiritual planes, has something of an apotheosis, even in the critical form which Mann's story finally took on. But this final form plays it down. No responsibility is taken by the author for the suggestion of an apotheosis, it is only given as the record of Aschenbach's feelings: 'Ihm war, als ob . . .' Mann never drew attention to his use of Platonic imagery—strange, since he liked his allusions to be known—and it has not to my knowledge been noticed before.[25] The scene stays, but in a story whose overt intention is to pass a moral judgement.

It is conceivable that the critical intentions were already there from the very first contact with Platonic material, but it seems on balance unlikely. Mann excerpted from Plato and Plutarch all the passages that are positive about love: they speak of the high potential of the lover's yearning, its fruitfulness for poetry especially, the acceptability in a lover of behaviour that would otherwise be outrageous, the high esteem in which love was held among respectably warlike peoples (a link here with Aschenbach's military ancestry), the many examples of lovers who were also heroes, the primacy of love over other obligations. One has a sense that greater understanding of the modern incident is being drawn from the ancient background. Moreover, if there had never been any intention to portray Aschenbach

[23] Cf. Kassner, pp. 37 f.: 'Jung ist der Gott, und seine Gestalt von zarter Bildung.' Underlined in Mann's copy and transferred to his notes.

[24] This is Mann's first use of a mythological figure who became a favourite later. The information about Hermes' function was provided by a footnote to the *Erotikos*, p. 26 of the German translation Mann used, as is confirmed by the wording on fol. 11 of the work-notes. This detail was brought to light by Manfred Dierks.

[25] Some attention has been given to the Greek echoes in Mann's text, but investigation of Plato has not gone beyond the *Phaedrus*, which is actually named there.

favourably in this Greek light, the collecting of so much matter calculated to do just this is odd; it is more plausible that a later decision turned the story in a different direction, while still perforce retaining the structural substance which it was too late to abandon.

When the change occurred (and it can be dated roughly as October 1911) this substance proved flexible; homosexual love, as all the Greek sources said, could be noble or debased.[26] Each episode which could yield a positive could equally yield a negative result. Nor (supposing a 'positive' interpretation which required to be changed) was it difficult to alter the stress. For instance, when Aschenbach thinks he recognizes beauty itself and the Platonic forms in Tadzio, a critical distance is created by the words: 'Das war der Rausch' (that was intoxication) and by the comment on his recollections from Plutarch: 'So dachte der Enthusiasmierte; so vermochte er zu empfinden' (thus he thought in his enthusiasm; thus was he capable of feeling). Similarly, his act of writing with Tadzio in sight, this 'seltsam zeugender Verkehr des Geistes mit einem Körper'[27] (strangely productive intercourse of the spirit with a body) can be shown in a less favourable light by the detail that Aschenbach's conscience afterwards accused him as if of a dissolute act. The increasing use of adjectival nouns as judgements—*der Verwirrte, der Starrsinnige*—are also a simple and economical way for the narrator to establish his position as a moralist. As much as anything else, the close-up view of Tadzio alters the work's whole import: not just his typically decadent bad teeth (p. 479), but the knowingness he increasingly shows, his coquetry, the smile which provokes Aschenbach's indignation even as it forces his avowal of love (p. 498). Tadzio is here far from the ideal, not a mere perfect statue, nor a miraculous epiphany akin (as he had earlier seemed) to Stefan George's Maximin. His beauty is skin-deep. Significantly, this climax of Chapter 4

---

[26] Kassner also emphasized just this point with a long epigraph from Pico della Mirandola on man's freedom to choose his own way of developing: 'poteris in inferiora quae sunt bruta degenerare, poteris in superiora quae sunt divina ex tui animi sententia regenerari'. One cannot of course be certain that Mann noticed this.

[27] This phrase is not in itself pejorative. *Zeugen* is Kassner's word for Plato's idea of 'begetting'—physical children physically, spiritual children in the spirit. Mann's excerpts from this section of the *Symposium* (208 c ff.) are headed 'Ruhm und Zeugung' (fame and begetting). (Work-notes, fol. 17.)

is preceded by the narrator's reflections on the delicate relationship between people who know each other by sight only. His conclusion removes the basis for a positive view of Aschenbach's passion, it draws its spiritual nerve, for it denies the value of yearning: 'die Sehnsucht ist ein Erzeugnis mangelhafter Erkenntnis' (yearning is a product of insufficient knowledge [p. 497]). We have returned to the principle of the analytical writer, *Erkenntnis*. Mann is, after all, an analytical writer.

How and why did the change of conception occur? Mann accounted for it by the 'necessities of his nature'. These produced their own objectivizing process which was 'painful' because it conflicted with his conscious will. His wishes were refused by his deepest nature as a writer. How this operated is ultimately impenetrable, but a mixed moral and aesthetic distaste for his first conception dictated changes of detail such as we have traced. One further important factor must be added.

Georg Lukács, or von Lukács, as at that time his name officially was, published in 1911 a book of essays entitled *Die Seele und die Formen*, with a strong neo-Platonic tendency. One essay in particular, 'Sehnsucht und Form', deals at some length with Socrates as the creator of a philosophy out of the human impulse for love and yearning. He did this in two senses, firstly in that he sublimated his own and his admirers' passions into a pursuit of truth, and secondly in that he developed a general theory in which love—the commonest form of yearning— became the motive power for all spiritual progress. The matter is put clearest, Lukács says, in the *Symposium*, which asks what the lover is and what he is really pursuing, why people yearn and what the true object of their yearning is. Sexual love, which Aristophanes in Plato's dialogue explains as the urge of two halves of a once undivided being to be reunited, is merely 'die kleine Sehnsucht, die erfüllbare' (the small, fulfillable kind of yearning). Higher forms of yearning can, by their nature, find no fulfilment in life. To yearn for something is to prove thereby how deeply foreign it is to oneself, and how impossible therefore any union with it must be. 'Was einem fremd ist, wird man nie ersehnen . . . Die Sehnsucht verbindet die Ungleichen, aber vernichtet zugleich jede Hoffnung auf ihr Einswerden . . . die wahre Sehnsucht hat nie eine Heimat gehabt' (Anything that is alien to one will never be attained by longing . . . Yearning links unlikes, but simultaneously destroys all hope of their union . . . true yearning has never had a home on earth).[28] These ideas are close to Mann's early themes, and even echo some of his formulations.[29] Lukács's bold interpretation of Plato puts in quintessential form the dilemma and mental condition of the Outsider and its ultimate grounds, and puts it in terms which were bound to catch Mann's interest. He had once called *Sehnsucht* his favourite word, a magic formula, a key to the secret of the world (to Katja Pringsheim, September 1904). He had shown that the desire to bridge an unbridgeable gap was the fruitful principle in Tonio Kröger's art. He had depicted Schiller's creativity in *Schwere Stunde* as the result of a yearning for form ('Sehnsucht nach Form, Gestalt, Begrenzung, Körperlichkeit . . .' [viii. 377]). Lukács's systematic account might well seem apposite to himself and also to his hero.

But the essay also gave a very definite angle on the Platonic philosophy, and struck the note of pessimism and tragedy which was finally to be dominant in *Der Tod in Venedig*. Lukács makes plain how precarious and rare was Socrates' achievement when he shaped men's longings into philosophy. In general, efforts at sublimation are almost bound to fail, because of the earthliness of the objects which first stimulate them:

Den Menschen und den Dichtern wird ein solcher Aufschwung immer versagt bleiben. Der Gegenstand ihrer Sehnsucht hat eine eigene Schwere und ein sich-selbst-wollendes Leben. Ihr Aufschwung ist immer die Tragödie, und Held und Schicksal müssen da zur Form werden . . . Im Leben muss die Sehnsucht Liebe bleiben: es ist ihr Glück und ihre Tragödie.

(Such spiritual flights will remain ever out of the reach of men and poets. The object of their yearning has its own gravity and a life which cares only for itself. Their aspiration is always tragedy, and hero and fate have to be turned into form . . . In life yearning must remain love: that is its happiness and its tragedy.)[30]

---

[28] Lukács, op. cit., p. 200.

[29] For example in *Fiorenza*, in the closing speeches of both Savonarola and Lorenzo: 'Wollt ihr ein Zeichen dafür, wann Unversöhnlichkeit und ewige Fremdheit gelegt ist zwischen zwei Welten? Die Sehnsucht ist dies Zeichen!' (Do you want a sign when irreconcilability and eternal alienation are set between two worlds? Yearning is that sign! [viii. 1061]). 'Wohin die Sehnsucht drängt, nicht wahr? dort ist man nicht, — das ist man nicht.' (Whither yearning urges, is it not so? there one is not, that one is not [1062].)

[30] Lukács, p. 203.

Formulations from this passage appear in the closing pages of the *Novelle*, in that mock-Platonic speech in which Aschenbach addresses Tadzio-Phaedrus and attains clear insight into his own downfall and its causes: '. . . Leidenschaft ist unsere Erhebung, und unsere Sehnsucht muss Liebe bleiben, — das ist unsere Lust und unsere Schande . . . wir vermögen nicht, uns aufzuschwingen, wir vermögen nur, auszuschweifen' (. . . passion is our elevation, and our yearning must remain love— that is our pleasure and our shame . . . we are not capable of spiritual flights, only of aberration [p. 522]). It is clear that Lukács's pessimistic view of Platonic possibilities decisively affected Thomas Mann's treatment of his theme. It provided a sterner, potentially moral view at a time when Mann was deeply dissatisfied with the story as he had begun it.

'At a time when': the timing is clearly important. The essay 'Sehnsucht und Form' first appeared in partial pre-publication form in the *Neue Rundschau* of February 1911. As a Fischer author, Mann not only contributed to the *Rundschau* but also read it. Did Lukács's suggestive title first catch his eye then? All we can be sure of is that the text he used when working on *Der Tod in Venedig* was the full text in *Die Seele und die Formen*.[31] And this volume came out, so far as can be ascertained, in the autumn of 1911.[32]

I would no longer wish to argue, as I have elsewhere, that Mann got his *positive* interest in Plato's theory of beauty and love via Lukács's essay, but then, having explored its possibilities, accepted Lukács's critical conclusions as confirmation for his own increasing resistance to the 'Greek' approach.[33] There is a less complicated alternative.

Mann's copy of the *Symposium* bears the date of acquisition

[31] The passage quoted above is the conclusion of § 1 and the first sentence of § 2. The *Rundschau* sample consisted of sections 1 and 4. Mann's copy of *Die Seele und die Formen*, with marginal markings, is in TMA.

[32] In the first half of October, according to Georg Lukács (private letter to the author of 20 July 1970). The accuracy of his recollection is not guaranteed, but it is a striking independent corroboration of the time scheme sketched above. Further evidence of the publication date of *Die Seele und die Formen* was not obtainable.

[33] As I suggested in my critical edition of *Der Tod in Venedig* (Oxford, 1971). The present account seems the more plausible. One could of course say that the *Rundschau* publication in February reminded Mann of Plato while only a closer look at Lukács's critical reservations in October had the effect described above. But at this point the argument would become unduly sophistical.

1904. There is little sign that it especially interested him in the years intervening (except that the letter singing the praises of *Sehnsucht* to Katja is also dated 1904). Nevertheless, it is quite conceivable that he turned to it when the 'hymnic' approach to his Venice subject was in full swing. Even when the very first intoxication cooled into a plan for a *Novelle* (to Witkop, July 1911), its declared qualities—purity, seriousness, propriety—suggest precisely the Platonic treatment, taking homosexual passion in an elevated sense, rather than the final moralistic treatment. The Plutarch text which Mann made such intensive use of also appeared in 1911,[34] and may itself have been the initial stimulus to a 'Greek' treatment. By October Mann's growing unease and the new light Lukács threw on Platonic aspirations came together to cast the story in its final form.[35] The critical view took over, but had to inform material which had been very differently intended. Precisely this negative reworking of what was at first a positive conception would account perfectly for the strange mixture *Der Tod in Venedig* actually is, of enthusiasm and criticism, classical beauty and penetration, elevation and sordidness.

The kinds of detailed change which resulted for the final text and the altered stress on episodes have already been illustrated. We can also see the change taking effect at its source, in the work-notes. Two consecutive notes[36] sketch the central issue the story has now come round to treating, and the passages in which it is to be made most explicit—the *Phaedrus* pastiche and Chapter Two. The first reads:

Aufstieg von der Problematik zur Würde. Und nun! Der Konflikt ist: von der 'Würde' aus, von der Erkenntnisfeindschaft und zweiten Unbefangenheit, aus antianalytischem Zustande gerät er in *diese* Leidenschaft. Die Form ist die Sünde. Die Oberfläche ist der Abgrund. Wie sehr wird dem würdig gewordenen Künstler die Kunst noch einmal zum Problem! Eros ist für den Künstler der

---

[34] Plutarch, *Vermischte Schriften*, translated Kaltwasser, Munich and Leipzig, 1911, 3 vols. Vol. 3 contains *Über die Liebe*.

[35] Is it significant that two months after the letter to Bertram (see above, p. 150) Mann speaks of his story only as '*vielleicht* eine unmögliche Konzeption' (my italics)? Letter to Wilhelm Herzog dated 8 Dec. 1911, in Herzog, *Menschen, denen ich begegnete*, Berne, 1959, p. 268.

[36] The present order of the work-notes is of course not an absolutely reliable guide to their relationship at the time they were written.

Führer zum Intellektuellen, zur geistigen Schönheit, der Weg zum Höchsten geht für ihn durch die Sinne. Aber das ist ein gefährlich lieblicher Weg, ein Irr- und Sündenweg, obgleich es einen anderen nicht gibt. 'Den Dichtern wird ein solcher Aufschwung immer versagt bleiben. Ihr Aufschwung ist immer die Tragödie. . . Im *Leben* (und der Künstler ist der Mann des Lebens!) muss die Sehnsucht *Liebe* bleiben: es ist ihr Glück und ihre Tragödie.' — Einsicht, dass der Künstler nicht würdig sein *kann*, dass er notwendig in die Irre geht, Bohemien, Zigeuner, Libertiner, und ewig Abenteurer des Gefühls bleibt. Die Haltung seines Stiles erscheint ihm als Lüge und Narrentum, Orden, Ehren, Adel fast lächerlich. Die Würde rettet allein der Tod (die 'Tragödie', das 'Meer' — Rat, Ausweg und Zuflucht aller höheren Liebe[)].

Der Ruhm des Künstlers eine Farce, das Massenzutrauen zu ihm eine Dummheit. Erziehung durch die Kunst ein gewagtes, zu verbietendes Unternehmen. Ironie, dass die Knaben ihn lesen. Ironie der Offizialität, der Nobilitierung.[37]

(Ascent from problematic state to dignity. And now! The conflict is: from 'dignity', from hostility to knowledge and from second innocence, from an anti-analytic position he gets involved in *this* passion. Form is the sin. The surface is the abyss. How deeply art once again becomes problematic for the artist who has attained dignity! Eros is for the artist the guide to things intellectual, to spiritual beauty, the path to the highest things goes, for him, through the senses. But that is a dangerous if delightful path, a wrong way and a sinful way, although there isn't any other. 'Such spiritual flights will remain ever out of the reach of poets. Their elevation is always tragedy . . . In *life* (and the artist is the man of life!) yearning must remain *love*: that is its happiness and its tragedy.'—Realization that the artist *cannot* attain dignity, that he necessarily goes astray, remains a bohemian, a gipsy, a libertine and eternal adventurer of the emotions. The discipline of his style appears to him lies and foolishness, decorations, honours, noble rank almost ludicrous. Dignity is rescued only by death (the 'tragedy', the 'sea'—solution, way out and refuge of all higher love[)].

The artist's fame a farce, popular trust in him idiotic. Education through art a risky undertaking which should be prohibited. Ironic that boys read him. Ironic that he is an establishment figure, with a title.)

In the phrase 'the conflict is:' one can sense the deliberate effort of clarifying complex issues, making a fresh start in the light of a new principle. Beginning at 'Eros' the Platonic

---

[37] fol. 4, continued on the (misnumbered) fol. 6.

material is then reinterpreted sceptically, and the authority for this view given—a quotation from Lukács. This is duly adjusted to fit the case—only poets, not men in general—and key words are underlined and glossed. Then follows the sketch for that final ironic, even sarcastic view of Aschenbach, the artist who seemed to have attained dignity but fell. This is where the theme which had been in Mann's mind so long, the precariousness of any status and recognition an artist might achieve, became established as the critical message of the Venice experiment. Only one way out was left—death. Not now as an apotheosis, but as an emergency exit from Aschenbach's dilemma: the 'tragedy' in which Lukács said all higher flights end; the 'sea', that borrowing of Plato's 'sea of beauty' at the close. Mann had difficulties finding the right ending for his *Novelle* (to Heinrich Mann, April 1912). It seems that an ending already envisaged in the 'hymnic' conception served after all the quite different 'tragic' purpose—served it all the better because it remains profoundly ambiguous, as does the wording of this work-note which still speaks of Aschenbach's passion as an example of 'higher love'.

The other note starts from the *Phaedrus* sentence 'Nur die Schönheit ist zugleich sichtbar und liebenswürdig' (only beauty is at the same time visible and worthy of love)[38] and from there spells out the paradox by which Aschenbach's resolute literary development placed him at risk:

Liebe zur Schönheit führt zum Moralischen, zur Absage an die Sympathie mit dem Abgrund, an die Psychologie, die Analyse, [added: d. h. zur Bejahung der Leidenschaft und des Lebens]; führt zur Einfachheit, Grösse und schönen Strenge, zur wiedergeborenen Unbefangenheit, zur Form. Aber eben damit auch wieder zum Abgrund.

Was ist moralisch? die Analyse? (Die Vernichtung der Leidenschaft?) Sie hat keine Strenge, sie ist wissend, verstehend, ohne Haltung und Form. Sie hat Sympathie mit dem Abgrund [Added: Sie *ist* der Abgrund.) Oder die Form? Die Liebe zur Schönheit? Aber sie führt zum Rausch, zur Begierde und also ebenfalls zum Abgrund.[39]

(Love of beauty leads to what is moral, to the rejection of sym-

[38] Platons *Phaidros* ins Deutsche übertragen von Rudolf Kassner, Jena, 1910[2], p. 44.　　　　　　　　　　　　　　　　　　　　[39] fol. 5.

pathy with the abyss, of psychology, analysis [added: i.e. to the affirming of passion and life]; leads to simplicity, grandeur, and beautiful austerity, to innocence reborn, to form. But precisely thereby to the abyss again.
What is moral? analysis? (The destruction of passion?) It has no austerity, it is knowing, understanding, it lacks discipline and form. It has sympathy with the abyss. [Added: It *is* the abyss.] Or form? Love of beauty? But that leads to intoxication, to desire, and thus equally to the abyss.)

The directness with which the crux of the story is given in this passage is the directness of Chapter Two, which was referred to above as an obituary and advance explanation of Aschenbach's fate. But if it is 'advance' in the order of the completed text, it seems likely that it was actually written late on in the experiment. The first of the two passages just quoted is preceded in the work-notes, on the same sheet, by a list of 'Beziehungen von Kap. II zu V' (links from Chapter II to V). The points listed are: Aschenbach's forebears and their courageous service; love of fame and ability to carry it; the motto *Durchhalten*, discipline, soldierly service; the production of great works in a state of tension; the principle of working against the grain (*das Trotzdem*).[40] This, coming as it does on the same sheet which works out the story's crucial issue as finally treated, suggests that Chapter Two is chronologically as well as essentially the conclusion of the experiment. For narrative purposes, to set the points for a reading of the work as a 'moral fable', it rightly stands near the beginning. But it was surely a simple matter to interpose it there, breaking the otherwise uninterrupted flow of the narrative from Chapter One to Chapter Three.[41]

Yet by a further twist the presence of a synoptic view of Aschenbach's development in Chapter Two again alters the story's moral impact. It may warn against the dangers of beauty and thus prepare us for a cautionary tale; but it also understands Aschenbach's behaviour as the product of his period and of his years.[42] In so doing, it surely goes beyond

[40] fol. 4.
[41] The phrase 'Links from Chapter II to V' does not necessarily suggest a long-standing Chapter Two (one might then expect 'Links back from Chapter V to II'); both chapters may well have been developed together, critically embracing the chapters (Three and Four) in which the earlier conception was most substantially contained.
[42] The letter to Weber (Br. i. 177) refers to the 'Klimakterium'.

those all too obvious condemnations which the narrator inter-
sperses in the later part of the action, and rises instead to the
plane of 'tout comprendre, c'est tout pardonner'. In this respect
too, Thomas Mann remains the writer he was.

## III

We are still not at the end of the complexities in Mann's story;
but those that remain are beneficial to the text as finally completed, not problems in the path of its completion. Indeed,
even the tortuous genesis so far discussed left enriching elements
behind it. For, when the intricate development is over, what
remains is a single text, which creates effects. Understanding
these fully may depend on some knowledge of the story's
genesis—our reading loses a dimension if we know nothing of
the specifically Platonic symbolism, or if we cannot connect the
details of Aschenbach's behaviour with Plutarch's description
of lovers who 'pursue by day and haunt the door by night'.[43]
But a proper standard for judging the text is the degree of unity
it finally has for the reader. The extent to which genetic difficulties and a variety of sources are reconciled in *Der Tod in
Venedig* into such a unified statement is remarkable.

Mann's actual experience, his latent preoccupations, philosophical theory, psychological analysis, mythology, and literary
parallels all came together and without any intervention on the
author's part offered suggestive connections, those *Beziehungen*
whose fascination Mann speaks of in the *Lebensabriss* apropos of
precisely this story (xi. 123 f.).

*Der Tod in Venedig* is about psychological decay finding in the
outside world pretext and occasion for its fulfilment. Aschenbach's creative discipline is essentially broken at the very outset.
The long years of too deliberate application and self-control
have begun to take their revenge. This is the psychological
premiss of the whole story. It is coloured specifically by
Nietzsche's theory of the components in artistic creation, the
Apolline and the Dionysiac: this second element is Aschenbach's 'geknechtete Empfindung' (p. 449). Nietzsche's terms
already led over into Greek mythology. On investigation,
Dionysus proved to be a foreign god originating in India and

[43] Cf. *Erotikos* 759 b: 'He loves when present and longs when absent, pursues by
day and haunts the door by night.'

superimposed on an older Greek deity. But the cholera epidemic, which in Naturalistic terms is what kills Aschenbach, also came from India. This coincidence between the external cause and a mythologically understood inner cause was suggestive, especially to a writer on the look-out for ways to elevate prose narrative above the literal Naturalistic level. If the epidemic was in Aschenbach's eyes a secret accomplice in disorder, for Thomas Mann the epidemic which broke out in Italy during his Venice stay was certainly an ideal accomplice in the creation of a symbolic pattern. Myth, psychology, and real events coincided in such a way that to state the one was simultaneously to allude to the others. Reality took on a new resonance.

The coincidental encounter with Tadzio takes its place in this complex as the stimulus to an insidious enthusiasm, which is related precisely to the aesthetic fashions of Mann-Aschenbach's time. The inspirer of Aschenbach's heightened condition is also a perfect embodiment of the coincidentally encountered, or re-encountered, Platonic theory of beauty. This gives ideal criteria against which Aschenbach can eventually be found wanting. His failure and degradation exactly illustrate the long-latent theme that the Artist's life is precariously based and should not lay claim to dignity too soon. Phrasing, images, and motifs are appropriately introduced from the Platonic dialogues and from the Plutarch dialogue coincidentally just to hand. Aschenbach's initially Platonic passion can be condemned as itself a form of *Rausch*: the general psychological theme of a Dionysiac reawakening subsumes the Platonic theme. Plutarch too spoke of a heightened condition—*enthousiasmos*[44]—which could take the form of literary inspiration; this, like Platonic love, fits into the scheme of Aschenbach's decline and can be finally rejected. But all these contributions, including the psychological framework itself, in turn fitted exactly the investigation of the artistic and intellectual problems which become clear in Chapter Two—the nature of artistic development, the problem of ageing for the artist, the problem of maintaining enough self-awareness to preserve himself from danger in his vulnerable existence. And these in turn are a generalized version of the problems of 'Geist und Kunst'.

[44] *Erotikos* 758 e, excerpted in work-notes, fol. 11. Hence the reference to Aschenbach as *der Enthusiasmierte* (p. 491).

The experiences of the Venice visit—apart from the coincidence of the cholera epidemic, with its Indian source, which aided the construction of a symbolic story—appear in the text in ideal integration with all these guiding themes and concepts. As Mann wrote in retrospect, they all had an innate symbolism, and only needed placing. So rich were they in symbolic potential, in fact, that they could have served the hymnic purpose just as well: the old disgusting dandy on the boat to Venice could have been an ignoble contrasting figure to set off Aschenbach's pure and serious passion; but in the critical history of a psychological break-up he becomes an omen. Omens of death itself, and figures whose features allude to the death's head or to the hat and staff of Hermes are numerous and by now common knowledge. The psychological process is converted into an apparently fated course, it is *realized* in symbolic figures and motifs. This is not to say that fate in any other sense than the psychological is being seriously put forward as the reality of Aschenbach's death: the end must be distinguished from the means. But they are brilliantly matched to each other. Despite the compositional difficulties his letters record, it is clear why Mann spoke of a feeling that, in writing *Der Tod in Venedig*, he was at times being borne along by it ('das Gefühl eines gewissen absoluten Wandels, einer gewissen souveränen Getragenheit' [xi. 124]). The meanings interlocked so remarkably. Mann's preoccupations and the varied materials which chance placed in his hands together created a wholly new suggestiveness, an art of rich ambivalence.

At the thematic level then, all ends well. At the symbolic level too, if one is prepared to accept the mingling of myths, the interplay of Eros and Hermes and Dionysus: for the writer in a sober age, myth is an exciting material which invites intensive exploitation. Criticism would have to start from the style, because here one can speak of ambiguity in the word's more dubious sense: not richness of meaning, but uncertainty of meaning, disunity.

Whose is the style? It has proved possible to detach Mann from the emphatic condemnations of the later pages. These formulations, despite the more critical view the author is by now taking of his character, are Mann's concession to more confident moralists than himself. But there are other features of the style, more firmly rooted in the text as a whole. There is its *gewollte Klassizität*, its deliberate classicism. In his response to early reviews which assumed the straight equation Aschenbach– Thomas Mann, and criticized it as presumptuous,[45] Mann stressed the element of parody in the writing, and this view has become popular among scholars. The extreme formality, the wording which contrives to be both elaborate and lapidary, the set-piece descriptions and evocations of Venetian setting and sea-shore, the symbolic externals which stand in place of analysis, all these are attributed to Aschenbach himself. They are part of his mode of experiencing which the author recreates from within, by a process he himself labelled 'mimicry'.[46]

But then is there not much else in this story which began by being part of Mann's own experiment and ended by being passed on to Aschenbach? May this not also be true of the style? Was Thomas Mann not concerned with the idea of a future classicism? His Venice article on Wagner shows he was. Was there not, among the temptations which Mann-Aschenbach underwent, a pressure to move away from the analytical to the beauties of the surface, to plastic re-creation and richness of external detail? We know there was. Was there not also a tendency to associate such ambitions with things Greek? Hauptmann's *Griechischer Frühling* shows it; and although Mann commented on this work ironically, his irony may have been open to revision, as were so many of the attitudes of 'Geist und Kunst'. It seems distinctly possible that the style of *Der Tod in Venedig* originally partook of ambitions which were discarded as part of the complex genesis, only coming to be a means to characterize Aschenbach at the last. After all, the critical placing of Aschenbach's style as a *gewollte Klassizität* occurs in Chapter Two, where the experiment's final conclusions are made clear. It questions the value of Aschenbach's literary manner when everything else about him has become questionable. The problem is, how conclusively has responsibility for that manner been transferred from Mann to Aschenbach?

The way the story affected contemporaries is relevant. Wilhelm Alberts, whose book on Mann[47] appeared the year after

---

[45] See the samples quoted in the appendix to the Amann correspondence, pp. 94 f.　　　　[46] To Paul Amann, 10 Sept. 1915 (Br. A. 32).
[47] Wilhelm Alberts, *Thomas Mann und sein Beruf*, Leipzig, 1913.

*Der Tod in Venedig* and dealt with the new work in a postscript, felt that the pursuit of beauty had now taken over from satire as the main aim of Mann's art. This seemed to Alberts clearly due to the influence of Greek art and outlook: Mann too, he says, seems to have experienced a 'Greek spring'. The allusion is significant. Had Hauptmann's example, his method of *sich arrangieren* with the changing tastes of the times, been in Mann's mind when he began to work with Greek motifs? Common ground seemed obvious to a perceptive contemporary. And did not Mann write to Heinrich of an *antikisierendes Kapitel* as one of the story's undeniable beauties? At that point in time, not long before publication, classical motifs and the highly wrought language in which they were introduced could still claim attention as special effects, although the heightened conception to which they originally corresponded had long been abandoned.

But if there was too much 'beauty' left in the text to be stylistically quite compatible with the changed conception, there was also too much 'criticism' for the earnest devotee of the Beautiful. At the opposite extreme from Alberts was Stefan George, who totally rejected Mann's *Novelle* because it had compromised the most elevated things with decadence ('das Höchste in die Sphäre des Verfalls hinabgezogen').[48] The classicizing externals were not enough to reconcile George to the Naturalistic pathological treatment of an emotion towards which he was austerely sympathetic.

Mann had sought to work out a changed conception in materials and language ideally suited to an earlier one. In the style of the resulting story, it can be argued, he managed to have his cake and eat it, arrive at critical conclusions about a certain kind of beauty while at the same time creating a literary equivalent of that beauty; just as it can be argued that he managed to construct from the sequence of hymnic and moral conceptions a single tragic vision of impulse and failure. Mann argued so himself, writing to Weber that he had striven for a synthesis of sensual and moral.[49] But equally it could be said

---

[48] Quoted in Mann's letter to Weber (Br. i. 179).
[49] 'Ein Gleichgewicht von Sinnlichkeit und Sittlichkeit wurde angestrebt, wie ich es in den 'Wahlverwandtschaften' ideal vollendet fand, die ich während der Arbeit am T.i.V., wenn ich recht erinnere, fünf mal gelesen habe' (ibid., p. 176).

that his story falls stylistically between two stools, that the classicizing element which went with the still perceptible hymnic origin remains at odds with the story's moral purport, leaving a disharmony between style and substance. When Mann represented the style as being a parody of Aschenbach's own, he made the one adjustment that could restore unity. But his suggestion is hard to bear out from the text. As a sweeping explanation applied to a whole story, parody is almost impossible to verify. *Der Tod in Venedig* remains to this extent ambiguous. It is perhaps revealing that Mann wrote to Bertram soon after the story was published that he did not know what to think of it: 'Ich bin noch heute völlig ohne eigenes Urteil' (Br. B. 12).

Mann's later retrospects offer other angles. In the *Betrachtungen* of 1918 he speaks of himself as one of those European writers who grew up in the age of decadence but are now at least experimenting with ways to overcome it ('mit der Überwindung von Dekadenz und Nihilismus wenigstens *experimentieren*' [xii. 201, Mann's italics]) and goes on to talk of *Der Tod in Venedig*. Their search is for new absolute values, some 'inner tyrant' controlling attitude and form: a need which, Mann says, he treated long before others were aware of it, not as a propagandist, but 'novellistisch, das heisst: experimentell und ohne letzte Verbindlichkeit' (in a *Novelle*, i.e.: experimentally and without final commitment [xii. 517]). This comes closer to the uncertainties at the core of the work. And that the experiment was essentially with Thomas Mann himself he makes explicit later, telling Graf Kessler that the hero of *Der Tod in Venedig* was 'more or less' himself,[50] and writing in his Princeton lecture that the story is not only a criticism of the artist in general:

zugleich werden die pädagogischen Ansprüche gegeisselt, die sich etwa ins Künstler-Selbstgefühl einschleichen sollten: Ansprüche, Neigungen, Ideen, die doch in meinem eigenen Leben, seitdem es aus seiner jugendlichen Einsamkeits- und Boheme-Epoche herausgetreten war, eine Rolle zu spielen begonnen hatte[n].

(at the same time the pedagogical pretensions are flayed which might perhaps infiltrate an artist's feeling about himself: pretensions,

[50] Harry Graf Kessler, *Tagebücher*, Frankfurt, 1961, p. 763.

inclinations, ideas, which had in fact begun to take on a significance in my own life since it had emerged from its youthful period of isolation and bohemianism.)[51]

In other words, it was an experiment with the condition and the risks of being a 'Master'.

Despite the ambiguities which are rooted in the genesis of *Der Tod in Venedig*, at least the direction of development is clear: in what it implies about the Artist, the story constitutes a moral victory which is nothing to do with the morality of homosexual love. Through Aschenbach Mann had experimented with a change in his literary ways, a decision to reject the values by which he had so far lived and worked. The forces influencing him in that direction were stated in 'Geist und Kunst'—a work which Aschenbach, significantly, had brought to completion, we can easily infer in what sense. Subjected to the temptation of swimming with the stream, and even for a time actively wishing to do so, Mann nevertheless remained true to himself. The nature of his talent asserted itself against his more superficial motives. In place of the new kind of form he yearned to achieve, it drew him back towards a soberer, more critical, still 'intellectual' work. This is surely what he meant when he spoke in the *Lebensabriss* of the surprises the work had in store for its author (xi. 123). The failure to achieve undeniable *Dichtertum*, which he still speaks bitterly of in *Gesang vom Kindchen*, was thus only a failure in a limited sense.

The ambivalent art which was first brought to maturity in *Der Tod in Venedig* was a permanent acquisition. It is the basis for many later ambiguities and for an adroit manipulation of levels of meaning. For example, the teasing description of Hans Castorp's heightened state in his early days on the mountain: is it caused by love? or by disease? or does love create disease? or vice versa? And are both these things mere external pointers to his intellectual destiny? The play with *Beziehungen* is akin to that in the Venice story: *Der Zauberberg* was conceived just before *Der Tod in Venedig* was completed, and was originally planned as a short pendant piece to it.

[51] 'On Myself', *Blätter* 6, p. 20. This retrospect is confirmed by a detail in the text of the *Novelle*. The passage from the Chamisso essay on 'settling down and becoming a master', for which we saw parallels in Mann's letters of the period, is used in the text (p. 456) almost unchanged.

G

Or again there is the Naturalistic surface of the Joseph novel, showing how all that 'really' happened, but with underlying suggestions of mythical re-enactment. And a yet more radical doubt and suggestiveness surround *Doktor Faustus*. Are Adrian Leverkühn's inspirations the product of syphilis or of a pact with the devil? The dubiousness itself parallels the two interpretations of Germany's descent into Nazism: pathological and mythical.

The creation of ambivalence was the breakthrough in Mann's long-standing programme to 'elevate' the novel. It rescued the novel of ideas from the mechanical methods of simple allegory. 'Allegory' still fairly describes some aspects of *Der Zauberberg* or *Doktor Faustus*; but the door has been opened to intellectual complexities of a quite different order from the encoded self-concern of *Königliche Hoheit*. From *Der Tod in Venedig* on, ambivalence is the central technique of Mann's art, suggesting, but not affirming, layers of meaning which lie beneath the surface of immediate experience.

Less permanent than the acquisition of this technique was Mann's commitment to critical intellect as the watchdog over human aberration. This had been reaffirmed after a testing experiment. It was soon to be swept aside by an enthusiasm less private and out of all proportion more powerful than the one provoked by a chance encounter in Venice.

# Unpolitics

To morals sententious adieu with good grace.

W. S. GILBERT

## I

WHAT Thomas Mann wrote during the First World War has
frequently been excused and extenuated, or romanticized, or
explained away as a kind of play-acting, or appreciated for the
piecemeal value of certain ideas taken from context. These
approaches are wrong, because they trivialize an episode which
Thomas Mann himself was unable to dispose of so easily. Only
by taking his war writings seriously as what they clearly were—
the expression of a whole-hearted emotional commitment
desperately seeking to rationalize itself—can we make sense
fully of the novels that refer back to them, critically and
tragically: *Der Zauberberg* and *Doktor Faustus*.

Analysis of Thomas Mann's position yields an unsympathetic
picture. The suddenness and vehemence of his national commitment in 1914 and the sophistical arguments he was driven
to in his own justification make this the low point of his career
as a critical intellectual. But his individual career is only one
context in which his war writings can be understood. The
attitudes they state are rooted unmistakably in his preceding
work and thought and in his private life, but they fit equally
well into other frames of reference: the reactions of German
artists and intellectuals as a group to the war; or the trends in
German society and thought, reaching back into the nineteenth
century, which helped determine those reactions. These are
not rival but compatible explanations of Mann's attitudes,
frames of reference different in scale but concentric. Examining
them in turn allows us to grasp with unusual completeness the
interlocking of personal and general, intellectual and social.
Mann is distinctively himself, his every thought closely related
to his own past evolution, yet he is also entirely representative.

This in turn argues the representativeness of that whole evolution and of the problems round which his work had revolved: something which could perhaps only emerge with full clarity at such a critical moment as the outbreak of war, when the deepest impulses of a national culture were forced to declare themselves.

What did Mann do in 1914? He took Germany's part against *Entente* propaganda, surprising himself and others by the violence of his patriotism. He then spent the rest of the war elaborating an argument to show that his commitment was consistent with everything he had previously written and thought. To prove this might seem a tall order. Nothing, at first sight, could be less applicable to politics than the themes of Mann's fiction—as the 'unpolitical' title of his main war essay accepts. His absorption hitherto in the problems of art and artists certainly did not seem a prelude to the kind of national involvement he rushed into when he added his voice to those who were exalting Germany and reviling England and France. The case which pacifists and pro-*Entente* writers brought against Mann, that he had gone back on all his earlier principles, seemed a strong one. Had he not been a cool and critical intellectual? How could he suddenly become a hot chauvinist?

Both sides were right. The same body of work could give support to both because of the inner tensions and divided allegiance which we have already seen. On the one hand, Mann had certainly set up an image of the artist as a natural protester and intellectual purist, a detached critic and gradual educator of his society in humane understanding, an incorruptible prober for truth. He had argued that good writing, clear thinking, and ethical behaviour were closely connected. His ideals, in some passages of 'Geist und Kunst' for example, were thus indistinguishable from those of the Enlightenment. His own writing had an exemplary clarity and psychological penetration.

So when, in April 1914, the pacifist writer Wilhelm Herzog proposed that European intellectuals should hold a conference and bring the voice of reason to the ears of governments which seemed bent on war, he naturally listed Thomas along with Heinrich Mann among the 'good Europeans' he could count on.[1] For those who saw Thomas Mann in this way, the *Gedanken im Kriege* were to come as a nasty shock.

[1] *Das Forum* I. 1, Munich, April 1914, p. 3.

But there was another side to Mann. In retrospect, it was not his critical intellectualism but his growing distaste for it which now seemed to him the essence of his past work. Tonio Kröger's reluctance to infect the healthy and innocent with the sickness of literature now appeared as an unconscious political conservatism (xii. 587). This interpretation, dubious at first sight, is a key to the way Mann transposed his earlier problems into political terms. His statement that anyone with eyes to see might have discerned in his work that he would stand by Germany in her hour of need is not just a provocative paradox. He genuinely came to think that the pointers to his allegiance were obvious. His reference to Tonio Kröger reminds us of the pull which normality and community had always exerted on the self-conscious outsider, and of the psychic strain which being always 'in opposition' meant. More recently, these attitudes had culminated in Aschenbach's (and Thomas Mann's own) experiment with the rejection of psychology for beauty, and of bohemianism for social acceptance. The outsider had never been at ease outside. August 1914 issued the most compelling invitation to return to the community—a national community which seemed regenerated by crisis.

In the other belligerent nations too the early days of the war produced an upsurge of idealism, a feeling of moral purity regained.[2] But in Germany this was turned into a systematic mystique, the so-called 'Ideas of 1914'. The practical causes and processes of war were ignored and Germany's 'defensive struggle' was seen as a higher conflict between the German mind, with its cultural and social forms, and the alien, essentially inferior mind and forms of her enemies. Britain was a non-culture based on commercialism, France a superficially rational civilization, Russia was barbarism. Germany alone had a profound culture which, linked with practical efficiency ('organization' was the keyword), justified her claim to the

---

[2] Cf. Rupert Brooke's 1914 sonnets 'Peace' and 'The Dead', especially the lines in the first:

> To turn, as swimmers into cleanness leaping,
> Glad from a world grown old and cold and weary,
> Leave the sick hearts that honour could not move . . .

And Romain Rolland in *Au-dessus de la mêlée*, p. 38, salutes the heroic youth of Europe and its 'guerre de revanche . . . revanche de la foi contre tous les égoïsmes des sens et de l'esprit, don absolu de soi aux idées éternelles . . .'.

world-power status which the rest of Europe had enviously denied her and which the war was a legitimate means of achieving—although she had not provoked war.

Far from being the work of a propaganda agency, this mystique sprang from the established intellectuals, historians, philosophers, cultural essayists.[3] It was not the work of any political wing—indeed, the transcending of political divisions by national unity was one of the miraculous results of the outbreak of war. It was the common coin of the majority of self-respecting intellectuals. Nowhere is this clearer than in the *Neue Rundschau* for the last four months of 1914. Since its origins in the socially radical Naturalist movement, the S. Fischer Verlag's *Rundschau* had been the organ of progressive artistic and intellectual circles. Nevertheless, in these months it states all the nationalist clichés and philosophical apologias for war. The 'ideas of 1914' could be reconstituted from this one source.[4] Its contributors are the usual distinguished names—Moritz Heimann, Julius Meier-Graefe, Samuel Saenger, Friedrich Meinecke, Max Scheler, Alfred Kerr, Emil Ludwig—but what they write is uniformly dominated by national enthusiasm and revolves around certain stock ideas.

Heimann speaks of the moral unity which 1914 has added to the external unity of 1870. Saenger celebrates the unity of Power and Mind (*Macht und Geist*) and revives Fichte's conception of the state as the 'unifying point for millions of moral wills', a framework from which it is impermissible for the individual to stand aside. Kerr, who had till now been a known pacifist, actually watches in himself the conflict between his old 'enlightened' principles and the upsurge of patriotic feeling. Even while he realizes that war is a relapse into the primitive, recognizes that Belgium is innocent, and is aware of the force of propaganda; even while he sceptically reflects that 'community', the word now on everyone's lips, is never offered to social inferiors except in time of crisis—still he feels an overriding

---

[3] See the brief summary and references in Fritz Fischer, *Germany's Aims in the First World War*, London, 1967, pp. 155 f. For a fuller account, Herman Lübbe, *Politische Philosophie in Deutschland*, Basle and Stuttgart, 1963, pp. 173–238.

[4] Since this chapter was completed, the wartime contents of the *Neue Rundschau* and the attitudes of Fischer's house-authors generally have received extended treatment in the chapter 'Ansichten des Krieges' of Peter de Mendelssohn's monumental *S. Fischer und sein Verlag*, Frankfurt, 1970, pp. 656–95.

patriotic commitment above social conflicts: 'alle letzte Liebe
für dies Land . . . trotz Krach und Zorn des Alltags'.

Ludwig similarly feels at last what it means to belong:
'dazugehören, einmal unter den Seinen sein, nicht unter vier
oder sechs — unter Millionen', and he records a 'thousand signs
of magnificent community', of great human beauty ('sagenhaft
schön'). Scheler speaks of Germany as a 'single arm' lifted in
defence, all partisan differences vanished before the 'sacred
requirement' of the hour. The broken contacts between
individual and nation and world (Scheler was a philosopher)
have been re-established. Individuals are no longer what they
had long been—alone.

The editor of the *Rundschau*, Oskar Bie, speaks of the simplification war brought, the relief of action after the tangles of
diplomacy, the relief of naked facts after the compexities of
overheated minds. War is at last something to be experienced
'without translation into the sphere of intellect'. It will clarify
the confused strivings of recent art, in which a 'will to organization . . . to new style and commitment' had long been evident,
prevented only by the 'danger of overrating the cerebral'. War
will provide the final impetus, German artists will have the
'courage to be simple' without being ashamed of it, and all
'cubisms and futurisms' will be laughed to scorn—an aesthetic
judgement which echoes the Kaiser's well-known pronounce-
ments on modern art.

But what is modern art at such a time? What, indeed, is any
art? Bie begins his essay with the revealing statement that
'writing seems superfluous', all writing stands in need of justification before 'naked life'. It is a 'time for immediacy'. Meier-
Graefe, in much the same vein, requires artists to accept fully
the experience of war for the benefit of their art; no other
profession is as 'warlike' as art. He welcomes war as a simplifying experience: 'wir werden besser, weil wir einfacher werden'.[5]

The unanimity of all these intellectuals—critics of literature,
art, and theatre, historians and biographers, essayists and
philosophers—is striking. As Bie said, they were a chorus all
singing one song. They celebrated 1914 as a *grosse Zeit*, as a
return to community after long disharmony, as a chance to act

[5] *Die Neue Rundschau*, 1914, Band 2. Heimann, p. 1191; Saenger, p. 1257; Kerr,
p. 1308; Ludwig, p. 1324; Scheler, p. 1327; Bie, pp. 1307 f.; Meier-Graefe, p. 1576.

simply after thinking complicatedly, as an injection of primitive experience which would revitalize culture. The war, in these early mo ths, seemed to have cut a number of Gordian knots simultaneously. It was the solution to long-standing social division, with all classes apparently sharing a new solidarity. It created a truce in party politics, with even the *vaterlandslose Gesellen* of social democracy abandoning socialist international-ism and voting war credits, so that Wilhelm II could say he saw before him no longer parties, only Germans. It even seemed it might promise an end to decadence in art, the growth of a new heroic poetry to match the military heroism. Above all, it simplified issues, it was a *force majeure* which relieved the individual of the need for thought and decision.[6] It was, in the word Thomas Mann chose, a visitation (*Heimsuchung*).

The protracted realities of war proved these solutions illusory. What had seemed regeneration turned out to have been only a feverish euphoria—although the memory remained dear to those who shared the enthusiasm.[7] In the course of the war, suppressed social and political conflict was intensified, unanimity turned into dissonance again.[8] There was no trans-cending of decadence by a new heroic art. At most, the dated 1813 imagery in which poets had greeted the war (the *Neue*

[6] This is exactly expressed in the first of Rilke's *Fünf Gesänge* of 1914, which begins with the apostrophe to the 'unbelievable War-God'. Boys are described looking at the young man who is off to fight:

> ihn, der noch eben
> hundert Stimmen vernahm, unwissend, welche im Recht sei,
> wie erleichtert ihn jetzt der einige Ruf; denn *was*
> wäre nicht Willkür neben der frohen, neben der sicheren Not?
> Endlich ein Gott.

Rilke, *Sämtliche Werke*, II, Insel, 1956, p. 86.

[7] e.g. Stefan Zweig, a cosmopolitan before and after, wrote in his memoirs: 'Trotz allem Hass und Abscheu gegen den Krieg möchte ich die Erinnerung an diese ersten Tage in meinem Leben nicht missen.' (*Die Welt von Gestern*, Frankfurt, 1962, p. 207). And there is a clear allusion to the 'community' of 1914 in Rudolf Alexander Schröder's poem 'Das Vaterland 1925':

> Weiss keiner mehr, was gestern war,
> als einmal doch der Hader schwieg?
> Arm Vaterland, dir droht Gefahr
> vom Frieden wie vom Krieg.

Quoted from the anthology *Deutschland, Deutschland*, ed. Helmut Lamprecht, Bremen, 1969, p. 343.

[8] See, for example, the chapter 'War and Revolution' in Agatha Ramm, *Germany 1789–1919, A Political History*, London, 1967.

*Rundschau* again offers some choice examples, by Hauptmann, the once progressive Dehmel, and Stehr) was abandoned, just as in English poetry Rupert Brooke faded away in the harsh light of Owen's and Sassoon's and Rosenberg's trench visions. Yet for all its unreality it is important to understand the mood of 1914. The decisive shifts of stress in Thomas Mann's thinking which are already complete in his first war essay, the *Gedanken im Kriege* of September 1914, where the pattern is set for all his wartime thinking, must be understood as part of the 'chorus', sharing its common impulse: to become a simple member of the community at war. This impulse was brilliantly analysed by Robert Musil in the one *Rundschau* essay of those early months which achieves a degree of objectivity.[9] Mind (*Geist*), Musil argues, had been the affair of an oppositional, 'European' minority in Germany. All the worthwhile intellectual products of the last thirty years had been directed against the existing social order. Literature had been made by and about exceptions. But war was a threat to that common basis of national life of which people are not normally aware. Suddenly, they were aware of nothing else, their one function became again the 'elemental' one of 'defending the tribe'.

This acute insight needs supplementing. The opposition stance Musil describes was reinforced by the official exclusion of 'modern' artists from favour in Wilhelmine Germany.[10] This in turn fed the desire to be accepted and, it seems, a paradoxical urge to conform. When war came, the desired community could be gained at once—though nothing less than war could have made sudden conformity feasible. And even war could only make it feasible because of the traitor within the intellectuals' gates, the ubiquitous belief that art and intellect were decadent, the products of over-refinement and deficient vitality. Exponents and opponents of modern art shared this popular Darwinian theory of its origins. They differed in the valuation they placed on the end product, yet even for artists themselves it was an uphill struggle to maintain the value of

[9] Robert Musil, 'Europäertum, Krieg, Deutschtum', *Die Neue Rundschau*, 1914, Band 2, 1303 ff.

[10] Examples of official attitudes to art in Wilhelmine Germany, and evidence of the outsiders' covert desire for official recognition, are given in the chapter 'Geist und Kultur' of *Das Wilhelminische Deutschland*, ed. G. Kotowski et al., Fischer Bücherei, 1965. See also above, p. 124.

their refinement against the natural implications of terms like 'vitality' and 'decadence'. Here is surely a further reason why they so whole-heartedly joined, albeit sometimes with a kind of horror,[11] the warrior community. Against this background, Thomas Mann's conformism becomes, if not estimable, at least less uniquely perverse. So does the unreality of his account of the issues war involved. For the problems to which the war appeared, in 1914, to have brought solutions dictated the terms in which it would be discussed. Hence throughout his war essays Mann scarcely refers to recognizably political causation, but is concerned, in line with the 'ideas of 1914', with the conflict of cultural ideals and with high-flown generalizations about historical development. This makes his considerations very much those of a non-political man, however real in effect his national commitment may have been.

## II

*Gedanken im Kriege*, published in the November *Neue Rundschau*, takes as its starting-point the contrast of culture and civilization with which European polemicists had already made some play. *Entente* journalism had tried to divide Germans by distinguishing barbarous militarism and its agents from the true Germany of culture, with which civilized countries had no quarrel. The war was between 'civilization' and 'militarism'. Mann counters by denying that civilization is an overriding value for Germans. It is a matter of politics and the superficial rational ordering of society. The German soul is too profound to make it an ideal, having always given precedence to a non-political, humane, purely moral culture—although Mann is careful to claim that Germany's educational, technical, and social achievements are well up to the standard of her military efficiency, and thus at least as good as those of the *Entente*.

Nevertheless, there is no necessary link between culture and civilization. Indeed, Mann says, they are opposites. Culture is

---

[11] Kerr, whose article was revealingly entitled 'Aus dem Kriegsbuch eines Hirn-wesens', registers 'ein Gefühl des Abrückens von einer Menschengattung, die Besseres noch nicht gelernt hat, als mit solchen Mitteln [viz. war] hiesige Dinge zu ordnen' (loc. cit., p. 1308).

compatible with all kinds of horrors—oracles, magic, pederasty, human sacrifice, orgiastic cults, inquisition, witch-trials, etc.— by which civilization would be repelled; for civilization is Reason, Enlightenment, moderation, manners, scepticism, disintegration—Mind (*Geist*).[12] Both these lists are familiar. The second contains the things which were set up in important notes of 'Geist und Kunst'[13] as the ideals of literature. The 'horrors' list comes from a later note in the same manuscript which already doubted the connection between literary values and culture, but in a quizzical, musing tone. In *Gedanken im Kriege*, the tone has become hard and dogmatic.[14] It triumphantly declares that culture has nothing to do with these and finally subsumes them all under *Geist*, once more a term with which Thomas Mann had identified his striving. Now he spurns it. This is the first indication of his changed attitudes. His allegiance is now whole-heartedly on the side of 'Nature', not 'Mind'. It is in Nature, he says, that culture has its roots. The relationship of Mind to art is one of irrelevance. It is a common modern tendency but an error to confuse intellectualism with art. Art has its real origins in a 'deeper, darker, hotter world' of 'demonic' forces.

Against this background, the cementing of German unity is completed when Mann adds one more to the elemental forces with which culture has affinities: religion, sexual love, and now war. Art and war—the imagery in which Gustav von Aschenbach's disciplined life was evoked now returns, the analogy of martial action and artistic creation which served to link him with his Prussian background now links Mann implicitly with the General Staff. War and art, he declares, both depend on systematic organization, that quality in which above all others Germans took pride in 1914 as their lesson to Europe. Logistics and the leitmotiv are both forms of connection with rear areas. The 'popular literary antithesis' of *Bürger* and

---

[12] *Die Neue Rundschau*, 1914, Band 2, 1473.

[13] Cf. 'Geist und Kunst', N 20 and N 41.

[14] N 118 of 'Geist und Kunst' reads: 'Der Geist ist zwar solidarisch mit der Kultur, sofern Kultur der Gegensatz von Natur ist. Aber das ist sie ja nur in einem gewissen Sinne, und es gilt hier, sich über die Begriffe der Kultur und der Zivilisation zu verständigen . . .' The corresponding passage of *Gedanken im Kriege* reads: 'Zivilisation und Kultur sind nicht nur nicht ein und dasselbe, sondern sie sind Gegensätze, sie bilden eine der vielfältigen Erscheinungsformen des ewigen Weltgegensatzes und Widerspieles von Geist und Natur.'

*Künstler* (one more which Mann had made his own) is rejected in favour of that between soldier and civilian.

Point by point, the essay is a reversal of Mann's known positions. Inevitably he was aware it would seem so, and he provides a hint of the double-think which he was consciously adopting. He sees the antithesis of *Gedanken im Kriege* embodied in two figures, Voltaire and Frederick the Great. The one was the father of the Enlightenment and all anti-heroic civilization; the other was also an Enlightenment dilettante. But though he was Voltaire's friend, and though he was doubtless amused by Voltaire's polemic against war, Frederick had no qualms about invading Saxony.

*Friedrich und die grosse Koalition*, written in December 1914 and published in January and February 1915, elaborates the parallel between the summer of 1756 and the summer of 1914, first stated in the words 'Deutschland ist heute Friedrich der Grosse'.[15] But the King's dual nature, as Enlightenment philosopher and *Realpolitiker*, becomes increasingly a symbol not just for Germany but for Thomas Mann. The identification of Frederick and Germany extends only to the two invasions and Europe's reaction to them. The identification with Thomas Mann is more complete. Both thrust philosophic subtlety aside in the critical hour. When Frederick came to the throne, those who knew his enlightened interests expected the reign of Literature (x. 78 f.). They were disappointed. Intellectuals in 1914 expected to find Mann in their ranks. They were disappointed. In both cases, a 'secret instinct' proved stronger than Literature (x. 135). And the secret is laid bare in words which describe Frederick's attitude and Mann's: 'er fürchtete den Geist nicht, denn seine Liebe zu ihm ward aufgewogen durch seine Verachtung für ihn — sofern er machtlos war' (he had no fear of intellect, for his love of it was balanced by his contempt for it—in so far as it was powerless [x. 89]).

Thus Frederick, who had once been the subject for a novel because Mann then saw literature in a heroic light, now comes to embody Mann's rejection of literature and all it stands for.

In another minor essay Mann goes further still. Not content with his confirmation from history for Germany's actions in 1914, he invokes philosophy to justify all 'practical' overcoming

[15] *Gedanken im Kriege*, loc. cit., p. 1475.

of scruple, invokes Kant, of all people, the most rigorous of moralists and a cosmopolitan political thinker. Mann speaks of Kant's 'practical reason' as if that meant the ability to ignore one's own insights and pursue a course of action 'beyond scepticism',[16] an appeal to tradition which uses ignorance to back up sophistry. No wonder the rationalist intellectuals, those few who had not been caught up in the mass emotions of 1914, were appalled.

Wilhelm Herzog was the first to castigate Mann's 'demented doctrine of the German soul, decked out as literature',[17] the glib generalizations from ignorance, and especially Mann's readiness to confirm his countrymen in their already powerful prejudices. The same charge was made in the same month by Romain Rolland as part of his attack[18] on the war delirium of German intellectuals, and is implicit in all Rolland's war essays, which state the principle that attachments or passions should not be permitted to cloud the mind's judgements. Support for national causes endangered the cause of the spirit, leading to 'murderous words' which were more criminal than the murderous deeds of war, because they sowed the seeds of future wars. The proper task of the 'lay church' of intellectuals was to prepare a future peace by ensuring bitterness did not destroy cultural communication.[19] In short, the intellectual's right place was 'au-dessus de la mêlée'.

Mann was later to deny that Rolland raised himself above the mêlée at all. But Rolland's essays and wartime diaries demonstrate how scrupulously he tried to do so and to what an impressive degree he succeeded. It is true that he believed in the moral superiority of the *Entente*, but only because of German

[16] *An die Redaktion des 'Svenska Dagbladet'*, *Stockholm*, repr. in the collection of Mann's shorter war essays *Friedrich und die grosse Koalition*, Berlin, 1916, p. 124. The text reads: 'Bismarcks Positivismus, seine "Realpolitik", sein Reichsgebilde — das korrespondiert auf tiefe und charakteristische Art mit Kants praktischer Vernunft im Gegensatz zur "reinen", — deutsch ist der kategorische Imperativ jenseits der abgründigsten Skepsis.' In his list of 'books for the times', Mann describes Kant and Nietzsche as 'die Moralisten des deutschen "Militarismus", — ja, sie zeigen, dass das deutsche Soldatentum ein Soldatentum aus Moralität ist'. In *Der Zeitgeist*, 9 Nov. 1914.

[17] 'diese literarisch manikürte Irrlehre der deutschen Seele'. *Das Forum*, December 1914, p. 452.

[18] 'Les Idoles', in *Journal de Genève*, 4 Dec. 1914. Later in the collection of Rolland's war essays *Au-dessus de la mêlée*, Paris, 1915 (referred to henceforth as M).

[19] See M 61; M 7; M 93 and 109; M 127 f.

responsibility for starting the war. This is a long way from the German belief in the essential superiority of all things German. Rolland was critical of the *Entente* powers whenever they compromised their moral position, as when France and England connived at the Russian domination of minority peoples.[20] His diary records instances of French as well as German sophistries and cynicism[21] in defence of ruthlessness. He attacked Christians and socialists in France for betraying their supranational creeds (M 49, 52 f.) and he acknowledged the younger German critics of the war even though this meant giving up the satisfying image of an enemy uniformly evil. One seeks in vain for any parallel in Thomas Mann's war writings, public or private. These are epitomized by his argument that, however noble it may be to criticize one's own side or speak up for the other, Germany just happens to be right.[22] This is what Rolland meant when he spoke of the 'thick wall of certainty' separating Germany from the rest of Europe (M 89).

It was probably Rolland who set Mann off writing his major war book, the *Betrachtungen eines Unpolitischen*. The collection of essays *Au-dessus de la mêlée* appeared in October 1915. By 7 November Mann was well into his new project.[23] It occupied him for the rest of the war, to the virtual exclusion of work on *Der Zauberberg*. It was not completed till March 1918, and published the following October.

The *Betrachtungen* was to benefit, if that is the right word, from one further stimulus. In November 1915, Heinrich Mann's essay *Zola* was published in *Die Weissen Blätter*. Like Thomas's essay on Frederick the Great, it treated the present under a thin disguise.[24] Thomas had found his attitudes anticipated, confirmed, and symbolized by Frederick the Great's disregard for scruple. Heinrich felt a similar bond with Zola, who had begun

---

[20] Rolland, *Journal des années de guerre 1914–1919*, Paris, 1952, p. 450.

[21] e.g. *Journal*, pp. 453, 457.

[22] *Gedanken zum Kriege*, in the *Frankfurter Zeitung*, 1 Aug. 1915.

[23] Letter to Amann of that date (Br. A. 38). Mann's references to Rolland suggest that he read his essays, with the exception of the title-piece (cf. to Amann 21 Feb. 1915) for the first time in their book form (Br. A. 40, Br. i. 130).

[24] The use of historic figures for support was common in a war which was widely felt to be a conflict of cultures. Hofmannsthal, for example, made much of Prinz Eugen, and evolved a theory of the value of quasi-historical legend. Rolland had used both Frederick and Zola before the Mann brothers adopted them, as types of the German and French traditions. See M 15, 30.

to describe the downfall of the French Second Empire before that downfall actually occurred, and whose intervention in the Dreyfus affair crowned a life devoted to criticism of society. Zola's *J'accuse*, 'the rarely heard truth of the Mind about the State', thus stood for Heinrich Mann's indictment of German war-guilt and of the society which had led logically to it, Zola's exile for Heinrich Mann's isolation. Germany's war-fever lay behind his description of the blind anti-Dreyfusard nationalism, the French nation's 'relapse into a subhuman state', its 'sudden urge to cheer the sabre'.[25] Reference to the present was transparent. It was made explicit by the prophecy of a yet greater historical crisis than the Dreyfus case, and by the generalization that Reason is fated to yield periodically to the 'orgies of a complicated *naïveté*, the outbreaks of a deep and ancient anti-reason' (*WB* 1380). Equally clear was the reference to German intellectuals in what Heinrich Mann said about their French counterparts who exploited anti-Dreyfusard nationalism for their own ends. This passage must be examined in full. It seeks the origins of their opportunistic commitment in their literary past:

Man müsste sie sich ansehen, ob es nicht auch sonst schon die waren, die das Profitieren verstanden. Waren sie etwa Kämpfer? Oder lag es vielleicht in ihrer Art, was die Macht — die Macht der Menschen und der Dinge — herbeiführte, zum Besten zu wenden, und auch zu ihrem eigenen Besten? Wie, wenn man ihnen sagte, dass sie das Ungeheure, das jetzt Wirklichkeit ist, dass sie das Äusserste von Lüge und Schändlichkeit eigenhändig mit herbeigeführt haben, — da sie sich ja immer in feiner Weise zweifelnd verhielten gegen so grobe Begriffe wie Wahrheit und Gerechtigkeit. Wir fanden nichts daran, in der ästhetischen Duldsamkeit der friedlichen Zeiten. Ihr Talent wirkte modern, ihr Geschmack war oft der zarteste. Gaben sie sich pessimistisch, leugneten sie geistreich den Fortschritt und gar die Menschheit, indes es ihnen nie beikam, zu leugnen, was bestand und gefährlich war: wir sahen gewollte Paradoxe darin, verwöhnten Überdruss am Einfachen und Echten, keineswegs stichhaltig, weder vor ihrer eigenen Vernunft, noch vor den Ereignissen. Im äussersten Fall, nein, dies glaubten wir nicht, dass sie im äussersten Fall Verräter werden könnten am Geist, am Menschen. Jetzt sind sie es. Lieber als umzukehren und, es zurückbannend, hinzutreten vor ihr Volk, laufen sie mit seinen abscheulichsten Verführern neben ihm her und machen ihm Mut zu dem Unrecht, zu dem es verführt wird. Sie, die geistigen Mitläufer, sind schuldiger als selbst die Machthaber, die fälschen und das Recht brechen. Für die Machthaber bleibt das Unrecht, das sie tun, ein Unrecht; sie wenden nichts ein als ihr Interesse, das sie für das des Landes setzen. Ihr falschen Geistigen dreht Unrecht in Recht um, und gar in Sendung, wenn es durch eben das Volk geschieht, dessen Gewissen ihr sein solltet.

(It's worth looking at them just to see if they were not the ones who always had an eye to the main chance. Were they fighters at all? Or was it perhaps more in their line to take whatever Power—the power of men and the power of things—decreed, and make the best of it, make it serve their own best interests? What if we were to tell them that with their own hands they have brought about this monstrous thing that is now reality, this ultimate in lies and infamy —by the way they always maintained their subtle scepticism about such crude ideas as justice and truth. We did not give it a second thought, in the aesthetic tolerance of peaceful times. Their talent felt modern, their taste was often of the most delicate. If they took a pessimistic stance, ingeniously denying progress and even humanity, while it never occurred to them to deny the existing—and dangerous —order: we saw deliberate paradoxes in their attitude, a pampered weariness with things that were simple and genuine. It would never stand up against their own reason or against events. When it really came to it, no, we never believed that when it really came to it they could betray Mind, betray Man. Now they have. Sooner than face about and step in front of their people, forcing it back, they run along beside it with its most hideous seducers and encourage it in the injustice to which it is seduced. They, the intellectual timeservers, are more guilty even than the rulers who falsify and break the law. For the rulers, the injustice they perpetrate remains an injustice; their only defence is their interests, which they identify with the national interest. You false intellectuals turn injustice into justice, even into a mission, when it is perpetrated by the people whose conscience you ought by rights to be. [*WB* 1369f.])

There is much here that could apply to Thomas Mann, in particular to his fastidious reservations about 'crude ideas' like justice and truth and his presentation of Germany's struggle as the fulfilment of a mission.[26] Heinrich's essay also contained clear private allusions—to Thomas's characteristic ideas, to the

---

[26] The closing sentence of *Friedrich und die grosse Koalition* reads: 'Er musste Unrecht tun und ein Leben gegen den Gedanken führen, er durfte nicht Philosoph, sondern musste König sein, damit eines grossen Volkes Erdensendung sich erfülle'.

chronology of his career and the nature of his talent.[27] Even though the *Betrachtungen* project was well under way before Thomas set eyes on *Zola*,[28] it was these thrusts that more than anything else were to make his war book what it is. In substance Heinrich's essay only repeated what Rolland and Herzog had said, but the formulation was immensely more savage. Heinrich, despite his later disclaimers, set out to wound and succeeded. He became not just the avowed symbolic target[29] but the ever-present accuser. Thomas, who had originally come to Germany's defence against the onslaught of *Entente* propaganda, was now forced personally on to the defensive. Without Heinrich's intervention, he would not have written as much or in as bitter a tone or probed as deeply as he finally did. The very massiveness of the *Betrachtungen* indicates not so much the solidity of his case as the urgency of his need for self-justification *vis-à-vis* his brother.

## III

Thomas's brotherly sensitivity has its own history. The accusations in Heinrich's *Zola* were the sharpest expression yet of a deep-rooted disagreement between the brothers over art, its function, and its relation to society. Their personal relationship had long been delicate.[30] There had been skirmishes and an uneasy peace. Now the issues were brought into the open. Understood in the light of this private history, the charges against Thomas in the *Zola* essay take us to the heart of the *Betrachtungen*.

Sketching Zola's achievement on the eve of his entry into the Dreyfus affair, Heinrich calls him an 'intellectual' and defines the term. It does not mean merely 'one who loves the things of the mind', nor 'one who is professionally concerned with them'. Least of all does it include a certain kind of 'profound' mind: 'jene Tiefschwätzer . . . die gedankliche Stützen liefern für den

---

[27] By an apt irony, the page preceding Heinrich Mann's essay in *Die Weissen Blätter* carries a woodcut of Saint Sebastian, the figure Lublinski chose, and Thomas Mann accepted, as epitomizing his ethos.

[28] He borrowed a copy of *Die Weissen Blätter* in January 1916. Cf. Br. i. 124.

[29] The term 'Zivilisationsliterat' generalizes Heinrich's qualities but in no way conceals his identity, since he is repeatedly quoted verbatim.

[30] Cf. to Amann, 27 Aug. 1917 (Br. A. 58), 'zart seit Jahren'.

Ungeist; die sich einbilden, sie hätten Erkenntnisse, und jenseits aller Erkenntnisse könnten sie die Ruhmredner der ruchlosen Gewalt sein' (those mouthers of profundities . . . who provide ideas to prop up the mindless; who imagine that they have insights, and that beyond all their insights they can be the panegyrists of brutal power [*WB* 1356]). Insights alone do not make an intellectual, they must issue in action. The intellectual is the man who has the courage of his convictions in practice:

Keineswegs die selbstgenügsame Erkenntnis macht den geistigen Menschen aus, sondern die Leidenschaft: die Leidenschaft des Geistes, die das Leben rein und die Menschen menschlich will. Der Intellektuelle erkennt Vergeistigung nur an, wo Versittlichung erreicht ward. Er wäre nicht, der er ist, wenn er Geist sagte, ohne Kampf für ihn zu meinen.

(Not by any means self-sufficient intellectual insight makes the man of the spirit, but passion: the passion of the mind which desires to see life pure and men human. The intellectual recognizes spiritual quality only where some moral effect has been achieved. He would not be what he is if he said 'spirit' without meaning the struggle for it. [ibid.])

Even minds as great as Nietzsche and Ibsen finally failed to live up to this requirement: they doubted and turned away. The 'spirit' they served was only their own; they mistrusted other men.

This critique of self-sufficient and self-enjoying intellect is directed at Thomas Mann by the phrase 'jenseits aller Erkenntnisse'. Thomas was later to complain that in referring to action 'beyond all insights' Heinrich had taken advantage of a single phrase which was typical of the 'hasty earthworks' put up at the beginning of the war (xii. 189),[31] and that such a method of arguing was neither sporting nor intelligent. But it is, on the contrary, very acute. Heinrich knew the self-doubtings of an intellectual which are plain in Thomas's works from *Tonio Kröger* on, and had long suspected what they meant in real life. He was right to see the search for some form of involvement beyond intellectual scruple as his brother's central problem. The yearning for a rebirth of simplicity 'beyond insight' was a central theme of *Fiorenza*. When, in *Der Tod in Venedig*,

---

[31] The sentence is the one quoted above (p. 189 n. 16). Despite his objection, Thomas Mann stands by the view that this attitude was 'typically German'.

Thomas Mann used that work as part of Aschenbach's corpus, he singled out the phrase for such rebirth—'wiedergeborene Unbefangenheit'—as a clue to Aschenbach's later development. And what was the essence of that development? The 'profound decision of a master to deny knowledge, to reject it and pass over it with head raised, in so far as it is in the least calculated to lame, to discourage, to degrade the will, action, feeling and even passion' (viii. 454 f.). The idea of action 'beyond insight' was thus anything but a hasty wartime invention. It was an underlying impulse of Thomas's early work. It could be called self-transcendence, or equally self-betrayal.

Besides the evidence of Thomas's works, Heinrich knew of his brother's impulses and temptations by directer means. He had watched Thomas's development from their earliest days as literary unknowns, when they spent eighteen months together in Italy staking their small means on proving their talent. At that time they shared basic assumptions: a mistrust and mockery of the society they had grown up in,[32] an axiomatically critical view of 'Life' in all its manifestations. Years later, Thomas was to call this phase the 'absolute bohemianism of our youth', a condition made up of 'freedom and unreality'.[33] This formula implies that the condition could not last; freedom and unreality could only be starting-points, not objects of permanent loyalty. The question was, what kind of 'reality' would take their place?

For Heinrich, criticism of the social order had itself increasingly become the writer's contact with real life. To have any other might mean losing the 'bohemian freedom' which was essential to this function. Social integration was not compatible with literary integrity. Thomas on the other hand suffered through his social detachment. While working on *Tonio Kröger* in 1901 he wrote to Heinrich that 'literature is death', adding that the best thing it had to teach him was to 'view death as a possibility of attaining to its opposite, *Life*' (Br. H. 13 f.). The terms seem vague and metaphysical. But the forms in which they were soon to be realized must have struck Heinrich as crudely concrete, to the point of betraying the brothers' original principles.

[32] Cf. *Lebensabriss* (xi. 99) on Thomas's early 'Spott und Hohn über "das Ganze"'.
[33] In a speech marking Heinrich's sixtieth birthday, repr. in Br. H. (p. 126).

For there were signs that in Thomas criticism of life had been partly sour grapes and might yield to other pressures. It was perhaps merely jocular when he wrote, at the height of his happy relationship with Paul Ehrenberg, that if he still sat at his desk negating and ironizing it was only from habit (Br. H. 20). But later, when their sister Julia and her banker husband disapproved of Heinrich's too direct portrayal of Munich personages, Thomas took their side. He was married himself now, into a rich and cultured Jewish family; social considerations weighed more heavily than the rights of literature—despite the fact that at just this time he was claiming literature's absolute rights for himself in *Bilse und ich*. Since Heinrich's early letters are not preserved, we can only guess what he made of that, or of the circumstances surrounding Thomas's marriage itself. Thomas's letters at this period must have appeared an unmistakable translation of 'death as a means of Life' into 'literary success as a means to social arrival'. A long letter of February 1904 describes Thomas's introduction into the Pringsheim family and conveys his situation with perhaps more clarity than he realized. It begins with a warm acknowledgement of Heinrich's latest story, but modulates into wonderment at Heinrich's new liberalism, which Thomas finds 'remarkable' and 'still a little unlikely'. He wonders whether the change is a sign of maturity, and whether he himself will reach such a stage. The question is largely rhetorical, allowing this negative answer:

Fürs Erste verstehe ich wenig von 'Freiheit'. Sie ist für mich ein rein moralisch-geistiger Begriff, gleichbedeutend mit 'Ehrlichkeit'. (Einige Kritiker nennen es bei mir 'Herzenskälte'.) Aber für politische Freiheit habe ich gar kein Interesse. Die gewaltige russische Literatur ist doch unter einem ungeheuren Druck entstanden? Wäre vielleicht ohne diesen Druck garnicht entstanden? Was mindestens bewiese, dass der Kampf für die 'Freiheit' besser ist, als die Freiheit selbst. Was ist überhaupt 'Freiheit'? Schon weil für den Begriff so viel Blut geflossen ist, hat er für mich etwas unheimlich *Un*freies, etwas direkt Mittelalterliches. . . Aber ich kann da wohl nicht mitreden.

(For the present I don't make much of 'freedom'. For me it is a purely moral, intellectual concept, equivalent to 'honesty'. (Some critics call it my 'lack of warmth'.) But in political freedom I have no interest. The mighty literature of Russia surely grew up under

an enormous pressure? Would perhaps not have grown up at all
without that pressure? Which would at least prove that the struggle
for 'freedom' is better than freedom itself. What is 'freedom' anyway?
The mere fact that so much blood has flowed for the concept gives it,
for me, something disquietingly *un*free, something positively medieval
. . . But I suppose I'm not an authority. [Br. H. 25 f.])

The interesting point here, aside from the precariousness of
Thomas's logic, is his insistence that intellectual freedom can
be self-sufficient, an abstract quality unimpaired by any social
substructure. This belief would clearly justify any degree of
social integration, and perhaps already rationalizes Thomas's
own in advance. Perhaps he is aware that this is how his
silent interlocutor will take it; when he goes on to describe the
dazzling circles he has begun to move in and confesses he
has thoughts of marrying into them, he offers this apologia to
the still free Bohemian:

Es ist müssig zu fragen, ob es mein 'Glück' sein würde. Trachte
ich nach dem Glück? Ich trachte — nach dem Leben; und *damit*
wahrscheinlich 'nach meinem Werke'. Ferner: Ich fürchte mich
nicht vor dem Reichtum . . . Auch ist alles Vergängliche mir nur ein
Gleichnis.

(It is idle to ask, whether it would be my happiness. Am I striving
for happiness? I am striving—after Life; and *thereby* probably after
my work. Further: I am not afraid of riches . . . Moreover everything transitory is for me only a symbol. [Br. H. 28])

The quotations here, from Nietzsche and Goethe,[34] are meant
to reassure Heinrich that Thomas's decision will be taken with
due regard to literary conscience. Yet the reassurance must
have been offset by the tone in which Thomas reported his
social advances—reported them, noticeably, with little after-
phrases to indicate a proper aloofness: his 'absorbing exertions'
to settle into his new family and 'adapt (as far as that is possible)';
he is 'managing quite nicely, so it seems' (Br. H. 31 f.). The
same letter contains some general reflections on 'happiness'
which try paradoxically to interpret 'happiness' as something
problematical, more moral than strict detachment, a duty
rather than a surrender:

Nie habe ich das Glück für etwas Leichtes und Heiteres gehalten,

---

[34] Respectively to *Also sprach Zarathustra*, the opening of Part 4 (Schlechta ii. 477);
and to *Faust* II, closing lines.

sondern stets für etwas so Ernstes, Schweres und Strenges wie das Leben selbst — und vielleicht *meine* ich das Leben selbst. Ich habe es mir nicht 'gewonnen', es ist mir nicht 'zugefallen', — ich habe mich ihm *unterzogen*: aus einer Art Pflichtgefühl, einer Art von Moral, einem mir eingeborenen Imperativ, den ich, da er ein Zug vom Schreibtisch *weg* ist, lange als eine Form von Liederlichkeit fürchtete, den ich aber mit der Zeit doch als etwas Sittliches anzuerkennen gelernt habe. Das 'Glück' ist ein Dienst — das Gegenteil davon ist ungleich bequemer. . .

(I have never considered happiness something easy and serene, but always as something as serious, difficult, and austere as Life itself —and perhaps it is Life itself that I *mean*. I haven't 'won' it, it hasn't 'fallen to my lot', I have *submitted* myself to it: from a kind of feeling of duty, a kind of morality, an innate imperative, which for a long time I feared as a form of indiscipline, since it drew me *away* from my desk, but which I have learnt with time to recognize as something ethical after all. 'Happiness' is service—its opposite is out of all proportion more comfortable . . . [Br. H. 30 f.])[35]

Literary liberty, it is implied, will remain unimpaired. But it would be appreciated if Heinrich would write the accepted few lines to his future sister-in-law—it is actually already a little late (p. 33).

Then from the honeymoon (Heinrich was not at the wedding, but their mother and younger brother 'at least' were there, and 'kept the family's end up') there comes a long letter marking the full acceptance of social integration after the long unreality of the Bohemian condition:

. . . ich wunderte mich den ganzen Tag, was ich da im wirklichen Leben angerichtet hatte, ordentlich wie ein Mann . . . Und alles das ist doch eigentlich noch immer die Folge davon, dass wir uns damals in Palestrina eine Art Gipper-Roman ausdachten . . . Aber nun ist es wahrhaftig dahin gekommen, dass ich von einem 'Roman meines Lebens' sprechen kann . . .

[35] This is the theme that was to be elaborated in the treatment of Klaus Heinrich's marriage to Imma Spoelmann, in *Königliche Hoheit*. An interesting document of the phase of 'adaptation' is the short story *Beim Propheten*, based on a visit by Thomas Mann and Katja Pringsheim's mother to a private reading by Ludwig Derleth. The closing page brings together the yearnings familiar from *Tonio Kröger* ('ein wenig Gefühl, Sehnsucht, Liebe'), and the rejection of loneliness and freedom as conditions for genius. The last line of the story, when the mother has hinted that the young writer's attentions to her daughter are welcomed, is: 'Er hatte ein gewisses Verhältnis zum Leben.' (He had a certain relationship to life.)

(. . . I could hardly grasp all day long what it was I had really set going, in real life, positively like a man[36]. . . . And all this is really still the consequence of our plans in those Palestrina days for a satirical novel. But now things have truly reached the point where I can speak of the 'novel of my life' . . . [Br. H. 34])

Thomas Mann speaks of having a conscience about these luxury hotels ('bei diesem Schlaraffenleben'—an appeasing reference to the title of one of Heinrich's social satires) and says how he yearns for a little more 'monastic peace and spirituality' (Br. H. 34). Yet it must have seemed to Heinrich that these were the last wavings of a drowning man. Was the real point of their literary apprenticeship, and of Thomas's immense achievement in *Buddenbrooks*, to have paved the way for social acceptance and a good marriage? What was now left, in these letters where uneasy self-justification alternated with hardly contained triumph and tactlessness,[37] of the incorruptible perceptiveness of *Buddenbrooks*? Was 'irony' reserved for literature?

This is the background to the brothers' war attitudes: to Heinrich's accusation of social opportunism and to Thomas's bitter self-defence. Whether Heinrich anticipated Thomas's *Verrat am Geist* is not certain. In *Zola*, we saw, he professed never to have believed it would happen. In a later letter, he claimed that Thomas's choice of side came as less of a surprise to him than to Thomas himself (Br. H. 111). It seems most likely that Heinrich was waiting uneasily to see. Long before the war he had formulated his criticism of Germany's artists and intellectuals which was to recur in *Zola*. Why did they maintain the radical separation of intellectual and practical matters which resulted in social stagnation, whereas the French from Rousseau onwards had provided armies of fighters for intellectual causes? German thinking went to the very limits of pure reason and into the nothingness beyond, yet left the social realm to be ruled by crude power. 'Ideas' were an elaborate game safely above reality. Lies and injustice were accepted desperately for fear of the abyss that might lurk behind truth. German intellectuals'

---

[36] Or conceivably: 'like a Mann'.

[37] Particularly the account of how Thomas Mann met Heinrich's publisher Langen at the Pringsheims', how Langen—for whom Thomas had once worked in the offices of *Simplicissimus*—behaved 'almost obsequiously', and how Thomas assured him that Heinrich was worth hanging on to because *one* day he *would* have a big success (Br. H. 28 f.) There is no trace of irony in this.

mistrust of the mind was at root a lack of self-confidence. Whatever the reasons for their non-involvement in the cause of reason—success-worship, ambition, vanity, fear of isolation, reaction against the nihilism of the free intellect, the 'perverse abdication of the all-too-knowing'—their eminence turned into a cult of the self, they were tempted to make up to the ruling caste and to 'betray Mind'. The people had no value for them except as a symbol for their elevated experiences, the real world had only a walking-on part in their dramas.[38]

These were clearly so many caps designed to fit Thomas.[39] But there was never at this stage an open declaration. Not till 1914 did Thomas answer his brother's question, abandon the 'lay church' for the national camp, and convince Heinrich that for all his talents he had been only an amusing parasite (*unterhaltsamer Schmarotzer*) on the society he had chosen to join. Where Aschenbach's abandonment of criticism had led to personal disaster and the orgies of Dionysus, Thomas Mann joined in the far greater 'orgies of a complicated *naïveté*', the 'outbreaks of a deep and ancient anti-reason'. 1914 was his rebirth into community.[40]

So Heinrich saw things. What was Thomas's view? Heinrich's message that the life of intellect must legitimize itself in action struck him as direct and unsceptical to the point of simple-mindedness. He probably always found Heinrich's social satire excessive. In 1907 he wrote of *Zwischen den Rassen* that it was

> das gerechteste, erfahrenste, mildeste, *freieste* Deiner Werke. Hier ist keine Tendenz, keine Beschränktheit, keine Verherrlichung und Verhöhnung, kein Trumpfen auf irgend etwas und keine Verachtung, keine Parteinahme in geistigen, moralischen, aesthetischen Dingen, — sondern Allseitigkeit, Erkenntnis und Kunst.

(the most just, the most experienced, the mildest, the *freest* of your works. Here there is no political message, no limitedness, no crying up and shouting down, no harping on anything, no contempt, no

---

[38] From the essay *Geist und Tat*, first published in 1910.
[39] Especially the last, which is surely an allusion to Thomas's prince-allegory *Königliche Hoheit* of the year before.
[40] In *Gedanken im Kriege* Thomas Mann epitomizes the mood in which Germany welcomed the war in the words of a young poet: 'Ich fühlte mich wie neugeboren' (p. 1473).

taking of sides in intellectual, moral, aesthetic matters—but rather universality, insight, and art [Br. H. 60])

The praise implies criticism of Heinrich's usual approach. It invokes the traditional German separation of art from all practical matters; the 'insights' art yields are self-sufficient. It gave vent to feelings which Thomas could only express fully in private notes which speak of Heinrich's political stance as verging on triviality and childishness.[41] There were no doubt less diplomatic exchanges in conversation, with Thomas defending the society Heinrich exaggeratedly attacked. As he says in the *Betrachtungen*, where other Germans learned what it felt like to be the outcasts of world opinion in August 1914, he was already at home in this situation, the 'Zustand der Abwehr und notgedrungenen national-geistigen Selbstbehauptung'. For he had lived for a long time

in brüderlicher Nähe einer bedeutenden und im naiv französischen Stil aggressiven Geistigkeit . . ., die längst mit schneidend unduldsamster Schärfe darauf bestanden hatte, dass man Deutschland, ausgerechnet Deutschland! als den moralischen Schandfleck der Menschenerde erkenne oder auf den Anspruch verzichte, ein Mann des Gedankens zu heissen.

(in fraternal proximity to a major intellectual, aggressive in the naive French style . . . who had long insisted with the most cutting and hostile intolerance that Germany, yes, just Germany! must be recognized as the moral abomination of the world—or one must give up all claim to be considered a man of the spirit [xii. 151 f.])

Thomas, it emerges, was aware all along of the caps Heinrich had prepared to fit him, and long before the war he had worked out his own rationale in conscious opposition to (and with a touch of contempt for) Heinrich's.

## IV

In 1914 each accused the other of opportunism—wrongly, to the extent that their attitudes had been long preparing. Heinrich said Thomas had sold out to militarism in order to be

[41] Cf. N 62 of 'Geist und Kunst', which gives a definition of the *Literat*: 'Bewusstheit, höchste psychologische Reizbarkeit, Reinheit, Güte, Humanität, was, bei politischer Teilnahme zu einem fast trivialen, fast kindlichen Radikalismus und Demokratismus führen kann. Heinrich.'

accepted as a 'national poet'.[42] Thomas said Heinrich was merely joining in the already massive chorus of recrimination against Germany. Their accusations are important because they make it clear that each thought he was defending the weaker side, the minority cause. Heinrich stood out for morality against the German majority's war fever, Thomas for isolated Germany against the weight of Europe. If it is respectable to set oneself against superior forces, both brothers' conscious motivation can be respected.

The helplessness of Germany, the unliterary land, under the onslaught of literate *Entente* journalism is the starting-point of Thomas's *Betrachtungen eines Unpolitischen*. It makes him see the war *à la* Fichte as only the latest stage of a long German struggle against Western domination, earlier phases of which were Arminius's defeat of the Roman legions, the medieval emperors' struggles with the papacy, Luther's revolt against Rome, the War of Liberation in 1813, and the Franco-Prussian War of 1870 (xii. 52). These historical references do not conceal the fact that Thomas Mann is now taking a positive view of things he had till recently criticized. The German 'lack of literature' had been a failing and a social danger, indicating a lack of sensitivity and scepticism. Now it is a noble innocence, the sign of an essentially higher culture than the facile verbalizing of the enemy. The word *Literat*, which Thomas Mann had tried to rescue from hostile misunderstanding, he now uses himself as a term of abuse.

He realized he must seem inconsistent, and his explanation is revealing. Anyone, he says, who underwent the school of Nietzsche and the experience of Wagner was bound to have a critical view of things German. But the very subtlety of the issues involved was bound to make such a person impatient of *crude* criticism of Germany, much as a connoisseur of Wagner who finally rejects him, for higher reasons, will be impatient of ignorant abuse of Wagner (xii. 78).[43]

[42] 'Durch Streberei Nationaldichter werden für ein halbes Menschenalter, wenn der Atem so lange aushält' (*WB* 1370 f.). Heinrich was probably exploiting his inside knowledge of how bitterly Thomas had always resented the *Dichter/Schriftsteller* dichotomy in the German view of literature.

[43] But it is also striking that Wagner is now accepted uncritically as a positive authority. That *Not* (necessity) was Wagner's favourite word is taken as sufficient reason to glorify it as a heroic concept; and in the chapter 'Bürgerlichkeit' the most provokingly reactionary passages from Wagner and Schopenhauer are quoted

Yet the charge that he had 'betrayed mind' still rankles, and will throughout the book. Mann is driven to prove the legitimacy of his 1914 patriotism, and of the 'unsimple man's becoming simple', as he wrote of Kleist. After a glance at the pro-*Entente* German writer and his ignoble mastery of words, in the chapter 'Der Zivilisationsliterat', he examines his own past work to see in what ways he contributed himself to Germany's *Literarisierung* and what reservations he had about it. In this discussion, entitled 'Einkehr', the seeker after the roots of his patriotism begins to get warm. He touches on Nietzsche's 'Leben' concept and on his own mode of appropriating it and sums up *Tonio Kröger* in words which already suggest a parallel to his war commitment, as 'eine verliebte Bejahung alles dessen, was nicht Geist und Kunst, was unschuldig, gesund, anständig-unproblematisch und rein vom Geist ist' (an enamoured affirmation of all that is not mind and art but innocent, healthy, decently unproblematical, and pure of any element of mind). This attitude he calls *sentimentalisch genug* (xii. 91).[44]

Mann gets warmer still towards the end of the chapter, where he mentions his minor essay *Der Literat* which, as recently as 1913, seemed to place him firmly on the side of the critical *littérateurs* he now opposes.[45] Mann rehearses from it the familiar points about the *littérateur*'s purity, insight, resistance to corruption, his educative and moralizing mission, the necessary link between good style and good actions—all this only to jeer at it in the words 'and so forth', and 'what a sermon!' (xii. 99 f.). Impossible though it is to talk himself out of what he then wrote, he quotes in extenuation words taken, he says, from his notes[46] of that time. They assert that the *Literat* is mistaken in

with approval. Of the critical view of Wagner in 'Geist und Kunst' there is hardly a trace.

[44] This parallels Mann's statement on his motives for writing *Gedanken im Kriege*. In December 1914 he wrote to Dehmel, who had volunteered for field service despite his age (he was twelve years older than Mann), that shame at staying at home had driven him to put his pen at the service of the German cause. When one stays at home, he says, one's relationship to war easily becomes *etwas sentimentalisch* (Br. i. 114 f.). Tonio Kröger at forty has given way to the longing to be one with Hans Hansen, now in uniform.

[45] It was one of two pieces which appeared in Wilhelm Herzog's journal *März*— a suggestively revolutionary name, as Mann remarks. They are reprinted in vol. x of the collected works as one essay under the title *Der Künstler und der Literat*.

[46] Not apparently preserved, certainly not as part of the 'Geist und Kunst' manuscript from which the ideas in *Der Literat* were drawn.

believing only *Geist* creates decency; on the contrary, there is decency only where there is no *Geist*. There are two sides to every thought, and he now regrets having printed the one he did. In fact, the essay in question was based on the 'Geist und Kunst' materials, and we already know how much contradictory statement and change they reveal. Mann's embarrassment over *Der Literat* resulted from using those materials, at a time when he had evolved beyond them. By 1913, his views on the *Literat* as put in the more positive earlier notes of 'Geist und Kunst' had been, to say the least, modified. On the other hand, his more critical views had not yet seen the light of day. Thus he had gone on maintaining old attitudes in public while preparing new ones in secret. When war precipitated his choice between the incompatible views which still to some extent coexisted, his change was bound to seem sudden, and the more shocking.

Mann's hint that there are two sides to every idea, and that commitment is therefore rash, is part of the central argument of his book: that all commitment involves oversimplification, and that political commitment is incompatible with art, which sees all things from all sides. Consequently it is Heinrich who is guilty of 'betraying mind'. His extremism (*Radikalismus*) lacks the saving grace of irony just as his art always exaggerated German reality, and just as his humanitarianism lacks true brotherly feeling—witness his vitriolic[47] attack in the Zola essay. Heinrich stands charged with distortion in art and doctrinaire narrowness in politics.

Thomas Mann then generalizes his distaste for doctrinaire democratic politics, claiming it is the typical attitude of the German burgher and of the true German artist.[48] This is the crucial and most dubious step in his whole argument. All the historical and constitutional reasons for the German tradition of non-involvement in politics are ignored. Abstention from politics is presented as an essential quality of the nation, praise-

47 Mann calls Heinrich's gibe in the opening paragraph of *Zola* 'ein kleiner Guss Schwefelsäure, en passant dem Nächsten ins Angesicht' (xii. 190).
48 Adopting Georg Lukács's conception of the German burgher-artist from the essay on Storm entitled 'Bürgerlichkeit oder l'art pour l'art' in *Die Seele und die Formen*. But Lukács's argument would have placed Mann among the modern ascetics like Flaubert, not among the old-style craftsmen of the nineteenth century like Storm and Meyer.

worthy for the same reason that the avoidance of one-sidedness is praiseworthy in an artist. So Thomas Mann's artistic ideal, evolved in opposition to his own more 'critical' self and in opposition to Heinrich's art, is identified with the character of the German nation. His support for the national cause thereby becomes consistent.

Yet was this support not itself a form of commitment? Yes, he has to admit it was. But it was justifiable by reason of that German 'many-sidedness' he has propounded. Commitment to such non-commitment cancelled itself out, became the opposite of extreme. Germany represented the broader human ideal, German beliefs, attitudes, and qualities made the nation nothing short of humanity in essence, Germans were the only truly supranational people (xii. 207), the unliterary, unextreme *Volk des Lebens* (xii. 83 f.). Where England was crude Commerce and France shallow Rationalism, Germany was Humanity. Given such a belief in the 'grotesque personification of the nations' (xii. 150)—by which Mann meant that in 1914 they really became these caricatures, not that propagandists imposed them—his commitment was not narrow politics. The nation he belonged to just happened to be ideal.

Of course the argument is naïve. Nevertheless it is worth looking further at the nature of Mann's commitment, this time in the terms he used of his brother's: *geistesgeschichtlich* terms which prove equally relevant to himself.

In attacking Heinrich, Thomas Mann does not say that he was of too limited an intelligence to rise above political commitment, or that he was unacquainted with complexity and subtlety, but rather that he turned his back on them; that to become a politician in the style Heinrich chose meant 'simplifying' himself. His 'resolute humanitarian love' was the deliberate self-stultification of an essentially aristocratic, artistic nature. As an artist, Heinrich must or should have known that Life (Thomas elsewhere calls it 'the heroic poem of life') was not that simple. Far from being a true *freier Geist* in the Nietzschean mould, Heinrich has simply borrowed the externals; if he ever had any inkling of the self-critical rigour of Nietzsche's tragic life, he has now transcended it—'er hat es "überwunden"' (xii. 311).

This is the key idea in Thomas's attack on his brother: that

Heinrich was trying a Nietzschean intellectual tactic—the transcending of a painful experience or a disturbing insight— at a debased level; that he was a Nietzschean nihilist looking for a pretext to escape from his nihilism; that the whole structure of his political argument was a cheap evasion of deeper truths he was really aware of. For to a true artist politics could only be a surrogate for the values which would be needed to transcend nihilism effectively. Where the true artist holds to his 'aestheticism', that grasp of many-sided life and abstention from judgement which is Thomas Mann's stated ideal, Heinrich has escaped into facile morality. His self-righteous 'virtue' is called an *Überwinderin* of aestheticism (xii. 389) and of the truly moral self-doubt which aestheticism entails. Politics is defined as the opposite of aestheticism and an escape from it (xii. 222). Is it not braver and more moral, asks Thomas Mann, to do without such facile beliefs? to live with dignity and composure in a godless world rather than escape from the profound and empty gaze of the sphinx into a blind faith in democracy? (xii. 543).

Heinrich's humanitarianism led to such things as protest against the horrors of war. The tough-minded aesthete with his grasp of many-faceted reality found this trivial. An artist must be capable of relapse into the primitive (xii. 150). He refused to condemn war as such; it is one of the great facts of life, and it would be a degenerate humanity which was not worthy of war. War has a positive function, which is to hold together national communities against 'rationalistic disintegration' (xii. 116). He refuses to exaggerate the sufferings war causes or to sentimentalize war-wounds, which are not necessarily all that bad, or to worry about Nurse Cavell's execution. He is sure that the mass experience in the trenches does not make the individual share any worse. And has it not been for many whose lives were narrow a form of spiritual liberation? Do they not write to him about how, in lulls or convalescence, they have discovered literature, his own works included? Such a mitigating circumstance only reinforces the essential rightness of war: the terrible aspects of life must be accepted, to accept them is the true artist's aestheticism, to believe they cannot be legitimately criticized is part of the true artist's critical scepticism.

This last is the *salto mortale* by which Mann can still claim all his old functions. He is still the 'born protestant' (xii. 491)—

protesting against the facile extremes of other intellectuals' protest; still the 'unreliable bohemian'—unreliable now not in the eyes of state and society, but of those who would organize artists and intellectuals to some practical purpose; still the moral and intellectual purist—criticizing now not reality itself, but others' attempts to purify it. Even doubt, once a progressive, subversive principle, has become conservative—*bürgerlicher Zweifel*, in Mann's paradoxical formulation, which one could almost translate as 'conformist doubt'. It questions all attempts to change the present forms of reality because such attempts are unworthy of artists.

For art is a metaphysical activity, and the only solutions that matter in the human sphere are metaphysical, not social. A concern to change social institutions is superficial and un-German. If art does have any social effect, this is an unintended and inessential bonus, for it should be 'essentially' critical—of Man, of Life, not of their particular forms. The less specific the reference, the more 'moral' the art, a principle whose logical conclusion is that *the* moral art is music (xii. 317).

Thus Mann's message at every point is acceptance: of the political *status quo*, because one should leave things to the experts and because it is wrong to meddle rationalistically with 'natural' forces;[49] of major catastrophes because they are part of the natural order of things; of social forms because only the metaphysical matters. The question is unavoidable: were not Thomas Mann's acceptances, behind the elaborate rationalizing theory about 'doubt' and 'scepticism', in fact a commitment sprung from the motives he imputed to his brother? Was he not fulfilling precisely Heinrich's description of the German intellectuals who supported existing power because they were sick of the process of critical rejection—'aus Ekel am Nihilismus'? Was he not rescuing himself from the morass of relativism by attachment to the national cause and was this not his own form of 'transcending' and (in another word frequently used in Thomas's argument) 'resoluteness'?[50] Was his whole argument

[49] On the need to leave politics to the *Fachmänner*, see xii. 149; on the 'natural' forms of politics, xii. 126; and on the contrast *à la* Burke between organic growth and rational intervention in society, xii. 307 f.

[50] The phrase Heinrich used for 'resolute humanitarian love' was *entschlossene Menschenliebe. Entschlossenheit* therefore becomes an alternative label for the attempt to 'transcend' aesthetic scruple and subtlety. But it also echoes the description in

not an intricate apology for his own escape from nihilism? And was it not precisely this that led him to couch his criticism of Heinrich's commitment in such terms? For the basis of all his critical insights, as he says in the *Betrachtungen* text itself, had always been introspection (xii. 296). And Thomas Mann has to step carefully indeed when he tries to show that *Heinrich's* present attitudes are critically foreshadowed in *his* works (*Fiorenza*, *Der Tod in Venedig*) but without recalling that such things as Savonarola's or Aschenbach's efforts to transcend nihilism originally related to impulses and temptations of his own.[51]

This is a *geistesgeschichtlich* view of Thomas's attitude of acceptance. There is also evidence in the *Betrachtungen* for a social view, in line with Heinrich's charge that integration affected his brother's judgement.

Take Thomas's attempt to reconcile the realm of culture with the state, and thereby to justify the artist's solidarity with the nation in time of crisis. He argues that just as Man is a metaphysical and not merely a social being, so too the people at large is not just society—an empirical political mass—but also a 'mythical personality', a 'metaphysical nation'. This personality is made up of the characteristics that distinguish it from other nations and is what is meant by its 'culture'. And in so far as the state embodies this culture and is the 'crystallization of the national life', it is itself a metaphysical entity and has interests which the artist shares and can therefore legitimately support (247 f.).

This argument leaves a gap between the metaphysical and the real state. How far did Wilhelm II's Germany truly express German culture? Of course, its non-political society seemed to match its non-political art; but this is not an adequate answer. For the state positively to express the national culture, the ideals of art—its breadth of vision, its understandingness, its

*Der Tod in Venedig* of Aschenbach's rejection of scruple—the 'tiefen Entschluss des Meister gewordenen Mannes, das Wissen zu leugnen' etc. (viii. 454 f.).

[51] Thus the idea from *Fiorenza* of 'morality becoming possible again' is applied to Heinrich's rebirth of political certainty, with the implication that at the time of writing the theme was purely an external observation of Thomas Mann's (xii. 95, 382).

Similarly, *Der Tod in Venedig* is interpreted as an experiment with the overcoming of decadence, but with the suggestion that it was Heinrich's type of activism that Aschenbach toyed with and that Thomas Mann was all along judiciously aware that overcoming decadence was impossible (xii. 517).

justice, its tolerance, all qualities which Mann associates with art in his argument—would have to appear demonstrably in society. The state would have to have absorbed these cultivating influences. Thomas Mann actually states that this has happened. Recalling Nietzsche's fierce attacks on the Bismarckian Reich, he declares that they simply no longer apply. Something has happened since Nietzsche's time to make the Reich a different place. And this something is the literary movement in which the young Thomas Mann participated. The essence of the 'revolutionary cultural epoch' around the turn of the century was resistance to the *status quo*, criticism of the state Nietzsche had scorned. This critical movement began a rebirth of idealism which is still in progress (xii. 239). In other words, society has absorbed the contribution of art, it has been transformed sufficiently for the artist to see his nation as 'metaphysical' and declare his solidarity with it. However merely practical an arrangement the modern state may have become, it still has a significant remnant of such dignity—'ein beträchtlicher Rest von metaphysischer Würde und Bedeutung' (xii. 252).

Yet only very few years before, in the ruminations of 'Geist und Kunst', Mann had doubted whether literature had made any impression on Germany. He had seen all the work still to be done. It had been an 'unliterary land' in a negative sense. Now, no longer committed to the kind of values he then upheld, he can contrive both to idealize that unliterary quality and to feel that Germany has somehow taken in the lessons of her recent culture. A little beneath the surface of these rationalizations, there surely lies the simple feeling that there cannot be much wrong with a condition of society which has allowed his own successful establishment. In *this* sense it is true that the 'revolutionary cultural epoch' of the turn of the century had been absorbed by society. The erstwhile extremists, like Gerhart Hauptmann, had become ornaments of the nation not because the social message of works like *Die Weber* had been taken, but because Naturalism was safely part of literary history and its exponents safely beyond the age of protest. War showed whether establishment was compatible with a critical spirit. The established men, the 'Aschenbachs', did not hesitate.[52]

---

[52] Rolland pointed out acutely that it was the older writers who, in all belligerent countries, were the most zealous knights of the pen. 'C'est un fait constaté

More important than any demonstration that the state was
'metaphysical' was the practical consideration, which Mann
also puts forward, that the state was a necessary framework
within which to unfold one's talents (xii. 252). Social status
entailed commitment. But it must not be thought that Mann's abdication of criticism was purely an instinctive thing, which needs to be probed
for psychologically. On the contrary, he states it as a principle.
In time of crisis, he says, self-criticism would be miserable
weakness. Self-knowledge must be self-affirmation. The demands
of truth are nothing beside those of life.[53] Yet if criticism has no
place in times of crisis, when has it a place? Can one ever be
wrong when it matters? Is intellectual integrity not thereby
confined to an area where it can have no practical effect? And
was this not Heinrich Mann's other charge, against German
culture generally, as well as against his brother, that in Germany
the life of the mind was axiomatically unreal: 'ein luftiges
Gespenst — und drunten trottet plump das Leben weiter', as he
put it in *Geist und Tat?* What Heinrich stated as an accusation,
Thomas affirms as a maxim. They are agreed about the facts
of German practice, just as Thomas and Romain Rolland were
agreed when they both declared that Germany in 1914 acted in
the tradition of Frederick the Great. But the agreement, in both
cases, gives the measure of the gulf between German thinking
and what can fairly be called the normal assumptions of
European culture because, in the valuations these men placed
on their identical observations, they were in different worlds.

dans tous les pays que partout les sentiments les plus exaltés se sont manifestés chez
les littérateurs ayant passé il mezzo del cammno.' M 193 f. The famous Declaration
of ninety-three intellectuals, Hauptmann among them, that Germany was not
guilty of causing war, or violating Belgian neutrality, or razing Louvain, is given
in Wilhelm Herzog, *Menschen, denen ich begegnete,* pp. 190 f. For an account of
what happened at Louvain, see the chapter 'The Flames of Louvain' in Barbara
Tuchmann, *August 1914,* London, 1962.

[53] '. . . und da in Notzeiten Selbstverneinung erbärmliche Schwäche wäre; da
in solchen Zeiten Selbsterkenntnis und Selbstbehauptung eins sind, eins sein
müssen; so ist kein Schritt mehr vom Bewusstsein seiner selbst zum Selbstbewusst-
sein, zur kriegerischen Freude an sich selbst, zum unpersönlichen Stolz, zum
"Patriotismus"' (xii. 150). '"Ist denn die Wahrheit ein Argument, — wenn es das
Leben gilt?" Diese Frage ist die Formel der Ironie' (xii. 568).

V

What did Thomas Mann's principles lead to in practice? We have seen him defy the charge of bias, arguing that, however estimable self-criticism might be, Germany just happened to be in the right; that her human substance was ideal; and that this ideal was reflected in her culture and the form of the state. His belief in these happy coincidences may seem suspect, but it was tenable all the time the writer knew of nothing to contradict it. Perhaps it makes him appear, for a one-time realistic social novelist, naïve; but nothing worse. It is when contrary evidence did present itself that his principles—the rejection of any self-criticism which is not also self-affirmation, and of 'truth' in the name of 'Life'—appear simply disreputable. In the course of his attack on Heinrich for seeing only German faults and closing his eyes to French and English shortcomings, he imagines the answer that self-criticism comes first; a patriot should look to his own country rather than criticize others. Mann flatly declares that, beside England's treatment of Ireland, he can find nothing to criticize: 'Aber ich finde nichts! Ich finde bei meiner Seele Seligkeit in deutscher Geschichte nichts, was sich dem Traktament Irlands durch England an die Seite stellen liesse'; he denies that the German annexations of Schleswig-Holstein and Alsace-Lorraine are comparable—for reasons which he says are sound (*stichhaltig*) but which he does not give (xii. 357). This already hints at an imperviousness to unfavourable evidence.

Two further instances are instructive. Both concern the question of Germany's guilt in starting the war. In 1914, Mann denied it. Wilhelm Herzog quickly pointed out[54] that Bethmann-Hollweg had admitted it himself in the Reichstag, on that day which also saw the famous 'scrap of paper' phrase. For Thomas Mann in the *Betrachtungen*, nothing was easier than to accommodate the Chancellor's admission and make positive capital out of it. Impolitic as it certainly was, he extols it as a stroke of genuine German unpoliticality, as 'beautiful' and 'appropriate to the suprapolitical, mighty ethical moment' (xii. 150).

The second and more important instance is Mann's reaction

54 *Gedanken im Kriege*, loc. cit., p. 1479. Herzog, *Forum* i. 9, Munich, 1914, 453.

to the Lichnowsky memorandum. On 6 February 1918 Mann
read the manuscript of this celebrated document[55] which was to
make such a stir when published the following month. In it, the
last German ambassador in London gave an inside account of
the diplomatic exchanges which led up to the war. He asserted
Germany's responsibility for war unequivocally and in particular presented a clear view, which other documents have
since confirmed,[56] of how Germany supported Austria and even
egged her on to follow a hard line against Serbia, thereby provoking Russian involvement. He painted a sympathetic picture
of Sir Edward Grey, up till then regarded by Germans as the
arch-villain in the plot to encircle Germany, and showed that
Grey had been untiring in his efforts to resolve the crisis peace-
fully. The policy-makers in Berlin appear as bent on provocation, ignoring both the overtures of foreign diplomats and the
reports of their own representatives when these conflicted with
their set views and set policy. Not surprisingly, the English
translation of the memorandum was sometimes entitled
'Germany's War Guilt', and it was claimed that it presented
'evidence which in normal times would convince even the
German nation that the whole basis of their beliefs [viz. in
Germany's blamelessness and the anti-German conspiracy of
the *Entente*] was a structure of deliberate falsehood'.[57]

When Mann read this account, his *Betrachtungen* text contained claims that Germany had restrained Austria while
Britain had done nothing to restrain the Russian government
(xii. 186). What effect did reading Lichnowsky have? Not the
one which might have been expected. Mann adds a reference
to Lichnowsky at the opening of the already completed chapter
'Einiges über Menschlichkeit' only to declare that the sympathetic human picture of Grey, with his little joke about how
clever the German children were to speak that difficult language, is irrelevant to the real issues. These are the impersonal

[55] Letter to Ernst Bertram of that date (Br. B. 58).

[56] See, for example, the exchanges between Moltke and Conrad von Hötzendorf quoted in the discussion of Hötzendorf which is part of Sir Lewis Namier's
'Men who floundered into the War', *Vanished Supremacies*, London, 1958.

[57] By Gilbert Murray, in: Prince Lichnowsky, *My Mission to London 1912–1914*,
Cassell, 1918, Introduction, p. x. For the full German text, including passages
Lichnowsky toned down in the final draft, see J. C. G. Röhl, *Zwei deutsche Fürsten
zur Kriegsschuldfrage*, Düsseldorf, 1971.

operations of power politics independent of morality, the blind processes whereby the status of nations changes, the international law of the jungle.[58] Against this background of forces vaster than individuals and nations, and not susceptible of moral judgement, Lichnowsky must be reckoned (Mann says) a mere *Aufklärer*, an Enlightenment man. His appeal to human sympathies is aimed at weakening the German people's belief in England's war-guilt, it will serve only 'das eigene Volk zu verwirren, zu entmutigen und zu lähmen' (xii. 429). Such insights—Mann does not even mention the detailed factual allegations in the memorandum which conflict with his own in the *Betrachtungen*—are a dangerous form of knowledge, which must be ignored.[59]

In thus deliberately choosing to ignore knowledge, Mann is close to the spirit of Aschenbach—how close, the wording of his text precisely shows. Aschenbach too resolved to reject knowledge 'insofern es den *Willen*, die *Tat*, das *Gefühl* und selbst die *Leidenschaft* zu *lähmen*, zu *entmutigen*, zu entwürdigen geeignet ist' (viii. 454 f.). The wording confirms the link between Aschenbach's spiritual dilemma and solution and Thomas Mann's. Mann's final critical view of Aschenbach in *Der Tod in Venedig* did not prevent his following in Aschenbach's footsteps.

It seems clear then that Mann's main intellectual effort went into keeping new evidence from upsetting his position. He was caught in the net of his own emphatic allegiance. So Bethmann-Hollweg's admission was turned to illustrate his argument. Lichnowsky's detailed evidence made Mann withdraw to a height from which historical forces appeared so impersonal as to cancel out the very idea of personal responsibility in politicians and nations. If the first impulse of the *verirrter Bürger* to rejoin the community in 1914 was understandable, his later efforts to maintain it were increasingly dubious.

Is it perhaps an anachronistic fallacy to expect him to have thought or written otherwise than he did? Was anyone in that

[58] '. . . mechanische, aussermenschliche, aussermoralische und also weder gut noch böse zu nennende Gesetze' (xii. 431).
[59] We can see the stages by which Mann ignored it. The letter to Bertram records that Lichnowsky's account has altered his view of Grey ('ich muss sagen, das bringt mich ihm näher'). Later he must have recognized that such sympathy was 'dangerous', and added the warning to the nearly finished *Betrachtungen*.

war free from the impulse to say 'my country, right or wrong' and then rationalize it as best he could? Mann was certainly typical of a generation whose attitudes may now seem alien. Yet there were exceptions—Hermann Hesse, for example, who remained genuinely 'au-dessus de la mêlée', from his first appeal in the language of Beethoven to his last in the language of Nietzsche.[60] More specifically, we know that to some writers the Lichnowsky revelations came as a profound shock and altered their attitudes. Ernst Toller, for example, was against the war because unlike the pen-warriors he had fought in it. But he had never stopped to consider the question of responsibility for the war, and had not consciously doubted the official version. He felt the force of Lichnowsky's evidence. Without becoming a starry-eyed supporter of the *Entente*, he drew the conclusion that, even if there was guilt on all sides, criticism and opposition must begin at home. 'Wir leben in Deutschland, wer die Wahrheit erkannt hat, muss in seinem Land beginnen'.[61] This was surely a proper position for a man of integrity. Thomas Mann had all along rejected it expressly. He had accepted gladly enough any self-criticism by the enemy—Romain Rolland's account of French society in *Jean-Christophe*, for instance—but felt no obligation to emulate it. Always sure of his and his nation's rightness and essential superiority, he was always able to put a favourable interpretation on any fact he did not prefer to ignore. The *Betrachtungen* is a piece of intellectual juggling, in the sense Romain Rolland gave to that term.[62]

## VI

It was common for *Entente* writers during the war to blame German traditions of thought for Germany's actions, as an

---

[60] 'O Freunde, nicht diese Töne!' of September 1914. The words are Beethoven's introduction of the choral text in the final movement of the Ninth Symphony, and that text itself is Schiller's 'An die Freude', with its call to human brotherhood. 'Zarathustras Wiederkehr' of 1919 calls on Germans to replace their old idols and hatreds by a mature acceptance of their fate and responsibility. Both pieces are reprinted in Hesse, *Krieg und Frieden*, Berlin, 1949.

[61] Ernst Toller, *Eine Jugend in Deutschland*, in Toller, *Prosa, Briefe, Dramen, Gedichte*, Hamburg, 1961, p. 82.

[62] See M 135 f.: 'Donnez à un intellectuel n'importe quel idéal et n'importe quelle mauvaise passion, il trouvera toujours moyen de les ajuster ensemble . . . Un intellectuel habile est un prestidigitateur de la pensée.'

alternative to separating German militarism from German culture. A favoured grouping was Nietzsche and Treitschke with General von Bernhardi, whose book on Germany and the next war was notorious for its frank anticipation of a conflict with England. The German response was to deride the incongruousness of that trio, and to deny that Treitschke was any longer or that Bernhardi ever had been an influence on German thought.[63] Nevertheless it was not in itself ridiculous to seek the roots of a nation's acts in its intellectual traditions, especially in the popular form in which these take effect beyond the circles of academic specialists. Bernhardi did make use of quotations from Treitschke, and his epigraph was a famous celebration of war from Nietzsche's *Zarathustra*.[64] Recent historians have returned to the idea that politicians' behaviour in 1914 was affected by underlying attitudes characteristic of their particular cultures.[65] The virtual unanimity of Germans at the outbreak of war and the prompt formulation of their feelings into the 'ideas of 1914' support this approach. That mystique has been traced to the school of historians dominated by Ranke's example,[66] which is accurate as far as it goes but can be taken further by seeing Ranke himself as only one of the thinkers who had created an optimistic belief in the rational processes of history which were bringing Germany to world-power status, by what means did not much matter.[67]

That such ideas had spread beyond specialist circles is shown

[63] Friedrich Meinecke, 'Kultur, Machtpolitik und Militarismus', in *Deutschland und der Weltkrieg*, ed. O. Hintze *et al.*, Leipzig and Berlin, 1915, p. 622. Bernhardi's book ran through six impressions totalling 6,000 copies between spring 1912 and February 1913.

[64] 'Der Krieg und der Mut haben mehr grosse Dinge getan, als die Nächstenliebe. Nicht euer Mitleiden, sondern eure Tapferkeit rettete bisher die Verunglückten. "Was ist gut?" fragt ihr. Tapfer sein ist gut.' 'Die Reden Zarathustras: Vom Krieg und Kriegsvolke' (Schlechta ii. 312).

[65] Most particularly James Joll in a stimulating inaugural lecture, '1914. The Unspoken Assumptions', London, 1968. Tuchman, op. cit., p. 33, writes that 'a hundred years of German philosophy went into the making of this decision' [viz. to violate Belgian neutrality]. Ernst Toller saw the connection clearly: 'Die Frage der Kriegsschuld ist nicht nur eine Frage der Kriegsschuldigen, die Herrschenden sind verstrickt in das feinmaschige Netz der Interessen, Ehrbegriffe, Moralwerte der Gesellschaft'. Toller, loc. cit.      [66] Fritz Fischer, op. cit., pp. 155 f.

[67] Cf. Friedrich Meinecke on the optimistic pre-war mood which resulted from a century of German historical theory and rising national status. Meinecke, *Die Idee der Staatsräson*, 3. Auflage, Munich, 1963, p. 482.

not just by the case of Bernhardi. Acquiescence in the amorality of political action and unquestioning belief in the 'rights' of a rising nation—the main pillars of historicist doctrine—are found repeatedly in the effusions of 1914. This unanimity, which helps to account for the glad acceptance of war in Germany and for the relative lack of public criticism over the invasion of Belgium, in practice lessens the problem of tracing the channels by which 'a hundred years of German philosophy' affected German action and response. Friedrich Meinecke, who was himself deeply marked by the historicist tradition and still in his *Staatsräson* of 1924 partly inclined to be its apologist, had no doubt of the reality or the direction of its influence. He was sure that Hegel's philosophy of history had been a strong element in the movement for German unification from the outset, countering its liberal tendencies by an emphasis on national power; that its effect had been to blunt moral feeling and make light of the excesses of power politics; and that Germany's ambitions for power had joined with Hegelian theory to open a gulf between her and Western Europe. Even while defending Treitschke against the use anti-German propaganda had made of his name, Meinecke granted that he led countless individuals who wanted a simple view of politics to overrate naked power at the expense of morality.[68]

Meinecke does not trace the spread of these ideas in detail. But it is plain they needed little simplifying or corrupting to produce the results observable in 1914. For example, Bernhardi's *Realpolitik* was not a phenomenon of the lunatic fringe. It was as easily derived in theory from German intellectual traditions as it was typical in practice of *alldeutsch* thinking.[69] Nor was there a flourishing rival philosophy of politics to complicate the formation of opinion. Kant's Enlightenment cosmopolitanism might never have been.[70] Add to all this the fact that ideas were never more 'in the air' than in the epidemic atmosphere of 1914, and it is evident that the nicer techniques of intellectual history are not called for.

[68] Meinecke, op. cit., respectively pp. 421 f., 432 f., 461, 468.

[69] Cf. Imanuel Geiss (ed.), *July 1914*, 1967, p. 39.

[70] Treitschke, in glorifying war, slated theories of 'eternal peace' but without mentioning their German proponent. He attributed them to French writers only. See Klaus Schröter, ' "Eideshelfer" Thomas Manns 1914—18', in: Schröter, *Literatur und Zeitgeschichte*, Mainz, 1970, pp. 59 f.

In fact, to trace individual influences on a writer at this time may falsify the picture of that crisis. Thomas Mann was in no mood to be influenced by new intellectual discoveries or to follow original arguments. His reading as he describes it was a hasty quest for support, for 'autoritäre Stützen für sein Gefühl' (xii. 281). He felt 'tempestuous gratitude' when he read Dostoyevsky's slavophil defence of 'loving community' against 'Westernizing politics'; it offered welcome confirmation of his own views. 'Exclamation-marks of profoundest assent' fell thickly in the margins (xii. 521 f.).

Thus, if there are echoes of Treitschke's central ideas in Mann's war writings,[71] they are not signs of an influence in the conventional sense. One could as easily find echoes of Hegel— in the idea of a metaphysical state and its identification with national culture, or in the denial of the individual's right to criticize the state of which he is part, or in the idea of Germany's historical mission, or in the small change of conservative rhetoric; and echoes of Ranke in Mann's view of the mechanisms of macro-politics, which recalls the God's-eye-view of *Die grossen Mächte*, or in his idea of German society as essentially different, or his preference for an organic patriotic state which needs no institutional guarantees, or his feeling for the mysterious German something which preceded and dictated particular social forms, all ideas anticipated in Ranke's *Politisches Gespräch*. Even Mann's analogizing, which makes so much of Frederick the Great, recalls Ranke's response to the Franco-Prussian war, the declaration that Germany was fighting Louis XIV.[72] But none of this makes Mann properly speaking a Hegelian or a Rankean. He was rehearsing a popular catechism in chorus with many others.

The catechism had two other well-known elements, once more almost impossible to trace exactly. One was popular Darwinism,[73] the other popular Nietzscheanism. Both in practice reinforced the amorality of historicism, improperly enough in

---

[71] Ibid., pp. 47 ff.
[72] Quoted by David Hackett Fischer, *Historians' Fallacies*, London, 1971, p. 250.
[73] e.g. Thomas Mann's idea that the 'function' of war was to hold together a community against the forces of rationalistic dissolution, or Musil's statement that 1914 forced the individual back into his 'elemental function of protecting the tribe', quoted above. Joll, op. cit., p. 18, quotes a choice example from Conrad von Hötzendorf's memoirs.

the first case, since Darwin had in no sense morally justified the natural processes he described. Nietzsche's case has ambiguities about which purists would argue, but the fact is that his saving subtleties went unheeded, his spiritual aims were ignored, and his ideas were absorbed in a simplified form which bore limited relation to his thinking. Thus Meinecke's wartime argument against the Nietzsche–Treitschke–Bernhardi cliché was all too sanguine. He claimed that, if Nietzsche had misled some weak minds into moral anarchy and megalomania, he had also sharpened Germans' moral judgement by his merciless criticism of conventional hypocrisy.[74] But how weak this influence had been is clear precisely from the case of Thomas Mann, a real connoisseur of Nietzsche in whom the impulse to 'transcend' such critical attitudes easily won out and left the way clear for him to become a 'popular' Nietzschean. For all the self-critical use he makes of Nietzsche in the *Betrachtungen*, he might have been one of that younger generation which 'had Nietzsche's results in them instinctively without needing to read him'.[75]

As a result it is often difficult to distinguish what is Nietzsche in the hotchpotch of Darwinism, historicism, and vitalism. The acceptance of war as a 'great fact of life', not to be criticized, might echo passages of Nietzsche like the one Bernhardi chose as his epigraph; or it might be acquiescence in a 'Darwinian' law of the jungle; or again it might be Hegelian shoulder-shrugging at the necessity of breaking eggs to make the omelette of History.[76] But a number of prominent ideas in the *Betrach-tungen* are drawn directly from a particular text of Nietzsche's, and it is illuminating to see what happens to them in the process. In April 1916, i.e. at an early stage in the writing of his book, Mann told Paul Amann that the one piece of Nietzsche he had reread, apart from much browsing, was the section 'Völker und Vaterländer' from *Jenseits von Gut und Böse* (Br. A. 43). This discussion of Germany in the context of European culture

[74] In *Deutschland und der Weltkrieg*, p. 622.
[75] 'Geist und Kunst', N 103.
[76] Meinecke's summary of popular assumptions of the period in his chapter on Treitschke reads: '. . . die sittliche Rechtfertigung des Sieges der Starken über die Schwachen konnte nun auch von solchen, die den tiefen sittlichen Ernst und zugleich die geistige Weite Treitschkes nicht mehr hatten, leicht gemissbraucht und mit Darwinistischem Naturalismus versetzt und vergröbert werden, — erst recht als die Nietzschesche Lehre vom Übermenschen hinzukam', *Staatsräson* p. 477. This comes close to reinstating the Nietzsche–Treitschke–Bernhardi trinity.

clearly provided Mann with stimulus. Nietzsche enthuses over Wagner's *Meistersinger* overture, just as Mann writes a set-piece evocation of his youthful emotions on hearing Wagner played before a partly hostile Italian audience.[77] Nietzsche discusses German 'profundity', as Mann was to do, and he speaks of the element of the barbaric in Wagner's art as the thing that helped secure its success among the culturally more refined French.

But Nietzsche puts all these statements in critical perspective. His *Meistersinger* enthusiasm is at once qualified as a 'relapse into old loves and narrownesses', a 'national excitation' such as good Europeans are still prone to. Later Nietzsche says that when great men become patriotic, it is as a temporary rest from their better selves. Similarly, German profundity is not just extolled, but declared a euphemism for 'unformedness'; Germans have great potential, but it has not yet taken firm shape. And the barbarism of Wagner is likewise of value only as a promise for the future. Germans are a people of the day before yesterday and the day after tomorrow. They have no realized present. The new Reich, with its aspirations to 'big politics' and its appeal to 'blood and iron' are emphatically a wrong answer to the question of how to give form to this German potential.[78]

In Mann's text, the basic ideas are there but the critical perspective is abandoned. Nietzsche is shorn of his reservations and thus becomes an authority of about the subtlety of Paul de Lagarde, whom Mann actually links with Nietzsche and Wagner as the 'great Germans' (xii. 276). German profundity and capacity for the primitive are taken simply as positive qualities, the political order which resulted from Bismarckian 'big politics' is accepted, and Nietzsche's criticism of the Reich is declared out of date. Nationalism has narrowed the horizon and purged away all irony. Mann's fall from the level of his intellectual master is evident.

Yet his replacement of the critical Nietzsche by a simpler, assertive, vitalist Nietzsche does eventually lead to valid insights into his own position and its place in intellectual history.

[77] xii. 80. Mann at this point sees the war as a struggle between 'the spirit of the Lohengrin prelude and international elegant society'.

[78] On *Meistersinger*, § 240; on the 'relapse', § 241; on patriotism as a 'rest from themselves', § 256; on German profundity, § 244; on the barbarism in Wagner's music, § 256; on 'grosse Politik', § 254.

Reflecting on his new position, in the *Vorrede*, he draws conclusions about the character of nineteenth-century thought which provide, at last, the proper context for his wartime attitudes.

In case the body of the book has not made it clear, he asks once more what he truly is. His answer is, a typical man of the nineteenth century, understood in the way Nietzsche once sketched it by contrast with the eighteenth. According to this formulation, the eighteenth century's humanism was a kind of wishful thinking which attempted to forget what was really known about man in order to pursue Utopian aims. It listened to the voice of Reason and the Heart rather than the truth about human nature. Nineteenth-century thinkers on the other hand tended to bow to realities, to be fatalistic, and thereby to liberate themselves from the 'domination of ideals'.

This 'realistic' attitude (Mann links its cultural exponents at once with Bismarck's anti-ideological *Realpolitik*) was the decisive legacy he himself received from the century whose last twenty-five years he lived through. Once again he quotes the episode of Hanno at school. Does it not dismiss the revolt of the exceptional, artistic nature against ordinary brutal life as decadent?[79] And he takes Nietzsche himself as an example of the self-denial of Mind in favour of Life, no longer just a fatalistic but an enthusiastic self-subjection to 'power'. Of this self-subjection, he says, his own work is a watered-down, ironic form, where 'Life' is not the brutal vitality of Renaissance heroes larger than life, but the pleasant normality of the Ordinary, untouched by Mind, which the representative of Mind can only half-heartedly try to convert, knowing in advance the vainness of the attempt.[80]

If the idea of a writer's spiritual background has any validity, this is surely as good an account as one could wish of Thomas Mann's. It stops short of actually saying that his own patriotism was itself a 'self-subjection to power' *à la* Nietzsche—Mann wishes only to make the negative point that a 'realistic' outlook kept him from following a radical political line like Heinrich's. But the connection is obvious. Mann's references to Hegel are similarly in place. Hegel and Nietzsche were eventually at

[79] Cf. xii. 575, where he similarly suggests that the school and its Prussianized ethos are in their way at least as 'right' as Hanno.
[80] This discussion xii. 21–6.

one, despite Nietzsche's early onslaughts on Hegel, in rejecting all forms of idealistic moral criticism, whether of historical processes and the state (Hegel), or of Man's vital basis and spontaneous acts (Nietzsche). Between them, these virtually exhaust the possibilities. The human mind is reduced to the status of a quibbling parasite.

In stressing the nineteenth century's 'realism' in that passage, Nietzsche was not arguing his own case alone. There is something of this attitude in all the major thinkers of the century. But it does have an alternative form which neither his nor Mann's account allows for, namely a recognition of harsh truths which still leaves open the question of how men are to act on their knowledge. In other words, an unfatalistic realism. Georg Büchner, Darwin himself, and at least the younger Marx are examples of this attitude. So is the younger Nietzsche, the author of the essays on history and on Schopenhauer. All these refuse to allow realities, however inescapable as *fact*, to determine their choice of *values*. This is an important alternative in its own right. It is also relevant to Thomas Mann because he was later to make it the foundation of his social and political thought, recognizing that the rejection of rational ideals because they do not correspond to 'realities' rests on an elementary confusion.

But in 1918 he was content to place himself in the anti-rational tradition. Perhaps this was a necessary first step towards freeing himself from it, for it meant he had grasped the principle which lay behind his war thinking. Typically, he grasped it in philosophical, not in social terms. But at least he was on the verge of realizing that traditions, for all the reassurance and sense of community they afford, can also make a 'freier Geist' into a 'gebundener Geist'.[81]

---

[80] Nietzsche, *Menschliches, Allzumenschliches*, Band 1, § 226 (Schlechta i. 585 f.). This does not exhaust the contexts in which Thomas Mann appears typical of general trends. Fritz Ringer's *The Decline of the Mandarins*, Harvard University Press, 1969, shows many of the leading German ideas on 'culture', 'civilization', and the factors differentiating Germans from all Western nations as the response of a social group, which derived its status in a pre-industrial country from its non-utilitarian cultivation, to the pressures of change in an increasingly technical and mass political society. Ringer's subject is the German academic community between 1890 and 1933, but the relevance of his discussion to Thomas Mann is no less striking for that.

## VII

If finally we return to the detail of Mann's war writings, we find that 'realism' in the ordinary empirical sense is what they lack. His assertions of fact and his generalizations have a marked, sometimes grotesque, unreality. Even in the most considered piece, the *Betrachtungen*, we learn such things as: that the war originated in German disgust with English and French ideas; that it was an intervention by the Bismarckian Reich to oppose the domination of Europe by literature; that all Europe was equally responsible for the war, but only Germany could accept her responsibility nobly, thanks to her superior culture; that she would, at an advanced stage of hostilities, at once withdraw from France if only the other nations of Europe would 'let her live'; that the world outside Germany was already totally democratized; that the failures of Germany's diplomats in 1914 were an index of their higher human qualities; that their error had been to mislead the world into thinking that Germany was unprepared for war; that sabre-rattling adventurers' wars were in practice not possible under the German social and political system and that there had never been any dominance of the military (*Säbelherrschaft*) in Germany; that the French national character as such had greater potential for hatred than the German, and had been morally degraded by war, whereas the German character had never appeared as more beautiful or more clearly deserving of mastery in Europe; that only a German victory could secure European peace because Germans were the only truly supranational people.

These propositions need no discussing, they are the propaganda clichés of the day. They are interesting only as evidence that so fastidious a writer as Thomas Mann could let his thinking be dominated by street-corner dogmas[82] to the point where they impaired his grasp of realities. And grasp of realities is a relevant criterion for judging a writer who purports to be writing about the world as it is. In this respect too, Mann's war essays are a pointer to the direction his work had been taking, a corollary of his aesthetic self-absorption.

[82] Literally. Oskar Bie, in his *Rundschau* article quoted above, refers to some of the typical 1914 antitheses between Germany and her enemies and says: 'Wir wollen diese Worte, die auf allen Plakaten stehen, getrost wiederholen' (loc. cit., p. 1306).

Heinrich Mann is the obvious comparison. We saw that the brothers brought identical charges against each other—of opportunism, of escaping from nihilism into easy allegiance. Which of them was in the right objectively, i.e. regardless of motivation, must be a matter of whose vision of Germany and Europe was nearer the truth. Heinrich undoubtedly was the greater realist. He saw a Germany of ambitions and illusions, of power and conformism, with no system of political or moral answerability. Whatever Thomas might say against him—that he idealized a France he never visited, or that he revelled in satiric viciousness for its own sake—his picture of Germany is closer to historical truth than his brother's. *Der Untertan*, allowing for the hectic colour of satire, is a description of Wilhelmine realities; the *Betrachtungen* is the record of an accommodation with them, based partly on wishful thinking and self-deception. Thomas's German Utopia was remote from what counted in 1914: the mechanics by which decisions were taken, the psychology which formed them and which accepted them. Where hard political causation was concerned, Thomas was, as Heinrich said, ignorant: 'unwissend über sie wie der Letzte' (*WB* 1371).

Thomas's first public critic, Herzog, made this point. Need a *poet* who wished to raise his voice in politics first have studied the relevant documents—the Blue Books, White Books, etc.? Perhaps not—but then he might at least refrain from sweeping judgements on national character.[83]

Romain Rolland similarly pointed out that intellectuals were prone to confuse ideas with realities. Working always in the realm of abstractions, which are only a convenient shorthand, they risked making them into oppressive forces and subordinating real things to them.[84]

The same criticism lay behind the opening of Heinrich's *Zola* which so wounded Thomas:

Der Schriftsteller, dem es bestimmt war, unter allen das grösste Mass von Wirklichkeit zu umfassen, hat lange nur geträumt und geschwärmt. Sache derer, die früh vertrocknen sollen, ist es, schon zu Anfang ihrer zwanzig Jahre bewusst und weltgerecht hinzutreten. Ein Schöpfer wird spät Mann.

[83] *Das Forum* i, p. 453.     [84] M 145 ff.

(The writer who was one day to encompass the greatest measure of reality of any was for long an enthusiastic dreamer. It is for those who are fated to dry up early to make their bow, self-aware and groomed for greatness, when they are scarcely into their twenties. A creator comes to manhood late.)[85]

This implies that Thomas Mann's brilliant early achievement *Buddenbrooks*, was a fluke of immaturity. If he has done nothing comparable since (here once more Heinrich exploits his inside knowledge of his brother's creative problems)[86] then this is because the precocious correspondence with reality of that first work has not since been consolidated.

The most radical form of the criticism comes in a letter Heinrich sketched in 1918 when Thomas had rejected his attempt at reconciliation. Starting from the extremely self-involved terms in which he knew Thomas saw things (an impression which the *Betrachtungen*, not yet published, would amply confirm), he says that Thomas is fundamentally unable to make contact with real people and events outside himself. So intense is his self-concern, so absorbed is he in his inner struggles that he cannot credit the spiritual reality of other people. They merely have the walking-on parts in his drama. Even major events in the outside world are important only for the way they bear on these inner concerns.[87] One reason why Thomas turned away Heinrich's overtures was his feeling that it was easy for Heinrich to condescend now, in his hour of triumph—for in 1918 the war was a very different one from those days of the successful German swing through Belgium. Triumph? Heinrich asks. Triumph at what? Europe in ruins and ten million slaughtered? What kind of man could be triumphant to have that as his justification? He is not the man, he says, to tailor the misery and death of peoples to fit his intellectual interests. Even if some improvement in the world should come of this war, it will taste bitter.[88]

The letter was never sent. Had it been, the brothers' eventual reconciliation would have been harder, for it is a perceptive

---

[85] *WB* 1312.

[86] Cf. e.g. the letter to Heinrich of 8 Nov. 1913, Br. H. 104: 'Ich bin ausgedient, glaube ich, und hätte wahrscheinlich nie Schriftsteller werden dürfen.'

[87] Thomas Mann speaks in the *Betrachtungen* of the way history has chosen to mark the turning-point of his reaching forty.

[88] Br. H. 117 f.

indictment of what resulted, in a broader social and human context, from the aesthetic Thomas had developed in the years leading up to the war. External realities had grown increasingly remote from intensely experienced private concerns, and were drawn into the works which stated those concerns as mere material, drained of independent existence and value, not imaginatively penetrated but acquired and manipulated.

At the end of that sketched letter Heinrich looks to Thomas's eventual return to realities: 'Du wirst, will Gott es, noch einmal 40 Jahre Zeit haben, Dich zu prüfen . . . Die Stunde kommt, ich will es hoffen, in der Du die Menschen erblickst, nicht Schatten, und dann auch mich.' (You will have, God willing, another forty years to examine yourself . . . The hour will come, I sincerely hope, when you will discern people, not shadows, and then I shall be among them). It is an accurate prophecy, not just in the span of years it predicts. Thomas Mann was indeed to continue his self-examination, which now included the new experiences of war; and increasingly he would seek realities with which to replace the shadows of the war years.

# Education

Man ändert hier seine Begriffe.[1]

JOACHIM ZIEMSSEN

## I

*Der Zauberberg* is Thomas Mann's most complex creation. It is the summa of his life, thought, and technical achievement to the age of fifty. It is spiritual autobiography, confession and apologia, an intricate allegory, a kind of historical novel, an analysis of Man and a declaration of principle for practical humanism. In appearance it is a parody of the German *Bildungsroman*,[2] the novel of education in which everything—characters, action, and material environment—acts primarily to form the hero's character. In reality it is a *Bildungsroman* in good earnest.

This is not a contradiction. Parody and playfulness result almost inevitably when an old literary formula is reused by a self-conscious modern writer. But in *Der Zauberberg* the playfulness is superficial, it is the ironist's gesture of sophistication which leaves him free to use the form he needs. The meeting of recurrent needs from the storehouse of its possibilities is the benevolent function of literary tradition.

The writer's need is not, however, abstractly literary. He did not, that is, choose to exploit this most traditional of German forms simply as a means to make more art. To no literary form is the purely aesthetic approach less adequate than to the *Bildungsroman*. The great examples in the genre—Goethe's *Wilhelm Meister*, Keller's *Der grüne Heinrich*—are records of a growth in their authors' understanding of life intimately linked with their own personal history. The development they achieved and especially the price they were aware of having paid for

---

[1] 'A man changes his ideas here' (iii. 16).
[2] Cf. to Ernst Fischer, 25 May 1926: 'Schon die Erneuerung des deutschen Bildungsromans auf Grund und im Zeichen der Tuberkulose ist eine Parodie' (Br. i. 257).

it compelled the literary record. So it was with Thomas Mann. *Der Zauberberg* is, as he said, a fragment of a greater whole, his life's work, indeed of the life and personality themselves.[3] True, it also aspires to the timelessness and self-sufficient perfection of art (ibid.). But these qualities and the serenity they imply are themselves part of the achievement which the novel records. The breadth of vision it contains was hard won, the aesthetic freedom with which it treats ideologies rests on Mann's own progress beyond them, not on the indifference and powerlessness of ideology as such. Hence to say that 'the ideologies . . . mean nothing as far as Thomas Mann's own beliefs are concerned' is to make the novel too trivial, too easy. They mean what our past involvements mean to us. To speak of them as 'intellectual pawns . . . to be pushed about for the sake of the composition'[4] ignores the question which is vital to the reality of a *Bildungsroman*, namely, why this composition demanded to be composed in the first place.

In the very first place, *Der Zauberberg* was not a *Bildungsroman* at all. To understand how it became one is to penetrate deep into the form and meaning of the finished novel, tracing the educative process it eventually describes. The moral and artistic issues of *Der Tod in Venedig* proved to be fully comprehensible only in the light of its genesis; and that was a brief work, written in scarcely more than a year, a year of peace, so that the story's evolution was an internal matter between the writer as a moral and artistic personality and his chosen material. In the case of *Der Zauberberg*, twelve years, a world war, deeply painful personal conflict, a revolution, and the turbulent beginnings of the Weimar Republic all intervened between conception and completion. No wonder Mann speaks in the *Vorsatz* to his novel of the 'extreme pastness' of its action, left behind on the far side of 'einer gewissen, Leben und Bewusstsein tief zerklüftenden Wende und Grenze' (a certain turning-point and frontier deeply cleaving life and consciousness [iii. 9]).

The material of *Der Zauberberg* is accordingly change, and compound change. For the story in its very first conception already set out to portray change. Then changes in the external world immensely broadened the issues Mann wished to treat.

[3] *Einführung in den Zauberberg. Für Studenten der Universität Princeton*, 1939, xi. 603.
[4] Theodore Ziolkowski, *Dimensions of the Modern Novel*, Princeton, 1969, p. 73.

He tried to work them out in the *Betrachtungen eines Unpolitischen*, realizing that the novel would otherwise be 'intolerably over-loaded';[5] the *Betrachtungen* show an apparently made-up mind. But he then began to change his mind about the matters his broader conception now encompassed, so that, instead of being able to refer back to a definitive treatment of the novel's themes, he eventually had to reject, relativize, and alter the import of his war book, drawing on it as material to the point where its 'unburdening' function was nullified. It is in this way, more complex than Mann originally intended, that the two books belong together.

But in its very beginnings, *Der Zauberberg* belongs with a quite different predecessor, *Der Tod in Venedig*, for it was conceived as a counterpart to the Venetian *Novelle*. Thomas Mann's visit to Davos, where his wife Katja was being treated for a lung complaint and where a specialist, with a 'profitable smile', declared Mann himself a tuberculosis sufferer in need of a prolonged stay,[6] fell in May and June 1912, immediately before *Der Tod in Venedig* was completed. Escaping from the mountains, Mann tried to resume work on *Felix Krull*, but evidently without much success. A year later he had again abandoned it in favour of a further *Novelle*, 'die eine Art von humoristischem Gegenstück zum "Tod i V" zu werden scheint'.[7] This is the first mention of *Der Zauberberg*.

As yet there is no hint of any *Bildungsroman*. What then was the point of the *Novelle* conception, and in what way did it already set out to portray change? In two later accounts, Mann spells out the parallel between *Der Tod in Venedig* and the 'humorous pendant', the 'satyr-play after the tragedy', which was how he saw his new story. Both works were to show the fascination with death and the triumph of disorder ('extreme disorder' or 'intoxicating disorder') over a life devoted to order. The tragic conflict and Dionysian intoxication in Aschenbach was to be

---

[5] 'Und die Betrachtungen muss ich nur deshalb schreiben, weil infolge des Krieges der Roman sonst intellektuell unerträglich überlastet worden wäre.' To Paul Amann, 25 Mar. 1917 (Br. A. 53).

[6] '. . . ich gewöhne mich mühsam an die 1600 m. Ein paar Tage lang machten sie mir sogar Fieber, so dass der Professor mich schon profitlich lächelnd für offenbar tuberkulös und einer längeren Kur bedürftig erklärte.' From an unpublished letter to Hans von Hülsen, quoted in Bürgin–Mayer, *Chronik*, p. 36.

[7] To Ernst Bertram, 24 July 1913 (Br. B. 18).

echoed in the comic conflict of bourgeois respectability and macabre adventures. As yet it was not clear how it would end, but something would no doubt turn up.[8]

What sort of change does this imply? Not the formation of a character, but its grotesquely comic undermining; not *Bildung* but, so to speak, *Entbildung*. And it is worth trying for once to read *Der Zauberberg* in this way, as the satyr-play originally planned, forgetting for a while its prestige as a novel of ideas. The lines of such a conception are still clear in the final text, and they are remarkably close (as Greek satyr-plays are sometimes thought to have been) to the lines of the tragic version, *Der Tod in Venedig*.

Both heroes begin by planning a brief interlude in their orderly lives, intending to return refreshed but essentially unchanged. Both find themselves in an enclosed but cosmopolitan society and are disoriented by climatic and cultural influences and meetings with strange, even grotesque characters.[9] Neither succeeds in escaping from the fateful milieu, though both are warned and consider or attempt it. They are held fast by a passion which is contrary in different ways to reason and conscience and therefore not avowed by their conscious minds, in each case for an exotic (Slavonic) beloved whom they live near yet only worship from a distance. Both find a perverse pleasure in their heightened state, psychological or physical, and the dissolute feelings which accompany it. Both finally admit they are in love and become the willing victims of intoxication, actually resisting being sobered down. Both are accompanied in their progress by Mercury, Aschenbach by the god in his various disguises, Hans Castorp by the rise and fall of 'Merkurius' in his thermometer. Aschenbach finally dies, Hans Castorp . . . but when the end of Hans Castorp's story comes to be decided, the satyr-play has long grown into something very different.

These striking similarities of motif are not all. There is a more fundamental coherence underlying each protagonist's experiences. A humorous manner may have replaced the tragic tones

---

[8] *Lebensabriss*, 1930 (xi. 125), *Einführung in den Zauberberg*, 1939 (xi. 607).

[9] The limping concierge of the Berghof, and the use of the name 'Rhadamanthys' for Behrens, are beginnings of a mythological second layer to Castorp's experience akin to the Hermes–Dionysus suggestions of *Der Tod in Venedig*.

of *Der Tod in Venedig*, but there is the same suggestion that the hero has a 'fate'. It is conveyed by means which are again familiar from the Venice story. Simple statements take on the ominous ring of potential dramatic ironies. The narrator records Hans Castorp's intention 'ganz als derselbe zurück-zukehren, als der er abgefahren war' (to return as entirely the man he was when he set out [iii. 12]), but then reflects how far his simple hero has left his native town and native order behind him and below him, and wonders whether it was quite wise to travel straight into these 'extreme regions' with no intermediate stopping-places to help him acclimatize (p. 12). Through these mild double meanings he is already winking at the reader. And when he tells how Hans Castorp declares himself 'entirely healthy, thank goodness',[10] or when he reflects in his own person how indubitably—indubitably?—normal a product of North German life Hans Castorp is (p. 47), the reader senses a gleeful rubbing of hands at complications to come.

Or there are those self-defeatingly straightforward explanations of cause and motive, used to hint at the true ones.[11] In particular 'chance' is again mentioned in order to suggest its opposite.[12] Is it really by chance that Hans Castorp looks across at Clawdia Chauchat while refusing Settembrini's advice to leave the mountain after only one day (p. 124)? Or that he and Joachim run into Behrens just when Hans Castorp is thinking of asking for a check-up (p. 244)?

*Der Tod in Venedig* created a similar sense that Aschenbach's course was a fated one. This was not meant with surface literalism: 'fate' was not really an outside agency as in Greek tragedy, and the figures along Aschenbach's route to death were not really 'sent to fetch' him. They were the formal means by

[10] See pp. 29 f. The idea of 'complete good health' is undermined, not just by Dr. Krokowski's sceptical reply, but also by the way Hans Castorp's declaration stands in indirect speech—both distanced and made slightly pompous—while Krokowski's question and comment are in simple direct speech.

[11] e.g. p. 117, on Hans Castorp's shivers; or p. 229, on the reason why he does not mention his departure—sympathy for Joachim. 'Herzliches Mitleid' becomes 'das stärkste Mitleid' and then 'ein geradezu brennendes Mitleid', which was 'denn auch wohl der Grund' etc., etc. By this point, the narrator has made 'Mitleid' the one motive it is impossible to accept.

[12] Cf. in *Der Tod in Venedig* the chance (*zufällig*) that the Munich tram-stop is deserted (viii. 444), or the chance (*es fügte sich*) that Tadzio comes into the breakfast room just as Aschenbach has at last risen to leave for the station and his abortive departure (viii. 482).

which the modern writer chose to externalize the character's inner decline, especially his slackened will. When Aschenbach rejoices at the misdirection of his luggage, or ecstatically welcomes the cholera epidemic as an aberration of the outside world to match and abet his own, he is acquiescing in what, by this very attitude, becomes his fate. He lives his life forwards, creating it in response to what he encounters. It is his author who views it in the light of its ending as complete and 'fated'.

But if *Der Tod in Venedig* used the idea of fate to externalize a moral process, what was to be the meaning of Hans Castorp's fate? Was it to be merely a comic echo of Aschenbach's— 'verkleinert und ins Komische herabgesetzt' (xi. 125)?

The humour is not that gratuitous. The inner precariousness to which Hans Castorp's fate points was meant to be a general truth: even North German normality has in it the seeds of abnormality, just as an artist's public dignity has in it the seeds of aberration and downfall. The satyr-play would have clearly been a *tour de force*: how much more piquant it would be to bring out the abnormality lurking in a healthily 'mediocre' young man, blond and correct, than to go on presenting the tediously familiar abnormality of 'outsiders' and artists.

True, even Thomas Mann cannot conjure abnormality out of thin air. Hans Castorp turns out to have a past which is not quite 'mediocre', although it takes an effort of his memory and the aid of an X-ray machine to uncover it. His family proves to have a history of tuberculosis and his early contacts with death have impressed him deeply.[13] His lungs bear traces of old infection, and his stay on the mountain activates a latent tendency.

This process needs to be traced carefully. With the technique evolved in *Der Tod in Venedig*, Mann keeps up a teasing ambiguity about causes. Thus, when Behrens has examined Hans Castorp, he gives the materialistic explanation that the mountain climate can be 'good for' the disease, can develop it as well as cure it (p. 253 f.). But for his psychoanalytic assistant, Krokowski, all organic processes are secondary, a view which is

---

[13] Hermann Weigand aptly called death one of Hans Castorp's primary experiences (*Urerlebnisse*) in ch. 3 of his study of *Der Zauberberg*, New York, 1933. This is still an indispensable study of the novel, and one of the best of books on Thomas Mann.

epitomized in his lecture course on love as a cause of disease, 'die Liebe als krankheitbildende Macht'.

Infatuation with Clawdia Chauchat is what keeps Hans Castorp on the mountain. His peculiar physiological state makes him think of leaving after only one day, but when Settembrini suggests this, he turns the idea down with the objection Joachim has already made: how can one judge after the first day? (pp. 118, 124). As he says this, his glance wanders 'by chance' to where Clawdia stands in the next room. What or whom does she remind him of? He remembers on the following day, when he asserts a visitor's freedom from Berghof routine and takes an energetic walk, to try and get back to normal— 'wir wollen doch sehen, ob ich nicht ein anderer Kerl bin, wenn ich nach Hause komme' (p. 165). He suffers a violent nose-bleed and during it has a memory breakthrough: Clawdia reminds him of Pribislaw Hippe, the schoolmate he was once so strangely attracted by (p. 169).[14] Returning to the Berghof, a 'different chap' indeed, he hears Krokowski's lecture, sitting (chance again) behind Clawdia.

From this point on, it is plain sailing. Repressed love determines his actions and, by implication, his physical state. He seems to produce the symptoms needed to keep him on the mountain because he needs them. Certainly, he is excited to have a temperature and as he waits to announce it to Joachim he smiles, as if to somebody in particular: 'es war, als lächle er jemandem zu' (p. 239). A lowered temperature puts him in two minds about whether after all to keep his appointment for an examination by Behrens. But a smile across the room from Clawdia's 'Pribislaw eyes' seems to say, 'It is time—well, are you going?' (pp. 247 f.). He goes. When his infection is confirmed he is filled with fear and alarm but also with joy and hope (p. 259). He can stay, the world of objective fact has fitted in with his passion—as it did with Aschenbach's. Clawdia will go on determining his physical state. She is the mistress of his temperature before she is of anything more, and the lowering effect of a snub from her can only be offset by a successful exchange of 'good morning', which makes his temperature soar again (pp. 327 ff.).

---

[14] See esp. p. 174: 'Darum also interessiere ich mich so für sie? Oder vielleicht auch: habe ich mich darum so für *ihn* interessiert?'

Despite all this, we are free up to a certain point to accept the Behrens view, and to see Hans Castorp's emotions contrariwise as the product of his infection (the erotically intensifying effect of sanatorium life is a minor theme of the book). We can even reject the link Hans Castorp makes between the old patches on his lungs and his love for Pribislaw Hippe, although we cannot so easily dispose of the link he makes between Hippe and Clawdia, since their resemblance makes it a psychic reality for him. We can object that the physiological reactions to high altitude began before he ever saw Clawdia. But these objections, besides going arguably against the grain of the narrative, can be accommodated in the 'fate' view of Hans Castorp's adventures. For in the decisive conversation with Clawdia during the Shrove Tuesday festivities, he not only tells her about Hippe,[15] he not only interprets his disease as 'really' his love for her, he also declares that love was what brought him to the mountain: 'c'était lui, évidemment, qui m'a mené à cet endroit . . .' (p. 475). Madness, says Clawdia. But Hans Castorp has the last word. What is love if not madness, a forbidden thing, an adventure with evil?

In this light, all the material and physical causes which have been put forward, and even the overt plot-motive of Hans Castorp's visit to his cousin Joachim, are overridden by a coherent pattern of 'fate' which echoes that of *Der Tod in Venedig*. Doubtless it is no more meant to be taken literally than that one was. But the parallel between the two conceptions is made complete.[16] The limitations of the original *Zauberberg* plan are clearly marked.

## II

But in the *Bildungsroman* which *Der Zauberberg* is, Clawdia and Hans Castorp's love for her are not the ultimate cause of his adventures, whatever he may say. They are enclosed within

---

[15] The death associations of the name 'Hippe' ('scythe') mean that love and death are intertwined in the best Romantic or Wagnerian manner, as early exploited by Thomas Mann in his 'burlesque' *Tristan*.

[16] As a last detail, Hans Castorp's realization of his fate-pattern occurs in a chapter of literary parody ('Walpurgisnacht'), thus echoing the pastiche Platonic dialogue (viii. 521 f.) in which Aschenbach perceives that his downfall was inevitable.

a yet more 'ultimate' explanation, provided by the narrator's authority at an early stage. Whatever the individual's private hopes and ambitions, we are told, they will not be enough to motivate an active life if the age in which he lives cannot tell him what the sense of his activity is, if the age itself lacks hopes and prospects. The 'laming' effect of the age's 'hollow silence' will actually affect the individual's 'organic part' via his spiritual and moral life. And even a person as unaware and uncritical as Hans Castorp will address those basic questions to his time, albeit unconsciously:

> Der Mensch lebt nicht nur sein persönliches Leben als Einzelwesen, sondern, bewusst oder unbewusst, auch das seiner Epoche und Zeitgenossenschaft . . . Wenn das Unpersönliche um ihn her, die Zeit selbst der Hoffnungen und Aussichten bei aller äusseren Regsamkeit im Grunde entbehrt, wenn sie sich ihm als hoffnungslos, aussichtslos und ratlos heimlich zu erkennen gibt und der bewusst oder unbewusst gestellten Frage nach einem letzten, mehr als persönlichen, unbedingten Sinn aller Anstrengung und Tätigkeit ein hohles Schweigen entgegensetzt, so wird gerade in Fällen redlicheren Menschentums eine gewisse lähmende Wirkung solches Sachverhalts fast unausbleiblich sein, die sich auf dem Wege über das Seelisch-Sittliche geradezu auf das physische und organische Teil des Individuums erstrecken mag. (p. 50)

This seems a radically different conception from the one we have been tracing. On the one hand, a narrative which implied that disease sprang essentially from emotions, which traced a spiritually adventurous destiny back to the search for erotic fulfilment, and the hero's erotic tastes back to a boyhood episode, finally allowing him to see his unconscious search as the real motive for his actions. On the other hand, an assertion that the real cause of his disease lay in the constitution of the age, getting at his physical via his unsatisfied spiritual part.

The two are compatible, but only just. The first explanation is deeply rooted in the story and was probably the basis of the satyr-play conception, but there is nothing to stop its being seen as only Hans Castorp's view. What then of Hippe, and the way he anticipates Clawdia, and the patches he left (if it was he) on Hans Castorp's lungs? Well, one has to say that even at that early stage in his life, Hans Castorp's proneness to the disease was already the result of the times working on his 'organic' via his 'spiritual' being. Any idea that love for Hippe actually caused the disease ('die Liebe als krankheitbildende Macht') and Hans Castorp's adventures is ousted by the new declaration of suprapersonal causes. We have moved from a Freudian theory of childhood eroticism and of repression creating disease to an even more non-materialistic (and implausible) one that individuals can get T.B. because the time is out of joint, even if they are neither aware nor critical of its being so. This change is an obvious extension of the art of ambivalence, in that one more layer of meaning is added beneath the existing ones. But the addition, apart from its implausibility, strains the capacity of that technique to keep the different layers compatible.

The strained relationship between the narrative and its new ultimate meaning is emphasized rather than eased when that meaning is restated. Hans Castorp has now become a resident and is giving himself up to the intoxication of love, with no desire to escape from it. At this advanced point of the Clawdia-motivated action the narrator might well feel the need to remind us of the suprapersonal meaning his plot now has. He duly interposes some remarks on Hans Castorp's love. It is composed, he says, of extremes with no link of warmer personal feeling between them. There is basic passion for Clawdia's body and there is also something scarcely tangible, 'etwas äusserst Flüchtiges und Ausgedehntes, ein Gedanke, nein, ein Traum, der schreckhafte und grenzenlos verlockende Traum eines jungen Mannes, dem auf bestimmte, wenn auch unbewusst gestellte Fragen nur ein hohles Schweigen geantwortet hatte' (something extremely fleeting and extended, an idea, no, a dream, the alarming and boundlessly alluring dream of a young man whose definite albeit unconsciously asked questions had been met only by a hollow silence [p. 321]). And he adds the opinion that Hans Castorp would not have stayed even the originally planned three weeks, had it not been for the lack of a satisfying explanation of the sense and purpose of life—a private opinion, he stresses: 'Wie jedermann, nehmen wir das Recht in Anspruch, uns bei der hier laufenden Erzählung unsere privaten Gedanken zu machen.' It seems excessive caution in a narrator to claim no more authority for his opinion than anyone else, and no doubt the circumlocution is ironic. But it also aptly reflects the way an original narrative is being moulded to carry a new meaning.

Is it perhaps arbitrary to pick out a new ultimate meaning within a single finished text? Two considerations make it less so. First, the exactness with which we can trace a self-sufficient first conception in which the influence of the age had as yet no place. Second, the virtual certainty that the passages just quoted were written with benefit of hindsight, at the earliest when the 1914 war broke out, perhaps not until after its end had shown a Europe changed for good whose pre-war form had therefore 'had no prospects'. This, in the context of a pre-1914 fictional world, could be stated 'prophetically', as something which even a simple man's psychophysical antennae could pick up. Hans Castorp's fate has become the means to present something far more serious and elevated than the sardonic message that abnormality is latent even in normal young men.

In other words, this was one of the changes which mark the growth of *Der Zauberberg* from the humorous sequel of *Der Tod in Venedig* to all those other things which it also is.

### III

It is time to start seeing what the war did to Mann's work in progress. The last chapter showed what it did to his thinking, and the two processes are closely related. But two other obvious things apply to the work. First, the war gave it an ending. 'Something would turn up' ('der Ausgang war vorderhand ungewiss, würde sich aber finden' [xi. 125]). Something had, with a vengeance. Thomas Mann quickly saw that war would bring Hans Castorp down from the mountain.[17] But the war also disturbed Mann's mood for creative writing, and then destroyed it altogether when it involved him in ever more bitter controversy and the massive task of writing the *Betrachtungen*. He had tried till then to continue with his story, but from November 1915 he added nothing more until after the war was over.[18]

[17] To Paul Amann, 3 Aug. 1915 (Br. A. 29).
[18] See letters of 1914 and 1915 (Br. i. 116 and 119 f.) and a letter to Julius Bab quoted in Heinz Saueressig, *Die Entstehung des Romans 'Der Zauberberg'*, Biberach an der Riss, 1965, p. 9. The letter to Paul Amann of 3 Aug. 1915 wonders whether he can go on with his fiction ('ob ich weiterfabulieren darf') or whether he should

But that does not leave a complete gap, thanks to the close relationship between *Der Zauberberg* and Mann's war thoughts. This means not only that there is much reference back from the novel to the war writings; it means also that one can trace in those writings the changing conception of the novel he was prevented from actually composing. If the *Betrachtungen* text was meant to keep the novel from being intellectually overloaded, it follows that it records the angle from which the novel's themes were to be treated. So the *Betrachtungen* and the accompanying wartime letters show us what the novel might have looked like had Thomas Mann been free to complete and publish it in those years.

In his letter to Paul Amann of 3 August 1915 he says:

Ich hatte vor dem Kriege eine grössere Erzählung begonnen, die im Hochgebirge, in einem Lungensanatorium spielt, — eine Geschichte mit pädagogisch-politischen Grundabsichten, worin ein junger Mensch sich mit der verführerischsten Macht, dem Tode, auseinanderzusetzen hat und auf komisch-schaurige Art durch die geistigen Gegensätze von Humanität und Romantik, Fortschritt und Reaktion, Gesundheit und Krankheit geführt wird, aber mehr orientierend und der Wissenschaft halber als entscheidend. Der Geist des Ganzen ist humoristisch-nihilistisch, und eher schwankt die Tendenz nach der Seite der Sympathie mit dem Tode. 'Der Zauberberg' heisst es, etwas vom Zwerg Nase, dem sieben Jahre wie Tage vergehen, ist darin, und der Schluss, die Auflösung, — ich sehe keine andere Möglichkeit, als den Kriegsausbruch.

(Before the war I had begun a longish tale, set in the mountains, in a T.B. sanatorium—a story with basically pedagogical-political intentions, in which a young man has to come to terms with the most seductive power, death, and is led in a comical and spine-chilling way through the spiritual antitheses of humanitarian and Romantic attitudes, progress and reaction, health and disease, but more for their intrinsic interest, for the sake of knowing about them, than with a view to decision. The spirit of the whole thing is humorous-nihilistic, and the tendency on the whole is rather towards sympathy with death. 'The Magic Mountain', it is called, it has something of Rip Van Winkle for whom seven years pass like seven days, and the ending, the resolution—I see no alternative to the outbreak of war.)

The satyr-play is plainly still there in this report, but overlaid

begin an essay on the problems of the times. By 7 November he has (Br. A. 38), and there are no more mentions of work on *Der Zauberberg* until September 1918.

by other elements. Death as the 'most seductive power', the 'comical and spine-chilling' effect of Hans Castorp's experiences, the 'humorous-nihilistic spirit' of the whole: so much is familiar. But if all this could just conceivably be connected with some (rather sardonic) 'pedagogical' intentions, it is hard to see how these could have been from the first political. This extension of their meaning was surely the war's doing. When Mann later wrote that he was aware 'early' of the 'dangerous richness of reference' his story potentially had, he was surely referring to an awareness which war brought.[19] The letter to Amann is not simply, as it purports to be, a description of the work as it was before the war,[20] but an account of broader meanings he can now see in it in the light of recent experience. He can call his intentions 'basically' political in much the same way as he could interpret *Tonio Kröger*, under the pressures of war, as a piece of political conservatism. Literary themes, that is, acquire the connotations of political issues with which they seem congruent. Specifically, the antithesis of health and disease on which the story was certainly based has two new antithetical pairs pressed into relation with it: 'humanitarian and Romantic attitudes', 'progress and reaction'. Why? Because this is a Thomas Mann who has been taking issue with the accusations of Germany's rationalistic, progressive enemies and inner critics, and has defiantly accepted their terms while inverting their values. Romanticism as the higher art born of disease, and reaction as a less facile outlook on life are opposed to humanitarian commitment[21] and shallow progressivism.

Now, because a story is a work of art and not a pamphlet, its essence can still be called 'mehr orientierend als entscheidend', a matter of intrinsic interest rather than decision. But the 'nihilistic humour' of the original plan, which showed a deepen-

[19] See xi. 125: 'Ganz im Grunde verhehlte ich mir die expansiven Möglichkeiten und Neigungen des Stoffes kaum und fühlte früh, dass er in einem gefährlichen Beziehungszentrum stand.'

[20] Mann's retrospects of the 1930s are more reliable on this point than his successive statements during the growth of the work. These latter reflect the phases in its complex genesis, but precisely for that reason tend to be inaccurate when recalling earlier stages.

[21] This is clearly what *Humanität* means here. Cf. the letter to Bertram of 17 Feb. 1915: 'die politischen Literaten, jene radikalhumanitäre Richtung französischer Observanz, mit der ich innerlich seit langem in Hader liege und die mich denn auch seit dem Erscheinen meiner 'Gedanken im Kriege' endgültig in Acht und Bann gethan hat'. (Br. B. 21).

ing of the mediocre individual by contact with death, could well be described as tending towards a 'sympathy with death'. And this motif could accommodate a sympathy with the newly associated terms romanticism and reaction, which had political implications. If not a polemical decisiveness, this conception had at least a firm basic attitude. But it is worth noting that 'sympathy with death' is given as the tendency of the work, not yet (or not explicitly) as the preference of the hero. He, after all, is merely being exposed experimentally to that 'most seductive power'.

In March 1917, again in a letter to Paul Amann, Mann digresses from gloomy musings on the future to mention *Der Zauberberg*:

Aber merkwürdig bleibt mir, wie ich schon vor dem Kriege, an den ich nicht glaubte, die Politik, und zwar die politischen Probleme des Krieges, im Blute und Sinne hatte: der Roman, in dem ich unter-brochen wurde, hatte ein pädagogisch-politisches Hauptmotiv; ein junger Mann war zwischen einen lateinisch-rednerischen Anwalt von 'Arbeit und Fortschritt', einen Carducci-Schüler — und einen verzweifelt-geistreichen Reaktionär gestellt, — in Davos, wo eine untugendhafte Sympathie mit dem Tode ihn festhält . . . Sehen Sie? Und die Betrachtungen muss ich nur deshalb schreiben, weil infolge des Krieges der Roman sonst intellektuell unerträglich überlastet worden wäre.

(But I still find it remarkable that before the war, which I did not believe possible, I had politics, and the political problems of the war at that, in my blood and in my mind: the novel in which I was interrupted had a pedagogical-political main motif; a young man was placed between an advocate of 'work and progress', a disciple of Carducci, eloquent in the Latin manner—and a desperate clever reactionary—in Davos, where an unvirtuous sympathy with death holds him fast . . . Do you see? And I must write the *Betrachtungen* simply because, as a result of the war, the novel would otherwise have been intellectually intolerably overloaded. [Br. A. 53])

Not much is left here of the 'satyr-play'. Gone are the 'seductive power', the 'comical and spine-chilling' effects, the 'nihilistic humour'. What was earlier a 'basically political intention' has become a 'political main motif', and the politics are explicitly those of the war. The antitheses are now personi-fied in figures we recognize as Settembrini and Naphta, although these—far from dating back to before the war—owe their existence to the much more powerful controversies Mann has lived through since his earlier letter to Amann. The most substantial component of Settembrini is Heinrich Mann and his ideas, and the adjective 'unvirtuous', here ironically applied to Hans Castorp's sympathy with death, takes its meaning from those passages of the *Betrachtungen* which argue the shallowness of Heinrich's rationalist 'virtue'.[22]

*Nota bene*, it is now explicitly Hans Castorp's sympathy with death, not just his author's. This much does appear to have been decided. From the almost neutral object of a sardonic joke, Hans Castorp has become a medium for the expression—albeit artistic rather than frankly polemical—of the work's inner tendency. His past contact with death has grown into his main positive quality. He has become much more his author's man.

Along with this growth in his significance, one can guess at a matching positive valuation of the sanatorium world. This too had acquired extra meanings from the clash of war ideologies and was not merely the milieu in which 'interesting' abnormality could be developed in a mediocre youth. Its major features, disease and timelessness, were both apt to express the positive terms which Thomas Mann opposed to Heinrich's 'virtue'. For how does he define that shallow quality? As

die unbedingte und optimistische Parteinahme für die Entwicklung, den Fortschritt, die Zeit, das 'Leben'; es ist die Absage an alle Sympathie mit dem Tode, welche als letztes Laster, als äusserste Verrottung der Seele verneint und verdammt wird. 'Ich habe die Gabe des Lebens', erklärt der Verfasser jenes lyrisch-politischen Gedichtes, das Emile Zola zum Helden hat, 'denn ich habe die tiefste Leidenschaft für das Leben! — [. . .]' Aus Vernunft ist man tugendhaft, schwört zur Fahne des Fortschritts, fördert als strammer Ritter der Zeit 'die natürliche Entwicklung der Tatsachen', verleugnet gründlich die Sympathie mit dem Tode, die einem *von Hause aus* vielleicht nicht fremd ist, und gewinnt so, sollte man sie ursprünglich nicht besessen haben, die Gabe des Lebens [. . .]

---

[22] It is just conceivable that a Settembrini figure could have been conceived before the war, say as a satire on Mazzini-type attitudes (cf. xii. 393 f.). But it must have come very close to an attack on Heinrich because of those Italian tastes of his which make Settembrini finall͙ such an apt vehicle for his style of thinking. Without the brothers' wartime breach, which made all fair, would Thomas have brought his full antipathy for Heinrich out of his notebooks and into the light of day?

Der kleine Herr Friedemann.

1. 1893: Beginnings.
Thomas Mann at 18

2. 1897: Misgivings. Portrait of
the artist as a misfit. A self-
caricature by Thomas Mann
in the copy of *Der kleine Herr
Friedemann* he gave to his
brother Heinrich

3. 1900: Achievement. The
author of *Buddenbrooks*

4. *Circa* 1903: the 'clear incorruptible vision'

5. 1909: Establishment. Thomas Mann with wife and children at their country house in Bad Tölz

**HERRN THOMAS MANNS NEUESTE WANDLUNG**

6. 1922: Transformation. The warlike nationalist turned republican as seen by a contemporary cartoonist

7. *Circa* 1947: the author of *Doktor Faustus*,
'the work which ate at my substance like no other'

Unzweifelhaft handelt es sich da um die Kunst, gesund zu werden. Aber das Problem der Gesundheit ist kein einfaches Problem . . .

(the absolute and optimistic siding with development, progress, the times, 'Life'; it is the renunciation of all sympathy with death, which is negated and condemned as the ultimate vice, the extreme of spiritual rottenness. 'I have the gift of life', declares the author of that lyrical-political poem which has Emile Zola as its hero, 'for I have the deepest passion for life! [. . .]' On the basis of Reason, one is virtuous, one takes the oath of allegiance to Progress, one furthers like a stalwart opportunist the 'natural development of things', one denies thoroughly the sympathy with death which one is perhaps not unacquainted with by virtue of one's *origins*, and by doing all this one achieves, in case one should not have had it from the first, the gift of life [. . .]

Without a doubt this is the art of becoming healthy again. But the problem of what 'health' means is not a simple one... [xii. 426 f.])

This onslaught on the *Zivilisationsliterat* makes plain who was behind the 'advocate of "work and progress"', the 'disciple of Carducci, eloquent in the Latin manner'. The attack on Heinrich Mann for his shoddy attempt to overcome decadence and nihilism[23] can be read as an account of the broadening conception of *Der Zauberberg*. The refusal to take sides with 'the times' and their development implies the ideal of rising above the times—an ideal which Thomas elaborated in his theory of non-social art, the 'many-sided' artist, and true 'aestheticism'. What better to stand for this detachment than the Mountain world, elevated and abstracted from time? And if Heinrich, by denying his nation and the brothers' common roots (*von Hause aus*), was taking an all-too-easy road to 'health', then the subtler world of disease acquired a positive value. So the sanatorium, with its height above life and its plumbing of the depths of disease, came to stand, in Mann's mind if not yet on paper, for the values he had formulated in the *Betrachtungen*.[24] The original sardonic story provided him with the thematic basis. War and the *Betrachtungen* gave the themes broader reference. And one other work had been a technical preparation: *Königliche Hoheit*,

[23] See above, pp. 205–6.
[24] The phrase *zur Fahne schwören* is itself part of the leitmotiv system of the finished novel, which further suggests that Mann had *Der Zauberberg* in mind when writing this passage.

the first attempt at allegory, at an 'intellectual work of art in which ideas could clearly show through' (xi. 574).[25]

Can we be sure that Mann was consciously forging the components for an allegory? Suggestive is the way he now gives the phrase *Sympathie mit dem Tode* a representative meaning. On the one hand, that original chink in the armour of Hans Castorp's normality has now become his prime quality; on the other, it has become Thomas Mann's catch-phrase for all those deeper characteristics which distinguish Germans from their Western enemies and critics. Hans Castorp stands for these characteristics; and when personal and general are linked in this way, allegory is the result.

The hero's allegorical status at this stage is confirmed by a small pre-publication from *Der Zauberberg*. For the fiftieth birthday of the novelist Adele Gerhard on 8 June 1918 a small volume appeared to which Thomas Mann contributed a 'speech by a simple young man and fragmentary novel-hero'. With minor variations, it is Hans Castorp's speech to Joachim on the beauty of coffins as pieces of furniture and on the edifying quality of funerals (iii. 155).[26] Mann later wrote Adele Gerhard an apology for using such a funereal piece to mark her jubilee. He comments that the fragment seems to him the 'schlicht stilisiertes Bekenntnis einer gewissen charakteristischen ethischen Grundstimmung' (confession, in unpretentiously stylized form, of a certain characteristic basic ethical attitude).[27] In other words, whenever and for whatever purpose the passage was first composed (and it must date from before autumn 1915) it now has a national significance. Hans Castorp shares what Thomas Mann found in Schopenhauer, Nietzsche, Wagner—the *Grundstimmung* he summed up in Nietzsche's formula 'Kreuz, Tod und Gruft' and 'ethische Luft' (xii. 79).

Equally revealing is the allegorical mode of a page from the *Betrachtungen* chapter on 'humanity' ('Einiges über Menschlichkeit'). Still intent on showing up the one-sided vision of life Heinrich expounded, Thomas Mann asked whether men's

---

[25] See above, pp. 98 ff. Mann later used the same formula for *Der Zauberberg* (xi. 612).

[26] It contains one sentence left out of the final text: 'Neulich war ich bei dem Begräbnis von Konsul Padde, — es hat mir sehr gefallen.' The publication is not noted in Bürgin's Thomas Mann bibliography or in Bürgin–Mayer, *Chronik*.

[27] Letter of 11 Sept. 1918 (Br. i. 147 f.).

dignity lay wholly in Promethean gestures of emancipation, whether the attitude of reverence was not aesthetically more acceptable. He then gives an example:

Ich brauche nur aufzublicken von meinem Tisch, um mein Auge an der Vision eines feuchten Haines zu laben, durch dessen Halbdunkel die lichte Architektur eines Tempels schimmert. Vom Opferstein lodert die Flamme, deren Rauch sich in den Zweigen verliert. Steinplatten, in den sumpfig-beblümten Grund gebettet, führen zu seinen flachen Stufen, und dort knien, ihr Menschtum feierlich vor dem Heiligen erniedernd, priesterlich verhüllte Gestalten, während andere, aufrecht, in zeremonialer Haltung aus der Richtung des Tempels zum Dienste heranschreiten. Wer in diesem Bilde des Schweizers, das ich von jeher wert und mir nahe halte, eine Beleidigung der Menschenwürde erblickte, den dürfte man einen Banausen nennen. Trotzdem ist der politische Philanthrop ohne Zweifel verpflichtet, dergleichen darin zu erblicken, — und soviel sei eingeräumt, dass es ein nur zu schlagendes Beispiel für die Unzuverlässigkeit der Kunst als Mittel des Fortschritts bietet, für ihren verräterischen Hang zur Schönheit schaffenden Widervernunft. Offenbar aber ist die Humanität des emanzipatorischen Fortschritts entweder nicht die wahre oder nicht die ganze Humanität ...'

(I need only look up from my desk in order to refresh my gaze with the vision of a moist grove through whose semi-darkness the architecture of a temple shimmers white. A flame burns on the sacrificial altar, its smoke is lost among the trees. Broad stones, set in the marshy flowered ground, lead to the altar's shallow steps, and there, solemnly humbling their humanity before the Holy, figures in priestly robes are kneeling, while others, erect, approach from the direction of the temple to perform the service. Anyone who saw in this picture by the Swiss artist, which I have long valued and felt an affinity with, an offence to human dignity, might be rightly called a philistine. Yet the political philanthropist is no doubt obliged to see it as just that—and so much may be admitted, that it offers only too striking an example of the unreliability of art as a means to progress, and of its treacherous proclivity to an anti-Reason which can create beauty. But obviously the humanity of emancipatory progress is either not the true or not the whole humanity ... [xii. 478 f.])

The Thomas Mann of 1917—he finished this chapter late that summer—is using Arnold Böcklin's *Heiliger Hain*[28] as an

---

[28] I owe this identification originally to the late Edgar Wind. The picture hangs in the Öffentliche Kunstsammlung in Basel, and is reproduced in Ostini, *Böcklin*, Berlin, 1909, p. 75. Heinz Saueressig, in *Die Bildwelt von Hans Castorps Frosttraum*,

allegorical medium to express his own ideas. But surely not for the last time. A temple, a sacrificial stone, hints of a terrible ceremony, all indicating that there is a side to humanity which rationalism ignores—these will recur in Hans Castorp's vision in the snow, in that second scene within the temple. Its mood and its meaning are close to this *Betrachtungen* passage and clearly owe much to Böcklin, just as the summer scenes outside the temple derive much of their detail from paintings by Ludwig von Hofmann.[29]

But the interesting thing is the difference of emphasis between the 'Schnee' vision and this forerunner. In the novel the dual nature of existence is again being presented in place of views which are 'either not the true or not the whole humanity'. But by this time, even if Settembrini's western rationalism is being corrected, so too is Naphta's extreme 'anti-Reason'—some of the detail for which comes verbatim from Thomas Mann's wartime arguments. As for Hans Castorp, he is more aware of the dangers of excessive 'sympathy with death' than of the need to integrate it into a mature view of life.[30] His author has gone beyond one correction to another, larger one. Hans Castorp's declared preference for Settembrini over Naphta, contrary to the balance of power in their disputations, is a symptom of this new attitude (p. 660). In other words, the central vision of the novel strives to restore balance in a different, very nearly opposite sense to the page of the *Betrachtungen* which anticipates it.

The reason is that by the 1920s Thomas Mann had changed his view of the themes his novel was committed to formulating. He himself had completed the education which *Der Zauberberg* relates. That is how the *Bildungsroman* became possible, and necessary. Beginnings of an education were of course implicit in those 'pedagogical intentions' he mentioned to Amann in 1915, and more strongly still in the personification of rival principles

Biberach, 1967, suspected the Böcklin source, but from Mann's earlier, far less suggestive mention of the picture (xi. 740).

[29] Saueressig, op. cit.

[30] Cf. the important letter to Josef Ponten of 5 Feb. 1925 (Br. i. 230 ff.) where this emphasis is interpreted: 'In seinem Schneetraum sieht er: Der Mensch ist *freilich* zu vornehm für das Leben, darum sei er fromm und dem Tode anhänglich in seinem Herzen. Aber *namentlich* ist er zu vornehm für den Tod, und darum sei er frei und gütig in seinen Gedanken.' (Italics mine.) Like other statements quoted, this marks only one phase in a tortuous development. But it is the phase in which the novel was given its final form and meaning.

which the 1917 letter to Amann records. If Mann did not yet use the term *Bildungsroman*, it was probably because he could not yet connect the fundamentally serious project his novel was becoming with a genre he could only imagine treating as parody: he called *Felix Krull* a parody of the novel of education and personal development, as part of a concession that he had contributed to Germany's 'dissolution by westernizing intellect' (xii. 101).[31] Nevertheless, the name matters less than the substance. What was lacking in the earlier stages to make the work truly a *Bildungsroman* was the element of error. As yet the issues were too clear-cut, Mann's assurance too great to achieve the half-rueful tone typical of the genre. The translation into art of his seemingly final *Betrachtungen* insights required nothing beyond the more direct and cocksure mode of allegory. But changing his mind meant changing his mode.

True, large elements of allegory remain in the finished novel. Settembrini's clothes for instance, old and worn yet carried with elegance, and Hans Castorp's nickname for him, Italian organ-grinder (always the same predictable old-fashioned tune) encode a judgement on his liberal-individualist views and their rhetorical delivery. When he switches on Hans Castorp's light, he is Enlightenment Man. More broadly, the sanatorium world itself has the meaning discussed above, although this will eventually appear in a critical light. Hans Castorp's vision in the snow, which contains what Mann called the 'result' of the novel,[32] is an allegory within an allegory, and the expedition leading up to it recapitulates Hans Castorp's whole Mountain adventure to date, the influences he has undergone, and their result.[33] In the closing pages of the novel, the moods of the Berghof inmates stand obtrusively for the moods of pre-war Europe, and the Naphta–Settembrini duel takes place in the spot where Hans Castorp had so often tried to think out the true yield of their endless word-battles.

---

[31] Mann's changing attitudes to the term *Bildungsroman* in this period are usefully documented in Jürgen Scharfschwerdt, *Thomas Mann und der deutsche Bildungsroman*, pp. 105–13.

[32] e.g. in *Fragment über das Religiöse* of 1931 (xi. 423 f.) Mann calls the words italicized in 'Schnee' the *Ergebnissatz* of the novel.

[33] e.g. p. 664: 'Vor ihm lag kein Weg, an den er gebunden war, hinter ihm keiner, der ihn so zurückleiten würde, wie er gekommen war'; or p. 670: 'Benommen und taumelig, zitterte er vor Trunkenheit und Exzitation, sehr ähnlich wie nach einem Kolloquium mit Naphta und Settembrini, nur ungleich stärker.'

But all these things are finally only means within a more complicated economy. Allegory does not learn as it progresses, it knows the answers from the start and they are relatively straightforward. But in *Der Zauberberg* the hero moves from being a normal young man, in whom bizarre experience then brings out qualities and interests undreamed of, back to being a normal young man again. His *penchant* for disease, which the story had to activate, has to be toned down again, offset, integrated. Hans Castorp's words to Clawdia on the two ways to life, one ordinary, direct, 'well behaved', the other bad, going via death, the way of genius (p. 827), interpret positively a development which has turned back on itself. They subtly convert into spiritual progress what might seem simple regress.

This is the very essence of the *Bildungsroman*. The temptation to say that Hans Castorp's author marched him up to the top of the hill only to march him down again is checked when we remember that such a movement can be accommodated uniquely in this genre, where past error becomes gain and gives shape to the story of a life.

The nature of the change of heart in Thomas Mann which shaped Hans Castorp's story will be discussed in a separate chapter on politics between the wars. Before that, three things remain to be shown: the way in which the *Bildungsroman* was developed, technically, from the original straightforward tale of love and death; the nature and result of the educative process and the status of the materials it draws on; and finally the complexity which arises from the relationship between Mann's and Castorp's spiritual biographies and from Mann's dual impulse to record past error and to convey present conviction.

## IV

Effective education begins with the need and hence the motive to learn. Hans Castorp is shaken by the exact repetition of Pribislaw Hippe's features in Clawdia and alarmed by the sense of an inevitable fate this gives him. He looks round for help (p. 207). Who can provide it? Not Joachim, he is himself too troubled by Marusja. Behrens? He is a figure of authority, and it is fatherly authority Hans Castorp feels the need of, but he also has problems of his own. The choice falls on Settembrini, a self-styled pedagogue; but provisionally and not uncritically, in the spirit of the *placet experiri* Hans Castorp has picked up from Settembrini himself (p. 210). He allows Settembrini not to convert or dominate him, but to lead him on intellectually and to prevent premature dogmatism—'berichtigend auf Sie einzuwirken, wenn die Gefahr verderblicher Fixierungen droht' (p. 281). Thus Hans Castorp's edifying exposure to the tradition of Western rationalism and liberalism (and in due course to its darker rival) goes back directly to his disorientation by Clawdia, and to the effects of love and disease.

So does his humanistic interest in the sciences of the body. This begins in that superb comic scene in which he infiltrates Behrens's flat together with a bemused Joachim, ostensibly to look at pictures but really to ferret out what there is between Behrens and Clawdia; and then ostensibly discusses the technique of Clawdia's portrait, but really wallows in talk about her physical attributes. Here he indulges in his first humanistic reflections, those shamelessly improvised associations of ideas which contrive to keep the ball of a secretly Clawdia-centred conversation rolling (362 ff.). Behrens's two roles as painter and medic, and a third role Hans Castorp suspects and envies, bring together the possible approaches to the body—lyrical, medical, technical. The substantial studies Hans Castorp then pursues, in anatomy, physiology, embryology, pathology, are a transposed eroticism. As Behrens punningly comments, Hans Castorp manifests an *ausschweifende Wissbegier* (p. 371).[34] His studies never lose this erotic incentive. Clawdia remains his mental image of organic life, his *Bild des Lebens* (pp. 385, 399) and his studies grade over, at the close of the chapter describing them, into a scientific-erotic dream of her (p. 399); this in its turn prepares the Walpurgisnacht declaration of love which contains, duly put into French, Walt Whitman's effusions on the body.[35] Much later, the expectation of Clawdia's return is the true reason why Hans Castorp declines to leave the

[34] 'An extravagant desire for knowledge' (i.e. not to be expected in a simple young man); but also 'a licentious desire for knowledge'. The uncertainty of how much Behrens means is part of Mann's humour.

[35] Whitman's poem 'I sing the body electric' (esp. section 9) in the part of *Leaves of Grass* entitled 'Children of Adam'. See H. Hatfield, 'Drei Randglossen zum *Zauberberg*', *Euph.* 56 (1962) 365 ff.

sanatorium when Behrens pronounces him cured (pp. 582 f.). The absent Clawdia, the *genius loci* (p. 486), is sufficient to keep him on the Mountain. She has played her role of setting his *Bildung* in motion so effectively that after the Walpurgisnacht her physical presence is not needed. She has not only led him to look for a mentor, she has also led him to show his independence of the mentor, in his Walpurgisnacht tasting of forbidden fruit —the Asiatic world of mystical quietism and 'sin' which she represents lies outside Settembrini's 'civilized' sympathies and is clearly meant to query these.[36] This establishes in good time Hans Castorp's right to expose himself to later dubious influences—Naphta's, Peeperkorn's. And his refusal to be sent back to the plains shows that self-education has now become a permanent accomplice of his erotic impulse. Only readers who insist on the purest motives for education will think that this need jaundice our view of the final results.

But what are the results? This brings us to our second, most substantial question: the essence of Hans Castorp's education and the nature and value of the means Thomas Mann employs for it. Misapprehension on this latter point is common. All appearances to the contrary, *Der Zauberberg* is not the creation of a brooding philosophical polymath, nor a paean to *Bildung* in its secondary sense of the inert materials of education, what Nietzsche once called the stony bits of knowledge that rattled loosely inside 'cultivated' nineteenth-century Man.[37] It is rather the work of one who, as a humanist and a humorist, is concerned to put the materials of culture where they belong: in the perspective of humane purposes. Once this is understood, the demands that *Der Zauberberg* makes on its readers prove less formidable than is usually supposed.

Those studies of the science of the body, for example. We have seen the student's motives humanize them and give them a personal colour. No claim is made that he becomes learned or expert, he seeks knowledge for which he has a direct personal need, and which for all its sketchiness is exactly suited to affect

---

[36] Clawdia thus stood allegorically for Mann's objections to 'virtue'. Cf. his statement in 1920 of the *Betrachtungen* problem as 'was förderlicher sei: die Tugend oder die Sünde, das heisst Zweifel und Erkenntnis, — wobei "Tugend" mir gleich galt mit der Vernunft, der humanitären Aufklärung, "Sünde" aber ein anderes Wort für Romantik war'. *Brief an Hermann Grafen Keyserling* (xii. 601).

[37] *Vom Nutzen und Nachteil der Historie*, § 4.

his outlook on life at a decisive moment. These are not scientific materials in all their neutral splendour, to be taken solemnly; they are, to borrow some words of Joachim's, 'weiss Gott, eine nette Gelehrsamkeit'—a fine sort of learning (p. 17). The fact that they still allow Hans Castorp to put together a coherent picture of human life in its cosmic setting is only to be expected in a story which is about *his* education. The limitations of his learning are made plain—in the hoariness of his philosophical musings (the universe repeated in the atoms of a dog's leg) or in his very commonplace reflections on the nature of time.[38] Far from being scientifically exhaustive, all this recalls the medical terms and social views which Tony Buddenbrook took over from Morten Schwarzkopf to do service for a lifetime, or the superficially acquired knowledge of Prince Klaus Heinrich (it is here that *Königliche Hoheit* proves its value as a finger exercise). But why not? It is only fitting that the materials in a work of fiction should be governed by the limitations of the main character. What we are to take seriously is the process of his *Bildung*, not the material *Bildung* which is its medium.

This is even more true of that other area of culture Hans Castorp pokes about in, the philosophy of Man and Society. The disputants in this field, Naphta and Settembrini, are meant to be taken as men of genuine and wide-ranging culture. As such, they operate above the heads of their pupil and the other Berghof residents. Even their most commonplace allusion to the standard knowledge of the 'educated' is misunderstood. Neat comedy results. Have you heard of the Lisbon earthquake? asks Settembrini. An earthquake? No, I don't take the papers up here, Castorp apologizes (p. 349). In respect of material culture, the gap which separates the mediocre hero from his mentors is beyond closing.

But the non-communication is not meant to ridicule Hans Castorp. The mediocrity on which his author so insists is a kind of norm, not a negative quality. For society is largely made up of 'mediocre' people, in the unpejorative sense Thomas Mann gives the word, and their education is at least as vital as the interests of high culture. That is why it is worth writing a novel, at first sight the most massively intellectual of all novels, about

---

[38] Ziolkowski, op. cit., p. 90, is rare in being ready to dismiss these as 'not really very original'. The usual response is to be deferentially awe-struck.

one of them. If in the story's beginnings Hans Castorp's mediocrity was that of an experimental object, it is finally more like the representative mediocrity of the atom in political society, the atom which in the Weimar Republic was formally responsible as it never had been before for the fate of the German nation. That is why Hans Castorp's story has a suprapersonal meaning. The Thomas Mann who completed *Der Zauberberg* had read and digested the poet of democracy, Walt Whitman.

So it is important to take notice when Hans Castorp asserts his independence, however inadequate his basis for doing so. It is his story, he is the essential point of reference for all we see and hear. From the first he is suspicious of Settembrini's rhetorical moralizing and even tries to catch Settembrini out in a contradiction: what objections can a humanist have to the body? (p. 347) or a rationalist to (psycho-)analysis? (p. 311). The simple man is already on the path to his final conclusions.

Settembrini, it is true, does not always take kindly to such interpellations. Though he is not a dogmatist, he is a pedagogue, aware of the confusions that result when a pupil tries to run before he can walk, leaps to conclusions, and prematurely applies (i.e. misapplies) past lessons. Interrupted after a 'firstly' by Hans Castorp's would-be knowing agreement, he sharply advises a passive attentiveness: Do not overrate your innate powers of thought, young man. Try to take in and digest—in your own interest and the interest of your nation and Europe— what I am about to impress upon you secondly (p. 711). It is as bad when Hans Castorp interrupts Naphta with a recollected analogy. Settembrini can only fling a hand over his head in dramatized despair and exhort his pupil to remain attentive and not confuse issues (p. 627).

But whose education is it? Why should Hans Castorp not put his spoke in? If the culture gap produces comedy, Hans Castorp's pertness also punctures the rhetorical balloon with the wholly serious point that, however intricate the matters treated, however complex the arguments they call forth from qualified people, the essential thing is what he—unqualified, ignorant, misapprehending—can manage to make of it all. The conflicting traditions of the Western world may be known in all their richness to scholars; but the future of the Western world is not in their hands. The 'mediocre' men who live out the continuation of those traditions do so from a hint here and a glimpse there, inevitably out of their depth with regard to the full picture. They are not to be scorned for that, nor are they any more likely to be wrong.

This is the heartening message—heartening for wilting readers as well as for Hans Castorp—which emerges ever more clearly from the fearsome chapters of argument in *Der Zauberberg*. And more than that: the problems which confront 'mediocre' men are not just too complex for them, they are actually incapable of being fully resolved by learning and intellect alone, however great. It is not simply that practical decisions cannot wait on far-off theoretical conclusions. The methods of verbalizing intellect are themselves inherently faulty—at least, as they appear in the novel. Left alone after the first duel between Naphta and Settembrini, Hans Castorp confesses his doubts to Joachim. He has tried hard, but the matter has not become clear, on the contrary, the result of the argument was confusion —'die Konfusion war gross, die herauskam bei ihren Reden' (p. 536).

This impression grows, and we are invited to share it. A later disputation on freedom states the conclusion emphatically. For all their masterly handling of abstractions—indeed, because of it—the speakers achieve no clarification, not even a 'militant' one, the clear-cut opposition of irreconcilables. For the terms expected on one side pop up on the other, so that both speakers seem to Hans Castorp to be contradicting themselves. It is impossible to decide between the opposita and equally impossible to keep these opposita pure and isolated from each other. It is once more 'the great confusion'—and essentially always one and the same confusion (pp. 644–6). That is, to the simple man words themselves seem to be the trouble. Unable to separate their many senses and the different levels of generality on which they function, he sees them as real entities, raising their heads now here, now there, unruly, unpredictable, making a chaos of the things they are supposed to clarify.

If this is an unduly despairing view, it is nevertheless a fair criticism of that traditional German mode of philosophizing in which verbal inflation and the hypostatizing of concepts are always at hand. From his earliest days Thomas Mann had been marked by it and suffered from the inflexibility which results from thinking in grand antitheses. The terms Naphta and Settembrini make free with—*Geist* and *Natur*, *Kunst* and *Kritik*— plainly echo his own past dilemmas. The effort to bring several sets of antitheses into line with each other in 'Geist und Kunst' had produced just such an intellectual impasse, and for just these reasons. And the same traditional method lay behind the verbal battles of the 1914 war, which were fought from antithetical positions just as fixed as the real trench-lines. Thomas Mann had fought one of the most bitter and prolonged of those verbal battles. He had bought dearly a scepticism which few Germans attained, either before or after him.[39] He passed this scepticism on to his hero.

It duly becomes one part of the message that the novel's central vision imparts. Reflecting on his dream in the snow, Hans Castorp aptly calls the two pedagogues' fight with antithetical weapons a 'confused din of battle' (*verworrener Schlachtenlärm* [p. 685]). Their learning and brilliance avail nothing, because their questions are false; their questions are false because the whole principle of antithetical argument is wrong; and this principle is wrong because antitheses are made by men and can be transcended and reconciled by men:

> Mit ihrer aristokratischen Frage! Mit ihrer Vornehmheit! Tod oder Leben — Krankheit, Gesundheit — Geist und Natur. Sind das wohl Widersprüche? Ich frage: sind das Fragen? [. . .] Der Mensch ist Herr der Gegensätze, sie sind durch ihn, und also ist er vornehmer als sie.

> (That aristocratic problem of theirs! All that business about nobility! Death or life—disease, health—spirit and nature. Are those contradictions, I wonder? My question is: are they questions? [. . .] Man is lord of the antitheses, they exist through him, and therefore he is nobler than they are. [p. 685])

It is clear that these conclusions rest on Hans Castorp's critical appraisal of his mentors.

---

[39] Hesse is again the exception. *Zarathustras Wiederkehr* (1919) faced young Germans returning embittered from the war with the diagnosis that their education was grounded on false antitheses: 'ihr habt, von irgendeiner schlechten Schulstube her, an gewisse Gegensätze geglaubt, von welchen die Sage ging, sie stammten von Ewigkeit her und seien von den Göttern erschaffen'. And he anticipated Mann's conclusions in the words: 'Sehet, es ist schwierig, einander zu verstehen, und gar sich selbst zu verstehen, wenn man immer so grosse Worte braucht.' Hesse, *Krieg und Frieden*, pp. 122, 118.

But they also rest on his own researches into human life. These are erotically motivated and intimately linked to the outward story and his experiences, so that even the origins of organic life and of matter itself appear as forms of 'Fall', anticipating the last and worst Fall into disease, with its associations of erotic pleasure and the 'advantages of disgrace'. But relative and personal though this makes them, they have given him the sense of a direct grasp on life. He has seen the proximity of life and death as different aspects of the same natural process, separated only by the slender barrier of continuing form. He has decided that only an interest in life validates the study of death and disease. Little though his studies may amount to, they bulk more solid than the pedagogues' words. It is a pardonable exaggeration when Hans Castorp declares that he 'knows everything about Man', because he has 'known' his flesh and blood— a knowledge in which his sexual experience also has an important part, as both the biblical word *erkannt* and the full context hint: 'Ich habe sein Fleisch und Blut erkannt, ich habe der kranken Clawdia Pribislaw Hippe's Bleistift zurückgegeben' (p. 684).

What of Hans Castorp's dream vision? It is a simple enough embodiment of his new intellectual independence and his scientific-cum-sensual interests, simple even to the point of crudity. But allegory is a crude mode. Sunny existence, represented in the Mediterranean landscape he first observes, has a darker side. The terrors of death in the temple lie behind the harmonious idyll. Rational humanism is wrong if it refuses to recognize and explore the areas of darkness. Romantic anti-Reason is wrong if it wallows triumphantly in them. The human ideal is a society in which respect and consideration among men spring from the constant awareness that all are threatened— indeed, doomed. Humanist compassion, unlike Christian compassion, springs from our common mortality. The 'sun people' are charming and polite to each other because of this awareness, which need not be spoken. 'Im stillen Hinblick'—'tacitly regarding' (p. 685): the message is difficult to mistake.[40]

---

[40] Ronald Gray (op. cit., p. 165) succeeds nevertheless by interpreting 'im stillen Hinblick' (which he cannot but translate as 'in silent recognition') to mean '*dis*regarding'. This allows him to indict Thomas Mann, as always, of amorality or worse. But inaccuracy of this order will allow anything.

Indeed, for all his subtlety Thomas Mann is simpler here than his critics are sometimes prepared to believe. The clear-cut allegory was meant to be read as a clear-cut allegory. The complexities which surround it are more the result of the novel's growth than of any intention to veil or qualify his meaning. He himself was quite clear that Hans Castorp undergoes a positive development whose essence is in the chapter 'Schnee', and that the meaning of that chapter is the novel's message, the already extra-literary thing that the reader takes away with him from his reading.

One cannot properly ignore this authorial view and still try to reinterpret the novel as the product of positive but subtler intentions. We know what Mann's means were, we know the meaning he set out to convey. If they do not fuse and jointly satisfy the reader, then the writer has failed, simply. If, for example, the reader finds Hans Castorp's vision *Kitsch*, it is wrong to conclude that Thomas Mann must therefore have meant it so, and was seeking a kind of alienation-effect.[41] It is true that the painters Mann drew on—Böcklin, Ludwig von Hofmann—are second-rate art. He perhaps had undistinguished taste, as well as avowedly little interest, in pictures. He was interested in them as models for description, receptacles for allegorical meaning.[42] But as such, he took them with full seriousness; and it is arguable that great painting would have been less accommodating for his purpose. In any case, an allegory is not meant to give a fully realized picture of an ideal, only to embody some truth or principle. The snow vision (which is also limited by being the relatively unsophisticated Hans Castorp's vision) does this with clarity.

Because *Der Zauberberg* is about spiritual change, it is worth reflecting on the workings of that process in author and text. How slight, for example, is the shift of emphasis which will make a new meaning out of old means. If he had executed the snow vision earlier (the seeds of the idea were in his mind as early as 1915,[43] Böcklin's contribution by 1917) then the 'inner temple'

---

[41] Scharfschwerdt, op. cit., p. 142.

[42] One other source for the idyllic vision is the section 'Von der Schönheit' of Gustav Mahler's *Lied von der Erde* (based on Chinese poems translated by Hans Bethge). See Michael Mann, 'Eine unbekannte "Quelle" zu Thomas Manns *Zauberberg*', *GRM* 46 (1965), 409 ff.

[43] Cf. to Bertram, 17 Feb. 1915 and 6 Aug. 1918 (Br. B. 21, 72).

idea would have shown up the superficiality of rationalist activism *à la* Heinrich Mann. Linked with this, Hans Castorp's studies of the body would no doubt have pointed to a 'Romantic' depth of understanding which the rationalist lacks, they would have borne out the remark he makes in Behrens's flat after the anatomy lesson, that an interest in life is really an interest in death ('Und wenn man sich für das Leben interessiert, so interessiert man sich namentlich für den Tod.' [p. 372]). Only a small adjustment was needed to make such arguments point the other way,[44] turn the central allegory into a declaration of devotion to life, and place the fascination with disease and death in perspective instead of giving it the pre-eminent value.

In an even more complex way, a writer can hold fast to a principle, yet change—perhaps imperceptibly to himself—by gradually giving it a different scope. The idea of 'transcending antitheses' is an old one in Mann's work. Long before Naphta and Settembrini's 'great confusion' and Hans Castorp's vision, it is implicit in the many-sided art to which the frustrated essayist of 'Geist und Kunst' turns. It recurs in the *Betrachtungen* as the German ideal, and the thing Mann longs to return to from the harsh conflicts of 'beliefs'. He can state there a hope for the future of Europe which seems very close to Castorp's conclusions: 'Undoktrinär, unrechthaberisch und ohne Glauben an Worte und Antithesen, frei, heiter und sanft möge es sein, dieses Europa.' (May it be undoctrinaire, without bigotry, no longer believing in words and antitheses, free, serene, and gentle, this Europe [xii. 488]).[45] It even seems that he has the Ludwig von Hofmann painting in his mind when he puts the ideal into artistic terms.[46]

[44] Cf. x. 219, where Mann quotes these words and goes on: 'Aber eine Zeit vergeht, und zu demselben Gedankenpunkte zurückgekehrt, *wendet* der Lernende das Aperçu; er sagt: 'Denn alles Interesse für Tod und Krankheit ist nichts als eine Art von Ausdruck für das am Leben.'''

[45] The passage was written late in the summer of 1917 and published separately under the title 'Weltfrieden?' in the *Berliner Tageblatt* of 27 Dec. 1917. But it is anticipated down to details of phrasing by a letter to Amann of 25 Feb. 1916 (Br. A. 39). An extolling of many-sidedness and a rejection of antitheses occurs at xii. 504; rejection of Heinrich's one-sidedness is linked with the names Erasmus, Voltaire, and Petrarch at xii. 499. The last is described as a melancholy artist and *Geniesser der Gegensätze*—surely the reason behind Hans Castorp's Petrarcan motto, *placet experiri*.

[46] He criticizes pre-war European art for its 'infantilism' and its return to primitive sculpture. All this is to be rejected with a *Gebärde vornehmer Ablehnung*, in

Yet the words occur in a work which is itself doctrinaire; its author was unable or unwilling to see his own one-sidedness, believing that he and Germany with him were uniquely free from one-sidedness—surely the essence of bigotry. It could be argued that, like some conciliatory notes later struck in the Foreword, this passage of the *Betrachtungen* is on the way to abandoning his false position. But it is only in the finished *Zauberberg* that the long-held ideal of freedom from antitheses is realized, by the act of playing with them.

Here, instead of turning away from harsh conflict, which is what 'free art' sometimes seemed to mean for Thomas Mann earlier,[47] he uses his and his opponents' views as material, treating them with equal irony. Again and again, we find statements from his past built into the speeches of the two disputants, and in such a way as to relativize them totally.

It would be tedious to list every case, but the twists and turns by which Naphta's and Settembrini's views came down to them are revealing. Passages from the *Betrachtungen* in which Mann summed up the *Zivilisationsliterat*'s position are put into Settembrini's mouth as rhetorical assertions.[48] He also speaks formulas which go further back still, ultimately to 'Geist und Kunst', to those notes in which the Thomas Mann of pre-war days himself defended an Enlightenment view of literature. In the meantime they have been published in *Der Künstler und der Literat* of 1913, still apparently endorsed, and in the *Betrachtungen*, where they are in disfavour.[49] Naphta's answers in each case paraphrase Thomas Mann's criticism of such simpleness in

favour of an art which will be 'reiner Ausdruck seines Zustandes: zart, schmucklos, gütig, geistig, von höchster humaner Noblesse, formvoll, massvoll und kraftvoll durch die Intensität ihrer Menschlichkeit' (xii. 488 f.). These remarks point forward to the snow vision, but they also point back to a mentality which could sneer at the 'cubisms and futurisms' which would be superseded by a German victory (cf. above, p. 183).

[47] Cf. *Betrachtungen* xii. 546: 'Künstlertum ist etwas, *wohinter man sich zurückzieht*, wenn es mit dem Sachlichen ein wenig drunter und drüber geht, — wohinter man heiter geborgen ist und von dem Drunter und Drüber noch Ehre hat.' The italics are Mann's.          [48] As noted by Weigand, op. cit., p. 114.

[49] The idea that 'fine writing' leads to 'good actions' is found in 'Geist und Kunst' N 41, then in *Der Künstler und der Literat* x. 64 f., recanted in *Betrachtungen* xii. 99 f., and given to Settembrini, iii. 224. 'Decency' as the quality of the *Literat*, who takes intellectual purism to absurd lengths, occurs in *Der Künstler und der Literat* x. 69, is spurned in *Betrachtungen* xii. 100, and then put into Settembrini's mouth, p. 549.

the *Betrachtungen*; at a later stage he also voices the counter-sentiment which Mann claimed always accompanied his own pro-intellectual attitudes: namely, that 'decency' is only to be found where there is *no* element of *Geist* (p. 745 = xii. 100). This much might, it is true, have been conceived by the novelist when he was still wholeheartedly opposed to his brother Heinrich's Enlightenment attitudes. It probably was. The original caricature of those views remains clear in the final text, as one element in a by now more complex picture. But the Thomas Mann who completed the novel had come round yet again to favouring something like his old views, at least to the extent of ironizing the attacks he made on them. When the *Zauberberg* narrator cuts short in despair a philippic of Naphta's against reason, justice, and the other liberal values, with the weary words: 'Wir haben da nur auf gut Glück aus dem Uferlosen ein Beispiel herausgegriffen dafür, wie er es darauf anlegte, die Vernunft zu stören' (we have only picked out at random from a vast ocean one example of the way he set out to undermine reason [p. 960]), what is he secretly alluding to but the 'vast ocean' of the *Betrachtungen*, whose arguments Naphta has been echoing?[50] And what is the narrator's judgement on these arguments now? That they are excesses, often verging on mental imbalance: 'dass sie nachgerade alles Mass und häufig genug die Grenze des geistig Gesunden überschritten' (p. 958).

This is self-ironizing indeed. True, there were signs from early in the genesis of the work that the rival pedagogues were both to appear as extremists—Naphta was never simply the 'good' side, opposed to Settembrini as the 'bad'. Both of them were 'oddities'.[51] But it is not likely Naphta was conceived then as a means to cut away from under Mann's feet the ground of doctrine he was still engaged in laying down.

'Etcetera, etcetera'; 'und so fort': the account of their speeches tails off into these weary dismissals of the predictable and futile. They cast off Mann's intellectual preoccupations of two decades, within the last five years of which he has moved from his most vehement commitment to his freest play with opposed concepts. The *Betrachtungen* did not as hoped lighten his novel, but did make his intellectual past ripe for the free play of art.[52] He learned long and painfully what he shows massively and at some aesthetic cost: that intellectual abstractions and involvements are to be taken with a pinch of salt.

Or even with a pinch of pepper, in so far as Peeperkorn is a positive figure. How positive is he? He remains the most enigmatic character in the book and the most controversial, eliciting flatly contradictory judgements—the novel's most successful creation,[53] or a 'travesty of the vision in the snow',[54] or even a sharp criticism of Gerhart Hauptmann down to the detail of Hauptmann's published works.[55] Yet Mann declared his love for the figure of Peeperkorn[56] and insisted, true to the principles of *Bilse und ich*, that he took over only Hauptmann's external features.[57] The case is complicated and is only falsely simplified if we exclude the whole Hauptmann issue as unwarranted biographism.[58] Of course, 'Peeperkorn is Gerhart Hauptmann' is wrong. But it is equally wrong to ignore the way his use of Hauptmann as a model affected first Mann's execution and then his interpretation of an original literary idea.

For the idea was there first as an intended element in the composition. The disputants were to be dwarfed but Mann was casting about in vain for the figure to do it.[59] Hauptmann provided him with apt externals for the forces he had in mind. What were these? We must assume that, whatever else happened, they are substantially present in the Peeperkorn episode and can be read from it. Yet this is itself not a straightforward matter. On a reader not pre-committed to a positive or negative view of Peeperkorn, he makes a curiously mixed impression. He is imposing yet precarious, majestic yet ludicrous: between

[52] Cf. *Lebensabriss* xi. 126, 'dem mühsamen Gewissenswerk . . . durch welches dem Roman das Schlimmste an grüblerischer Beschwerung abgenommen oder doch zu seinen Gunsten spiel- und kompositionsreif gemacht wurde'.

[53] Heller, op. cit., p. 208, and many other critics.

[54] Ziolkowski, op. cit., p. 86.

[55] Scharfschwerdt, op. cit., pp. 125 ff.

[56] To Herbert Eulenburg, 6 Jan. 1925 (Br. i. 224).

[57] To Gerhart Hauptmann, 11 Apr. 1925 (Br. i. 234 f.).

[58] Oskar Seidlin, 'The Lofty Game of Numbers. The Mynheer Peeperkorn episode in Thomas Mann's *Der Zauberberg*', PMLA 86 (1971), 924. Seidlin throws out a number of babies with a little bath-water.

[59] To Eulenburg, loc. cit.

Hans Castorp's first and last comments—'robust und spärlich' (p. 760) and 'eine königliche Narretei' (p. 867)—all else is equally ambiguous.[60] Reverence mingles with irony, awe with mockery.

Nowhere is this clearer than in the religious allusions in which some critics see unmixed affirmation. It may not be blasphemous but it is surely ironic that Peeperkorn speaks Christ's words to the sleeping disciples—'Könnet ihr denn nicht eine Stunde mit mir wachen?' (p. 789)—as an appeal to flagging carousers. As to his more incoherent mumblings: '"Der Wein" — sagte er, "— Die Frauen — Das ist — Das ist nun doch — Erlauben Sie mir —Weltuntergang—Gethsemane—."' (p. 793), they are difficult to take seriously, let alone solemnly, as religious symbolism.[61] The same is true of the Bacchic, or more properly Dionysiac element. This is more substantial. The Bacchanal Peeperkorn supervises does have, under its modern social surface, traditional features of a Dionysiac gathering.[62] Yet Peeperkorn-as-Dionysus is amply ironized as well. At first sight, it seems he ought to confirm the lesson of devotion to life which Hans Castorp learns. But 'life' is a vague term, and there are many ways of being devoted to it. Beside Hans Castorp's vision of harmony and form—which can itself be read as a reconciling of Dionysiac and Apolline forces—Peeperkorn sets an all-too-deliberate cult of feeling (*Gefühlsdienst*, pp. 779 f.), a dogmatic insistence on certain sacred, simple things, an anxious forcing of appetite, and a panic fear of cosmic disaster if the sensual celebrant cannot screw up his manly powers to the act of enjoyment. He positively drives others on to enjoy ('im Genuss überwacht von ihm', p. 781). The very name Peeperkorn declares the desperate spicing which his declining powers rely on.

This is a strained vitalism. Even before Peeperkorn's suicide

[60] Cf. e.g. p. 765, 'eine Persönlichkeit, aber verwischt', and p. 819, 'dies torkelnde Mysterium'.

[61] For Seidlin, Peeperkorn is 'the figure in whom the earthy and the noumenal meet' (p. 928), a Christ-figure (p. 927) but also a Peter-the-Apostle figure (p. 931). For Winfried Kudszus, 'Peeperkorns Lieblingsjünger', *Wirkendes Wort*, 20 (1970), the Peeperkorn episode is a confrontation with 'fremd gewordene, ursprungsnahe Kräfte' (p. 325).

[62] The details on pp. 790 ff. can be read as allusions to Dionysiac experience— the general 'irresponsible condition' of the participants, their feeling of intensified life ('Frau Magnus gestand, sie fühle, wie Leben sie durchrinne')—and to Dionysiac practices—the greater activity of the women, their baring of teeth and tugging at male ear-lobes.

proves it, it has been effectively questioned, by Hans Castorp himself, in that cheeky speech which defends decadent 'refinements' as ultimately a true homage to the cult of feeling. Of course they are artificial, 'stimulantia, wie man sagt' (p. 785); yet from the praise of wine into which he modulates to avoid Peeperkorn's rising wrath, the conclusion emerges unmissably that Peeperkorn's own stimulants, emotional and material, are of the same order (p. 787). Peeperkorn is himself one-sided and extreme, even if he is beyond the kind of purely intellectual antitheses Naphta and Settembrini cultivate (p. 819). Hans Castorp tells him so, politely: his idea that Man is God's organ for consummating a marriage with Life is 'eine höchst ehrenvolle, wenn auch vielleicht etwas einseitige religiöse Funktion'; his outlook generally shows 'eine gewisse Rigorosität . . . die ihr Beklemmendes hat' (p. 837).

Still, Peeperkorn is a great experience for Hans Castorp. Despite ironic reservations, he speaks of him positively, even as an absolute: '*absolut* positiv, wie das Leben, kurzum: ein Lebenswert' (p. 809). It is this attitude and the premiss that what Hans Castorp judges positively must be positive that have led critics to take Peeperkorn so seriously. Yet Hans Castorp is a character in a novel judging another character; and the novel treats the intellectual life of a particular period. The terms of his judgement, like other terms and images that occur in the episode—the bird of prey (*Raubvogel*, p. 820) with which Peeperkorn is associated, the idea of life as a demanding woman, the reference to stimulantia, the allegorically diseased woodland on the walk to the Flüela waterfall—all suggest a recognizable current of thought of the period. The form in which 'devotion to life' was available to a son of that time was the emphatic vitalism which was ostensibly a reaction to decadence but at root one of its manifestations. And its main author was, for Mann at least, Nietzsche, in whose life the religious terms of the Peeperkorn episode—Dionysus and the Crucified—come together.[63] No picture of intellectual life in Europe before 1914 would have been complete without this

[63] Nietzsche's concern with Christ and Dionysus culminates in the letters of his madness signed 'Der Gekreuzigte' and 'Dionysos'. The bird of prey incident also recalls the anecdote of Tolstoy and the hawk from *Goethe und Tolstoi* (ix. 110 f.). Tolstoy, we shall see, first interested Mann anew in the twenties as a specimen of vitalism in culture. See below, pp. 286 f.

element. That does not mean it was an ideal. It was real; it was available to Hans Castorp; its exponent was calculated to relativize Naphta and Settembrini more strikingly than a mere dream vision; yet it also had its questionable side, as we know Mann was aware. All this is in the Peeperkorn episode. Hauptmann, in whom there were elements of Christian compassion and of vitalist 'regeneration', was an apt model.

Apter than Mann was free to admit. Choosing as his model a man he was attached to already made the treatment of his literary idea subtly more positive than it might have been. But once Peeperkorn had been 'recognized' as Hauptmann, diplomacy limited Mann's interpretations of the figure to the wholly positive; for the public, he knew, never believes that it was only the externals that were borrowed. Not till much later, in the retrospects of *Die Entstehung des Doktor Faustus* and the 1952 speech on Hauptmann could he speak openly of the correspondence between Peeperkorn and the real-life *schmerzhaften Dionysier* (ix. 815), conceding how much the fictional character really was a characterization of Hauptmann and also linking him explicitly with Nietzsche.[64] In the meantime, he accepted the verdict of readers who were bowled over by Peeperkorn's *verwischte Persönlichkeit*: rather than go into the detail of what he stood for, it was simpler to accept that he was an 'irrational' poetic figure—and as such no mean achievement for an 'intellectual' novelist in the context of a very intellectual novel.

All this tells us something about the problems of allegorical writing. More important, it brings us back to the nature of the *Bildungsroman*. For if, instead of seeing Peeperkorn as simply positive or negative, we read him as one thing for Hans Castorp and a somewhat different thing in the over-all patterns of the work, this is possible precisely because the *Bildungsroman* presents trials and errors and leaves us free to judge the hero's judgements. A picture emerges of his situation in his time, a lesson emerges from his experiences. We do not have to endorse him uniformly throughout. His snow vision is part of the novel's positive message not just because it carries conviction for the hero but because it epitomizes what is shown repeatedly at other stages. Peeperkorn is, in contrast, an episode.

---

[64] 'Der Gekreuzigte und Dionysos waren in dieser Seele mythisch vereinigt, wie in derjenigen Nietzsche's . . .' (ix. 812).

This leads to our third problem: the relation between the educations of author and character. It is not surprising that Hans Castorp and his author are not consistently at one. A simple fact complicates matters. The action of the novel ends in 1914, but it was completed in 1924. Hans Castorp's education is ended by the war, yet as Mann presents it it owes much to the experiences of war and the years beyond, which educated Thomas Mann. From the standpoint of 1924[65] Thomas Mann strove to make the novel convey his most recent conclusions— a didactic intention. Yet it was also a record of the trial and error by which he arrived at them and thus inevitably had a confessional and self-critical intention. So the hero has a dual role. He is both the bearer of a message and the object of criticism. Developing at a preternaturally rapid rate in the experimental conditions of the abstracted Mountain world, he reaches valid conclusions before (fictional) 1914. This gives him a clear lead over his author—the overcoming of a perilous 'sympathy with death' was not something Mann could look back on as part of his pre-war past, it was a later lesson built in retrospectively. On the other hand, Hans Castorp also represented some of his author's aberrations before (real) 1914 and thus comes in for criticism. Nor was the sequence inherent in an education by itself enough to get over this duality, since Hans Castorp, for all his ideal visions, was needed as a negative figure right up to the 1914 limit.

These quite distinct roles of his hero are surely the key to understanding the structure of the novel. Mann may not have fully realised the ambiguity in his relationship to Hans Castorp —he only ever refers to the two roles separately, speaking now of the *Bildungsroman* narrator as identical with yet superior to his other self, the fictional character;[66] now of Hans Castorp as an anticipator, a young German who has learned the lessons of war before war came.[67] But whether or not he grasped this

---

[65] Mann later referred to the book as a document of Europe's intellectual problems in the 'first third' of the twentieth century (xi. 602).

[66] '... ein Du, an welchem das dichterische Ich zum Führer, Bildner, Erzieher wird — identisch mit ihm und zugleich ihm überlegen ...' *Goethe und Tolstoi* (ix. 150).

[67] 'Hans Castorp is am Ende ein Vortypus und Vorläufer, ein Vorwegnehmer, ein kleiner Vorkriegsdeutscher, der durch "Steigerung" zum Anticipieren gebracht wird. Das ist in der Entlassungsrede direkt ausgesprochen, und während der Arbeit

technical problem in the abstract, he solved it in effect by placing (or leaving) the chapter 'Schnee' in the middle. This, together with the realistic touch that Hans Castorp has already begun to forget his dream and can no longer understand what he thought about it by that very evening, allows him to convey the message of the snow vision while still not turning Hans Castorp into a paragon of humanistic virtue, beyond the reach of eventual criticisms. His subsequent actions—or inaction— are free to belie the revelation he has had; he can return from the world of allegory within allegory, which embodies the author's positive insight, to the world of simple allegory, which embodies the author's critical insight.

Criticism is the keynote of the novel's last five sections. It is directed at more than just the hero, because increasingly towards the end the novel tries to represent the pre-war condition of Europe in the guise of the enclosed Berghof society. This is a shift from earlier chapters, which reconstructed essentially private experiences, of European relevance only in so far as Thomas Mann believed that his private experiences were representative.[68] The 'great stupor' (*grosse Stumpfsinn*) which results from the monotony of sanatorium life and gives rise to frivolous and sensational pastimes, and the 'great irritability' (*grosse Gereiztheit*) which derives directly from the stupor (p. 947) stand for the pointlessness and lack of organic prospects of pre-1914 Europe and for the aggressive moods which purposeless existence fostered. When war comes, it is the detonation of these moods, which have built up dangerous pressures (p. 985). Whatever one may think of this as a historical diagnosis, it is the burden of the allegory in this last phase.

Burden indeed, for by now the Mountain world has already had to stand for a number of things. If they are not wholly compatible, this is due first to the novel's complex genesis and secondly to the mixture of positive didacticism and critical

sagte ich immer: "Ich schreibe von einem jungen Deutschen, der vorm Kriege schon über den Krieg hinauskommt".' To Julius Bab, 23 Apr. 1925 (Br. i. 239).

[68] Cf. to Bertram, 25 Nov. 1916 (Br. B. 43): 'Es ist nicht Grössenwahn . . . wenn ich dies Verhängnis [Deutschlands] längst in meinem Bruder und mir symbolisiert und personifiziert sehe . . . Europäische Kriege würden nicht mehr auf deutschem Boden geführt? Und ob sie es werden! Es werden immer sogar deutsche Bruder-kriege sein.'

confession which it finally became. The world of disease was originally the means to a sardonic dissolution of apparently healthy North German normality, and doubtless had the sympathies of a *fin de siècle* artist who scarcely believed in health. It then became the allegorical means to set off the subtlety and profundity of the Romantic tradition against the superficiality of the Enlightenment and all rationally inspired activism. Even more generally, its abstraction and elevation above the practical Flatlands world fitted it to stand for Art itself, 'many-sidedness' as the Thomas Mann of the *Betrachtungen* conceived it. But then Hans Castorp's humanistic investigations came round ever more to a wholeness of vision 'beyond antitheses' which superseded the 'Romantic' *Betrachtungen* arguments too, and began to overcome the traditional temptations of the Romantic sphere. The Mountain world in which these temptations lurked accordingly took on a negative colour. If it could be seen positively at all, then only because the education it provoked finally led, against the odds, to a rejection of its temptations. Now, finally, the Berghof was to stand for a whole doomed political society, not because of the disease as such which it housed, but because of the style of life it permitted: a life without time, carefree, hopeless, stagnant, vicious, dead[69]—the European way of life which hindsight now adjudged 'without prospects'.

Of this life Hans Castorp, for all his earlier visions, has to be shown as part. He had managed to rise above *die grosse Konfusion*; but *der grosse Stumpfsinn* and *die grosse Gereiztheit* seize hold of him, like any other inhabitant of Berghof/Europe. He participates in the crazes which sweep his society, he cannot escape the irritation which produces symptomatic duels, until the Great Duel puts an end to them. Criticism and apocalyptic prophecy begin with the crass contrast of a worried Settembrini expounding the dangers of Balkan politics and a carefree Castorp too 'busy' playing patience to pay any attention (p. 880). But the pupil knows he is being irresponsible. His eyes, Settembrini tells him, try in vain to conceal his knowledge of how things are with him. Left alone, Hans Castorp is afraid:

[69] Cf. p. 872: 'Er sah durchaus Unheimliches, Bösartiges . . . Das Leben ohne Zeit, das sorg- und hoffnungslose Leben, das Leben als stagnierend betriebsame Liederlichkeit, das tote Leben.'

Ihm war, als könne 'das alles' kein gutes Ende nehmen, als werde eine Katastrophe das Ende sein, eine Empörung der geduldigen Natur, ein Donnerwetter und aufräumender Sturmwind, der den Bann der Welt brechen, das Leben über den 'toten Punkt' hinwegreissen und der 'Sauregurkenzeit' einen schrecklichen Jüngsten Tag bereiten werde.

(He felt as if 'all this' must come to a bad end, as if it would end in a catastrophe, a protest of patient Nature, a thunderstorm and violent wind which would clear the air, break the spell on the world, carry life beyond the point where it had 'got stuck', and bring a terrible Day of Judgment upon this 'silly season'. [p. 881])

Castorp's belated urge to flee is diverted, first by Behrens, who has in hand some new experimental approaches to his disease, then by the richer diversions of the crazes—for music, for spiritualist seances. These latter grow out of Krokowski's lectures, which have moved on from psychoanalysis to psychic phenomena. The narration hints that the motives for this may have been as much sensationalist as scientific. For all that, Krokowski is—once again—a useful ally for the allegorist. The preamble to this 'most questionable' episode of the novel canvasses a general theory of 'pathological idealism', an anti-materialist approach to the chicken–egg problem of causal priority between spiritual and material phenomena; more specifically the idea of a *super*-conscious (*Überbewusstsein*) or universal soul which may have access to knowledge which is beyond the individual (pp. 908 f.). This echoes the non-materialistic ultimate explanation of Hans Castorp's disease and adventures, and prepares us for the prophetic apparition which is to come.

Which is not to say that it convinces. The conjuring up of Joachim remains questionable, not just morally as the section title 'Fragwürdigstes' implies, but as art. What is its explanation? Nothing in Mann's experiences of the occult, startling though these may have been,[70] gave any ground for that look into the future which is vouchsafed when Joachim materializes wearing a helmet from the First World War. Mann said later

---

[70] See to Bertram, 25 Dec. 1922: 'ich habe okkulte Gaukeleien des organischen Lebens gesehen (mit meinen unbestochenen Augen gesehen), die sich mehr als zwanglos in den Kreis meines Romans fügen' (Br. B. 116). An account of the Schrenck-Notzing seances Mann attended is given in the essay *Okkulte Erlebnisse*.

that the scene went beyond his experience in kind.[71] He protested nevertheless that he did not think such things 'in principle' impossible, and wondered whether something as 'dirty' as war might not announce itself in this 'dirty way'. These are feeble answers. The real point was, as the same letter admits, that the scene fitted the intellectual pattern—'es steht gut in der Composition'. Allegory has taken over to the point of doing violence to the surface realism which carries it. Nowhere in Mann's work is the manipulation of reality to make an argument less acceptable.

More important is the musical section, apparently a digression but in fact leading back to the novel's deepest themes. The account of Hans Castorp's favourite records restates these in little, right down to that awkward duality of his negative and positive roles.

Musical allusion has slyly interpreted his experience long before the section 'Fülle des Wohllauts'. When the distressing episode of Clawdia's snub has ended happily with Castorp regaining his high temperature, he is exuberant and proposes to Joachim a trip to the Kurhaus. Perhaps there will be music, perhaps even the aria in which José swears his continued faithfulness to Carmen. Like him, Castorp rededicates himself to his dubious beloved (pp. 329 f.). Accordingly, when much later he explains to Peeperkorn how he has stayed on the Mountain all these years, lost to home, family, and duties for Clawdia's sake, he is reminded of *Carmen*. It is anything but irrelevant ('eine ziemlich beziehungslose Geschichte' [p. 848]). Arias from *Carmen* are third in the list of favourite pieces and they repeat that first parallel, with their conflict between duty— the call of the military bugle—and irresponsibility, love, freedom, desertion. The other records are close kin. The last scenes of *Aida* repeat the dilemma: love leading to dereliction of duty, love overriding the claims of honour and fatherland and leading to death, the hero entombed alive with his beloved, a hideous death which only the 'victorious ideality' of art makes acceptable. Then, after the terrors and idealization of *Aida*,

[71] To Julius Bab, 22 Feb. 1926 (Br. i. 233). Weigand's explanation of this episode (op. cit., pp. 143 ff.) is ingenious, but unnecessarily assumes that the author must mean what he says. Mann thus becomes a 'mystic', where he was simply a too energetic allegorist.

Hans Castorp relaxes with the *Prélude à l'après-midi d'un faune*, becomes himself a flute-playing faun, happy in his summer meadow: he enjoys 'die Liederlichkeit mit bestem Gewissen, die wunschbildhafte Apotheose all und jeder Verneinung des abendländischen Aktivitätskommandos' (dissipation with the best possible conscience, the ideal apotheosis of every kind of negation of the Western injunction to activity [p. 898]).[72] Then there is Valentin's song from Gounod's *Faust*, dear to Hans Castorp because he hears in it Joachim's soldierly voice and a benign promise to look down protectingly on him from heaven.[73]

The reference to Hans Castorp's situation on the mountain is clear in all these pieces, and identical in the first three. Hence his 'sympathy for these situations' (p. 893). His musical tastes reflect his *Urerlebnisse*,[74] but they do more, they also reflect his dilemma—the rival claims of 'duty' in the Flatlands and 'freedom' on the Mountain.

And what values are given to these? What do the musical versions tell us about Castorp and his state of mind? For the most part, little enough. A gentle humour constantly reminds the reader that these are only records, the conflicts are there in a box; still, they retain their beauty, and Hans Castorp is enthralled. But what does he *think* about them? He enjoys the licence to relax of Debussy, but to the gipsies' invitation to 'freedom' in *Carmen* he responds with a non-committal and perhaps ironical 'Ja, ja!' (p. 902).

Like so much in the novel, all this is ambiguous. Like so much, it probably existed, in conception at least, at an early stage in the process of genesis and education we have followed. For in the opening pages of the *Betrachtungen* 'music' was made to stand for many-sided German humanity, and opposed to the more articulate 'Western' art of literature. For Germany, the 'unliterary land', was the land of music (which included

[72] Mann makes no reference to the erotic element which this piece shares with the two operas. Did he not know what the faun in Mallarmé's poem has on his mind? Or were nymphs too idyllically healthy to parallel the diseased woman in Castorp's life?

[73] The association Joachim–Valentin has already been suggested in the words from Goethe's *Faust* 'als Soldat und brav' which head the section in which Joachim dies.

[74] Weigand, op. cit., p. 113.

the higher, freer form of writing, *Dichtung*). For 'virtuous' Latin civilization, music was unreliable, suspect (xii. 50 f.). These become Settembrini's sentiments, expressed in the section 'Politisch verdächtig'. He likens such clarity as music has to the mere clarity of Nature, of a stream—a 'clarity without consequences'; and even though music appears to be movement, it leads only to quietism (p. 160), it is an opiate (p. 162). It is the art that goes with the contemplative ideal; it is at odds with activity, let alone activism. The accents of a chapter devoted exclusively to music will thus depend on the author's attitude to the rights and wrongs of the contemplative life.

In the closing phases of *Der Zauberberg*, the contemplative life and all that goes with it is being critically questioned. It had once seemed an abstraction from life and activism akin to that of pure art, but it has come to seem a refusal of responsibilities. The *vita contemplativa* now looks more like accidie. So where music might, once, have been celebrated as a 'negation of the Western injunction to activity', it is so no longer. These temptations still have to be spelled out, for the sake of the confessional record; hence the full and non-committal description of those favourite pieces in which Hans Castorp rightly sees (even while he enjoys them as art) his own dilemmas repeated. But a judgement is also entered. This is done in the description of Hans Castorp's fifth favourite, the song *Am Brunnen vor dem Tore*.

Unlike the other four, Schubert's *Lindenbaum* song has affinities with Hans Castorp beyond its situation. It does have this affinity, since it evokes the temptation of death for a man who has been rejected in love. But that is barely a beginning. Alone of the five pieces it is from the same Germanic world Castorp comes from—'etwas besonders und exemplarisch Deutsches' (p. 903)—and is thus not just coincidentally allusive. The narrator begins by insisting on its representative status as 'Ausdruck und Exponent eines Geistig-Allgemeineren, einer ganzen Gefühls- und Gesinnungswelt' (p. 904), and on the significance of Castorp's love for it. If the song is typically German, and if Castorp loves it, it follows that he 'must love' the German world it stands for. In the wording—'eine ganze Welt, und zwar eine Welt, die er wohl lieben musste'—we

hear a man uncovering by logic the allegiance of his emotions.
The text continues:

Wir wissen, was wir sagen, wenn wir — vielleicht etwas dunkler-
weise — hinzufügen, dass sein Schicksal sich anders gestaltet hätte,
wenn sein Gemüt den Reizen der Gefühlssphäre, der allgemeinen
geistigen Haltung, die das Lied auf so innig-geheimnisvolle Weise
zusammenfasste, nicht im höchsten Grade zugänglich gewesen wäre.

(We know what we are saying when we—perhaps somewhat
darkly—add that his fate would have taken a different shape if
his mind had not been in the highest degree open to the charms of
that emotional sphere, the general spiritual attitude, which the
song epitomized in such an intimate, secret way. [p. 905)]

These words apply to Hans Castorp, not darkly but clearly.
The 'somewhat darkly' is a typical device of Mann's to make the
reader check for concealed meanings. Sure enough, what he
says of his *alter ego* Hans Castorp applies to himself and his own
education: without the attraction to the 'emotional sphere'
he is speaking of, there would not have been the fascination
with death and decay which marks the sequence from *Buddenbrooks* to *Der Tod in Venedig*. Nor would there have been that
fateful commitment of the artist in 1914 to the German cause,
based on a naïve equation of that 'emotional sphere' with the
Wilhelmine Reich.

But these things educated him, and through him Castorp.
Precisely the adventures of their fate made them capable of
criticizing the Germanic world, its artistic product, and the
love this inspired. For this is what the narrator asserts, knowing
it may meet incredulity ('Will man glauben, dass . . .', p. 904):
that Hans Castorp is aware of what that song and his love for it
mean. His conscience tells him that the *Lindenbaum* song stands
for a world of forbidden love, a world of death. The narrator
anticipates the flood of objections—that nothing could be more
magnificent, more masterly and pure as art, more typical of the
popular soul, or more immediately lovable than Schubert's song
—and stands by what he has said. He hints at the song's
associations in Castorp's mind with Naphta's ethos, with inhumanity in Spanish black and medieval ruffs, with cruelty,
all the unintended result of a piety obsessed with death such as
the song ultimately speaks of. He links it with medievalism
and with Settembrini's warnings against medievalism. He

sees behind its apparent health a threat. Perfect if 'enjoyed at the right moment', at the next it threatens to spread sickness among mankind. The highest of achievements if judged as beauty without conscience, it must appear untrustworthy to anyone with a responsible attitude to life. For anyone who loved it, the song was thus a challenge to self-education, stated in the Nietzschean word 'self-transcendence' (*Selbstüberwindung*). It is in short, though the words are not used at this point, 'politically suspect'.

In the closing paragraph of the section, Hans Castorp sits before the musical coffin (*Musiksarge*) and duly goes over the historical realities which grew from the Romantic impulse and its fascination with the past. So powerful was the ethos of the *Lindenbaum* that it could inspire in its sons works of great power; a large-scale talent could give it gigantic proportions and aspire to conquer the world; it could even serve as the basis for more earthly empires, robust and pushful and not very artistic, with music reduced to a small voice from an electrical instrument. But the best of its sons was surely the man whose life was consumed in the effort to overcome its temptations, who died with the new word of love and the future on his lips, a word which as yet he knew not how to speak.

As a history lesson, this is sweeping and vague, its terms not fully to be grasped unless we go beyond the context of the novel. It links together a century of German art and Thomas Mann as its descendant ('wir alle waren seine Söhne, und Mächtiges konnten wir ausrichten auf Erden, indem wir ihm dienten' [p. 907]), the dubious side of Wagner's achievement, the ostentatious Bismarckian–Wilhelmine Reich, and Nietzsche's criticism of both as *irdisch, allzuirdisch*. Who then is the 'best son' of the emotional sphere from which all this came? Is Hans Castorp meant? Yes, in so far as he bears Mann's message and has attained at least a fleeting clarity. Or is it Thomas Mann himself? Again yes, in so far as he drew conclusions, from his private counterparts of Hans Castorp's experience, about the way Germans should live with their past and the European present. Is it anyone else besides? Perhaps Nietzsche, apropos of whom Mann used the full wording of this peroration in 1924.[75]

---

[75] *Vorspruch zu einer musikalischen Nietzsche-Feier*, a speech delivered 15 Oct. 1924; the passage in question x. 183. The correspondence was first noted by Weigand.

It is not the first nor the last time Nietzsche is linked with Thomas Mann and a major fictional character in common suffering or striving.[76] At this late stage then, long after he has seemingly forgotten his vision in the snow, Hans Castorp is once more the positive hero, the young man who has learned the lessons of the war before it breaks out. Perhaps at a subconscious level he never totally forgot the vision, as his words at the time hinted he would not ('Mein Traum hat es mir deutlichst eingegeben, dass ich's für immer weiss' [p. 686]). Yet however deep and full his education has been, however praiseworthy the truths he has glimpsed, he has not acted on them. The conflict between duty in the Flatlands sense and the adventurous freedom of the Mountain is unresolved. If, as Hans Castorp once said to Joachim, they were there to become cleverer *and* healthier (p. 535), at what point does the combination issue in activity? This is the last critical question the book asks about its hero, and it gets no proper answer, because it is the 'elemental powers' of war that take him back to the Flatlands, not any decision of his own. By then, in fact, he is beyond taking decisions, his watch is broken, his place has been moved to the poorer-class Russian table, and the authorities no longer even bother to find distractions for him. Settembrini, the tireless pedagogue, has tried to the last to inform him about events down there in the real world, but gets no response from a pupil

der sich zwar von den geistigen Schatten der Dinge regierungsweise[77] das eine und andere träumen liess, der Dinge selbst aber nicht geachtet hatte, und zwar aus der Hochmutsneigung, die Schatten

---

[76] Both Tonio Kröger and Aschenbach are too delicate for the burdens they have to bear, 'called' but 'not born' to the pains of insight, the strain of creation. The formula echoes Nietzsche's account of Hamlet in *Die Geburt der Tragödie*, and is later applied by Mann to Nietzsche himself in the essay of 1947.

[77] *Regieren* is the word Hans Castorp uses of his meditations. It may be connected with the prince-imagery recurrent since *Königliche Hoheit*, but more specifically it is a Goethe quotation. Mephistopheles says of the Emperor:

'Und ihm beliebt' es, falsch zu schliessen,
Es könne wohl zusammengehn
Und sei recht wünschenswert und schön,
Regieren und zugleich geniessen.'
(*Faust II*, ll. 10248 ff.)

Mann quotes the last line in a letter to Max Rychner of 26 July 1925: 'Und doch habe ich längst gelernt, dass es das nicht gibt: regieren und zugleich geniessen.' *Blätter* 7, p. 11.

für die Dinge zu nehmen, in diesen aber nur Schatten zu sehen, — weswegen man ihn nicht allzu hart schelten darf, da dies Verhältnis nicht letztgültig geklärt ist.

(who allowed himself, it is true, to dream this and that about the spiritual shadows of things, as an administrative exercise, but had paid no attention to the things themselves, from the arrogant tendency to take shadows for things, but to see in things only shadows— for which one should not scold him too severely, since the relationship between the two is not finally cleared up. [p. 985])

This eleventh-hour criticism threatens to negate what has long since become the novel's point. Is the value of Hans Castorp's education itself to be questioned? Is all that he (and we) have gone through now to be dismissed as not good enough? Surely he has done his best—has seen through the claims of *Bildung* and abstract argument, has studied Man, has possessed Woman, has mused, queried, dreamt, has opened his mind to all possible influences . . . Perhaps in that last summary lies the ground of his author's criticism. At some stage in personal development, the open mind has to be closed, richness and many-sidedness are not the final aim. They may in some form be the ideal for art, but Hans Castorp is not an artist, and should aspire to a different condition.[78] Even his author, who is an artist, is now uneasy about the old ideal of many-sidedness in its extreme form. It is this self-critical awareness that makes him use Hans Castorp once more, before abandoning him for good, as whipping-boy for his own faults. The elevation of the Mountain, sometime symbol of pure art, is now the symbol of that divorcing of art from realities which has been the chief social characteristic of German art since the age of Weimar Classicism. 'Aestheticism' is the word for both, but the valuation has changed. It is a radical change. By locating the 'hopelessness' and 'lack of prospects' of pre-1914 Europe in aestheticism, Thomas Mann had come fully round to his brother's view and stated it in identical terms. For in *Zola* Heinrich had written that 'aestheticism is a product of times without hope, of states which kill hope'.[79] Hans Castorp, though in so many ways he has reached the conclusions his author had reached,

[78] Heller, op. cit., p. 213, nicely suggests that Hans Castorp is now fit only to be a novelist.

[79] 'Ästhetizismus ist ein Produkt hoffnungsloser Zeiten, hoffnungtötender Staaten' (*WB* 1326).

is left torpid on the Mountain as a warning against the sloth and quietism which *Bildung* in some circumstances may lead to. When he descends, it is not from any inner initiative; and he is last seen in the midst of his countrymen at war, fulfilling a primitive form of duty. He has the *Lindenbaum* song again on his lips, his love for it stronger now than his intuition of its perils.

And if this is where Hans Castorp is left, once again the object of criticism, where does the novel leave its author? He has certainly achieved, more than in any previous work, his ideal of richness and many-sidedness—even while coming to be critical of that ideal. Many-sidedness resides in the sheer complexity of the record, and what makes the record complex is above all the sequence of changes which history, private and public, dictated. No easy answer emerges from the novel's pages—the divergent interpretations it has had prove, if nothing else, that Mann did not fall into 'inartistic' explicitness.

Still, he believed that he had made his meaning clear. If it is not unequivocally plain to all, this is partly because art, especially the art of the novel (and even more especially Thomas Mann's art) is not made for the conveying of simple messages; and more specifically because ambiguities are increased when a work has the dual role of recording what was and declaring what should be.

The record of complexity has of course considerable value in itself, certainly greater value than a facile clarity based on superficial presentation.[80] And in addition to recording change in the perspective of Hans Castorp's education, Mann placed pointers to his meaning in certain key episodes—the snow

---

[80] An illuminating contrast is the sanatorium novel *Sanatorii Arktur*, written in the thirties, in part as a riposte to Thomas Mann's novel, by the Soviet novelist Konstantin Fedin (now in Fedin, *Sobranie Sochinenii*, Moscow, 1960, vol. 5). It presents with full explicitness the message that will-power and concentration on the work and society one has to return to can overcome disease. This non-materialist thesis is not different in essentials from Mann's. Where they differ is in the way Fedin simplifies: a healthy, brotherly society inspires devoted labour, leaving its members with no problems but their bacilli. That this society had gone through upheavals even more total than twentieth-century Germany could not be guessed from the text. Mann on the other hand registers allegorically all the negative forces—the long arm of tradition, the temptations his hero is exposed to—and brings out of this a positive and humane, if still apparently vague principle. Even by some such practical criterion as the broadening of social understanding, this is out of proportion more valuable.

K

vision, the musical digression. Pointers, it is true, can be missed in a work of the volume of *Der Zauberberg*. They often have been. Accordingly, Mann added his own explicit commentary. In the face of wilful misunderstanding, he explained his own allegory. When occasion offered, he stated that the italicized words of the snow vision were the book's message. He even seems to have wished that he had placed that chapter, for emphasis, at the end instead of in the middle.[81] All this is typical of the dilemma of an artist who wishes both to remain an artist and to influence the world outside art.

Yet even if it is accepted that the meaning of *Der Zauberberg* resides in those italicized words—that for the sake of goodness and love Man shall grant death no dominion over his thoughts (p. 686)—for today's reader this still lacks concreteness. It is metaphysical, if not in the pejorative sense other nations often apply to things German, then in the sense that it states a principle of utmost generality. This need not be a criticism— the whole *Zauberberg* conception is anything but concretely social. Still, if we are to assess Thomas Mann's increased grasp of realities and his claims to be considered a 'higher' realist, it is important to know what social realities he had in mind when he used those very general terms, and why the principle he stated seemed so vital.

He certainly did have particular realities in mind. To find out what they were, we have to go outside the pages of the novel, into the between-wars crisis in German public life; just as Thomas Mann himself went outside the traditionally self-sufficient sphere of German art to help rescue what could be rescued from the past and the coming catastrophe.

[81] Cf. Thomas Mann–Robert Faesi, *Briefwechsel*, Zürich, 1962, p. 16.

# Republic

Do I contradict myself?
Very well, I contradict myself.
WALT WHITMAN, *A Song of Myself*

## I

THE wartime commitment of the 'unpolitical' Thomas Mann typified the highly political consequences of ideals which Germans who cherished them believed were purely cultural. Mann's political involvement after the First World War is not typical in this way, but it is in another. What he experiences and struggles with in the years of the Weimar Republic is a recurrent problem of German political history, in the particular form it took at that time. His response is not that of the majority of Germans, but it is, *mutatis mutandis*, that of a distinguished minority in the past.

The problem is the disjointedness and historical discontinuity of German national life, and the uncertainty and overcompensation which resulted. Germany's long fragmentation, her never more than loose political groupings and eventual belated nationhood, the subordination of the small German states to old established European powers, the nineteenth-century struggle between Prussia and Austria, *kleindeutsch* and *grossdeutsch*, which was a struggle over what 'Germany' was to mean, and then the sudden status of a great power—all this hardly allowed nationality to be taken for granted and forgotten. Nationality became a problem in itself, brooded over with a hypersensitivity which sometimes appeared as self-doubt, sometimes as self-assertion.

A much-favoured solution was the construction of a national identity from the materials of the past. In 1813 the co-operation of the German states in the overthrow of Napoleon was inspired by and interpreted through the poetic legends of the Germanic past, which were readily turned into heroic simplicities. A dangerous habit was inaugurated of drawing historical parallels, creating historical connections and developments, choosing an ancestry to emulate—dangerous because of the arbitrary way choice might operate and because of the easy supremacy offered to myth. Even aside from the 1813 episode, German Romantic attitudes rested on myth but issued in politics. The Romantic cult of the 'organic' society, and hence of the Middle Ages, was an expedient of complicated modern men seeking a soothing simplicity. Its influence extended beyond poetry and counteracted all openness to reform in a society which was already far behind its European neighbours in political development. The effects can still be seen in 1871. Ignorance and a willingness to live with legends made the Hohenzollerns who were to rule the new Germany appear as the essential continuation of the medieval Hohenstaufens. The 'Second' Reich could be inaugurated in a cloud of glory and illusion.

The only antidote to all this lay in the arts of history and literature. Historians might show up the falseness of the myths and trace the realities of the past. Writers might show up the self-indulgence of heroic myth by soberly portraying the present. For both tasks, critical detachment was needed.

It is now commonly agreed that the historians failed.[1] German historiography in the nineteenth century has its glories, but they do not include acts of clarification and national self-criticism. The principle of *Historismus*—that uniqueness of character and development was the category under which historical phenomena could most fruitfully be studied—led to a narrowing concern with the uniqueness of German character and development, and to an uncritical acceptance of the order of things and the course of events.[2] 'Uniqueness' seemed to

[1] See Eckart Kehr, 'Neuere deutsche Geschichtsschreibung', in *Der Primat der Innenpolitik*, Berlin, 1965; the discussions of historians scattered through Hans Kohn's *The Mind of Germany*, repr. 1965; and the fully documented account by G. G. Iggers, *Deutsche Geschichtswissenschaft*, Munich, 1971. Peter Gay, *Weimar Culture*, 1968, pp. 86–96, gives a polemical summary from the viewpoint of the Weimar years.

[2] 'Aber aus der individuellen Fülle der Volksgeister wurde die Verachtung der allgemeinen Menschheitsidee . . . aus der romantischen Revolution ein sattes Behagen am Gegebenen . . . aus dem Drang des deutschen Geistes zu einem staatlichen Leibe derselbe Imperialismus wie überall sonst in der Welt.' Ernst Troeltsch, 'Naturrecht und Humanität in der Weltpolitik' (1922), a lecture printed posthumously in *Deutscher Geist und Westeuropa*, Tübingen, 1923, pp. 17 f. This lecture was an important influence on Mann's thinking. See below.

justify abandoning all general moral criteria on which dissenting judgements might have been based. Hegel had furnished dubious formal arguments for this. In the introduction to his *Philosophie der Geschichte* he went beyond an attack on the philosophically vulnerable doctrine of Natural Law and revelled in the amorality of historical forces which Natural Law had been a means to keep in check. He was not alone in thus disposing of the moral function of historiography. The young Ranke's famous claim to have rendered his subject 'wie es eigentlich gewesen' is, taken in its context, less a claim to total accuracy than a disclaimer of the role of moral judge.[3] These attitudes formed the central tradition of German historical writing in the nineteenth century. Only after 1918 did some German historians realize that there were responsibilities the guild had failed to meet.

Writers did a little better. Goethe in 1813 by eloquent non-participation; Heine by a lifelong polemic against Romantic self-deception and its practical consequences; Nietzsche by his attacks on the Bismarckian Reich and its non-culture, starting with his philippic against the illusion that victory over France in 1870 was the victory of a superior culture; Fontane more gently but in the end unmistakably, by his analysis of Prussia's hollow ethos. Their teaching is that Germans should not become uncritically absorbed in their own culture, especially when this means an unhealthy cultivation of illusion. (As Heine made plain, the Romantics' 'Middle Ages' had precious little to do with the real thing.)

But these were isolated voices, two of them exiles. Far more writers abstained from comment, following what they took to be the tradition of Weimar Classicism, that Art should remain above reality. Nevertheless, in the periods of national success, literature in practice rallied to the flag, reflecting popular heroic assumptions, monumentalizing myths in a way which matched Wilhelmine styles in art and architecture—themselves a product of the uneasy search for a historical identity,

---

[3] 'Man hat der Historie das Amt, die Vergangenheit zu richten, die Mitwelt zum Nutzen zukünftiger Jahre zu belehren, beigemessen: so hoher Aemter unterwindet sich gegenwärtiger Versuch nicht: er will bloss zeigen, wie es eigentich gewesen.' *Vorrede* to *Geschichte der romanischen und germanischen Völker von 1494 bis 1514, Werke*, vol. 33, p. vii.

*Verlegenheitshistorismus.*[4] Only late in the century, with the rise of Naturalism, did an opposition literature assert itself; and how that fared in 1914 we have observed.

The defeat in 1918 brought back the problem of discontinuity, more acute now because for half a century the nation had tasted unity and power. Defeat brought loss of power, and also a new form of state. Theatrical and irresponsible as Wilhelm II had been (criticisms which became commonplace after the war) the loss of the monarchy left a 'gaping void in the national life of the German people'.[5] Intelligent observers saw that the new start was too abrupt, and tried to build intellectual bridges from the Old to the New Germany.[6] Others were more inclined to live in the past and cherish myths in place of the unpleasant reality.

The temptation was strong. Germans were resentful of the Versailles treaty and outraged by the war-guilt clause. They were lulled by legends into believing that Germany had been neither guilty at the start of the war nor defeated at the end; that disunity on the home front had let the army down decisively; that the humiliation of surrender and a dictated peace was the responsibility of Republicans, especially Social Democrats, who took up the trailing reins of government in 1918—the 'November criminals'; they saw Germany reduced to secondary status and excluded from world councils as a moral leper. The Republic itself hazily appeared to have been imposed by the enemy; certainly it was not 'truly German'. It reduced the role of authority and such authority as it had lacked all prestige. Universal suffrage and parliamentary sovereignty invited private citizens and political parties to participate responsibly, something equally novel for both. The constitution was designed by an academic and accepted by a Constituent

[4] Helmut Plessner, *Das Schicksal deutschen Geistes im Ausgang seiner bürgerlichen Epoche*, Zürich, 1935, p. 81. Plessner's book elaborates, and the title of his second edition—*Die verspätete Nation* (Stuttgart, 1959)—epitomizes, the trends here discussed. On the literary climate of the early Empire, see Jost Hermand, 'Zur Literatur der Gründerzeit' in *Von Mainz nach Weimar*. Stuttgart, 1969, pp. 211–50.

[5] Winston Churchill, *The Second World War*, vol. 1, *The Gathering Storm*, 1948, p. 9. Churchill thought a constitutional monarchy was in the circumstances the thing for Germany—a view anticipated on more general grounds of national psychology by Heine.

[6] e.g. the historians Ernst Troeltsch and Friedrich Meinecke. In this chapter, I take their attitudes and insights as representative of the minority Ringer terms 'modernist mandarins', i.e. those who strove to adapt themselves to a changed social and political world.

Assembly meeting in Weimar, not because Weimar symbolized past cultural greatness but because Berlin was unsafe. From this intimidated start the Republic remained almost constantly in a state of crisis, political or economic, unstable within, vulnerable without. The fall from the obvious glories of the Wilhelmine Reich was too painful; the present was not a fit place to live in.

Thomas Mann's *Betrachtungen*, begun when the military struggle was evenly balanced and ended before the defeat, already contained an appeal to the German past, which he saw as an ideal threatened by the European present. That past comprised the traditional German disengagement of art from practical matters; the long-standing German resistance to the disintegrating influence of the rational West; and most specifically Romanticism. The very existence of culture at all was made to appear dependent on preserving these past values. They were duly represented in *Der Zauberberg* as Mann conceived of it early in the war, epitomized in the definition of Romanticism as 'sympathy with death'—a cryptic formula[7] meant to suggest a knowledge of 'deeper' truths, superior to any optimistic activity in the cause of mere life.

In the early years of the Weimar Republic, this view changed, so diametrically that the key term—'sympathy with death'— was kept, but its valuation reversed. It came to mean the dangerous and destructive tendency to escape from reality into a (dead) past. The change in the value Mann gave this formula is the axis on which his political life turned. The process is worth studying for itself, because of the importance of Mann's political role. But it also gives substance to our understanding of *Der Zauberberg*.

Mann's change was not sudden or facile. Troeltsch and Meinecke had an equally conservative past, but they accepted Weimar reality, traced its historical necessity, and chose to support the Republic far sooner than Mann did. He had no immediate thought of adapting himself to the new circumstances. If he did not remain a conservative for long, it was not for want of trying.

[7] The term first appears in the letter to Paul Amann of 3 Aug. 1915 (discussed above, pp. 237 f.). By mid-1917, when he was astounded to hear Hans Pfitzner use the identical phrase apropos his own opera *Palestrina* (cf. xii. 423 f.), Mann is speaking of it as a 'thematic component of the composition' of his novel.

## II

In August 1919 Thomas Mann received an honorary doc-torate from Bonn. His letter of thanks points to a probable reason. He is proud to have his work recognized by this par-ticular university—'gerade durch die Universität Bonn, die rheinische' (xi. 351). In a less obtrusive way than the later withdrawal of the same degree from Mann the anti-Nazi exile, the award was a political gesture: an institution in the occupied Rhineland was honouring a champion of the lost national cause, the author of the *Betrachtungen eines Unpolitischen*. Further signs of Mann's public image just after the war are the reviews his *Betrachtungen* received. The journal *Hochland* speaking for 'Catholic youth' felt able to claim him as 'wholly one of them in the struggle against the modern spirit', that is against 'Enlightenment and utilitarianism';[8] another reviewer pointed out Mann's affinities with the extreme anti-modernism of Julius Langbehn's *Rembrandt als Erzieher*. It was clear that Mann's basic allegiance (*Grundpathos*) was to the past; his book was the 'manifesto of a dyed-in-the-wool reactionary mind'.[9]

Mann would scarcely have demurred from the substance of this, though he might have disputed the term 'reactionary'. The events of these months in late 1918 and early 1919—Ger-many's plea for peace, Wilhelm II's abdication, the revolution, the declaration of the Republic, the Spartakist rising, the Bavarian Soviet episode—were not calculated to alter his position. Government and society seemed to be sliding irresistibly towards the abyss of Bolshevism. Some form of conservatism appeared imperative. Even those intellectuals who adapted themselves to the new circumstances and accepted the demo-cratic republic as a historical necessity did so at least in part because it was more 'conservative' than the red alternative. They spoke of the 'ideal of conservative democracy', even of 'conservative socialism', they saw the much-scorned rules of

---

[8] Repr. in Schröter, *Dokumente*, p. 82.

[9] Ibid., p. 85. The correspondences are more substantial than the 'antithetical method' the reviewer points to. Langbehn anticipates Mann's objections to democratic levelling, his cult of individualism, celebration of 'Germanness', and use of 'German' as an adjective of quality; his belief that the Germans are an 'art people' (*Kunstvolk*) and the quintessence of humanity; and his appropriation of historical ideal figures. See the opening sections of Langbehn's *Rembrandt als Erzieher*, 'Leitgedanken', Neuausgabe Leipzig, 1922, pp. 45–58.

'formal democracy' as a bulwark against 'Bolshevistic chaos' and a means to prevent the Imperial class-structure from being inverted into a dictatorship of the proletariat.[10]

At the same time, they did also begin to probe the causes of catastrophe and the flaws and divisions in Imperial society from which it had sprung. There are only slight hints of this in Thomas Mann's formal statement on these matters, the meditation on Germany's defeat in *Gesang vom Kindchen*. He speaks of German self-accusation, of the contrast between individuals' heroic self-sacrifice and the ignoble realities they served, of the *hubris* of Germany's bid for world power. But the dominant notes are a brooding stoicism, which sees defeat as a 'warning fall' for the ultimate good of the 'most significant soul', and a deep resentment at the hypocrisy of the *Entente* powers,[11] whose high morals have proved compatible with a blockade of Germany. The closing line of the poem explains the frugality of the christening supper by this act of the 'cold imperious Angles'. The harmonious idyll, meant as a kind of spiritual retreat after the polemics of war and before resuming work on the *Zauberberg* project, thus has deeper dissonances. Mann's bitterness was to be increased by the Versailles treaty and the evident vindictiveness of the Allies.

So his wartime outlook seemed doubly confirmed—his mistrust of Western 'virtue' by the acts of the *Entente*, his fear of a politicized society by the instability of the new order in Germany. What could be done? Probably nothing. The 'verdict of history', however surprisingly, had gone against the side with deeper values. One had to accept this fatalistically— here Spengler's modish philosophy of history offered a sort of solace—and see Germany's defeat as part of the total decline of the Occident.[12]

---

[10] 'Heute ist demokratisch gleich konservativ, und ist ein richtiger, die Planwirtschaft fördernder Sozialismus staatserhaltend'; '. . . das einzige Mittel, die umgekehrte Klassenherrschaft, die Herrschaft des Proletariats, in die Bahnen einer gesunden und gerechten Staatsbildung hineinzuführen.' Ernst Troeltsch, *Spektator-Briefe, Aufsätze über die deutsche Revolution und die Weltpolitik 1918—1922*, Tübingen, 1924, pp. 117, 303. Cf. also Friedrich Meinecke, *Nach der Revolution*, Munich, 1919, pp. 114 ff.

[11] *Gesang vom Kindchen*, final canto, esp. viii. 1096 f.

[12] Cf. to Gustav Blume, 5 July 1919: 'Man muss sich kontemplativ stimmen, auch fatalistisch-heiter, Spengler lesen und verstehen, dass der Sieg England-Amerika's die Civilisierung, Rationalisierung, Utilitarisierung des Abendlandes,

Mann's instinct was to devote himself entirely to art, to whose free dimension he had longed throughout the war to return. He writes to Kurt Martens in June 1919 that he has no inclination to involve himself in yet another political book. Quite apart from the fact that it is not the right moment, things being very much in flux, he is wholly concerned 'mich in den "Zauberberg"-Roman wieder einzuspinnen' (Br. i. 163 f.). The cocoon image is telling.

Nevertheless, if he should come to speak on political questions again, it is clear that it would be as a conservative. Hermann Graf Keyserling, a kindred spirit and admirer of the *Betrachtungen*, encouraged him to believe that conservatism was dormant, not dead. If this was true, Mann could see a political function for himself, eventually. He writes to Keyserling in January 1920:

> Sehr hat mich Ihre Äusserung interessiert, dass in Kurzem die Konservativen wieder am meisten in Deutschland zu sagen haben werden. Ich glaube es selbst; die Natur stellt sich am Ende irgendwie wieder her, und 'der Deutsche *ist* konservativ', — Wagner wird damit ewig recht behalten. Nichts ist aus diesem Grunde wichtiger, als die Vergeistigung des deutschen Konservatismus . . .

> (I was very struck by your suggestion that in a little while the conservatives will have the main say again in Germany. I believe it myself; Nature eventually restores itself somehow, and 'Germans *are* conservative'—Wagner will always be right there. For just that reason, nothing is more important than the task of giving German conservatism an intellectual element . . . [Br. i. 173])

Keyserling set out to serve this cause by founding a 'School of Wisdom' at Darmstadt. Mann's open letter to him supporting this remarkable idea clarifies his position. It restates the essentials of his *Betrachtungen* argument for 'deeper' values: 'organic bonds' (*Bindung*) opposed to 'emancipation' (*Befreiung*), Romantic 'sin and doubt' opposed to Enlightenment 'virtue'; and it then defines the work of spiritual reconstruction which needs doing as the 'reconciliation of antitheses on the level which Mind has reached'. There must be no slipping

die das Schicksal jeder alternden Kultur ist, besiegelt und beendigt' (Br. i. 165). Mann had no doubt read Spengler since May, when he wrote to Philipp Witkop that he intended to (Br. i. 161). He later rejected Spengler, in line with his general change of attitude: but it is clear that, contrary to what he says in *Von deutscher Republik* (xi. 841), he began by taking him wholly seriously.

back to lower, earlier levels of consciousness. That is, what cannot any longer stand up to criticism has in the long run no prospect of dominating. The argument eventually becomes specific enough for us to identify what he means:

Jeder Versuch, das Alte, das durch Kritik Tote aus sich selbst, aus der Autorität und von Gemüts wegen wieder zu beleben, ist Obskurantismus, und in ihm haben weder Geist noch auch Seele ein gutes Gewissen, während doch eben nur dieses einer Lebens- und Seelenform Dauer verbürgt. Man verwechsle auch nicht Gemüt und Roheit! Denn Reaktion und Obskurantimus sind Roheit — sentimentale Roheit; und wenn ich mich in den 'Betrachtungen' auf die Seite der Romantik schlug, so ist es nur darum unnötig, unsere Pogrom-Monarchisten und Patriotenlümmel vor Verwechslungen zu warnen, weil sie die 'Betrachtungen' nicht lesen können.

(Every attempt to take what is old and killed off by criticism, and revive it from its own resources, from authority, and by appeal to 'the German cast of mind', is obscurantism, and such attempts can never make intellect or spirit feel easy in conscience—which is precisely what is needed to guarantee the permanence of a way of life or spiritual form. Nor must we confuse 'German Mind' and mere coarseness. For reaction and obscurantism are coarseness—sentimental coarseness; and the only reason why I need not warn our pogrom-monarchists and bumpkin-patriots against such confusions in the case of my 'Betrachtungen', where I plumped for Romanticism, is that they are incapable of reading the book. [xii. 601 f.])

The fastidious artist is very aware that all that blusters is not true conservatism; there are claimants to the name with whom he does not care to be associated; and certain conservative aims like the restoration of the monarchy are now out of the question, past for good, 'reaction'. These are vital reservations, which were to lead Mann far away from his original conservatism. But for the present, his position is clear: he is a conservative looking about for the beginnings of constructive conservatism to which he can add his effort. Will Keyserling's project fit the bill? Or the circle around Moeller van den Bruck, whose cultural and political attitudes for a time 'soothed his nerves' and inspired his sympathies?[13] Or was there even, perhaps, some chance of a conservative *coup* succeeding?

[13] Mann appears to have used these words to Moeller van den Bruck at some unspecified date soon after the war: 'Die politische und kulturelle Haltung Ihres

Mann's response when one came is illuminating. The conservative hopes and the fastidious reservations are clear. So is his uncertainty about the true mood of the country. He wrote to his equally conservative friend Ernst Bertram in March 1920, three days after the Kapp Putsch:

Ich möchte wohl wissen, was Sie zu den Ereignissen sagen. Diktator Kapp wird auch Ihnen persönlich kaum willkommen sein; und im Ganzen habe ich doch, bei aller Sympathie mit gewissen Tendenzen der augenblicklichen Machthaber ('Ehre und Ehrlichkeit' wollen sie herstellen, — nun, bravo!) den Eindruck einer verfrühten, den ruhigen Gang der Dinge störenden Aktion und fürchte eine schwere Kompromittierung der konservativen Idee, die im ganzen Lande wieder so sehr an Boden gewonnen hatte. Die Staatsstreichler haben offenbar sogar den Grad ihrer Ausbreitung überschätzt und auf eine Miterhebung des ganzen Volkes gegen das bisherige Regime gerechnet, die aber nun, so viel ich sehe, nicht statt hat. Nicht nur der organisierte Sozialismus,[14] auch alles Parlamentarisch-Demokratische steht ihnen entgegen, — wobei freilich die Gesinnung des eigentlichen Volkes schwer zu erkennen ist.

(I should much like to know what your view of these events is. Dictator Kapp is hardly, I imagine, personally welcome to you either; and on the whole my impression, despite some sympathy for the present rulers (they want to restore 'honour and honesty'—well, good for them!) is one of a premature act which will disturb the steady trend of things and, I fear, do considerable damage to conservatism, which had gained so much ground in the whole country. The men behind the coup have evidently overestimated the spread of conservative attitudes and reckoned on a spontaneous rising by the whole people against the previous regime, but so far as I can see this hasn't happened. Not only organized socialism, but the whole parliamentary democracy is against them—though of course the real feelings of the people proper are hard to make out. [Br. B. 88 f.]])

The same letter epitomizes the spiritual power vacuum of the Weimar Republic, its failure to command men's inner allegiance, in the words: 'Dass die Deutschen ihre Fürsten verjagt haben, ist als Glück vollkommen, als Unglück aber bei Weitem

---

Kreises schmeichelt unmittelbar meine geistigen Nerven und damit auch wirklich meine physischen; was geistige Sympathie ist, ich erfahre es immer bei der Berührung mit Ihrer Welt.' At all events, Moeller's paper *Das Gewissen* printed them in 1928 without provoking any denial by Thomas Mann. See Kurt Sontheimer, *Thomas Mann und die Deutschen*, Munich, 1961, p. 56.

[14] The socialist organizations had met the coup with a general strike.

noch nicht ermessen.' (That the Germans drove out their princes is the very height of good fortune, but as ill-fortune has still some way to go.) But he was right to have doubts about Kapp; the Putsch collapsed the following day.

Clearly, up till this point there is no sign of a new Mann. His later statements that the *Betrachtungen* had worked conservatism out of his system ignore these first post-war years of conservative expectancy. In line with this unchanged allegiance, *Der Zauberberg* was still very much the conception which it had been in mid-war, when he was prevented from working on it. In September 1920 Mann writes to Julius Bab that the *Zivilisationsliterat* appears as an Italian freemason, and he implies that the novel will soon be finished (Br. i. 183). More than a year later, poor Settembrini is still being pilloried, this time in an essay on Franco-German relations where he is the culturally bankrupt but still highly verbal representative of the powers whose victory was such a paradox of history. Nothing more comical, Mann says, than the rhetorical Western bourgeois, with his advocate's jargon and his classical blah-blah about virtue: he should be put on the stage, or in a novel, where he might be contrasted with a sphere of sinful Romanticism (xii. 621).[15] The essay rehashes yet again the cultural conservatism of the *Betrachtungen*, declaring in particular that the gap between the *Entente*'s moral propaganda and its ruthless behaviour inspires even in more educated Germans (*das höhere Deutschtum*) a general doubt of Western *ratio* (xii. 616). The situation is nothing less than a crisis of European humanism. People now sense that it is 'ausgelaugt, obsolet, sterbenshinfällig' (washed out, obsolete, on the point of collapse) along with its panoply of concepts—Enlightenment, Civilization, Democracy, Liberalism (xii. 619). But this need not be a fatal crisis for Germany, because her affinities lie elsewhere, with the East, where the 'Sarmatic radicalism' of Tolstoy had first prophesied the decline of the humanist tradition, with its Graeco-Roman basis, within a hundred years.

Playing off Russia against the West, despite the fact that Russia too had been at war with Germany—which was viewed as a kind of blunder of History—is another stock argument in the

[15] Work on this essay, *Das Problem der deutsch-französischen Beziehungen*, can be dated to December 1921 (Br. i. 106).

German analysis of culture at this time. It rested on a 'kind of ideological geography in which technical progress, along with spiritual decay, appeared to increase to the west, while an apparently inseparable mixture of economic backwardness and spiritual profundity was associated with the easterly portion of the map'.[16] Mann's renewed interest in Tolstoy originates here. And in between the two disparaging references to Settembrini, he had written and delivered his paper *Goethe und Tolstoi* in which the same prophecy of the death of humanism occurs.

In its original form,[17] Mann's paper is largely confined to the question of education. Its title was at first to be 'Die Idee der Erziehung bei Goethe und Tolstoi' (Br. B. 100). It closes with the question of Europe's future. Are its classical foundations not crumbling? Tolstoy's prophecy has already come true in Russia, with the revolution. Will it come true in Germany as well? The question seems more rhetorical than open. Mann only hints in his peroration at what will replace the humanist tradition. But a German audience at a 'Nordic Week', hearing these reflections from the author of the *Betrachtungen*, will have filled in the details effortlessly, taking its cue from the markedly *völkisch* phrasing used to praise or blame: the connection of Tolstoy's talent with 'das Mythisch-Wurzelhaft-Volkstümliche', or the gloss on Tolstoy's distaste for city life which refers to 'der Wortgeist der Stadt, Geist des Gassengeschwätzes, der Anmassung und der halbgebildeten Maulgeläufigkeit ... der deutscher Sachlichkeit so wenig gemäss ist'.[18] If Goethe rather than Tolstoy is finally set up as the German ideal, it is for his greater success in moulding and ordering the irrational forces, the 'Grösse und Kraft' he shared with Tolstoy. No doubt is left where Germany's affinities lie—with Russia. There is a 'hohe Verständigungsmöglichkeit . . . zwischen russischem und deutschem Wesen'.[19]

All this is typical of the cultural self-appraisal of German conservatives. Since early in the nineteenth century German culture had grown away—in actuality and even more in its

---

[16] Fritz Ringer, *The Decline of the German Mandarins*, p. 187.

[17] Delivered in Lübeck on 4 Sept. 1921, first published in the conservative *Deutsche Rundschau* in March 1922, pp. 225–46. The later expansion corresponds to the text of ix. 79–149.

[18] loc. cit., pp. 243 f., 245.        [19] loc. cit., p. 245.

image of itself—from Western influences and traditions, developing a compensatory superiority complex. Manifestos from the Romantics down to 1914 preached it as an alternative tradition. Thus it is not a paradox that a German conservative should blithely suggest that the whole of Western humanism was in decline. In 1921 this was a gesture of higher *Schadenfreude* towards Germany's conquerors. What true German would wish to conserve *that* tradition, when he had his own 'deeper' one, untouched by the decay which was clearly ruining its neighbour?

This is the *Goethe und Tolstoi* of 1921. Put beside it the corresponding passage of the expanded version completed less than four years later,[20] and a total reversal in Mann's outlook and in the direction of his effort becomes dramatically clear. In place of the *Schadenfreude*, the rhetorical question, the invitation to see a conservative German culture as the true path of the future, we find this:

Es ist für Deutschland nicht der Augenblick, sich anti-humanistisch zu gebärden, Tolstoi's pädagogischen Bolschewismus zum Vorbild zu nehmen [. . .] Im Gegenteil ist es der Augenblick, unsere grossen humanen Überlieferungen mit Macht zu betonen und feierlich zu pflegen — um ihrer selbst willen nicht nur, sondern auch, um so die Ansprüche der 'lateinischen Zivilisation' recht sichtlich ins Unrecht zu setzen.

(It is not the moment for Germany to go in for anti-humanistic behaviour, or to follow the example of Tolstoy's pedagogical Bolshevism [. . .] On the contrary, it is the moment to put all possible emphasis on our great humane traditions and solemnly cherish them—not just for their own sake, but also in order to give a clear demonstration that the claims of 'Latin civilization' are unjustified. [ix. 169 f.])

Why this change? Because the half-prophecy of 1921 has come all too true, but in a form which fails to meet the ideals of a fastidious conservative. The question he asked in his Lübeck paper stands unchanged in the later text: is the Mediterranean, classical humanist tradition something eternal, rooted in Man, or was it merely an appendage of the bourgeois

---

[20] It was published in *Bemühungen* in October 1925, but had been completed before April, since it refers (ix. 167) to the Herriot government in France as still in office.

period, now at an end? Europe has meanwhile given the answer: 'Der anti-liberale Rückschlag ist mehr als klar, er ist krass. Er äussert sich politisch in der überdrussvollen Abkehr von Demokratie und Parlamentarismus, in einer mit finsteren Brauen vollzogenen Wendung zur Diktatur und zum Terror.' (The anti-liberal reaction is more than clear, it is glaring. It finds political expression in the disgust with which people turn away from democracy and parliamentarism, turning faces of dark resolve towards dictatorship and terror. [ix. 166])

Italy and Spain are obvious examples, but the waters of nationalism are rising everywhere; in Germany it takes the form of a fascism avowedly anti-Christian as well as anti-Jewish, an ethnic religion of Wotan cults and solstice celebrations—to put it in hostile terms (and that is what Mann wishes to do) 'romantic barbarism'. All of which plays into the hands of germanophobes like Poincaré and Barrès, because it justifies their claim that civilization ends at the Rhine and beyond the Roman *limes* lies barbarism;[21] and thereby encourages policies of repression towards Germany, in place of the policies of reconciliation and reintegration for which Germans like Stresemann were working (ix. 168 f.).

Hence Mann's exhortation. Not only is the fascist version of 'Germanic culture' a ludicrous caricature, it is also a political liability. Yet because of the view of German culture that more than a century of dogmatic assertion had ingrained, fascist nationalism was winning hands down. How could it be resisted? Only perhaps by an even older, more venerable tradition, a common European humanism. So he is now openly resisting the cultural and political tide. He was to maintain this stance for the remaining years of the Weimar Republic, driven increasingly leftwards by the excesses of a 'conservatism' he could not accept, and speaking in ever more sober, clear, realistic terms for what was ever more obviously the losing side.

The two versions of *Goethe und Tolstoi* give the measure of Mann's change of heart and place it in a European political context. But the point between them at which he saw the light

---

[21] Cf. *Der 'autonome' Rheinstaat des Herrn Barrès*, esp. xii. 626: 'die Kulturpropaganda . . . die aus diesem Gebiete durchaus ein Glacis der lateinischen Zivilisation machen will . . .'

can be stated precisely: June 1922. The decisive factor was the assassination of Walther Rathenau.

Rathenau had proved himself as wartime organizer of military raw materials. In May 1921 he chose to place his abilities, in a conscious spirit of self-sacrifice, at the service of the Republic; he became associated with a policy of fulfilling the Versailles reparations clause; and he was a Jew purporting to represent Germany. All good reasons why nationalists should hate him. He was murdered on 24 June by simple-minded youths fed on stories about the Elders of Zion and the secret communist connections behind Rathenau's policies,[22] and inspired by the 'myth of the Prussian-German past.'[23]

It was a disturbing event, even by the standards of the Weimar Republic, and its effects were considerable. It led to the reunion of the split Social Democratic Party; to the resignation of a number of Nationalists who saw that their party's propaganda methods had helped create the climate for murder; to a Law for the Protection of the Republic. It was a factor in the accelerated fall of the mark.[24] Far from being a random event, it clearly struck many people as a turning-point, a symbol, an omen, a sign of Germany's spiritual condition. Albert Einstein called it the fruit of fifty years of German education.[25] It was thus no trivial thing that changed the course of Thomas Mann's political life. Nor was his response purely an emotional one to the fact of murder, as his political opponents later suggested.[26] (The murder of Matthias Erzberger in 1921, a few days before Mann delivered the original *Goethe und Tolstoi*, had gone unmentioned.) A letter of 8 July, once more to Bertram, shows Mann's complex reaction:

Sie streiften die Politik. Ein heilloses Wirrnis. Die Sozialisten schreien nach Ausnahmegesetzen und die Konservativen klagen über den Verfall der Demokratie. Rathenaus Ende bedeutete auch für mich einen schweren Choc. Welche Finsternis in den Köpfen

[22] See Erich Eyck, *A History of the Weimar Republic*, Harvard University Press, 1967, vol. 1, p. 214.
[23] See James Joll, *Intellectuals in Politics*, 1960, p. 128.
[24] Cf. Eyck, op. cit., 1. 215 ff.
[25] In the August number of the *Neue Rundschau*, p. 816. The wording is: 'Denjenigen aber, welche die ethische Erziehung des deutschen Volkes in den letzten fünfzig Jahren geleitet haben, möchte ich zurufen: An ihren Früchten sollt ihr sie erkennen.' The figure might have been doubled.
[26] See Schröter, *Dokumente*, p. 104.

dieser Barbaren! Oder dieser idealistisch Verirrten. Nachgerade bekomme ich Einsicht in die Gefahren der Geschichte, die durch falsche Analogieen die Einzigartigkeit der Situation verdunkelt und eine gewisse Jugend zum Wahnsinn verführt. Ich leide unter der Verzerrung des deutschen Antlitzes. Ich denke daran, einen Geburtstagartikel über Hauptmann zu einer Art von Manifest zu gestalten, worin ich der Jugend, die auf mich hört, ins Gewissen rede. Ich verleugne die 'Betrachtungen' nicht und bin der Letzte, von der Jugend Enthusiasmus für Dinge zu verlangen, über die sie innerlich hinaus ist, wie Sozialismus und Demokratie. Aber die mechanische Reaktion habe ich schon einmal sentimentale Roheit genannt, und die neue Humanität mag denn doch auf dem Boden der Demokratie nicht schlechter gedeihen, als auf dem des alten Deutschland. Es ist ein Scheuen und Ausbrechen vor Worten. Alsob nicht 'die Republik' immer noch das deutsche Reich wäre, das thatsächlich heute weit mehr, als zur Zeit, da ins banal Theatralische entartete historische Mächte darüber thronten, in unser Aller Hände gelegt ist, — und das eben ist die Demokratie.

(You touched on politics. A wretched confusion. The socialists are crying for exceptional laws and the conservatives are lamenting the decay of democracy. Rathenau's death was a great shock for me too. What benighted minds these barbarians have! Or are they misguided idealists? I am gradually coming to see the dangers of history, the way it obscures the uniqueness of a situation by false analogies and leads a certain kind of youth astray into mad acts. The distortion of the German countenance causes me acute suffering. I am thinking of turning a birthday article on Gerhart Hauptmann into a kind of manifesto in which I appeal to the conscience of the young people whose ear I have. I am not going back on the 'Betrachtungen', and I am the last to demand that young people should be enthusiastic about things like democracy and socialism which their inner development has left far behind. But I have already on a previous occasion called mechanical reaction sentimental coarseness, and the new humanity may perhaps after all flourish no worse on the basis of democracy than on that of the old Germany. It is all a matter of shying and rebelling at words. As if 'the Republic' were not still the German Reich, which is in fact today placed in all our hands to a much greater extent than it was when historical forces which had generated into banal theatricality throned over it—and that precisely is democracy. [Br. B. 112 f.])

Every proposition and nuance of phrasing here reflects the dilemma of the conservative—his natural sympathies and hopes ('idealistisch', 'Geschichte', 'deutsches Antlitz', 'altes Deutschland'), his disillusionment ('Barbaren', 'Verirrten', 'Verzerrung'), and his self-criticism ('Gefahren der Geschichte', 'falsche Analogieen'). He shows no great sympathy for democracy or socialism, but only a dawning sense that democracy may after all ('denn doch') be no worse a foundation for humane existence than any other. Yet this alone, together with his dismissal of mere slogan opposition to the Republic ('Scheuen und Ausbrechen vor Worten') is an immense advance. It is a realization which others achieved immediately after the war: that the form of the state need be no more than an organizational technicality, in no way diminishing the quality of life and culture.[27] At least democracy is for Mann no longer the unfeeling monster which, with Heinrich triumphant on its back, was to tread German culture underfoot. It is accepted in its simplest terms, as participation and responsibility. Finally, a single sentence puts his development in a nutshell, by linking a quotation from his first post-war utterance with the pro-Republican message he now has in mind: 'Aber die mechanische Reaktion . . .' is that important reservation which the Unpolitician retained about the forms conservatism sometimes took,[28] while the rest of the sentence is his first, half-reluctant commitment to democracy. The would-be Germanic conservative's quest has ended in disillusionment. It has found no worthy object. What turns out to be worth conserving—indeed, urgently in need of conserving if a basic decency of life is to be preserved—is the three-year-old Republic whose constitution was the work of a Jewish intellectual.[29] But behind this there stands something much older, the Western humanist tradition and all those 'obsolete' concepts, Enlightenment, Reason, Civilization, Liberalism, whose probable demise Mann had recently viewed with unconcern. From now on, he sees his task as breathing life back into them. Inevitably this turns him into an ally of the Settembrini he had mocked.

---

[27] Cf. Troeltsch, *Spektatorbriefe*, p. 310, on the state as a mere technicality, and p. 312 on the undiminished quality of culture: 'Im übrigen aber bleiben Geist und Kultur, bleibt die Tiefe der Seele doch genau das, was sie war . . .'
[28] xii. 601 f. Discussed above, p. 283.
[29] Hugo Preuss. See Eyck, op. cit., i. 54 ff.

### III

Rathenau's death shows Mann becoming a *Vernunftrepubli-kaner*—that grudging concept of the Weimar period which speaks volumes about German attitudes to reason, as well as to the Republic.[30] He takes his place, a little belatedly, beside Troeltsch and Meinecke. More interestingly, he has arrived at this position by a development which is stage by stage identical with that of Gustav Stresemann. Stresemann too was originally a conservative and a monarchist. Feeling no compulsion to accept the legitimacy of the Republic he too sympathized with the Kapp Putsch. Experience of moderate government in the Republic gradually convinced him that the Republic as such need not mean only socialism and the death of the old Germany. He was shocked by the political assassinations, of Erzberger as well as Rathenau, and committed his anti-Republican Deutsche Volkspartei first to defending the constitution, then to participating in the government, and later to supporting the Law for the Defence of the Republic, which was anathema to all true conservatives. Eventually, as Foreign Minister, he became the most statesmanlike and respected representative of German policies of reconciliation in Europe.[31]

In part this development was a realistic response to political pressures: Stresemann saw how right-wing extremism produced shifts to the left. But in part it was a genuine conversion, via the stage of *Vernunftrepublikaner*, into a devoted servant of the Republic. His was a 'history of ideas broadening under the pressure of insistent reality', he 'began as a typical, he ended up as an extraordinary German'.[32] Exactly the same is true of

---

[30] The term is used by Meinecke as early as January 1919 (*Politische Schriften*, Darmstadt, 1968, p. 281), in contrast to the term *Herzensmonarchist*. Cf. also the final section of Meinecke's *Nach der Revolution* of 1919, a dialogue in imitation of Ranke, where two historians discuss the proper attitude to adopt to the new state. The more open-minded Reinhold grants that democracy offers reliable 'rules of the game'; the more conservative Eberhard objects that these are 'still only barren rational grounds, nothing to warm the heart [nichts innerlich Erwärmendes] for democracy'. Op. cit., pp. 119 f.

[31] On Stresemann's development, see Henry Ashby Turner, *Stresemann and the Politics of the Weimar Republic*, Princeton, 1963, especially ch. 3.

[32] Gay, op. cit., p. 25. On the other hand Gay calls Thomas Mann's conversion 'a little late, and not particularly impressive' (p. 74). This offhand judgement is not explained, unless the rest of the sentence—'there were many who interpreted Mann's change of front as treason or sheer irresponsibility . . . and refused to follow him'—is meant to be an explanation. It clearly is not one. Why should

Thomas Mann, whose progress beyond the stage of *Vernunft-republikaner* we shall now trace.

The showpiece in accounts of Mann's republicanism is normally the speech *Von deutscher Republik*, first mentioned in the letter to Bertram after Rathenau's death. It is certainly important as Mann's first public statement of support for the Republic; and it was exemplary as a known conservative's declared change of heart.[33] It also makes some good points—on the essence of the Republic as individual responsibility, for writers and for other citizens: 'wir sind der Staat' (xi. 823); on the perils of historical analogy, of seeing post-1919 as a time for secret military reconstruction like the years which followed the Prussian defeat in 1806; on the irresponsible way nationalists were exploiting the present crisis to glorify a past they had not the least practical means of restoring; on the stupidity of cultural nationalism, which could lead only to provincial mediocrity; and on the dangers of 'sentimental obscurantism' which practised terrorism (the Rathenau murder) under the mask of Germanic *Gemüt*. This last he calls a perversion of Romanticism which could drive the most inveterate Romantic into the Enlightenment political camp—for the present emergency. The allusion to himself is obvious, the declared limitation of his commitment a proviso not often noticed.

Yet valuable though this stand was as an example, as a piece of political writing it was only a first groping towards realities. It was perverse of Mann to date the Republic 'essentially' from the enthusiasm of August 1914. (It was scarcely even good propaganda, since that enthusiasm had so soon proved to rest on illusions.) It was naïve of him to suggest that the true aim of all political parties (in the Weimar Republic, of all places) was the 'good of the state'. It was little short of ludicrous to expand on Whitmanesque homosexual feeling as a force binding society, 'Eros als Staatsmann'.[34] In fact, all the play he makes in this speech with cultural materials, the

failure to impress his benighted contemporaries entail failure to impress a responsible historian?

[33] Cf. the *Vorwort* to the printed text: '. . . dieser kleinen Aktion, die zur Aktion eben dadurch werden mochte, dass ich es war, der sie unternahm' (xi. 810).

[34] Mann was here guided by Hans Blüher, whose book *Die Rolle der Erotik in der männlichen Gesellschaft* he was much impressed by. Cf. Br. i. 177 and esp. x. 196, where Blüher's idea that the state sprang from 'this sphere' is taken seriously.

discovery of equally democratic vistas in (of all people) Novalis
and Whitman, well intentioned though it was as an endeavour
to give the Republic a 'warming' association with Romanticism,
is wasted effort. For unliterary reactionaries, it would have
no meaning; while the more literate would be aware—as
Mann really was himself[35]—of the cavalier way he was manipulating these oddly assorted quotations. The mode of operating is still very much that of the *Betrachtungen*. The change of
heart has not yet brought a change of method. Time, contact
with political affairs, and further disturbing events were needed
before a piece could be produced of the exemplary realism and
clarity of the 1930 *Deutsche Ansprache*.

If we are not just to follow Mann's political evolution in the
Weimar years, but also to see how it shaped the formulations of
*Der Zauberberg*, another document is more important, though
briefer and less celebrated, than *Von deutscher Republik*. In 1922
Ernst Troeltsch gave a lecture to the Deutsche Hochschule für
Politik on the subject of 'Natural Law and Humanity in World
Politics'. Thomas Mann wrote a notice of the printed version
which sums up his position as the national preceptor he now
consciously strove to be, and is an invaluable gloss on the novel
which was by now[36] approaching completion.

Troeltsch had set out to trace back the conflicts in Weimar
society, which he described as the 'slogans of war transferred
into our midst', to their ultimate roots in European intellectual history. The concept of Natural Law, of an 'eternal
rational and God-given order as the common basis for morality
and law', was a general European tradition reaching back to
earliest Christian times and further still into antiquity. Germany had become estranged from it in her Romantic period,
which 'sought to unmake the foundations of Western European
thought', and erected 'in state and society the "organic" ideal
of a communal aesthetic and religious spirit informed by an
idealism which was opposed to mere civil society (*antibürgerlich*)'.

---

[35] Cf. to Ernst Bertram on 25 Dec. 1922, where Mann describes the speech he
has just given (October) as a 'pedagogical action' and confesses 'mit dem Geistigen
nehme ich es darin nicht sonderlich genau' (Br. B. 115). Just how cavalier he was
with Novalis has been shown by Hans Eichner, 'Thomas Mann und die deutsche
Romantik', in Wolfgang Paulsen (ed.), *Das Nachleben der Romantik in der modernen
deutschen Literatur*, Heidelberg, 1969.
[36] The notice appeared in the *Frankfurter Zeitung* on 25 Dec. 1923.

Against Natural Law with its universal claims, Romantic thought set the principles of historical uniqueness and free individual development untrammelled by moral prescript—in other words (Troeltsch does not use the word) *Historismus*. To those who accept such criteria, Natural Law seems 'aridly rational and shallow'; to those who are rooted in the Natural Law tradition, the German view seems compounded of 'mysticism and brutality'. The more so since its workings in reality have not matched its higher claims: in serving as an ideal to base a nation-state on, it has been distorted 'bis zur völligen Selbstentfremdung'.

Two points were particularly important for Thomas Mann. Firstly, the older pedigree of the Natural Law tradition. It is the Western idea that is shown to be the original tradition, and it is the German idea which is 'new, modern, unelaborated, not yet tested by time, theoretically incomplete'. Conservatism lies with the West—a paradox, Troeltsch says, when Germans tend to see themselves as conservative. In historical perspective, the things they have been resisting for a century—liberalism, humanitarianism—turn out not to be the 'revolutionary' elements they are commonly supposed.

Secondly, the recognition that the German position may need correcting. Troeltsch proposes a *rapprochement* with Western ideas; it can be done without denying what is 'essentially German'. He warns Germans against a self-indulgent and rigid adherence to tradition ('sich nicht auf Tradition, Gewohnheit und Selbstliebe versteifen'), thus implying a much more radical critique of the German position than he is prepared to spell out.[37]

The new historical perspective which reversed the terms 'tradition' and 'revolution', and thus turned the tables on German conservatives; and the notion of an intellectual self-correction and *rapprochement* with the West to match the reconciliation needed on the political level: these clarified and confirmed Mann's ideas. He could now see his Germanic

[37] The editor of the posthumous volume (cited above) in which the lecture appeared actually placed it under a heading 'Development of a new German intellectual world *in the struggle against* the Enlightenment and Natural Law' (my italics). Troeltsch was clearly anxious to conciliate: a fatal flaw of moderates under the Weimar Republic was to make concessions to national traditions which made none in return. Appeasement began at home.

conservatism as an aberration from an older 'conservative' tradition. At the same time, having shared the aberration gives him authority to preach the change Troeltsch advocates, it entitles him to the *praeceptor Germaniae* role which so many Germans resented as priggish. Wrongly, since Mann had learned the hard way before he began to preach. This is what he meant by his frequent allusions to the growth of pedagogic impulse from autobiography and self-education.

His notice of Troeltsch begins with the argument that defending democracy need not be Republican party politics; it may be a higher form of national self-correction, a recognition of spiritual necessities no German, for his health's sake, should ignore. He recommends people to read Troeltsch's pamplet to find out what these necessities are—as well as to see (conciliation again) the 'by no means simply contemptible resistance' Germans have traditionally put up against them.

He sketches Troeltsch's argument briefly, stressing that it does not remain purely contemplative, but issues in the 'pedagogical' programme of *rapprochement* without self-betrayal. He then gives, in one sentence, a characteristic blend of autobiography, apologia, polemic, and allusion to work in progress:

Was ... hier von einem gelehrten Denker mit stärkender Bestimmtheit ausgesprochen wurde, das war, gefühlsweise, als dunkle Gewissensregung, seit Jahr und Tag in manchem Deutschen lebendig gewesen — in solchen vielleicht sogar, die im Zauberberge des romantischen Ästhetizismus recht lange und gründlich geweilt — und hatte zu Bekenntnissen geführt, die von einer Zukunftslosigkeit, die sich treu dünkt, als Zeugnis des Überläufertums und der Gesinnungslumperei übel begrüsst worden waren.

(What has here been put into words with strengthening precision by an academic thinker had also been present for some time as an emotion, an obscure stirring of conscience, in many Germans—perhaps even in some among them who have dwelt long and thoroughly in the magic mountain of Romantic aestheticism—and had led to commitments which caused an outcry among that group which has no future but believes it is being loyal, where they were seen as a sign of apostasy and lack of principle. [xii. 628])

The 'magic mountain' as symbol of irresponsible aestheticism; his *mea culpa* for lingering there; the change of heart in *Von deutscher Republik*; the conservatives who reviled him for his change; his diagnosis that they are living in the past: all the threads come together. Another is added when he argues that the degenerate Romanticism cast by Troeltsch as the villain of the piece is not essential to Germans as a race—the racially German Swiss and Austrians have escaped it. Not that they need be exactly envied for that: it is a sickness they have not had, and they are bound to seem a bit innocent to Germans who have: 'ein wenig tragen unsere Empfindungen für ihre bewahrte Tugend vielleicht den Akzent des "Kinder, was wisst denn ihr!"'. Simple virtue or deeper experience: this is the voice of the residual Romantic, proud of his spiritual perils. It echoes a motif of the novel, those 'two ways to life' which Hans Castorp expounds to Clawdia: 'der eine ist der gewöhn-liche, direkte und brave. Der andere ist schlimm, er führt über den Tod, und das ist der geniale Weg!' (iii. 827).

But to be proud of one's adventures and one's fascinating destiny is all very well provided one can be sure of surviving them. The danger lies in taking that one dangerous stage of German destiny (*Schicksalsgang*) as the permanent essence of 'Germanness'. There are great temptations to cherish Romantic anti-rationalism, as an act of defiance to the rest of Europe whose rational Natural Law tradition has not prevented the victors of 1918 from behaving outrageously. Their anti-German measures have deeply compromised the foundations of their own civilization, hardened German resistance to change, and stimulated the heroics of Romantic pessimism.[38] But the temp-tation must be withstood. The regulative truths of the Western tradition remain valid even if the Western nations have failed to live up to them. Indeed, precisely this is the German oppor-tunity: to keep pure an idea which others have allowed to become corrupted. Is this not *more* German than the cult of German ideas which themselves have turned bad? Is it not the chance of a new start? Is not the proper reaction to the great catastrophe of 1918 that it should educate the nation?—'ein Unglück, das würdelos wäre, wenn es uns nicht zu bilden vermöchte' (xii. 629).

Mann's notice ends on this appeal to *Bildung*. It points not

[38] As typified by the dour Eberhard in Meinecke's dialogue of 1919, who quotes von Roon—'besser verbluten als verfaulen'—and parallels the defeated Germans with the downfall of the Nibelungen. Op. cit., pp. 130 f., 142.

only to his own *Bildungsroman*, but to the tradition of German writing in which the narrowly national was criticized in a European perspective. It echoes the more elevated patriotism of Goethe, Heine, Nietzsche. Mann has come a long way since *Gedanken im Kriege*, which closed with the thought—oddly bathetic in the context of wartime—that now at last the other nations of Europe would have to *study* Germany. This was a demand, born of political isolation and the consciousness of superior culture, to be taken as one was and taken seriously. It was for others to adapt themselves to the German presence. Now, less than ten years later, the same writer exhorts his countrymen to adapt themselves to Europe. From 'uns zu studieren' to 'uns zu bilden': this is a transformation of his claims for German culture and character, a shift from enclosed self-sufficiency to cosmopolitanism. Cosmopolitanism, a dirty word to nationalists, means openness to change, flexibility, education:[39] giving up the cherished values of a national tradition, but moulding and integrating them into a larger whole. An internationally accepted German artist was still a *German* artist.[40] Mann's visit to Paris in 1926 in the cause of cultural relations was not for him a betrayal of German dignity; he went as a German and was respected as a German. Once again, there is a parallel with Stresemann, whose speech at Geneva when Germany became a member of the League of Nations transformed the conflict between national and cosmopolitan into a process of natural growth by the formula 'im Nationalen wurzelnd, über das Nationale hinauswachsend'.[41]

IV

Golo Mann duly called *Der Zauberberg* the 'representative' novel of the Stresemann era.[42] Yet he also saw it as politically indecisive,[43] and this is a common opinion, shared by historians

---

[39] Cf. the essay *Kosmopolitismus* of 1925: 'Gehört es vielleicht . . . zum Begriff des Kosmopolitismus, dass der Charakter eines Volkes nichts Starres, unwandelbar Feststehendes und Endgültiges ist, sondern bildsam, sondern erziehbar?' (x. 188). The echoes of Nietzsche's *Völker und Vaterländer* are plain.

[40] Cf. *Von deutscher Republik*, on Hauptmann (xi. 813 f.), and *Kosmopolitismus*, on Wagner (x. 189 f.).    [41] Recorded on contemporary newsreel.

[42] Golo Mann, *Deutsche Geschichte des 19. und 20. Jahrhunderts*, Frankfurt, 1961, p. 704.

[43] He calls it 'ein Werk, aus dem Anregung und Unterhaltung die Fülle, nicht aber belehrende Entscheidung zu gewinnen war', loc. cit.

and literary critics.[44] It is quite wrong, and can be explained only by the failure of each group to practise in a modest way the other's craft. Historians have been scared off by the complexities of a literary text which it is easiest to shelve respectfully as 'ironic'. Critics have not been prepared to trace in detail Mann's evolution, and that of his novel, as a response to the particular events of the times.

Yet not much knowledge of politics and society in the Wiemar Republic is needed to make the formulations which seemed vague in the novel emerge as epitomes of the vital issues of those years, and as unmistakable contributions to the inner-German debate. It is in this sense that *Der Zauberberg* is a political statement, and not at the obvious level of treating political realities directly. Another novelist might have portrayed the parties in the Reichstag, the influence of the Centre in a German village, the hesitations of a young working man between communism and the trade unions, the activities of the Reichswehr always quietly at work in the background, or industrialists in the Ruhr.[45] A documentary novelist like Theodor Plivier could graphically reconstruct the events of the German revolution in his *Der Kaiser ging, die Generäle blieben* (1932). Not to have done any of these things does not disqualify Thomas Mann from the title of 'political novelist'. Using narrative materials which antedated the ideas he now

---

[44] e.g. Sontheimer, op. cit., p. 69, says that the novel is neither for nor against democracy, which is 'not properly a theme' in it. This ignores the potential of allegory. Hans Kohn, *The Mind of Germany*, p. 256, outdoes literary formalists with the opinion: 'It is a criterion of the artistic value of the novel that it is impossible to say where Mann's sympathies lie'—a plain misreading. Ferdinand Lion in *Thomas Mann in seiner Zeit*, Zürich, 1935, sees precious little connection between the two terms of his title when analysing *Der Zauberberg*. Ulrich Karthaus in '*Der Zauberberg* — ein Zeitroman' (another promising title until 'time' proves yet again purely metaphysical) opines that the novel is ideologically undecided, and thinks that this is 'perhaps' its political importance for and beyond its time (*DVjs* 44, 1970, 305). Scharfschwerdt, op. cit., denies any move towards democracy as part of his general denial of development and education in the novel. These are random examples which could be multiplied. Marxist critics tend as a group to assign political meaning to the novel, but not by close analysis of Weimar realities or the text. The dogmatic generality of Marxist social analysis does not help here. Hence a recent comment by an East German critic on the 'Schnee' vision that it is beautiful but abstract, withdrawing from social realities into pure ethics. Günter Hartung, 'Bertolt Brecht und Thomas Mann. Über Alternativen in Kunst und Politik', *Weimarer Beiträge*, 12 (1966), 411.

[45] These possibilities are listed by Lion, op. cit., p. 137.

wished to communicate, he moulded them so as to illustrate the principles at stake in contemporary politics.

Thus the problem of reconciling past and present in a synthesis acceptable to conservative instincts is the basic problem of Weimar, and has echoes in other commentators.[46] The solution offered in Hans Castorp's dream is plain. He vows, in accordance with the message which stands in italics, to 'keep faith with death in his heart but wakefully remember that loyalty to death and the things which have been [*dem Gewesenen*] is only malice and dark lust and misanthropy if it determines our thinking and ruling' (iii. 686). Allegorical as the passage is, it invites translation into other terms. Indeed, by stepping outside the life/death allegory and alluding to 'things which have been', Mann explicitly guides the translation. 'Death' has come to have almost its literal meaning: those things which are past and should no longer hold men's minds in thrall. The reader is compelled to reflect on the danger of allegiance to the past. The reader in Weimar Germany knew what political role appeals to the past were playing; he could have a shrewd idea what Mann meant.

Similarly with Hans Castorp's vision of harmony. Read ahistorically, its classical features may seem only a matter of 'idyllic' convention. But for a thinking contemporary the depiction of an ideal community in classical terms stood in eloquent contrast to the pervasive Germanic obsessions of the day. Mann was attempting to counter these by suggesting that the classical

---

[46] For example, Meinecke's essay of 1919, *Verfassung und Verwaltung der deutschen Republik*, regrets the lost monarchy because 'es atmet sich zu dünn, zu leicht, man friert in einem politischen Dasein, das ganz von Vergangenheitswerten gereinigt ist'. Nevertheless, he declares: 'Ich bleibe, der Vergangenheit zugewandt, Herzensmonarchist und werde, der Zukunft zugewandt, Vernunftrepublikaner.' *Politische Schriften*, Darmstadt, 1968, p. 281. By 1926, the Congress of Republican University Teachers is still taking as its theme 'Die geschichtlichen Werte unserer Vergangenheit und der heutige Staat' (Meinecke, *Ausgewählter Briefwechsel*, Stuttgart, 1962, p. 123). And in 1929, Meinecke is still cherishing the plan for a compromise political party to paper over precisely this ideological crack: 'eine grosse bürgerliche Partei, die den nationalen Imponderabilien und den rationalen Staatsnotwendigkeiten immer zugleich und synthetisch gerecht würde . . .' (*Ausgewählter Briefwechsel*, pp. 129 f.). Similarly Troeltsch regretted the lost monarchy because it would have been a bridge between the old and a new social order; and he stressed possible links between German Classical culture and a higher conception of democracy ('Auch unsere klassische Geisteswelt bietet Verbindungslinien zu einer geistig-ethischen Auffassung der Demokratie genug'). *Spektatorbriefe*, pp. 302, 312.

tradition was (what he had till recently doubted it was) a permanent part of European man. That is how Hans Castorp can have a vision of scenes he has never visited. He seems to be—the narrator is emphatic—*remembering*, recognizing them: 'Dennoch *erinnerte* er sich. Ja, das war eigentümlicher-weise ein Wiedererkennen, das er feierte' (iii. 678). The appeal to a countervailing tradition is clear. Nor was Mann alone in looking to classical humanism for support and a new start.[47]

And if Hans Castorp's classical 'remembering' affirms Mann's belief in common European traditions, that is only part of his yet broader belief in a common humanity, very much in the spirit of the Enlightenment. From their differing viewpoints, both nationalists and historical pessimists (or as Mann preferred to call them, defeatists) like Spengler poured scorn on such faded ideas, and denied the very possibility of an understanding between alien cultures. Mann's retort was that such a negative theory collapsed at a stroke before a 'single work of love' which successfully linked one culture with another. He instances Mahler's *Lied von der Erde*, with its combination of modern music and ancient Chinese lyric.[48] The example is not a random one, but has deeper associations for him, since the *Lied von der Erde* was one of the sources on which he drew for the 'Schnee' vision. His creative practice, in a small way, had thus borne out his belief.

An approach to works of art via the realities of their time may provoke the stock charge of 'explaining away' an artistic structure. On the contrary, it is the only way to do justice to this particular work. Formal and intellectual analysis of the novel's structure can show how it reaches certain conclusions, but cannot alone make these seem more than generalities. As the lessons of Hans Castorp's complicated education they seem inadequate truisms; they are well meant but have no practical application. Unless we relate them to the social and intellectual conflicts of the Weimar years as a contemporary could, the novel's stature is diminished. Mann's humanism seems more

[47] Cf., for example, 'Humanismus als Initiative', the final chapter in Ernst Robert Curtius's *Deutscher Geist in Gefahr*, Stuttgart, 1932.

[48] *Über die Lehre Oswald Spenglers*, 1924 (x. 175). Mann also makes the nice debating point that, despite his disbelief in inter-cultural understanding, Spengler seemed to think that he had understood other cultures pretty well.

wishy-washy than it was, he pays too high a price for avoiding
too explicit a statement. For of course he did avoid it. He was
consciously an artist, and consciously an odd man out, writing
an immense novel in a period which, as he said, demanded
manifestos.[49] He had something to say to his contemporaries
about their actual situation, but it concerned the ultimate
ground of political attitudes, not day-to-day party tactics.
He said it allegorically, but this does not mean he failed to say
it, or did not say it decisively. If nevertheless his message could
and can be missed, the reason lies not in any ironic abstention of
the author's, but in the complexity of his subject and his
record, and in the demands the novel consequently makes on
its readers. But then the novelist's art *is* demanding. Criticisms
of *Der Zauberberg* as politically inadequate imply a more sweeping rejection of that art as such, because its exhaustiveness,
conscientious recording, and subtle probing for truth are out
of place in an age of manifestos.

Yet the manifestos with which Mann met the demands of
the age themselves owe much to those subtler modes of art. He
had worked out his convictions in the ample space of a novel—
they were the firmer for being sprung from such painstaking
analysis. His novel traces the process by which he arrived at
them—they were the more persuasive for the exhaustiveness of
the account.

Mann's response to the problems of his society was thus at
root that of a novelist, but the political propagandist was then
able to draw on the lessons of the novel. The author of Hans
Castorp's story and the author of *Von deutscher Republik*, he wrote,
were the same. The speech was composed in the spirit of,
against the background of the novel: 'Sein Autor . . . ist derselbe,
der, aus dem Roman heraus, den Aufruf "Von deutscher Republik" verfasste.' This is Mann's explanation to the conservative Josef Ponten.[50] And he continues, explaining his political
position in the terms of the novel: 'Er ist in seinem Herzen
kein Settembrini. Aber er will in seinen Gedanken frei, ver-
nünftig und gütig sein.' (In his heart he is no Settembrini. But
he is resolved to be free, rational, and benevolent in his mind.)
The form of the explanation is tailored to the conservative

---

[49] To Ernst Bertram, 21 Feb. 1923 (Br. B. 117.)
[50] Letter of 5 Feb. 1925 (Br. i. 232).

recipient, the tone half-apologetic. But the shift of allegiance from *Herzen* to *Gedanken* — in Weimar terms, from 'national' to 'rational'—is plain.[51]

Thorough artistic treatment of human nature thus issues in decision and practical action. And why not? The artist's devotion to richness and 'many-sidedness', properly understood, was not the pretext for abstention Mann had previously made it, but a reluctance to accept anything less than truth. In theory this seemed at first sight to rule out partisan commitment, since the truth was bound to be subtler than any party line. It seemed to rule out action itself, since—in theory again—the artist's vision of the truth must always remain incomplete. Yet it was ironic that these scruples should inhibit practical commitment and thus leave the field of action to those who saw at best a very small facet of truth and had no scruples whatever. In practice, the conscientious artist had sufficient basis for opposing nationalist fanatics. To say otherwise was to turn artistic perfectionism into political defeatism.

In practice, moreover, the right course in the Weimar situation lay nearer to Settembrini *tout pur* than to any synthesis such as Republicans hoped for and the chapter 'Schnee' enjoined. Here the paths of Mann's art and his developing political activity do diverge. His novel, which grew to its final form in the first five years of Weimar, typifies the appeal of those years for synthesis, balance, conciliation. These were not only ideals worthy to be appealed to in a work of art, they were the principles which the Republic had set out to embody. By the time *Der Zauberberg* was published, the attempt had already failed. The pattern of the Republic's development was set, its failure to command the whole nation's allegiance was plain, its inner divisions were unbridgeable. If it was to preserve itself at all from now on, it would not be through conciliation.

Arguably, that ideal had never been practical politics. The idea of 'reconciling' a German historical essence and a new political form had been held—could be held—only by one side in the projected reconciliation, since it was a rational idea,

[51] Gay, op. cit., p. 127, expressing his 'doubts' about Thomas Mann, says: 'he would not, could not, take the last step. "In his heart", the author of *Der Zauberberg* said about himself, "he is no Settembrini"'. Such partial quotation (not to mention the ignoring of Mann's political speeches of the late twenties) is a serious misrepresentation.

requiring a realistic and undoctrinaire grasp of history and a degree of intellectual detachment. These were not qualities of the nationalist extremists in the Republic. For them reconciliation within a Republic could have no value because the Republic itself had none. Value lay wholly in the past they revered, whether in the form of the *Obrigkeitsstaat*, the monarchy, military glory, the Germanic ethos, colonial acquisitions, or simply the status of a feared power. If the Republic made concessions to them and their ideals, that was all to the good, but it inspired contempt, not co-operation. Sweet reasonableness met implacable hostility.[52] Their attitude is epitomized in the closing words of Gottfried Benn's essay welcoming the new era which put an end to the Republic: 'Halte dich nicht auf mit Widerlegungen und Worten, habe Mangel an Versöhnung, schliesse die Tore, baue den Staat!' (Do not waste time over words and refutations, set your faces against reconciliation, close the gates, build the state!)[53]

This rejection of compromise was something Republican intellectuals only gradually understood. For Mann or Meinecke it was possible, soon or late, to accept the new order and try to link it with the national past so as to give flesh to the bare bones of new political forms. But what it was like to live wholly in the past, in the blinkered way of the true reactionary, was at first beyond their comprehension. It created a political problem quite different from their own and far more acute. *Von deutscher Republik* makes it plain that by 1922, despite the murder of Rathenau, Mann had not grasped the difference. His increasingly partisan speeches in the years which followed, culminating in the *Deutsche Ansprache* of 1930, make it plain that he later did.

Der *Zauberberg*, then, grasps the issues of its time correctly and arrives at a reasonable solution. But by the time it did so the situation had changed radically for the worse. Thus in a sense the novel embodies political solutions which had already failed. Yet its diagnosis remains accurate, and was indeed strikingly confirmed the year after it was published by the

---

[52] One example for many is the way the Reichstag's Investigating Committee on the war yielded to Ludendorff's insistence that Hindenburg should testify with him. This provided a perfect platform for launching the 'Dolchstosslegende'. See Eyck, op. cit., 1. 136 ff.

[53] Gottfried Benn, *Der neue Staat und die Intellektuellen*, in *Gesammelte Werke*, ed. Wellershoff, i. 449.

German electorate's flight into the past in choosing Hindenburg—Junker, monarchist, war hero, the epitome of the
Wilhelmine era—to succeed the Social Democrat Ebert as
President of the Republic. Hindenburg's candidature, Mann
wrote before the election, was 'Lindenbaum'[54]—in other
words, the product of that misplaced attachment to the past
which Schubert's song stands for in the chapter of *Der Zauberberg*
most sharply critical of things German and their political
aspect.

Clearly, the artistic diagnosis was insufficient to affect the
practical issues. More direct speaking and less conciliatory
measures were called for. They are contained in Mann's
political speeches and essays up to the end of the Republic:
*Kultur und Sozialismus, Deutsche Ansprache, Rede vor Arbeitern in
Wien, Die Wiedergeburt der Anständigkeit*; and in the essays in
literary and cultural criticism which ran parallel to them—
on Lessing, on Freud, on Goethe. It is on this body of work
that his political role must be assessed.

## V

Two qualities of these writings impress: their persistence in
stating a small number of simple propositions, and the coherent
view of politics, culture, and society on which those propositions rest.

The most important propositions are: that Europe was living
through a reaction against reason which began in philosophy
and had spread into art, learning, and politics; that it was
irresponsible to revel in irrationalism when this meant en-
dangering basic freedoms and decencies; that in Germany
irrationalism had merged with the bitter national feeling provoked by Versailles and subsequent anti-German measures;

---

[54] 'Die Kandidatur Hindenburgs ist "Lindenbaum' — gelinde gesagt.' To Julius
Bab, 23 Apr. 1925 (Br. i. 239). Mann goes on to quote an article he has published
in the *Neue Freie Presse* attacking the exploitation of the German people's Romantic
impulses and urging them not to elect a Knight of Olden Times ('Recken der Vor-
zeit'). He closes his letter with the words 'Soweit hat der kleine Hans es gebracht'
('progress indeed for little Hans'). The comment is apt, since in the *Betrachtungen*
he had himself proposed Hindenburg for Chancellor, and in just such Olden
Time Knightly terms ('eine Eckart-Gestalt an monumentaler Treue und Sachlichkeit [xii. 366]).

that the mind of Germany was dangerously diseased,[55] unable to see present realities in its blind striving to restore past 'values'; that to avoid the destruction of society and the renewal of war, the Republic must be defended against its inner enemies and reinstated as part of a reconciled Europe; that to these ends a non-doctrinaire social democracy was appropriate at home and the gradualist policies of Stresemann abroad; that in all spheres it was time to right the balance in favour of reason in the control of human affairs. It was a programme Settembrini would have endorsed.

The coherence of Mann's view is summed up in the principle: 'in jeder geistigen Haltung ist das Politische latent' (every intellectual attitude is latently political [x. 267]). Putting it into practice, he treats the most disparate themes—cosmopolitanism, marriage, historiography, education, the literary status of Lessing, the psychotherapy of Freud—as parts of the overall struggle between reason and unreason.[56] All are convincingly related to the general phenomenon whose political form he attacks in his specifically political speeches.

The result is an unusual view of politics, and this is one reason why as a political writer he has sometimes been undervalued. Even a political scientist who praises Mann's position as exactly right in the circumstances does so with the proviso that, being an intellectual, he inclined to overstate the intellectual element in politics.[57] But it could as easily be argued that usual accounts of political crises pay too little attention to the spiritual and intellectual factors which were at work. (The same political scientist later found it worthwhile to devote a valuable book to them.)[58] It is true they are harder to trace or to quantify than, say, economic factors. But here, precisely, is where Mann had a unique advantage. He was tracing the further development of impulses he had shared, diagnosing a disease he had had. When he spoke of *geistesgeschichtlich* factors

[55] To the pro-Enlightenment attitude Mann has now revived he adds the element of Freudian psychology as a modern means to analyse political reaction and extremism. Cf., for example, x. 207.

[56] *Kosmopolitismus* (1925); *Über die Ehe* (1926); *Über die Lehre Spenglers* (1924); *Ansprache an die Jugend* (1931); *Zu Lessings Gedächtnis* (1929); *Die Stellung Freuds in der modernen Geistesgeschichte* (1929).

[57] Cf. Sontheimer, *Thomas Mann und die Deutschen*, pp. 48, 98.

[58] Kurt Sontheimer, *Anti-demokratisches Denken in der Weimarer Republik*, Munich, 1962.

in politics between the wars, he was not turning political realities into idealist abstractions, he was analysing with the aid of personal experience what the historian finds so hard to reconstruct: the climate of thought and feeling in which popular movements arose. Mann was sensitive to the general trends because his work had been part of them. He could recognize the sources of those trends in thinkers whom he revered, who had helped to form his work—Schopenhauer, and especially Nietzsche. Seeing these affinities, he could also measure the falling off—of authentic pessimism, which had become Spengler's facile defeatism; of nineteenth-century vitalism, which had degenerated into the pseudo-psychology of Ludwig Klages (*Der Geist als Widersacher der Seele*); of the Romantic interest in myth and the national past, which had become Bäumler's mythical nationalism.[59]

It was these intellectual factors that he was almost uniquely qualified to describe. They were not his exclusive concern: by 1930 he could set them realistically in their place among more concrete factors. *Deutsche Ansprache* pays due attention to the economic crisis and its sources in European and world politics, to the recent Nazi election successes, to questions of German frontiers and reparations, to the uncertain status of parliamentary democracy in Germany, to the dictatorial alternatives in Russia and Italy, to the resolution of recent labour troubles and the success of Stresemann's foreign policies, to the principles of Social Democracy and the errors of the last Social Democratic budget. Still, at the heart of Mann's 'appeal to reason' lies his analysis of unreason, his explanation of the decline of bourgeois values like freedom and justice not in economic terms (although he is aware of the economic decline

[59] As one of his sources for the Joseph-novel Mann used Bachofen, in an edition by Alfred Bäumler—*Der Mythus von Orient und Occident. Aus den Werken von J. J. Bachofen*, Munich, 1926. Mann's annotations of the introduction by Bäumler are as implicitly political as is the text itself. They culminate in the note to p. cxliii: 'Das Ganze schmeckt arg nach Dunkelmännerei und ist in historischer Form auf kleine Art zeit-tendenziös und feindselig. Den Deutschen heute all diese Nacht-schwärmerei vorzureden ist abscheulich.' These criticisms were expanded in Mann's *Pariser Rechenschaft* of 1926 (xi. 48). Bäumler counter-attacked in a 1931 Reclam selection of Nietzsche, vol. 4, p. 86. Much of Mann's work for his 1947 essay on Nietzsche was then done on this edition, with its Nazi emphases and arrangement—aptly enough, since he was considering above all the intellectual consequences of Nietzsche.

of the *Bürger*) but as part of the modern irrationalism, obscurantism, and chthonic mysticism which in Germany has blended all too easily with Nordic nationalism.[60] In historical perspective these are the things which, more than its political and economic occasions, give Nazism its distinctive stamp.

Yet Mann the politician is usually dismissed as out of place, out of his depth in politics, naïve, unrealistic, ineffectual. The assertion often rests simply on the fact that he was a mere writer, rather than on analysis of what he wrote. No critic has yet shown that Mann's assessment of the intellectual climate was wrong, that his warnings were irrelevant, that his appeal had no effect.[61]

In fact, most criticism of Mann's politics at the time came from opponents, whether Nationalists or Marxists. They are thus rival, not superior viewpoints. Brecht's celebrated stanza attacking *Der Zauberberg*,[62] his failure to recognize German realities in Mann's allegorical presentation, his contempt for Mann's political role are judgments on him rather than on Mann. The *Zauberberg* stanza is vulgar Marxism at its worst; the man who could write that was not qualified to deny anyone else's political understanding. Party doctrine and, even more, personal prejudice[63] prevented Brecht from approving—or even observing—the way Mann had transcended irony and artistic detachment, very much as preached in Brecht's own poem 'Lob des Zweifels':

[60] Cf. xi. 878: 'Philologen-Ideologie, Germanisten-Romantik und Nordgläubigkeit aus akademisch-professoraler Sphäre'. Mann probably here had his friend Ernst Bertram in mind.

[61] The SPD were certainly eager to secure him as a speaker. See the letters of 1932–3 from the SPD Minister of Education in Prussia Adolf Grimme to Thomas Mann in Schröter, *Dokumente*, pp. 196 f. and 500.

[62] 'Der Dichter gibt uns seinen Zauberberg zu lesen. / Was er (für Geld) da spricht, ist gut gesprochen! / Was er (umsonst) verschweigt: die Wahrheit wär's gewesen. / Ich sag: der Mann ist blind und nicht bestochen.' 'Von der Billigung der Welt', stanza 16. In line with this orthodox materialist approach, Hartung, op. cit., p. 413, states that what distinguished Brecht from Mann was the 'unerring insight' that human existence could not be reduced to intellectual and spiritual experiences. Mann did not, of course, so reduce it; and whether the insights of *Der Zauberberg* err more than those of (say) *Die Massnahme* cannot be taken as settled. Incidentally, if Hanns Eisler is to be believed, Brecht never actually read *Der Zauberberg*. See Hans Bunge (ed.), *Fragen Sie mehr über Brecht*, Munich, 1972, p. 61.

[63] Cf. Klaus Schuhmann, *Der Lyriker Bertolt Brecht*, expanded edition, Munich, 1971, pp. 371 f.

Was hilft Zweifeln können dem
Der nicht sich entschliessen kann!
Falsch mag handeln
Der sich mit zu wenigen Gründen begnügt
Aber untätig bleibt in der Gefahr
Der zu viele braucht.

The charge against the substance of Mann's political writing is thus the least damaging. Those who brought it have doubtful claims to authority, and many of them have been adequately answered by subsequent German history. Two other criticisms are worth considering. The first is that Mann was motivated by self-interest, not in the sense of Brecht's crude accusation that *Der Zauberberg* was corruptly written for money (all one thousand pages of it, with their twelve-year genesis), but in the sense that at every stage of his career Mann strove to conserve whatever form of society he lived in, as the necessary basis for his career.

In its most damaging form, this charge was brought by Kurt Hiller, who explained Thomas Mann's political swing in the Weimar years by a temperamental conservatism incapable of rebelling against anything. Mann was a '*bel esprit* with a passionate affinity with whatever the status quo was', Prussian to the core when Liebknecht was in gaol, every inch a democrat under Ebert. There was 'no more busily representing representative of German culturedness' than Thomas Mann, the appointed 'purveyor of metaphysics to cultured captains of commerce', 'decorating the *status quo* and its happy acceptance with the significant arabesques of profound contemplation'. But acceptance, Hiller says, is immoral. Thomas Mann is the most conservative, the most immoral writer Germany has.[64]

It is a virtuoso attack and a plausible one. Is it true? Appearances were against Thomas Mann on the evidence available in 1925. Not only was he once again the established figure he had been under the Empire, it could be shown that what he once said to justify supporting the old order he was now saying to justify support for the new. The conviction that ultimate metaphysical unity is possible between culture and

---

[64] In a 1925 addition to his account of Thomas and Heinrich Mann, *Taugenichts — Tätiger Geist — Thomas Mann*, Berlin, 1917, repr. Schröter, *Dokumente*, p. 73.

state appeared in the *Betrachtungen* and reappears in *Von deutscher Republik*.[65]

Admissions of Mann's own might seem to confirm Hiller's view. How often did he not say that he was a *Mann des Gleichgewichts*, leaning one way when the boat threatened to capsize the other (Br. i. 354.) But a predisposition to keep the boat on an even keel is not yet immoral conservatism. Our behind-the-scenes view of Mann's political development in the twenties reveals more respectable motives. Social concern and a responsive intelligence are more evident than time-serving. Striking though the conservative habit may have seemed to a critical onlooker, Mann's Weimar conservatism was not a psychological recurrence but part of a genuine growth of understanding. Hiller's psychocriticism allows for no such real reorientation.

Then there is the evidence of the Nazi period. As early as 1931 people were adjusting to the anticipated Nazi regime.[66] On Hiller's principle, Mann would at least have been preparing to change horses. Instead he continued to defend the Republic whose days were clearly numbered. He attacked the Nazis in blunt language.[67] At no time did he make concessions to them. True, he later made some tactical errors (who in Europe at that time did not?) which have been interpreted as concessions, dissociating himself from his son Klaus's journal *Die Sammlung*,[68] refraining from attacks on the Nazis in the first period of his exile. In this last, his aim was simply to preserve a German readership as long as he could by not provoking a ban on his writings. There was sense in his tactics, because the more fanatical and inhuman the regime, the more political in effect the most apparently unpolitical piece of humane literature

---

[65] Cf. xii. 247 f. (discussed above, p. 208) and xi. 821.

[66] Cf. Meinecke's letter of 4 December to Walter Goetz on the failure of an anti-Nazi appeal to the student body of Berlin University: 'Jeder bisher Gefragte hat Gegengründe wie Brombeeren. Im Hintergrunde richtet man sich eben auf die kommende Naziregierung ein.' *Ausgewählter Briefwechsel*, p. 131.

[67] e.g. in *Was wir verlangen müssen*, in the *Berliner Tageblatt* of 8 Aug. 1932, reprinted in *Sinn und Form* 22 (1970), 347–9: 'Das Deutschland, das diesen Namen verdient, hat es satt, endgültig satt, sich tagaus, tagein durch Prahlereien und Drohungen der nationalsozialistischen Presse und durch das halbnärrische Geifern sogenannter Führer, die nach Köpfen, Hängen, Krähenfrass und Nächten der langen Messer schreien . . . die Lebensluft im Vaterland vergiften zu lassen.'

[68] On this and related matters see the account in Gottfried Bermann Fischer, *Bedroht — Bewahrt. Der Weg eines Verlegers*, Frankfurt, 1967, pp. 96 ff., and the documents in Schröter, *Dokumente*, pp. 259 ff.

becomes. The effect is even greater if the work is, like the Joseph novel then in progress, a loving re-creation of Jewish prehistory to set against anti-Semitism and an ironic treatment of myth to set against the Nazis' Germanic mythicizing. Meanwhile, Mann was also contemplating a full-scale political work which, if an open breach was to come, would at least hit the Nazis hard.[69] But his temporary silence undoubtedly suited the Nazis, who were anxious to avoid a final break[70] and might even have welcomed him back as a figurehead for their fast sinking culture. Eventually it was a literary attack by a Swiss neutral that provoked Mann to a public stand.[71] Loss of his German citizenship promptly followed and by 1936, with his letter to the Dean of the Philosophical Faculty of Bonn University, he had found his path. At no time was there any question that he might come to terms with the Nazi regime.

Hindsight may argue that, if for once Mann did not conform, then it was because not much discrimination was needed to see the Nazis for what they were. Yet there are cases enough— Benn, Bertram, Ernst Jünger, Hauptmann, and many other literary intellectuals—to show that even that much discrimination was often not to be had. Obsessed as their whole culture had long been with ideas of new vigour and vitality, they could take January 1933 for the millennium, Nazism for a spiritual rebirth,[72] the Nazis for a new genetic type.[73] Mann on the other hand had outgrown his vitalist leanings. He saw clearly

[69] Cf. Br. i. 370 f.

[70] The Gestapo pressed for Mann's *Ausbürgerung*, the Foreign Office strove to delay it because of the bad effect it would have on world opinion. See the documents quoted in Peter Stahlberger, *Der Zürcher Verleger Emil Oprecht und die deutsche politische Emigration 1933—1945*, Zürich, 1970, pp. 236 ff.

[71] Eduard Korrodi, 'Deutsche Literatur im Emigrantenspiegel', *Neue Zürcher Zeitung* 26 Jan. 1936, repr. in Schröter, p. 266. Mann's reply, *NZZ* 3 Feb. 1936, repr. Br. i. 409.

[72] Cf. the speech *Deutscher Aufbruch* with which, instead of a lecture, Bertram opened his summer lecture course at Cologne on 3 May 1933. Fusing and confusing the literary past and the political present, he sees Hitler as a repetition of the 'great leader of the pre-Romantic spiritual revolution in Germany' (Herder? Goethe?) and as the historic rescuer who fulfils Hölderlin's words 'Wo aber Gefahr ist, Wächst das Rettende auch'. Quoted in Franz Schonauer, *Deutsche Literatur im Dritten Reich*, Freiburg, 1961, pp. 54 f.

[73] Cf. Benn, *Der neue Staat und die Intellektuellen*, 'Für den Denkenden gibt es seit Nietzsche nur *einen* Massstab für das geschichtlich Echte: sein Erscheinen als die neue typologische Variante . . . als der neue Typ, und der, muss man sagen, ist da . . . [Die Geschichte] lässt nicht abstimmen, sondern sie schickt den neuen biologischen Typ vor . . .', ed. cit., i. 443 f.

in Nazism a culmination of tendencies in the national culture which had once attracted, but now alarmed him, and about whose organized political form there could be for him no mistake.

The misapprehension of sophisticated minds about Nazism is relevant to the last and most fundamental criticism of Mann the politician. It is that, not simply are his positions inadequate when judged by some notion of political realism, but politics as such, especially rationalist melioristic politics, is unworthy of the artist. It is simple where art is complex, shallow where art is deep, credulous where art is sceptical, optimistic where art is pessimistic. On this principle as brilliant a piece of writing as Heinrich Mann's *Zola* is dismissed for its 'catastrophic platitudes' and Thomas Mann's political writings as mere 'paper currency'.[74]

We have been here before. These are the arguments Thomas Mann himself used in the *Betrachtungen*. Their persistence proves the tenacity of the tradition Mann then drew on—the tradition of German 'aestheticism' which was insidious because it led not to abstention from politics, but to acquiescence in a certain kind of politics. Because time has shown that the results of that acquiescence were out of all proportion more 'catastrophic' than any word or deed of Heinrich Mann's, the point can now be made only in a melancholy tone, as if it were regrettable, but a fact of life, that artistic vision is incompatible with political vision, and that in the modern age 'all profundities tend to be sinister, and shallow all the friendlier thoughts about man'.[75] Thomas Mann's political stance is here not so much criticized as patronized.

The argument is no more valid for having outlasted Mann's own better judgement—or for ignoring the way the art of *Der Zauberberg* leads via 'profundities' to 'friendlier thoughts'. At root, it is a circular argument, resting on a simple preference for art over politics, and on a particular way of describing art. 'Profundity' is only a metaphor used to express approval of certain things found in art: subtlety of psychological analysis, unusual spiritual experience, the fascination of original speculation, free exploration beyond conventional morality. Set

---

[74] Erich Heller, *The Ironic German*, pp. 127, 118.
[75] Heller, op. cit., p. 127.

crudely beside these, the more constant principles which secure basic decencies in society may well seem platitudinous and not interesting. Yet in politics it is not a matter of being interesting,[76] and only the aesthete will judge politics in these terms. Politics is not an inferior but a different activity, an art with complexities of its own, which the saner aesthete recognizes (did not Schiller speak of political freedom as the most perfect work of art?)[77] and to which Thomas Mann strove, despite the tradition he sprang from, to do justice. The failure to distinguish between art and politics in any but aesthetic terms led in Germany to much more than a facile aristocratic scorn for democracy; it led men of culture who were enamoured of 'profundity' to welcome the apparent introduction of cultural values into politics. They had feared for the life of culture within the all-too-rationally ordered Republic. The state which succeeded it was allegedly ordered so as to promote cultural health and community, a spontaneity free from 'intellect', a characteristic national expression; it led to unheard-of brutality and repression. The 'profound' cultural ideas coursing in Germany since the turn of the century made evil politics. As Mann later said of Nietzsche's irrationalism, the worst form of popularization of an idea is its realization.[78]

Like his dictum of the twenties that all intellectual attitudes are latently political, this is sober truth beside the 'profound' unwisdom of so many of his contemporaries. Nobody who achieved these two insights from his experience and observation of German history in the twentieth century can be convicted of 'blue-eyed innocence' or of 'robust dilettantism'.[79]

---

[76] Cf. Mann's letter of 13 Mar. 1952 to Ferdinand Lion: 'Ich fühlte immer, dass ich zur Zeit meines reaktionären Trotzes in den 'Betrachtungen' viel interessanter und der Platitüde ferner gewesen war. Freilich scheint mir, dass es beim direkten Umgang mit der Menschenbedürftigkeit auf Interessantheit nicht so sehr ankommt.' (Br. iii. 248).

[77] '... das vollkommenste aller Kunstwerke, der Bau einer wahren politischen Freiheit ...' Schiller, *Ästhetische Briefe* 2.

[78] 'Die drastische Form der Popularisierung einer Idee ist ihre *Verwirklichung*.' In the notes for the 1947 Nietzsche essay, Mp. ix. 199, fol. 6.

[79] Heller, op. cit., p. 121. The particular occasion for these phrases was the foreword to *Altes und Neues* of 1953, with its reference (xi. 696) to the way the democracies connived at fascism before 1939 and were now furthering its post-war forms. In view of the appeasement policies leading up to Munich, and American attitudes in the Cold War and McCarthy era (to which Mann's later letters

One other dismissive phrase from the same critic is worth quoting for a different reason. Heller speaks of the 'deliberate well-meaningness and studied simple-mindedness'[80] of Mann's political utterances. The terms point precisely to Mann's achievement. Given the German traditions we have been examining and the attachment to them of Mann the artist, his position was 'deliberate' to the point of heroic self-correction. He repeatedly emphasized, in a crudely dualistic way, that his political development was due to 'will' rather than 'nature'.[81] And simple-mindedness? Simplicity and how to regain it are a constant theme in Mann's work, rooted as it was in a period of relativism. In face of unmistakable evil, the subtle analyst and erstwhile disciple of the immoralist Nietzsche was prepared to assert that knowledge of good and evil were innate in men (xi. 896). This is no adequate answer to Nietzsche's critique of morality, nor did Mann imagine it was. It was a rejection of certain kinds of scepticism because they were dangerous, just as humanism itself meant going beyond any knowledge of man which might inspire pessimism, to a new optimism, an 'Optimismus quand même'.[82] This deliberate simple-mindedness—a turn very much in the spirit of Nietzsche himself—was the intellectual's riposte to the *terribles simplifications* of the enemy. Mann summed it up in May 1941, when he spoke of a new moral epoch and of

eine gewisse Vereinfachung und Verjüngung des Geistes im Gegensatz zu allem müden und skeptischen Raffinement, — es ist *seine* Art, sich zu 'rebarbarisieren'. Wir sind des Bösen in so niedriger abschreckender Gestalt ansichtig geworden, dass Nietzsche's Unterscheidung von Böse und *Schlecht* uns nichts mehr zu sagen hat . . .

(a certain simplification and rejuvenation of the intellect in contrast to all weary and sceptical refinement—it is *intellect's* way of 'rebarbarizing itself'. We have seen Evil in such a vile and repellent

provide a detailed commentary), it is not clear on what superior political judgement the disparagement rests.

[80] Ibid., p. 118.

[81] On the message of *Der Zauberberg* as a transcendence of his nature, cf. xi. 423 f. The contrast of 'nature' and 'will' in his political evolution is drawn in *Kultur und Sozialismus* (1928)—'wenn nicht wesentlich, so doch willentlich' (xii. 640; cf. also 647). Reusing the latter passage in *Rede vor Arbeitern* (xi. 894), Mann omits the *Wesen/Willen* distinction, perhaps significantly: in the four intervening years, the situation has worsened, his own commitment has hardened, and subtle distinctions no longer matter.    [82] Manuscript note *c.* 1931. TMA Mp. ix. 173, fol. 52.

form that Nietzsche's distinction between Evil and *Bad* no longer means anything to us . . .)[83]

As the familiar phrasing makes plain, this was one more phase, and not the least admirable, in Mann's lifelong search for values which could command assent.

Equally important is the social aspect of Mann's achievement, his escape from the limitations of the *Bürgertum* and mandarin culture. He became one of the few 'modernists' who saw that the old self-sufficient culture was an anachronism, that its supposed neutrality let political issues go by default, that it must find a relation with modern society. Few mandarins adapted themselves as radically as Thomas Mann did—for one of his background to speak for the Social Democrats is, even in the Germany of the Weimar period, breath-taking—and none to such effect. If his language always remained mandarinesque, it must be remembered that this was the language of his intended audience, the *Bildungsbürgertum*, whose support for the Republic would have been decisive. At least he was making a combative use of his culture. He had taken to heart Naphta's mockery of 'mandarinism',[84] just as he took to heart the example of Settembrini, however ridiculous the 'eradication of human suffering by means of an encyclopedia' may have been made to sound in the context of fiction.

Setting Mann's record against that of the German academic and cultural world generally, Karl Kerényi later wrote:

Der alte statische Begriff der stofflichen 'Bildung' ist längst antiquiert, er hat sich moralisch unmöglich gemacht, indem er nicht die mindeste Widerstandsfähigkeit gegen totalitäre Angriffe der Unbildung oder Scheinbildung aufgebracht hat oder heute noch aufbringt.

(The old static concept of material culture has long been outdated, it has made itself morally impossible by not raising the least power of resistance to totalitarian attacks by un-culture or pseudo-culture. It does no better today.)[85]

---

[83] In a speech for Heinrich Mann's seventieth birthday, repr. in Br. H. 210. In Nietzsche's genealogy of morals, 'evil' is the moral condemnation the weak use to avenge themselves on the strong and spontaneous, with whom their own poor quality ('bad') cannot stand comparison. In Nazism, Mann argues, it is precisely the 'bad' who are responsible for 'evil'.

[84] Cf. iii. 720. Naphta's word is *Bildungsmandarinentum*. He claims it is a laughing-stock among the People, who have long known where to go for the culture their struggle requires.     [85] To Thomas Mann, 31 Dec. 1954 (Br. K. 200).

By contrast with 'static culture', Kerényi admired Mann's for being flexible, adaptable, mobile. One may well speak of the mobilization of culture as Thomas Mann's achievement alike in fiction, essay, and polemic. The inner mechanics of this process will concern us next.

# Identities

Denn dem Menschen ist am Wiedererkennen gelegen; er möchte
das Alte im Neuen wiederfinden und das Typische im Individuellen.
Darauf beruht alle Traulichkeit des Lebens, welches als völlig neu,
einmalig und individuell, ohne dass es die Möglichkeit böte, Altver-
trautes darin wiederzufinden, nur erschrecken und verwirren könnte.

THOMAS MANN[1]

## I

'SUDDENLY this happened: *Hans Hansen and Ingeborg Holm
went through the room.*' With a shock the italics hint at, the
mature Tonio Kröger sees again the two young people he
loved in childhood. It is of course not really Hans Hansen or
Ingeborg Holm. The girl is only 'a little more grown up than
before', the boy is 'exactly as he was'; perhaps they are brother
and sister (viii. 327, 333). The text is as plain as literary delicacy
allows. Then why that dramatic statement of identity? Because
literal statement is the most striking metaphor to convey the
point: that there are patterns of recurrence into which personal
experience fits. Identity is real, not at the personal, but at this
typical level: '. . . Hans und Ingeborg. Sie waren es nicht so
sehr vermöge einzelner Merkmale und der Ähnlichkeit der
Kleidung, als kraft der Gleichheit der Rasse und des Typus.'
(Hans and Ingeborg. It was they not so much through individual features and similarity of dress as through identity of race
and type [p. 331].) The episode is the culmination of a typology
which the story's leitmotivs have established, and it is also a
beginning of myth as Mann understood it. Here, long before
his systematic interest in myth, he already uses what he was
later to call the characteristic formula for asserting mythic

---

[1] 'Recognizing things is important to men; they want to find again the old in
the new and the typical in the individual. That is the basis of feeling at home in
life; for life as something wholly new, unique and individual, with no chance of
finding old familiar features in it, could only alarm and confuse.' *Freud und die
Zukunft* (ix. 492).

identity:[2] not 'they were *like*', but 'they *were* Hans and Inge' 'Sie waren *es* . . .' Leitmotiv, type, myth: all three terms are associated with Mann's technique and the substance of his thought, all three use recurrence to give a sense of meaning. This chapter will analyse their origins and nature and look at their use in fiction and essay.

As with Mann's ironic style, the roots lie in the insecurity of the young writer still unsure of his talent, the burgher still unsure of the value of art, and the man far from at home in life generally. His early letters to Heinrich Mann show the 'problematic existence' behind the façade of ironic superiority and literary polish. In 1900 after his release from military service he writes that all has turned out well, at least for the present moment—and that must suffice: 'so problematische Existenzen wie ich sind gewöhnt, sich an den Augenblick zu halten' (Br. H. 5). A few months later, after a winter of emotional upheaval which had led him to contemplate suicide, another letter welcomes spring sardonically as one more of the changes which prove life's inconstancy—'den Mangel an Treue und Dauer . . . den ich am Läben mehr fürchte und hasse als alles Übrige'. This 'lack of fidelity and permanence' is 'feared and hated' by an individual whose ego, according to a notebook entry of 1897, lacks clarity and firm grasp (*unklar und haltlos*).[3]

The gloomfulness may seem self-conscious in the man who was mature enough to write *Buddenbrooks*. One is tempted not to take it too seriously, in the spirit of Mann's own comment when his talk of suicide alarmed Heinrich: 'Das Ganze ist Metaphysik, Musik und Pubertätserotik: — ich komme nie aus der Pubertät heraus' (the whole thing is metaphysics, music, and adolescent sexuality:—I don't seem to get beyond puberty [Br. H. 16]). Metaphysics certainly sprouted readily from mundane pressures, like the threat of further military service.[4] Nevertheless, the ideas of incoherence and impermanence must

---

[2] ix. 496. Mann had clearly forgotten his usage in *Tonio Kröger*, which he would surely have been delighted to adduce.

[3] Quoted in Hans Wysling, '*Mythos und Psychologie*' bei *Thomas Mann*, Zürich, 1969, p. 8.

[4] 'Freilich, was einmal wird, dafür kann ich nicht einstehen, und ob ich zum Beispiel, die fixe Idee vom "Wunderreich der Nacht" im Herzen, die Widerholung des Militärdienstes aushalten werde, ist eine Frage, die michselbst beunruhigt' (loc. cit.).

be taken seriously because Mann's characteristic literary forms are a response to them.

The Naturalism of his day accepted that life had no coherent 'higher' meaning. Its exponents were aware, as Mann was, that religious and other idealist doctrines had been shaken by modern thinkers and especially by positivist science. But this led them to concentrate on immediate realities, which they rendered with a painstaking technique analogous to scientific observation. In contrast, Thomas Mann from the first uses leitmotiv and recurrent episode to create a sense of coherence and meaning. The real world does not show this kind of coherence; the artist is impelled to compensate through the patterns of his work. The original *Buddenbrooks* epigraph says as much. It states the autonomy of art not just as the retreat of a wounded spirit, but as a means to create an order for experience:

> Ihm werde die gewaltige Natur
> Zum Mittel nur,
> Aus eigner Kraft sich eine Welt zu baun.[5]

This is matched by the autonomy of language, which at about this time Mann was giving licence to order its self-sufficient world.[6] In Nietzsche's phrase, art was a 'metaphysical activity', replacing transcendental beliefs with its own patterns of meaning. Mann's attempt to supersede Naturalism was partly aimed at raising the status of the novel, but partly also a way of filling a spiritual vacuum.

Paradoxically, Nietzsche, who did most to undermine old meanings, helped him create his patterns. Where Mann treats his most intimate theme, the genesis of the artist, recurrent formulas become more than a formal technique. He expresses the alien nature of art by a visual code probably first derived from the contrast of his own appearance and the type more common in his Lübeck milieu. These externals became associated with Nietzsche's ideas of sickness and abnormality

---

[5] Quoted in full above, p. 52. This is a good example of what Hermann Bahr described in 1891 in his article 'Die Überwindung des Naturalismus': 'Es war ein Wehklagen des Künstlers im Naturalismus, weil er dienen musste; aber jetzt nimmt er die Tafeln aus dem Wirklichen und schreibt darauf seine Gesetze.' Reprinted in Hermann Bahr, *Zur Überwindung des Naturalismus*, ed. Gotthart Wunberg, Stuttgart, 1968, p. 89.

[6] See above, p. 29

as the determining factors in the growth of art.[7] The result was a narrowly based but seriously held typology. The externals and the ideas have had a lot of critical attention. What has had less is the question, what kind of meaning they create. Their point is to give a sense of necessity; type means fate. *Der Bajazzo* first develops the theme of typological determination. The hero believes his will is free, he can choose between affinity with his father or his mother, his life outside society is the result of his decision. He finally recognizes that he was born what he is and that his fate was a necessary one.[8] In *Tonio Kröger*, this is already a firm assumption of the narrator, and is eventually accepted by the character. Tonio goes the way he must; he feels in himself the potentiality for a thousand ways of life, yet secretly knows that they are all impossibilities (viii. 288 f.). The episode in Denmark, where his childhood experience is re-enacted, is decisive and consoling. There are fixed patterns of fate. It is no use wishing one could begin again—everything would be the same. Some men must go astray, because there is no right way for them (332). No normal right way, that is, for there is always the one labelled art. In its melancholy way, this is already a kind of destiny; it becomes more positive later in Krull and Joseph. We are on the way to myth.

Another path led in the same direction. In 1899, Mann wrote a Platenesque meditation on his literary ambitions and uncertainties. It begins:

Ich bin ein kindischer und schwacher Fant,
Und irrend schweift mein Geist in alle Runde,
Und schwankend fass' ich jede starke Hand.

(A childish and a feeble fop, I stand
And in perplexity cast all about me,
And faltering catch at every stronger hand. [viii. 1106])

Whose strong hand could the artist clutch, and how? The first answer is rather surprising. By declaring the burgher character

---

[7] e.g. 'Es sind die Ausnahme-Zustände, die den Künstler bedingen: alle, die mit krankhaften Erscheinungen tief verwandt und verwachsen sind: so dass es nicht möglich scheint, Künstler zu sein und nicht krank zu sein' (Schlechta iii. 715). Mann was still speaking of himself as 'krank' in his notebooks after 1900. See Wysling, *Quellenkritische Studien*, p. 43.    [8] Cf. viii. 108, 138, 140.

of his art, as he does in *Tonio Kröger*, Mann appealed to the very ethos from which he appeared to have cut himself off. However genuine his preference for decent dress over bohemianism and for regular working hours rather than 'inspiration', announcing it was a brilliant tactic. Transposing the workaday virtues of Lübeck into art was ultimately, as he said in his speech for the city's 700th anniversary, a case of *the* psychological identification, with the father (xi. 385 f.).

The real father was only a beginning. Besides that life-line to his social past, the writer needed ancestors in his art. Hence the cult of Tolstoy and Turgenev, who gave him strength in his early work (x. 592). But he did not stop at models to emulate, he sought to identify with the predecessors he admired. They became 'substitute father-figures of a higher and spiritual kind', his education the process of being 'formed and stamped by love, admiration and childlike identification with a father-image chosen from intimate sympathy'.

This is the 1936 speech on Freud (ix. 498 f.). Mann is looking back on a practice which has become second nature and when he also calls it 'infantile', this is a technical term, not a criticism. Yet identification does have its problematic side, in the way 'intimate sympathy' operates. There is an early clue in the autobiographical *Der Bajazzo* (1897), where the hero describes his literary enthusiasms: 'Jede dichterische Persönlichkeit verstand ich mit dem Gefühl, glaubte in ihr mich selbst zu erkennen und dachte and empfand so lange in dem Stile eines Buches, bis ein neues seinen Einfluss auf mich ausgeübt hatte.' (I understood every poetic personality intuitively, believed I could recognize myself in each, and went on thinking and feeling in the style of a particular book until a new one had exerted its influence on me [viii. 114].)

What he identifies with is not the characters and events in the story, but the personality revealed in the style. He is not concerned with literary technique; his intuition reaches out to the human being behind the style and sees the world temporarily through his eyes. Is something external modifying the reader? Or is he being confirmed in what he already is? Or is he jumping to conclusions about what he is or what he reads?[9]

[9] Cf. the revealing generalization in *Geist und Kunst*, N 3: 'Abgesehen davon dass Jeder in Büchern nur sichselbst findet.'

It is hard to distinguish. The Bajazzo speaks of 'influence', yet he believes that it is himself he finds in each new author. His intuitive approach blurs the borderline between subject and object. He meets each influence half-way. This is the way Thomas Mann, with his impulse to find confirmation of himself, 'caught at every stronger hand'.

There are two important consequences. First for his fiction: the intuitive recognition of himself in others is a step towards Mann's later belief that others had objectively anticipated his experience, laying down patterns for him to relive. This eventually combines with the other products of his formulaic intelligence, leitmotiv and typology, in the theory of myth on which the Joseph novel rests. Secondly for his evocations of past artists and thinkers in his essays and fiction: all are questionable as objective accounts because of the way subject and object are fused, analogies contrived, conclusions leapt to. This is not to dismiss them—far from it. It means that they must be read primarily as the self-expression and self-assertion of their author. His purposes and hence the uses to which he put the past vary through his career. To trace them is to recapitulate the development of his thought and art, at that most personal level where an individual looks at other individuals and asks what tradition can give him.

## II

Historical chance led to Mann's first major identification with a literary figure. He was commissioned by *Simplicissimus* to write a piece for the centenary of Schiller's death in 1905. The result was *Schwere Stunde*.

The story sustains emotional intensity by a discreet rhetoric working through *erlebte Rede*; but this technique in turn is inspired by the affinity with Schiller which Mann's sources made him feel. The sources were slender, but disproportionately stimulating. A volume of biographical details gave him the necessary grasp of *realia*—physical descriptions, milieu, facts—and an essay in a centenary volume suggestively sketched Schiller's character, aims, and difficulties.[10]

---

[10] Respectively Ernst Müller, *Schiller, Intimes aus seinem Leben*, Berlin 1905; and Adolf Baumeister, 'Schillers Idee von seinem Dichterberuf', in *Marbacher Schiller-*

Scarcely a material detail in the story cannot be traced to these sources. They allowed Mann to create an impression of total familiarity with Schiller and his situation. Scholars have accordingly often treated *Schwere Stunde* as if it were a scholarly reconstruction from primary sources. In fact, it is a triumph of delicate montage. This is not a quibble. For one thing, it is foolish to ignore the realities of an Alexandrian age and the way writers' relations with the past are affected by the general diffusion of culture. More specifically, to see] *Schwere Stunde* as a reconstruction is to miss its real point, and Mann's point of contact with Schiller. His story is governed by a quite un-Schillerian conception. The materials are authentic, but their phrasing and assembling leaves room for an expressive purpose.

This begins to work in the process of selecting from among the materials pre-selected by the sources, in the choice of details which suggest affinity and the discarding of counter-suggestions.[11] It goes further in the rephrasing by which details are assimilated to Mann's intellectual world—the translation, for example, of the Schillerian 'Reflexion und Produktion' into 'Erkennen und Schaffen';[12] or in the stylizing of Schiller's merely technical problem of a 'Bedürfnis nach Stoff' into a 'Drang nach Stoff',[13] in harmony with the story's heroic mode.

For heroism is the dominant idea: the heroism of weakness, of achievement under pressure, of the *Trotzdem*, the struggle with artistic sterility. It is not just Schiller the reflective, *sentimentalisch* poet, Schiller the ambitious, the poet with affinities to music, the erstwhile intellectual libertine now settled to bourgeois society and marriage that inspires Thomas Mann to identify, although all these connections can be traced from his underlinings in the sources to the formulations of his text. It is above all the sickly Schiller whose will wrings greatness from

*buch*, Zur hundertsten Wiederkehr von Schillers Todestag herausgegeben vom Schwäbischen Schillerverein, Stuttgart and Berlin, 1905. Mann's copies in TMA. For a full analysis of the relation of text to sources, see H. J. Sandberg, *Thomas Manns Schillerstudien*, Oslo, 1965, ch. 3.

[11] e.g. Baumeister, p. 20 on Schiller's ambition rather than Wilhelm von Humboldt to Mme de Staël ('la gloire même n'avoit jamais un attrait visible pour lui') in *Marbacher Buch*, p. 3, which Mann appears to have read. Baumeister, p. 19, on Schiller's lack of interest in music is unnoticed, while the famous passage on 'das Musikalische eines Gedichtes', quoted by Oskar Walzel in *Marbacher Buch*, p. 43, is heavily marked with marginal lines and exclamation marks.

[12] Baumeister, p. 18; viii. 377.          [13] Walzel, loc. cit.; viii. 377.

suffering. And this strength of will appears in the text as 'der Wille zum Schweren', which is followed immediately by a reference to the *Selbstüberwindung* demanded by creation (viii. 377). We are once more unmistakably in Nietzsche country. An act of *Selbstüberwindung* is the turning-point of the story, when Schiller resolves to affirm his pain and misery and mask their banal reality in names which give them a positive value: 'Man war noch nicht elend, ganz elend noch nicht, solange es möglich war, seinem Elend eine stolze und edle Benennung zu schenken.' This is a Nietzschean ruse, though it uses the Schillerian term *naiv*: 'Nur hierin naiv sein, wenn auch sonst wissend in allem!' (375). What is at stake is nothing less than a demand for greatness and spiritual world-conquest as compensation for suffering. Literary ambition is revealed as a form of the Will to Power, duly ennobled by the spirit of service and self-sacrifice which was part of Nietzsche's conception: 'Denn tiefer noch als diese Ichsucht lebte das Bewusstsein, sich dennoch bei alldem im Dienste vor irgend etwas Hohem, ohne Verdienst freilich, sondern unter einer Notwendigkeit, uneigennützig zu verzehren und aufzuopfern.' (For deeper still than this egotism there lived the consciousness that he was yet at the same time consuming and sacrificing himself in the service of something noble, altruistically, albeit by no merit of his own but from necessity [376 f.].)[14] This Schiller is close kin to the Savonarola of *Fiorenza* in whom Mann had embodied Nietzsche's psychology of the Ascetic Priest.[15]

Thus Schiller has not been reconstructed as an act of centenary piety but assimilated to a modern view of the artist compounded of Mann's experience and his reading of Nietzsche. The historical figure provides support because his successor reads so much of himself into it.

Less dramatically than *Schwere Stunde*, all Mann's essays on

[14] Cf. e.g. 'Ecce homo', no. 62 of the poems which introduce *Die fröhliche Wissenschaft*:

> Ja! ich weiss, woher ich stamme!
> Ungesättigt gleich der Flamme
> Glühe und verzehr ich mich.'

[15] Cf. their almost identically phrased demands for fame and greatness, viii. 376 and 1064. On Savonarola, a note in Mp. xi. 13b Mat. reads: 'Er verlangt im Kloster niedrige Dienste zu tun . . . Aber diese Erniedrigung ist Selbsttäuschung. Schon beginnt sich in ihm der Wille zur Macht zu regen.'

artists find ways of alluding to his own situation. Even Fontane, aged, mellow, and a far cry from the 'heroism of weakness' or the vehement demand for fame, can serve. Mann calls his work heroic because it was achieved through persistent plodding despite discouragement (ix. 12). His modesty came from a scepticism about art and artists which can be linked (just) with Nietzsche (17 f.). He can typify the writer as Mann then saw himself, too independent a critic to become part of the establishment (30). Again, Fontane's effects depend on hard work and cultivated taste, an 'awareness of the ideal' (a phrase from *Schwere Stunde*)[16] which can be realized not by inspiration but through critical insight (20). His prose had a poetic quality which should by now have made the German novel a less philistine thing (24). And if Fontane never completed *Die Likedeeler*, perhaps the time was not ripe for the truly poetic historical novel Germany still lacks (25). This is 1910; Mann was hoping that the time would be ripe soon, for his novel on Frederick the Great.

The essays abound in such self-reference, and to catalogue it fully would be tedious. They are self-centred in the technical sense that they respond to all subjects with the antennae of personal interests. They have duly been criticized as if a coy egotism were their whole point;[17] but what in a late collected volume can look like the self-indulgence of an established master is a record of the reassurance he went on needing over the years. The fact of being established itself led to a conflict with rival, even hostile positions which made up the literary scene. Allies were wanted as much as ever in this public phase, as the writer's private interests began to merge with his idea of the right development of the national culture.

This is first clearly reflected in 'Geist und Kunst', where Mann invokes the analytical Nietzsche, the reasoning constructor Lessing, the *Schriftsteller* Schiller, the un-naïve, selfconscious Romantics. To strengthen his position, he links these intellectual artists by the term *Kritik*. He was right to see them

[16] 'In der Wurzel ist [das Talent] *Bedürfnis*, ein kritisches Wissen um das Ideal, eine Ungenügsamkeit, die sich ihr Können nicht ohne Qual erst schafft und steigert' (viii. 376). The identical words occur in Mann's letter to Katja Pringsheim of late August 1904 (Br. i. 53).
[17] e.g. L. A. Fiedler, 'The Sufferings and Greatness of Self-Love', a review of the American edition *Essays of Three Decades* in *Partisan Review*, 5 (1947).

as a tradition,[18] and to place himself in it. Not because they all necessarily influenced him, but because their struggles were historically connected with each other, and with his, and sprang from the same causes: the late development of German literature, the intellectual effort which went into its creation, and the suspicion with which intellect, reason, even consciousness itself were regarded from the later Enlightenment on.[19]

Over the next two decades, Mann's identifications take on an ever larger function. If his technique remains self-centred, the self was by now at the centre of much else. The narrowly personal themes of his fiction which once provoked Heinrich's charge of self-centredness took on public reference. The figures he treats in his essays explain him to himself in a longer perspective, they offer historical analogies, their attitudes and ideas become exemplary or prophetic. When in the Weimar Republic politics dominates all else, figures from the past, or rival interpretations of one single figure, are set up by opposed parties as champions of their position. Culture becomes frankly political ammunition.

That was true, in a less naked way, of the 1914 controversies, although Mann's identification with Frederick the Great and through him with Germany shows that crisis can make mere cultural figures and their nuances irrelevant. That episode would need no re-examining, but for the way it led to a new identification, or rather to a more comprehensive phase of an old one. Nietzsche, besides being a source of ideas, had also done much to confirm Mann's attitudes—critical, analytic, ironical. That was the Nietzsche of 'Geist und Kunst'. But there was more to him than that. There was also the vitalist and *anti*-intellectual who rejected analysis, philosophy, history, truth, because they destroyed the illusions necessary to life or weakened men's vital and creative powers.

In 1910 Mann knew about this paradox ('Geist und Kunst' N 32, N 103). But by 1918 he had relived a version of it himself. In defence of Germany's vital interests, he had turned against 'psychology', 'literature', 'criticism'. His experience had thus emulated more nearly the whole Nietzsche. And as he worked

---

[18] See above, p. 129.

[19] For the early history of this tradition, see my article 'Critical Consciousness and Creation: the Concept *Kritik* from Lessing to Hegel', in *Oxford German Studies* 3, 1968.

on the *Betrachtungen eines Unpolitischen* where all this took place, Nietzsche was set before him again in the work which grew alongside his, Ernst Bertram's *Nietzsche, Versuch einer Mythologie.* Mann's long letter to Bertram[20] after reading the finished book is dominated by his sense of identity with Nietzsche and the relevance of everything in the book to himself—'wie nahe es mir ist; wie mein ganzes Wesen beständig darin mitschwingt'. To be actually *named* in such a book comes as a shock—yet it has its rightness, and it could have occurred, he says, at many other points.[21] In fact he doubts whether Bertram could have written of Nietzsche with quite this 'spiritual intimacy', had he not personally known a small version of its great subject: 'wenn Sie den grossen Gegenstand nicht, gewissermassen, in gewissem Umfange, im Kleinen noch einmal erlebt hätten'.[22] Not that Mann's appreciation was only flattered vanity. Bertram's book gave him encouragement and consolation, showed him his own life and its deeper necessity from a higher standpoint, gave him new stimulus to live it out:

die Empfindung wahrhaft tröstlichen, freundschaftlich wissenden Zuspruchs, eine Rückblick-Ergriffenheit beim Betrachten dieser geistigen Landschaft, Übersicht des eigenen Lebens, Einsicht in seine Notwendigkeit, ein Verständnis meiner selbst, so intensiv, wie meine eigene tastende Schreiberei es mir nicht hatte gewähren können, etwas wie Todeswehmut und doch auch wieder ein starker Antrieb und Auftrieb des Selbstbewusstseins, neue Lust, mich zu Ende zu führen, weiter auszuführen . . .

How had Bertram done all this? By taking as his theme Nietzsche's ambiguity, the inner contradictions which made him a myth of the believing sceptic (*Mythos des glaübigen Zweiflers*)— or, as Mann puts it, his 'intensity of lived antithesis' (*antithetische Lebensintensität*). Each chapter relates this theme to some

[20] 21 Sept. 1918 (Br. B. 74 ff.).

[21] Bertram names Mann in the chapter on Venice (p. 266) along with Nietzsche and Byron as men conscious of an 'incurable tragic dualism at the very root of their being'. Marginalia in Mann's copy of the book show the points at which he felt an affinity, e.g. p. 236 in the account of *Ecce Homo* against which he notes 'Btrchtgen'.

[22] It does seem likely Mann contributed something during the symbiosis of the two books. Because it was he who borrowed the out-of-the-way quotations common to both (cf. Br. B. 230), it does not follow that in all other respects he was the taker, as assumed by Walter and Inge Jens, '"Betrachtungen eines Unpolitischen": Thomas Mann und Friedrich Nietzsche', in *Das Altertum und jedes gute Neue.* Festschrift Wolfgang Schadewaldt, Stuttgart, 1970, pp. 237–56.

person, place, or concept which evoked Nietzsche's ambivalent reactions. The last, 'Eleusis', treats that most fundamental conflict between the urge to analyse and the instinct to preserve mysteries by rejecting knowledge. Mann calls it the 'crowning conclusion' of a skilfully ordered series. If ever there were grounds for him to identify, it was here. Unquestionably, Nietzsche—the whole Nietzsche—was the proper medium through which to understand himself. He had come near to this in the pages of the *Betrachtungen* which discuss Nietzsche's two sides, the vitalist philosopher and the European intellectual (xii. 83 ff.). But Bertram provided a new dimension. Not only did he remind Mann of much that reinforced the affinity, in his mosaics of quotation. He stated as a method of understanding what Mann had practised instinctively; and he linked it with myth.

Bertram's approach, typical of the historiography of the George-Kreis, is stated in an introduction entitled 'Legende'. He takes the problems and limitations which historians commonly recognize and exalts them into a mystique. Objectivity is unattainable; historians empty the past of the reality it had in order to set up their own values or those of some force they unconsciously serve; a historic personality can only live as a myth or image capable of affecting the present. History is not a report, reproduction, or preservation of the past, but the active creation of such images. Knowledge is only raw material. The historical record is made up of the myths which changing perspectives have created.

Mann must have felt at home here. He found objectivity dismissed, knowledge patronized, subjective understanding approved as the way to 'vision'.[23] He found it accepted as inevitable that we create in our own image the historical figures who are to influence us.[24] Bertram's formulas are dubious prescriptions for cultural history but accurate descriptions of what often happens, and they fitted Mann's practice like a glove. It is true Bertram does not speak of mythic recurrence. But clearly the creator of each myth finds himself in it (as how could

[23] '. . . wir wissen nur, was wir schauen, und wir schauen nur, was wir sind und weil wir es sind' (p. 5).

[24] 'Ein grosser, das ist "bedeutender" Mensch ist immer unvermeidlich unsere Schöpfung, wie wir die seine sind' (ibid.).

he not?) and therefore has a sense of recurrence. If Bertram's had been a critical account and not a rather heady celebration of this process, it might have cut away the ground from under Mann's feet. As it was, it gave his approach to the past academic blessing. Indeed, for Bertram, myth is the condition to which all reality positively aspires: 'Alles Geschehene will zum Bild, alles Lebendige zur Legende, alle Wirklichkeit zum Mythos' (p. 6).

The ground had also been prepared in Mann's fiction. From leitmotiv and type he had gone on to exploit mythology. In *Der Tod in Venedig* ancient patterns served to underpin modern meanings, were congruent with them and helped create a sense of fate. Still, no belief in any particular myth was necessarily entailed. But myth as a principle—that is, identification interpreted as recurrence and called myth—was different. To treat historical figures as anticipations of the present did involve belief. Or at least a willing suspension of disbelief; for Mann was too intelligent not to see that the 'myth' perspective needed insulating from the sceptical part of his mind. In 1919 he contrasts myth with psychology as incompatible ways of looking at the same thing.[25] He cites Fontane's two views of Bismarck, the sceptical, irreverent letters as against the reverent mythic vision of the dead Bismarck being received by the legendary Germanic warrior:

> Widukind lädt ihn zu sich ein:
> Im Sachsenwald soll er begraben sein.

The poet, Mann comments, is conservative as the guardian of myth, whereas psychology is the sharpest undermining tool at the disposal of democratic enlightenment. The *aperçu* fits Fontane and Bismarck, and also the conservative Thomas Mann of 1919. But not the later Mann. His fascination with myth grew, but so did his democratic involvement; and he placed myth in the service of his no longer so conservative politics.

The clearest example is his speech for the Lessing bicentenary in 1929. Lessing had been one of the champions of intellectual art in 'Geist und Kunst'. Two decades later, the trends Mann recorded there had shown their political colours. Anti-intellectualism was a plank of the *völkisch* platform. On the

---

[25] In a passage added to his essay on Fontane of 1910, now ix. 32 f. ('Auf welchen wohl?' down to 'demokratischer Aufklärung').

conciliatory principle of the Weimar Republic, *völkisch* writers sat alongside republicans in the Sektion für Dichtkunst of the Prussian Academy of Arts and preached their crypto-political ideals of *Landschaft* against *Grossstadt*, the German *Dichter* with his roots in the *Volk* against the rootless, international *Schriftsteller*.[26] The conflicts of the Republic can be read in these antitheses; as Joseph Ponten said of the opposition between city and countryside, 'Das sagt alles, für den, der verstehen mag'.[27] Mann's speech was given before the Academy where this controversy was being fought out, and it is part of it.

It celebrates Lessing as the archetypal *Schriftsteller*, the classic exponent of critical clarification and poetic intelligence (*kritische Klärung, dichterischer Verstand*, ix. 231 f.). But Mann squeezes a special meaning out of 'classic'. A classic is *vorbildlich* not just in the common meaning of 'ideal', but in that it prefigures. It is the original form laid down for later re-enactment, it is the first foundation of a way of life, a 'patriarchal prototype' ('erzväterlich geprägter Urtypus'), a myth in whose tracks later life will follow. Lessing is the 'patriarch'—the language insistently recalls *Joseph*[28]—of the intellectual poet: 'Erzvater alles klugen und wachen Dichtertums' (232).

A Lessing myth once established, its authority backs Mann's attack on the *Dichter*-worship of the *völkisch* 'fanatics of simplicity'. There follows a polemical attempt, much as in 'Geist und Kunst', to broaden the *Dichter* concept and appropriate it for Lessing. Also, of course, for Thomas Mann, since all he says about Lessing applies to himself and is based on his experience.[29]

---

[26] Thomas Mann was one of the original electors who practised this conciliation. But when inner dissension virtually paralysed the Sektion, he decided he had been wrong; 'dass unser damaliger guter Wille zur Unparteilichkeit falsch war' (letter to Oskar Loerke of 26 Nov. 1930, quoted in Inge Jens, *Dichter zwischen rechts und links*, Munich, 1971 p. 129). This epitomizes the original Weimar situation and Mann's hardened line.

[27] Jens, op. cit., p. 97. Ponten also supplied a detailed gloss on how the *völkisch* group understood the terms *Dichter* and *Schriftsteller* in an open letter to Thomas Mann in 1924, repr. Schröter, *Dokumente*, pp. 110 ff.

[28] Cf. esp. ix. 231 with iv. 9 f.

[29] Cf. 233, the denial that sobriety disqualifies for the title *Dichter*, since sobriety may have been preceded by creative intoxication (the reference is clearly to *Der Tod in Venedig*—there are verbal echoes of the confession in *Gesang vom Kindchen*, viii. 1069); 233 f. on the self-critical impulse which plays into the hands of hostile critics; and 235 f. on an art not of invention and action but of elaboration and craftsmanlike motif-work.

The tone gradually sharpens. Into light sarcasm: 'Und also wird es denn auch wohl dichterisch sein' (237). Into contempt: 'wenn dieses Deutsch nicht dichterisch war, so war es so vieles andere, dass es auf den verschwommenen Ehrentitel verzichten kann' (238). And into open contemporary polemic, when he comes to speak of Lessing's polemical habit, so unforgivable in a *Dichter*:

Reizbarkeit gegen die Zeit, die Welt, das Schlechte, Dumme, Niederträchtige und Geistwidrige in ihr,[30] . . . das degradiert, das entehrt den Dichter . . . Ein Dichter, wie er sein soll, das ist nach ihrer Meinung ein Wesen, das nichts sieht, nichts merkt, von nichts etwas ahnt, und dessen reine Torheit sich bequem als Vorspann der Schlechtigkeit und des Interesses missbrauchen lässt. Sieht und merkt er etwas, lässt er sich in Harnisch jagen durch Heuchelei, Rechtsbruch und Volksverdummung, durch die betrügerische Vermengung etwa von Industrie und Heldenlied, so ist er kein Dichter, sondern bloss ein Schriftsteller, und zwar ein unvaterländischer . . .

(Sensitivity to his times, the world, what is base, stupid, villainous and ignoble in it . . . that degrades, that dishonours the poet . . . The poet as he is supposed to be is, in the common opinion, a being that sees nothing, notices nothing, has no inkling of anything, and allows his pure *naïveté* to be misused in the service of baseness and private interests. If he does see and notice something, if he gets worked up about hypocrisy, contempt for law, the brutalizing of the nation, about—let us say—the deceitful way industrial interests are disguised under heroics, then he isn't a poet, just a writer, and an unpatriotic one at that [239])

The savage close breaks the double reference and comes firmly into the Weimar present.

The rest of the speech celebrates Lessing's passionate scepticism, and claims the title *Dichtung* even for his theological polemics. Mann allows that Lessing's rationalism may seem abstract and outmoded to the twentieth century, only to switch to his usual attack on the excesses of irrationalism which 'deeper' modern views have led to. Reaction has gone too far. The Lessing of today would be fighting to right the balance again. Eighteenth and twentieth centuries are drawn together in a peroration which quotes Lessing's belief in a future

[30] An interesting expansion of the more abstract *psychologische Reizbarkeit* of 'Geist und Kunst'.

'manhood of mankind' and the famous words expressing hope of progress even in periods of reaction: 'Geh deinen unmerklichen Schritt, weise Vorsehung! Nur lass mich dieser Unmerklichkeit wegen an dir nicht verzweifeln, wenn selbst deine Schritte scheinen sollten zurückzugehen! — Es ist nicht wahr, dass die kürzeste Linie immer die Gerade ist.' (Go thy imperceptible step, wise Providence! Only let me not despair in thee because thou art imperceptible, not even if thy steps should seem to go back! It is not true that the shortest line is always the straight one.)[31]

Peroration indeed, for this is a speech in more than name. It is an accomplished piece of rhetoric in its organization and phrasing but also by virtue of Mann's eye for the analogies and debating-points which will make a case. Here and there rhetoric even tips over into sophistry, especially in the arguments which strain after the *Dichter* title. Was this so important? Why be so sensitive to Lessing's (or his own) rating? Brecht called himself flatly a *Stückeschreiber* and was even ready to set his own value on the pejorative *Asphaltliteratur* when it was used against him.[32] In another piece on Lessing in the same month, Mann himself dismissed the whole question as a 'querelle allemande'.[33] But there was the rub. However unreal the concepts, the 'German quarrel' was real, and reached far beyond literature. To shrug it off was to allow the opposition its tendentious usage and lose by default some of the prestige which gave weight to one's public statements. Tactics dictated an attempt to capture some of the enemy's pet concepts and give them one's own meaning, just as tactics dictated turning the opposition's Nietzsche into a kind of socialist.[34]

Tactics were also a reason for making Lessing into a myth. It would have been possible to speak of him as history: the 'patriarchal times' in which the 'myth' originated lay less than two centuries back, 'an dem Anfange des Weges . . . auf dem wir heute noch fortgehen' (230). The situation of 1929 was part of a traceable historical process. But the idea of myth gave Lessing an authority history would not have done. His qualities were made timeless, ever-present, part of the natural order.

---

[31] Lessing, *Die Erziehung des Menschengeschlechts*, § 91.
[32] Cf. Hartung, op. cit., p. 427.      [33] Cf. x. 252, *Zu Lessings Gedächtnis*.
[34] Cf. ix. 243, 245; xii. 673; xi. 898.

This justified his modern counterpart. Myth simplified an intricate story and converted facts and causes into an 'essential' meaning. It was an effective way to present history, just as it was a comforting way to experience it. Serious distortion of historical truth was not necessarily involved in either.

Of course Mann took liberties with the past, selecting what gave him a sense of affinity, sometimes interpreting anachronistically. This bears out Bertram's theory of 'legend' and illustrates Nietzsche's theory of 'monumental history'—the heroic use of the past in a present struggle.[35] But between Mann and his chosen allies there was often some connection via the mazes of history, or at least a fair analogy. 'Monumental history deceives through analogy', Nietzsche wrote. But there are degrees of deception, and of self-deception. To put Mann's practice into perspective, one must remember the way history and literature were being falsified in the twenties and thirties. His historical analogies were innocent beside their rivals— the view of post-1919 as post-1806,[36] of Hindenburg as a trusty Eckhart (xii. 749), of Hitler as a second Luther[37] or the fulfilment of Hölderlin's visions;[38] his myth of Lessing was a benign thing compared with what was stirring in the Germanic depths, or with the propaganda legends the Nazis built up round figures like Schlageter and Horst Wessel.

In such political myths Mann saw a total destruction of truth and the logical conclusion of something ingrained in the Germans—the Will to Legend: 'Der deutsche Wille zur Legende, zum Mythos, zu dem, was nicht wahr, aber "schöpferisch" ist, ein Wille gegen die Wahrheit, gegen die geistige Reinlichkeit' (xii. 748). He saw, his wording leaves no doubt, the links with Germany's higher intellectual traditions. Events had shown what happens when ideas that were exciting in Nietzsche, and still the property of a civilized mind in the Bertram of 1918, get into the political gutter. And he probably also saw the connection with his own creative use of the past, which

---

[35] Cf. *Vom Nutzen und Nachteil der Historie für das Leben*, § 2, esp.: 'Die Geschichte gehört vor allem dem Tätigen und Mächtigen, dem, der einen grossen Kampf kämpft, der Vorbilder, Lehrer, Tröster braucht und sie unter seinen Genossen und in der Gegenwart nicht zu finden vermag' (Schlechta i. 219).

[36] Cf. above, p. 293.

[37] Joseph Ponten's suggestion, quoted xii. 731.

[38] Bertram's suggestion. Cf. above, p. 311.

had equally led to myth. Here yet again he was of his time and place but achieved a critical perspective and put something characteristically national to a corrective purpose. What in the end distinguishes him from the Bertrams and the Pontens is the irreducible fact of saner judgement. We do well to remember that distinction when Mann's analogies seem fanciful, his literary portraits subjective, his identifications most questionable. Which brings us to Goethe.

## III

We saw how *Goethe und Tolstoi* changed its political import between 1921 and 1925. The German conservative watching Western decline with unconcern became the prophet warning against the loss of common European traditions. The body of the essay alters along with the conclusion. The stage is no longer held by Goethe and Tolstoy alone, heathen nature-gods whose *Volkhaftigkeit* is meant to shame a more superficial civilization. A spiritual countertype is treated extensively.[39] Which is nobler is left formally undecided, indecision is insisted on as a virtue,[40] *Humanität* as a problem.

This already corrects the leanings of the 1921 speech, but without flying to the other extreme. It neither rejects the 'natural' Goethe nor reinterprets him as a 'spiritual' type. Instead there is a gentle shift of emphasis. The themes of the original speech stand, but say something rather different.

The original celebrated the elemental national power which Goethe shared with Tolstoy. It discounted Goethe's abstention from public patriotism in 1813 and warned against confusing that with the anti-patriotism of the *Zivilisationsliteraten* in 1914. Was not Goethe's Germanness proved by his works? A man who had written *Götz*, *Faust*, *Wilhelm Meister*, *Hermann und Dorothea*, could allow himself a little 'cosmopolitan unreliability'. So genuine was his *Volkhaftigkeit*, it could even cast doubt on his humanism. Was the Olympian image not a mere surface stylization? Was Goethe not really an ethnic deity like Tolstoy, an eruption of that aristocratic Germanic paganism

[39] The original refers only briefly to Schiller and Dostoyevsky. *Deutsche Rundschau*, March 1922, p. 232.
[40] See ix. 60 f., 77, 95, and especially 170 ff.

which produced Luther and Bismarck as well, and which it was Germany's mission to defend against the Christianity of the *Entente* democracies in the last war?[41]

This and much like it was a continuation of *Betrachtungen* polemics. In 1925 these things are again referred to, but the tone has changed. The 'ethnic core' beneath Goethe's humanism is traced in a humorous spirit (ix. 125). The idea that it was a surface stylization is prefaced by the words: 'Dangerous to relate—because one fears it will be pleasing to the cave-bears of nationalism.' The 'aristocratic Germanic paganism' is now only something 'exploited by both sides in the ideology of the last war' (ix. 135). Goethe's 'cosmopolitan unreliability' is now something to be not excused but defended: the author of *Von deutscher Republik* has meantime had the gibe 'un-German' flung in his own face, and is implicitly claiming with Goethe that his works prove his 'national nature' and give him a right to 'speak up for *Geist* without for that becoming a rootless *littérateur*' (138).

Mann is trying to take into account all the things his original speech made much of, and still harmonize them with his changed political beliefs. This is both fair—he faces up to his former convictions and the evidence they were argued from—and necessary: if the harmonizing fails, then the greatest figure in German culture is available to be used against him. But something more than fair argument and tactical necessity holds him to his original themes. He could not present a radically different Goethe because that would have meant sacrificing beliefs which, unlike his political views, had not changed.

This is the heart of Mann's dilemma in the twenties. He was still convinced that art, civilization, society, really did have their roots in the natural, the unconscious, the irrational. In a balanced art (or civilization, or society), what grew from those roots was formed and controlled by the conscious mind, the Dionysiac by the Apolline. If the balance was disturbed, as in a period of irrationalism, the values of reason and control had to be insisted on. But an artist who spoke out for reason risked being taken for a mere rationalist whose art had no deeper impulse. Mann's image had always been intellectual; he had struggled to persuade himself and others that he was not only

[41] Loc. cit., p. 244.

that. Those who did not wish to be persuaded could now use his rationalism in politics as a stick to beat his artistic work with—and, if they were his ideological opponents, use the reduced status of his work in turn to discredit his politics. It was not difficult to make a crude case of this sort out of *Von deutscher Republik* and the very obviously 'intellectual' *Zauberberg*.[42] This is why in the 1925 version of *Goethe und Tolstoi*, published the year after *Der Zauberberg*, Mann tries to establish the broader picture of his full beliefs and declare a compromise peace between so many of his old antitheses. Within this framework his rational politics might appear as what they were: a corrective for the times, not an embracing cultural ideal.[43]

Hence the ostentatious sitting on the fence and the praise of indecision. Hence a statement like: 'Worauf es ankommt ist aber, dass nichts zu leicht falle. Mühelose Natur, das ist Roheit. Müheloser Geist ist Wurzel- und Wesenlosigkeit.' (The important thing is that nothing should come too easily. Effortless nature is mere crudity. Effortless spirit is a lack of root and substance [ix. 138].) Hence in particular the reconciliation of both elements in Goethe, in whom culture grew out of nature and social responsibility out of powerful individualism.

That point too was made in the 1921 speech.[44] But there it was the elemental nature rather than the refinement which made that culture an ideal. In 1925 the stress has moved to the controlling of nature because of its dangerous potential. The self-discipline which achieved this in Goethe's life and work now appears as a mission, a moral example to the nation: 'seine besondere nationale Sendung, die eine wesentlich *sittigende* Sendung war'. Perhaps educating the nation is the mission of *all* German men of the spirit who have progressed,

---

[42] See the note of December 1924 thanking Korfiz Holm for his comments on the novel: '. . . dass Sie von den 'lebendigen Gestalten' des Buches sprechen, tut mir wohl; denn wo Leben und Gestalt ist, da ist ja Irrationales, Dichterisches, und so bin ich wohl nicht der restlos durchrationalisierte 'Schriftsteller', als der ich neuerdings angesprochen werde. Die wechselseitige Durchdringung von Plastik und Kritik, die ich anstrebe, oder nicht anzustreben brauche, da sie in meiner Natur liegt, verführt dazu'. Quoted in Saueressig, *Entstehung des 'Zauberberg'*, p. 5.

[43] Cf. Mann's letter of September 1935 to Harry Slochower (Br. i. 397 f.).

[44] 'Vergeistigung wird ihm Kultur, d. h. die Läuterung, Erhöhung und Vermenschlichung des Natürlichen'; loc. cit., p. 246.

like Goethe, from a loving self-absorption via autobiographical confession to 'educative responsibility' (ix. 123). Unexpectedly in a section of the argument which started by equating things national with Nature and cosmopolitanism with Spirit, the 'natural' Goethe has turned into the reverse of a narrowly national ideal.

This and other changes of emphasis do not make *Goethe und Tolstoi* mere cultural politics. It is Mann's most balanced treatment of large cultural themes and his richest essay on Goethe. But the effort to display his full sympathies and beliefs was ignored. Hostile simplifiers went on attacking the 'conscious' Thomas Mann with sayings of Goethe's about the 'creative unconscious'.[45] It was not a climate for balance and fairness. The approaching Goethe centenary was unlikely to rise above these conflicts.

By 1932, renewed political and economic crisis made this certain. A unified national celebration was out of the question. Goethe was used as partisan feeling required. Mann's centenary essays show a clear movement in this direction, away from the balanced contemplation of *Goethe und Tolstoi* to a firm, often polemical argument. Goethe is again the exemplary synthesis, not just of greatness and control, but of demonic and rational, Mediterranean and Nordic, German and European. Goethean *Weltliteratur* is set against nationalism in culture, and readiness for social change against bourgeois individualism and worship of the past. Sharp formulation and some brilliantly chosen quotations[46] direct these points at obvious contemporary targets. The essay themes are themselves broadly social: in *Goethes Laufbahn als Schriftsteller* it is the writer as educator of a nation which sorely needs it, in *Goethe als Repräsentant des bürgerlichen Zeitalters* it is the urgent need to transcend the limitations of bourgeois society in a new form of democracy which will forestall its more violent enemies. By skilful selection and presentation, Goethe can be made to endorse these themes.

If this is 'monumental history', at least the monument has

---

[45] See xii. 664. The assailant there quoted could go further still in using literature for political ends. He turned Rilke's reflections on the abolition of torture (*Sonette an Orpheus*, ii. 9) into a proposal for reintroducing it, along with such other 'naturhafte Gesetze des Lebens' as the burning of witches and Jews (xii. 668 f.).

[46] See ix. 353, 359 f.

much Goethean substance. One need only compare the constructs of the *völkisch* opposition in 1932. For example, Wilhelm Schäfer's speech for the Frankfurt Goethe-Feier which calls the Goethe-year an 'act of defiance by the slighted German people', claims Goethe is a focus of national feeling as Schiller was in 1859, and sets up a 'heroic Goethe'—'weil wir ohne Heroismus nicht aus dieser zerrütteten Gegenwart kommen'.[47] The ideology behind argument and quotations would be plain even without the thrust at Thomas Mann for his insufficiently irrational Goethe.[48] Even cruder is E. G. Kolbenheyer's Weimar address *Goethes Weltbürgertum und die internationale Geistigkeit*,[49] which tries to deny modern cosmopolitans the support of Goethe by reducing *Weltbürgertum* to the mere recognition abroad of works which grew out of and were created for one people. Goethe's contacts with the non-German world, like the Italian journey, are seen as necessary evils; the message of *Iphigenie* becomes 'the vital bond of a great soul with its people'; Goethe in Weimar appears as a *Heimatkünstler* in his narrow province. The 'international intellectuals' on the other hand are the products and parasites of modern communications, whose channels they block for 'genuine' national literature ('der Raum angesichts der Welt, der dem wesenhaften Schrifttum eines Volkes gebührt, ist besetzt von der internationalen Geistigkeit').[50] Goethe is made the champion of an anti-cosmopolitanism compounded of self-sufficiency, envy, and a myth of international conspiracy whose parallel is not far to seek. This can no longer be classed as subjective interpretation, nor even distortion, since nothing of the historical figure is left at all. The speech is political cliché in cultural disguise.

Mann's need to make Goethe speak to the times had results outside politics. It intensified his interest in Goethe, directed it urgently to the experiences they had in common, and gradually persuaded him of their over-all identity. Suggestions of affinity

---

[47] *Festgabe zum Goethejahr 1932* of the Freies Deutsches Hochstift, Halle, 1932, pp. xxxv–xliii.

[48] '. . . dass dem angeblichen "Repräsentanten des bürgerlichen Zeitalters" die dunklen Untergründe . . . retuschiert sind . . .', ibid., p. xl.

[49] E. G. Kolbenheyer, *Gesammelte Werke*, Munich, 1939–40, vol. 8, pp. 135 ff. The address was given on 22 March, the day after *Goethes Laufbahn als Schriftsteller*.

[50] Ibid., pp. 139 f.

in *Goethe und Tolstoi* were discreet. In the 1932 essays they are marked, ranging from the governing concepts of the two major pieces, *Bürgertum* and *Schriftstellertum*, which are closer to Mann than to Goethe and were plainly meant to provoke,[51] down to the minor points of contact which can be contrived by choices of phrase or date, by calling Goethe's *Werther* phase one of 'sympathy with death', or by dating the German anti-political attitudes which repeat Goethe's between 1916 and 1919. Late in 1932, an opportunity offered to announce his conclusions. In a letter thanking Käte Hamburger for her book on him, he explains his interest in *Geistesgeschichte* by Goethe's dictum that 'an artist must know where he comes from'; and he continues:

> *Goethe* — Sie notieren ganz mit Recht meine Zugehörigkeit zum 'sentimentalischen' Gegentyp. Und doch — lassen Sie mich dem kritischen Freundesgeist unter vier Augen gestehen: Das Verwandt-schaftsgefühl, das Bewusstsein ähnlicher Prägung, einer gewissen mythischen Nachfolge und Spurengängerei ist sehr lebhaft und hat in den Reden dieses Goethejahres innigversteckten Ausdruck gefunden. Es ist unmöglich etwas misszuverstehen. "Ich bin kein Goethe, aber einer von seiner Familie", schrieb Stifter.

> *Goethe*—you note quite rightly that I belong to the other, the 'sentimental' type. And yet—let me confess it privately to a friendly critical mind: the feeling of affinity, the consciousness of similar stamp, of a certain mythical imitation and following in footsteps is very acute and has found hidden but heartfelt expression in the speeches of this Goethe-year. It is impossible to mistake my meaning. "I am no Goethe, but one of his family", wrote Stifter. [Br. i. 323])

So Goethe too now appears in a mythical light—a 'Vor-Bild' like Lessing, an 'Ur-Bild' and 'Über-Bild' into the bargain (x. 328), and a source of 'mythusbildende Kräfte' (ix. 299). But this time mythic identification has snags. Mann is declaring his affinities with Goethe, the classic *naiv* poet, while still admitting he is typologically the very opposite. He does not resolve the contradiction, he merely leaves the revelation vouchsafed him in 1932 to outweigh the old view. The contradiction can be explained, if not resolved. As with Lessing, the legitimate parallels between Mann and Goethe are historical:

---

[51] Especially the use of the term *Schriftsteller* for Goethe, the most sacrosanct of *Dichter*. Mann's original title was more provoking still: 'Goethe der Schriftsteller' (Mp. ix. 180, fol. 1). The provocation is not removed by his explanation of the title (ix. 334 f.).

their *bürgerlich* background, their response to German nationalism, their increasing *Weltbürgertum*. And in this phase of Mann's
work it is these larger patterns of history he is concerned with;
beside them, the narrowly typological affinities between artists
which once made him identify with Schiller are less important.
It is in fact scarcely the artist Goethe who interests Thomas
Mann. None of his essays has much of substance to say about
the works, and he never approaches the thing which makes
Goethe unique, the quality of his poetry. For Mann's purpose,
it is enough that Goethe was an artist and that he is one too.
This assures him that their experiences are kin, and that he
has intuitive access to Goethe's life and inner problems. In a
phrase of Nietzsche's which he often quoted, he has 'regained
the consciousness of the master'.[52] And since it is the life that
matters, the sense of identity can be confirmed by combing
through biographical sources. These exist in such mass and
variety in Biedermann's great collection—which Mann used
intensively[53]—that a search for common experiences, moods,
or ideas can hardly fail.

This makes Mann's most celebrated identification questionable (the criticism which has taken it literally even more so).
Imitation, identification, *unio mystica*—he used all these terms
for his relationship to Goethe, and they have established an
orthodoxy which ignores his own reservations. He stated the
essential one in 1930 when, contemplating a book on Goethe
for the centenary, he wrote to Bertram on the pros and cons:
it would interrupt his work on *Joseph*, and he is not sure he has
the equipment (*Bildungsvoraussetzungen*) for the job. But these
objections then paradoxically unite in favour of the idea:
'mir wird nichts übrig bleiben, als aus *Erfahrung* zu reden,
über Goethe aus Erfahrung: eine mythische Identifikations-
Hochstapelei, mit der vielleicht die Brücke vom "Joseph" zum
"Goethe" geschlagen wäre' (the only thing left will be for me to
speak from *experience*,—on Goethe from experience: a mythical
confidence trickster's identification with which perhaps the
gap between "Joseph" and "Goethe" would be bridged [Br. B.

[52] Cf. 'Geist und Kunst' N 22; Br. A. 32; ix. 361. The source is a note from the
period of *Menschliches*, GOA *Allzumenschliches*, Grossoktavausgabe xi. 51.
[53] The differing pagination of references in his notes for the 1932 essays on
Goethe and in his notes for *Lotte in Weimar* shows that he worked through
Biedermann at least twice.

172]). Speaking from experience is his only resort, and also a way of staying close to his major work in progress. Both works involve identification, and in both it is not to be taken at face-value.

## IV

The insight was soon buried under discovered 'affinities', but it is illuminating, for the essays and for *Joseph*. Seen in this light, the novel is not just an expansion of the biblical story, or a benevolent *Menschheitsbuch*, but a fictional parallel to Mann's experience with cultural tradition in his time. It celebrates the use of tradition under the guise of the myths Joseph exploits. And although it presses Joseph's not wholly engaging presumption on us with a coyness which may fall short of the intended humour, it does in the end tell us the truth about this kind of achievement. We even glimpse the abyss beneath Joseph's success.

Mann repeatedly calls Joseph a confidence-man.[54] His confidence trick is the conscious reliving of myth in a world of 'open identities', where people do not distinguish clearly between themselves and the predecessors they resemble. He hoodwinks them by first consciously influencing himself: 'auf dem Wege bewusster Selbstbeeinflussung die Leute . . . zu blenden' (iv. 582).[55] That is, he uses the myth to express and confirm his self-confidence and thereby inspires confidence in others. But the origin of his confidence is his natural endowment; and these real qualities ensure his success when, trickster-like, he has set up a situation to profit from. Success in turn confirms his belief that his role is authentic, so the two kinds of confidence progressively strengthen each other.

Thus, Joseph's sense of superiority inspires self-love, an expectation that others will love him more than themselves, and the 'crass immodesty' of his dreams (iv. 460). This provokes his brothers and sets off an action which he can recognize. He knows the story of Tammuz, the Torn God (*der Zerrissene*) and he knows the festive nature of myth-enactment (iv. 448). Jaakob too, in whom mythical associations are 'almost an affliction' (iv. 93 f.), thinks of his obviously exceptional son in

[54] Cf. Br. i. 261, 262 f., 271; Br. K. 50; ix. 498; xi. 628.
[55] Cf. iv. 819 'fromm verblendende Selbstverwechselungen'. Both passages take up the *blenden/verblenden* motif from *Krull*. Cf. above, p. 112.

the same terms. So when cast into the pit, Joseph becomes to his own satisfaction Tammuz, the 'true son' returned to the earth, the sacrificial god, *der Zerrissene.* Or approximately:

> Zerrissen? Sie hatten ihm nur die Lippe zerrissen und die Haut da und dort, aber das Kleid hatten sie ihm abgerissen und es zerrissen mit Nägeln und Zähnen, die roten Mörder und Verschwörer, seine Brüder, und würden es in das Blut eines Ziegenbocks tauchen, das für sein Blut gelten sollte, und es vor den Vater bringen.

> (Torn? They had only torn his lip, and his skin here and there, but they had torn his coat from him and rent it with nails and teeth, the red murderers and conspirators, his brothers, and would dip it in the blood of a goat, which should seem to be his blood, and bring it before their father [iv. 583 f.])

Joseph brings this first descent about by the way he treats his brothers, then stylizes it into a myth. The myth promises resurrection, and Joseph's first career, in Potiphar's household, fulfils the promise. His disgrace and imprisonment in Lower Egypt are a second descent of the 'true son' into the pit: the mythic parallels are spelt out once more in full (v. 1295) They need to be, if Joseph is to keep up his courage. He scans his experience for signs of recurrence and allusions to a higher coherence (*höhere Stimmigkeit*). For it takes effort to rise above immediate experience to the higher perspective. Though the myth-pattern gives him hope amounting to certainty, it leaves room for moments of despair: 'Seine Hoffnung war sogar gewissestes Wissen; aber er war ein Kind des Augenblicks, und er weinte' (v. 1296). Joseph manages to read even his tears mythically, as part of the story of Gilgamesh. Nevertheless, this second low point is a test of his faith, and it reveals that living a myth is not that easy.

It never has been. Keeping experience in step with some higher coherence involves constant effort, in contriving and in interpreting events.[56] Joseph has to work as hard for his 'resurrection' as he did for his 'descent', seeing his chances and taking them. His dreams need help in coming true—'man musste nachhelfen' (iv. 811). When he is first sold into Potiphar's

---

[56] Not only for Joseph. Jaakob was well aware that even God's promises could not be fulfilled without a bit of assistance (iv. 273). Myth-patterns likewise: when one scented recurrence, one hastened to add extra similarities to confirm it (iv. 528).

house, he sizes up the situation like a practised opportunist—
'wie jemand, der sich so schnell wie möglich zum geistigen
Herrn der Umstände und Gegebenheiten zu machen sucht,
in die er von ungefähr versetzt worden und mit denen er zu
rechnen hat' (iv. 810). He is always out to impress—'die
Menschen stutzen zu lassen' (v. 1330). He is a born passer of
exams and putter of best feet forward. He backs up the immediate impression he makes by tendentious interpretations
of his past, virgin birth and all (v. 998). He defends opportunism openly (v. 1082). He is a social and political climber, as
clearer heads like Pharaoh's politically experienced mother
soon see (v. 1471).

The narrator is aware that this might all be distasteful, and
he adds the religious dimension which the sources place to hand.
Joseph's ambition is repeatedly excused as ultimately ambition
'for God' (e.g. iv. 812, 883). The ruthless single-mindedness
which might 'dampen our sympathies' springs from an obligation to further God's intentions (v. 1499 f.). Joseph does indeed
act his Tammuz role on the broader stage of divine providence,
in the belief that God is looking after him through the events of
his myth, has resurrected him, and brought him to Egypt by
means of the Ishmaelites (iv. 811).

But what sort of God is this? From the first he has been the
creation of Abraham, Jaakob, the whole Israelite community
(iv. 130). He is the product of men's developing sense of what
has become spiritually right in changing circumstances.[57] He
is mildly patronized as a promising theological idea: 'diesem
. . . Gotteswesen [war] eine grosse theologische Laufbahn
vorbehalten' (iv. 131). He is not an intervening agent, and one
of the book's moments of deeper feeling is Jaakob's grief at the
death of Rahel, when God is silent and incomprehensible (iv.
388). He is called much later the author of all occurrence
(*Verfasser alles Geschehens*, v. 1691) but this cancels out intervention by making it general, and leaves—as the metaphor
suggests—only reality and its earthly narrator. Where direct

---

[57] This is part of the novel's political message. Attachment to the past is called
*Frömmigkeit zum Tode* and the necessary balancing factor *Freundlichkeit zum Leben* (v.
1508) so that it is easy to recognize the themes of *Der Zauberberg* and of the speeches
and essays of the Weimar period. In addition, *Geist* is equated with the future and
*Seele* with the past (iv. 48) and the *Vorspiel* elaborates a fable of the mission of *Geist*
to rescue *Seele* (iv. 42 f.).

intervention is positively asserted by the Bible, the narrative
dissolves the idea. If the Lord 'shewed mercy' (*Huld*) to the
imprisoned Joseph 'and gave him favour in the sight of the
keeper of the prison', as stated in Genesis 39: 21, the mercy
lay in no direct influencing of the keeper but in the unfailing
effect of Joseph's person: 'sondern die Sympathie und das
Vertrauen, mit einem Wort: der Glaube, den Josephs Erscheinung und Wandel jenem einflössten, ging vielmehr aus dem
untrüglichen Gefühl eines guten Mannes für die göttliche Huld,
das heisst: für das Göttliche selbst hervor, das mit diesem Zücht-
ling war . . .' (v. 1328 f.). The Bible's simple paratactic style
leaves a loop-hole, and the divine act is deftly relocated in the
hero's earthly form. The gloss is part of the parody of learned
style which Mann meant humorously, but its substance is
serious enough. Joseph's faith in God is one more projection of
his self-confidence.[58] The unvarnished truth has already been
stated by Potiphar's wife. Joseph's success cannot be the work
of his gods; the cause is in himself that he has not stayed an
underling: 'In ihm selbst müssen die Gaben sein, die ihm dazu
verhalfen' (v. 1066).

The situation is a familiar one. In earlier works—*Der Tod
in Venedig*, *Der Zauberberg*—Mann created teasing ambiguities,
offering a choice between natural explanation and some 'higher'
meaning. Similarly in *Joseph*, with personal qualities and
calculation on the one hand, divine grace and mythic pattern
on the other. But there is this difference: the natural materials
are here arranged into patterns not just by the author, but by
the character. The Joseph–Tammuz equation is found in
Mann's sources and goes back at least to 1700.[59] But it had
never been suggested that Joseph himself was aware of the
parallels, much less that he engineered them. This is Mann's
contribution. It is a problematic one. While retaining the idea
of myth, Mann destroys its essential quality, its *naïveté*.

It was difficult enough to keep his own psychological method
from doing this and merely rendering a psychology *of* myth.
Till now he had been remarkably successful in handling a

[58] Mann's notes for the 1932 Goethe essays include this: 'Als Psycholog an
Nietzsche erinnernd: "Glaube ist nur Selbstvertrauen, objektiv gefasst und
objektiviert".' Mp. ix. 180, fol. 8.
[59] See Willy R. Berger, *Die mythologischen Motive in Thomas Manns Roman 'Joseph
und seine Brüder'*, Cologne and Vienna, 1971, pp. 106 ff.

material which has brought many modern writers to grief. Myth fascinates because it seems to offer an escape from the limitations which modern ways of thinking impose on the imagination. In primitive times it was the imagination's way of explaining mysterious patterns. But it is almost impossible to switch off the modern consciousness and regress to the pre-rational vision of myth; what results is usually a quite un-mysterious surface-story heavily hinting at a piece of mythology.[60] *Der Tod in Venedig* kept the primal suggestiveness of myth by not bringing it into direct contact with the other ways of seeing which are present in the work. The levels of meaning are parallel and self-contained. They meet only outside the work in the coincidental links between their sources. As with those visual figures for which two mental interpretations are possible but can never be seen at the same moment,[61] the mind cannot entertain myth and psychology as true explana-tions of Aschenbach's fate simultaneously.

In *Joseph* there is a similar attempt to keep both options open. The image of the 'rolling sphere' obscures the question of whether myths originate on earth or in heaven (iv. 189 f.). The narrator in his role as commentator does his best, as we saw, to maintain a religious and mythic view of Joseph, although his efforts are themselves a sign that the narrative proper points the other way. Still, a balance might just have been kept had it not been for Joseph's self-consciousness. He believes with one part of his mind that he is 'in a story', but with the other part he is working as a confidence-man to bring that story about. Inescapably therefore, he inherits his author's problems. In character as well as author, myth and psychology have met. Myth cannot survive. What is left is mythology, which Joseph manipulates.

In all Mann said over two decades on the question, this conclusion is at hand. Answering the irrationalist amateurs of myth who denied the two elements could go together, he falls back on a description of his approach as a 'psychology of myth', a mixture of sympathy and reason, an 'irony which need not

---

[60] The problem is clearly stated and some specimen novels analysed by John J. White, *Mythology in the Modern Novel*, Princeton, 1971.

[61] e.g. the duck–rabbit figure reproduced in E. H. Gombrich, *Art and Illusion*, 1962, p. 4.

be unholy' (xi. 137). That is 1930. In 1933 he discovers deeper psychological (i.e. Freudian psychoanalytic) meaning in Wagner's Germanic myths (ix. 368 ff.). In 1936 he draws parallels between Freudian psychoanalysis which probes the depths of the soul and mythic interest which probes the depths of man's past (ix. 492 f.). In 1941 he asserts that the 'combination' of myth and psychology is his element (xi. 651). None of this manages to square the circle and resolve the conflict between myth and psychology which he stated clearly in 1919 in his remarks on Fontane and Bismarck. Why did Mann try so hard to reconcile them? Because he was torn two ways. He was fascinated by myth and theories on myth.[62] He saw in myth yet another hope of achieving that old artistic aim of a restored simplicity.[63] But he was also aware that mythical thinking could be politically dangerous and needed to be opposed by rational clarity—by psychology, in fact. Hence his insistence in the Freud essay on conscious control and clinical treatment of the 'powers of the underworld' (ix. 500). The episode which drove Mann into exile had shown how myth and psychology could come into political conflict, bearing out what he said in 1919 about their opposed political roles. For it was the discovery of psychoanalytic meanings in Wagner (a 'wertbeständigen deutschen Geistesriesen') and in his heroic characters ('Ausdruck tiefsten deutschen Gefühls') which led to the 'Protest of the Richard-Wagner-City of Munich'.[64] Despite the cliché of the 'deep' German soul, *Gemüt*, feeling, etc., it apparently would not do to search out what actually lay in the depths. Analysis was not just abhorrently rational and Western, it was a threat. There is some symbolic truth in Mann's later suggestion that Hitler's invasion

---

[62] For details of Mann's mythological source studies for *Joseph*, see Berger, op. cit., and Manfred Dierks, *Studien zu Mythos und Psychologie bei Thomas Mann*, Berne and Munich, 1972.

[63] Cf. the letter of 8 Jan. 1932 to an unknown correspondent: 'Ich' halte in der Dichtung eine Wendung weg von allem Extremen, Abenteuerlichen, stofflich Sensationellen und Exotischen und hin zum menschlich Ursprünglichen und Einfachen für wahrscheinlich, eine Neigung zum menschlich Urmythischen und Reinen, zu einer neuen Klassik also, die auf anderer später Ebene wiederkehren und, da die Kunst unterdessen durch manches hindurchgegangen ist, natürlich ein anderes Gesicht zeigen wird, als auf einer früheren Lebensstufe. Ich rede hier gewissermassen aus Erfahrung . . .' (Br. i. 312).

[64] The protest, from which these phrases are taken, is reprinted in Gottfried Bermann-Fischer, op. cit., pp. 92 f.

of Austria was aimed at the city where Freud worked (xii. 850). By 1941, the political relevance of the conflict between myth and psychology, and of the Joseph novel in particular, is even clearer. Psychology is the means to take myth from its evil fascist users and give it a humane function ('den faschistischen Dunkelmännern aus den Händen zu nehmen und . . . ins Humane umzufunktionieren' [xi. 651]). The combination of myth and psychology is the sign of a future humanity which will be doubly blessed—'gesegnet . . . oben vom Geist herab und "aus der Tiefe, die unten liegt"'; the words restate Joseph's attributes. Yet the roots in the 'depths which lie beneath' are not myth, but a *knowledge* of myth, and Mann himself duly calls this 'mythology' in an immediately following passage (xi. 653). If he nevertheless clung to the term 'myth', it was for familiar reasons. As with those other cult terms of the irrationalist opposition *Plastik* and *Dichter*, it was necessary to claim one's own version of it. He was especially delighted to hear that there were 'mythic' features in his work which he had not consciously put there.[65] And if he also maintained that the schemata of myth represented a higher truth, 'die höhere Wahrheit, die sich im Wirklichen darstellt' (ix. 493), this was the old impulse to see his experience as typical of a general pattern. His belief in mythic schemata seems even to deny individual experience any independent value. He speaks of the

Schema, in dem und *nach* dem das vermeintlich ganz Individuelle lebt, nicht ahnend in dem naiven Dünkel seiner Erst- und Einmaligkeit, wie sehr sein Leben Formel und Wiederholung, ein Wandeln in tief ausgetretenen Spuren ist.

(schema in which and *according* to which what is mistakenly thought to be individual leads its life, not realizing in the naïve presumption of its own novelty and uniqueness to how great an extent its life is formula and repetition, a treading in footsteps which have been trodden deep by others [ix. 493 f.]).

The desire for *Gebundenheit* beneath individual *Freiheit* here reaches an extreme which disregards logic. Whatever creates patterns of regularity and typicality in human life, it is not the

---

[65] As the works and letters of his mythologist friend Karl Kerényi often suggested. See e.g. Br. K. 44, 94. And when a critic read Lotte in *Lotte in Weimar* as a mother-myth, Mann commented: 'das Mythische ist bei mir nachgerade "selbsttätig" geworden' (Br. ii. 179).

existence of mythical schemata, much less schemata men are unaware of. For such patterns of determination myth is at best a decorative term. And where there is actual awareness of mythic schemata, there is already choice rather than determination. In neither case does myth truly bind. Nowhere is this clearer than in Joseph's own account of the relation between mythic schema and personal freedom. The mythical tradition comes from the depths and binds, he tells Pharaoh, while the individual ego comes from God and the spirit and is free. The ideal of a civilized life (*gesittetes Leben*) is that the one should be filled out by the other—'dass sich das Bindend-Musterhafte des Grundes mit der Gottesfreiheit des Ich erfülle' (v. 1421). How does this happen? About to prophesy and interpret Pharaoh's dreams, Joseph has to ease him out of his traditional expectations: that there will be a trance, that the prophecy will end in the prophet's sudden death. Why not? Is he a prophet at all? Yes and no. There are details of his background which fit the traditional picture, but a gap remains:

ich bin's und bin's nicht, eben weil *ich* es bin, das will sagen: weil das Allgemeine und die Form eine Abwandlung erfahren, wenn sie sich im Besonderen erfüllen, also, dass unbekannt wird das Bekannte und du's nicht wiedererkennst. Erwarte nicht, dass ich tot umsinken werde bei meinem letzten Wort, weil es sich so gehört. Dieser dein Knecht, den du aus der Grube riefst, erwartet es nicht, denn es gehört zur Form, nicht aber zu mir, in dem sie sich abwandelt.

(I am and am not, precisely because *I* am involved, that is to say: because the General and the Form undergo an alteration when they are fulfilled in the Particular, in such a way that the familiar pattern becomes unfamiliar and you do not recognize it. Do not expect that I shall sink down dead at my final word because it is proper so. This your servant, whom you called from the pit, does not expect it for it is part of the Form but not part of me, in whom the Form is realized.)

In other words, the individual finally decides what to take from tradition.[66] His fulfilment of the pattern may be approximate. The depths do not 'bind', they offer modes of behaviour to be chosen and moulded. The life in myth is creative, guided not

---

[66] Cf. Mann's lapidary formula: 'Auf eigene Art einem Beispiel folgen, das ist Tradition.' *Deutsche Hörer!*, broadcast of April 1942 (xi. 1035).

by the schemata themselves but by the spiritual *Forderung des Tages* in whose light they are adapted. It insists on the schemata only for reassurance and authority.

This is religion as shown in *Joseph*, not a transcendental but a humanist religion. Like other great humanisms—the Christian humanism of Lessing which accepts Christ's teaching because it is good rather than because it is authenticated, or the hypothetical deism of Goethe's 'Das Göttliche' which aims to re-create Man in a higher image of his own making—it rests on rational discrimination. The parallel with Thomas Mann's use of tradition and its 'myths' is obvious.

But like all Mann's heroes, Joseph is chastised as well as celebrated, because like them all he is a general confession. His success in using myth is only the happy outcome which justifies the rest. In his education from self-love to maturity he resembles the figures in whom Mann worked out his humanism, Tolstoy and Goethe; and resembles through them Thomas Mann, who also developed from self-absorption through auto-biography to education, of himself and others. Self-love seemed to Mann a guarantee that life would have the significant pattern of a story: 'Liebe zu sich selbst ist immer der Anfang eines romanhaften Lebens.'[67] He had rejoiced to see his personal life becoming a 'novel' more real than the one he had merely written.[68] Like Joseph, he was 'in a story'; to other people it sometimes seemed that they were reduced to the walking-on parts in it. The self-involvement which issued in creativity could appear plain egoism, as it did to Heinrich Mann in 1918; the minor actors in the story were exploited, their private existences appropriated as the means through which the writer worked out his problems in literature. Similarly with Joseph. The Ishmaelite traders are only a means to get him to Egypt; when Potiphar's steward Mont-Kaw dies, he is 'abdicating' (v. 997); Potiphar's wife suffers torments of desire; Joseph's father suffers intense grief and is left for years ignorant that his dearest son is alive; Joseph's brothers are thrust into the role of villains in what they do not know is a story. Only Joseph

[67] x. 559, adapting Oscar Wilde's *mot* that 'to love oneself is the beginning of a lifelong romance' (*An Ideal Husband*, opening of Act III). The whole passage, written in 1913 as 'Vorwort zum Roman eines Jungverstorbenen', was later taken over into the section 'Erziehung und Bekenntnis' of *Goethe und Tolstoi* (ix. 69).

[68] See above, pp. 198 f.

knows. At the close of the novel, he wonders if such knowledge was after all wrong: 'Man kann sehr wohl in einer Geschichte sein, ohne sie zu verstehen. Vielleicht soll es so sein, und es war sträflich, dass ich immer viel zu gut wusste, was da gespielt wurde' (v. 1821). The question becomes more pressing if one accepts that the 'story'—whose outcome is certain only in the sense that the Bible guarantees it—is in its actual mechanics largely the hero's work. His triumph leaves grounds for unease. He has achieved much and risen high, but many have suffered. Though he imitated Tammuz, he has not really been sacrificed. They have.

## V

In *Goethes Laufbahn als Schriftsteller*, Mann mentions Goethe's plan for a novel 'Der Egoist'. Egoism, he comments, was an obvious charge against Goethe, and he was well aware of it. What a novel Goethe might have made out of the insight that the great master appears, in human terms, as an egoist (ix. 356).

*Lotte in Weimar* attempts to make good the loss. That means going against the traditional reverence which sees Goethe's life and character in the transfiguring light of his art. Where a standard biographer was pleased that the women Goethe loved were worthy of him—'Goethe hat sein Herz niemals an eine Unwürdige geschenkt'—Mann queries the perspective: 'Weiter ist nichts zu sagen?'[69] What about the women's angle? Goethe expected of Marianne Willemer a renunciation like his own: 'Ja, warum nicht?' is the sarcastic marginal note.[70] It was the end of the Napoleonic upheaval that allowed Goethe to enjoy that Rhineland summer of 1814 with Marianne—and to forget meanwhile the fate of the man he revered: 'Und dass sein Held zugrunde geht?'[71] The whole episode produced the *West-Östlicher Divan*, in which Marianne was 'honoured' to have her poems to Goethe included. 'Eine schwindelnde Ehre', notes Mann.[72] Every fact in Bielschowsky's innocent relation is looked at with a jaundiced eye.

---

[69] A. Bielschowsky, *Goethe*, Munich, 1905, vol. 2, p. 361.
[70] Ibid., p. 354.                                          [71] Ibid., p. 352.
[72] Mp. xi. 14, fol. 30, apropos Bielschowsky 2. 364.

Mann's marginalia state the novel's critical themes: art is self-centred, demands sacrifices, and is an unreal thing when measured by the simpler commitments it evades. The action is a series of meetings between Goethe's victims: Lotte, whose private life was exposed to all Europe in *Werther*; Riemer, who has given up a university career to be Goethe's assistant; August, who is fated to be merely the great man's son and will marry Ottilie von Pogwisch despite their evident incompatibility because she is Goethe's type, and suitable to run his household. Riemer, August, and Ottilie's friend Adele Schopenhauer can speak their resentment and frustration to Lotte because she too is the great man's intimate and victim, albeit of a generation ago. Her 'historic' character is a unique pretext for her callers; also incidentally for their high articulateness. She is forced to compliment Riemer on his fluency with 'Sie sprechen vortrefflich' (ii. 438)—he is after all at times repeating passages of Mann's own essays on Goethe—and cannot but notice her own *vis-à-vis* August: 'Aber was rede ich? Es fliesst mir heute nur so zu' (ii. 589). Thus, in a spirit of *qui s'accuse s'excuse*, the claims of realism are recognized—and dismissed.[73] As Lotte says when a third visitor comes between her and her lunch and she resigns herself to another massive monologue: 'ich bin nun einmal keine Privatperson, sondern muss höhere Ansprüche anerkennen als ein wartendes Mittagessen' (ii. 559). The claims of this fictional meditation on the artist keep her hungry for fifty more pages.

But Lotte resigns herself less easily to Goethe's art than she does to Thomas Mann's. Her relationship with Goethe has tormented her all her life as an old unsettled score (455). It has accumulated compound emotion—resentment at the mixture of truth and untruth in *Werther*, a touching bewilderment at the way her simple words have been immortalized in Goethe's text, a sense of injury that Goethe has ignored her in her married state and preferred scissor-profiles of her children, mere shadows of reality, to meetings with them. She has always sensed unreality and unreliability in him—'etwas Unwirkliches und

---

[73] This allows among other things free use of anachronism. August can tell Lotte that the *West-Östlicher Divan* contains poems by Marianne (590), something which became known only after Goethe's death and which he is unlikely to have communicated; Goethe can quote from his poem 'An Werther' (655) which was not written till eight years later.

Lebensunzuverlässiges in seiner Natur' (393). In all this, a real person struggles against the encroachments of art. Encroachments, because her literary role is a threat to her natural being. Her immortality, on which in a human and amusing way she likes to insist, is hurtful when it is taken more seriously than she is. The hotel porter gropes for words to make sure she is *the* Lotte: Lotte Kestner, *née* Buff, the erstwhile . . . Not erstwhile, she corrects him, but present and waiting to be shown her room: 'ich bin gar nicht ehemalig, ich bin hier sehr gegenwärtig und wünschte wohl, auf das mir zugewiesene Zimmer . . .' (373). What Mager states is the viewpoint of art: her reality is in *Werther*, in the world of beauty, 'droben im Schönen' (390). It is the viewpoint of the artist too. His love for her produced art, was (in Mann's presentation) only a means to that end. She then passed out of his life, became erstwhile. She has acted her role in the creation of something timeless, and is left to the mercies of time. Her role is filled by someone else, and it is the role that matters to the poet. Only in parenthesis is he disturbed by what has become of its actress:

Die Geliebte kehrt wieder zum Kuss, immer jung, — (eher apprehensiv nur freilich, zu denken, dass sie in ihrer der Zeit unterworfenen Gestalt, alt, auch daneben noch irgendwo lebt, — nicht eben ganz so behäglich und billigenswert, wie dass auch der 'Werther' fortbesteht neben dem 'Divan').

(The beloved returns for the kiss, ever young—(only a bit disturbing, it is true, to think that somewhere she still goes on living too in a shape subject to time, aged—not exactly quite so comfortable and acceptable as that 'Werther' too goes on existing alongside the 'Divan'). [ii. 649])

In Marianne—married, inaccessible, inspiring poetry—Lotte has recurred. She 'is' Lotte (Mann's notes call her 'Lotte rediviva')[74] and her husband 'is' Albert: 'Albert schlief ein,

---

[74] Mp. xi. 14, fol. 27. Bielschowsky (2. 350) suggested that Goethe found in Marianne 'vieles *von früheren Geliebten* wieder' (Mann's underlining). More suggestive still were Goethe's words to Lotte: 'Wir werden uns wiedersehen, unter allen Gestalten werden wir uns erkennen' (Bielschowsky 4. 167. Thomas Mann: !). Since these words with only a slight addition occur in *Werther*, in the final paragraph of Part I, Mann can find a pretext for the well-read Mager to speak them (ii. 381), thus stating the theme of recurrence in authentic words. It is a typical creative appropriation: Goethe and Werther were assuring Lotte of an after-life in which she would see her mother again.

Willemer schlief ein', Goethe recalls the scene at the Gerber-
mühle (ii. 630). Goethe having 'recognized' her, she has no
business to return literally, least of all wearing her timeless
*Werther* frock on her ageing person. It throws the relation of
art and life, recurrent pattern and uniqueness, into confusion.
Mann's deceptively simple title epitomizes this. Weimar should
never have seen Lotte.

For art brooks no competition, not even from life's organic
processes. Goethe long evaded marriage (*Ehescheu*, 654); when
he dallied with Lotte he was really about the business of his
poetry (647); for him, marriage and procreation are a pointless
labour beyond the goal, their products are poor things:
August is a *Nachspiel* and if he has offspring in his turn they
will be shadowy creatures inspiring no hope or faith (654).
Perhaps Goethe even sucked the vital force from his four siblings,
only one of whom reached maturity: 'Bin ich so egoistisch, so
lebenshungrig, dass ich mördrisch an mich zog, wovon ihr
hättet leben können?' (655). These are not reproaches of the
resentful but Goethe's own musings in the interior monologue
of the seventh chapter. They are of a piece with the terms
other characters use of the artist's life—metaphors either of
incomplete or of aberrant natural processes: poetry is self-
sufficient like the mere kiss by which alone children are not
made (456); the poet who involves himself with a girl already
engaged is a parasite, his feelings are a cuckoo's egg (464 f.).

The case against art and the artist—against Goethe—is
grave. It goes well beyond the negative pages of Mann's
Goethe essays, and is even more questionable than they were
in its use and interpretation of sources[75] and its reduction of
Goethean phenomena to fit Mann's experience.[76] But one

[75] The recurrent account of Goethe the nihilist (e.g. ix. 316 ff.) is so much more
Nietzsche and Thomas Mann than Goethe that it is false. H. Stefan Schultz,
'Thomas Mann und Goethe' (in Pütz, *Thomas Mann und die Tradition*, pp. 150 ff.)
analyses Mann's falsifications and shifts of emphasis in transferring materials from
source to fiction. How far what the characters say is their responsibility, is a
delicate question. Riemer's jaundiced view repeats passages of Mann's essays,
which thus seem relativized by the fictional context. Yet they occur in Mann's
post-war essays on Goethe—a point which Meyer (*Das Zitat in der Erzählkunst*, p. 237)
is aware of but does not adequately meet.

[76] e.g. the idea of culture as parody (622), or of Goethe's relation to the learning
of his age as superficial acquisition (426 f., 662). For a hint of the depth and range
of Goethe's interests at the time Mann treats, see Max Rychner's edition of the
*West-Östlicher Divan*, Zürich, 1963, p. 582.

should no more be outraged at this than gulled into accepting the novel as an objective portrait of Goethe. We have seen enough of Mann's purpose and method in identifying with his subjects to accept that it is himself he is speaking of. The case against Goethe is a self-indictment.[77] Mann constructs it with the energy of a devil's advocate, knowing that Goethe's victims will not have the final word.

Neither charge—that art is an evasion of the responsibilities of real life, and that art takes a toll of human sacrifice—is denied. Each is taken further in its own terms until it changes into a positive view. Lotte's comparison of poetry to a kiss of which nothing is born took up consciously (and again anachronistically) an aphorism of Goethe's.[78] Coming from the real Goethe, it was a wilful provocation; Mann's Goethe elaborates it into a philosophy of art. What the fertile Lotte scorns, he defends.

Ist die Liebe das Beste im Leben, so in der Lieb das Beste der Kuss, — Poesie der Liebe, Siegel der Inbrunst, sinnlich-platonisch, Mitte des Sakraments zwischen geistlichem Anfang und fleischlichem End, süsse Handlung, vollzogen in höherer Sphäre als das da, und mit reinern Organen des Hauchs und der Rede,—geistig, weil noch individuell und hoch unterscheidend, —. . . da das Zeugen anonym creatürlich, im Grund ohne Wahl und Nacht bedeckts . . . flüchtiger Besuch der wissenden Inbrunst auf rasch verderblicher Schönheit . . .

(If love is the best thing in life, then the best part of love is the kiss —poetry of love, seal of ardour, sensual and Platonic, middle of the sacrament between religious beginning and fleshly end, sweet act consummated in a higher sphere than that down there, and with purer organs of breathing and speech—spiritual, because still individual and in high degree distinguishing—. . . whereas procreating is anonymous and creatural, at root undiscriminating and night covers it . . . fleeting visit of ardour and awareness on swift-decaying beauty . . . [ii. 647])

'Poetry of love' is no empty metaphor, and 'Platonic' has more than its popular meaning. The parallel with art is already

---

[77] Cf. to Agnes E. Meyer, 12 Jan. 1943: '. . . die unheimliche Atmosphäre, mit der ich Goethe im Roman bis zur Komik umgab [war] eine Selbstzüchtigung und Selbstverspottung . . . Ich habe Goethe, mein Vater-Imago recht recht schlecht gemacht' (Br. ii. 290).

[78] It dates from autumn 1825. Cf. Biedermann, *Goethes Gespräche*, 5 vols., vol. 3, Leipzig, 1910, p. 240.

clear and the next words make it explicit. Then at the dinner-party, Goethe tells the story of a young man so charmed by a picture that, alone in the gallery, he kisses it on the mouth. His breath freezes on the glass, leaving the impress of his lips as the 'chance materialization of a warm-blooded caress imposed upon icy unresponsiveness' (742).[79] But the point of the story is not the illusionism of art—art, Goethe says, is not an illusion, *keineswegs ein Blendwerk*. It is the dual affiliation of art to the heavenly and earthly spheres, its mixture of the sensuous and the spiritual, of (in Platonic terms) the divine and the visible,[80] its appeal to the spirit through the senses (741 f.). As the kiss was a mid-way stage in the consummation of love, at once spiritual discrimination and physical expression, so art is midway between the extremes of coldly abstract spirit and warm animal existence.

The value of this middle position is stated fully in the scene where August brings his father Lotte's note. Goethe reads it and at once creates a diversion by showing August a hyalite just received for his mineral collection. In content the diversion is a response to the challenge of Lotte's return,[81] prompt and elaborate as only the suprarealism Mann works with in *Lotte in Weimar* will allow. This time, art is placed between the extremes of cold crystalline perfection and a woman's fulfilled natural life, in a dimension of its own. The crystal has form, precision, a transparent structure. It is a work of art or rather, Goethe corrects himself, it is a projection of the geometry of the spiritual realm into matter. It is perfect, but it has a fault: it is

[79] This is again authentic material worked into a motif-pattern of Thomas Mann's. He takes over the story from Goethe's Annals because it will continue the association between mere kissing and poetry already set going by a Goethe quotation. Lest the fictional Goethe seem too obliging in choosing to raise the subject, Mann even motivates this turn in his thoughts: a raspberry cream has just been served for dessert, and raspberries/kisses are an association of ideas reaching back to the beginning of the novel and the young Goethe's relations with Lotte. Cf. ii. 739, 647, 390; and Bernhard Blume, *Thomas Mann und Goethe*, Berne, 1949, p. 110.

[80] The words echo Aschenbach's (viii. 521), and ultimately Kassner's translation of *Phaedrus* 250 d.

[81] Another fine example of creative adaptation of sources. Goethe's Annals for 1816 note additions to his mineral collection including 'Hyalit von Frankfurt' (Mann's notes xi. 14, fol. 8). A reference was perhaps originally planned only as authentic detail—Goethe was to show August the hyalite *before* reading Lotte's note ('Zeigt August den *Hyalit*, bevor er das Billet liest' [ibid. fol. 9]). The transposition turns appropriated material once more into artistic meaning.

dead. Complete at the moment it formed, it can last indefinitely through time—*in die Zeit*—but without change, development, 'biography'. This is a false victory over time. Its duration would be enviable if only it had life: 'es wird nicht älter, was ja nicht übel wäre, aber es ist tote Beständigkeit, und dass es kein Zeitleben hat, kommt daher, dass ihm zum Aufbau der Abbau fehlt und zum Bilden das Einschmelzen, das heisst: er ist nicht organisch' (it gets no older, which wouldn't be at all a bad thing, but it is a dead constancy, and the reason it has no life in time is that there is no destruction to follow the construction, it is formed but never broken down again, in other words it isn't organic [686]).

But neither is organic life an ideal state. Man is a structure that lives in time—*in der Zeit*—but even this is only an outer, not yet a true, 'inner' biography. As in animals, the processes of nourishment and propagation are repeated mechanically, inadequate ends in themselves. Matter has not yet acquired meaning, only its own—tedious—form of timelessness, *öde Dauer*; for

öde und sterbenslangweilig, mein Lieber, ist alles Sein, das in der Zeit steht, statt die Zeit in sich selber zu tragen und seine eigene Zeit auszumachen, die nicht geradeaus läuft nach einem Ziel, sondern als Kreis in sich selber geht, immer am Ziel und stets am Anfang,[82] — ein Sein wäre das, arbeitend und wirkend in und an sich selber, so dass Werden und Sein, Wirken und Werk, Vergangenheit und Gegenwart ein und dasselbe wären und sich eine Dauer hervortäte, die zugleich rastlose Steigerung, Erhöhung und Perfection wäre.

(tedious and deadly boring, my dear boy, is all being that stands in time instead of carrying time in itself and constituting its own time, a time which does not run straight forward towards a goal but goes in a circle of its own, ever at the goal and always at the beginning— that would be a Being worth the name, working to some effect in and upon itself, so that development and being, the labour and the

---

[82] The wording echoes Goethe's poem 'Unbegrenzt' from the *West-Östlicher Divan*, especially the lines 'Dein Lied ist drehend wie das Sterngewölbe, / Anfang und Ende immerfort dasselbe, / Und was die Mitte bringt, ist offenbar / Das, was zu Ende bleibt und anfangs war.' What Goethe wrote as a characterization of Hafiz's poetry and the Persian ghazal form has been appropriated as a philosophy of life. As a commentary on this passage, cf. 'Lob der Vergänglichkeit' of 1952 (x. 383 ff.).

result, past and present would be one and the same and produce a
duration which was at once restless intensification, elevation, and
perfection [687].)

Art and the artist's life are indeed the escape from organic
process Lotte suspected, but not for despicable motives, and
not into a cold timelessness. They know change, but it is inner
change as the artist labours at his own perfection, which is
indistinguishable from that of his works. If he succeeds, the
artist's life is his greatest masterpiece, of more value than any
single work. This is an apologia for art as egocentricity.

Even if it is accepted, it leaves the second charge standing:
that the egocentricity sacrifices others to its purposes. They
suffer in situations which to them are unique, though for the
artist they are the milestones of recurrence in his creative pattern. The fact that they are themselves little egoists, proud of
their roles in his life and jealous of each other, does not absolve
him. But here the philosophy of art passes over into a myth of
art. When Lotte first let fall to Riemer the word 'parasite', he
replied that there was a divine parasitism, the 'passion of the
prince of gods for the wife of a man' (466): Lotte is invited to
cast herself as Alkmene to Kestner's Amphitryon and Goethe's
Zeus. Earlier, Goethe's failure to visit his mother during the
eleven years before she died led Riemer to quote Christ's rejection of his mother: 'Weib, was habe ich mit dir zu schaffen?'
(453). And after painting a picture of the all-too-human Goethe,
Riemer leaves Lotte with the thought that she and he are
immortal in history and legend, like the figures about Jesus
(474).

This last allusion redirects the idea of sacrifice. If the small
actors suffer, so does the protagonist. This is Goethe's theme
in his imaginary second meeting with Lotte which ends the
book. He admits his guilt towards her and the others who
played her role—'ihr alle seid nur Eine in meiner Liebe —
und in meiner Schuld' (762)—and when she still speaks of the
bitterness of being a sacrifice, he answers her with the mystery
of transformation by which the receiver of sacrifice becomes
the sacrifice himself: 'Den Göttern opferte man, und zuletzt
war das Opfer der Gott.' For if his victims are like moths
drawn to the candle-flame, as Lotte says, is he not the candle
which consumes itself as well as them to produce light, 'die

ihren Leib opfert, damit das Licht leuchte'? His sacrifice burns his substance into spirit: 'Einst verbrannte ich dir und verbrenne dir allezeit zu Geist und Licht.' Transformation is all—'Wandlung ist alles'. Sacrifice is made acceptable by the imagery and theme of Goethe's *Divan* poem 'Selige Sehnsucht'.[83]

Lotte is conciliated. But the conclusion does more. In justifying Goethe, it justifies the modern artist to whom he has been subtly assimilated. What Thomas Mann has found in Goethe's life is a version of the separation from normal living which Tonio Kröger lamented; that is what Goethe's *Entsagung* has turned out to mean. What he has found in Goethe's art is something very like his own method for solving the technical problem such separation entailed: *Contactnahme*, a technique of appropriating others' work as literary material which repeats Goethe's parasitism in love.[84] So, as the culmination of two decades of fashioning and using Goethe, Mann draws on him for the most sweeping vindication of all. And because he has finally read Goethe's way of life as a myth, the power of myth is added to the vindication.

We are still not done with myth and identification. They have yet to perform their greatest task, radically different from what went before. Schiller, Nietzsche, Lessing, Goethe, Joseph were all affirmations. Through them Mann celebrated the artist he knew himself to be, found support in polemic, discerned larger meanings for his experience. The mode was heroic. Even the fictional play of *Lotte in Weimar* was a retort to the regime which had withdrawn his German citizenship, bearing out his words in exile, 'Wo ich bin ist die deutsche Kultur'. But war created a different problem. Who was the enemy? Was it Germany? If so, a German exile could only lose, whatever the outcome. Or was it only the 'bad' Germany of Nazism? The distinction was impracticable. The Nazi defeat was a German catastrophe. Moreover, Mann had all along said that Nazism had its roots in German culture. In however crude a way, it drew on distinctive modern German ideas in anthropology and

---

[83] Perhaps also of Nietzsche's poem 'Ecce Homo' (quoted above, p. 324) as suggested by Blume, op. cit., pp. 114 f. The combination would have a symbolic aptness since the novel blends Goethean materials and a Nietzschean vision.

[84] See Riemer's comments, ii. 425 ff., and Goethe's reflections, 662. For examples of the montage method as Mann used it in *Lotte in Weimar*, cf. Reed, 'Clarifications', pp. 168 ff.

philosophy, it showed the same impulses as much German art of this century, including (as Mann knew) his own. As the war neared its end and the strain eased, not triumph but self-questioning began. Myth and identification moved into the tragic mode.

# Reckoning

> One day someone will venture to embark upon a pathology of cultural communities.
>
> FREUD, *Civilization and its Discontents*

## I

*Doktor Faustus* attempts the impossible: to encompass and explain the German catastrophe. What happened to Germany and what was done by Germans under Hitler was horrible on such a scale that it defies the resources of artistic imagination to formulate it and perhaps even casts doubt on the possibility of an adequate tragic art in modern times. But to defy means to challenge. How could Thomas Mann have refused the challenge? He had spent a lifetime evolving means for just such a task, learning to say the general—by allegory, symbol, myth—through the particular. In *Der Zauberberg* he had embodied complex truths about an earlier phase of German history and society in the fate of a single individual. Besides, he was at root an *Erlebnisdichter*. He had put too much of his substance into the fight against Hitler, brooded too much over what made Hitler possible, suffered too much from the distortion of his country and its culture to be able to leave the account artistically unsettled. What literary subject could he have turned to with a quiet mind, leaving that immense task unattempted? He toyed, as often before, with *Krull*. It was comfortingly familiar, but its themes were no longer live.[1] What was live was the idea of a 'Faust'—'wenn gestaltungsfähig' (xi. 160).

'If it could be given form': this is the first of many doubts recorded in Mann's diaries of the time and quoted in *Die Entstehung des Doktor Faustus*. No work of his had produced such moods of despondency since *Der Tod in Venedig*—the links between these two works are many and not chance. But his doubts

---

[1] Cf. *Entstehung*: '... verjährt und überholt durch den "Joseph"'; but 'Vorteil, auf einer alten Grundlage weiterzubauen' (xi. 158).

were practical. Could he do the job? Was his thematic material
not exhausted? Had he the creative energy? And later, was the
work failing? Was the material swamping the structure?[2]
Critics have had more radical doubts and asked whether the
Faust subject was *permissible*. For some it is too transcendental,
for others not transcendental enough. Their queries will help
to clarify our problems later. But one point can be made clear
at the outset, and it will lead to the heart of the matter: the
choice of the Faust theme was not arbitrary or facile. It was not
a case of the most eminent German writer taking up the
most prestigious German myth. Nor was it a case of hasty
recourse to a diabolic explanation for the rise of forces Mann
hated. This was a possible reaction in minds accustomed to
analysis but stunned by the catastrophe of Nazism. Meinecke,
for example, called Hitler's doings a 'breakthrough of the
satanic principle in world history'.[3] Mann's satanic idea had
roots further back, in time and in his characteristic themes.

*Doktor Faustus* grew from a note of 1905[4] to which Mann
returned in 1943. It reads:

Novelle oder zu 'Maja'. Figur des syphilitischen Künstlers: als
Dr. Faust und dem Teufel Verschriebener. Das Gift wirkt als
Rausch, Stimulans, Inspiration; er darf in entzückter Begeisterung
geniale, wunderbare Werke schaffen, der Teufel führt ihm die Hand.
Schliesslich aber *holt ihn der Teufel*: Paralyse. Die Sache mit dem
reinen jungen Mädchen, mit der er es bis zur Hochzeit treibt, geht
vorher.

(Story or for 'Maja'. Figure of the syphilitic artist: as Dr. Faust
who has sold himself to the Devil. The effect of the virus is intoxication, stimulus, inspiration; in transports of exaltation he is allowed
to create wonderful works of genius, the Devil guides his hand. But
in the end *the Devil carries him off*: paralysis. The business of the pure
young girl he goes to the point of marriage with is before this.)[5]

The note bears the stamp of those years after *Buddenbrooks*

[2] C. xi. 156, 192.
[3] '. . . während das Werk Hitlers zu den Durchbrüchen eines satanischen
Prinzips in der Weltgeschichte gerechnet werden muss'. *Die deutsche Katastrophe*,
Zürich and Wiesbaden, 1946, p. 26.
[4] Mann says 1901 (xi. 155) but was taking the date inside the cover of notebook 7 where the idea is recorded on p. 155. Cf. Wysling, *Studien*, pp. 37 and 329,
n. 29.
[5] The reference is to a note on p. 138 of the notebook. The 'syphilitic artist',
impelled by yearning, becomes engaged but shoots himself just before the wedding.

when Mann was vainly seeking means to follow up his first
success and felt uneasy about the future of his work. *Schwere
Stunde* dramatized his struggle with discouragement and inhibition. It sought comfort in the idea that writing only came
easily to bunglers and dilettantes ('nur bei Stümpern und
Dilettanten sprudelte es'); true talent was self-critical, exacting
('kritisches Wissen', 'Ungenügsamkeit')[6] and this was bound to
be experienced as inhibition. Inhibition was therefore a proof
of talent. It was even the writer's ally because it ensured work
of quality. This is the sense of another tribute Mann paid to
Schiller in 1905:

> Die Hemmung ist des Willens bester Freund.
> —Den *Helden* grüss' ich, der Friedrich Schiller heisst.[7]

(Inhibition is the will's best friend. I greet the *hero* whose name is
Friedrich Schiller.)

These were brave assertions, but they did not reduce the
practical threat of sterility. Mann's standards, he wrote, were
becoming so 'desperately exacting' that they would probably
one day prevent his writing altogether.[8] This was the period
when he was unable to get started on a major project. There
were plans enough—'Maja', the Frederick novel, stories—
but he consumed his energies in planning and could not make
a beginning.[9] Meanwhile, in painful contrast, Heinrich Mann
was producing book after book, of a standard which proved
to his secretly fuming brother that he at least was not one to
suffer over his art.[10] He was one of the dilettantes. Finally,
Mann's fears of literary sterility were intensified by his marriage plans. Marriage was a risky experiment for one who
believed that art arose in suffering and isolation and that
happiness was forbidden fruit for the artist. These doubts produced the idea for a story about a pessimistic writer whose
marriage makes him so happy that he can no longer write,

---

[6] viii. 375 f. and Mann's letter of August 1904 to Katja Pringsheim (Br. i. 53).

[7] Supplement to the newspaper *Die Zeit*, Vienna, 23 Apr. 1905, p. iv, col. 3.
The aphorism is from *Fiorenza* (viii. 1063). Cf. Sandberg, op. cit., p. 41.

[8] Cf. to Kurt Martens, 16 Apr. 1906 (Br. i. 66).

[9] Cf. to Heinrich Mann, 11 June 1906 (Br. H. 57).

[10] Cf. to Heinrich Mann, 7 June 1907 (Br. H. 59) and the section '*Anti-Heinrich*'
in notebook 7, which includes such comments as: 'Ich halte es für unmoralisch,
aus Furcht vor den Leiden des Müssigganges ein schlechtes Buch nach dem andern
zu schreiben' and 'vielleicht ist Produktivität nur eine Form des Leichtsinns'.
Quoted in the introduction to Br. H, p. xxxiv.

until he finds that his wife is unfaithful.[11] Ominously enough, the year of Mann's engagement and marriage proved 'tormentingly unproductive'.[12]

The 'Dr. Faust' plan fits into this picture, right down to the radical way it poses the alternative art/marriage. Between the lines must be read the artist's *need* for abnormal stimulus. Devilish (or syphilitic) inspiration would overcome self-critical scruple. This is hardly a practical solution but a projection of personal difficulties into the further realms of fiction. Not surprisingly, the self-critical artist went on in practice with his slow labours. He settled to work again after the upheavals of 1905 and instead of executing the Faust story wrote *Königliche Hoheit*, which allegorized his more sober solutions and managed after all to reconcile artistic isolation and marriage. Yet the problem was not disposed of. Exacting standards remained a mixed blessing and periods of frustration and despair recurred. One such led to Mann's Venice journey and an experience of inspiration which, as formulated in the story of Aschenbach, paralleled the more crudely produced effects of syphilis. Both were cases of intoxication—*Rausch*. The word begins to stand out as marking an alternative area of experience, tempting, even fruitful, but dangerous. It is the area ruled by an alien god, Dionysus.

If the Faust note reflects the problems of 1905, in a technical sense it points far beyond them. Its parallel realistic and legendary meanings anticipate Mann's later use of ambivalence. As yet the parallel is not subtle, no more so than the one Hauptmann had used to move beyond straight Naturalism in *Hanneles Himmelfahrt*. It is not much more than decorative— the italics of 'holt ihn der Teufel' suggest a satisfaction that the legend would stay in step with reality right to the end. The Devil does no more than add a traditional *frisson*. The disease element is equally melodramatic, a caricature of Mann's interest in pathology and Nietzsche's theory that genius springs from abnormality. The whole has an arbitrary, anecdotal character. In Mann's later judgement, it was 'inadequate and vague':[13] 'vague', because there was no substantial meaning

---

[11] Notebook 7, p. 101. Quoted by Wysling, *Studien*, p. 35.
[12] Cf. to Heinrich Mann, 17 Oct. 1905 (Br. H. 38).
[13] '. . . den dürftigen und vagen thematischen Kern' (xi. 156).

behind the sensational elements. It could hardly be foreseen that history would provide one.

For the Devil, obviously; but also for the disease. In 1905, linking them as alternative explanations was only a clever literary idea. Over the years it acquired point. In Mann's reading of history, the temptations an artist was exposed to by his times were identical at their source with those which endangered political society. It is this that allowed him to write the 'novel of his epoch' (xi. 169) in the guise of an artist's biography. The artist's development could be, as Zeitblom declares, a paradigm of human fate (vi. 37), and music could be a paradigm of the broadest issues: the situation of art, of culture, of Man and his mind in the modern age—an age of critical reflection, 'unserer durch und durch kritischen Epoche' (xi. 171). An artist who sought escape from the inhibitions of his conscious mind could stand for a society which sought escape from the inhibitions men normally impose on their primitive instincts. And the form of escape, syphilitic infection, could stand for the history of Germany under Nazism—the responsibility for contracting it, the period of triumphs and exaltation, the final collapse. An intoxicated artist, an intoxicated nation.

This is what the Faust conception had become by 1943. In his work-notes Mann copies out the old plan and continues:

Habe diese Idee lange mit mir herumgetragen . . . Gedanken moralischer Vertiefung fanden sich hinzu. Es handelt sich um das Verlangen aus dem Bürgerlichen, Mässigen, Klassischen, [added: Apollinischen,] Nüchternen, Fleissigen und Getreuen hinüber ins Rauschhaft-Gelöste, Kühne, Dionysische, Geniale, Über-Bürgerliche, ja Übermenschliche — vor allem subjektiv, als Erlebnis und trunkene Steigerung des Selbst, ohne Rücksicht auf die Teilnahme-Fähigkeit der Mitwelt. . . .

(Have carried this idea about with me a long time . . . Deeper moral associations accumulated. It is really a desire to escape from everything bourgeois, moderate, classical, [added: Apolline,] sober, industrious, and dependable into a world of drunken release, a life of bold, Dionysiac genius, beyond society, indeed superhuman— above all subjectively, as experience and drunken intensification of the self, regardless of whether the world outside can go along with it. . . .)[14]

[14] TMA MS. 33, fol. 8.

The artist's disease is the symbol of his escape from the bourgeois context. And the escape has this political parallel:

Die Sprengung des Bürgerlichen, die auf pathologisch-infektiöse und desintegrierende Weise vor sich geht, zugleich *politisch*. Geistig-seelischer Faschismus, Abwerfen des Humanen, Ergreifen von Gewalt, Blutlust, Irrationalismus, Grausamkeit, dionysische Verleugnung von Wahrheit und Recht, Hingabe an die Instinkte und das fessel-lose 'Leben', das eigentlich *der Tod* und als Leben *nur Teufelswerk, gifterzeugt* ist. Der Faschismus als vom Teufel vermitteltes Heraus-treten aus der bürgerlichen Lebensform, das durch rauschhaft hochgesteigerte Abenteuer des Selbstgefühls und der Übergrösse zum Gehirn-Collaps und zum geistigen Tode, bald auch zum körperlichen führt: die *Rechnung* wird präsentiert.

(The bursting of social bonds, which occurs as a disintegration by infectious disease, at the same time *political*. Intellectual-spiritual fascism, throwing off of humane principle, recourse to violence, blood-lust, irrationalism, cruelty, Dionysiac denial of truth and justice, self-abandonment to the instincts and unrestrained 'Life', which in fact is *death* and, insofar as it is life, only the *Devil's work, product of infection*. Fascism as a Devil-given departure from bourgeois society which leads through adventures of drunkenly intense sub-jective feeling and super-greatness to mental collapse and spiritual death, and soon to physical death: the *reckoning* is presented.)[15]

These notes show how Mann connected what went on in art with what went on in politics. If a writer's intention counts for anything, they rule out the more superficial criticisms of *Doktor Faustus*: that the story of a musical genius cannot say anything about the crude evils of Hitler's Germany—unless he were a representative fellow traveller of Nazism, which Lever-kühn is not; that the novel is therefore a slur on music; or that it is further proof Thomas Mann could not get outside the charmed circle of art about art and write about reality. These objections stay at the work's literal surface or assume too di-rect a secondary reference. Mann's intention goes deeper. It is possible to question his premises—the quasi-anthropological reading of Nazism, or the theory that art is a paradigm of

[15] MS. 33, fol. 9. Cf. xi. 163: '. . . der Durst eines stolzen und von Sterilität bedrohten Geistes nach Enthemmung um jeden Preis und die Parallelisierung verderblicher, in den Kollaps mündender Euphorie mit dem faschistischen Völker-rausch'. It is notable that neither here nor, with one minor exception, in the text of the novel, does Mann use the term *dionysisch*.

responsible human activity, or the typicality of his own experience as an artist which is the novel's nerve-centre. But at least the critic must take account of the level Mann is operating at. The 1905 plan appears in retrospect an allegory waiting for meaning. Mann's notes state so plainly what its elements have now come to mean that there seems no choice but to treat *Doktor Faustus* as allegorical. Certainly it has the total awareness and the calculated execution typical of the mode. For the first and only time in a major work, Mann knew in advance what he wanted to do, planned the large scope, worked with the full range of motifs from the first page (xi. 168 f.). This makes a striking contrast with his other attempt to grasp political issues, *Der Zauberberg*. There a story already in progress had to accommodate matters not thought of when it was begun; and his view of these went on changing as he wrote. The wonder is that so integrated a work was finally achieved. With *Doktor Faustus* no such complicating circumstances arose.

Complication enough, however, lay in the material, and in the ways Mann was drawn to present it. Clear though his central thesis was, he was writing the novel of his epoch. So much seemed relevant, demanding to be included. Once he had decided to set the story literally in the period whose political catastrophe it was to parallel,[16] the reality of the period made its claims: his personal reminiscences, of individual people or of social groups, could be fitted into the narrative pattern. Indeed they had to be. If the central themes were to be realized, Mann needed support for his imagination, *Anschauungsstütze* (xi. 160). Hence the montage of old acquaintances, Hans Reisiger as Rüdiger Schildknapp, Paul Ehrenberg as Rudi Schwerdtfeger, or of eminent musicians like Otto Klemperer and Bruno Walter under their own names. But this was also more than a technical necessity. It sprang from an urge alien to allegory, to grasp the time direct and to people it in the novel with its real inhabitants.[17] The members of the

---

[16] A diary note from the early days of composition reads: 'Welche Form könnte das annehmen?   Der Geist des Vortrags ist fraglich. Selbst Zeit und Ort . . .' (xi. 159).

[17] Cf. xi. 165 on 'das eigentümlich *Wirkliche*, das [dem ganzen Buche] anhaftet'.

Kridwiss circle are similarly identifiable.[18] But here the depiction goes beyond mere montage of persons. The views Zeitblom records from their meetings are typical between-the-wars irrationalism, symptoms of Germany's intellectual disease, preparing its political form—'erzfaschistische Unterhaltungen' (xi. 245). Zeitblom is retailing direct the thing Leverkühn's art was to parallel, analysing factors in the larger events his career was to stand for. Realism operates alongside allegory.

The directness is not accounted for by the fact alone that for this and related sections Mann had to hand the materials gathered long ago for projected social novels—'Die Geliebten' and 'Maja'.[19] They only suggested one approach to a subject whose scope compelled him to try many. This compulsion was the crucial factor in the composition of *Doktor Faustus*. Mann left no technical means untried in the hope that finally, through allusion, analogy, parallel, symbol, plain presentation, and analysis, the subject would be enmeshed. For the reader it is a major task merely to discriminate which of these methods is embodied in a given detail, episode, or theoretical digression, and by what hook or crook it bears on the main theme. It may leave him unsure whether such intensity of effort and diversity of means produced a self-defeating complexity or a new standard of literary mastery.

The problem is plainest in the major motif which works with several of these methods at once and thereby relates their different levels: the use of Nietzsche's life as the pattern for Adrian Leverkühn's.

## II

By the time Mann expanded the old Faust idea in the thematic sketches we have seen, Nietzsche had become associated with it. Before turning up the 1905 note, before he had even finished writing the last part of *Joseph*, Mann was re-reading familiar books on Nietzsche, including Podach on Nietzsche's collapse

[18] See Gunilla Bergsten, *Thomas Manns Doktor Faustus. Untersuchungen zu den Quellen und zur Struktur des Romans*, Lund, 1963, pp. 33–42.
[19] Cf. xi. 155. The Faust subject brought with it memories of these plans. Wysling, 'Zu Thomas Manns "Maja"-Projekt", *Studien*, pp. 23–47, reconstructs their content and interrelation from early notebooks.

(xi. 151). The phrasing of his sketches ('ins Dionysische . . .
Übermenschliche') means more than that Nietzsche's theories
were being drawn on as tools of analysis. Nietzsche was becoming part of the subject. The parallel between the course
of syphilis and the course of Nazism had given meaning to the
1905 plan. But Nietzsche too was thought to have had syphilis.[20]
And Nietzsche was the source of German irrationalism, in which
Mann saw the prime cause of fascism. By introducing him
substantially into the novel, Mann gave the merely formal parallel between individual and political disease a further meaning.
Cause and effect could be portrayed together—a Nietzsche-
figure against the background of what he helped bring about,
the course of his personal life a tragic parallel to it. Causal
explanation could be compressed into a symbol, an immense
historical subject scaled down into a peculiarly appropriate
individual fate.

A Nietzsche-figure, not simply Nietzsche. To have written
directly about Nietzsche[21] (possible in theory—Mann had after
all written a novel about Goethe) would have excluded other
possibilities. It would have prevented so direct a treatment of
music, which for Mann was *the* German art and was relevant
to his political subject because of its changing role in his past
work—as the archetypal non-social art of the *Betrachtungen*,
then as the 'politically suspect' art of *Der Zauberberg*. It would
have excluded the personal confession which could be achieved
through a fictional figure partly fashioned in Mann's own
image. So Adrian Leverkühn simply lives a Nietzschean life

---

[20] If Mann knew this in 1905 (the first suggestion of Nietzsche's pathological
state was made in 1902 by P. J. Möbius and caused some stir) there is no sign that
his Faust plan of that year was meant to allude to Nietzsche. This may have been
another case of coincidence adding point to a symbolic system, as happened so
strikingly with *Der Tod in Venedig*. Mann's library contains Möbius's *Nietzsche* in
an edition of 1909.

[21] It has been argued that Mann planned a German mythic novel with Nietzsche
in the leading role as early as the 1930s. See Bengt Algot Sörensen, 'Thomas
Manns "Doktor Faustus", Mythos und Lebensbeichte', *Orbis Litterarum* 13 (1958).
The evidence is insufficient to bear this out. In particular, when Mann told Kerényi
that he had long contemplated an essay on Nietzsche (Br. K. 68), he did not say
a '*dichterischen* Versuch' (Sörensen, 85). But Sörensen usefully draws attention to
passages which may have helped prepare Mann's later use of Nietzsche in *Doktor
Faustus*, especially a letter from Kerényi in 1934 which states a paralell between the
collapse of the German intelligentsia and the madness of Hölderlin and Nietzsche
(Br. K. 60).

in general outline and some characteristic details. He has
Nietzsche's background and education, his brothel adventure,
his infection, his inspiration, his bizarre courtship arrangements, his madness, collapse, and death at the identical age on
the identical day.[22] To make sure that the meaning comes
across, the disguise is thin, the allusions far from cryptic, the
identity and common hubris of the two men are hinted at in
the name Leverkühn.[23]

This is not to be taken as an 'imitation' of Nietzsche by
Adrian. If we are to believe his final confession, he has lived
his life consciously on the Faustian model (thus fulfilling
Mann's Faust plan). Besides, many of the decisive similarities
with Nietzsche's life are beyond Adrian's control to arrange.
It is his author who has used Nietzsche's life as a legendary
pattern, for purposes of his own and with complications we
shall see.

The Nietzsche motif has several functions. First, incidentally
to larger purposes, it helps 'realization' by providing substance for the fictional hero's life and even for the (rare) evocation of his appearance.[24] It works out the parallel between
pathological and political collapse which is an implied judgement on German politics. It also links the Devil theme to
politics in another way: not only has Germany 'sold her soul
to the Devil', but the individual Faust (Adrian) also 'is' the
thinker whose ideas set the fateful movement going. In addition,
the retracing of Nietzsche's life is a reminder that the later
extreme elements of his thought were in part the products of
(literal) disease, which to say the least casts a shadow over them.

[22] For the similarities between the two lives, cf. Maurice Colleville, 'Nietzsche
et le *Doktor Faustus* de Thomas Mann', *Études germaniques* 3 (1948), pp. 343–54.
Aside from externals, the inspiration the Devil promises Adrian (vi. 316 f.) quotes
and paraphrases Nietzsche's account of the heightened state in which he wrote
*Zarathustra* (*Ecce Homo*, on *Zarathustra*, §3; Schlechta ii. 1131 f.).

[23] Cf. *Die fröhliche Wissenschaft*, Bk 4, §283, headed '*Vorbereitende Menschen*', esp.
the words: 'das Geheimnis, um die grösste Fruchtbarkeit und den grössten Genuss
vom Leben einzuernten, heisst: *gefährlich leben!*' (Schlechta ii. 165 f.). The link
with the Faust idea is implicit.

[24] Cf. vi. 675, which renders a famous picture of Nietzsche: 'Tief lagen die
Augen in den Höhlen, die Brauen waren buschiger geworden, und darunter hervor
richtete das Phantom einen unsäglich ernsten, bis zur Drohung forschenden
Blick auf mich . . .' The ambiguous phrase 'ein Ecce homo-Antlitz' on the pre-
ceding page ('the face of a suffering Christ', or 'the face of the man who wrote
*Ecce Homo*') helps to guide the reader in the right direction.

The *Beziehungen* this sets up and their different levels can be shown in a diagram:

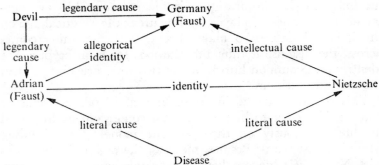

This is complex enough. But complexity does not end there. Giving so much of Nietzsche's biography to Adrian meant that within the novel Nietzsche himself could no longer be allowed to exist: 'eben weil der euphorische Musiker an seine Stelle gesetzt, so dass es ihn nun nicht mehr geben darf' (xi. 165). This was awkward. Nietzsche's influence on the society which the novel portrays was pervasive. It was easy enough to avoid mentioning his name, but his effects could not be so easily disposed of. To have ignored them would have been to undo the thesis of his influence which was what made his symbolic presence apt. In practice, ignoring them proves impossible. Nietzsche is present in the attitudes of the social groups who make up Adrian's significant background (the theological students of his Halle days, the Schlaginhaufen salon, the Kridwiss circle) and he is present in Adrian's response to the dilemma of modern music—not because Adrian 'is' Nietzsche and can therefore have his ideas, but because Adrian lives in a period pervaded by Nietzsche's thoughts on culture and society. The real Nietzsche thus affects his symbolic counterpart. Complexity here begins to be confusion, of the kind which is born of mixing literary methods. It recalls the scene in *Königliche Hoheit*, which Mann realized was dubious, where the prince meets a poet and 'reality converses with its own symbol'.[25]

Yet Mann ignored his own prohibition to the novel's benefit. It could not have become the historical document it is without

[25] Cf. Br. i. 76 f. and above, p. 102. But Mann called the mixture of reality and fiction in his Nietzsche motif an 'eigentümlich träumerische und reizvolle Vermischung der Sphären' (xi. 166).

full freedom to portray the intellectual currents of the time, Nietzschean ones above all. Its depiction of ideas in society is direct and powerful. In contrast to *Der Zauberberg*, it anchors abstractions in individuals with real social roles and it gives ideas the firm shape which springs not from tentative exploration but from moral judgement. For that shape is the shape of political things to come.

The links here are deftly made and worth examining: for their relation to the central Nietzsche motif, for the way they draw together Adrian's art and the intellectual climate it grows from, and for the political relevance of both.

Adrian's fellow students are full of the need for a new order of values to overcome modern disintegration,[26] a problem stated most radically and given most extreme solution by Nietzsche. They see the only possible social *Bindungen* as socialism and *völkisch* nationalism. Neither was an alternative acceptable to Nietzsche; but as if to hint that his thinking lies behind the discussion, he is alluded to as an example of tragic misunderstanding, a deeply German figure who yet rejected national commitment.[27] With the discussion of nationalism, we are obviously on political ground. *Völkisch*-minded students, appropriately named Teutleben and Deutschlin,[28] rehearse the usual ideas on German 'depth'. When this assumption of national superiority is criticized as a 'demonically threatened philosophy', the defiant answer—'Dämonische Kräfte stecken neben Ordnungsqualitäten in jeder vitalen Bewegung' (p. 167)—sounds a sequence of leitmotivs: the quest for order, the quest for vital force, the acceptance of a demonic element. The only other reply heard before the scene closes, to the effect that 'the demonic' is a euphemism for human instincts, illuminates the motives behind some kinds of new order and reminds us that, at least for some theologians, the instinctive and especially the sexual sphere is the Devil's domain.[29]

[26] 'Die Ausschau aus der Zersetzung nach Ansätzen zu neuen Ordnungskräften ist allgemein' (p. 167).

[27] Cf. p. 165, from 'Wir haben aber Fälle . . .' down to 'Widerstreit von Sein und Bekenntnis'.

[28] The names like many others in the novel were taken from a selection of Luther's letters. Cf. Bergsten, op. cit., pp. 41, 51. Some of the jargon-ridden student discussion was taken over verbatim from a right-wing pamphlet of the thirties, *Die freideutsche Position* (ibid., pp. 49 f.). [29] Cf. Schleppfuss's lectures, pp. 140 f.

Adrian too has a private craving for order. At the novel's realistic level, he chooses to study theology because it is a possible source of order and value for his too sharp mind which sees through and relativizes everything. He compares it to entering a strict monastic order (p. 175). He has been seeking some such value since schooldays. His comment on mathematics, which gave him some satisfaction, lays bare the nature of his quest. 'Die Ordnung ist alles. Römer dreizehn: "Was von Gott ist, das ist geordnet"' (p. 64).[30] In Beissel, the Pennsylvanian sect-leader who invented his own musical system, Adrian respects the desire for order: even a foolish order is better than none at all (p. 94). When Adrian turns seriously to music, this general unease of a free ironic mind becomes the dilemma of a late-comer in cultural history. He sees through the tricks and conventions of the past so completely that his own creativity is jeopardized. All means seem fit only for parody (pp. 178, 180), and parody the only escape from artistic sterility. His first work, 'Meerleuchten' is a masterpiece without belief (p. 202), his opera on *Love's Labour's Lost* the play of art on the verge of impossibility (p. 290).

At first sight it hardly seems that order will help to solve these problems. Order is a form of restriction, and Adrian is restricted enough already by his fastidious sense that so many of the tricks of the trade are no longer possible. But order is what he desires, a 'schoolmaster in objectivity and organization', a means to reconstitute the strict compositional methods (*strenger Satz*) of church music.[31] The point is that an order in some way imposed externally would rescue the modern artist from the most difficult convention of all, which grew from the rejection of conventions and has dominated music since Beet-

---

[30] Romans 13 in fact says the converse: that (the civil) order is to be regarded as of God. The misquotation, whether Adrian's error or Thomas Mann's, has no obvious significance; but the allusion itself, to the classic text on obedience to civil authority, already touches on the question how cultural order and political order are related.

[31] The term *strenger Satz* is not a new one in Mann's work. Hanno Buddenbrook's music teacher, Edmund Pfühl, is a devotee of organ music which has the 'moralisch-logische Würde des strengen Satzes' (i. 496). Most significantly, it is in Wagner (whose music he at first abhors as chaos, demagogy, and blasphemy) that Pfühl finds a revival of the method, which obliges him to add to his book on church music a section 'Über die Anwendung der alten Tonarten in Richard Wagners Kirchen- und Volksmusik' (i. 498 f.).

hoven: that the substance of his art must come from within him, must be subjective. In technical terms, the organization of a work of music was taken over increasingly by the development, which originally had only limited scope within a work organized in accepted formal ways. Free creation became possible, and freedom was at first productive. But it has now become an intolerable strain, affecting talent like a mildew and leading to artistic sterility. The artist despairs of creating from his own substance and seeks shelter in an objective order. Freedom (Adrian generalizes) always tends to such a 'dialectical reversal', and is happy to fulfil itself within a system of compulsion.[32]

Zeitblom is sceptical and at once makes the political objection, that freedom is then no longer freedom, any more than the dictatorship born of revolutions is freedom. Adrian brushes politics aside and goes on to speak of the beginnings of system in his work—the *h–e–a–e–es* sequence in his Brentano settings. But the political parallel has been suggested. Nor is it merely a formal analogy. Adrian's view of the crisis of music has itself a social aspect. While still at school and under the influence of Wendell Kretzschmar's lectures on music, he conceived of art one day regaining its role in the service of some higher corporation (*höherer Verband*). For alongside music's technical evolution away from convention towards free subjective expression, it has also evolved socially, away from a religious role (*Kultus*) to become free and self-sufficient (*Kultur*). Though Adrian declines to think about the political parallel to his ideas, they contain a political potential.

He does not specify what kind of corporation music might one day serve, and he does not postulate a revival of religious belief to undo the self-sufficiency of culture. At this stage, all he conceives of is some new source of primitive energy to counter culture's over-refinement and lack of vitality. When he queries the value of culture, the good Zeitblom is shocked and objects that the opposite of culture can only be barbarism. Adrian is not disturbed. 'Barbarism' is only the pejorative term which modern culture uses for what it cannot accept. But how genuine is 'modern culture'? Doesn't it talk about itself too much to be the real thing? Should culture not have

[32] This discussion pp. 252 ff. of the novel.

more *naïveté* and unselfconsciousness? Culture, even advanced culture, has been known to coexist with what would now be called barbarism. The present would need to be a good deal more barbaric if it were to become capable of real culture once again.[33]

Acceptance of barbarism, abandonment of the artist's social and technical freedom for disciplines restoring the past: how sinister are these things meant to sound? Inevitably they are chilling. They echo Nietzsche's question—where are the barbarians of the twentieth century?[34]—in a work written in full knowledge of the political answer. Of course, nothing practical comes of Adrian's social ideas in his own case, nothing connects him directly with Fascism. But it is with parallels, not direct connections that Mann is working. For this purpose, even Adrian's technical innovation, his invention of the twelve-tone system of composition, is enough, because at the deepest level it bears the signature of his times, combining primitivism and acceptance of order. A manuscript note[35] states the parallel in these words:

> *In der Musik vorkulturelle Neigungen denkbar*, zurückgehend *vor die Tonstufen-Ordnung und gesanglich wie instrumental das heulende, kreatürliche Gleiten über mehrere vorschreiben[d]*. (Posaunen-Glissandi.) 'Rückkehr zur Natur' in einem sehr unrousseauischen, unsentimentalen, eben 'barbarischen' Sinn.
>
> Nach der völligen Befreiung der Musik zur Atonalität: der eiserne Konstruktivismus des 12-Ton-Systems. Restaurativ im revolutionären Sinn und insofern faschistisch.

(*In music, pre-cultural inclinations conceivable*, going back *to before the tonal order and prescrib[ing]*, *vocally and instrumentally*, *the howling, creatural slide over several*. (Trombone *glissandi*.) 'Back to Nature' in a very un-Rousseauian, unsentimental, in fact 'barbaric' sense.

After the total liberation of music in atonality: the iron constructivism of the 12-tone-system. Restorative in the revolutionary sense and to that extent fascistic.)

[33] This discussion pp. 82 f. of the novel.

[34] Nietzsche, reflecting on a future Europe of decadence and cultural chaos, inquired how a stronger species might arise with 'classical' taste, which he defines as a will to strength and simplification (*Vereinfachung*). On the implied analogy of the barbarian invasions of Rome, which swept over a decadent culture, he asks: 'Wo sind die *Barbaren* des zwanzigsten Jahrhunderts?' *Aus dem Nachlass der Achtzigerjahre* (= 'Der Wille zur Macht'), Schlechta iii. 690.

[35] MS. 33, fol. 4. Immediately preceding is a reference to examples of *antihumane Vereinfachung* in other spheres, including the bizarre example from dentistry (see below).

In the novel, this parallel is made explicit (one of Zeitblom's functions is to help a fastidious novelist be explicit) in Chapter 34, which describes the Kridwiss circle alongside Adrian's 'Apocalipsis cum figuris', where the trombone *glissandi* occur. The date is 1919 and the Kridwiss discussions show the effects of the war on men's thinking. Belief in the value of the individual and in the old bourgeois liberal concepts of culture, enlightenment, humanity, and progress has been shaken—or rather, shaken yet more, since war only brought out more drastically what had long been felt: 'was längst vorher sich angebahnt, einem neuen Lebensgefühl sich zugrunde gelegt hatte' (p. 484). Indeed, the ideas of the circle are familiar from pre-war days within the novel. One of the Kridwiss *habitués* is Chaim Breisacher, a man with a fine flair for fashions in *Zeitgeist* who shocked the Schlaginhaufen salon by his preaching of barbarism and the primitive. The episode is a beautifully observed vignette of old-fashioned conservatism outflanked far to the right by a new way of thinking which paradoxically combines revolutionary effect and ultra-conservative appeal.[36]

The Kridwiss meetings are very different from that salon; not a social background for intellectual solos, but a gathering of like-minded academics for the purpose of giving those war-damaged ideals a *coup de grâce*. They are all representatives of the *Bildungsbürgertum* among whom contempt for the Weimar Republic was normal and flirtation with extreme right-wing ideas common. They quote Tocqueville on the two possible developments from revolution, towards free institutions or absolute power. They scorn the former and opt for the latter, with 'blithe satisfaction' (pp. 485 f.). They quote Sorel on the coming cataclysms of Europe and the replacement of parliamentary democracy in a mass society by propaganda manipulation and 'mythic fictions' which need have nothing to do with

[36] Cf. p. 372: '"Das heisst ... pardon ... der Barbarei?" krähte Herr von Riedesel, der wohl gewohnt war, in der Barbarei eine, wenn auch leicht kompromittierende Form des Konservativen zu sehen'; p. 373: 'Diese Namen [Bach, Palestrina] besassen für ihn den Nimbus konservativer Autorität, und nun wurden sie dem Bereich modernistischer Zersetzung überwiesen'; and p. 377: 'Der Baron tat mir wahrhaftig leid. Seinen Kavalierskonservativismus übertrumpft zu sehen durch das fürchterlich gescheite Ausspielen des Atavistischen, durch einen Radikalismus der Bewahrung, der ... etwas Revolutionäres hatte und zersetzender anmutet als jeder Liberalismus, dabei aber doch, wie zum Hohn, einen löblich konservativen Appell besass ...'

truth in order to be 'creative' and 'dynamic'. Truth has gone the same way as the individual, both are subordinated to the exigencies of the Community (p. 487). The circle even mounts a grim game in which a mythic fiction is put on mock trial, only to prove that by nature it is impervious to rational argument. Intellectuals themselves, they are hugely amused at the 'despairing onslaughts of criticism and reason'. The verdict goes to the myth; justice itself has no regard to truth but must judge, fashionably, in favour of what is 'false but fruitful' (p. 488). When Zeitblom observes that truth, even unpleasant, may serve the community better than its denial, which insidiously undermines true community, his remark is frostily received.

Parallels are already obvious with Adrian's ideas on music. The Kridwiss circle's eagerness to accept violence, distortion of truth, dictatorship is a case of what Adrian called the 'dialectical reversal' inherent in all freedom. (It is an idea familiar to political theory as the 'paradox of freedom.')[37] The members illustrate that 'freedom within a system of compulsion' which Adrian suggested and Zeitblom questioned. As academics, they feel their research is free, even though it functions under an objective obligation to justify violence, just as once it was the task of the 'free' mind to justify religious faith (p. 490). A bizarre detail underlines the similarity of their and Adrian's situations. As one sign of a welcome new barbarism, the circle note a return in dentistry to the practice of extraction, despite the refined techniques of conservation which have gradually been developed (p. 491). Years before, Adrian compared the refinements of late musical impressionism with the conservation of a dead tooth by delicate root-treatment. 'Dead tooth' or 'root-treatment' became his and Zeitblom's shorthand term for any 'late' works, including his own 'Meerleuchten' (pp. 201, 238). By implication, what Adrian turns to as a way out of the dilemma of being a latecomer—his quest for an analogue of archaic musical order to reconstitute a *strenger Satz*—is revolutionary primitivism: primitive because inspired by the past, revolutionary because calculated to bring about change in the present. Both his musical theory and the intellectual world of the Kridwiss circle are 'eine alt-neue, eine revolutionär

[37] Cf. Karl Popper, *The Open Society and its Enemies*, repr. 1963, vol. i, p. 123.

rückschlägige Welt' (p. 489). Both involve the abandonment
of cultural achievements for the sake of simplification or 'rebarbarization'.[38]

In case the parallels are not clear enough, Zeitblom seeks
them out in the work which was composed at the time of the
Kridwiss meetings, Adrian's 'Apocalipsis cum figuris'. He
points to its use of pre-classical strict forms to express absolute
binding obligations (*das Absolute, Bindende und Verpflichtende*,
p. 494), its turn back from 'harmonic subjectivity' to 'poly-
phonic objectivity', its use of the *glissando*, a barbaric rudiment
from pre-tonal times—in sum, its revolutionary regressions.
He admits to the suspicion that these recherché musical means,
far from being a true return to 'community', were aestheticism
—which is a harbinger of barbarism. The comment would be
obscure but for the preceding account of the Kridwiss circle,
whose values are pure aestheticism, as the poet among them,
Daniel Zur Höhe, clearly demonstrates.[39]

He then as Adrian's friend tries to deny the charge of barbarism. He would bite off his tongue before conceding it (p.
499). But he uses the word repeatedly in his denial (pp. 496,
500, 501); he admits the *anti-humane Dämonie* of the *glissandi*
and the 'disturbing, dangerous, malicious' effect of making
orchestra and voice interchangeable (pp. 497, 498). By protesting too much, he rams the point home. We hear only the
accusation, not the increasingly desperate defence. It is the
old technique of persuasion by contraries.[40]

What we are persuaded of is of course only the parallel. No
direct equation is intended between Adrian and the intellectual
renegades of the circle. Dubious though his ideas may themselves be, he has not sunk to their level. The 'Apocalipsis', as
Zeitblom says, 'confirms and realizes' their discussions 'on

[38] The phrasing here—'Bereitschaft . . . sogenannte kulturelle Errungenschaften
kurzerhand fallenzulassen, um einer als notwendig und zeitgegeben empfundenen
Vereinfachung willen, die man, wenn man wollte, als intentionelle Re-Barbari-
sierung bezeichnen konnte' (p. 491)—echoes Nietzsche on the 'barbarians of the
twentieth century', quoted above.
[39] Cf. p. 483 on Zur Höhe's poem which ends with a vision of soldiers plunder-
ing the world: 'Dies alles war "schön" und empfand sich selber als "schön"; es
war "schön" auf eine grausam und absolut schönheitliche Weise, in dem unver-
schämt bezuglosen, juxhaften und unverantwortlichen Geist, wie eben Dichter
ihn sich erlauben, — der steilste ästhetische Unfug, der mir vorgekommen.'
[40] Cf. above, p. 230.

a higher, creative plane' (p. 470). Something similar is true
of the circle's relation to Nietzsche. Dubious though his ideas
may themselves be, they are present here in a debased form
much closer to Nazi practice than to their speculative origins.
There is a gap between the mythic fictions which Nietzsche's
theory of monumental history allowed for and the cynical use
of myths in the word's pejorative sense which the circle take
over from Sorel.[41] Theirs is already that total rejection of truth
which Mann summed up as the German Will to Legend, in
full flower after 1933.[42] Again, in the principles underlying the
mock-trial, Nietzsche's belief that justice is not neutral but
presupposes values and purposes has been crudened into the
'decisionist' principle of Nazi law that Right is what serves
Germany's interests and vice versa.[43] And in the ideas of community, tyranny, and violence, it is easy to recognize not so
much Nietzsche's answer to the problem of values (which
certainly used images of violence and domination) as the
right-wing ideologies of the Weimar Republic as Mann analysed them at the time.[44]

Nor—and this is what makes *Doktor Faustus* a historical
document—did Mann have to create this advanced stage in the
perversion of Nietzsche out of his imagination. Sorel needed no
inventing. Nor did Spengler, who lurks behind the Kridwiss
attitudes, unnamed for some reason, but unmistakeable. His
ideas were at least as fashionable as Sorel's in the *Götterdäm-
merung* atmosphere after Germany's defeat in 1918. He outdid
Nietzsche in pronouncing Europe decadent and accepted
future catastrophe with a fatalism which provoked Mann, as
the Kridwiss circle's fatalism provokes Zeitblom.[45] Spengler
himself considered Nietzsche one of his forerunners. To

[41] Mann makes the connection, and implies the distinction, in his Nietzsche
essay of 1947 (ix. 689 f.).
[42] xii. 748. Cf. above, p. 333.
[43] In *Leiden an Deutschland* Mann quotes a German Minister of Justice as saying:
'Recht ist, was Deutschland nützt, und umgekehrt' (xii. 698). On decisionism, see
Hans Kohn, op. cit., p. 337.
[44] Cf. *Geist und Wesen der deutschen Republik*, esp. xi. 859, on the decline of liberal
values and the rise of new absolutes—community, iron discipline, terror—to
replace the relativism of a liberal society.
[45] Zeitblom's comments, vi. 492 f. Cf. Mann's *Über die Lehre Spenglers*, esp. x.
176: 'Und wenn es etwas noch Schauderhafteres gibt als das Schicksal, so ist's
der Mensch, der's, ohne ein Glied dagegen zu rühren, trägt.'

Thomas Mann, once the first impressions of his grandiose thesis had worn off, he was merely Nietzsche's ape.[46] Then there were Mann's personal contacts. His group portrait of treacherous clerks was done from life, drawing together recollections from pre- and post-war Munich society[47] and using old sketches.[48] The members of the circle had real-life counterparts, whose work carried Nietzsche's ideas to extremes. Breisacher is based on Oskar Goldberg, whose book *Die Wirklichkeit der Hebräer* (1925) pursued Nietzsche's idea of an age before 'slave morality' into primitive times (for Goldberg David and Solomon were late decadent liberals).[49] Daniel Zur Höhe is based on the poet Ludwig Derleth, one of whose works did conclude with the injunction to his soldiers to 'plunder the world'.[50] Derleth was a member of the George circle which had turned Nietzsche's intellectual rigour into intellectual snobbery and his intermittent prophetic gestures into a permanent pose. In Georg Vogler it is not hard to recognize Joseph Nadler and his racially based literary history in which Nietzschean vitalism is narrowed into the dogma that true poetry must spring from a *Stamm* and a *Landschaft*.

Thus as a group and as individuals the Kridwiss circle shows that Nietzsche's influence was pervasive in a distorted form. Few intellectual influences operate without undergoing some change, but Nietzsche's was peculiarly open to debasement. In everything Mann wrote about Nazism and its relation to German culture, the idea of debasement (*Verhunzung*) recurs. Showing how it happened is an important part of his subject. Nietzsche's images of conquering warriors and blond

---

[46] To Ida Boy-Ed, 5 Dec. 1922: 'ich habe mich von Nietzsche nicht abgewandt, wenn ich auch freilich seinen klugen Affen, Herrn Spengler, billig gebe' (Br. i. 202).

[47] Cf. to Agnes E. Meyer, 11 Oct. 1944: 'ich krame in meinen gesellschaftlichen Erinnerungen an das München von 1910 . . . dieses einfältige Capua, das dann zur "Wiege der Bewegung' werden sollte" (Br. ii. 394).

[48] Cf. notebook 7, p. 117 (Wysling, *Studien*, p. 37) on *skurrile Eindrücke* in literary circles, and an unexplained allusion to the 'last things', which is perhaps the seed of the 'Apocalipsis' idea.

[49] Cf. xii. 743 and Bergsten, op. cit., p. 40.

[50] *Beim Propheten* (1904) describes a reading in 'Daniel's' obscure top-floor room (hence the later full name 'Zur Höhe') by a disciple. A picture of Nietzsche hangs on the wall with other conquering heroes. At this stage, humour seemed an adequate response. As the lengthy ceremony moves to the final vision of 'world-plundering', the writer nurses his stiff back and has his own visions of a ham roll.

beasts were fatally easy to take in a literal sense, but it was not only their intrinsic nature which made them so. It was their separation from the context of moral purpose which nobody who reads Nietzsche can mistake. Even in that context, they are often excessive and at odds with Nietzsche's fastidious intellect. But outside it they become merely sensational. The elements which are difficult enough to reconcile into a unity at their source have the potential for a dubious independent life.

As early as 1910 Thomas Mann read the German cultural scene as a reflection of the two distinct Nietzsches, the militant psychologist and the triumphant vitalist. Of the two, vitalism was the message he thought would last, the effect which the younger generation had in them instinctively. Nietzsche was for them, significantly, a prophet they hardly needed to have read.[51] The conditions for misunderstanding and distortion were ideal.

If the Kridwiss circle shows Nietzsche being turned into an ideology which would help transform society, the separation of Nietzsche's influence into two currents has appeared earlier in a private context, the tragic disharmony between Helmut Institoris and his bride Ines Rodde. He, despite (or because of) physical feebleness, is a devotee of the Renaissance as Nietzsche evoked it—all beauty and unscrupulous power *à la* Cesare Borgia, 'eine Zeit, die "von Blut und Schönheit geraucht" habe' (p. 382). She is pessimistic and introspective. The contrast of his immoralism and her moralism reflects for Zeitblom the salient conflict of the times:

der Gegensatz zwischen Ästhetik und Moral, der ja zu einem guten Teil die kulturelle Dialektik jener Epoche beherrschte . . . der Widerstreit zwischen einer schulmässigen Glorifizierung des 'Lebens' in seiner prangenden Unbedenklichkeit — und der pessimistischen Verehrung des Leidens mit seiner Tiefe und seinem Wissen. Man kann sagen, dass an seiner schöpferischen Quelle dieser Gegensatz

---

[51] In N 103 of 'Geist und Kunst'. Quoted in full above, pp. 136–7. Mann's remark is borne out by one of the best accounts of the intellectual scene around 1900: 'Die Wirkung Nietzsches auf die Literatur um 1900 ist unabsehbar gross. Dabei ist es nicht eigentlich der philosophische Gehalt seiner Schriften, der rezipiert wird. Dieser bleibt weithin unentdeckt. Was wirkt, sind die Grundpositionen, in dreissig oder vierzig Sätzen erkennbar.' Wolfdietrich Rasch, 'Aspekte der deutschen Literatur um 1900', in Rasch, op. cit., p. 40.

eine persönliche Einheit gebildet hatte und erst in der Zeit streitbar
auseinandergefallen war.

(the antithesis between the aesthetic and the moral outlook which
in fact to a great extent dominated the cultural dialectics of that
epoch . . . the conflict between an orthodox extolling of 'Life' in its
glorious spontaneity—and the pessimistic veneration of suffering
with its depth and its knowledge. One can say that at its creative
source this antithesis was a personal unity and only in the course of
time became two conflicting elements. [p. 384])

Mann's rule prohibits any mention of Nietzsche's name, but
the reference is unmistakable. Tragedy in private life, ominous
shifts in ideas: Nietzsche is ubiquitous, casting his shadow over
the uneasy epoch—'die alles verändernde und unterwühlende
Epoche' (p. 381).

It needs no saying that his shadow fell on Thomas Mann in
the epoch he is describing. The conflict between the moral and
the aesthetic in Mann has been documented in this study.
*Doktor Faustus* retraces it, adding to the complex of relationships the identification of Thomas Mann and Adrian Leverkühn which makes the novel a confession and tempers its
judgements with charity.

### III

What Adrian's biography does not have from Nietzsche, it has
from Thomas Mann.[52] Here too borrowed externals point to an
intrinsic connection. Adrian's problems are, *mutatis mutandis*,
his author's. He has the same critical intelligence, the same
exacting standards. He has also inherited a similar situation.
What is said of music since Beethoven applies to literature since
Goethe, in which subjective experience has taken over the task
of organizing the artistic work (*Erlebnisdichtung*). Here too the

---

[52] *External circumstances*: the Kaisersaschern background which 'never released'
Adrian, i.e. as a *geistige Lebensform* (p. 113); residence and social contacts in Munich;
stay in Rome and Palestrina; between-wars visit to Switzerland experienced as
breaking out of German provincialism into Europe. *Personalities and relationships*:
Senatorin Rodde based on Mann's mother, Clarissa Rodde's death on Carla
Mann's, Ines Rodde's marriage partly on Julia Mann's to the banker Löhr; Adrian–
Rudi Schwerdtfeger and Ines–Rudi Schwerdtfeger relationships both versions of
Thomas Mann's relations with Paul Ehrenberg. *Personal motifs*: especially the isolation and coldness of Adrian, and his need for a personal 'breakthrough'. Details
could be multiplied.

originally fruitful subjective freedom has itself become a convention, imposing a strain on the artist, and as a result the
'spontaneous work' has become impossible, an illusion in the
sense of a deception and no longer in the sense Classical aesthetics gave to the term. Only conscious management, *Kunstver-
stand*, creates the appearance of natural flow (pp. 240 f.).

This view of musical and literary history[53] elevates to a
general significance the two problems Mann faced around 1905,
and which are at the root of all his subsequent work. First his
inhibitions. These now appear not just as signs of talent, but of
the particular talent needed in a late culture if art is to go on
making revolutionary progress. The distaste Adrian is sure he
will feel for a whole range of musical means turns his talent
into a positive calling; his sense of what is no longer possible
makes him the chosen instrument of the age. So Kretzschmar
sees matters (pp. 181 f.). Secondly, Mann's inability to mount
a new major work in those years. This can now be seen as the
strain of subjectivity at the end of its historical tether. He was
avowedly a subjective writer—'ein Lyriker (wesentlich)' (Br.
i. 62)—and in *Buddenbrooks* and *Tonio Kröger* he had formulated
his most intimate material exhaustively. Subjectivity could not
structure an epic unsupported; imaginative invention was not
Mann's forte and he rejected it in principle in *Bilse und ich*.
There was every appearance of an impasse.

So far, the correspondence is as close as the nature of the
two arts allows. It cannot continue so direct throughout—partly
because Mann is showing the response to that initial situation
through a fictitious career, but more importantly because, for
all the confession he intends through Adrian, there is from a
certain point a divergence. In Adrian are sketched temptations
Mann knew. Adrian fell, he did not. He came near enough to
it to give the confession point, but the fact remains that
Adrian is an extrapolation into the tragic, a 'there but for the
grace of God' figure. Only Aschenbach in all Thomas Mann's
work is comparable. It is no chance similarity; Adrian repeats
Aschenbach's fate on a larger stage.

---

[53] On the literary side, Mann had been developing this view for a long time.
Theodor Adorno, who has had much credit for his part in the composition (perhaps too much—see Br. iii. 226) was responsible for its translation into musical
terms and for some of the musical detail. But as a philosophy of culture, it was
Mann's own ideas that were fed back to him in different form.

What possibilities are open to Adrian? From the first there are hints that he will create a radically new musical order, but it is not clear what this can be. Meanwhile, there is parody, which turns the hypercritical intelligence to constructive use, as in 'Meerleuchten'. But it cannot absorb his mind fully or do anything to make an art of conviction possible again. Its only value lies in the fact that any work is a victory in the permanent struggle an artist like Adrian lives with, between inhibition and the productive impulse, between (Zeitblom adds) chastity and passion.[54]

This apposition is casual but crucial. All along, the sensuous, even sensual, nature of music has been suggested: in the dairymaid's singing with the children, which has animal warmth; in Elsbeth Leverkühn's abstention from singing despite her attractive voice, once more out of a 'kind of chastity' (pp. 41, 673); in Adrian's remark that the human voice is 'almost a pudendum' (p. 95); in the way Adrian has for years after his first experiments with music, which began in puberty, withheld himself (p. 47) from the art he is destined for and which needs him. The word Kretzschmar uses to make this point—'die nach ihm verlange' (p. 181)—itself has sexual associations,[55] confirmed when he calls Adrian's theological studies a 'virgin state', and ends his letter by quoting Angelus Silesius:

> Die Jungfrauschaft ist wert, doch muss sie Mutter werden,
> Sonst ist sie wie ein Plan von unbefruchter Erden.
>
> (Virginity is sweet, but must one day give birth,
> Else will she ever be a field of fruitless earth. [p. 182])

Music itself, involvement with it, the act of musical creation—all are spoken of in sexual imagery.

Music is not of course merely sensuous; it is a dual art in which sense is a necessary component. So Kretzschmar explains it in one of his lectures. In an extreme conceit, he suggests that music's 'deepest wish' may be to communicate without passing through the senses: 'überhaupt nicht gehört,

---

[54] 'Der fast unschlichtbare Konflikt zwischen der Hemmung und dem produktiven Antriebe mitgeborenen Genies, zwischen Keuschheit und Leidenschaft' (p. 203).

[55] It also accommodates a hint of the long-range plans to trap Adrian which the Devil later admits.

noch selbst gesehen, noch auch gefühlt, sondern, wenn das möglich wäre, in einem Jenseits der Sinne und sogar des Gemütes, im Geistig-Reinen vernommen und angeschaut zu werden'. But bound to the world of sense, it also has to strive for a seductive sensuous form ('berückende Versinnlichung'). It is like Kundry in Wagner's *Parsifal*, embracing the Pure Fool with the 'soft arms of pleasure' (p. 85).

What fascinates Adrian in music, overtly at least, is the spiritual component, its intellectual order which is akin to mathematics. For him it is not an element which can harmonize with sense, but a means to control sense. Music's duality is a conflict. The 'strict moralism" of its form must excuse the 'seductions of its sound' ('Berückungen ihrer Klangwirklichkeit'); the 'cow-warmth' of music needs formal laws to cool it (pp. 94 f.). But if the means to realize music's abstract structures are suspect, they are also indispensable. Spirit or intellect alone will not make art. His intellectuality, with its implied element of repression, is after all what has brought him to his creative impasse. The artist's way to the Spirit has to pass through the senses: that, and the dangers which may result, was the message of *Der Tod in Venedig*. There too, as in Kretzschmar's analysis of music, the problem was put in Platonic terms.

In Aschenbach's case, awareness of the danger came too late; he draws the moral after his fall, in the scene of pastiche Platonic dialogue (viii. 521 f.) Adrian in contrast has foreknowledge. Aschenbach slips gradually from his aesthetic admiration of Tadzio into sexual infatuation. Adrian knows what he is doing and chooses to do it. Both are throwing off a repression, but Adrian more deliberately. When he insists on possessing Esmeralda despite her warning that she is infected, it is a symbolic act of self-abandonment to forces he has so far resisted. There is an intention, real if obscure, to come by artistic inspiration, a 'tief geheimstes Verlangen nach dämonischer Empfängnis, nach einer tödlich entfesselnden chymischen Veränderung seiner Natur' (p. 206). Aschenbach too travelled to find regeneration of his flagging poetic powers, but his case can be read at most as a wholly subconscious search for the Dionysiac inspiration he finds.

This differing degree of consciousness in the two artist-figures typifies the relation between the two works, extending to their whole treatment. *Doktor Faustus* restates the themes of *Der Tod in Venedig* in the light of later experience, especially of the gradually acquired conviction that what occurs in art is linked at the roots with what occurs in society. It consciously makes Adrian a representative figure whereas Aschenbach was not. His fate pointed a moral but it had at the time no specific reference other than to the private case of an artist who, like Thomas Mann, shared his problems and experiences. When Aschenbach joins the worshippers of the alien god, he does so as one individual and in the privacy of a dream. He does not stand for the society which produced him. The Thomas Mann of 1912 was only just beginning to see that the issues of the time—and they were still only cultural issues—were contained in his own personal dilemmas, in the conflict between his desire for regeneration and reborn spontaneity and his mistrust of the means which might provide them; in the conflict between his ambition to achieve the forms and public status of a *Dichter* and his temperamental obligation to go on practising psychology and *Kritik*. Out of these conflicts came the story of Aschenbach, in its final form a warning of the danger which lies in appreciating beauty without regard to moral criteria—of aestheticism, that is; and of the destructive power which is latent in the 'mania' of Dionysiac feeling. In the retrospect of *Doktor Faustus*, these things appeared typical and a portent. They could be reduced to the one underlying conflict between aestheticism and morality, the 'Gegensatz von Ästhetik und Moral' which the narrator sees as 'largely dominating the cultural dialectics of that epoch'. *Der Tod in Venedig* formulated unknowingly what *Doktor Faustus* pursues by design into every recess of personal, social, and artistic life: the 'danger of a barbaric underworld latent in German civilization as its necessary complementary product'.[56]

*Doktor Faustus* thus repeats a confession Thomas Mann had made thirty years before. Why was his conscience still troubled? Even *Der Tod in Venedig* confessed temptations rather than sins

---

[56] The phrase is from George Lukács's essay 'Auf der Suche nach dem Bürger', quoted in *Entstehung* (xi. 240). Mann accepts the implied link between *Der Tod in Venedig* and *Doktor Faustus* and the theory on which it rests, that the writer is a seismograph recording things which at the time he has no clear understanding of.

—Mann clearly parted company with Aschenbach by taking a cool critical view of his Dionysiac *Rausch*. If this rules out a straightforward equation Mann–Aschenbach, it rules out all the more an equation Mann–Leverkühn, because Adrian is Aschenbach taken further, a *gesteigerter Aschenbach*. He lives to enjoy the fruits of intoxication whereas Aschenbach died almost at once. He has the promised inspiration for the span of time which the Faust legend (or: the known course of syphilis) allows. His 'Apocalipsis' takes four and a half months to compose, the time it would take merely to copy out the score. Compositional problems are solved the instant they are posed (p. 477). All his inhibitions are gone, he has full creative freedom and power—'höchste Freiheit, staunenswerte Macht' (p. 468). There is no hesitation, only a glorious spontaneity, 'prangende Unbedenklichkeit': the Devil describes his inspiration in the same words (p. 316) which elsewhere (p. 384) sum up Nietzschean vitalism. Aptly. Adrian has escaped from the inhibitions of his critical mind into an absolute creativity which at times produces 'triumphal' well-being (p. 641). His work may draw on all available musical means, but it is no longer parody (p. 648). The 'spontaneous work' is reborn, just as the order he aspired to is reborn—in the archaic styles which correspond to his 'archaic' inspiration[57] and in the invention of serial methods which restore a *strenger Satz*. And though he remains an intellectual composer, this is not in contradiction to his heightened state. We have seen that order, any order, can serve to lift the burden of rational or imaginative freedom. Adrian's is no exception. It is paradoxically a way of abdicating rational control, as Zeitblom objects; something vaguely demonic, akin to astrology, games of chance, and the like, a system calculated to 'dissolve human reason into magic' (p. 258). What is more, it is actually born of intoxication, not just in that Adrian's serial method is invented after he infects himself, but because it stems direct from the source of his infection, Esmeralda: the first experiment with the method is the cryptic celebration of her name in the *h–e–a–e–es* note sequence.

---

[57] Cf. p. 316: 'erst das Rechte und Wahre . . . nicht mehr das Klassische [sondern] das Archaische, das Urfrühe, das längst nicht mehr Erprobte'. The idea of primitive inspiration goes back to the passage of Nietzsche's *Ecce Homo* cited above.

Author and character thus diverge on the crucial point. Their lives and problems show parallels. So do their techniques —it is now common knowledge that *Doktor Faustus* uses literary equivalents of the methods it discusses and is in many respects analogous to Adrian's last work, 'Doktor Fausti Weheklag'.[58] But if the Faustian guilt or Dionysiac self-abandonment is not shared; if there is nothing in Mann's work like the birth of order from intoxication in Adrian's (which parallels the rise of the Nazis' so-called 'New Order' from the diseased state of German society); if this link is missing, how can *Doktor Faustus* be the 'radical confession' Mann said it was (xi. 247)?

Logically it cannot. But emotions have a logic of their own. Even a distant association with the causes of catastrophe— aspirations unfulfilled, temptations not yielded to, all long past and long confessed—can induce guilt. Even to have ventured near an abyss may trouble the conscience when European civilization has subsequently fallen into it.

This was Mann's case. He had flirted with irrationalism, chafed at the limitations of mere intellect, turned in disgust from relativism and psychological clear-sightedness, and hoped for a new, simpler order in art and ethics, 'eine neue Schönheit, eine Vereinfachung der Seele'.[59] This was the Aschenbach syndrome. By the late thirties Mann read it as fascism *avant la lettre*. The tendencies which produced *Der Tod in Venedig*, he wrote to Mrs. Meyer, were perhaps scarcely recognizable in their later political form, but they had none the less prepared it morally and intellectually. Mann had also given irrationalism his own political form in the writings of 1914–18 when he joined in what Heinrich Mann, anticipating the Dionysiac reading of society, called 'orgies of a complicated *naïveté*, outbreaks of a deep and ancient anti-reason'.[60] His reflections at that time even anticipate the Kridwiss circle.[61]

---

[58] Cf. the systematic account in Bergsten, op. cit., ch. 5; and for minute details of correspondence in technique the articles by V. A. Oswald mentioned below.

[59] Unpublished letter of 30 May 1938 to Agnes E. Meyer, quoted in Wysling, *Studien*, pp. 121 f.

[60] See above, p. 191.

[61] An entry in notebook 10 predicts the demise of political freedom and sees a new acceptance by intellectuals of absolute commitment: 'Freiheit ist ein bis zum Nihilismus geistiges Prinzip und kann daher auf die Dauer—länger als 100 Jahre— kein *politisches* Prinzip sein. Umso weniger kann es den Anspruch auf absolute, ewige politische Geltung erheben in einem Augenblick, wo der Geist selbst in eine

But this phase was no longer so near the quick of conscience—perhaps because it had been disposed of in *Der Zauberberg*[62]—as were the earlier symptoms in *Der Tod in Venedig* and *Fiorenza*. It was these Mann stressed to Mrs. Meyer. It was these he stressed again when he turned the historical connection between his work and fascism into the incongruous personal one of *Bruder Hitler*. These statements are the seeds of Mann's confession in *Doktor Faustus*.

But *Der Tod in Venedig* was only one case in an epidemic, typical of the 'inclinations and ambitions of the time' (xii. 850). Reflecting in these years on the art and philosophy of the recent past, Mann saw related impulses at every turn—irrationalism, anti-intellectualism, anti-idealism. Nietzsche, Bergson, Klages, George, Hamsun, were linked in his mind by the one feature which was now his prime concern: the danger latent in their ideas when transferred from a cultural to a political context. For reality, Mann says, cannot understand the revolt of idealism (that is, purist critics) against 'idealism', or of intellectuals against 'mind'. Pure motives and fine nuances go by the board in the practical world; the intellectual revolution becomes a political *carte blanche* for abolishing all humane standards. Doubtless none of those writers dreamt of such consequences; they thought their daring thoughts in a secure society—'in jenen bürgerlich gesicherten Zeiten'. They hardly considered consequences at all, believing culture to be insulated from reality.[63] It was Thomas Mann's mature experience that this is not so. In the light of events, those who acted as if it were so appeared irresponsible.

Yet Mann had once believed as firmly as any in the artist's freedom to explore and experiment. He was still, for all his

Periode neuen *Bindungs-* und nicht Auflösungsbedürfnisses tritt.' Quoted in the introduction to Br. H., p. 1 (where the 'nicht' is mistakenly omitted).

[62] See above, p. 257. In *Doktor Faustus* Mann's old wartime formulas are put at the appropriate moment in the mouth of Serenus Zeitblom (p. 405), probably less as a confession than as a means to historical authenticity.

[63] This discussion is in *Leiden an Deutschland* of 1933–4 (xii. 696 ff.). It could be objected that Nietzsche very much envisaged his own effects, which he spoke of in melodramatic terms in his later, shriller works. Mann's point remains valid that he never really conceived the terrible form they would take, and that his thought was out of touch with political reality and essentially a kind of aestheticism, the product (as Mann argues in the 1947 essay *Nietzsche im Lichte unserer Erfahrung*) of a 'theoretical man'.

activism, primarily an artist and unable in some moods to take his own political involvement seriously.[64] Even his confession that he was implicated in the roots of fascism, overscrupulous though it seems, also strikes a note of resentment at being compromised *ex post facto*. He distinguishes the political phenomenon from the intellectual antecedents which, however relevant, are 'scarcely recognizable' in it. He hates the gutter version precisely because it debases what he once took seriously as an artist. This does not mean that he would have continued to be influenced by those ideas if they had retained a purer form. (Conjecture here is idle since they did not, and the decisive fact of Mann's career was his readiness to grasp what *was* happening outside culture and adjust to it.) But it does mean that his sympathies remain with artists and thinkers even though what they write can be perverted. Indeed, this gives the sympathy a higher quality. If the originators of ideas were ultimately responsible for their effects, it was not responsibility of a legal kind, since the perversion was the work of others. At least in the case of the greatest among them, Nietzsche, there was something more like tragic guilt. To the tragedy of his conflict-ridden life was added the tragedy of his consequences.

Yet the sympathies he concentrated on a fictional Nietzsche-figure could not be allowed to mitigate judgement on those consequences. Mann's ambivalence can again be put the other way round: if he was a reluctant politician, he was a passionate anti-Nazi; if he was primarily an artist, he was now challenged by political catastrophe about which no artistic ambiguity could be countenanced. The old-fashioned liberal humanism on which his politics were based demanded to be given a voice in art, simple and explicit. This is the key to the narrative structure of *Doktor Faustus*.

For whichever is stressed, artistic individualism or social responsibility, there is a conflict, ultimately the same Nietzschean conflict between aestheticism and morality which runs through all Mann's work. *Doktor Faustus* is its extreme expression, locating Mann's two souls in separate bodies: the daring artist and his worthy, worried friend. This was crucial. A conflict unresolved left no standpoint for narration. Mann

---

[64] Cf. to Ferdinand Lion 13 Mar. 1952 (Br. iii. 248), partially agreeing with Philip Toynbee's judgement that his politics were 'almost too good to be true'.

projected its elements into two contrasting figures[65] and let one tell the other's story, with a mixture of love and horror. An 'inconsiderable background figure' Zeitblom calls himself (p. 470). On the contrary, he is responsible for the novel's most striking effects. Indeed, he made the novel possible. For he allows his author to do what was impossible without an intermediary. As an old-fashioned humanist, Zeitblom can make explicit moral judgements on German history within an artistic work;[66] as a man avowedly untouched by the Dionysiac ('Serenus'), he is the perfect foil to Leverkühn; as an old-fashioned *Bildungsbürger*, he can use an elaborate style which is sometimes taken to caricatural extremes but is as frequently what Mann needs, especially in the creation of period atmosphere in the Munich social scenes; as a biographer he can analyse exhaustively each incident and document of a life whose meaning, in this most serious of Mann's books, must at all costs be made clear; as a newcomer to literary construction, he can draw attention to his own clumsiness and problems of arrangement at just those points his author wants us to notice; and as a mind free from inhibitions about what is 'no longer possible' in literature, he can use classic, hackneyed epic conventions— the portentous anticipation, the melodramatic chapter-ending, the direct attack on the emotions culminating in Nepomuk's death—to get the emphasis his subject requires.[67] Alongside all this and flatly inconsistent with the limited viewpoint he embodies, he is a virtually omniscient narrator, knowing things which Adrian of all people would never have communicated to him—the second visit to Esmeralda, her warning, his infection, the mysterious removal of the two syphilis specialists,

[65] In the *Entstehung* Mann cannot recall when he first thought of his fictional narrator and suggests only that he may have been influenced by the parody of autobiographical style in *Krull*, completing which was the rival project of this period (xi. 164). But among his reading in the earliest stages of planning, mentioned in a diary entry but not emphasized (xi. 156), was the classic of split personality, R. L. Stevenson's *Doctor Jekyll and Mr. Hyde*. On the ultimate identity of Zeitblom and Leverkühn, see xi. 204.

[66] e.g. vi. 638 on German guilt for atrocities, which is identical in substance and frequently in phrasing with Mann's 'Die Lager' of 1945 (xii. 952).

[67] Not only his main subject. The account of Clarissa Rodde's death and of Adrian's last conversation with Rudi Schwerdtfeger are very direct treatments of emotional crises in Mann's early life, the death of his sister Carla (cf. xi. 120 f.) and the break with Paul Ehrenberg; and in the pathos of Leverkühn's isolation we are sometimes back to the latent emotionalism of *Tonio Kröger*.

the use of Esmeralda's name as a musical motif—and meeting possible objections with diversionary tactics or plain rebuff.[68] In technique as in ethics he thus restores what was otherwise unattainable to an artist of Mann's sophistication: simplicity and direct expression. The subject needed these: does not Zeitblom himself say that some things are too serious for art? —'wenn es ernst wird, verschmäht man die Kunst und ist ihrer nicht fähig' (p. 235).

But Zeitblom is not Thomas Mann. He expresses part of him, but he is his literary means, not his limitation. Mann's own narrative is far more complex than Zeitblom's and is better described by another aphorism from the text, Kretzschmar's 'Zuletzt wirft immer die Kunst den Schein der Kunst ab' (p. 75): in late works, it is not art but the appearance of art that is thrown off. The subtleties of Mann the artist underlie the simplicities of Zeitblom–Mann the humanist. The creation of Zeitblom and the novel's simple surface is itself a skilful and intricate piece of art. Then beneath the plain man's biographical account there is the calculated layout with the pact scene at the numerical centre in chapter 24;[69] or such details as the way those gathered in the Manardi house in Palestrina spell out with their initials the words 'he-ra esmeralda',[70] which fulfils for *Doktor Faustus* what is said of Leverkühn's 'Doktor Fausti Weheklag', that the motif *h–e–a–e–es* recurs when the pact is referred to; or the allusions to Dürer which are packed in and interwoven with Mann's number games.[71] Then there are the clues which Mann slips into the information Zeitblom

[68] Some of these things are alluded to (though still not described fully) in the interview with the Devil; but Zeitblom has some of this information during the course of the story, long before he comes into possession of Adrian's record of the interview. Adrian does point out the *h–e–a–e–es* motif to him, but with no word of its origin. For diversionary tactics see p. 199, which begins as if to explain Zeitblom's exact knowledge but wanders away from the point and never answers the question; for plain rebuff, see p. 576, where Zeitblom simply insists on his right to the convention of omniscience he needs.

[69] One can count the tripartite chapter 24 as three and add the unnumbered epilogue; or discount the epilogue because it is unnumbered. The first yields fifty chapters with the pact scene inevitably off centre; the second—as suggested by Seidlin, 'The Lofty Game of Numbers'—yields forty-nine, a multiple (indeed, the square) of Mann's favourite 'mystical' number seven, and brings the pact to dead centre.

[70] Cf. V. A. Oswald, '"Full Fathom Five"; Notes on Some Devices in Thomas Mann's *Doktor Faustus*', GR 24 (1949), 275. Oswald points out too that Manardi was the name of a pioneer syphilologist.

[71] Cf. J. Elema, 'Thomas Mann, Dürer und *Doktor Faustus*', Euph. 59 (1965).

gives us about Esmeralda and Madame de Tolna which establish an identity Zeitblom never dreams of.[72] And on a larger
scale there are the fundamental correspondences—Leverkühn–
Nietzsche, Leverkühn–Mann—which Zeitblom inevitably
serves unawares. Everywhere a simple surface and a rebirth of
old-fashioned conventions, resting on an intricacy not equalled
even by Mann's other works.[73] In *Doktor Faustus* as in Leverkühn's music, there are no free notes, every detail is determined
by a thematic order. But Leverkühn's order accommodated
archaic inspiration and Dionysiac release; Mann's was the
product of a technique he had evolved over decades as an
alternative to such insidious regeneration. It serves the moral
concern of an Apolline artist.

## IV

The expression of that concern came in for bitter criticism.
Early German reviewers saw in *Doktor Faustus* a work of hatred
and a besmirching of German culture. Non-German critics
have sometimes seen the reverse—an incorrigible love of
German culture and a tragic apologia for its consequences.
The contradiction itself suggests that in both cases something
unduly simple has been abstracted from something complex.
To anyone with eyes it is evident that *Doktor Faustus* expresses
ambivalent feelings corresponding to Mann's argument in
*Deutschland und die Deutschen* that there were not two Germanys,
a good and a bad, but a single Germany in which good ele-

---

[72] Cf. V. A. Oswald, 'The Enigma of Frau von Tolna', *GR* 23 (1948). Oswald's
fine detective work is confirmed if one reads Mann's comment on the episode in the
*Entstehung*—'ein Beispiel tiefster Diskretion' (xi. 272)—as a *double entendre*, referring
to Madame de Tolna's behaviour and his own art. Oswald missed only the clue to
how Esmeralda escaped from prostitution, the adjective *ritterlich* in the description
of Madame de Tolna's husband (vi. 519).

[73] Oswald, in 'Thomas Mann and the Mermaid; A Note on Constructivist
Music', *MLN* 65 (1950), 172, speaks of an 'elaborate and impenetrable' constructivism and is unsure 'whether it was Thomas Mann's love of the intricacy of his
designs or a despair of being understood' that prompted some of the revelations in
*Entstehung*. It should be remembered that the musical discussions in the novel exclude
the possibility that the twelve-tone order could actually be heard as such. By
analogy, the intricacies of *Doktor Faustus* cannot be part of the reader's immediate
experience. But the artist in Mann was proud of his patterns, and the critic in the
artist had always been quick to point out what others did not notice. *Die Entstehung des Doktor Faustus* allowed him to have his cake and eat it.

ments had been turned into bad. Given such a belief, ambivalent feelings were inevitable. Criticism owes impatient readers no further answer.

But the other ambivalence, the technique Mann had used since *Der Tod in Venedig*, does need further discussion. It matters very much how we read the parallel layers of meaning and which we take to be the real explanation, which merely the means to convey it. It mattered less with earlier works: the question whether Aschenbach's death was brought about by disease, psychological breakdown, or a transcendental agency hardly went beyond literary criticism. But the question whether Germany was 'really' a tragic Faust, or the willing victim of a vile disease, or something different again is a choice between historical judgements. Can we ascertain what Mann was saying? Was ambivalence a defensible way to say it? Is what he says true? Is his whole conception adequate to the subject? These fundamental questions must be asked of a work which was the culmination of his technique and the synthesis of his life's experience.

Two criticisms mentioned at the outset help to locate the problem. Both are aimed at Mann's use of Faust. To one Christian critic it seemed a misappropriation because it is backed by no belief in God. The legend makes no sense in a world without transcendence.[74] For a Marxist the same holds true, with different emphasis: the modern writer should not use a myth like Faust, not just because of its specifically religious background but because more generally it implies individual freedom and moral choice, a personal fate, a meaningful tragedy. These are illusory. What happens to modern man must be understood rather by sociological analysis in which statistical trends are more important than the micro-effects of individual decisions. Fascism above all was an impersonal mechanism, the amplification of a banal evil which should not be explained, much less ennobled, by reference to a mythical devil. It wrought wholesale senseless destruction; so personal a thing as tragedy was a luxury. To use myth in describing it is to bestow meaning on what was meaningless, make static what was dynamic, and relate what the writer does not understand, falsely, to a traditional Higher Order. Myth, in short, is

[74] Hans Egon Holthusen, *Die Welt ohne Transzendenz*, Hamburg, 1949.

regressive, evasive, and obscurantist.[75] Where the Christian denies Mann's right to something which has a higher value, the Marxist deplores his resort to what has none.

Both are wrong, for a similar reason: they will not accept that myth can be a vehicle to carry meaning and need not be a literal assertion of its own truth. Holthusen will not have it reduced to mere use by a writer who does not share his belief in its religious elements. Lem will not have it used lest it be taken literally. Both are in different ways reducing the available means of communication. Holthusen is ultimately doing no more than declare the gap between himself and an unbeliever. He need concern us no more since the gap is unbridgeable (although to anyone not set on destructive criticism, *Doktor Faustus* is evidently a work of religious feeling).[76]

On the other hand, the Marxist sociologist might have paused to observe how the myth is used, especially how its literal force is relativized by other layers of meaning. Lem's argument is conceptually very impressive but he pays too little attention to what actually goes on in the novel. He speaks of Faust as, in the most general terms, a myth of the choice between good and evil. Mann does not use it in any such clear-cut way. Far from portraying such a choice in a space artificially cleared for individual tragedy, he in fact approaches the sociological account Lem would have. When Adrian infects himself, it is from a subconscious desire for inspiration and release. This is a paradigm of the way German society yielded to a current of the times, irrationalism, not as a clear-cut choice but as a trend. The trend is further illustrated by the social groups we are shown, especially the Kridwiss circle. They also answer Lem's further criticism, that Mann's work has in it no place for anything so banal as stupidity, which is what the analyst of fascism should start from.[77] Yet stupidity is just what the circle does represent—the historically specific and socially influential stupidity of cultured Germans between the wars.

On examination then, Mann is doing what he has been

---

[75] Stanislaw Lem, 'Über das Modellieren der Wirklichkeit im Werk von Thomas Mann', in *Sinn und Form*, Sonderheft Thomas Mann, 1965.

[76] Holthusen's negative and often unfair essay can now only be read, charitably, as a product of a time of inevitable resentments. Karl Kerényi by contrast called *Doktor Faustus* a 'Christian novel' (Br. K. 26). The term is imprecise, but the substance of the insight is sound.          [77] Lem, op. cit., p. 175.

criticized for failing to do. We can take this further. Lem argues that a Devil myth cannot be applied to society; that we can speak, at a pinch, of the 'Devil in man', by which we mean the dark forces of the psyche; but that we cannot speak of the 'Devil of society' or the 'Devil of the Germans'. If we insisted on doing so, it would have to be a quite new type of devil, since the traditional one is something quite different.[78] Yet all this is precisely what Mann achieves by the way he adapts the Faust legend. He does portray the Devil of society, and specifically of German society; he does underlay the traditional Devil with a different conception. Not, it is true, a 'new' one, but one much older than the Faust legend itself.

The Devil Adrian talks with is admittedly traditional enough. That is part of his private imitation of the chap-book Faust and is only the first layer beneath the story's Naturalistic surface. It does not mean that German society's metaphorical 'pact with the Devil' has the same character. Even in Adrian's private world, the Devil is nearly superfluous. He is put together—by Adrian, and, following him, by Zeitblom—from a sense of personal fate, from omens and chances and correspondences, from resemblances of individuals and recollections of doctrine. (Fate in *Doktor Faustus* and the technique used to suggest it recall *Der Tod in Venedig*, often down to minute detail.)[79] The interview with the Devil in Palestrina is only a confirmation, the real 'pact' is Adrian's self-infection. Aptly, one of the Devil's names is Sammael, 'angel of poison' (p. 304). Mann's is thus, significantly, the only Faust story which leaves no distinct function to the Devil. His involuted arguments at the interview, like the ones Ivan Karamazov's devil uses, struggle to prove himself not just a figment of the fevered imagination. The adequate and undeniable explanation of Adrian's fate remains, despite the 'systematic ambiguity'[80] of a conception which must keep the Devil fictionally in play, his disease.

[78] Ibid., p. 174.

[79] e.g. Schleppfuss, who disappears from the university scene with the same suggestive unobtrusiveness as the stranger in the monumental mason's yard like him in the Leipzig guide and in the Devil in Palestrina. The figures of the two works even share the distinctive reddish hair. The Devil's language and ideas are drawn from Adrian's theological days and the aesthetics of Kretzschmar.

[80] 'Die Zweideutigkeit als System' is one of Adrian's definitions of music (p. 66). It is also the most accurate and succinct of Mann's implied commentaries on his own work.

The hold of the literal myth is thereby weakened. Even more so when we consider the novel's larger meaning. This is not specifically Faustian. It lies less in the traditional associations of the legend than in the new ones which disease—already the real basis in Mann's earliest two-layer conception—had acquired by the forties. Dionysiac intoxication in the individual symbolized Dionysiac release and violence in society. This is the bedrock of *Doktor Faustus*: not the Faust myth, but the theory of the Dionysiac. This is the level which invites serious belief. The Faust story is a myth *ad usum populi*, an exoteric surface. From first to last, the dark powers are spoken of in a way which allows the Dionysiac meaning to show through. The most frequently used term is 'demonic' (*das Dämonische*) which mixes Christian and Greek connotations. Zeitblom knows of its essential role in life and especially in art, though he has always held it at arm's length, which is why he doubts whether he is the right man to tell the story (pp. 9 ff.). Before he relates the second visit to Esmeralda, he is moved to invoke Apollo and the Muses, only to realize how much they are at odds with the specific tone (*Eigenfärbung*) of his story (p. 204). The allusion only stops short of using the word Dionysiac.[81] Descriptions of the Dionysiac condition are never far away, couched either in the language of cult celebration or in the standard metaphor of drunkenness. The Devil promises Adrian 'sacred ecstasy' (p. 316). His inspiration will be an inebriation (*Beschwipsung*, p. 305); the music he produces will be against reason and sobriety (p. 331); his confession speaks of a 'hellish drunkenness' (p. 662). At this late point, the two myths are impressively joined in a single quotation: 'Denn es heisst: Seid nüchtern und wachet!' The apostle's warning against the Devil who walketh about seeking whom he may devour[82] fits perfectly into a Faust story; but its wording—be sober, be vigilant—also reads as a warning against the power of Dionysus. The two myths are joined again in the novel's closing paragraph, when Zeitblom contrasts an earlier triumphant Germany with a Germany now fallen into the hands of demons. The demons are those of a Faustian hell, come to claim their due. The triumph

---

[81] The word itself only occurs once, in a minor context. The Munich of pre-1914 is characterized by its *ästhetische Lebensunschuld* and *dionysische Behaglichkeit* (p. 378).                        [82] 1 Peter 5: 8.

Reckoning 397

was that of a Dionysiac celebrant, reeling drunkenly with flushed cheeks.

It can be objected that a mixture of myths is confusing or that another surface story might have carried this Dionysiac meaning more plainly. Conceivably so. The fact is that means and meaning were already linked for Mann in an old conception which history brought alive. No idea of separating them arose —the artistic imagination, even in so intellectual a writer as Thomas Mann, is not that calculating. It can be objected thas Mann risked ennobling what was base and flattering Germans with the idea of their own tragic destiny by feeding them their most characteristic myth in his overt narrative. The risk occurred to him at the time.[83] Yet the novel simply will not allow this reading. If Adrian's is a tragic fate, the events in the world outside Zeitblom's study are never given the least colouring of tragedy. There is acid comment on the Germans' habit of reading a tragic national destiny into the catastrophes in which they involve their European neighbours.[84] What is tragic in the individual—this much the technique of paradigm and parallel allows—can still be seen as base in its social, political form. But for individual and society together, the Faust myth has the function Mann needs: to produce an atmosphere of foreboding and a sense of grim retribution. One need only ask what other traditional story could have competed, what German myth had the same suggestion of hubris. The question answers itself.

It may still seem that we have merely exchanged one myth for another, which would fail to meet the radical objection that all myths evade or distort the plain truth. But the Dionysiac is not a myth like Faust. It is a way of describing forces observable in man and society which were strikingly present in the cult of Dionysus and which are not yet explained in other terms. It is not a red herring just because it is taken from mythology. Nietzsche, who gave the term currency, was no more concerned than Freud was to hide objective truth under mythic superstructures. He used 'Dionysiac' as a convenient label for

[83] Cf. *Entstehung*: '[Bruno Franks] emotionelle Anteilnahme am "Faustus" . . . wollte als Warnung erfasst sein — vor der Gefahr, mit meinem Roman einen neuen deutschen Mythos kreieren zu helfen, den Deutschen mit ihrer "Dämonie" zu schmeicheln' (xi. 181).

[84] See vi. 232 and 401. Both passages place responsibility with Germanic myths in the form Wagner made popular.

psychological constants in man, as the opening paragraph of *Die Geburt der Tragödie* makes clear.[85] And throughout that book it is equally clear that the Dionysiac in art is the end of a thread which leads back to something more fundamental still in man: the urge to break the bonds of individuation, to experience oneness with a god, with other men, with nature, to give up rational for instinctual life. But Nietzsche's concern was with culture only, with the origins, decline, and possible rebirth of tragedy. He was not interested in social consequences, though he knew of medieval parallels to the Greek orgies.[86] He read Euripides' *Bacchae* as a monument to a cultural force whose loss he deplored, not as a depiction of what can happen in any society. He was a theoretic man, invoking Dionysus for the large but limited purpose of revivifying, hand in hand with Richard Wagner, the culture of nineteenth-century Germany.

Later scholars, alerted by later events, have seen the Dionysiac more broadly as a social force and the original rituals as a purgation of irrational impulses which can endanger society. They argue that the ritual is older than the myth which explains it and rooted in an understanding of individual and mass psychology. The *Bacchae* is read as an analysis of mass emotion and fanaticism in revolt against the restraints of civilization. Dionysiac phenomena are discovered not just in the medieval cases Nietzsche knew of, but in the eighteenth, nineteenth, and twentieth centuries. In each case they appear linked with disturbed social conditions, just as in Greece they were linked with the breakdown of an old social structure and the emergence of an unfamiliar need for individual responsibility.[87]

---

[85] 'Diese Namen entlehnen wir von den Griechen, welche die tiefsinnigen Geheimlehren ihrer Kunstanschaung zwar nicht in Begriffen, aber in den eindringlich deutlichen Gestalten ihrer Götterwelt dem Einsichtigen vernehmbar machen. An ihre beiden Kunstgottheiten, Apollo und Dionysus, knüpft sich unsere Erkenntnis . . .'

[86] 'Auch im deutschen Mittelalter wälzten sich unter der gleichen dionysischen Gewalt immer wachsende Scharen, singend und tanzend, von Ort zu Ort: in diesen Sankt-Johann- und Sankt Veittänzern erkennen wir die bacchischen Chöre der Griechen wieder . . .' Op. cit., § 1.

[87] This paragraph is based on: E. R. Dodds, *The Greeks and the Irrational*, Berkeley, 1951; Euripides' *Bacchae*, ed. E. R. Dodds, 2nd edition, Oxford, 1960; R. P. Winnington-Ingram, *Euripides and Dionysus*, Cambridge, 1948; and Euripides, *The Bacchae and other plays*, translated and introduced by Philip Vellacott, Harmondsworth, 1961.

When scholars make suggestions like these about the reality and social effects of the force they call 'Dionysiac', it is hardly overimaginative in a novelist to read Nazism as such a phenomenon. He is certainly not sacrificing truth to myth. At worst he is giving symbolic status to a single truth about man and society, making it the root explanation of an immensely complex process. To condemn this is to reject not the deception of myth, but the intuitions of art—intuitions which agree strikingly with accounts of Nazism by political philosophers and sociologists.[88] Mann's explanation, like theirs, is not exhaustive in the way historical research may eventually be exhaustive; it is a perspective within which hard historical evidence may become coherent.

In *Doktor Faustus* then, myth is not in conflict with psychology but transformed into it. The novel rests on the idea that political and social phenomena, in Germany at least, are psychological in origin: 'Das Seelische [ist] immer das Primäre und eigentlich Motivierende; die politische Aktion ist zweiter Ordnung, Reflex, Ausdruck, Instrument' (p. 408). And that origin is shown to be Dionysiac. This begins in the unobtrusively skilful chapter 6, where Zeitblom evokes Adrian's home town, Kaisersaschern, with its medieval atmosphere and latent medieval mentality, such that an outbreak of group hysteria—'eine Kinderkreuzzug-Bewegung, ein Sankt-Veits-Tanz, das visionär-kommunistische Predigen irgendeines "Hänselein"'—would have come as no surprise (p. 52). From this conceit to the essentially medieval group-acts which actually have since happened, book-burnings and worse ones that Zeitblom will not name, is an easy step. The people retain an 'archaic' layer in them, superstitious and irrational beneath their modern surface. This is what is stimulated whenever the

[88] Cf. the chapter 'The Technique of the Modern Political Myths' in Ernst Cassirer's *The Myth of the State* (Yale University Press, 1946), with its stress on the role of the collective, the reversion to primitivism, and the abandonment of reason, all deriving from a 'much older stratum' than the social forms they overthrow; and Roger Caillois, *Instincts et société*, Paris, 1964, esp. the chapters 'L'Esprit des sectes' and 'Le Pouvoir charismatique'. That other artists had similar intuitions to Mann's is shown by D. H. Lawrence's remarkable *Letter from Germany* of 1924, with its sense of the primitive stirring and of time 'whirling to the ghost of the old Middle Ages of Germany, then to the Roman days, then to the days of the silent forest and the dangerous, lurking barbarians'. *A Selection from Phoenix*, Harmondsworth, 1971, p. 120.

crowd is appealed to by the name *Volk* and such appeals are
always for purposes of atavistic evil (*das Rückständig-Böse*, p. 53).
As 'the people' they would look on inactive at witch-burning,
a thing which (so Zeitblom reflects with the relative *naïveté*
of his 1943 standpoint and the bitter irony of Mann's factual
knowledge)[89] is once again quite conceivable, though it would
be justified by different official reasons. And yet, to speak of
the *Volk* reminds him that there is that primitive layer, *die
altertümlich-volkstümliche Schicht*, in all of us. It is the potential
for even worse conflagrations.

It was the potential from which Nazism produced the
'national rebirth' which was also a Dionysiac outbreak, 'den
Aufstand, den Aufbruch, Ausbruch und Umbruch . . . die
völkische Wiedergeburt von vor zehn Jahren, diesen scheinbar
heiligen Taumel'—an 'apparently sacred transport', falsified
from the first by its baseness and its evident delight in sadism
(p. 233). The same impulses, only on another social level, underlie German beliefs from which Nazism also drew strength, the
old assumptions about Germany's youthful vitality and re-
generative role which Adrian's fellow students professed:
'Jung sein heisst . . . den Quellen des Lebens nahe geblieben
sein, heisst aufstehen und die Fesseln einer überlebten Zivilisation abschütteln können' (p. 159); they underlie the acceptance of a necessary rebarbarization of culture in the Kridwiss
circle. Then, at the highest level, politically uninvolved yet
a paradigm of those same impulses and temptations,
Adrian Leverkühn, striving to escape from the strain of creative
freedom back into a tyrannical order, from the modern into
the archaic, from isolation into cultural community. 'To the
*thiasos* [service] of Dionysus everything is surrendered, including the intellect and the individuality; while it enables the
individual to transcend his limitations, it is indifferent to the
direction of that transcendence; it allows the lowest to set its
easy and uncritical standard.'[90]

Late in the novel, Zeitblom returns to his idea of the primitive layer in all men. Although its 'dark possibilities' are part
of universal human nature, it was in fact Germans, he says,

[89] Although full knowledge of the extermination camps came only later, Mann
reported atrocities against Jews in his broadcasts to Germany as early as January
1942. See *Deutsche Hörer!* xi. 1015 on the experimental gassing of Dutch Jews.
[90] Winnington-Ingram, op. cit., pp. 176 f.

who did such things as these which are the horror of mankind. How can such a people show its face again? (p. 638). From such sentiments and from Mann's use of the Faust legend some have inferred that *Doktor Faustus* is a myth of Germanness, carrying the message that national character is a fated and fateful thing.[91] Mann's text says something less simple. Each of Zeitblom's late solemn judgements refers emphatically to Germany's *history*: 'wie wird es sein, einem Volke anzugehören, dessen Geschichte dieses grässliche Misslingen in sich trug?' (p. 638); and again, 'uns Deutschen, deren tausendjährige Geschichte widerlegt und ad absurdum geführt, als unselig verfehlt, als Irrweg erwiesen durch dieses Ergebnis' (p. 599). German history, not a unique German capacity for evil, is what produced this terrible result.

Yet to blame history in the abstract would be no more precise than blaming the national character with which, in ways too complex to analyse fully, it must interact. Nor does Mann leave it at that. From the course of German history which Zeitblom rejects, he picks out culture. He sees in the Nazi regime itself the same traits which can be observed in great Germans, albeit now in a vulgarized, distorted, ghastly form— 'verzerrt, verpöbelt, verscheusslicht' (p. 639). Responsibility for atrocities rests on all things German and therefore on culture too—'alles Deutschtum, auch der deutsche Geist, der deutsche Gedanke, das deutsche Wort' (p. 638). Is this hypochondria? asks Zeitblom. Reviewing all Mann had written from the 1920s on, and even further back in the pre-political analyses of 'Geist und Kunst', one must answer: no. Of course, the rejection of German history and culture is too sweeping—it is born of an apocalyptic mood and it ignores the immense range of German literature, music, and thought which bears no relation to the *Irrweg* of later German politics. Yet enough of it did bear such a relation—at this stage the list need not be recapitulated—for the charge to have some truth.[92] There were

---

[91] e.g. Sörensen, op. cit., p. 95: 'ein mythisches Deutschtum, wie Th. Mann das nun einmal auffasste'; p. 96: 'nachromantische Auffassung des Volkes als eines corpus mysticum'; p. 97: 'mythisches Werk vom Deutschtum'.

[92] Holthusen, op. cit., p. 15, objected to Mann's selection within German culture: he had left out the Classical, the rational and humane, Mozart, Goethe, Kant, Schiller, Lessing, Hölderlin, Mörike, etc., etc. Such incomprehension is hardly credible. The analyst of disease does not concentrate on the healthy tissue.

indeed cultural traditions in Germany, as rarely in any other country, which had in them seeds of peril for society. It was justifiable to arraign them in a time when the 'Lindenbaum' had thrown its most poisonous blossom.[93]

Zeitblom and his author are here at one. The responsibility of culture and the debasement of culture; genuine impulses, false fulfilment; in place of true community, a travesty of community; diseased intoxication producing an 'apparently sacred transport'. It is an impressive diagnosis. It does not dress horror and catastrophe in the comfortably distant terms of culture, it tries to grasp the connection between psychological impulse in the individual and the collective, cultural aspirations and intellectual traditions, and disastrous political events. The problem is too immense for one man, one work to encompass. In the attempt, Mann understandably pressed his technique to extremes, creating a density of cross-reference among themes and motifs, an interpenetration of private and public experience, a multiplicity of modes—literal, allegorical, symbolic—which is in the end excessive. These flaws could be spelt out. Yet in fairness one would then have to spell out the successes, the adroit correspondences and subtleties of detail. Both procedures would be lengthy; this chapter has done little more than raise the novel's main themes to the surface. Neither procedure would decide the Common Reader's verdict, which is swayed by simpler things. To have created simpler things out of a compulsive and fearsome complexity is the triumph of the book. Its almost art-for-art's sake intricacy is masked under Zeitblom's naïve narration, its material mass is moulded and brought alive by the direct expressiveness he mediates. If *Doktor Faustus* is a failure, it is more impressive and more moving than most literary successes. What work on this subject achieves so much? Faults and all, it is the greatest of Thomas Mann's works.

[93] An old linden tree at Hof Buchel is a symbol of tradition (p. 19); when Zeitblom visits Leverkühn there in his last years, he is sitting under the linden, which is in full bloom (p. 674). It is 1935.

# Pattern and Perspective

*. . . jene Einheit — und dass es immer dasselbe ist . . .*
*Joseph in Ägypten*[1]

WHAT came after was a coda. Where *Doktor Faustus* is the grand and painful synthesis of a lifetime's themes, *Der Erwählte* is a mechanical restatement. It uses an extreme montage technique[2] no longer to master a compelling subject but to create the old illusion of substance. *Königliche Hoheit*, though distant in time, is its essential neighbour. True, Mann's last work *Felix Krull* has given much delight. But its best scenes had been written long before; Mann considered its themes superseded and surpassed by *Joseph* before he returned to it.[3] Completing it struck him as somehow unworthy, a mere pastime after his real task, *Doktor Faustus*.[4] That novel is the terminal peak from which to look back over the whole range of his work and try to make out its basic pattern and meaning.

These may not be the ones he discerned himself. For the critical reader, an author's conclusions are part of the problem, not its solution. We saw that beneath Mann's belief in myth and recurrence there lay needs and tactics which made a coherent picture; the theories he evolved are surface decoration. Nevertheless, a self-scrutiny as unremitting as Mann's was bound to glimpse patterns which were not those of his conscious literary ideas. Setting out to write of Mut-em-enet's passion for Joseph, he was struck by the way his writing returned to one idea, that of visitation (*Heimsuchung*), of drunken destructive forces breaking into a life of composure and relative happiness: 'Das Lied vom errungenen, scheinbar gesicherten Frieden

---

[1] '. . . that unity—and the fact that it is always the same thing' (v. 1085).

[2] Cf. Wysling, *Studien*, pp. 258–322.

[3] See above, p. 360, Mann's opinion in 1943. He felt the same in 1951. Cf. to Otto Basler, 8 Jan. 1951, *Blätter* 5, p. 10.

[4] Cf. to Ferdinand Lion, 28 Apr. 1952: 'Nur war ich im Grunde wohl nach dem "Faustus" fertig. Schon der "Erwählte" war ein scherzhaftes Nachspiel, und was ich jetzt treibe, ist nur noch Zeitvertreib' (Br. iii. 251 f.).

und des den treuen Kunstbau lachend hinfegenden Lebens, von Meisterschaft und Überwältigung, vom Kommen des fremden Gottes war im Anfang, wie es in der Mitte war.' (The song of an achieved, seemingly secure peace and of life sweeping away with a laugh the careful structure of art, the song of control being overpowered, of the coming of the Alien God, was in the beginning as it was in the middle [v. 1086].)

Little Herr Friedemann in 1897, Aschenbach in 1911; and now, in 1935, Potiphar's wife: all are victims of Dionysus.[5] The unity was to be confirmed a decade later. Yet the preamble to Mut-em-enet's story does more than just support a Dionysiac reading of *Doktor Faustus*. It makes us look elsewhere for other signs of that unity. Not in vain. They are there, first in the recurrent Dionysiac imagery which runs through all Mann's work; and then, underlying the imagery, in the psychological constants which made it apt.

*Der kleine Herr Friedemann* does indeed begin it. Mann was not reading back a late mythological interest into an early story. Not only is the work built on the contrast of anxious control and helpless surrender to passion which can be called Apolline and Dionysiac; at the close, the humiliated Friedemann feels a 'thirst to tear himself in pieces' (viii. 105), which is hardly apt to the realistic context—he commits suicide by drowning—but matches the inner theme. For it transposes into psychological impulse the fate which, in the Dionysus legend, befell those who resisted the god's power. Little Herr Friedemann fills the role of Pentheus, like Aschenbach after him.[6]

At this stage, Mann is exploring the psychology of repression and sublimation, using Nietzsche's aesthetic-psychological terms as tools.[7] He is not yet declaring a position—the Apolline is at least as questionable in its precariousness as the Dionysiac is in its violence. But in other contexts he did declare himself. A review in 1895 of a now-forgotten poet starts and ends

[5] The term 'Alien God' is plain enough. For confirmation, see Mann's letter of 29 Sept. 1935 to Kerényi: '. . . gerade bin ich im Begriff, die Passion der Frau des Potiphar aufs Dionysische, Mänadenhafte zu stilisieren' (Br. K. 66).

[6] The Aschenbach–Pentheus equation has been suggested by Dierks, op. cit., pp. 21 ff.

[7] The Grossoktavausgabe, vol. 1, with *Geburt der Tragödie*, did not come out till 1899. But Mann had apparently acquired a separate edition of it in 1893. Notebook 1 of that year has a list of planned purchases which includes it. See Sandberg, op. cit., p. 23.

with polemic against the new fashion for 'Dionysiac art'. This for Mann is a contradiction: no one is an artist who, instead of standing victorious over his mastered feelings, merely gives vent to them in helplessly inarticulate sounds. The task of art is to put the seemingly unsayable into severe form; bacchantic howling only proves incompetence.[8] This is already close to the aesthetic which Tonio Kröger expounds to Lisaweta. And in 1902, the year Mann wrote *Tonio Kröger*, the key term recurs. Reviewers of *Buddenbrooks* had compared him favourably with D'Annunzio. He writes with satisfaction: 'That people of my sort are to be taken more seriously than this false Dionysus is what I want to hear.'[9] This is the first hint that the Dionysiac, besides being dangerous, may also be false.

Thus far, the Dionysiac as a metaphor for passion and as an issue of literary method are separate. It was unlikely they would remain so since Mann's writing concentrated increasingly on his own artistic problems; the aesthetic discussion and the psychological theory which shared the same terms were almost bound to effect a junction. In *Der Tod in Venedig* they do. It is artistic discipline that has so long repressed Aschenbach's feelings. He has lived in an Apolline manner for the sake of art. Ironically, it is his recently intensified Apolline taste for beauty of external form that leads to his downfall. Tadzio's Apolline appearance casts an insidious spell, leading with remorseless logic to Dionysiac self-surrender. The boy is the 'instrument of a mocking god' (viii. 515)—Dionysus. And since Aschenbach's new taste goes with a refusal to probe beneath surfaces, especially of his own motives, he has no chance of escape.

Behind this tragedy of one artist, it will be remembered, there lies not just Mann's Venice experience and his own flirtation with anti-intellectualism, but his fears—expressed earlier in *Fiorenza* and 'Geist und Kunst'—for a society which will not look into its own depths, which scorns and dismisses psychology, analysis, and understanding. It is a paradox that Mann's first analysis of a society which was destined for

---

[8] 'Ostmarkklänge, Gedichte von Theodor Hutter', in *Das Zwanzigste Jahrhundert* 6, H. 3, December 1895, p. 282.

[9] To Georg Martin Richter, 15 Jan. 1902. From an extract in translation in Sotheby's sale catalogue of 22 Oct. 1968, p. 18.

Dionysiac destruction should show it turning resolutely Apolline. A paradox, not a contradiction. For precisely this is the meaning of the Venice fable: that the too exclusively Apolline is an easy prey to Dionysiac *Heimsuchung*. Denying the forces which lie beneath the surface is more insidiously dangerous than simple self-abandonment. That is why, for his own art, he set up the principle of maintaining contact with the depths, not through self-surrender but through the instrument of the conscious mind: 'tief erkennen und schön gestalten' is the aspiration of artists from the school of Nietzsche; so he says in *Bilse und ich* (x. 19), restating the Apollo–Dionysus theory without its mythological figureheads.

The image of *Heimsuchung* is common to *Der Tod in Venedig* and the war writings.[10] The war itself was a *Heimsuchung*. For Mann as for the never repentant Aschenbach, the visitation, however terrible, brought inspiration, release from his personal limits, a kind of rebirth. Dionysus was after all the god of regeneration, something German culture and Mann himself had been seeking. In 1914 he joined the seemingly regenerated national community, enthusiastically merging his critical individuality into a unanimous collective. His first move into politics confirms the pattern we are pursuing—not this time as a theme he consciously treats, but as a motif he enacts. The whole episode was, in Heinrich Mann's words, an orgy, an outbreak of ancient anti-reason.

Intoxication passed and critical balance was restored. It rested now on a discrimination between feeling and responsible action. This is first sketched, significantly, in the interpretation Mann gave of *Der Tod in Venedig* in 1920, some time before his political change of heart. He explains the critical impression his story leaves by the distinction between the Dionysiac spirit of irresponsible and individualistic lyrical outpouring and the eventually victorious Apolline spirit of responsible epic writing, with its obligations to society and morals ('Unterschied zwischen dem dionysischen Geist unverantwortlich-individualistisch sich ausströmender Lyrik und dem apollinischen objektiv

---

[10] Venice is the *heimgesuchte Stadt* (viii. 515), Aschenbach immediately after his Dionysiac dream *der Heimgesuchte* (viii. 517). War is called a *Heimsuchung* in *Gedanken im Kriege*, loc. cit., p. 1475, and in Mann's letter to Paul Amann of 25 Feb. 1916 (Br. A. 38).

gebundener, sittlich-gesellschaftlich verantwortlicher Epik').[11] From this, it is no great step to the acceptance of a general social responsibility by the writer. By the time Mann wrote these words, he had already returned to work on *Der Zauberberg*, which poses the problem of social responsibility ever more insistently, through a hero who like Aschenbach has known and welcomed intoxication of body and spirit.[12] And from the fable of Hans Castorp, apparently vague in the conventional German 'artistic' manner but in fact referring precisely to Weimar realities, it was no distance at all to a direct political appeal for sobriety—'die grosse Ernüchterung'[13]—or to the later praise of Freud as a sobering agent for a Germany sick in mind (xii. 850).

Throughout this sequence runs Mann's suspicion, fear even, of the Dionysiac. Whatever benefits were claimed for it as a source of new life, its perils seemed greater. Nazism and the ravings of its supporters were enough to 'destroy all reverence for the sources of life'—'ein Treiben, das einem die Ehrfurcht vor den Quellen des Lebens verleiden könnte' (xii. 850). Of course it could be argued that Nazism was not a 'true' but a 'false' dionysiac phenomenon. Mann's friend Kerényi saw it so,[14] and the falseness of everything the Nazis claimed to be and do was one of the most persistent of Mann's themes. *Doktor Faustus* makes plain that they and all their works were pathological. Yet the novel's Dionysiac imagery itself draws no distinction between true and false. Surely this is right. If 'Dionysiac' stands for the deepest of human psychic impulses and energies, these are not themselves good or bad in their inchoate state. Only the form they take, the directions in which they are channelled by individual or society, decides whether they will be creative or destructive, transcend rationality or fall horribly short of it. The form they took in the 1930s and

[11] To Carl Maria Weber, 4 July 1920 (Br. i. 176). There is the seed of this idea in an unpublished letter of 1912 to a Herr Goldschmied, where Mann says he would not dream of reading from *Der Tod in Venedig* in public (as he did from other works) for fear of creating a false impression. Original in the Landes- und Stadtbibliothek, Dortmund.

[12] Cf. iii. 317 and 334: 'ein kolossal Beschwipster und Hochilluminierter'.

[13] At the close of the speech *Goethe als Repräsentant des bürgerlichen Zeitalters* (ix. 331).

[14] Kerényi described the madness of German youth which he observed in 1934 as a 'schlimmen, nicht dionysischen (dysdionysischen, könnte ich sagen) Wahnsinn'. To Thomas Mann, 13 Aug. 1934 (Br. K. 60).

1940s justified Mann's increasing withdrawal to an Apolline position, justified Zeitblom's doubt whether it would ever again be possible to teach the integration of that dark force with the cult of light and reason (vi. 669). Like Euripides in the *Bacchae*, Mann had come to ask himself the radical question: should the Dionysiac be allowed to exist at all?[15] He doubted it. Apollo and Dionysus were no longer elements of a possible artistic harmony, fruitful impulse from the depths clothing itself in beautiful dream, but elements of a permanent conflict, destructive instinct needing a curb. The more the one appeared brutal, the more exclusively the other came to stand for rational control.

This then was the position Mann had reached long before *Doktor Faustus*. In 1935 he wrote that he was coming to feel himself more and more Apolline (*als Apolliniker*) and to find the Dionysiac more and more unpalatable. He is speaking of Wagner, whom he finds 'as a mind and as a man' confused, helpless, driven every way by impulse and yearning, too much the *object* of life for Mann's taste.[16] 'Zu sehr Objekt des Lebens': the formula expresses the most fundamental of Mann's spiritual characteristics, the refusal to be dominated by blind alien forces, the insistence on detached appraisal, the need for conscious control—in short, the withdrawal from Life understood as instinctual existence.

We are approaching that basic pattern which the all-too-vague *Leben–Geist* antithesis tries to state and which the imagery of Dionysus and Apollo expresses so aptly. Underlying all Mann's work is a tension between withdrawal and involvement, recognizably the same in changing contexts. He presents art itself, his own art, as a withdrawal from the normal processes of life. *Tonio Kröger* already makes this generalization from its simple social episodes. *Lotte in Weimar* goes deeper with its distinction between repetitious organic life and a self-sufficient creative order which frankly accepts the need to inhibit natural processes. Adrian Leverkühn in his early days meets the seductions of music with a puritan abstention. What gives these situations their tension is the countervailing fascina-

---

[15] Cf. Nietzsche, *Geburt der Tragödie*, § 12: 'Euripides selbst hat am Abend seines Lebens die Frage . . . vorgelegt. Darf überhaupt das Dionysische bestehen?'
[16] To Karl Vossler, 4 May 1935 (Br. i. 387).

tion of the thing withdrawn from, which tempts the character to give up his detachment. Tonio Kröger yearns for normality, Goethe was drawn repeatedly to the candle-flame of erotic experience, Leverkühn is subconsciously drawn to music's dangerously sensual medium and succumbs to his desire in a symbolic sexual act.

In the artist's relation to society, the same pattern recurs. The tension now is between isolation and community, detached criticism and acceptance—of society and by society. We saw the pressures and temptations to conform to society's ideals which built up from *Tonio Kröger* on, were richly documented in 'Geist und Kunst' and culminated in the crisis of 1914. But from the 1920s on, this problem no longer exists. A decision has been taken once for all. Mann's allegiance to Weimar was of a new kind. There was no cosy animal warmth about that community. Supporting the Republic was a rational choice, an act of detached judgement, even if it was stimulated by the emotionally disturbing outrage of Rathenau's murder. Mann's attitude to politics and society did not again substantially change. He remained a political rationalist, incurring all the facile scorn which the appeal to reason in human affairs always provokes.

And what of the basic pattern within the works? Because Mann was an autobiographical writer, it is inevitable that those tensions he became aware of—Tonio Kröger's dilemma, for instance—appear in his fiction. Yet he never realized the consistent picture his fiction as a whole built up: Friedemann anxiously withdrawing from the areas of life where no fulfilment could be hoped, Tonio Kröger eternally behind glass doors looking in, Savonarola the ascetic priest, aspiring to break the wings of the bird of life, Aschenbach denying emotion in the cause of art and then denied fulfilment by the nature of his passion, Joseph the classic case of withdrawal from erotic entanglement, Goethe twisting the patterns of human fulfilment into the patterns of poetry, Leverkühn fulfilling his desire but in the service of an ill-omened art, and at what a price—all these by their success or their downfall imply the same thing, that instinct and passion are destructive and that there exists an alternative order which it is better to serve, either art or some analogue of art like the faithfulness to his god which makes Joseph leave his garment in Mut-em-enet's hands. Even the most trusting devotee of natural processes, Frau von Tümmler in *Die Betrogene*, is mocked by Nature's response; what seemed the symbolic return of her fertility is a uterine cancer. Hans Castorp knows a fulfilment of his passion, but only briefly and as a necessary part of his education; even then it is presented as an illicit excursion.

So the pattern appears overwhelmingly in sexual terms— unforcedly, since that is the language Mann uses. It is a wearisomely familiar idea that our basic patterns are sexual. Does it follow that the 'real', the deepest meaning of Mann's work is a set of Freudian truisms? It is certainly possible to take this kind of analysis further, finding the impulses of withdrawal from normal relations in the sexual particularities which recur in Mann's work, especially the obsession with incest which is plain in *Wälsungenblut* and *Der Erwählte* and more striking still when it is not, as there, part of the given material—in *Königliche Hoheit*, whose hero insists on calling his bride 'little sister', and in *Lotte in Weimar*, which goes to remarkable lengths to introduce the idea.[17] It is possible to bring out a thread of narcissism, even virtual solipsism, running through Thomas Mann's novels.

Such analysis has been done, and well.[18] Yet, however sensitively it is carried out, there is inescapably the suggestion that we are dealing with personal inadequacies, interesting and even valuable as a stimulus to literary creation, but inadequacies just the same. This is an unfortunate prejudgement. If there was a streak of narcissism in Thomas Mann, a final judgement might more properly stress the degree to which he overcame it. More important, a 'negative' impulse may come to have a function we can judge positive in situations beyond the merely

[17] Lotte reflects that August could be her son, might have been if she had married Goethe. She also half-confuses him with the Goethe of about his age whom she once knew (ii. 564 f.). August tells her that his intended fiancée, Ottilie, could well be her daughter, not just in age but because she repeats Lotte's type (ii. 611 f.). Thus for Lotte August's marriage to Ottilie would make up for the omissions of the past—'Goethe' (through his son) marrying 'her' (a girl repeating her type). Yet the marriage would also be quasi-incestuous because both could be her children. She can only hint at this and then cover up for her bizarre and socially impossible remark by pleading the strain she is under (ii. 615). Her and Thomas Mann's bizarre notion is prepared for by the allusions to Goethe's own novel of bizarre relationships, *Die Wahlverwandtschaften* (ii. 611).

[18] See Peter Szondi, 'Versuch über Thomas Mann', *Neue Rundschau* 67 (1956) and Peter Dettmering, *Dichtung und Psychoanalyse*, Munich, 1969.

personal. Withdrawal from natural process may be prima facie a psychological failing. But where the impulse has a broader bearing—say, in the context of culture, where 'natural process' means the forces that shape society and 'withdrawal' means the critical detachment of the writer—it is invaluable. In other words, psychological impulses cannot be judged except by their results in the field of action where they are realized. Withdrawal from 'Life' is no more axiomatically wrong than total involvement in 'Life' is right. Precisely such wholesale affirmation is the flaw in the vitalist philosophy of Nietzsche and later writers who took Dionysus as their patron god.[19] In the very act of establishing an overriding value, vitalism begs the question of values by failing to say what quality of life is meant beyond the baldest biological sense. Why anything so undiscriminated should be a value remains obscure, as Mann objected.[20] His own career was a steady progress away from such crude metaphysics towards sober discriminations in the light of what seemed good for human society. In a cliché, he learned from experience, the experience of history, and acted on what he learned. It is in the perspective of history that we have to see and appraise the patterns his work displays.

How does he appear in that perspective? Historical circumstances pressed him into a role he would hardly have adopted in less disturbed times. He conducted, as a sympathetic colleague wrote in 1925, one of the most brilliant rearguard actions of Enlightenment against barbaric credulities.[21] The terms are apt. The remnants of Enlightenment principles were indeed in retreat before irrationalism and the political

[19] For a survey of this subject, see J. H. W. Rosteutscher, *Die Wiederkunft des Dionysos*, Berne, 1947; and, bringing it up to date ('Dionysiac' thinking persists in Germany into the 1960s), Max L. Baeumer, 'Zur Psychologie des Dionysischen in der Literaturwissenschaft', in W. Paulsen (ed.), *Psychologie in der Literaturwissenschaft*, Heidelberg, 1971.

[20] Cf. *Nietzsche im Lichte unserer Erfahrung*: 'Das Leben über alles! Warum? Das hat er nie gesagt' (ix. 694).

[21] '... eines der glänzendsten Rückzugsgefechte der Aufklärung gegen ... die barbarisch-ursprünglichen Gläubigkeiten'. Alfons Paquet in the *Berliner Tageblatt* of 31 May 1925, repr. in Schröter, *Dokumente*, p. 124. For a rare and excellent view of Mann as an *Aufklärer*, see Eberhard Wilhelm Schulz, 'Thomas Mann und der Geist der Aufklärung', in Schulz, *Wort und Zeit*, Neumünster, 1968; and in a similar spirit, Walter Jens, 'Der Rhetor Thomas Mann', in Jens, *Von deutscher Rede*, Munich 1969.

extremism linked with it. The crisis strengthened Mann's instinct for control to the point where he revived old and philosophically vulnerable doctrines. He defended Natural Law for its 'core of regulative truth' (xii. 629); he declared that Good and Evil were not relative or obscure but absolute and present in men's consciences (xi. 896); he rejected Nietzsche's arguments against the claims of the human mind to make judgements which were not determined by instinctual need; he reasserted a simple idealism: the mind was a wholly independent agent (ix. 694 f.).

If these positions seem naïve, we must remember they were emergency measures. The restoration of old values was not an ideal answer to relativism; it was the only practical one Mann could propose against its militant alternative, the cult of irrational rebirth. Mann was not naïve. He believed his humanism was deeper than the eighteenth century's because it had assimilated all that was now known of Man. It was not sentimentally optimistic, but at most an 'Optimismus quand même'. He also knew that some of its props were hypothetical. Sometimes he admits it: it may not be true that Man is the final aim of creation, but it would be well if he behaved as though it were (x. 385). Sometimes the admission is veiled in a reference to the abyss which lay beneath the positive beliefs of writers he admired: Tolstoy found values for others, but never escaped negation himself (ix. 117); Lessing the brilliant dialectician could easily have been a nihilist and a mocker but for his goodness of heart, which Mann insists is not to be confused with optimism (x. 253). He himself remained too much the child of a relativistic age, too much a pupil of Nietzsche and later of Freud, ever to be a naïve optimist. One may indeed suspect that, if his appeal to old beliefs was dictated by the struggle against Nazism, the years of that struggle were also paradoxically comforting, 'moralisch gute Zeit' as he afterwards said (xi. 253 f.), because they allowed the relief of a return to simple principles. Confusion came into its own again, and with it disillusion, in the years of the lost peace and the Cold War. Mann could now speak ironically of the thirties as the heyday of his democratic optimism.[22] At the end of his

[22] '. . . meines demokratischen Optimismus Maienblüte'. To Ferdinand Lion, 13 Mar. 1952 (Br. iii. 248).

essay on Chekhov, written the year before he died, he is again the sceptic with no answers to mankind's questions, the artist with at best an obscure faith in the power of artistic truth and form to edge the world slowly in a favourable direction.[23] His last task, celebrating the greatest of German idealists, Schiller, could produce only wistful admiration for the unbroken enthusiasm of a lost age. At the end of his life, Mann's idea of art is predominantly that of a consoler of men, a bringer of mirth and higher serenity—*höhere Heiterkeit*.

To make this a final judgement on Mann's own art would be inadequate. If he achieved this, he also achieved much more. In a unique degree he combined a participation in the movements of German thought and culture with an ability eventually to see them clearly and critically. This makes his work, as document and as analysis, a picture of modern Germany which stands unrivalled for scope and penetration. It is rarely a direct portrayal in the conventional realistic manner— society, the very element of the novel, was avowedly not Mann's forte[24]—but this detracts little from its ultimate realism. The kind of novel Mann made for himself[25] performed a task no conventional novel could have performed. If after *Buddenbrooks* it lacks the feel of social immediacy, it makes us intimate instead with the spiritual and intellectual forces which lie beneath the social surface, giving it its shape, slowly bringing about change, occasionally erupting. Mann concentrates on what near the end of *Der Zauberberg* he calls the 'spiritual shadows of things', not as an escape from reality but because he sees in those shadows the true reality of ultimate causes. He is an idealist in the technical sense, believing that spiritual forces come first—at least in Germans and German affairs.

Critics who do not share this unfashionable view do see Mann's work as an escape from reality, into an art which modern events have rendered impermissible. In the 'epoch of the ovens', Mann's world seems too cosy, too much of a

[23] Cf. ix. 869.
[24] 'Dass das Soziale meine schwache Seite ist, — ich bin mir dessen voll bewusst . . .' To Julius Bab, 23 Apr. 1925 (Br. i. 238).
[25] 'So habe ich mir aus meinen Begabungen und profunden Unbegabungen einen eigenen Roman zurechtgemacht . . .' To Karl Kerényi, 5 Dec. 1954 (Br. K. 199).

carefully preserved bourgeois anachronism, it purifies horrors into history, it maintains 'beautiful semblance' in a world which declares such semblance a lie, it even finds comfort in recognizing and accepting the course of the inevitable.[26]

But even in the epoch of the ovens, need all art be direct portrayal? Leaving aside the risk that such portrayal may itself create an aestheticism of horror, is it so certain that value cannot reside in an art which alludes? Leaving aside, again, the very direct statement which Mann contrives in *Doktor Faustus*, is there to be no value allowed to an art which speaks through the symbolic means stored up by culture?

Perhaps it is precisely culture, Mann's use of traditional means, which sticks in the throat. For the critic harrowed by harsh realities, Thomas Mann's cultural language may seem too coherent, too readily disponible, his technique too sovereign. Altogether he has something too much like mastery. And mastery is unpalatable in a world the critic believes is unmastered.

Yet the mastery was not easy. It was an achievement, demanding all the creative effort that word implies. Mann's culture was not complacent—only the legend of the solemn polymath makes it seem that—nor was it exhaustive or static. It was purposefully acquired, personally turned, and subtly used. Over a long lifetime it also acquired, inevitably, its own coherence of theme and substance; but this personal synthesis was incidental to Mann's work as an artist, using materials like any other artist. If the result is open to objection in principle, then it is doubtful whether any culture can subsist. The order established by art seldom rests on an ideally ordered world. It nevertheless has a value in proportion as the artist has taken issue with the disorder of the real world—we have seen how conscientiously Thomas Mann did that—and contributed, by whatever means, to understanding it. For understanding is the first small step towards control.

[26] See the paragraphs headed 'Verzauberung', in the *Sinn und Form* Thomas Mann number of 1965, by the East German poet and novelist Günter Kunert.

# Bibliography

EXCEPT for the sub-section 'correspondence', which lists all substantial publications, what follows is exclusively a check-list of titles cited in the text and footnotes. It thus represents a fraction of the materials I have used and a much smaller fraction of what exists—the most recent and exhaustive bibliography, Harry Matter's *Die Literatur über Thomas Mann 1898–1969* (Berlin and Weimar, 1972) contains some 15,000 items. The subject is not as exhausted as this mass of secondary writing might suggest. Besides the more ephemeral journalism and other superficial treatments, a good deal even of the serious critical and scholarly work was done before important documents became available. Much early conjecture and controversy is superseded. Thomas Mann scholarship is still, paradoxically, in its beginnings.

## I. PRIMARY SOURCES

  (i)   Writings by Thomas Mann
  (ii)  Correspondence
  (iii) Manuscripts
  (iv)  Sources used by Thomas Mann
  (v)   Biographical and historical documents and other primary texts

## II. SECONDARY SOURCES

  (i)   Literature on Thomas Mann
  (ii)  Early reviews of Thomas Mann's works
  (iii) Historical studies
  (iv)  Other

## I. PRIMARY SOURCES

(i) Writings by Thomas Mann

*Gesammelte Werke in zwölf Bänden*, Frankfurt am Main, 1960.

'Ostmarkklänge', review in *Das Zwanzigste Jahrhundert*, Jg. 6, Heft 3, Dec. 1895.

Contribution to *Kritik der Kritik. Monatsschrift für Künstler und Kunstfreunde*, Bd. 1 (1905), Heft 2.

'Aphorismus über Schiller', *Die Zeit*, Vienna, 23 Apr. 1905.

'Geist und Kunst', notes for a projected essay *c.* 1910; printed by Wysling, *Quellenkritische Studien* (see below, Secondary sources i).

Contribution to *Geistiges und künstlerisches München in Selbstbiographien*, Munich, 1913.

'Gedanken im Kriege', *Neue Rundschau* 1914, Bd. 2.

'An die Redaktion des "Svenska Dagbladet"', 11 May 1915, reprinted in *Friedrich und die grosse Koalition*, Berlin, 1916.

'Gedanken zum Kriege', *Frankfurter Zeitung*, 1 Aug. 1915.

'Weltfrieden?' *Berliner Tageblatt*, 27 Dec. 1917, reprinted in Thomas Mann–Heinrich Mann, *Briefwechsel* (see below, section ii).

'Rede eines einfältigen jungen Mannes und fragmentarischen Romanhelden', in *Adele Gerhard als Festgabe zum fünfzigsten Geburtstag, 8. Juni 1918*.

'Goethe und Tolstoi', original version, *Deutsche Rundschau*, Mar. 1922.

'Was wir verlangen müssen', *Berliner Tageblatt*, 8 Aug. 1932, reprinted in *Sinn und Form* 22 (1970).

'On Myself', text of two lectures given at Princeton University in May 1940, *Blätter der Thomas-Mann-Gesellschaft* 6, Zürich, 1966.

(ii) Correspondence

*Briefe 1889–1936*, *Briefe 1937–1947*, and *Briefe 1948–1955 und Nachlese*, all edited by Erika Mann, Frankfurt am Main, respectively 1961, 1963, and 1965. Cited as Br. i, Br. ii, Br. iii.

Thomas Mann–Heinrich Mann, *Briefwechsel 1900–1949*, edited by Hans Wysling, Frankfurt am Main, 1968. Cited as Br. H.

*Briefe an Paul Amann 1915–1952*, edited by Herbert Wegener, Lübeck, 1959. Cited as Br. A.

*Thomas Mann an Ernst Bertram. Briefe aus den Jahren 1910–1955*, edited by Inge Jens, Pfullingen, 1960. Cited as Br. B.

Thomas Mann–Karl Kerényi, *Gespräch in Briefen*, edited by Karl Kerényi, Zürich, 1960. Cited as Br. K.

Hermann Hesse–Thomas Mann, *Briefwechsel*, edited by Anni Carlsson, Frankfurt am Main, 1968.

Thomas Mann–Robert Faesi, *Briefwechsel*, edited by Robert Faesi, Zürich, 1962.

*The Letters of Thomas Mann 1889–1955*, selected and translated by Richard and Clara Winston, 2 volumes, London, 1970. (This edition has a number of letters not contained in any of the above.)

*Thomas Mann, Briefwechsel mit seinem Verleger Bermann Fischer 1932–1955*, Frankfurt am Main, 1973.

Smaller sets of letters are periodically published in the *Blätter der Thomas-Mann-Gesellschaft*—to Emil Preetorius (1963), Otto Basler (1965), Max Rychner (1967), Hans Reisiger (1968), Bruno Walter (1969), Erich von Kahler (1970), Kuno Fiedler (1971 and 1972).

Mann's correspondence with Hugo von Hofmannsthal was printed in the *Fischer-Almanach 82* (1968).

(iii) Manuscripts

TMA Mp. xi. 13 Mat., the notes for *Buddenbrooks*.

TMA Mp. xi. 13b Mat., the notes for *Fiorenza*.

TMA Mp. ix. 168, the notes for 'Geist und Kunst'.

TMA Mp. xi. 13e, the notes for *Der Tod in Venedig*.

TMA Mp. ix. 173, notes *c*. 1930 for political speeches and the Goethe essays.

TMA Mp. ix. 180, notes for the 1932 Goethe essays.

TMA Mp. xi. 14, notes for *Lotte in Weimar*.

TMA Mp. ix. 199, 1 and 2, notes for the Nietzsche essay.

TMA MS. 33, notes for *Doktor Faustus*.

I have not been able to use Thomas Mann's early notebooks, held in the TMA, since they are no longer open to scholars. Quotations from them in my text are from work done by others before the bar was imposed. Nor have I used the manuscript of rejected and reworked passages from *Der Zauberberg*, deposited in the Beinecke Rare Book and Manuscript Library at Yale. From descriptions it appears not to affect decisively the reconstruction of the novel's genesis, and in any case it cannot be quoted because exclusive rights are claimed by a Mr. Joseph Angell, who has been intending to publish it since 1937.

(iv) Sources used by Thomas Mann

Volumes marked * are preserved, with Mann's annotations, in TMA.

*BACHOFEN, J. J., *Der Mythus von Orient und Occident. Eine Metaphysik der alten Welt*. Aus den Werken von J. J. Bachofen. Herausgegeben von Alfred Bäumler, Munich, 1926.

*BERTRAM, Ernst, *Nietzsche. Versuch einer Mythologie*, Berlin, 1918.

*BIELSCHOWSKY, Albert, *Goethe*, Munich, 1905.

BLÜHER, Hans, *Die Rolle der Erotik in der männlichen Gesellschaft*, Jena, 1917–19.

*GOETHE, *Gespräche*, herausgegeben von Woldemar Freiherr von Biedermann, Leipzig, 1889–91.

*HUCH, Ricarda, *Blütezeit der Romantik*, Leipzig, 1899.

LUBLINSKI, Samuel, *Die Bilanz der Moderne*, Berlin, 1904.

*LUKÁCS, Georg von, *Die Seele und die Formen*, Berlin, 1911.

*Marbacher Schillerbuch*. Zur hundertsten Wiederkehr von Schillers Todestag herausgegeben vom Schwäbischen Schillerverein, Stuttgart and Berlin, 1905.

*MÜLLER, Ernst, *Schiller. Intimes aus seinem Leben*, Berlin, 1905.

*NIETZSCHE, Friedrich, *Werke*, 20 volumes, Leipzig, 1894 et seq. (The Grossoktavausgabe, cited as GOA.)

*—— *Werke in Auswahl*, herausgegeben von Alfred Bäumler, volume 4, Leipzig, 1931.

*PLATO, *Das Gastmahl*, verdeutscht von Rudolf Kassner, Jena, 1903.

—— *Phaidros*, ins Deutsche übertragen von Rudolf Kassner, Jena, 1910$^2$.

PLUTARCH, *Über die Liebe* (= *Erotikos*), in *Vermischte Schriften*, translated Kaltwasser, Munich and Leipzig, 1911, volume 3.

*ROHDE, Erwin, *Psyche*, Tübingen, 1907⁴.

*SPENGLER, Oswald, *Der Untergang des Abendlandes*, Munich, 1918–22.

(v) Biographical and historical documents and other primary texts

BENN, Gottfried, *Essays, Reden, Vorträge* (*Gesammelte Werke*, volume 1) herausgegeben von Dieter Wellershoff, Wiesbaden, 1965.

BERMANN FISCHER, Gottfried, *Bedroht, Bewahrt. Der Weg eines Verlegers*, Frankfurt, 1967.

BERNHARDI, Friedrich von, *Deutschland und der nächste Krieg*, Stuttgart, 1912.

BUNGE, Hans (ed.), *Fragen Sie mehr über Brecht. Hanns Eisler im Gespräch*, Munich, 1972.

BÜRGIN, Hans and MAYER, Hans-Otto, *Thomas Mann. Eine Chronik seines Lebens*, Frankfurt, 1965.

CURTIUS, Ernst Robert, *Deutscher Geist in Gefahr*, Stuttgart, 1932.

DEHMEL, Richard, *Dichtungen, Briefe, Dokumente*, Hamburg, 1963.

EINSTEIN, Albert, 'In memoriam Walther Rathenau', *Neue Rundschau* 1922, Bd. 2.

EURIPIDES, *The Bacchae and other plays*, translated and introduced by Philip Vellacott, Harmondsworth, 1961.

FEDIN, Konstantin, *Sanatorii Arktur*, in Fedin, *Sobranie Sochinenii*, Moscow, 1960, volume 5.

FLAUBERT, Gustave, *Œuvres de jeunesse*, Paris, 1910.

FREYTAG, Gustav, *Ingo und Ingraban*, Leipzig, 1873.

HAUPTMANN, Gerhart, *Griechischer Frühling*, in Hauptmann, *Gesammelte Werke*, Berlin, 1921, volume 6.

HERZOG, Wilhelm, contributions to *Das Forum*, Munich, 1914.

—— *Menschen, denen ich begegnete*, Berne, 1959.

HESSE, Hermann, *Krieg und Frieden*, Berlin, 1949.

HOFMANNSTHAL, Hugo von, *Aufzeichnungen*, Frankfurt, 1959.

—— and STRAUSS, Richard, *Briefwechsel*, Zürich, 1955.

KERR, Alfred, *Caprichos*, Berlin, 1926.

KESSLER, Harry Graf, *Tagebücher*, Frankfurt, 1961.

KOLBENHEYER, Erwin Guido, 'Goethes Weltbürgertum und die internationale Geistigkeit', in Kolbenheyer, *Gesammelte Werke*, Munich, 1939–40, volume 8.

KOTOWSKI, Georg, et al., *Das Wilhelminische Deutschland*, Frankfurt, 1965.

LANGBEHN, Julius, *Rembrandt als Erzieher*, Neuausgabe, Leipzig, 1922.

LAWRENCE, D. H., 'Letter from Germany', in *A Selection from Phoenix*, Harmondsworth, 1971.

LICHNOWSKY, Prince Karl Max, *My Mission to London 1912–1914*, London, 1918.

LIENHARD, Fritz, *Neue Ideale*, Stuttgart, 1920⁵.

MANN, Heinrich, 'Geist und Tat', in Mann, *Politische Essays*, Frankfurt, 1968.

—— *Zola*, in *Die Weissen Blätter*, November 1915.

—— *Sieben Jahre*, Berlin, 1929.

—— *Ein Zeitalter wird besichtigt*, Stockholm n.d. [1946].

MANN, Viktor, *Wir waren fünf*, Konstanz, 1949.

MEINECKE, Friedrich, 'Kultur, Machtpolitik und Militarismus', in O. Hintze *et al.*, *Deutschland und der Weltkrieg*, Leipzig and Berlin, 1915.

—— *Nach der Revolution*, Munich, 1919.

—— *Die deutsche Katastrophe*, Zürich and Wiesbaden, 1946.

—— *Die Idee der Staatsräson*, Munich, 1963³.

—— *Politische Schriften und Reden*, Darmstadt, 1968³.

—— *Ausgewählter Briefwechsel*, Stuttgart, 1962.

*Neue Rundschau* 1914, Bd. 2. Articles by Bie, Heimann, Kerr, Ludwig, Meier-Graefe, Musil, Saenger, Scheler.

NIETZSCHE, Friedrich, *Werke in drei Bänden*, herausgegeben von Karl Schlechta, Munich, 1960².

OSTINI, Fritz von, *Böcklin*, Leipzig, 1909.

PLATO, *The Dialogues*, translated by B. Jowett, Oxford, 1967⁴.

PLIEVIER, Theodor, *Der Kaiser ging, die Generäle blieben*, Berlin, 1932.

ROLLAND, Romain, *Au-dessus de la mêlée*, Paris, 1915.

—— *Journal des années de guerre 1914–1919*, Paris, 1952.

SCHÄFER, Wilhelm, speech printed in *Festgabe zum Goethejahr 1932* of the Freies Deutsches Hochstift, Halle, 1932.

SCHRÖTER, Klaus, *Thomas Mann im Urteil seiner Zeit, Dokumente 1891–1955*, Hamburg, 1969.

SPEYER, Wilhelm, *Wie wir einst so glücklich waren*, Munich, 1909.

TOLLER, Ernst, *Eine Jugend in Deutschland*, in Toller, *Prosa, Briefe, Dramen, Gedichte*, Hamburg, 1961.

TOLSTOY, Lev Nikolayevich, *Ispoved'* [*Confession*], in Tolstoy, *Sobranie Sochinenii*, volume 16, Moscow, 1964.

TROELTSCH, Ernst, *Spektatorbriefe. Aufsätze über die deutsche Revolution und die Weltpolitik 1918–1922*, Tübingen, 1924.

—— 'Naturrecht und Humanität in der Weltpolitik', in Troeltsch, *Deutscher Geist und Westeuropa*, Tübingen, 1923.

ZWEIG, Stefan, *Die Welt von Gestern*, Frankfurt, 1962.

## II. SECONDARY SOURCES

(i) Literature on Thomas Mann

ALBERTS, Wilhelm, *Thomas Mann und sein Beruf*, Leipzig, 1913.

ALKER, Ernst, 'Über den Einfluss von Übersetzungen aus den nordischen Sprachen auf den Sprachstil der deutschen Literatur seit 1890', in *Stil- und Formprobleme in der Literatur*, Heidelberg, 1959.

420    *Bibliography*

BAUMGART, Reinhart, *Das Ironische und die Ironie in den Werken Thomas Manns*, Munich, 1966.

BERENDSOHN, Walter, 'Ein Blick in die Werkstatt', *Neue Rundschau* 56 (1945).

BERGER, Willi, 'Thomas Mann und die antike Literatur', in Pütz, q.v.

—— *Die mythologischen Motive in Thomas Manns Roman 'Joseph und seine Brüder'*, Cologne and Vienna, 1971.

BERGSTEN, Gunilla, *Thomas Manns 'Doktor Faustus'. Untersuchungen zu den Quellen und zur Struktur des Romans*, Lund, 1963.

BERTRAM, Ernst, 'Das Problem des Verfalls', repr. in Bertram, *Dichtung als Zeugnis*, Bonn, 1967.

BLUME, Bernhard, *Thomas Mann und Goethe*, Berne, 1949.

COLLEVILLE, Maurice, 'Nietzsche et le "Doktor Faustus" de Thomas Mann', *Études germaniques* 3 (1949).

DETTMERING, Peter, *Dichtung und Psychoanalyse*, Munich, 1969.

DIERKS, Manfred, *Studien zu Mythos und Psychologie bei Thomas Mann*, Berne and Munich, 1972.

EICHNER, Hans, 'Thomas Mann und die Romantik', in Wolfgang Paulsen, ed., *Das Nachleben der Romantik in der modernen deutschen Literatur*, Heidelberg, 1969.

ELEMA, J., 'Thomas Mann, Dürer und *Doktor Faustus*', *Euphorion* 59 (1956).

FIEDLER, LESLIE A., 'The Sufferings and Greatness of Self-Love', *Partisan Review* 14 (1947), 5.

GRAY, Ronald, *The German Tradition in Literature*, Cambridge, 1965.

HARTUNG, Günter, 'Bertolt Brecht und Thomas Mann. Über Alternativen in Kunst und Politik', *Weimarer Beiträge* 12 (1966).

HATFIELD, Henry, 'Drei Randglossen zum "Zauberberg"', *Euphorion* 56 (1962).

HELLER, Erich, *The Ironic German*, London, 1957.

HENNECKE, Hans, 'Der vollkommen gemeisterte Satz', in Hennecke, *Kritik*, Gütersloh, 1958.

HOLTHUSEN, Hans Egon, *Die Welt ohne Transzendenz*, Hamburg, 1949.

JENS, Walter, 'Der Rhetor Thomas Mann', in Jens, *Von deutscher Rede*, Munich, 1969.

—— and JENS, Inge, 'Betrachtungen eines Unpolitischen: Thomas Mann und Friedrich Nietzsche', in *Das Altertum und jedes neue Gute*, Festschrift Wolfgang Schadewaldt, Stuttgart and Berlin, 1970.

KARTHAUS, Ulrich, '*Der Zauberberg* — ein Zeitroman', *Deutsche Vierteljahrsschrift* 44 (1970).

KAUFMANN, Fritz, *Thomas Mann. The World as Will and Representation*, Boston, 1957.

KUDSZUS, Winfried, 'Peeperkorns Lieblingsjünger', *Wirkendes Wort* 20 (1970)

KUNERT, Günter, 'Verzauberung', in *Sinn und Form*, Sonderheft Thomas Mann, 1965.

LEHNERT, Herbert, *Thomas Mann. Fiktion, Mythos, Religion*, Stuttgart, 1965.

LEM, Stanislaw, 'Über das Modellieren der Wirklichkeit im Werk von Thomas Mann', in *Sinn und Form*, Sonderheft Thomas Mann, 1965.

LION, Ferdinand, *Thomas Mann in seiner Zeit*, Zürich, 1935.

MANN, Michael, 'Eine unbekannte "Quelle" zu Thomas Manns *Zauberberg*', *Germ.-roman. Monatsschrift* 46 (1965).

MEYER, Herman, *Das Zitat in der Erzählkunst*, Stuttgart, 1967².

NICHOLLS, R. A., *Nietzsche in the Early Work of Thomas Mann*, Berkeley, 1955.

OSWALD, V. A., 'Full Fathom Five: Notes on Some Devices in Thomas Mann's *Doktor Faustus*', *Germanic Review* 24 (1949).

—— 'The Enigma of Frau von Tolna', *Germanic Review* 23 (1948).

—— 'Thomas Mann and the Mermaid: A Note on Constructivist Music', *Modern Language Notes* 65 (1950).

PEACOCK, Ronald, 'Much is Comic in Thomas Mann', London, 1964.

PRINGSHEIM, Klaus, 'Ein Nachtrag zu "Wälsungenblut"', *Neue Zürcher Zeitung*, 17 December 1961.

PÜTZ, Peter (ed.), *Thomas Mann und die Tradition*, Frankfurt, 1971.

REICHART, Walter A., 'Thomas Mann: An American Bibliography', *Monatshefte* 37 (1945).

REED, T. J., 'Mann and Turgenev—A First Love', *German Life and Letters* 17 (1964).

—— 'Thomas Mann and Tradition. Some Clarifications', in P. F. Ganz, ed., *The Discontinuous Tradition*, Festschrift Ernest Stahl, Oxford, 1971.

—— (ed.), *Der Tod in Venedig*, Oxford, 1971.

RILKE, R. M., 'Thomas Manns "Buddenbrooks"', in Rilke, *Sämtliche Werke*, ed. Zinn, vol. 5, Frankfurt, 1965.

SANDBERG, Hans-Joachim, *Thomas Manns Schillerstudien*, Oslo, 1965.

SAUERESSIG, Heinz, *Die Entstehung des Romans 'Der Zauberberg'*, Biberach an der Riss, 1965.

—— *Die Bildwelt von Hans Castorps Frosttraum*, Biberach an der Riss, 1967.

SCHARFSCHWERDT, Jürgen, *Thomas Mann und der deutsche Bildungsroman*, Stuttgart, 1967.

SCHERRER, Paul, 'Vornehmheit, Illusion und Wirklichkeit', *Blätter der Thomas-Mann-Gesellschaft* 1, Zürich, 1958.

—— 'Bruchstücke der Buddenbrooks-Urhandschrift und Zeugnisse zu ihrer Entstehung 1897–1901', *Neue Rundschau* 69 (1958).

—— 'Aus Thomas Manns Vorarbeiten zu den "Buddenbrooks". Zur Chronologie des Romans', in Wysling, *Studien*, q.v.

SCHRÖTER, Klaus, *Thomas Mann*, Reinbek, 1964.

—— '"Eideshelfer" Thomas Manns 1914–18', in Schröter, *Literatur und Zeitgeschichte*, Mainz, 1970.

SCHULTZ, H. Stefan, 'Thomas Mann und Goethe', in Pütz, q.v.

SCHULZ, Eberhard Wilhelm, 'Thomas Mann und der Geist der Aufklärung', in Schulz, *Wort und Zeit*, Neumünster, 1968.

SEIDLIN, Oskar, 'Stiluntersuchung an einem Thomas-Mann-Satz', in Seidlin, *Von Goethe zu Thomas Mann*, Göttingen, 1963.

—— 'The Lofty Game of Numbers. The Mynheer Peeperkorn episode in Thomas Mann's *Der Zauberberg*', *PMLA* 86 (1971).

SONTHEIMER, Kurt, *Thomas Mann und die Deutschen*, Munich, 1961.

SÖRENSEN, Bengt Algot, 'Thomas Manns "Doktor Faustus". Mythos und Lebensbeichte', *Orbis Litterarum* 13 (1958).

SZONDI, Peter, 'Versuch über Thomas Mann', *Neue Rundschau*, 67 (1956).

WEIGAND, Hermann, *Thomas Mann's Novel 'Der Zauberberg'*, New York, 1933.

WEYDT, Günther, 'Thomas Mann und Storm', in Renate von Heydebrand and Klaus Günter Just (eds.), *Wissenschaft als Dialog*, Festschrift Wolfdietrich Rasch, Stuttgart, 1969.

WILKINSON, Elizabeth M., 'Aesthetic Excursus on Thomas Mann's *Akribie*', *Germanic Review* 31 (1956).

WYSLING, Hans, *Mythos und Psychologie bei Thomas Mann*, Zürich, 1969.

—— *Quellenkritische Studien zum Werk Thomas Manns*, Berne and Munich, 1967.

—— 'Thomas Manns Pläne zur Fortsetzung des "Krull"', *Fischer-Almanach* 1967.

ZIOLKOWSKI, Theodore, *Dimensions of the Modern Novel*, Princeton, 1969.

(ii) Early reviews of Thomas Mann's works[1]

Review of the volume *Der kleine Herr Friedemann*, *Bonner Zeitung*, 26 June 1898.

Report of a public reading by Mann, *Münchener Neueste Nachrichten*, 20 Nov. 1901.

Review of *Buddenbrooks*, *Münchener Neueste Nachrichten*, 24 Dec. 1901.

Review of *Buddenbrooks*, *Der Tag*, 11 Jan. 1902.

Max Lorenz, review of *Buddenbrooks*, *Preussische Jahrbücher*, 1902.

Review of the volume *Tristan*, *Leipziger Tageblatt*, 22 Apr. 1903.

Edgar Steiger, review of the volume *Tristan*, *Freistatt*, 17 (1903).

Eduard Goldbeck, 'Der Kampf mit dem Leben', *Leipziger Tageblatt*, 11 Apr. 1904.

Report of a public reading by Mann, *Lübecker General-Anzeiger*, 4 Dec. 1904.

Maurice Murat, review of *Buddenbrooks*, *Journal des débats*, 24 Mar. 1908.

Georg Martin Richter, review of *Königliche Hoheit*, *Münchener Neueste Nachrichten*, 28 Oct. 1909.

---

[1] These items are contained in the Ida Herz Sammlung, TMA, the nucleus of which was Mann's own cuttings of early reviews. The collection is invaluable for documenting the way the writer's reputation grew, the more so since Schröter, *Dokumente*, has little to show for this earliest period.

(iii) Historical studies

(Unless otherwise stated, place of publication is London.)

EYCK, Erich, *A History of the Weimar Republic*, 2 vols., Harvard University Press, 1967².

FISCHER, Fritz, *Germany's Aims in the First World War*, 1967.

FISHER, David Hackett, *Historians' Fallacies*, 1971.

GAY, Peter, *Weimar Culture*, 1969.

GEISS, Imanuel, *July 1914*, 1967.

IGGERS, Georg G., *Deutsche Geschichtswissenschaft*, Munich, 1971.

JENS, Inge, *Dichter zwischen rechts und links*, Munich, 1971.

JOLL, James, *Intellectuals in Politics*, 1960.

—— '1914. The Unspoken Assumptions', Inaugural Lecture at the London School of Economics, 1968.

KEHR, Eckart, 'Neuere deutsche Geschichtsschreibung', in Kehr, *Der Primat der Innenpolitik*, Berlin, 1965.

KOHN, Hans, *The Mind of Germany*, repr. 1965.

LÜBBE, Hermann, *Politische Philosophie in Deutschland*, Basle and Stuttgart, 1963.

MANN, Golo, *Deutsche Geschichte des 19. und 20. Jahrhunderts*, Frankfurt am Main, 1961.

MENDELSSOHN, Peter de, *Der S. Fischer Verlag*, Frankfurt am Main, 1970.

NAMIER, Lewis, *Vanished Supremacies*, 1958.

PLESSNER, Helmut, *Das Schicksal deutschen Geistes im Ausgang seiner bürgerlichen Epoche*, Zurich, 1935.

RAMM, Agatha, *Germany 1789–1919. A Political History*, 1967.

RINGER, Fritz, *The Decline of the Mandarins. The German Academic Community 1890–1933*, Harvard University Press, 1969.

RÖHL, J. C. G., *Zwei deutsche Fürsten zur Kriegsschuldfrage*, Düsseldorf, 1971.

SCHONAUER, Franz, *Deutsche Literatur im Dritten Reich*, Freiburg, 1961.

SONTHEIMER, Kurt, *Antidemokratisches Denken in der Weimarer Republik*, Munich, 1962.

STAHLBERGER, Peter, *Der Zürcher Verleger Emil Oprecht und die deutsche politische Emigration 1933–1945*, Zurich, 1970.

TUCHMAN, Barbara, *August 1914*, 1962.

TURNER, Henry Ashby, *Stresemann and the Politics of the Weimar Republic*, Princeton, 1963.


(iv) Other

ALEWYN, Richard, *Hugo von Hofmannsthal*, Göttingen, 1958.

AUERBACH, Erich, *Mimesis*, Berne, 1946.

BAEUMER, Max, 'Zur Psychologie des Dionysischen in der Literaturwissenschaft', in Wolfgang Paulsen (ed.), *Psychologie in der Literaturwissenschaft*, Heidelberg, 1971.

BAYLEY, John, *Tolstoy and the Novel*, London, 1966.

CAILLOIS, Roger, *Instincts et société*. *Essais de sociologie contemporaine*, Paris, 1964.

CASSIRER, Ernst, *The Myth of the State*, Yale University Press, 1946.

DODDS, E. R., *The Greeks and the Irrational*, Berkeley, 1951.

—— (ed.), Euripides' *Bacchae*, Oxford, 1960².

FRYE, Northrop, *Anatomy of Criticism*, Princeton, 1957.

GOMBRICH, E. H., *Art and Illusion*, London, 1962.

HELLER, Erich, 'Imaginative Literature 1830–1870', in *Cambridge Modern History* vol. x.

HERMAND, Jost, 'Zur Literatur der Gründerzeit', in Hermand, *Von Mainz nach Weimar*, Stuttgart, 1969.

KAYSER, Wolfgang, *Das Groteske. Seine Gestaltung in Malerei und Dichtung*, Oldenburg, 1961.

LÄMMERT, Eberhard, *Bauformen des Erzählens*, Stuttgart, 1967.

LEWES, G. H., *The Life and Works of Goethe*, repr. London, 1938.

LORENZ, Konrad, *On Aggression*, London, 1966.

LUBBOCK, Percy, *The Craft of Fiction*, London, 1921.

POPPER, Karl, *The Open Society and its Enemies*, repr. 1963.

RASCH, Wolfdietrich, *Zur deutschen Literatur seit der Jahrhundertwende*, Stuttgart, 1967.

REED, T. J., 'Critical Consciousness and Creation. The Concept *Kritik* from Lessing to Hegel', *Oxford German Studies* 3 (1968).

REUTER, Hans-Heinrich, *Fontane*, Berlin, 1969.

ROSTEUTSCHER, J. H. W., *Die Wiederkunft des Dionysos*, Berne, 1947.

RYCHNER, Max (ed.), Goethe, *West-Östlicher Divan*, Zürich, 1963.

SCHUMANN, Klaus, *Der Lyriker Bertolt Brecht*, Munich, 1971².

SCHWERTE, Hans, 'Deutsche Literatur im Wilhelminischen Zeitalter', *Wirkendes Wort* 14 (1964).

SOERGEL-HOHOFF, *Dichtung und Dichter der Zeit*, Düsseldorf, 1964.

STARKIE, Enid, *Flaubert. The Making of the Master*, London, 1967.

# Index

No fictional characters are included. References to Thomas Mann's works will be found under 'MANN, Thomas, writings'. The alphabetical arrangement disregards umlauted vowels.